AMERICAN LEGISLATIVE PRACTICE

■ ■ ■

Legislative counsel
↳ *·general*
·comittee specific
·person specific

Advocate
· activist
· lobbyist
↳ *outside org*
citizen

Sean J. Kealy

Clinical Associate Professor of Law
Director, Legislative Experiential Programs
Boston University School of Law

WEST
ACADEMIC
PUBLISHING

© 2021 LEG, Inc. d/b/a West Academic
    444 Cedar Street, Suite 700
    St. Paul, MN 55101
    1-877-888-1330

West, West Academic Publishing, and West Academic are trademarks of West Publishing Corporation, used under license.

Printed in the United States of America

ISBN: 978-1-68328-211-2

For my wife Susan and our daughters Nell, Norah & Maeve.

ACKNOWLEDGMENTS

My thanks to Professor Louis S. Rulli from the University of Pennsylvania Carey Law School and Professor Marilyn Marchello Bautista from Stanford Law School who were indispensable in getting this project off the ground.

Thank you to Professor Emeritus Michael E. Libonati, who was my Legislation professor at Temple University's Beasley School of Law—not only for reviewing draft chapters of this book, but for being a mentor and a friend. My thanks to Toby Dorsey and Delegate David Toscano, the former Democratic Leader of the Virginia House of Delegates, for reviewing draft chapters and offering their valuable insights.

Thank you to Massachusetts Senate Majority Leader Cynthia Stone Creem for giving me the opportunity to work in the Massachusetts Legislature, and to my many colleagues there, especially Richard Powell, Catherine Anderson, Josh Krintzman, Mark Fine, Lisa Sears, Wendy Levine, Rob Schwartz, Alexis LeBlanc, Elisabeth Stein, and Rachal Aronson.

Thank you to John Moen, Moriah Hamstad, Gregory Olson, and Laura Holle of West Academic for all of their help, support, and edits.

Finally, thank you to all of my students at Boston University School of Law, from whom I have learned so much. A special thanks to my research assistants: Nabaa Khan, Kate Lipman, Lillian Feinberg Scott, Patricia Jo, Jennifer Yoo, Alex Intile, Sarah Simkin, Lakeisha Applegate, Stephen Gomez, and Christopher Hair.

SUMMARY OF CONTENTS

TABLE OF CONTENTS

———

TABLE OF CASES

The principal cases are in bold type.

AMERICAN LEGISLATIVE PRACTICE

CHAPTER 1

LEGISLATION & THE LEGISLATURE

■ ■ ■

"Civil Society being a State of Peace, amongst those who are of it, from which the State of War is excluded by the Umpirage, which they have provided in their Legislative, for the ending all Differences, that may arise amongst any of them, 'tis in their Legislative, that the Members of a Commonwealth are united, and combined together into one coherent living Body. This is the Soul that gives Form, Life, and Unity to the Commonwealth: From hence the several Members [of society] have their mutual Influence, Sympathy, and Connexion. . . . For the Essence and Union of the Society consisting in having one Will, the Legislative, when once established by the Majority, has the declaring, and as it were keeping of that Will."—John Locke, *Two Treatises of Government*

For most of America's history, statutory law—created and passed by a legislature, was considered inferior to the judge-made common law. Starting with the Progressive Era (1890–1920) and gaining steam during the New Deal (1933–1936), this dynamic changed significantly during the 20th century. Legislatures dramatically increased the output of new statutes, began writing statutes to comprehensively change areas of the law and how society was ordered, and to create the administrative state. Although statutory law has come to dominate the American legal system, the old biases can still be seen—especially in law schools. During the first year, most law students are immersed in the common law system, reading judicial opinions and almost exclusively discussing the role and operations of the court system.

Writing in 1908, Dean Roscoe Pound saw not just the emergence of statutory law but proclaimed the potential superiority of legislation. Pound was one of the most influential legal thinkers of the early 20th century. From 1903–1911 Pound served as dean of the University of Nebraska College of Law. He began teaching at Harvard Law School in 1911 and served as Harvard Law's dean from 1916 until 1937. Pound was an early adherent of the new discipline of sociology and was a founder of the "sociological jurisprudence" movement. Dean Pound was also an early leader in the American Legal Realism movement, which focused on how legal processes actually worked and argued for a more pragmatic and

1

public-interested interpretation of law. In this visionary article, Dean Pound argues that in the future problems would be solved in the "sociological laboratory" of the legislature.

COMMON LAW AND LEGISLATION
Roscoe Pound, 21 *Harvard Law Review* 383 (1908)

NOT the least notable characteristics of American law today are the excessive output of legislation in all our jurisdictions and the indifference, if not contempt, with which that output is regarded by courts and lawyers. Text-writers who scrupulously gather up from every remote corner the most obsolete decisions and cite all of them, seldom cite any statutes except those landmarks which have become a part of our American common law, or, if they do refer to legislation, do so through the judicial decisions which apply it. The courts, likewise, incline to ignore important legislation; not merely deciding it to be declaratory, but sometimes assuming silently that it is declaratory without adducing any reasons, citing prior judicial decisions and making no mention of the statute. In the same way, lawyers in the legislature often conceive it more expedient to make of a statute the barest outline, leaving details of the most vital importance to be filled in by judicial law-making. It is fashionable to point out the deficiencies of legislation and to declare that there are things that legislators cannot do try how they will. It is fashionable to preach the superiority of judge-made law. It may be well, however, for judges and lawyers to remember that there is coming to be a science of legislation and that modern statutes are not to be disposed of lightly as off-hand products of a crude desire to do something, but represent long and patient study by experts, careful consideration by conferences or congresses or associations, press discussions in which public opinion is focused upon all important details, and hearings before legislative committees. It may be well to remember also that while bench and bar are never weary of pointing out the deficiencies of legislation, to others the deficiencies of judge-made law are no less apparent. To economists and sociologists, judicial attempts to force Benthamite conceptions of freedom of contract and common law conceptions of individualism upon the public of today are no less amusing— or even irritating—than legislative attempts to do away with or get away from these conceptions are to bench and bar. The nullifying of these legislative attempts is not regarded by lay scholars with the complacent satisfaction with which lawyers are wont to speak of it. They do not hesitate to say that "the judicial mind has not kept pace with the strides of industrial development." They express the opinion that "belated and antisocial" decisions have been a fruitful cause of strikes, industrial discord, and consequent lawlessness. They charge that "the attitude of the courts has been responsible for much of our political immorality."

There are two ways in which the courts impede or thwart social legislation demanded by the industrial conditions of today. The first is narrow and illiberal construction of constitutional provisions, state and federal. "Petty judicial interpretations," says Professor Thayer, "have always been, are now, and will always be, a very serious danger to the country." The second is a narrow and illiberal attitude toward legislation conceded to be constitutional, regarding it as out of place in the legal system, as an alien element to be held down to the strictest limits and not to be applied beyond the requirements of its express language. The second is by no means so conspicuous as the first, but is not on that account the less unfortunate or the less dangerous. Let us see what this attitude is, how it arose, and why it exists in an industrial community and an age of legislation.

Four ways may be conceived of in which courts in such a legal system as ours might deal with a legislative innovation.

(1) They might receive it fully into the body of the law as affording not only a rule to be applied but a principle from which to reason, and hold it, as a later and more direct expression of the general will, of superior authority to judge-made rules on the same general subject; and so reason from it by analogy in preference to them.

(2) They might receive it fully into the body of the law to be reasoned from by analogy the same as any other rule of law, regarding it, however, as of equal or coordinate authority in this respect with judge-made rules upon the same general subject.

(3) They might refuse to receive it fully into the body of the law and give effect to it directly only; refusing to reason from it by analogy but giving it, nevertheless, a liberal interpretation to cover the whole field it was intended to cover.

(4) They might not only refuse to reason from it by analogy and apply it directly only, but also give to it a strict and narrow interpretation, holding it down rigidly to those cases which it covers expressly.

The fourth hypothesis represents the orthodox common law attitude toward legislative innovations. Probably the third hypothesis, however, represents more nearly the attitude toward which we are tending. The second and first hypotheses doubtless appeal to the common law lawyer as absurd. He can hardly conceive that a rule of statutory origin may be treated as a permanent part of the general body of the law. But it is submitted that the course of legal development upon which we have entered already must lead us to adopt the method of the second and eventually the method of the first hypothesis. . . . .

American courts, unrestrained by any doctrine of parliamentary supremacy, such as was established in England in 1688, found themselves opposed to legislatures, just as English courts of the sixteenth and seventeenth centuries had been opposed to the crown. They found in the books, over and above express constitutional limitations, vague doctrines of inherent limitations upon every form of law-making and of the intrinsic invalidity of certain laws. They soon wielded a conceded power over unconstitutional legislation. The great American institutional writer was an ardent federalist and had little faith in a popular legislature. The greatest of American judges, a man of like political sentiments, was not sure that "by general principles "legislatures were not bound to respect a *bona fide* purchaser for value as would a court of equity, and refuse to assert against him the rights of a defrauded people. Thus American courts were predisposed to look doubtfully upon legislative innovations.

But the determining factor in the attitude of our courts toward legislation is doubtless to be found in the coincidence of a period of development through judicial decisions with one of great legislative activity. Usually legislative activity has succeeded juristic or judicial activity. With us they happened to be coincident. Roughly speaking, the first century of American judicature was taken up with determining the applicability of the several doctrines of the common law to this country and working out the potential applications of common law principles to American conditions. Hence it was marked by fresh and living juristic thought and vigorous judicial law-making. For once, legislation had to contend with living and growing law of the discursive type instead of with the feeble offspring of a period of juristic decadence.

If, however, we should concede that an attitude of antipathy toward legislative innovation is a fundamental common law principle, we should have to inquire whether that principle is applicable to American conditions and is a part of our American common law. "The capital fact in the mechanism of modern states is the energy of legislatures." American legislatures have been conspicuously active from the beginning. Moreover, our constitutional polity expressly contemplates a complete separation of legislative from judicial power. And this is in accord with the whole course of legal history. Not only is a doctrine at variance with that polity inapplicable to American conditions, but if it ever was applicable, the reasons for it have ceased and it should be abandoned. For one thing, the political occasions for judicial interference with legislation have come to an end. In the sixteenth and seventeenth centuries the judiciary stood between the public and the crown. It protected the individual from the state when he required that protection. Today, when it assumes to stand between the legislature and the public and thus again to protect the individual from the state, it really stands between the public and what the public needs and desires, and protects individuals who need no protection against society which does need it. Hence the side of the courts is no longer the popular side. Moreover, courts are less and less competent to formulate rules for new relations which require regulation. They have the experience of the past. But they do not have the facts of the present. They have but one case before them, to be decided upon the principles of the past, the equities of the one situation, and the prejudices which the individualism of common law institutional writers, the dogmas learned in a college course in economics, and habitual association with the business and professional class, must inevitably produce. It is a sound instinct in the community that objects to the settlement of questions of the highest social import in private litigations between John Doe and Richard Roe. It is a sound instinct that objects to an agricultural view of industrial legislation. Judicial law-making for sheer lack of means to get at the real situation, operates unjustly and inequitably in a complex social organization. One might find more than one illustration in the conflict between judicial decision and labor legislation. But Dicey has pointed out a striking example in the operation of the equitable doctrines of separate property prior to the married women's acts. "The daughters of the wealthy," he says, "were when married, protected under the rules of equity in the enjoyment of their separate property. The daughters of workingmen possessed little property of their own. The one class was protected. The other would, it seemed, gain little from protection." Whether the state exists only to secure "the individualistic minimum of legal duty," or to interfere with the activities of sane adults along paternal or even socialistic lines in the interests of the community at large, legislative law-making must be the chief reliance of modern society.

But it is objected that statutes "have no roots" and are "hastily and inconsiderately adopted"; that they are crude and ill-adapted to the cases to which they are to be applied, and are unenforced and incapable of enforcement; and that they "breed litigation," whereas, supposedly free from the foregoing defects, judge-made laws "rest on principles of right" and "are the slow fruit of long-fought controversies between opposing interests." Very little reflection is needed to show how ill-founded these oft-repeated statements are in fact. Dicey has shown that the married women's acts had very deep roots in the equity doctrines as to separate property. Can we say that homestead and exemption laws, mechanics' lien laws, bankruptcy laws, divorce laws, wills acts, statutes abolishing the common law disqualifications of witnesses, permitting accused persons to testify, and allowing appeals in criminal causes, had no roots? Do any judge-made doctrines rest more firmly upon principles of right than these statutes, or than Lord Campbell's Act or Lord St. Leonards' Act or the Negotiable Instruments Law? Do the refinements of equity and the ultra-ethical impossibilities which the chancellors imposed upon trustees have deeper roots or represent right and justice better than trustees' relief acts? Are any judicial decisions more deliberately worked out or more carefully adjusted to the circumstances to which they are to be applied than the draft acts proposed by the Conference of Commissioners on Uniform State Laws or the National Congress on Uniform Divorce Legislation? What court that passes upon industrial legislation is able or pretends to investigate conditions of manufacture, to visit factories and workshops and see them in operation, and to take the testimony of employers, employees, physicians, social workers, and economists as to the needs of workmen and of the public, as a legislative committee may and often does? Failures are not confined to legislative lawmaking. The fate of the fellow servant rule, of the doctrine of assumption of risk, and of the whole judge-made law of employers' liability, the Taff-Vale case in England, and the fate of judicial adjustment of water-rights in America should make lawyers more cautious in criticizing the legislature: Freaks of judicial law-making are abundant. Spendthrift trusts are as out of line with right and justice as any statute-made institution ever was. The Exchequer rule as to reversal for error in admission of evidence, our American judge-made law of instructions to juries, our practice of new trials on the slightest provocation, and our whole pitfall-bestrewn practice in appellate courts are warnings of the evil possibilities even of judicial law-making. In short, crudity and carelessness have too often characterized American lawmaking both legislative and judicial. They do not inhere necessarily in the one any more than in the other.

Formerly it was argued that common law was superior to legislation because it was customary and rested upon the consent of the governed. Today we recognize that the so-called custom is a custom of judicial decision, not a custom of popular action. We recognize that legislation is the more truly democratic form of lawmaking. We see in legislation the more direct and accurate expression of the general will. We are told that law-making of the future will consist in putting the sanction of society on what has been worked out in the sociological laboratory. That courts cannot conduct such laboratories is self evident. Courts are fond of saying that they apply old principles to new situations. But at times they must apply new principles to situations both old and new. The new principles are in legislation. The old principles are in common law. The former are as much to be respected and made effective as the latter—probably more so as our legislation improves. The public cannot be relied upon permanently to tolerate judicial obstruction or nullification of the social policies to which more and more it is compelled to be committed.

NOTES & QUESTIONS

1.   Why have lawyers (and law schools) traditionally focused on the court system as the main source of law?

2.   Professors William N. Eskridge and Phillip P. Frickey continued to point out the legal academy's shortcomings when it came to legislation in their

article, "Legislation Scholarship and Pedagogy in the Post Legal Process Era," 48 *U. Pitt. L. Rev.* 691 (1987):

> Legal academe's approach to the systematic study of 'legislation' resembles Congress' attitude toward balancing the federal budget: everyone agrees that it is a good thing, but laments that it is not done. A growing body of opinion bemoans legislation's 'second class' status as an academic discipline and advocates substantially enhanced scholarly interest in the subject. We join this collective lament and endorse a more systematic and creative approach to teaching and writing about legislation."

Twenty-two years later, Professor Michael E. Libonati continued to find the study of legislatures "marginalized" in law school: "The topic of this Essay, the comparative study of state and federal legislatures, is doubly marginalized in the legal academy. First, it has to do with the legislative branch of government. Second, it has to do with the legislative branch of state government." "State Constitutions and Legislative Process: The Road Not Taken," 89 *B.U. L. Rev.* 863 (2009). In fact, the symposium where Prof. Libonati delivered his paper was entitled: "The Most Disparaged Branch: The Role of Congress in the Twenty-First Century."

3.   During your legal education so far, how have legislatures been portrayed in readings and in class? Have most of the perspectives on legislatures and statutes come from reading judicial opinions? Is this problematic?

4.   In his very influential book LAW'S EMPIRE (1986), Professor Ronald Dworkin portrayed his ideal judge as Hercules—a wise, all knowing, and powerful decision maker. Prof. Jeremy Waldron in "The Dignity of Legislation," 54 *Md. L. Rev.* 633 (1995) wrote, "My point then is not that legislatures are suffering from overall academic neglect, but that, in jurisprudence at any rate, we have not bothered to develop any idealistic or normative picture of legislation. Our silence here is deafening compared to our philosophical loquacity on the subject of courts. There is nothing about legislatures or legislation in modern philosophical jurisprudence remotely comparable to the discussion of decision-making by judges. No one seems to have seen the need for an ideal type or theoretical model that would do for our understanding of legislation what, for example, Ronald Dworkin's "Hercules" purports to do for adjudicative reasoning."

What would be the metaphor for the ideal legislator?

5.   What is needed for the "sociological laboratory" to work properly in addressing society's problems?

THE DIGNITY OF LEGISLATION

Jeremy Waldron, 54 *Maryland Law Review* 633 (1995)

I began with the familiar fact that everywhere legislatures consist of hundreds of members. These throngs of people do not simply assemble from time to time and vote on laws.

It is surely part of our normative image of legislatures that they are bodies where deliberation takes place. Think back to the John Adams's idea outlined in Part I: A representative legislature "should be an exact portrait, in miniature, of the people at large," so that when the legislators talk to one another, different parts of society can be taken, through their representation, to be talking to one another.

The importance of deliberation was also emphasized by John Stuart Mill:

> Representative assemblies are often taunted by their enemies with being places of mere talk and bavardage. There has seldom been more misplaced derision. I know not how a representative assembly can more usefully employ itself than in talk, when the subject of talk is the great public interests of the country, and every sentence of it represents the opinion either of some important body of persons in the nation, or of an individual in whom some such body have reposed their confidence. A place where every interest and shade of opinion in the country can have its cause even passionately pleaded, in the face of the government and of all other interests and opinions can compel them to listen and either comply or state clearly why they do not, is in itself, if it answered no other purpose, one of the most important political institutions that can exist anywhere.

But we saw earlier that Mill did not entertain a particularly rosy view of parliaments as places for action. It is not clear that he regarded this business of "talking" as anything other than an expressive opportunity to vent a variety of grievances and complaints.

There is, however, an older tradition in political theory which assigns an important synthetic function to talking in the context of practical deliberation. That tradition has its most explicit origin in the Politics of Aristotle. For, although Aristotle inclined to the view that the law-giver in an ideal society would be "the one best man," he conceded that

> There is this to be said for the Many. Each of them by himself may not be of a good quality; but when they all come together it is possible that they may surpass—collectively and as a body, although not individually—the quality of the few best. Feasts to which many contribute may excel those provided at one man's expense. In the same way, when there are many [who contribute

to the process of deliberation], each can bring his share of goodness and moral prudence; and when all meet together the people may thus become something in the nature of a single person, who—as he has many feet, many hands, and many senses—may also have many qualities of character and intelligence. This is the reason why the Many are also better judges [than the few] of music and the writings of poets: some appreciate one part, some another, and all together appreciate all.

What lies behind this is the idea that a number of individuals may bring a diversity of perspectives to bear on issues under consideration, and that they are capable of pooling these perspectives to come up with better decisions than any one of them could make on his own. That, after all, is why Aristotle took it as the mark of man's political nature that he was endowed with the faculty of speech. Each can communicate to another experiences and insights that complement, complicate or qualify those that the other already possesses; and when this happens in the deliberations of an assembly, it enables the group as a whole to attain a degree of practical knowledge that surpasses even the coherently applied expertise of the one excellent legislator.

We may or may not buy Aristotle's view that the many can in this way come up with better results than the one. But the existence of diverse perspectives in the community and the helpfulness of bringing them to bear on proposed laws are surely important features in any account of why the task of legislating is entrusted to assemblies. I believe that these features in turn frame the way in which we should think about the deliberative process itself, and in particular how we should regard the relatively high level of formality associated with debate and action in a legislative assembly.

I said a moment ago that Aristotle's view about the wisdom of the multitude is connected intimately with his teaching that the mark of man's political nature is his capacity for reasoned speech. It is worth pausing at this point to notice a renewed emphasis on speech, discourse and conversation in political and legal theory, particularly in theory that has been influenced by the work of Jurgen Habermas. Jurists influenced by Habermas have suggested, for example, that a commitment to the United States Constitution is "less a series of propositional utterances than a commitment to taking political conversation seriously.... [T]he Constitution is best understood as supportive of such conversations and requiring a government committed to their maintenance." They suggest too that the authority of judicial decision-making is "sustained less by the perceived correctness of the result than by the coherence of the result, for coherence permits conversation, and it is ultimately a faith in our ability to converse morally that holds us together."

Much of this is far-fetched in ways I cannot go into here—in its aestheticism, for example, or in its conception of discourse as an end in itself. But one point is particularly important for our purposes. There is a constant temptation in modern discourse jurisprudence to take as an implicit procedural ideal the model of an informal intimate conversation among friends. Certainly, an informal conversation among friends has attractive features of equality, openness and mutual respect. But it also tends to be predicated upon the idea that participants share implicit understandings and that their interaction is oriented towards the avoidance of adversarial disagreement and the achievement of consensus. These, I think, are qualities which are quite misleading so far as our models of political deliberation are concerned.

Suppose, then, that instead of a conversation among friends we were to take the following as our ideal type of legislative deliberation. A large number of persons have assembled in a hall as representatives from different parts of a diverse society. Let us suppose that it is a radically diverse society—so that the members of the assembly represent not only different interests and regions, but come from completely different backgrounds, ethnic and cultural, as well as whatever political differences divide them. Imagine, for example, the national legislature in India or some other vastly diverse modern state. The representatives may belong to various religious traditions; they may be familiar with quite different social forms; they may have disparate senses of what gives meaning to life. They may not even speak the same language. Perhaps there is a state language stipulated for their proceedings in the legislature; if so, we may think of it as a second language for most of them, and one that they must use carefully and hesitantly. Certainly, their presence together in the chamber attests to the fact that they share some sense of common purpose—though it may not be much more than a foreboding that any attempt to disentangle their diverse interests into more homogenous "nation" states, each with a legislature of its own whose members really do understand each other, would be fraught with the most frightful dangers and difficulties.

To the extent that such a body seeks to legislate on common problems, there is a need for the members to be able to talk to one another, so that each can contribute insights and perspectives that would otherwise be quite outside the experience of the other legislators. However, the very reasons that make this interaction desirable and necessary also make it quite unlikely that the members can proceed with their deliberations as though they were conducting an open-ended conversation among friends. They are not transparent to one another as friends are, and they do not have a great deal of common ground on which confidences could be shared, premises assumed, and nuances taken for granted. Indeed, the prospects for mutual misunderstanding and for talking at cross purposes are greatly enhanced by the very features of their situation that make it important—

on Aristotelian grounds—for them to talk to one another. These representatives cannot deal with one another in the way that members of a tightly-knit gemeinschaft or an "old-boy's network" are often thought to be able to deal with one another. They share very little beyond an overlapping sense of common problems, and the rather stiff and formal language that they address to one another in their debates about those problems. If any one of them says, in the rather cozy way that people have who share tacit understandings, "Come on, you know what I mean," the answer is as likely as not to be: "No, I don't know what you mean. You had better spell it out for me."

Of course this is an extreme example. The membership of the United States Congress is less diverse than this, and the British House of Commons is more homogenous still. There are reasons for dwelling on the more extreme model nonetheless.

First, as we have seen, the less diverse the body of representatives, the weaker the case for legislation by an assembly as opposed to legislation by a single representative individual. Both John Adams's case, the "microcosm" model, and the Aristotelian case for legislation by the multitude rely on the fact that different members will bring to the process differing perspectives and experiences.

Second, and more generally, exaggeration offers certain methodological advantages in ideal type analysis. By highlighting the diversity associated with the sheer plurality of a modern legislature, the model I am framing may help us understand the challenges and techniques that come along with diversity, so far as deliberation and decision-making are concerned. True, in a more homogenous legislature, these concerns can be discounted *pro tanto*.

There is, nevertheless, some theoretical advantage in using an exaggerated model to focus our attention on diversity among legislators, particularly when—as I shall argue—they offer a plausible basis for understanding certain features of modern legislation which are otherwise somewhat bewildering: for example, the high degree of formality associated both with legislative deliberations and with legislative outputs.

Third, there are normative reasons for taking this approach. We pride ourselves on having not only a diverse society, but a political philosophy—particularly liberal political philosophy—oriented specifically to the challenges and difficulties of that diversity. Analytic jurisprudence should participate in that orientation, while in its philosophical assumptions about the sources of law, it should not err on the side of social homogeneity. Even if the diversity which we actually face is somewhat less extreme, the liberal instinct is that we should not be counting on that. Indeed, it is an important criticism of recent communitarian theories that they implicitly presuppose and rely upon on a degree of cultural and ethical homogeneity to an extent that is really quite reckless in the circumstances of the modern world.

We should be careful, in other words, to avoid building in any premise of ethnic and cultural homogeneity as a prerequisite in our models of politics and legislation. The narrow and intolerant impulses of communitarianism, tribalism and nationalism are wreaking enough havoc in the world as it is, without the encouragement of liberal jurisprudence. If there is a conception of law that makes no such assumption—or that celebrates diversity or, at any rate, comes to terms with it—we should try to state that conception clearly and make it central in our jurisprudence if we can.

We left our diverse legislators in their chamber, a little unsure of each other and a little tongue-tied. We might imagine that from time to time one of them will stand up and make a proposal to her fellow representatives. When she does, it may evoke a flurry of responses. Some she will recognize as opposing her idea; some will appear to misunderstand it. Others may put forward a different proposal or a counter-proposal, which in turn will evoke similarly confusing responses. Some members may stand up and make speeches on quite different matters. They may tell stories of tenuous or indeterminate relevance about the problems and experiences of their constituents. Others may interrupt by chanting slogans, singing hymns, telling jokes, or shouting threats. Matters that various members conceive as having great urgency will cut across one another. Responses to one idea will be taken as responses to a different idea, and no one will be able to keep track of where they have got to on any particular front.

In circumstances of this kind, we see the importance of deliberative formality, parliamentary procedures, and rules of order. It is clear from the scenario just outlined that an assembly like the one we are imagining needs to structure and order its deliberations if it is to achieve any of the advantages that the Aristotelian theory suggests may accrue from legislation by the many. The members of our assembly need to establish rules and procedures that address issues such as the following: How are debates initiated and how are they concluded? Who has the right to speak when, how often, and for how long? Who may interrupt, who may exact an answer to a question, who has a right of reply? How is a common sense of relevance maintained or how are members assured that they are not talking at cross purposes? What issues, subjects, or details may be addressed at various stages in the proceedings? How are topics for debate selected, how are subject matter priorities set, and how is an agenda determined? How is the conduct and conclusion of a deliberative session related to the assembly's powers of resolution and action? How is debate brought to an end? How are decisions taken?

Blandly stated, these matters might seem obvious and beneath notice in jurisprudence. It is tempting to regard such procedural rules as arbitrary conventions, with no intrinsic philosophical significance of their own. That would be a mistake. Political scientists have noted the remarkable similarity in parliamentary procedures around the world. There are no doubt historical reasons: for example, the global influence of the Westminster tradition, largely as a legacy of British imperialism. But the similarity can also be understood as a common human response to a similar set of problems: the circumstances of procedure, so to speak. Wherever there is a felt need for common action as an upshot of deliberation in circumstances of diversity and disagreement, then needs of the kind outlined in the previous paragraph are bound to be felt.

VII

I have focused so far on what the ideal model of a diverse legislature contributes to our understanding of procedural formality in lawmaking. I now want to turn to the relative formality of legislation—i.e., statutes—considered as products of processes of this kind.

My hunch is that textual canonicity and the procedural formality discussed in the previous parts are connected. At first glance, however, there is no obvious reason that procedural formality should necessarily issue in output—or interpretive—formality. We might imagine a proclamation made by a legislator-monarch with all sorts of formal pomp and ceremony, and yet it might be understood that the purpose of the occasion's formality is to impress upon subjects the personal authority of the ruler rather than to evince any commitment on his part to the particular linguistic expressions that were used. Indeed, it might follow from the fact that the procedural pomp highlights the personal authority of the monarch, that we should orient our behavior to what we think he intended rather than the words he happened to say. In these circumstances, one might want to say, with Hobbes, that "it is not the Letter, but the Intendment, or Meaning ... (which is the sense of the Legislator,) in which the nature of the Law consisteth." By itself, then, procedural formality is not sufficient to make sense of output formality.

It is possible, however, to relate output formality to procedural formality, when the later is undertaken for certain reasons. Think back to the predicament of the radically diverse legislature we imagined in Part VI. The members of that body found it necessary to order their deliberations with formal rules governing the setting of an agenda, the initiation and conclusion of discussion, the right to speak, the structure of debate, and the basis of voting and decision-making. Those familiar with parliamentary procedure, whether in national legislatures or small-scale public meetings, will know that debating rules are largely oriented towards and ordered by the idea that at any given time there is a specified proposition under discussion. Even in the most basic forums, propositions are moved and seconded, and once a motion is on the table, the deliberative body has a specific form of words which is open for discussion, and the organizing principle of debate becomes (roughly) that all and only contributions to the consideration of that proposition are to be heard, until either the time set for debate runs out or until the question defined by that proposition has been resolved. This insistence that there be a formulated motion, and that speakers observe norms of relevance in regard to that motion, are the primary basis on which parliamentary procedure seeks to avoid the nightmare of people talking endlessly at cross-purposes and the failure to make the sort of contact with one another's contributions (synthetic or dialectic) that practical deliberation requires.

No doubt, in the course of discussion, someone may feel that it would be wiser for the assembly to discuss a somewhat different proposition than the one specified, perhaps worded in a subtly or substantially different way. But if they want to press the point, the parliamentary rule is that they must move an amendment, changing the wording of the motion under discussion, once again in a specifically formulated way. Proceedings are then devoted to a discussion of the virtues of the amendment, qua amendment, and a vote is taken on that, before the substantive discussion is resumed. And again, we see the virtue of this way of doing things in a diverse assembly. In conversation among friends, the topic may shift in an open-ended way, and people familiar with one another have both the willingness and the ability to keep track. But in an assembly consisting of people who are largely strangers to one another, deliberation would be hopeless if there was a sense that the topic might or might not have shifted slightly after every contribution. So, although amendment processes exist, their formulaic character and the rules governing their proposal and adoption provide a way of keeping track of where the discussion is, a way of keeping track which does not depend upon implicit understandings that some of the members may not share.

When discussion is exhausted, a vote may be called for, and—if my experience of law faculty meetings is any indication—someone will immediately leap to their feet and say: "I'm confused. What exactly are we voting on?" In a well-run assembly, the clerk or secretary will be in a position at that stage to read out the proposition (as amended) which now is the focus of the final vote. Once again, the determinacy of that proposition, as formulated and as amended, is important to establish a sense that we are all orienting our actions in voting to the same object. It is important for me to know, for example, that what I take myself to be voting against is exactly what my opponent takes himself to be voting in favor of. Otherwise, the idea that our votes, on a given occasion, are to be aggregated and weighed against one another becomes a nonsense.

What I have just described is rudimentary by comparison with the processes employed in actual legislative assemblies such as the Congress of the United States. Bills are longer and more complex than the sort of motions one hears at faculty meetings. They have usually been drafted—more or less competently—in advance, and there are many stages of deliberation (including committee stages, whose proceedings may be much less formal) that bills must go through before they are adopted. And, this is to say nothing of the vicissitudes of bicamerality, conference committees, and the rest.

For the most part, however, these complications enhance the need for a determinate text to focus and coordinate the various stages of the legislative process. Without a text to consider, to mark up, to amend, to confer about, and to vote upon, the process of law-making in a large and unwieldy assembly would have even a greater air of babel-like futility than that which is currently associated with Congress.

Thus, whether we are talking about a small scale meeting or a large-scale legislative process, the positing of a formulated text as the resolution under discussion provides a focus for the ordering of deliberation at every stage. The existence of a verbalized bill, motion, or resolution is key to norms of relevance, and key to the sense, which procedural rules are supposed to provide, that participants' contributions are relevant to one another and that they are not talking at cross purposes. Maybe, a one-person deliberative body can do without this—though even there, many of us are familiar with the mnemonic virtues of a formulated proposition in our own solitary decision-making. And maybe, decision-making in a small group of oligarchs or in a junta of familiars can do without this as well, if they can move toward consensus on the basis of conversational informality. But the sense of a determinate focus for discussion—something whose existence is distinct from the will or tacit understandings of particular members—seems absolutely indispensable for a large and diverse assembly of people whose knowledge and trust of one another is limited.

VIII

If there is anything to this hypothesis, then we might want to start thinking about the textual canonicity of legislation in a slightly different way. I said in Part I that one of the values most commonly associated in the modern world with legislation is democratic legitimacy: We should defer to statutes because they have been enacted by a democratically elected entity. Just as the idea of democracy is insufficient to explain why we prefer a large elected legislature to a single elected legislator, so the democratic principle is insufficient to explain the particular way in which authority is accorded to legislation in the modern world, viz., by taking seriously the exact words that were used in the formulations that emerged from the legislative chamber. If I am right, we now have an explanation for the importance of the *ipsissima verba* which is oriented primarily to the legislators' dealings among themselves, rather than directly to the issue of their collective authority vis-a-vis the people.

The final step, then, in pursuit of this hypothesis would be to show how this account of the importance of a text to the legislators is connected with the authority of the text for its intended audience. Here there are a couple of lines to pursue. First, as we have seen, the existence of orderly discussion is necessary to secure whatever Aristotelian advantages accrue from deliberation in a large and diverse group. Unless the diverse experiences and knowledge of the various legislators can connect and be synthesized, it is unlikely that their interaction will produce standards that are superior to those that any individual citizen could work out for herself.

The conditions for orderly discussion, then, are indirectly conditions for the legislature's authority, in the Razian sense. In other words, authority requires superior expertise; superior expertise comes from deliberation among those who are different from one another; deliberation among those who are different from one another is possible only on the basis of formal rules of order; and crucial to rules of order is the postulation of an agreed text as the focus of discussion.

Second, respect for statute law is partly a matter of respect for the legislature as a forum whose representativeness is an aspect of the fairness of the way a community makes its decisions. To the extent that representativeness requires diversity in the assembly, respect for that fairness is a matter of respecting the conditions under which diverse representatives can deliberate coherently. Thus, fairness-based respect for the legislature as a body may require not only that we respect the standards which it posits, but also that we respect these more formal aspects of the way in which its posited standards are arrived at—and thus that we respect the standards in question under the auspices of text-based formality.

NOTES & QUESTIONS

1.   Professor Waldron creates a legislature with great diversity—one that extends to language and religion. How much diversity among members should a legislature have? What kind of diversity is desirable?

2.   Professor Waldron's legislature is brand new and starting from scratch, making debate difficult. How would you anticipate that will change over time?

3.   According to this article, legislation is "dignified" by the fact that a legislature with many diverse people debating and voting on a formal document that can be scrutinized and amended under formal rules. What other conditions are needed for a society to accept legislation as legitimate?

Metaphors for the Legislative Process

The best-known saying about legislation is attributed to German Chancellor Otto von Bismarck:

"There are two things you don't want to see being made—sausage and legislation."

Political scientist Alan Rosenthal examined this metaphor while studying state legislatures. In fact, he took it a step further by touring an actual sausage factory and comparing what happened there to what he saw in legislatures. Rosenthal found some similarities between sausage making and legislative process, but also some significant differences:

- While sausage factories are hard to get into for a tour, the state capitol is typically very accessible, and the work of the legislature is well publicized. Further, citizens can actively participate in law-making, and their involvement is considered a positive rather than a contaminant.

- The team making sausage all had defined roles to create several well-defined products. In contrast, legislators are all working, individually or in groups which may change depending on the issue, with different goals in mind. The is no single product or purpose, but many competing outcomes.

- Sausage making is highly regular because the company wants uniform products, and the government strictly regulates the industry. Every piece of legislation is unique and even seasoned political observers have difficulty predicting exactly how a bill will emerge from the process.

- A sausage factory has to be efficient to make a profit and the product must leave the factory as quickly as possible. Legislation takes time—often far more than anticipated. Rosenthal states, "Legislatures are hardly efficient in any economic sense. Nor should we expect them to be."

- Even the complex process of making sausage is comprehensible, whereas the "legislature is too human, too democratic and too messy to be totally comprehensible."

Rosenthal concludes that the sausage metaphor should be retired, perhaps to replace by another metaphor. Still, he doubted an adequate metaphor could be found, "We can search for another metaphor, although I doubt that we will find one. The legislative process in Congress and the states is *sui generis*, incomparable, not like anything else in our experience—and pretty much the way it ought to be." See, Alan Rosenthal, "The Legislature as Sausage Factory: It's About Time to Examine This Metaphor," *State Legislatures* (September 2001).

William K. Muir Jr's book *Legislature: California's School for Politics* (1982) examined of the California Legislature during he called its "golden age" during the mid-1970s. Muir uses the metaphor of a very exclusive school where legislators are the students and lobbyists are the professors:

> Two of our most original political theorists, James Madison (1751–1836) and John Stuart Mill (1806–73), were drawn to the analogy of the legislature as a school. They both insisted that legislative institutions in a free society must teach their members to govern well. In fact, the preparation of political leaders was—or ought to be—a central event in a legislature.
>
> . . .
>
> Madison understood that this legislative medium needed to be carefully cultivated. He had no illusions about the low caliber of the individual representatives, selected as they would be from parochial circumstance, deficient in the theory and practice of public affairs, and lacking 'due acquaintance with the objects and principles of legislation.
>
> Madison hoped legislators would learn three "fundamental competencies:"
>
> Patriotism: a sympathy for the circumstances of all of their constituents—not just of their supporters, but also opponents and strangers;
>
> Justice: how to manage legislation fairly, openly, and in the face of opposition; and
>
> Wisdom: legislators needed to take personal responsibility for some portion of the legislative agenda, and by specializing in a subject, to develop an expert's competence, allowing the legislator to produce well developed policy proposals in their particular field.
>
> . . .
>
> Madison saw a second advantage in increasing the competence of all the representatives. As legislators improved their skills in conducting the public business, their commitment to the vocation of politics would harden. As a result, they would stand for reelection. Their competence, if they had taken the trouble to nurture it, would stand out boldly against the inexperience of any challengers. The electorate would discern the differences and tend to return incumbents to office, thus giving the legislature an institutional continuity.

NOTES & QUESTIONS

1.   Other suggested metaphors for the legislative process are a circus; a casino; a marketplace; a zoo, an auction, several basketball games taking place, at different stages, on the same floor, with teammates constantly changing.

2.   What metaphor would you apply to a legislature? Or do you agree with Rosenthal that a good metaphor is elusive?

Analyzing Case Studies

This book includes several case studies and fact specific exercises. Although a staple of business schools, this type of exercise is not typical in law school. Students reading through case studies should make a point of reading these case studies actively to identify the most relevant evidence, develop discussion questions, and hypotheses. As you read the studies, identify the most important actors and aspects of the given situation and ask why the actors are behaving as they are and how they may respond to the challenges before them. Bringing thoughtful hypotheses to class will enrich our class discussions.

There are different types of cases:

- "Problems" cases focus on situations where there is an outcome or a performance, which could be either positive or negative, without further explanation. Ask, "why did things turned out this way?" There may be no explicit problem and the reader may have to both define the problem and test various hypotheses as to why the problem existed and how it was or can be resolved.

- "Decisions" cases ask an actor to make a decision and require students to identify the relevant evidence within the case study, what options exist, and consider what factors will influence an actor's decision. As is true in real life, "right" answers are exceedingly rare. Instead, think about what decision will maximize benefits and minimize negative effects.

- "Evaluations" cases ask the student to evaluate an actor's performance or the outcome. The student might assess the actions of a single legislator, a person or group trying to influence the legislature, or the legislature itself. Students should identify both the positive and negative aspects of the actors' decisions.

- Students may need to read a case several times and find talking about the case with classmates particularly helpful. This approach helps students identify the main issues, relevant evidence, formulate working hypotheses, and come to possible conclusions.

A suggested process for working through a case is:

1. Ask what is the situation these characters are facing?

2. Once the situation is identified, spend some time asking relevant questions: what is the problem? who, if anyone, created the problem? What are the available options? Do the actors have the information they need? Who is being evaluated? What are the potential outcomes?

3. Students should spend significant time thinking about hypotheses for what happened or what should happen. Keep track of your theories as your understanding of the situation deepens—this is very valuable during class discussions.

4. Devote another significant amount of time to identifying evidence that supports or undermines your hypotheses. What other evidence would you like to have? What should the actors do? Be practical—what would work in a real-world setting?

5. Finally, identify alternatives. What negative outcomes could come from your proposed solution? What else could the actor(s) do?

For more information see, William Ellet, *Reading and Writing Case Studies* pp. 19–35 (Harvard Business School Press, 2007).

CHAPTER 2

THE MAKE-UP & STRUCTURE
OF THE LEGISLATURE

■ ■ ■

A. THE CHANGING LEGISLATURE

THE PARTY'S OVER: THE RISE AND STALL OF
LOUISIANA LEGISLATIVE INDEPENDENCE
Wayne Parent, Michael B. Henderson, 48 *Loyola Law Review* 527 (2002)

Any visitor to the Louisiana State Capitol who paid attention to the tour guide will remember that the original leadership offices flanking the desks of the Speaker of the House and the President of the Senate are minuscule. Governor Huey Long designed them that way; he did not want the heads of the chambers to have room to maneuver.

Capitol visitors also notice that in between the two chambers, across the hallway from the Long assassination bullet holes, lies the spacious original Office of the Governor, where Long had been minutes before he was fatally shot. The symbolism and practical effect of the disparity in accommodations for the governor, on the one hand, and the heads of the legislative chambers, on the other hand, are obvious. The huge Office of the Governor was situated right in the middle of the two legislative chambers, whereas the leaders had only modest space. The Office of the Governor was to dominate state politics.

Today, however, the office arrangements are different. The tiny offices at the rear of the House chambers hold snack machines and a private elevator to modern, high-tech offices and committee rooms. The offices in the Senate Chamber have elevators to well-appointed quarters downstairs for the President of the Senate and for all thirty-nine senators. In addition, there is ample space for committees to meet as well as for large conferences of senators. The governor has been moved upstairs away from the two chambers. The roomy first floor governor's office is now home to the Speaker of the House.

Appearances indicate that times have changed dramatically. Perhaps they have. For decades, the legislature had little independence from the governor and little credibility. Thus, reform seemed almost inevitable. When reform finally began in the late 1960s, the changes were dramatic, fundamental, and promising. Forty years later, however, the effects of the legislative revolution are decidedly mixed.

In the first half of the twentieth century, Governors Huey and Earl Long towered over the Louisiana Legislature. Even in their most noted defeats, Huey's impeachment and Earl's banishment to a mental hospital, they rose victorious and even stronger. The Louisiana Legislature, simply extending legitimacy to the latest whims of the governor, was an executive tool in this period.

However, legislative reform was sweeping the nation during the latter part of the twentieth century. Louisiana, a state in which the culture of power was tilted firmly on the side of the executive branch, was a prime candidate for calls for greater legislative independence from the governor. It is important to note that, while the formal structural powers of the governor of Louisiana were not particularly strong when compared to those of other states, it was the ability of the Louisiana governor to have his way with a weak legislature that made the balance of power in the state so distinctively lopsided.

When change came, it arrived with a vengeance. All the pieces came together in the course of a decade, and the Louisiana Legislature was poised for a much stronger role in legislative-executive relations. The actions of legislators, legislative staff, and even the governor all aligned to produce dramatic legislative reform designed specifically to raise the stature of the House of Representatives and Senate in relation to the Office of the Governor. The main legislative players in the legislative reform movement were a group of legislators, elected mainly in 1967, but also in 1971, who called themselves 'The Young Turks.' Behind the scenes was a legendary Clerk of the House, David Poynter. Finally, and perhaps only because of his lack of resistance to the reforms, was the man who, after Huey and Earl Long, would be the third towering figure of Louisiana politics in the twentieth century, Governor Edwin W. Edwards.

YOUNG TURKS AND LEGISLATIVE REFORM

In 1967, a small group of about ten legislators were elected to the House of Representatives and set about to unsettle the normal workings of the chamber. Initially, no real leader emerged from the group, but E.L. 'Bubba' Henry, a young representative from Jonesboro, located in rural north Louisiana, later became best known for the actions of this group. These legislators, who dubbed themselves 'The Young Turks,' intentionally tried to challenge the status quo of a lackadaisical legislature that capitulated to the will of the governor through sheer disorganization and structural weakness.

The Young Turks saw a problem. The legislature was weak because it was run from the outside. A long succession of governors was adept at assuring that the organization of the legislature did not come from within, but rather from the executive. A weak, chaotic legislature allowed the governor to fill the vacuum. In their first four-year term, 1968–1972, these new representatives called attention to their cause by learning the minutia of the rules and then using procedure to challenge points, overrule the leadership, and generally create parliamentary standstill. It attracted attention and it worked. Between 1968 and 1972, at the impetus of these Young Turks, several changes were made that affected rules, procedures, and actions of the House of Representatives. Several resolutions and laws were passed to strengthen the chamber. These actions affected the leadership and gave more power to individual legislators. The changes enabled legislators to elect some members of the Appropriations Committee, install microphones at every legislator's desk, and hire and fire one's secretary.

The Young Turks also worked to strengthen the committee system and the legislative staff. They reduced the number of standing committees, regularized when and where the committees met, and enacted stricter jurisdictional rules. Formerly, the standing committees had vaguely worded areas of jurisdiction that allowed for easy political manipulation of bills by the leadership, and by extension, the governor. In addition, the legislature created a research division to assist both committees and individual legislators in information gathering and processing.

All of these structural changes added solid organizational characteristics to a fluidly organized body. The changes were significant and expanded upon in the next legislative term; but their impact on legislative independence may have paled in comparison to a simple housekeeping resolution that was passed in 1970, the second year of the Young Turk disruptions.

House Resolution Number Four of the 1970 Regular Legislative Session restricted those persons allowed on the floor of the House Chamber and required identification permits for those who were admitted. While it was hailed as a measure that kept lobbyists from the desk of the representatives, it also kept members of the Governor's staff from the floor. It effectively insulated the House of Representatives and created an environment for independence and reform. By the end of the 1968–1972 Young Turk term, the conditions existed for a major transformation of legislative-executive relations.

At the beginning of the 1972 legislative term, the politics of the legislature had turned upside down. In the previous term, the Young Turks were outsiders who shrewdly passed small but key procedural reforms. In 1972, the outsiders became insiders, and the overhaul of the legislature could proceed in earnest.

This extraordinary situation was the result of the unique character of the 1971 legislative and gubernatorial elections.

These legislative elections were the first where all members were elected from single member districts. As a result, over half of the House of Representatives membership was replaced. With many of the older status quo legislators out of office, the majority of the newcomers sided with the Young Turks, who were generally successful in their reelection campaigns.

Perhaps as significant as the new legislative membership was the gubernatorial side of the equation. In retrospect, the result of the 1971 race for governor was a particularly inopportune time for the legislature to try and assert itself. The winner of that election was Edwin W. Edwards, the man who would be elected an unprecedented three more terms and dominate the Louisiana political landscape for the next twenty-five years. In 1971, however, the circumstances did not appear to be daunting at all. In fact, Edwards had campaigned on a theme of governmental reform, promoting his idea for a constitutional convention to write a new document to replace the confusing, convoluted 1921 document that had over five hundred amendments. In addition, many legislators had already secured their electoral victories while Edwards was still struggling to secure his razor-thin margin of victory in the Democratic primary run-off election with future United States Senator J. Bennett Johnston, and then launching a further effort in the general election. Edwards's energy was more on electoral strategy and consolidating his success than on procedural machinations of the Louisiana legislature.

The Young Turks and their allies seized the opportunity presented by a novice legislature and a pre-occupied, reform campaigning governor to capitalize on their efforts of the previous term. E.L. 'Bubba' Henry was elected Speaker of the House and, two years later, Chair of the 1973 Constitutional Convention. Henry worked with David Poynter, the Clerk of the House, and promulgated a series of wide-ranging reforms that would give the Louisiana legislature unprecedented independence. Most of the measures passed the House fairly easily, made it through the Senate, and were then signed by newly elected Governor Edwin Edwards. The next year, with Henry at its helm, the Constitutional Convention re-enforced the letter and the spirit of reform. By the end of the 1972–1976 legislative term, massive procedural and structural changes to the legislature were written into legislative rules, statutes, and the just-adopted 1975 Constitution.

The results were dramatic. The changes made in the previous term were built up on and several provisions for direct oversight of the executive branch were added as well. The internal strength of the legislature was the subject of several new rules and acts. The committee system was further strengthened by abolishing the previous interim committees, replacing them with the relevant standing committees, and defining jurisdictional rules more extensively. Individual legislators not only received a microphone, but also a legislative assistant and district office space.

Provisions were made for space for individual offices for Senators and committee rooms and offices in both chambers. Greater restrictions were made on access to the floor of the Senate and House.

The centerpiece of the oversight provisions was the creation of a Legislative Fiscal Office that would monitor the spending of executive departments. The office of the Legislative Auditor was given greater authority as well. Together, these two offices could be used as an effective check on the governor and other statewide elected officials' power over the bureaucracy. With the political skill of Speaker E.L. "Bubba" Henry, the time and intellectual commitment of Clerk David Poynter, and the acquiescence of the Senate and the Governor, the House of Representatives had in eight short years given the Louisiana Legislature an enormous boost in structural power.

While the changes were made in Louisiana and carried out by Louisiana officials, they did not occur in a national vacuum. Indeed, many of the provisions were part of a national movement to make all state legislatures more effective. In order to evaluate the significance of the legislative reform movement in Louisiana, it is imperative to analyze it in terms of its actual impact on legislative independence, which is the focus of the next section.

UNDERSTANDING LEGISLATIVE STRUCTURE AND CAPABILITY

The activities and effects of a legislative body are not simply the products of individual member behavior. To be sure, individuals in a legislative body play an important role in shaping the legislature's effectiveness; nevertheless, organizational attributes of the institution powerfully impact legislative capability.

A legislature would be unable to make collective decisions if it were merely an assemblage of men and women from all over the country who met at intervals in the nation's capital. What converts these individuals into a body able to act is a structure for the organization of work and a set of rules by which it can proceed. The same can be said of state legislatures. Specifically, organizational characteristics in a state legislature establish its patterns of operation, shape policy outcomes, mold the divisions of power and channels of activity, and extend its legitimacy. '[O]rganizational characteristics are important features of a legislature because they define the situation in which legislative activity takes place, structure legislative behavior and activity, and establish the ways in which legislatures operate .... The impact of such organizational factors has been seen in both direct and indirect ways ....'

Chief among an institution's organizational characteristics are its structural attributes. Three examples suffice to illustrate the possible impact of structural arrangements on legislative capability. First, chamber size can affect procedural aspects. As the number of legislators in a chamber increases, greater hierarchical organizational structure, limited floor debate, and increased specialization among members follows. Second, committee system characteristics can also manage a legislature's effectiveness. The delineation of committee jurisdictions, the number of committees, the number of committee assignments per legislator, and inter-session committee stability impact the legislative decision-making process by affecting the time and information available for legislators. Finally, a sizable professional legislative staff is often understood to promote a legislature's effectiveness. 'The ability of [legislative] leaders to be effective depends in no small part on the size, professional skills, and experience of their staff.'

In order to move away from a system dependent on external sources of information, national trends in legislative improvement over the last few decades have stressed increasing in-house staff resources. From 1979 to 1996, total state legislative staff in the United States rose from just under 27,000 to 34,400. Permanent staff rose by almost 10,000, while session-only staff dropped by 2,500. Total number of staff employed increased in 36 legislatures.

One consequence of institutional reforms in the 1970s was an increased professionalism of state legislatures nationwide. An often used term to categorize and rank legislatures, 'professionalism' provides a 'concept that summarizes the differences between legislative institutions in terms of session length, size of legislative operations, and salary.' John G. Grumm's index of legislative professionalism established a 'summary score for each state based [upon] . . . biennial compensation of legislators; expenditures for legislative staff, services, operations, and printing; number of bills introduced in a session; length of session in calendar days; and a score measuring legislative services.' Based on data gathered in the 1960s, Grumm's index ranked the Louisiana Legislature as the sixteenth most professional in the country.

. . .

Professionalism and capability refer to different concepts and, therefore, involve measurement of different characteristics. While factors affecting professionalism, such as chamber size and session length, may also impact capability, an adequate measure of legislative capability based on structural characteristics demands a broader scope. For instance, measures of professionalism often do not include many reforms that occurred in Louisiana—characteristics of committee systems, terms of office for legislators, regulations regarding special legislation, municipal home rule laws, sunset laws, types of staff employed, or oversight and consent powers. These characteristics of a state's political institutions determine the power the legislature may exert in the political arena. Most importantly, professionalism fails to include a structural comparison of legislative characteristics vis-á-vis other political institutions, particularly the governor's office and executive branch.

. . .

Legislative capability in the context of [the CCSL report *State Legislatures: An Evaluation of Their Effectiveness* (1971)] denotes such abilities as the collection, analysis, and application of information, the ability to represent effectively the various interests and values held by a state's citizens, the ability independently to contribute to the formulation and review of state policies, the ability to conduct the basic activities necessary to function as a legislative body, and the ability of constituents to hold legislators and legislatures accountable for their actions.

The group established five major criteria to cover legislative capability and rank legislatures: Functional, Accountable, Informed, Independent, and Representative. 'Functional' involves the ability to carry out various activities basic to legislative performance.

. . .

'Accountable' involves the degree to which the body and its members can be held responsible for their actions. In evaluating legislative accountability, the study looks at the following: comprehensible forms and procedures; public access to legislative functioning; and ability of individual members to exert influence within the legislature.

'Informed' involves the ability to collect, analyze, and utilize information without depending on external sources. To measure this the study examines: adequacy and use of time; structure and use of standing committees as devices for specialization; use of interim periods; adequacy of bill documents; adequate professional staff; and capability to handle fiscal information.

The measure for 'Independent' involves the legislature's control over its own activities, including independence from the executive branch, powers for review, oversight and auditing, control of lobbyist activity, and rules regarding conflict of interest. The measure for 'Representative' involves: identification of members and constituents through use of single-member districts and establishment of district offices; reflection of population diversity in legislative membership; and rules and procedures that determine the effectiveness of individual legislators.

The Louisiana Legislature was ranked thirty third among the fifty state legislatures. The legislature ranked somewhat high on two of the criteria—thirteenth on Independent and fourteenth on Representative. However, the legislature scored fairly low on the remaining three criteria, forty-seventh on Functional, thirty-ninth on Accountable, and thirty-third on Informed. . . .

The LES has particular relevance for any historical analysis of the capability of the Louisiana Legislature because from this study the CCSL initiated The Program for Legislative Improvement (hereinafter 'PLI'). PLI was designed to study more intensively seven state legislatures, including Louisiana's, make specific detailed recommendations for improvement in each of the seven state legislatures, and work closely with state authorities toward implementation of these recommendations.

This program contributed to the trend of legislative reforms for Louisiana in the 1970s. Some significant recommendations presented to the Louisiana Legislature included: removal of constitutional restrictions on session subject matter; establishment of legislative power to call special sessions and to add subjects to the call of the governor; establishment of pre-session budget review; establishment of organizational and annual issue seminars; joining of standing committees for joint interim committees; election of the Senate's presiding officer by that body; and implementation of program review and evaluation. All in all, PLI in Louisiana included sixty-eight recommendations. Of these, nineteen were fully implemented, and seven were partially implemented.

. . .

THE POLITICS OF LEGISLATIVE INDEPENDENCE IN LOUISIANA

There is evidence that the reforms had some impact on legislative independence. For example, the new constitution authorized the legislature to carry out the massive restructuring of the executive branch of government in the late 1970s. This complete reorganization of state departments, offices and agencies was exempt from gubernatorial veto.

More telling, however, were some political ramifications. E. L. 'Bubba' Henry, the 'Young Turk' Speaker of the House and Chair of the Constitutional Convention, was not a gubernatorial pick. A little more than a decade later, several of Governor Roemer's choices for leadership positions were removed and replaced with the legislators' more independent choices.

Indeed, a dramatic coup occurred two years into Roemer's term when the Presidency of the Senate fell from his influence and was filled by an ally of his political nemesis, former and future governor Edwin Edwards. Finally, in perhaps the most dramatic episode of legislative autonomy, the Senate and House were able to muster and override Governor Roemer's veto of a bill, the first successful attempt at least since the implementation of the 1921 Constitution. Under the next administration, two of Governor Edwards's vetoes suffered the same fate.

However, these instances of legislative capability are notable mainly because they appear to be exceptions to the norm. Indeed, there is a preponderance of evidence to suggest that despite all reforms to invigorate the structural mechanisms of the state legislature, little demonstrable progress toward legislative independence has materialized. In fact, there are many indications to the contrary.

The spirit of reform clearly failed to sustain a critical mass of sympathetic legislators through the 1990s, as structural changes during this period reversed the direction of legislative improvement and markedly set back the movement toward a stronger legislative institution. Among the major achievements of the era of increasing legislative strength were significant changes in the legislatures' control of legislative sessions. During this period, several key recommendations that appeared in The Program for Legislative Improvement's 1973 report, *Louisiana Agenda for Legislative Improvement*, were put into the new constitution and had the effect of dissolving some of the governors' control over legislative sessions. The report recommended eliminating constitutional restrictions on session length and subject matter. Additionally, the report recommended legislative authority to call itself into special session and to add to the governor's call for a special session. These changes were considered critical by the PLI and by those legislators and convention delegates who wanted to make the legislature a coequal branch of government. However, a 1993 constitutional amendment did away with annual general sessions and restored the subject matter limitations on sessions. The limitations on fiscal sessions in even numbered years provided by the amendment are even more restrictive than were the provisions of the prior constitution. In addition, the necessity for more special sessions resulting from these restrictions has greatly enhanced the power of the governor to control what subject matters the legislature considers. Many legislators and observers of the legislature would agree that the impact of this reversal of legislative independence cannot be overstated.

Another structural setback to legislative capability was enacted in 1995, when legislators restricted themselves to a three-term limit. Scholarship on term limits points out that these limits on legislators weaken the legislature vis-á-vis the governor and executive branch agencies.

NOTES & QUESTIONS

1.   This article points out three ways in which legislatures can change: 1) chamber size, 2) the structure of committees, and 3) the size and make-up of legislative staff. What difference do these changes for the role of the representatives? How does it change the way the body operates?

2.   How could Congress or your legislature become more effective?

B. BICAMERALISM

Why is nearly every legislature divided into two chambers, a house and a senate? This was barely even a debate during the Constitutional Convention on this point. At the federal level having two chambers made the "Great Compromise" possible—the House would represent the people and would be elected proportionate to the population of each state. The Senate, however, was a living manifestation of the Union—each state equal in representation with two senators selected by the state's legislature.

There was no need for such a compromise when the various states adopted their constitutions. John Adams wrote the Massachusetts Constitution and there was no question of having a senate. For Adams, it was a matter of preventing a "natural aristocracy" from coming to dominate the population. He quoted James Harrington's *The Commonwealth of Oceana*:

"A commonwealth is but a civil society of men; let us take any number of men, as twenty, and immediately make a commonwealth. Twenty men, if they be not all idiots, perhaps if they be, can never come so together, but there will be such a difference in them, that about a third will be wiser, or at least less foolish, than all the rest. These, upon acquaintance, though it be but small, will be discovered, and (as stags that have the largest heads) lead the herd: for while the six, discoursing and arguing one with another, shew the eminence of their parts, the fourteen discover things that they never thought on, or are cleared in diverse truths that formerly perplexed them: wherefore, in matters of common concernment, difficulty, or danger, they hang upon their lips, as children upon their fathers; and the influence thus acquired by the six, the eminence of whose parts are found to be a stay and comfort to the fourteen, is the authority of the fathers—*auctoritas patrum*."

IN DEFENSE OF THE CONSTITUTIONS OF THE UNITED STATES
JOHN ADAMS (1790)

If there is then, in society, such a natural aristocracy as these great writers pretend, and as all history and experience demonstrate, formed partly by genius, partly by birth, and partly by riches, how shall the legislator avail himself of their influence for the equal benefit of the public? and how, on the other hand, shall he prevent them from disturbing the public happiness? I answer, by arranging them all, or at least the most conspicuous of them, together in one assembly, by the name of a senate; by separating them from all pretensions to the executive power; and by controuling, in the legislature, their ambition and avarice, by an assembly of representatives on one side, and by the executive authority on the other. Thus you will have the benefit of their wisdom, without fear of their passions. If among them there are some of Lord Bolingbroke's guardian angels, there will be some of his instruments of divine vengeance too: the latter will be here restrained by a three-fold tie; by the executive power, by the representative assembly, and by their peers in the senate. But if these were all admitted into a single popular assembly, the worst of them might in time obtain the ascendancy of all the rest. In such a single assembly, as has been observed before, almost the whole of this aristocracy will make its appearance; being returned members of it by the election of the people: these will be one class. There will be another set of members, of middling rank and circumstances, who will justly value themselves upon their independence, their integrity, and unbiassed affection to their country, and will pique themselves upon being under no obligation. But there will be a third class, every one of whom will have his leader among the members of the first class, whose character he will celebrate, and whose voice he will follow; and this party, after a course of time, will be the most numerous. The question then will be, whether this aristocracy in the house will unite or divide? and it is too obvious, that destruction to freedom must be the consequence equally of their union or of their division. If they unite generally in all things, as much as they certainly will in respecting each others wealth, birth, and parts, and conduct themselves with prudence, they will strengthen themselves by insensible degrees, by playing into each others hands more wealth and popularity, until they become able to govern elections as they please, and rule the people at discretion. An independent member will be their aversion; all their artifices will be employed to destroy his popularity among his constituents, and bring in a disciple of their own in his place.

But if they divide, each party will, in a course of time, have the whole house, and consequently the whole state, divided into two factions, which will struggle in words, in writing, and at last in arms, until Cæsar or Pompey must be emperor, and entail an endless line of tyrants on the nation. But long before this catastrophe, and indeed through every scene of the drama, the laws, instead of being permanent, and affording constant protection to the lives, liberties, and properties of the citizens, will be alternately the sport of contending factions, and the mere vibrations of a pendulum. From the beginning to the end it will be a government of men, now of one set, and then of another; but never a government of laws."

NOTES & QUESTIONS

1.   For James Madison, the point of the Senate was to slow down the legislative process. Senators were to be older, more experienced, chosen indirectly by the state legislators, and would serve long six-year terms. The Senate would provide "a necessary fence" against sudden shifts in public opinion. "The use of the Senate," he wrote, "is to consist in its proceeding with more coolness, with more system, & with more wisdom, than the popular

branch." See, "Madison, June 25, 1787," Adrienne Koch, ed., NOTES OF DEBATES IN THE FEDERAL CONVENTION OF 1787 REPORTED BY JAMES MADISON (Athens: Ohio University Press, 1966/1984).

2.   The following story may be apocryphal, but it gives a sense of how the Founders saw the Senate:

It is said that on his return from France after the framers had completed the U.S. Constitution, creating two houses of Congress, Thomas Jefferson called Washington to account for having agreed to a second chamber, the Senate, in the U.S. Congress.

"Of what use is the Senate?" he asked Washington, as he stood before the fire with a cup of tea in his hand. As he asked the question, Jefferson poured some of the tea into his saucer, swirled it around a bit, and then poured it back into the teacup.

"You have answered your own question," Washington replied.

"What do you mean?" Jefferson asked.

"Why did you pour the tea into your saucer?"

"To cool it," said Jefferson.

"Just so," said Washington, "that is why we created the Senate. The Senate is the saucer into which we pour legislation to cool."

THE SENATE AS A SAUCER—(Statement of Senator Robert Byrd (D-WV), Senate—April 24, 2006; GPO's PDF Page: S3408).

3.   "The bicameral structure of Congress serves a number of familiar values and purposes. Fundamentally, this structure creates different levels of representation. The House of Representatives provides a direct and immediate connection to the people through popular election every two years. Originally selected by state legislatures, the Senate provides for equal representation of each state. The Senate also serves as an upper chamber with more statesmanlike views as reflected in longer, staggered, six-year terms. . . .

With a bicameral legislature, lawmaking requires separate deliberation in the House and Senate and agreement between the two branches before presentment to the President. Article I, Section 7, reinforces that all bills and "[e]very Order, Resolution, or Vote to which the Concurrence of the Senate and House of Representatives may be necessary (except on a question of Adjournment)" must be presented to the President for his approval.

Bicameralism provides an internal check within Congress that ensures each branch restrains the other. As James Wilson argued, "If the Legislative authority be not restrained, there can be neither liberty nor stability; and it can only be restrained by dividing it within itself, into distinct and independent branches." The two branches represent different constituencies and therefore have somewhat different interests, further reinforcing the checking mechanism. Bicameralism raises the cost of legislating and checks factionalism, promoting legislation aimed at the general good and with due regard for the multitude of interests in society." "Why Congress Matters: The Collective Congress in the Structural Constitution," Neomi Rao, 70 *Fla. L. Rev.* 1 (2018).

4.   "The Constitution creates a collective Congress, but it also carefully specifies the structure, powers, and limits for the two branches of Congress and for individual senators and representatives. Moreover, the internal structure of Congress reflects values promoted by collective decision making, such as the minimization of factional influence, the fiduciary duty of members to the people, and the enactment of laws that promote the general good." See, "Why Congress Matters: The Collective Congress in the Structural Constitution," Neomi Rao, 70 *Fla. L. Rev.* 1 (2018).

As Prof. Rao points out, "The Constitution creates a bicameral Congress and provides the House and Senate with separate institutional dignity, but with no separate legislative powers." What are the distinct powers of each House, which the Supreme Court called "narrow, explicit, and separately justified" in *INS v. Chadha*?

Constitutional Power	House of Representatives	Senate
Impeachment	"the sole Power of Impeachment"	"the sole Power to try all Impeachments."
Nominations		Power to provide advice and consent for the officers, judges, and other officials nominated by the President.
Treaties		President has the power to "make Treaties, provided two thirds of the Senators present concur."
Money Bills	"All bills for raising revenue must start in the House of Representatives, but the Senate may propose or concur with amendments as in the case of other bills." U.S. CONST. Article I, Section 7, Clause 1	

Rules	Sole power over internal proceedings	Sole power over internal proceedings
Elections of members	Sole judge of elections to House U.S. CONST. ARTICLE I, SECTION 5	Sole judge of elections to the Senate U.S. CONST. ARTICLE I, SECTION 5
Punishment of members	Sole power to expel House members for "disorderly Behaviour."	Sole power to expel Senate members for "disorderly Behaviour."

5.   Bicameralism seems to be a bedrock of American legislatures, with 49 states and Congress having two chambers. Still, many nations and most municipalities have a unicameral legislature. In 1937, Nebraska became the only state to adopt a unicameral and non-partisan legislature. In this article, the former Lieutenant Governor of Nebraska extols the benefits of the non-partisan unicameral legislature, but also argues that other states will not adopt the format. Kim Robak, "The Nebraska Unicameral and its Lasting Benefits," 76 *Neb. L. Rev.* 791 (1997).

At the state level, some have argued that bicameralism lost its main purpose after the Supreme Court ruled in *Reynolds v. Sims*, which stated representation could not be based on geography, but must be proportionate: "Legislators represent people, not trees or acres. Legislators are elected by voters, not farms or cities or economic interests." The Court claimed that bicameralism would not be rendered "anachronistic and meaningless" with houses elected based solely on population, since a prime reason for that structure was "to insure mature and deliberate consideration of, and to prevent precipitative action on, proposed legislative measures."

Lt. Gov. Robak counters that legislative rules can allow for sufficient debate and gubernatorial review acts as a check and balance. Two houses act as a redundancy that "slows the process and allows members to conceal their own actions and to shift responsibility to the other house."

Lt. Gov. Robak also argues that "the most innovative feature" of the Unicameral Legislature is "its nonpartisan nature." She states, "Nonpartisanship in the Unicameral requires senators to focus their constituent base rather than party platforms making the effect of legislation on their constituency the primary, if not the sole factor and motivation for legislative action. Legislative leaders are elected based on ability, "leadership becomes personal rather than party-based. When confidence and credibility are established, the Speaker can be and is a dynamic and effective force." Further, committee chairs are selected by the entire membership based on specific expertise, reducing leadership turnover because it is not based on party membership.

Lt. Gov. Robak admits there are some legitimate criticisms of the Unicameral, including a lack of strong leadership. "When everyone is equal, everyone is in charge, and thus no one is in charge." Legislation may stall and legislators often lack the power to push bills to completion. Legislative coalitions may break down due to a lack of party discipline, and overall, the legislative process may take longer. On the other hand, this defused power structure requires senators and interest groups to build a consensus to reach agreement, and potentially, "better reasoned and more thoroughly debated legislation."

In a bicameral system, a lack of leadership can be replaced by partisanship. In the Unicameral, therefore, a lack of leadership may be more apparent, and the vacuum is often filled by "the governor, coalitions of urban, rural, or ideological viewpoints, or public sentiment."

The Unicameral also makes lobbyists work harder, because they have to concentrate their efforts on all 50 unaffiliated senators rather than on a majority leader or powerful chair.

Lt. Gov. Robak also claims that the Nebraska Legislature will remain the sole Unicameral. First, it would be hard to find a chamber willing to vote itself out of existence. Second, the public is "leery of governmental innovation."

C. "PROFESSIONAL" V. "CITIZEN" LEGISLATURES

Different states have adopted different types of legislatures. Some states have legislatures that meet often enough where the members may consider themselves full-time, or "professional," legislators. Members are relatively well paid, and they are supported by a large full-time staff. Congress would certainly fall into this category. Other states retain the American tradition of part-time, so-called "citizen legislatures."

In 2017, the National Council of State Legislatures (NCSL) categorized 14 state legislatures as "part-time" and nine as "full-time." The other 26 were a hybrid of the two forms.

Part-time legislatures	Full-time Legislatures
Idaho	Alaska
Kansas	California
Maine	Illinois
Mississippi	Massachusetts
Montana	Michigan
New Hampshire	New York
New Mexico	Ohio
North Dakota	Pennsylvania

Part-time legislatures	Full-time Legislatures
Rhode Island	Wisconsin
South Dakota	
Utah	
Vermont	
West Virginia	
Wyoming	

Smaller more rural states tend to have part-time legislatures. Although part-time legislators may work on constituent issues year-round, they may devote perhaps less than half of the time of a full-time job legislating. In fact, states with so-called "citizen legislatures" celebrate the idea that its legislators must spend most of their time with their constituents. The Wyoming Legislature meets for just 40 days in odd numbered years for their general session. In even numbered years the Legislature meets for 20 days to conduct a budget session. Committee work takes place before and after the daily general sessions, and sometimes during the noon recess.

Because they are not paid very much, on average around $18,000, these legislators often must have another regular job. An extreme example of "citizen legislature" pay is New Hampshire, where legislators receive $200 per term plus milage costs. The Speaker of the House and the Senate President receive $250 per term. These legislatures also have relatively small staffs. The NCSL found that part-time legislatures had an average of 160 staff members. In Wyoming, legislators do not have individual staff. Instead, there is a small permanent, central, and non-partisan staff agency that is supplemented with temporary staff during sessions.

The *Citizen's Guide to the Wyoming Legislature* points out that a citizen legislature may keep legislators in closer touch with their constituents. On the other hand, its legislators do not have the same accommodations of a full-time legislature. For example, only a few legislators even have offices—most legislators get a desk on the floor of the House or Senate and perhaps a few file cabinet drawers in a committee meeting room. For most of the year Wyoming constituents contact their legislators either at home or place of business.

Full-time legislatures are the preference of several of the more-populous states. These legislators spend more than the equivalent of 80% of a full-time job on legislative matters and are paid, on average, over $82,000. This relatively high salary allows the legislator to view legislating as their job or profession. These legislatures employ, on average, 1,250 staff members. As of 2009, the New York Legislature employed 2,700 staff. Just one committee, the Assembly Ways and Means Committee, employed over 100 people with a $5 million budget. In contrast, in 2020 Wyoming appropriated $8.7 million to staff the entire legislature. The argument in favor of full-time legislatures is that legislatures with longer sessions and larger staffs are better able to make independent and informed policy decisions and balance the power of the executive branch.

According to the NCSL, the legislatures in just over half of the states fall somewhere in between, although many will continue to style themselves "citizen legislatures." These hybrids pay legislators, on average, $41,000 and employ an intermediately sized staff with an average of 469.

Texas fell into the NCSL's hybrid category. Despite the Lone Star State's size and population, its legislature is part-time, and legislators are paid $7,200 a year. The Texas Legislature was likely categorized as a hybrid because of its lengthier regular session—140 days spread over five months every other year. The Constitution only requires the Legislature to meet every other year because of the difficulty of bringing legislators together from such a large state before modern transportation. One commentator notes, however, that this short session results in logjams of legislation requiring special sessions called by the governor. Still, there seems to be little interest in expanding the legislative calendar.

The low salary is set by the Texas Constitution. To change legislators' salary requires a recommendation from the Texas Ethics Commission and the voters amending the Constitution. The current salary dates back to 1975, before which legislators made $4,800. Lawmakers also receive $190 per day during the session ($5,600 total) to cover their expenses.

Sources:

- *Citizen's Guide to the Wyoming Legislature* (https://wyoleg. gov/leginfo/guide98.htm#citizen).

- *New Hampshire Almanac* (https://www.nh.gov/almanac/ government.htm#:~:text=New%20Hampshire%20takes%20 pride%20in,homemakers%2C%20students%2C%20and%20 lawyers.)

- Brian Weberg, "Full- and Part-Time Legislatures," National Council of State Legislatures, June 14, 2017.

- Jacob Gershman, "NY's bloated Legislature," New York Post, November 25, 2009 (https://nypost.com/2009/11/25/nys-bloated-legislature/)

- Alex Samuels "Hey, Texplainer: Why does a state as big as Texas have a part-time Legislature?" Texas Tribune (2017)

(https://www.texastribune.org/2017/12/08/hey-texplainer-
why-does-texas-have-part-time-legislature/)

D. WHO SHOULD BE IN A LEGISLATURE?

"The principal Difficulty lies, and the greatest Care should be taken in constituting this Representative Assembly. It should be, in Miniature, an exact Portrait of the People at large. It should think, feel, reason, and act like them."—John Adams, letter to William Hooper, 27 March 1776

BOND V. FLOYD
Supreme Court of the United States
385 U.S. 116 (1966)

MR. CHIEF JUSTICE WARREN delivered the opinion of the Court.

[Note: Julian Bond was elected to the Georgia House of Representatives in 1965. Bond was the communications director for the Student Nonviolent Coordinating Committee (SNCC). Shortly before Bond was sworn in as a legislator, SNCC issued a statement opposing the war in Vietnam:

'We believe the United States government has been deceptive in its claims of concern for freedom of the Vietnamese people, just as the government has been deceptive in claiming concern for the freedom of colored people in such other countries as the Dominican Republic, the Congo, South Africa, Rhodesia and in the United States itself.

'We, the Student Nonviolent Coordinating Committee, have been involved in the black people's struggle for liberation and self determination in this country for the past five years. Our work, particularly in the South, has taught us that the United States government has never guaranteed the freedom of oppressed citizens, and is not yet truly determined to end the rule of terror and oppression within its own borders.

. . .

'We are in sympathy with, and support, the men in this country who are unwilling to respond to a military draft which would compel them to contribute their lives to United States aggression in Viet Nam in the name of the 'freedom' we find so false in this country.

'We recoil with horror at the inconsistency of a supposedly 'free' society where responsibility to freedom is equated with the responsibility to lend oneself to military aggression. We take note of the fact that 16 per cent of the draftees from this country are Negroes called on to stifle the liberation of Viet Nam, to preserve a 'democracy' which does not exist for them at home.

'We ask, where is the draft for the freedom fight in the United States?

'We therefore encourage those Americans who prefer to use their energy in building democratic forms within this country. We believe that work in the civil rights movement and with other human relations organizations is a valid alternative to the draft. We urge all Americans to seek this alternative, knowing full well that it may cost their lives—as painfully as in Viet Nam.'

Although Bond claimed to a reporter he did not participate in the drafting of the statement, he endorsed the message telling a reporter that he was he was against the war and the draft. When asked by the reporter if he could take the oath of office required by the Georgia Constitution, he stated that he saw nothing inconsistent between his statements and the oath.]

Before January 10, 1966, when the Georgia House of Representatives was scheduled to convene, petitions challenging Bond's right to be seated were filed by 75 House members.

These petitions charged that Bond's statements gave aid and comfort to the enemies of the United States and Georgia, violated the Selective Service laws, and tended to bring discredit and disrespect on the House. The petitions further contended that Bond's endorsement of the SNCC statement 'is totally and completely repugnant to and inconsistent with the mandatory oath prescribed by the Constitution of Georgia for a Member of the House of Representatives to take before taking his seat.' For the same reasons, the petitions asserted that Bond could not take an oath to support the Constitution of the United States. When Bond appeared at the House on January 10 to be sworn in, the clerk refused to administer the oath to him until the issues raised in the challenge petitions had been decided.

Bond filed a response to the challenge petitions in which he stated his willingness to take the oath and argued that he was not unable to do so in good faith. He further argued that the challenge against his seating had been filed to deprive him of his First Amendment rights, and that the challenge was racially motivated. A special committee was appointed to report on the challenge, and a hearing was held to determine exactly what Bond had said and the intentions with which he had said it.

. . .

Tapes of an interview Bond had given the press after the clerk had refused to give him the oath were also heard by the special committee. In this interview, Bond stated:

'I stand before you today charged with entering into public discussion on matters of National interest. I hesitate to offer explanations for my actions or deeds where no charge has been levied against me other than the charge that I have chosen to speak my mind and no explanation is called for, for no member of this House, has ever, to my knowledge, been called upon to explain his public statements for public postures as a prerequisite to admission to that Body. I therefore, offer to my constituents a statement of my views. I have not counseled burning draft cards, nor have I burned mine. I have suggested that congressionally outlined alternatives to military service be extended to building democracy at home. The posture of my life for the past five years has been calculated to give Negroes the ability to participate in formulation of public policies. The fact of my election to public office does not lessen my duty or desire to express my opinions even when they differ from those held by others. As to the current controversy because of convictions that I have arrived at through examination of my conscience I have decided I personally cannot participate in war.

'I stand here with intentions to take an oath—that oath they just took in there—that will dispel any doubts about my convictions or loyalty.'

The special committee gave general approval in its report to the specific charges in the challenge petitions that Bond's endorsement of the SNCC statement and his supplementary remarks showed that he 'does not and will not' support the Constitutions of the United States and of Georgia, that he 'adheres to the enemies of the * * * State of Georgia' contrary to the State Constitution, that he gives aid and comfort to the enemies of the United States, that his statements violated the Universal Military Training and Service Act, and that his statements 'are reprehensible and are such as tend to bring discredit to and disrespect of the House.' On the same day the House adopted the committee report without findings and without further elaborating Bond's lack of qualifications, and resolved by a vote of 184 to 12 that 'Bond shall not be allowed to take the oath of office as a member of the House of Representatives and that Representative-Elect Julian Bond shall not be seated as a member of the House of Representatives.'

. . .

While this appeal was pending, the Governor of Georgia called a special election to fill the vacancy caused by Bond's exclusion. Bond entered this election and won overwhelmingly. The House was in recess, but the Rules Committee held a hearing in which Bond declined to recant his earlier statements. Consequently, he was again prevented from taking the oath of office, and the seat has remained vacant. Bond again sought the seat from the 136th District in the regular 1966 election, and he won the

Democratic primary in September 1966, and won an over-whelming majority in the election of November 8, 1966.

The Georgia Constitution sets out a number of specific provisions dealing with the qualifications and eligibility of state legislators. These provide that Representatives shall be citizens of the United States, at least 21 years of age, citizens of Georgia for two years, and residents for one year of the counties from which elected. The Georgia Constitution further provides that no one convicted of treason against the State, or of any crime of moral turpitude, or a number of other enumerated crimes may hold any office in the State. Idiots and insane persons are barred from office, and no one holding any state or federal office is eligible for a seat in either house. The State Constitution also provides:

> 'Election, returns, etc.; disorderly conduct.—Each House shall be the judge of the election, returns, and qualifications of its members and shall have power to punish them for disorderly behavior, or misconduct, by censure, fine, imprisonment, or expulsion; but no member shall be expelled, except by a vote of two-thirds of the House to which he belongs.'

These constitute the only stated qualifications for membership in the Georgia Legislature and the State concedes that Bond meets all of them. The Georgia Constitution also requires Representatives to take an oath stated in the Constitution:

> "Oath of members.—Each senator and Representative, before taking his seat, shall take the following oath, or affirmation, to-wit: 'I will support the Constitution of this State and of the United States, and on all questions and measures which may come before me, I will so conduct myself, as will, in my judgment, be most conducive to the interests and prosperity of this State.' "

The State points out in its brief that the latter part of this oath, involving the admonition to act in the best interests of the State, was not the standard by which Bond was judged.

The State does not claim that Bond refused to take the oath to support the Federal Constitution, a requirement imposed on state legislators by Art. VI, cl. 3, of the United States Constitution:

> 'The Senators and Representatives before mentioned, and the Members of the several State Legislatures, and all executive and judicial Officers, both of the United States and of the several States, shall be bound by Oath or Affirmation, to support this Constitution; but no religious Tests shall ever be required as a Qualification to any Office or public Trust under the United States.'

Instead, it argues that the oath provisions of the State and Federal Constitutions constitute an additional qualification. Because under state law the legislature has exclusive jurisdiction to determine whether an elected Representative meets the enumerated qualifications, it is argued that the legislature has power to look beyond the plain meaning of the oath provisions which merely require that the oaths be taken. This additional power is said to extend to determining whether a given Representative may take the oath with sincerity. The State does not claim that it should be completely free of judicial review whenever it disqualifies an elected Representative; it admits that, if a State Legislature excluded a legislator on racial or other clearly unconstitutional grounds, the federal (or state) judiciary would be justified in testing the exclusion by federal constitutional standards. But the State argues that there can be no doubt as to the constitutionality of the qualification involved in this case because it is one imposed on the State Legislatures by Article VI of the United States Constitution. Moreover, the State contends that no decision of this Court suggests that a State may not ensure the loyalty of its public servants by making the taking of an oath a qualification of office. Thus the State argues that there should be no judicial review of the legislature's power to judge whether a prospective member may conscientiously take the oath required by the State and Federal Constitutions.

We are not persuaded by the State's attempt to distinguish, for purposes of our jurisdiction, between an exclusion alleged to be on racial grounds and one alleged to violate the First Amendment. The basis for the argued distinction is that, in this case, Bond's disqualification was grounded on a constitutional standard—the requirement of taking an oath to support the Constitution. But Bond's contention is that this standard was utilized to infringe his First Amendment rights, and we cannot distinguish, for purposes of our assumption of jurisdiction, between a disqualification under an unconstitutional standard and a disqualification which, although under color of a proper standard, is alleged to violate the First Amendment.

We conclude as did the entire court below that this Court has jurisdiction to review the question of whether the action of the Georgia House of Representatives deprived Bond of federal constitutional rights, and we now move to the central question posed in the case—whether Bond's disqualification because of his statements violated the free speech provisions of the First Amendment as applied to the States through the Fourteenth Amendment.

First Amendment rights, the State may nonetheless apply a stricter standard to its legislators. We do not agree.

Bond could not have been constitutionally convicted under 50 U.S.C.App. s 462(a), which punishes any person who 'counsels, aids, or abets another to refuse or evade registration.'—Bond's statements were at worst unclear on the question of the means to be adopted to avoid the draft. While the SNCC statement said 'We are in sympathy with, and support, the men in this country who are unwilling to respond to a military draft,' this statement alone cannot be interpreted as a call to unlawful refusal to be drafted. Moreover, Bond's supplementary statements tend to resolve the opaqueness in favor of The State argues that the exclusion does not violate the First Amendment because the State has a right, under Article VI of the United States Constitution, to insist on loyalty to the Constitution as a condition of office. A legislator of course can be required to swear to support the Constitution of the United States as a condition of holding office, but that is not the issue in this case, as the record is uncontradicted that Bond has repeatedly expressed his willingness to swear to the oaths provided for in the State and Federal Constitutions. Nor is this a case where a legislator swears to an oath pro forma while declaring or manifesting his disagreement with or indifference to the oath. Thus, we do not quarrel with the State's contention that the oath provisions of the United States and Georgia Constitutions do not violate the First Amendment. But this requirement does not authorize a majority of state legislators to test the sincerity with which another duly elected legislator can swear to uphold the Constitution. Such a power could be utilized to restrict the right of legislators to dissent from national or state policy or that of a majority of their colleagues under the guise of judging their loyalty to the Constitution.

Certainly there can be no question but that the First Amendment protects expressions in opposition to national foreign policy in Vietnam and to the Selective Service system. The State does not contend otherwise. But it argues that Bond went beyond expressions of opposition, and counseled violations of the Selective Service laws, and that advocating violation of federal law demonstrates a lack of support for the Constitution. The State declines to argue that Bond's statements would violate any law if made by a private citizen, but it does argue that even though such a citizen might be protected by his legal alternatives to the draft, and there is no evidence to the contrary. On the day the statement was issued, Bond explained that he endorsed it 'because I like to think of myself as a pacifist and one who opposes that war and any other war and eager and anxious to encourage people not to participate in it for any reason that they choose.' In the same interview, Bond stated categorically that he did not oppose the Vietnam policy because he favored the Communists; that he was a loyal American citizen and supported the Constitution of the United States. He further stated 'I oppose the Viet Cong fighting in Viet Nam as much as I oppose the United States fighting in Viet Nam.' At the hearing before the Special Committee of the Georgia House, when asked his position on persons who burned their draft cards, Bond replied that he admired the courage of persons who 'feel strongly enough about their convictions to take an action like that knowing the consequences that they will face.' When pressed as to whether his admiration was based on the violation of federal law, Bond stated:

'I have never suggested or counseled or advocated that any one other person burn their draft card. In fact, I have mine in my pocket and will produce it if you wish. I do not advocate that people should break laws.

What I simply try to say was that I admired the courage of someone who could act on his convictions knowing that he faces pretty stiff consequences.'

Certainly this clarification does not demonstrate any incitement to violation of law. No useful purpose would be served by discussing the many decisions of this Court which establish that Bond could not have been convicted for these statements consistently with the First Amendment.

Nor does the fact that the District Court found the SNCC statement to have racial overtones constitute a reason for holding it outside the protection of the First Amendment. In fact the State concedes that there is no issue of race in the case.

Times case disposes of the claim that Bond's statements fell outside the range of constitutional protection. Just as erroneous statements must be protected to give freedom of expression the breathing space it needs to survive, so statements criticizing public policy and the implementation of it must be similarly protected. The State argues that the New York Times principle should not be extended to statements by a legislator because the policy of encouraging free debate about governmental operations only applies to the citizen critic of his government. We find no support for this distinction in the New York Times case or in any other decision of this Court. The interest of the public in hearing all sides The State attempts to circumvent the protection the First Amendment would afford to these statements if made by a private citizen by arguing that a State is constitutionally justified in exacting a higher standard of loyalty from its legislators than from its citizens. Of course, a State may constitutionally require an oath to support the Constitution from its legislators which it does not require of its private citizens. But this difference in treatment does not support the exclusion of Bond, for while the State has an interest in requiring its legislators to swear to a belief in constitutional processes of government, surely the oath gives it no interest in limiting its legislators' capacity to discuss their views of local or national policy.

The manifest function of the First Amendment in a representative government requires that legislators be given the widest latitude to express their views on issues of policy. The central commitment of the First Amendment, as summarized in the opinion of the Court in *New York Times v. Sullivan*, 376 U.S. 254 (1964), is that 'debate on public issues should be uninhibited, robust, and wide-open.' We think the rationale of the New York of a public issue is hardly advanced by extending more protection to citizen-critics than to legislators. Legislators have an obligation to take positions on controversial political questions so that their constituents can be fully informed by them, and be better able to assess their qualifications for office; also so they may be represented in governmental debates by the person they have elected to represent them. We therefore hold that the disqualification of Bond from membership in the Georgia House because of his statements violated Bond's right of free expression under the First Amendment. Because of our disposition of the case on First Amendment grounds, we need not decide the other issues advanced by Bond and the amici.

NOTES & QUESTIONS

1.   Why did the Georgia House work so hard to prevent Bond from taking his seat?

2.   How else could the House have dealt with a member like Bond?

3.   Contrast *Bond v. Floyd* with *Wheatley v. Secretary of the Commonwealth*, 439 Mass. 849 (2003), where the incumbent representative won the election by twelve votes, which increased to 17 votes after a recount. At that point, the Governor issued the incumbent a certificate of election and the challenger filed suit in the Superior Court. After an evidentiary hearing, the judge found three instances of voting irregularities, which he believed cast doubt on the outcome of the election. These included: voters who received the wrong ballot, a voting location that ran out of ballots causing three-dozen people to leave the voting area, and eight absentee ballots that were not counted because they contained votes for candidates in the wrong district. The judge ordered new election. Before a new election could take place, the House of Representatives assembled for the 2003–2004 session and the incumbent presented the certificate of election issued by the Governor. The House seated the incumbent while a special committee reviewed the election. The committee held a hearing to hear from the two candidates and their attorneys and reviewed the pleadings, exhibits, and transcripts of the court proceedings. A few months later, the House seated the incumbent on the recommendation of the special committee.

The Supreme Judicial Court reversed the superior court order finding a court's power to remedy election irregularities is limited by the Massachusetts Constitution Part II, c. 1, § 3, art. 10, which provides that "[t]he house of representatives shall be the judge of the returns, elections, and qualifications of its own members. . . ." The meaning of that provision was firmly settled as a matter of State constitutional law; "The constitutional authority of each branch of the Legislature to judge the elections, returns, and qualifications of its members is exclusive, comprehensive, and final." *Opinion of the Justices to the Senate*, 375 Mass. 795, 815, 376 N.E.2d 810 (1978). Where there is no allegation of a violation of Federal law, "[n]o other department of the government has any authority under the Constitution to adjudicate upon that subject." *Dinan v. Swig*, 112 N.E. 91. . . . The Court concluded that even if the challenger won a special election, the House's decision to seat the incumbent would still stand.

1. GERRYMANDERING

Gerrymandering has been a part of the American lexicon since its earliest days. The story is that Massachusetts Governor Elbridge Gerry re-drew legislative districts to protect his political allies. One newspaper reporter looked at the new district and said it looked like a salamander. Another reported allegedly said, "No, it's a Gerrymander." Some allege that gerrymandering allows representatives to pick their constituents, rather than the other way around.

Gerrymandering to deprive racial minorities any political power was common in the southern states during the "Jim Crow Era" from 1870–1965. The Voting Rights Act of 1965 prohibited such redistricting. In the 1980s, Congress required states to redraw maps if they had a "discriminatory effect."

The Voting Rights Act of 1965 also required nine states, mostly in the South, to get federal approval from the Justice Department before making changes to state voting laws. In 2013, however, the Supreme Court struck down those sections of the Act by a 5-to-4 vote in *County of Shelby Alabama v. Holder*. The law had applied to nine states—Alabama, Alaska, Arizona, Georgia, Louisiana, Mississippi, South Carolina, Texas and Virginia—and several counties and municipalities in other states, including Brooklyn, Manhattan and the Bronx.

The Court weighed whether racial minorities continued to face barriers to voting in these historically discriminatory states. Chief Justice John G. Roberts Jr. wrote for the majority, "Our country has changed. . .While any racial discrimination in voting is too much, Congress must ensure that the legislation it passes to remedy that problem speaks to current conditions."

The Act's preclearance requirement was originally scheduled to expire in 1970, but Congress repeatedly extended it. In 2006 Congress renewed the act after holding extensive hearings on the persistence of racial discrimination at the polls, extending the preclearance requirement for 25 years. Still, Congress relied on data from the 1975 reauthorization to decide which states and localities were covered. Chief Justice Roberts objected because localities were targeted "based on 40-year-old facts having no logical relationship to the present day."

Justice Ruth Bader Ginsburg vigorously dissented citing the words of the Rev. Dr. Martin Luther King Jr., "The great man who led the march from Selma to Montgomery and there called for the passage of the Voting Rights Act foresaw progress, even in Alabama. . .'The arc of the moral universe is long,' he said, but 'it bends toward justice,' if there is a steadfast commitment to see the task through to completion."

Immediately after the decision, Texas announced that a voter identification law that had been blocked by courts would go into effect immediately, and that its redistricting maps would no longer need federal approval. See, Adam Liptak, "Supreme Court Invalidates Key Part of Voting Rights Act," *New York Times*, June 25, 2013.

The Supreme Court has also held that the Equal Protection Clause prevents jurisdictions from drawing district lines to favor racial groups. The Court struck down this so called "affirmative racial gerrymandering" in *Shaw v. Reno* (Shaw I) 509 U.S. 630 (1993). The Court held that plaintiffs "may state a claim by alleging that [redistricting] legislation, though race neutral on its face, rationally cannot be understood as anything other than an effort to separate voters into different districts on the basis of race, and that the separation lacks sufficient justification". Such redistricting "reinforces racial stereotypes and threatens to undermine our system of representative democracy by signaling to elected officials that they represent a particular racial group rather than their constituency as a whole."

In 2003, the Republican controlled Texas Legislature redrew the state's congressional districts to maximize the number of Republicans sent to the House. Typically, such redistricting is only done after the decennial federal census. In *League of United Latin American Citizens v. Perry*, 548 U.S. 399 (2006), the U.S. Supreme Court upheld most of the new congressional map. The 7–2 decision allows state legislatures to redraw and gerrymander districts as often as they like (not just after the decennial census). Justice John Paul Stevens, joined by Justice Stephen Breyer, dissented and pointed out that there was evidence that the only reason for the new map; former Texas Lt. Governor Bill Ratliffe, stated, "political gain for the Republicans was 110% the motivation for the plan." Justice Stevens opined that a plan whose "sole intent" was partisan could violate the Equal Protection Clause.

In recent years, partisans have used computer programs to redraw districts to maximize the number of seats in Congress for that party. After the 2010 census, several states did this, resulting in a 234 to 201 seat advantage for the Republicans, despite the Democrats getting 1.5 million more votes that year. In 2018 the Supreme Court considered two partisan gerrymandering cases—*Gill v. Whitford*, 138 S.Ct. 1916 (2018), dealing with the entire Wisconsin map and *Benisek v. Lamone*, 138 S.Ct. 1942 (2018), which challenged one district in Maryland. Part of the problem with partisan gerrymandering is that the Court has struggled to come up with a metric to determine the dividing line between districts that are politically motivated, and those that are so politically designed that they disenfranchise voters and violate the Equal Protection Clause. Ultimately, the Supreme Court avoided making a decision in both *Gill* and *Benisek* on technical reasons.

In the summer of 2019, the Court decided in *Rucho v. Common Cause*, 139 S.Ct. 2484 (2019) that the courts are powerless to hear challenges to partisan gerrymandering. In a 5–4 decision, Chief Justice Roberts wrote that the Constitution's drafters understood that politics would influence redistricting when they gave the task to the state legislatures. Therefore, partisan gerrymandering was a political question "beyond the reach of the federal courts."

2.   DIVERSITY OF LEGISLATORS

Bond's constituents—and even his former opponents—thought Bond would be a good representative of his district. If judged by race, priorities, and political outlook he would fit into Adams' conception of a "portrait in miniature" of the population sitting in the House. In other ways, he was different from many of his constituents if judged by education or socio-economic status. In reality, how much are representatives like the populations they represent?

a.   Race

The 117th Congress, which was sworn in on Jan. 3, 2021, was the most racially and ethnically diverse Congress ever, continuing a 12-year trend of greater diversity. Nearly a quarter of voting members (23%) were racial or ethnic minorities. Congress had 124 lawmakers that identified as Black, Hispanic, Asian/Pacific Islander or Native American, which is a 97% increase over the 107th Congress of 2001–03, which only had 63 minority members.

Despite these gains, Congress remains disproportionately White compared to the U.S. population. Whereas just 60% of the U.S. population is non-Hispanic White Americans, 77% of voting members of the 117th Congress fall in that category. In the House of Representatives, however, some races and ethnicities have become reflective of the country as a whole—13% of House members are Black, and Native Americans make up about 1% of both the House and the U.S. population. See, Katherine Schaeffer, "Racial, ethnic diversity increases yet again with the 117th Congress," Pew Research Center, January 28, 2021, (https://www.pew research.org/fact-tank/2021/01/28/racial-ethnic-diversity-increases-yet-again-with-the-117th-congress/)

While the racial and ethnic make-up of the House is catching up to the US population as a whole, the Senate remains overwhelmingly White. This chart shows all of the Senate members belonging to various groups since the direct election of senators in 1914.

Black	Asian/Pacific Islander	Hispanic	Native Americans
Edward W. Brooke (R-MA), 1967–1979	Hiram L. Fong (R-HI), 1959–1977	Octaviano Larrazolo (R-NM), 1928–29	Charles Curtis (R-KS), 1907–13; 1915–29 (Kaw)
Carol Moseley-Braun, (D-IL), 1993–1999	Daniel K. Inouye (D-HI), 1963–2012	Dennis Chavez (D-NM), 1935–1962	Robert Owen (D-OK), 1907–1925 (Cherokee)
Barack Obama (D-IL), 2005–2008	Samuel I. Hayakawa, (R-CA), 1977–1983	Joseph M. Montoya, (D-NM), 1964–77	Ben Nighthorse Campbell (R-CO), 1993–2005 (Northern Cheyenne)
Roland Burris (D-IL), 2009–2010	Spark M. Matsunaga, (D-HI), 1977–1990	Ken L. Salazar (D-CO), 2005–2009	
Tim Scott (R-SC), 2013–present	Daniel K. Akaka (D-HI), 1990–2013	Melquiades R. Martinez (R-FL), 2005–2009	
William "Mo" Cowan (D-MA), 2013	Mazie Hirono (D-HI), 2013–present	Robert Menendez (D-NJ), 2006–present	
Cory A. Booker (D-NJ), 2013–present	Tammy Duckworth, (D-IL), 2017–present	Marco Rubio (R-FL), 2011–present	
Kamala Harris (D-CA), 2017–2021	Kamala Harris (D-CA), 2017–2021	Ted Cruz (R-TX), 2013–present	
Raphael G. Warnock (D-GA), 2021–present		Catherine Cortez Masto (D-NV), 2017–present	

	Ben Ray Lujan (D-NM), 2021– present	
	Alex Padilla (D-CA), 2021– present	

Besides race, there are other differences, notably gender, education and wealth.

b.   Wealth

In 2019, the median net worth for a U.S. family was $121,760 according to the Federal Reserve. In 2015, the 535 members of Congress had a total net worth of $7 billion. The top five senators were worth over $200 million each. The median senator or representative had a net worth of $1.03 million.

c.   Gender

In a letter dated March 31, 1776, Abigail Adams wrote to her husband, John Adams, urging him and the Continental Congress not to forget about the nation's women:

> "I long to hear that you have declared an independency. And, by the way, in the new code of laws which I suppose it will be necessary for you to make, I desire you would remember the ladies and be more generous and favorable to them than your ancestors. Do not put such unlimited power into the hands of the husbands. Remember, all men would be tyrants if they could. If particular care and attention is not paid to the ladies, we are determined to foment a rebellion, and will not hold ourselves bound by any laws in which we have no voice or representation."

The first woman elected to Congress was Jeannette Rankin of Montana, who was elected to the House in 1916, four years before the ratification of the 19th Amendment in 1920. Rebecca Felton of Georgia became the first woman to serve in the Senate in 1921.

In 2018, there were 23 women serving in the Senate (23%); 84 women from 33 states were in the House (19.3%).

In 2021, there were 147 women serving in the 117th Congress: 24 in the Senate and 123 in the House.

As of 2018, California had sent more women to Congress than any other state—41. New York is second with 28. As of 2021, Vermont had never sent a woman to either the House or the Senate.

d. Education

According to the Census Bureau, in 2018, 35% of American adults had a bachelor's degree or more education, and 13% reported an advanced degree, such as a master's, professional, or doctorate degree.

In contrast, 93.8% of House Members and 100% of Senators of the 117th Congress (2021) have earned at least a bachelor's degree. Sixty-seven percent of House Members and 76% of Senators hold educational degrees beyond a bachelor's. A disproportionate number of members are lawyers: 144 House members (32.7%) and 50 Senators (50%). Twenty-two Representatives and 4 Senators have doctoral degrees. Twenty House members and 5 Senators have medical degrees.

— STOP!

NOTES & QUESTIONS

1.   What qualities would you want in a representative?

2.   If the Legislature is "a portrait in miniature of the population," there will be all types elected to the legislature. If you were a member of a legislature, how would you deal with a colleague that was of lower intelligence? Who was an ideologue? Who is corrupt?

3.   How important is legislative experience to the answer to question 1? The longer someone serves in a legislature, the person becomes more knowledgeable about politics and process, grows in influence, has institutional memory of what worked and what did not. On the other hand, spending many years in the legislature could mean that the representative grows out of touch with her constituency, makes decisions based on self-preservation, and becomes too close to special interests and party leadership. One way to deal with this is term limits.

Starting in 1990, several states imposed legislative term limits, typically through initiative campaigns, beginning with Oklahoma, California, and Colorado. In 2018, fifteen states imposed term limits. In nine states the limits are consecutive, meaning once a legislator has served the maximum number of terms in office, the person can either leave the legislature or run for a seat in the other legislative chamber. After a period of time, often two years, the person is again eligible to run for their former seat. This is the practice in Arizona, Colorado, Florida, Louisiana, Maine, Montana, Nebraska, Ohio and South Dakota.

In six term limit states, there is a lifetime limit; once a legislator has served the maximum number of terms in a legislative chamber, they are ineligible to run for or hold that seat again. This is the practice in Arkansas, California, Michigan, Missouri, Nevada and Oklahoma.

4.   Term limit advocates claim they prevent legislatures from being dominated by career politicians focused on attaining and keeping power. Others argue that term limits open up the legislature to new ideas and to women and minorities.

Political science professor Thad Kousser examined the effects of term limits and concluded that term limits has undone many of the benefits of the 20th Century trend toward legislative professionalism.

Prof. Kousser first considered how professionalism and term limits affect internal organization and dynamics. He concluded that whereas professionalization stabilizes legislative leadership, term limits encourage challenges to leadership. Whereas professionalization leads to greater independence for legislative committees, term limits make committees less active. Finally, term limits lead to greater polarization over claims of legislative achievement.

Prof. Kousser found professionalization strengthened the legislature against the governor and term limits gave the governor an advantage when it came to budget and operational operations. Finally, Prof. Kousser finds professionalism increases innovative policy, while term limits decrease innovation. He concludes, "[W]hatever a higher level of professionalism produces more of, term limits has reduced." See, Thad Kousser, *Term Limits and the Dismantling of State Legislative Professionalism* (Cambridge University Press, 2004).

5.   One criticism of Prof. Kousser's book states that that undoing the effects of legislative professionalism was the main goal of the term limits movement. One commentator states that Prof. Kousser is biased and prefers professional legislatures, and "writes as though the imposition of term limits had inadvertently destroyed the work of professionalization." Still, term limits are meant to check the undesirable effects of professionalism. See, Michelle S. Friedman, "Legislative Term Limits and Professionalism: Examining the Obvious Link," 16 *U. Fla. J.L. & Pub. Pol'y* 635 (2005).

6.   In 2014, physics Professor Michael S. Lubell decried the lack of scientists in Congress. In 2008, the House of Representatives included five Ph.D. holding scientists: three physicists, one chemist and one mathematician. By 2014, that number was down to two. In contrast, 60 percent in the Senate and about a third in the House were lawyers. Prof. Lubell argues that a law degree is "no longer a sufficient credential for legislating on science," and "In a world in which science and technology increasingly control the roll of the dice, we simply cannot afford to gamble solely on lawmakers who don't fully understand the rules of the science game or the odds of the next bet." For example, he points out that the FIRST Act, which the House Science, Space and Technology Committee offered to "prioritize 'science investments to keep America first,'" but which some scientists argued would do the opposite. For example, the bill seemed to assume typical research projects would be completed within five years, "Yet in the fields of high-energy physics, nuclear physics and astronomy, many projects require a decade or more to reach

fruition." See, Michael S. Lubell "Scientists Are Becoming a Rarer Congressional Breed, and That's Not a Good Thing," *Rollcall*, Mar 25, 2014.

E. LEGISLATIVE LEADERSHIP

1. THE SENATE

"The Vice President of the United States shall be President of the Senate, but shall have no Vote, unless they be equally divided."— U.S. CONST, Article I, Sec. 3, clause 4.

Connecticut delegate Roger Sherman said, "if the vice-President were not to be President of the Senate, he would be without employment, and some member [of the Senate, acting as presiding officer] must be deprived of his vote." The first two vice presidents, John Adams and Thomas Jefferson, helped shape the President of the Senate office and set many Senate precedents. During the 18th and 19th centuries, the Vice President was seen as a primarily legislative officer, and some exerted influence over the body by personality, parliamentary skill, and interest in the operations of the Senate. Some found the job boring, could not maintain order, or left the job to the president pro tempore. During the 20th century, the vice president was increasingly viewed as an important part of a president's administration and presides over the Senate only on ceremonial occasions or when a tie-breaking vote may be needed.

"The Senate shall chuse their other Officers, and also a President pro tempore, in the Absence of the Vice President, or when he shall exercise the Office of President of the United States." U.S. CONST. Article I, Sec. 3, clause 5.

The president pro tempore (Latin meaning "for the time being") is an elected member of the Senate and may speak and vote on any issue. Since the mid-20th century, the senior member of the majority party has been elected president pro tempore. Since 1947, the order of succession for a presidential vacancy has been: the vice president, the speaker of the house, the president pro tempore, the secretary of state, and after that, the cabinet members in order in which the office was created.

U.S. Senate Leadership

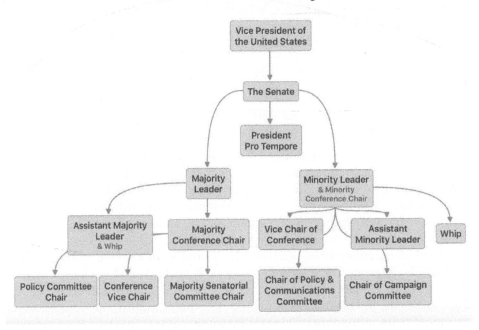

Party floor leaders are not mentioned in the Constitution but was an innovation of the 20th century. The Democrats first elected a floor leader in 1920, and in 1925 the Republicans followed suit. The Majority and Minority Leaders are elected by the Senate members of their party at the beginning of each Congress. The leaders are spokespersons for their party's positions on issues. The majority leader schedules the daily legislative program, and (with unanimous consent) sets the time for debate. The majority leader has the right to be called upon first in debate, which allows the leader to control the agenda by offering motions or amendments before any other senator.

Senate leaders have few defined powers but work together to seek to balance the needs of senators to express themselves fully while moving bills toward enactment. Lyndon Johnson, a successful Senate majority leader during the 1950s, said that the majority leader's greatest power was "the power of persuasion."

Whips assist the leaders and are elected by the party caucuses. "Whip" is a hunting expression, to "whipper-in," which is the hunter responsible for keeping the dogs from straying while chasing an animal. These assistant leaders are mainly responsible for counting votes and persuading members to vote with leadership. Occasionally, the whip may stand in for the majority or minority leaders in their absence.

Conference chairs lead the closed sessions of party members known as party conferences (or party caucuses). The conference or caucus elects floor leaders, makes committee assignments, and sets legislative agendas. The position developed for both parties in the mid 19th century. The Democratic floor leader serves as conference chair, while the Republican party separates the positions.

Policy Committee Chairs are elected by each party's caucus to help set policy. The post was first created in 1947.

Case Study: Senate President Mike Miller

Until his death in January 2020, Maryland Senate President Thomas V. "Mike" Miller Jr. was the longest-serving Senate president in the country and offered an example of how to successfully run a legislative chamber. A moderate Democrat, in 2018 Miller faced a strong challenge by progressives, due in part to a belief that Miller thwarted efforts to impose a $15 minimum wage and sanctuary protections for immigrants. After the primaries, several of his top allies in the Senate lost their seats. These losses and the nomination of a progressive Democrat for governor threatened "to drive a wedge through Miller's carefully calibrated chamber."

Miller was elected to the Maryland House in 1971 and to the Senate in 1975. He served as the senate president for 33 years—from 1987 until 2020 when he resigned his seat for health reasons. Some observers said his leadership "offers a master class in diplomacy, adaptation and the cultivation of political power."

While some people claimed Miller was an autocratic ruler, others pointed out that Miller worked hard to court the loyalty of his colleagues— treating other senators like family, understanding their districts and learning the details of their personal lives. Miller credited learning lessons on customer-service by working at his family's community liquor and general store.

Miller was a practicing Catholic, which tended to make him more conservative than many of the other senators in his caucus. For instance, in 2012 he opposed—and voted against—same-sex marriage. Still, a leader of the Senate, he paved the way for the law to pass. Miller said he understood his personal views were "on the wrong side of history."

Miller was also very good at adjusting to new circumstances. The 2018 "Take a Hike Mike" campaign by the Service Employees International Union (SEIU) was specifically aimed at ousting Miller from the senate presidency by defeating his allies. Miller won his primary by 40 percentage points, but several of his top lieutenants lost. Miller, however, welcomed the new nominees to his office and started to learn about them personally and professionally. He reportedly bonded with the new members over a common love of political history or the university they both attended. Miller also appointed a new group of committee chairs and vice chairs for what would be his last legislative session with an obvious effort to give leadership positions to women and racial minorities.

See, Erin Cox & Ovetta Wiggins, "His Top Lieutenants Lost Their Jobs. So Senate President Mike Miller Dug In," *Washington Post*, August 24, 2018.

2. THE HOUSE OF REPRESENTATIVES

"The House of Representatives shall chuse their Speaker and other Officers. . ."—U.S. CONST. Article I, Section 2.

U.S. House Leadership

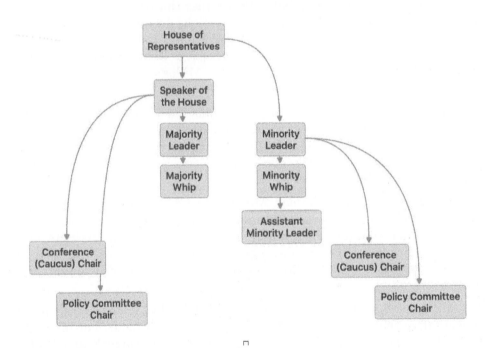

The **Speaker** is the political and parliamentary leader of the House of Representatives. While the speaker does not have to be a member the House to serve, only members have been elected speaker so far. The speaker, therefore, has the same obligations to their constituents, but holds an extraordinary amount of power. In a new Congress, the majority and minority caucuses each select a candidate for speaker and the entire body votes and elects—almost always—the majority candidate. By Constitutional amendment, the Speaker of the House is second in line to succeed the President, after the Vice President.

The **Majority Leader** works with the speaker to conduct legislative business and as the second officer of the majority caucus, works to enforce party discipline. During the last half of the 19th Century, the majority party depended on influential chairmen; often from the Ways and Means or Appropriations Committees to manage debate for the majority. By 1919, the majority leader became a formal office.

The **Minority Leader** speaks for minority party members and the party's policies and works to protect the minority's rights.

Whips assist the leadership in managing their party's legislative program on the House Floor. The whip provides a communications network for the members of their conference and mobilizes them for important party measures coming up for a vote. First created by the Republican caucus in 1897, the whips have grown in importance. Whips are elected by their party caucus at the start of a new Congress. When in the majority, the whip is the third highest position in the caucus, behind the majority leader and the speaker. When in the minority, the Whip is the second highest position behind the minority leader. Several members in each caucus may be elected as deputy whips.

The House **Caucus (or Conference) Chairs** preside over caucus meetings, which are composed of all members of a party. The caucus elects party leaders and meets on a weekly basis to discuss party policy, pending legislative issues, and other matters of mutual concern. The chair is elected by the caucus.

The **House and Senate Policy Committees** are formal councils to meet regularly with leadership and the Administration to formulate and carry out national policy.

Case Study: The US Speaker of the House & the Austin-Boston Connection

Some may argue that the House of Representatives was most effective as an institution during the so-called "Austin-Boston Connection" that produced a string of speakers while Democrats dominated the institution from the 1930s until 1995.

The Austin-Boston Connection was essentially an apprenticeship program where House leaders identified younger members with leadership potential and groomed them to potentially assume the speakership in the future. When the House elected a speaker during this period, they came to office with years of training and experience in the specific tasks needed to run the large and rule-bound chamber. These speakers understood how to use the levers of power to pass legislation, control their own caucus, and how to deal with the opposing party. In contrast, speakers after 1995 had significantly less experience in leadership, partisanship dominated the House, and the productivity of the chamber dropped off dramatically.

In a quirk of history, the speakers during this six-decade run of the Austin-Boston Connection came from a select number of districts near northeastern Texas or around Boston, Massachusetts.

- When Sam Rayburn (D-TX) first became speaker in 1940, he had not only been the majority leader for nearly four years, but he had also been the speaker of the Texas House for two years—starting at the age of 29. When he retook the speakership for the last time in 1955, he had over 10 years previous experience as speaker and 4 more years as minority leader.

- John McCormack (D-MA)(1962–1971), was the Majority Leader for 18 years before being Speaker.

- Carl Albert (D-OK) (1971–1977) was majority whip for seven years and majority leader for nine years before taking the gavel.

- Thomas "Tip" O'Neill (D-MA) (1977–1987) was previously the Massachusetts House Speaker for four years, served two years as majority whip and spent four more years as majority leader before becoming Speaker.

- Jim Wright (D-TX) (1987–1989) was majority leader for 10 years before his two-year speakership.

- Tom Foley (D-WA) (1989–1995) became speaker, he had been majority whip for six years and majority leader for two and a half years.

From 1995–2018; half of the time the Austin-Boston era, there have been five speakers with a combined five years of prior experience running the House as either the majority whip or leader:

- Newt Gingrich (R-GA)(1995–1999) was a minority whip for five years.

- Dennis Hastert (R-IL)(1999–2007) was majority whip for four years.

- Nancy Pelosi (D-CA)(2007–2011) was minority whip for only one year.

- John Boehner (R-OH)(2011–2015) was majority leader for one year, minority leader for four years and a committee chairman for five years.

- Paul Ryan (R-WI)(2015–2019) was a committee chairman for five years before being drafted by his caucus to be speaker.

The difference in productivity between the two groups of leaders is stunning. From 1973–2015, nine of the ten most productive Congresses, according to a 2015 analysis by Alex Greer, were led by Albert, O'Neill, Wright, and Foley. The lone post Austin-Boston speaker is Hastert at #10 from 1999–2001. The least productive Congresses during that time were the two led by Boehner—2011–2015.

Many factors could contribute to this fall off in productivity. Many point to the rise of the Tea Party and the "Freedom Caucus" within the Republican Conference. Still, the caucuses have rarely been ideologically coherent. When Speaker McCormack shepherded through maybe the most significant law of the 20th Century, the Civil Rights Act of 1964, 91 members of his caucus strongly opposed to the bill.

NOTES & QUESTIONS

1.   For an interesting history of this era, see, Anthony Champagne, Douglas B. Harris, James W. Riddlesperger Jr., & Garrison Nelson, *The Austin Boston Connection: Five Decades of House Democratic Leadership, 1937–1989* (2009). Why do you think the "Austin-Boston Connection" develop and exist for so long?

2.   What are the advantages and disadvantages of the Austin-Boston system?

3.   How are the challenges faced by a speaker different from those of a senate president or majority leader?

3.   CASE STUDY: THE KANSAS EXPERIMENT

In the Spring of 2017, Senate President Susan Wagle and Majority Leader Sen. Jim Denning faced some difficult decisions. In 2012, at the request of Governor Sam Brownback, the Kansas Legislature passed sweeping tax cuts. This included reducing the three income tax brackets to two and making pass through income from certain businesses untaxed. The purpose of the tax cuts was to spur economic growth, creating jobs and attracting people to the state. Ultimately, Gov. Brownback and his conservative allies in the Legislature wanted to eliminate the income tax altogether. This example of pure supply-side economics became known as the "Kansas Experiment." Over the next four years, however, the budget deficit exploded while the Supreme Court required substantial increases in school funding. During the 2016 elections, several conservative legislators lost their primaries to more moderate Republicans who were willing to undo the tax cuts. Still, the moderates and Democrats alone could not override the Governor's certain veto. This put the Senate President and the Majority Leader in a predicament. They were both tax cutting conservatives and staunch allies of the Governor. How would they react to this effort to undo the Governor's signature issue?

The Kansas Legislature

The Kansas Legislature consists of a 125-member House of Representatives and a 40-member Senate. Representatives are elected for a two-year term and Senators are elected for a four-year term. The Legislature convenes on the second Monday in January for an annual session and generally adjourns in early May.

While the Democrats are officially the minority party in the Legislature, the real power struggle over the past several decades has been between the conservative and moderate factions of the Republican Party. For many years, Kansas was represented in Congress by moderate Republicans such as Sen. Nancy Kassebaum and Sen. Bob Dole. Conservatives often chaffed as they saw moderates betray what they considered the core principals of the Republican Party, or worse, work across the aisle with Democrats.

What had been tense relationship became an all-out war by the 2012 elections. The conservatives gained a powerful champion when Sen. Dole's successor in the U.S. Senate, and arch conservative, Sam Brownback, was elected governor in 2010. During the 2012, the Kansas legislative elections gained national attention as Gov. Brownback, the Kansas Chamber of Commerce and Industry and the Koch Brother's PAC Americans for Prosperity primaried several moderate GOP members of the state senate. Former two-term Gov. Bill Graves, a moderate Republican, along with labor and teacher unions, worked to support moderate candidates.

In 2010, along with electing Gov. Brownback, conservative Republicans won a majority in the Kansas House of Representatives—around 70 of 125 seats. During the 2011 session, 14 moderate Republicans and 8 Democrats often voted together to the dismay of conservatives—especially when moderate members of the GOP caucus criticized Gov. Brownback's plans to steeply cut taxes. By the 2012 primaries, fighting between the moderates and conservatives had become nasty. Prof. Burdett A. Loomis, a political science professor at the University of Kansas, said, "The conservatives, they hate the moderate Republicans. They think they really have conspired with Democrats and have prevented conservative forces from their rightful place of dominating the government." Conservatives pointed to the previous session when moderates and Democrats passed a 1% sales tax increase, opposed tougher voter identification laws and for not repealing in-state tuition rights for illegal immigrants. Moderates responded that conservatives were too preoccupied with ideology and purity tests even when their approach is impractical.

Entering that primary, conservatives needed just three or four more seats to control the Senate. A total of nine Republican senators were defeated in the primary, eight of whom were targeted by conservatives for being too moderate.

Two of the beneficiaries of this conservative wave were Susan Wagle and Jim Denning.

Jim Denning earned a bachelor's degree in finance from Fort Hays State University and worked as the chief executive officer and on the board of directors of the Discover Vision Centers and was a financial analyst at the Dallas Federal Reserve Bank. Denning served in the House of Representatives from 2010–2012. In 2012, he defeated one of the moderate senate incumbents in the primary with the help of Gov. Brownback. In 2017, Sen. Denning became the Senate Majority Leader.

Senate President Susan Wagle had been a member of the Kansas Legislature representing Wichita since 1991. She spent a decade as a member of the House, and in 2001, was elected to the Senate. In 2011 Wagle became the Senate President. She is a 1979 graduate of Wichita State University and worked as a teacher for the Wichita Public Schools from 1979–1982. Later she became a business owner and real estate investor. She is a board member of the American Legislative Exchange Council. When running for reelection to the Senate in 2012, Sen. Wagle received large donations from the Kansas Chamber of Commerce and the Americans for Prosperity PAC.

The 2012 Tax Cuts

In his 2012 State of the State Message, Gov. Brownback made tax policy a centerpiece of his legislative agenda,

> Last session the Legislature gave our rural communities a new tool to help them reverse their population loss—and they have embraced the Rural Opportunity Zone program, offering no income tax and buying down of student loan debt to new or returning residents.
>
> . . .
>
> Still—the economy remains one of our most pressing issues. While there are certainly factors a state cannot control when it comes to its economy, taxes are one area we do control. And when it comes to taxes, we have some of the highest in the region. This hurts our economic growth and job creation.
>
> To address this, I'm proposing a major step in overhauling our state tax code to make it fairer, flatter, and simpler. My tax plan will lower individual income tax rates for all Kansans. It brings the highest tax rate down from 6.45 percent to 4.9 percent, the second lowest in the region—and lowers the bottom tax bracket to 3 percent. My plan also eliminates individual state income tax on most small business income.

As we modernize our tax code and lower everyone's rates, it is also time to level the playing field and simplify state taxes by eliminating income tax credits, deductions, and exemptions— while expanding assistance to low-income Kansans through programs that are more effective and accountable. I firmly believe these reforms will set the stage for strong economic growth in Kansas—and will put more money into the pockets of Kansas families and businesses. Growth that will allow us to further reduce tax rates and increase our competitiveness. Growth that will see people move to Kansas instead of leaving our state.

With that in mind, I ask the legislature to limit further growth in government expenditures to no more than 2 percent a year—and devote all additional revenues to reductions in state tax rates. This will get us ever closer to the pro-growth states with no state income taxes—which are among the country's strongest economic performers.

It also will enable us to keep the lid on state sales tax and property tax rates by providing robust economic growth. Let's put our "lost decade" in the rear view mirror and speed ahead—at 75 miles per hour—to make this decade the decade of growth and job creation.

The 2012 Tax Cuts

Gov. Brownback's call to the legislature for deep tax cuts on the way to no state income tax at all was not universally popular. As the Wall Street Journal noted, "Kansas effectively has two political parties: conservative Republicans and liberal Republicans." Despite a huge 31–9 majority in the Senate, Senate President Steve Morris opposed the Brownback plan. The *Wall Street Journal* characterized the Senate as trying to paint the Governor and the more conservative House into a corner by passing a giant tax cut with a huge cost to the state, which backfired. The path was a bit more complicated.

The tax scheme Gov. Brownback outlined in his state of the state address seemed politically unviable because it would eliminate many popular tax credits and exemptions and would disproportionately hurt low-income Kansans while giving tax cuts to wealthier residents and business owners.

When the governor's plan was first considered by a Senate committee, senators voted to retain many of the credits and deductions Brownback wanted to cut, which drastically increased the cost. Senators changed the bill even more on the floor before rejecting the bill by a vote of 20–20. The Administration pleaded with the Senate to approve the bill "so that House and Senate negotiators could work out a better plan." In a new vote, the Senate approved the amended bill 29–11. The vote was taken, however, with many senators believing Brownback would not sign the bill without significant changes. When asked if the bill could pass the house and be signed as it was, Senate President Steve Morris said flatly, "That won't happen."

Even though legislative negotiators worked out a less-expensive alternative plan during the next few weeks, House members feared the Senate might reject it. The House took the initiative and quickly passed the original Senate bill. The bill went to the governor, who tried to use the enacted bill as leverage to get lawmakers to approve an alternative tax bill. The Senate, however, voted 21–18 against debating an alternative plan. Gov. Brownback then signed the tax bill.

The new tax scheme made major changes. The law collapsed the state's three tax brackets (3.5, 6.25 and 6.45%) to two (3% and 4.9%). According to the Department of Revenue, the change was projected to result in a $570 a year benefit for married couples with a child filing jointly and earning $65,430 after federal deductions. A single parent with a child and an adjusted income of $20,000 would see a benefit of $43 a year.

The bill also

- Eliminated taxes on the profits business owners get from limited liability companies, subchapter S corporations, and sole proprietorships;

- Increased the standard deduction to $9,000 from $4,500 for single head-of-household taxpayers and $6,000 for married couples;

- Eliminated about 20 tax credits, including the food sales tax refund;

- Eliminated the child and dependent care credit.

The *Wall Street Journal* lavished praise upon the new Kansas tax scheme stating, "some enlightenment reigns in the American heartland." The Journal opined that the "tax cut will force state politicians to restrain spending, and above all it sends a signal to businesses and taxpayers that Kansas wants more of both."

While proponents claimed the tax cuts would spur economic growth within Kansas, opponents worried about the dramatic loss of revenue on programs such as education, health, and social programs as well as equity concerns. First, the nonpartisan Legislative Research Department prepared an estimate of the bill's costs for the Legislature:

Fiscal Year	(Millions of Dollars)
2013	231.2
2014	802.8
2015	824.3
2016	854.2
2017	892.9
2018	933.7

Kansas had a 2012 revenue of $6.4 billion. The Legislative Research Department predicted an annual reduction in revenue of approximately 12%–15% from 2014 through 2018. The Brownback Administration claimed that the tax regime would attract new businesses to Kansas, causing greater capital investment and hiring. By expanding the wage base, the State would offset most of the potential revenue loss. Gov. Brownback's press release claimed that, "Dynamic projections show the new law will result in 22,900 new jobs, give $2 billion more in disposable income to Kansans and increase population by 35,740, all in addition to the normal growth rate of the state." Still, The Kansas Economic Progress Council, a nonprofit group of businesses and chambers of commerce, estimated that it would take more than 550,000 new jobs paying $50,000 a year by 2018 to pay enough taxes to fill the expected budget gap that year; growth of 50% over six years.

The second argument against the tax cuts was one of equity. Before the enactment of the tax cuts, Kansas had one of the least regressive state and local tax systems in the United States. The new law not only eliminated most of the progressive elements of the income tax but created a regime that some predicted would likely be regressive and may be "among the most regressive in the nation."

The "Kansas Experiment" Fails

Although Gov. Brownback sought to boost the Kansas economy, create jobs and increase population, instead Kansas suffered sluggish growth, lower than expected revenues, and brutal cuts to government programs. In fact, the Kansas economy fared worse than neighboring states, or the country itself.

Immediately after the Kansas tax cuts went into place, Gov. Brownback's revenue secretary, Nick Jordan, promised great benefits for

Kansas. These included the creation of 22,000 more jobs over 'normal growth' and 35,000 more people moving into the state in the next five years. Jordan also expected a five-year increase in disposable income by $2 billion.

None of these predictions came true. In one analysis, Kansas averaged job growth of approximately 1.2% annually before the tax cuts, which would project to 1,437,000 jobs created by April 2017. With Jordan's projected added jobs, there should have been 1,456,000 new jobs. In reality, In April 2017, Kansas had added just 1,409,000 jobs. Further, job growth in Kansas's four neighboring states, Colorado, Nebraska, Missouri, and Oklahoma, increased slightly in the 2013–2017.

The tax cuts also did not positively affect population growth. From 2008 through 2012, Kansas' population grew by an average of about 0.8% each year. At that rate, there would be 2,909,000 people in Kansas by 2016 plus the bonus promised by the Administration that should have brought the population close to 3 million. Instead, in 2016, the population in Kansas totaled 2,852,000.

Disposable income growth also lagged in Kansas. Prior to the tax cuts, disposable income in Kansas grew by an average of about 5.5% each year. At the same rate over the next four years Kansas would exceed $144 billion by 2016. The Administration's predicted $1.6 million due to the tax cuts would have brought that number to $146 billion. In fact, disposable income in Kansas in 2016 totaled less than $127 billion.

There was a regional slowdown in the growth of disposable income after 2012. Still, Kansas was in a worse position after the tax cuts in comparison to its neighbors. Neighboring states saw growth slow from a 4.8% average annual growth before 2012 to 3.4% afterwards. Kansas, however, saw its average annual growth rate drop from 5.5% to 2.1%.

One of the great lessons of the Kansas Experiment was that the favorable business income tax rates could be manipulated. By cutting the rate on pass-through income to zero, Gov. Brownback expected rapidly grow the economy. Not only did the economic activity not materialize, many Kansans simply re-characterized income from labor into the right business-form to avoid paying taxes. The massive tax sheltering combined with weaker than expected growth led to tremendous deficits, lower bond ratings, and the Legislature had to cut central services such as education and infrastructure.

By April 2015, The Kansas City Star led off an article, "The path for digging Kansas out of a deep budget mess could end up paved with broken promises." The 2012 tax cuts, which did not result in the expected growth, led to a "massive budget hole." In 2015 the state was $48 million below revenue estimates for the year, and the 2016 budget required $200 million in new taxes to balance.

The budget situation was so dire that Gov. Brownback asked legislators to pass higher taxes on cigarettes and alcohol, along with a $136 million tax increase on health maintenance organizations.

Despite the budget crisis, about a third of Kansas House members, and nearly half of the Senate, signaled an unwillingness to raise taxes, in part, because moderate Republicans drew conservative challengers for raising taxes during past budget difficulties.

A survey of legislators showed that 36 House members said they would cut spending and not raise taxes. Another seven House members said they would only consider a tax increase if spending was cut more than 5%. Eleven senators said they would prefer to cut spending over raising taxes. Another six senators, including Senate President Wagle, signed pledges with the anti-tax group Americans for Tax Reform promising to oppose new taxes.

Cutting spending was equally difficult. House Speaker Raymond Merrick stated, "The Legislature is not equipped effectively to identify savings in the rest of the budget. Lawmakers do not have time or resources to go into the agencies and identify places for cuts or where duplication of efforts may exist."

School Funding

While the "Kansas Experiment" tax cuts were creating problems for the state's economy, the Kansas Supreme Court was weighing in on education funding. The series of cases entitled *Gannon v. State of Kansas* resulted in the Legislature being ordered to spend hundreds of millions of dollars more on public education.

School funding had been litigated in Kansas since 1972. When a county court found the education funding system unconstitutional, the Legislature responded by passing the School District Equalization Act (SDEA). In 1991, another court found that the Kansas Constitution mandated that the Legislature give all students "an educational opportunity equal to that owed every other child." In 1992, the Legislature passed the School District Finance and Quality Performance Act (SDFQPA), which placed most school finance decisions in the hands of the state government.

In the 2001 case *Montoy v. State*, some school districts successfully challenged the SDFQPA, claiming the state was underfunding the schools. In 2004, the Supreme Court ordered the Legislature to spend more on public education.

Despite allocating more money for schools, the school districts returned to court and the Supreme Court ordered the Legislature to spend another $290 million on education. During the 2006 session, lawmakers appropriated another $466 million to be spent over the next three years.

Due to an economic recession, in 2010 the Legislature deeply cut most state spending, including per pupil state aid. As a result, various school districts filed *Gannon v. State of Kansas,* alleging the Legislature's funding of public education was unconstitutional. The plaintiff alleged two constitutional deficiencies: equalization and adequacy. Under the Kansas Constitution, the state is required to provide the same educational opportunity to all children in the state and trial court suggested it may take another $50 million to attain equalization. In addition, the court held that Article 6 of the Kansas Constitution requires an adequate education, and like several other states, adopted the adequate education standard established by the Kentucky Supreme Court in *Rose v. Council for Better Educ., Inc., 790 S.W.2d 186, 212 (Ky. 1989).*

In another decision, the Kansas Supreme Court opined that if the Legislature in 2015 intended to "fully fund the capital outlay and supplemental general state aid entitlements, supplemental appropriations would be necessary."

In 2015, however, the Governor and Legislature changed the funding scheme for schools. Faced with a request for $54.1 million more in state aid, Gov. Brownback called for legislative repeal of the existing school finance formula and appropriation of money directly to the school districts for the next 2-year budget cycle. In addition, lower than expected sales tax revenues meant a loss of $28.3 million in operating funds for the districts. The governor recommended the legislature reform the formulas for capital outlay state aid and supplemental general state aid, i.e., "equalization aid," and "stall" the increase of the $54 million required to fully fund those formulas for fiscal year 2015.

The 2015 legislature passed two bills—S.B. 4, which stalled the increase in equalization aid and transferred $25.3 million to the capital outlay state aid fund, and S.B. 7, which appropriated an additional $27.3 million in general state aid to approximately restore the cuts that would have been made to districts' operating funds because of the SB 4 allotment. S.B. 7 also reduced districts' capital outlay state aid and supplemental general state aid entitlements for that year by approximately $54 million by revising the formulas for capital outlay state aid and supplemental general state aid.

For fiscal years 2016 and 2017, S.B. 7 repealed the 20-year-old school formula and replaced it with a block grant system—freezing school funding at the 2015 level for two years. This funding system was known as the Classroom Learning Assuring Student Success Act (CLASS). The Court held that this was not a "substantial shift in the way funds are distributed for public education" and gave the Legislature until the end of the fiscal year, June 30, 2016, to demonstrate to the court that it had met its constitutional obligation to provide an adequate and equal education.

Despite the Legislature's use of a block grant to attempt a work around of the Courts, the *Gannon* case continued. Some Kansas conservatives claimed that the Supreme Court had no say in how much should be spent on education and even proposed changing the method for choosing Supreme Court justices.

In March 2017, the Court issued *Gannon IV*. The Court noted the declining education outcomes, especially for students of color. For example, in 2011–2012, 22.1% of all Hispanic students did not meet the state's minimum standards for proficiency in reading. By 2016, that percentage was 36%. The Court noted that during the last school year more than 33,000 Hispanic students and 15,000 African American students in Kansas performed below grade level in reading. From 2012 to 2016, the percentage of all students performing below grade level climbed from 12.4% to 23.3%. An even higher percentage of all students, 26.3% were below grade level in math.

Once again, the Court gave the Legislature until the end of the fiscal year, June 30, 2017, to demonstrate that its K–12 public education financing system was capable of meeting the adequacy requirements of Article 6. Otherwise, the Curt would declare the education financing system "constitutionally invalid and therefore void."

Although the Court did not give the Legislature a specific amount needed to satisfy its ruling, an attorney for the plaintiff districts suggested a cost of roughly $800 million. The director of school finance for the Kansas Department of Education offered a more conservative figure of $535 million.

Gov. Brownback disputed the idea that more money would fix the education problem, "The Kansas Legislature has the opportunity to engage in transformative educational reform by passing a school funding system that puts students first. Success is not measured in dollars spent, but in higher student performance." Brownback suggested spending less on administrative costs as well as allowing vouchers and other school choice measures as part of a new school funding formula.

The 2016 Election

Governor Brownback's "Kansas Experiment" was dealt a blow even before the 2016 general election. Moderate Republicans had a great deal of success against several of Brownback's key allies in the Legislature in the primaries that year; moderates gained 11 seats in the House and eight in the Senate Among the conservatives to lose was Senate Majority Leader Terry Bruce who lost his primary to a moderate Republican by 14%. Sen. Bruce had been one of Governor Brownback's closest allies in the Senate. The results all but assured a Legislature dominated by moderate Republicans in concert with the Democratic minority.

The moderate Republicans made the primaries a referendum on Gov. Brownback's tax policies. Roger Elliott, who won the Republican primary for an open Wichita House seat, said of the Governor's tax policies, "After four years of the failed experiment, people ran out of patience."

A key supporter of the tax cuts, the Kansas Chamber of Commerce, campaigned for the conservative lawmakers. Washburn University Professor Mark Peterson said many of chamber's preferred candidates "went down in flames."

Rep. Melissa Rooker, R-Fairway, a moderate who mentored some of the primary challengers, said the state was no longer able to cover its financial problems with "accounting tricks" and that she was "optimistic we can have that debate we've been denied" about finances when the Legislature reconvened in 2017. Despite all of the success, Rooker admitted that the moderates, even with the help of the Democrats, would not have a veto-proof majority.

Senate President Susan Wagle also acknowledged voter frustration and stated she wanted "a return to fiscally-responsible balanced budgeting" and "a tax code that is fairer to all Kansans while keeping taxes low."

Conservative Rep. Gene Suellentrop, R-Wichita, who won the right to run for an open Senate seat, said conservatives still had an "opportunity to hold taxes low."

HB 2178

In February 2017, the Legislature came within three votes of undoing the Kansas Experiment. Early in the new session, the Legislature faced a projected budget gap of over $1 billion through June 2019. In response, the House Taxation Committee produced HB 2178, which would have restored approximately $1 billion in income tax revenues over two years.

HB 2178 eliminated the tax exemption for small businesses that allowed more than 330,000 business owners to pay zero state tax on their income. The bill increased the income tax rates beginning in tax year 2017 and utilized a three-bracket system of 2.70 percent, 5.25 percent, and 5.45 percent, as opposed to the current two-bracket system with rates of 2.70 and 4.60 percent. The bill also repealed future automatic rate reductions based on future tax receipt growth. Finally, medical expenses would again be allowed as itemized deductions beginning in tax year 2017.

The Legislature received testimony in favor of the bill from the Kansas Association of School Boards, neutral testimony from the Kansas Center for Economic Growth, and negative testimony from the Kansas Chamber of Commerce and the Kansas Policy Institute.

The Kansas Department of Revenue forecast the bill to increase tax revenues as follows:

- FY 2018: $590.2 million
- FY 2019: $453.8 million
- FY 2020: $458.6 million
- FY 2021: $463.4 million
- FY 2022: $468.2 million

The morning after the Legislature presented Gov. Brownback with HB 2178, he vetoed the bill. Gov. Brownback's veto message read:

> My veto of Substitute for House Bill 2178 is based in my belief that, as the elected public servants of Kansas, we must not choose to resolve budget challenges on the backs of middle income Kansans with retroactive personal income tax increases.
>
> We should be clear about what this bill will do. The proposed tax increase will raise income tax liability for married Kansans filing jointly earning at least $30,000 per year from 4.6% to 5.25%, and from 4.6% to 5.45% for those married filers earning more than $100,000 per year. At the same time, income tax rates for small businesses will increase from 0% up to 5.45%, depending on income. More to the point, any single full-time worker earning more than $9.74 per hour will see an income tax increase.
>
> Working families and small businesses are the backbone of our economy, and we should not punish them.
>
> Moreover, applying a retroactive tax increase on our citizens is irresponsible and will ultimately harm families and individuals who are working to make ends meet. Were this bill to become law, the majority of Kansans would see a significant reduction in their pay check immediately. This is unfair.
>
> I also reject the idea that we must choose to either make large cuts to public education or burden every hard working Kansan with a higher tax rate. This dichotomy is false. In my budget proposal, I suggested modest revenue measures on targeted consumption and taxes paid by businesses. I have also proposed adoption of efficiencies recommended by the study commissioned by the Legislature, all of which result in a structurally balanced budget by Fiscal Year 2019. It is irresponsible to raise taxes on low and middle income Kansans without first ensuring we are doing everything we can to keep the cost of government low.
>
> Kansas has pioneered new ground to generate small business growth and thus create jobs and economic opportunity for more

Kansans. We have seen record levels of new business formation and consistently low unemployment. These efforts have been successful, and reversing course now will have a long term negative impact on growing business and opportunity in Kansas. Instead, this bill would raise the tax burden on every small business in the state, create a new tax bracket, raise the income tax liability of Kansans, and would result in undermining the economic health of our state and the opportunity for every Kansan to provide for themselves and their families.

It is our responsibility to make the decisions to build a brighter future for Kansas and to ensure that we do everything we can to provide high quality government service at the lowest cost to Kansans.

Over the coming weeks, I will remain committed to working with legislative leadership to develop a plan that structurally balances our budget without permanently harming hard working Kansans.

Accordingly, pursuant to Article 2, Section 14(a) of the Constitution of the State of Kansas, I hereby veto House Bill 2178.

Vetoed: February 22, 2017

Signed, Sam Brownback, Governor of Kansas

After Gov. Brownback vetoed the bill, HB 2178 went back to the Legislature and two hours later the House voted 85–40 to override the veto. The Senate override vote, however, was 24–16 vote—three votes short of the required two-thirds majority. Two senators switched their votes from "nay" to "yea" between enactment and consideration of the override: Sen. Elaine Bowers (R-Concordia), who was the Senate Majority Whip and Sen. Tom Holland (D-Baldwin City), the top Democrat on the Senate Assessment and Taxation Committee.

Key to the Senate outcome was that both Senate President Susan Wagle, and Senate Majority Leader Jim Denning spoke against the bill. Two of the newly elected Senate moderates, Barbara Bollier, (R-Mission Hills), and Dinah Sykes (R-), thought the override measure would have passed if Wagle and Denning had supported the bill.

Sen. Denning had no regrets about voting against the override because of the retroactive provision that would have increased taxes from the beginning of the year. Sen. Denning stated, "I did everybody a favor, actually." The Senate Minority Leader Anthony Hensley (D-Topeka), however, claimed the Republican leader told him that if the House were to override the veto, he would vote to override it as well. Sen. Denning would not comment on Hensley's claim. Further, Senate President Wagle disagreed that she and Denning were the deciding factor in the vote.

Sen. Wagle also seemed upset with Gov. Brownback, in that legislative leaders had asked him for a new tax proposal before vetoing HB 2178, but they never received one. Wagle stated, "I do believe the Senate and the House will have to come up with a plan to fix the budget." In a later statement Sen. Wagle called for a "holistic approach" to the budget with both spending cuts and revenue increases.

Some House members remained committed to the vetoed tax plan. Rep. Stephanie Clayton (R-Overland Park) said the House should "remain steadfast" and continue to push for the legislation, which she said "represents the will of the people, even if that means the session lasts for months." Meanwhile, Sen. Laura Kelly (D-Topeka) predicted that Senate leadership would use the failed override to justify further cuts to public schools, "I think they'll concoct something that won't work and will not be progressive, and they'll try to ram that down our throats."

SB 30

Several months after the Senate failed to override the Governor's veto, a new tax bill worked its way through the Legislature. The original SB 30 was a minor change to the statute concerning the North Central Association of Colleges and Schools, which had no fiscal impact on the budget. The Senate passed the bill, but when the House made minor changes to the bill, SB 30 ended up in a conference committee.

On May 2, 2017, the SB 30 conferees reported a very different bill—one that would accomplish the HB 2178 tax reforms. Once again, the bill would

- Repeal, effective for tax year 2017, the exemption for non-wage business income;

- Taxpayers could begin claiming certain non-wage business income losses in conformity with federal tax law;

- Medical expenses deductions would become available in tax year 2018;

- In tax year 2018, the low-income exclusion threshold (below which any positive income tax liability is otherwise eliminated) would be reduced from $12,500 to $5,000 for married filers and from $5,000 to $2,500 for single filers;

- In tax year 2017 there would be a three-bracket system of 2.85%, 4.9%, and 5.1%;

- Starting in tax year 2018 the tax rates would be 3.0 percent, 5.25 percent, and 5.6 percent; and

- Automatic rate reductions based on tax receipt growth were repealed.

The Department of Revenue predicted the bill would be expected to increase revenues by:

- FY 2018: $514.0 million;

- FY 2019: $548.7 million;

- FY 2020: $554.2 million;

- FY 2021: $559.8 million; and

- FY 2022: $565.4 million.

This Senate and House, however, did not take up the conference report and the conferees went back to work. A few weeks later, the Conference Committee issued a new proposal putting a moratorium on new capital improvement projects for a year and further increasing the tax brackets.

For tax year 2017 the brackets would be: 2.9%, 4.9%, and 5.2%. For tax year 2018 and after, brackets would be 3.1%, 5.25%, and 5.7%

According to the Department of Revenue, these changes would raise an additional $39 million over the next five tax years beyond the previous conference committee proposal. The House rejected the committee report by a vote of 53–68.

On June 5, 2017, the conference committee issued its third report on SB 30. The report came on the 109th day of the session—among the longest legislative sessions in state history. The legislature desperately needed to close a projected $900 million budget deficit over the next two years and enact a new school funding plan by the June 30 deadline set by the Kansas Supreme Court.

The conference committee's next proposal, like previous versions, repealed the non-wage business income exemption for 2017 and taxpayers could begin deducting certain non-wage business income losses. Also, the low-income threshold was lowered for both married and single filers. The tax brackets would be set at the same levels as the previous report that the House rejected.

The conference committee also agreed to several new changes regarding tax deductions:

- Allowed a medical expense deduction for 50% in 2018, which increased to 75% in 2019 and 100% starting in 2020;

- Increased the deductions for mortgage interest and property taxes paid from 50% of the federal allowable amounts, to 75% for 2019 and to 100% beginning in tax year 2020;

- Restored the child and dependent care tax credit that had been repealed in 2012: 12.50% of the allowable federal amount in 2018; 18.75% in 2019, and 25% (the level that had been utilized prior to the 2012 repeal) in 2020.

Individual Income Tax Brackets, Married Filing Jointly

Taxable Income	Tax Year 1992–2012	Current Law Tax Year 2017	Proposal Tax Year 2017	Current Law Tax Year 2018	Proposal Tax Year 2018
$0–30,000	3.50%	2.70%	2.90%	2.60%	3.10%
$30,001–$60,000	6.25	4.60%	4.90%	4.60%	5.25%
$60,001 and above	6.45%	4.60%	5.20%	4.60%	5.70%

The Department of Revenue projected an increase in tax receipts significantly:

FY 2018 $591.0 million

FY 2019 $633.0

FY 2020 $617.4

FY 2021 $584.4

FY 2022 $590.3

The total package, therefore, was projected to increase revenues by over $3 billion over the next 5 years. Significantly, the new plan was projected to raise revenues by nearly $582 million more than HB 2178 that the Legislature failed to override the Governor's veto.

The day the Conference Committee issued its report, Gov. Brownback again vowed to veto the bill, "Senate Bill 30 is a $1.2 billion tax hike, making it the largest in state history. This is bad for Kansas and bad for the many Kansans who would have more of their hard-earned money taken from them."

Senate President Wagle and Majority Leader Denning know that the new proposal will have a veto-proof majority in the House. What are their possible courses of action in the Senate? What should they do to resolve this budget crisis?

Sources:

• Kansas Legislature Website, (http://www.kslegislature.org/li/about/).

• John Elibon, "In Kansas, Conservatives Vilify Fellow Republicans," *NY Times*, Aug. 5, 2012.

- https://ballotpedia.org/Kansas_State_Senate_elections,_ 2012.

- Scott Rothschild, "End may be coming for GOP moderates," *Lawrence Journal-World*, July 22, 2012.

- "What's Right with Kansas," *Wall Street Journal*, May 30, 2012 (https://www.wsj.com/articles/SB100014240527023040 70304577394340998558490).

- Brent D. Wistrom, "Governor signs bill for massive tax cuts," *The Wichita Eagle*, May 22, 2012, (https://www.kansas.com/ news/politics-government/article1092592.html).

- Martin B. Dickinson, Stephen W. Mazza & Michael R. Keenan, "The Revolutionary 2012 Kansas Tax Act," 61 *Kansas Law Review* 332.

- Barb Shelly, "Sam Brownback Signs Budget-Busting Income Tax Bill," *KansasCity.com,* May 2012).

- William G. Gale, "The Kansas Tax Cut Experiment," *Brookings*, July 11, 2017 (https://www.brookings.edu/blog/ unpacked/2017/07/11/the-kansas-tax-cut-experiment/).

- Michael Linden, "Kansas' experiment with tax cutting failed spectacularly—on its own terms," *Business Insider*, Jun. 14, 2017 (https://www.businessinsider.com/kansas-experiment- with-tax-cutting-failed-on-its-own-terms-2017-6).

- Brad Cooper, "Fixing Kansas budget problems could undo no-tax promises," *Kansas City Star*, April 13, 2015 (https://www. kansascity.com/news/politics-government/article18463949. html).

- Sam Zeff, "A Primer On The School Funding Case Before The Kansas Supreme Court" *KCUR*, November 5, 2015 (https:// www.kcur.org/post/primer-school-funding-case-kansas- supreme-court#stream/0).

- *Gannon v. State of Kansas*, 298 Kan. 1107 (2014).

- *Gannon v. State of Kansas (II)*, 303 Kan. 682 (2016).

- *Gannon v. State of Kansas (III)*, 304 Kan. 490 (2016).

- *Gannon v. State of Kansas (IV)*, 305 Kan. 850 (2017).

- Bryan Lowry, Hunter Woodall, Katy Bergen, "Kansas Supreme Court rules the state has failed to ensure adequate education funding," *KansasCity.com*, March 2, 2017, (https:// www.kansascity.com/news/politics-government/article13594 9108.html).

- Bryan Lowry, "Brownback's support in Legislature weakens after moderates' big gains," *Wichita Eagle*, August 3, 2016.

- Hunter Woodall and Bryan Lowry, "Gov. Brownback's tax policies barely survive after Kansas Senate vote" *Kansas City Star*, February 22, 2017, (https://www.kansas.com/news/ politics-government/article134395734.html).

- Kansas Legislative Research Department, "Supplemental Note On Substitute For House Bill No. 2178," 2017 (http:// www.kslegislature.org/li_2018/b2017_18/measures/ documents/supp_note_hb2178_01_0000.pdf).

- 2017 Permanent Senate Journal, February 22, 2017, p. 199 (http://www.kslegislature.org/li_2018/b2017_18/chamber/ documents/permanent_journal_senate_2017.pdf).

- Kansas Legislative Research Bureau, Summary of SB 30, (http://www.kslegislature.org/li_2018/b2017_18/measures/do cuments/supp_note_sb30_00_0000.pdf).

- "Conference Committee Report Brief for Senate Bill 30," May 22, 2017 (http://www.kslegislature.org/li_2018/b2017_18/ measures/documents/ccrb_sb30_02_may22ccr.pdf).

- "Third Conference Committee Report Brief Senate Bill 30," June 5, 2017 (http://www.kslegislature.org/li_2018/b2017_18/ measures/documents/ccrb_sb30_04_ccrjune55pm.pdf).

- Jonathan Sherman & Daniel Salazar, "Brownback vows veto of tax increases approved by Legislature" *Wichita Eagle*, June 5, 2017.

F. COMMITTEES

The workhorses of the legislative system are the committees. Committees conduct hearings, gather information, research issues, consider bills, make amendments to legislative language, oversee the executive branch, conduct investigations into wrongdoing and manage the legislature's operations. There are several types of committees at the federal level:

1. STANDING COMMITTEES

The House and Senate standing committees consider bills and oversee agencies, programs, and activities within their jurisdictions. The committees are created by the rules of each chamber. The committees were created as needed and evolved over time to meet the country's different challenges. The current committee structure came about in 1947, as a part of the Legislative Reorganization Act of 1946 (60 Stat. 812). In 1974,

Congress again changed the committee structure to formally create subcommittees for each committee. Before members are assigned to committees, the size and party make-up of each committee must be decided by the party leaders. The total number of committee slots allotted to each party is approximately the same as the ratio between majority party and minority party members in the full chamber.

2.   JOINT COMMITTEES

A joint committee consists of both Senate and House members with jurisdiction over matters of joint interest to both chambers. For instance, the Joint Committee on the Library oversees the Library of Congress.

House Standing Committee	Senate Standing Committees	Joint Committees
Agriculture	Agriculture, Nutrition, and Forestry	Joint Committee on Budget and Appropriations Process Reform
Appropriations	Appropriations	Joint Economic Committee
Armed Services	Armed Services	Joint Committee on the Library
Budget	Banking, Housing, and Urban Affairs	Joint Select Committee on Solvency of Multi-employer Pension Plans
Education and the Workforce	Budget	Joint Committee on Printing
Energy and Commerce	Commerce, Science, and Transportation	Joint Committee on Taxation
Ethics	Energy and Natural Resource	
Financial Services	Environment and Public Works	
Foreign Affairs	Finance	

Homeland Security	Foreign Relations	
House Administration	Health, Education, Labor, and Pensions	
Judiciary	Homeland Security and Govern. Affairs	
Natural Resources	Judiciary	
Oversight and Government Reform	Rules and Administration	
Rules	Small Business and Entrepreneurship	
Science, Space, and Technology	Veterans' Affairs	
Small Business		
Transportation and Infrastructure		
Veterans' Affairs		
Ways and Means		

The jurisdiction of the various committees is established by rule. For instance, the Rules of the House of Representatives, Rule X (Establishment and Jurisdiction of Standing Committees) establishes the jurisdiction of the Agriculture Committee as follows:

COMMITTEE ON AGRICULTURE

Adulteration of seeds, insect pests, and protection of birds and animals in forest reserves. Agriculture generally. Agricultural and industrial chemistry. Agricultural colleges and experiment stations. Agricultural economics and research. Agricultural education extension services. Agricultural production and marketing and stabilization of prices of agricultural products, and commodities (not including distribution outside of the United States). Animal industry and diseases of animals. Commodity exchanges. Crop insurance and soil conservation. Dairy industry. Entomology and plant quarantine. Extension of farm credit and farm security. Inspection of livestock, poultry, meat products, and seafood and seafood products. Forestry in general, and forest reserves other than those created from the public domain. Human nutrition and home economics. Plant industry, soils, and agricultural engineering. Rural electrification. Rural development. Water conservation related to activities of the Department of Agriculture.

3. SPECIAL AND SELECT COMMITTEES

The House and Senate will sometimes form a special or select committee for a short time period and specific purpose, frequently an investigation.

House Select Committees	Senate Select Committees
Permanent Select Committee on Intelligence	Aging (Special)
	Ethics (Select)
	Indian Affairs
	Intelligence (Select)

4. HOUSE PRESTIGE COMMITTEES

Some committees are particularly powerful—a seat on the committee is considered very prestigious, and the chair of the committee wields considerable power within Congress and the government as a whole.

The House is Constitutionally empowered to have greater control over the finances of the United States: Article I, section 7 states, "All Bills for raising Revenue shall originate in the House of Representatives; but the Senate may propose or concur with Amendments as on other Bills." Therefore, the House's prestige committees include the **Appropriations**, **Budget** and **Ways & Means** Committees. In addition, House floor debate is governed by a rule created for each debated bill, making the **Rules** Committee very important to House operations.

a. Appropriations

The Appropriations Committee draws its power from the Constitution, Article I, section 9, Clause 7, "No money shall be drawn from the treasury, but in consequence of appropriations made by law; and a regular statement and account of receipts and expenditures of all public money shall be published from time to time." The committee is responsible for passing appropriation bills which must also be passed by its Senate counterpart.

These bills regulate all expenditures of money by the United States government.

The Committee has 12 Subcommittees that appropriates for various parts of the government:

- Agriculture, Rural Development, Food and Drug Administration, and Related Agencies
- Commerce, Justice, Science, and Related Agencies
- Defense
- Energy and Water Development, and Related Agencies
- Financial Services and General Government
- Homeland Security
- Interior, Environment, and Related Agencies
- Labor, Health and Human Services, Education, and Related Agencies
- Legislative Branch
- Military Construction, Veteran Affairs, and Related Agencies
- State, Foreign Operations, and Related Programs
- Transportation, Housing and Urban
- Development, and Related Agencies

The Appropriations Chair and the 12 subcommittee chairs are collectively called the "Cardinals," after the highest-ranking Catholic bishops who elect the Pope and run the Roman Catholic Church.

b.   Ways & Means

The U.S. Constitution Article I, Section 8 states, "The Congress shall have Power To lay and collect Taxes, Duties, Imposts and Excises, to pay the Debts and. . .To borrow Money on the credit of the United States." The Committee on Ways and Means is the oldest committee of the United States Congress and is the chief tax-writing committee in the House of Representatives. The Committee's jurisdiction is vast:

Raising revenue through individual and corporate income taxes, excise taxes, estate taxes, gift taxes, and other miscellaneous taxes; authority of the Federal Government to borrow money; oversees the U.S. Department of the Treasury's management of the Federal debt; jurisdiction over most of the programs authorized by the Social Security Act, including the old-age and disability insurance, Medicare, Supplemental Security Income, Temporary Assistance for Needy Families (TANF), child support enforcement, child welfare services including foster care and adoption, unemployment compensation programs, reimbursement to states for social services; responsible for international trade policy including tariffs, international trade agreements, customs administration and enforcement.

c. Budget

The Congressional Budget and Impoundment Control Act of 1974 (the Budget Act) established the Budget Committee and required an annual budget resolution on the budget to set levels of spending, revenue, the surplus or deficit, and public debt. The House rules require the Budget Committee's membership to be: five members from the Committee on Ways and Means, five members from the Committee on Appropriations, one member from the Committee on Rules, a member designated by the majority party leadership and one member designated by the minority party leadership. The Budget Committee currently has 39 members.

d. Rules

The Rules Committee does not have a specific area of policy but determines the rule under which other bills will come to the floor. Since the Committee regulates the flow of bills to the House floor, it is often considered part of leadership. A rule is typically a short resolution of the House to permit consideration of bill or resolution, and to prescribe conditions for debate and how the bill may be amended

5. SENATE PRESTIGE COMMITTEES

The Senate's prestige committees include Appropriations, but also those that play a major role in that chamber's "advise & consent" role for treaties and nominations. The Constitution Article II, section 2 states, "He [the President] shall have Power, by and with the Advice and Consent of the Senate, to make Treaties, provided two thirds of the Senators present concur; and he shall nominate, and by and with the Advice and Consent of the Senate, shall appoint Ambassadors, other public Ministers and Consuls, Judges of the supreme Court, and all other Officers of the United States, whose Appointments are not herein otherwise provided for, and which shall be established by Law. . . ."

a. Armed Services

The Constitution in Article I, section 8 gives Congress the power to declare War, raise and support Armies, provide and maintain a Navy; regulate the land and naval Forces; and provide for organizing, arming, and disciplining of the state Militia when called into federal service. The Committee's jurisdiction includes:

Air and space activities related to the development of weapons systems or military operations; oversee the Department of Defense; military research and development; and the pay, promotion, retirement, and other benefits of members of the Armed Forces.

The Armed Services Committee considers approximately 50,000 nominations each year for civilian and military officials in the Department of Defense, Army, Navy, Marine Corps, and Air Force.

b. Foreign Relations

Established in 1816, the committee has been instrumental in developing and influencing United States foreign policy. The committee has considered, debated, and reported important treaties and legislation. The Committee holds jurisdiction over all diplomatic nominations. Members of the committee have assisted in the negotiation of treaties, and at times have helped to defeat treaties they felt were not in the national interest. The Committee considers the nominations for State Department officers, including the ambassadors who represent the United States in other countries.

c. Finance

The Committee's jurisdiction includes:

taxation and other revenue measures generally; bonded debt; customs, collection districts, and ports of entry and delivery; reciprocal trade agreements; tariff and import quotas; the transportation of dutiable goods; deposit of public moneys; general revenue sharing; health programs under the Social Security Act, including Medicare, Medicaid, the Children's Health Insurance Program (CHIP), Temporary Assistance to Needy Families (TANF) and other health and human services programs financed by a specific tax or trust fund; and national social security.

The Committee considers nominees for: the Treasury Department, the Federal Reserve, Tax Court, the Internal Revenue Service, the Department of Health & Human Services, and the International Trade Commission.

d. Judiciary

The Judiciary Committee oversees both the Department of Justice its agencies, including the Federal Bureau of Investigation, and the Department of Homeland Security.

The Committee considers nominations for positions in the Department of Justice, Office of National Drug Control Policy, the United States Parole Commission, the United States Sentencing Commission, and the State

Justice Institute, as well as select nominations for the Department of Homeland Security and the Department of Commerce are referred to the Senate Judiciary Committee.

The Committee considers all Article III judicial nominations, including Supreme Court nominations, appellate court nominations, and district court nominations. The Committee also considers nominations to the Court of International Trade.

e. Appropriations

Works closely with its House counterpart to pass appropriations.

NOTES & QUESTIONS

1.   In Massachusetts, the substantive committees that address policy are all joint committees with 6 senators and 11 representatives. The speaker and senate president each appoint the members and a committee chair. The co-chairs then run the committee jointly.

- What are the advantages of this type of committee structure?

- What difficulties would you anticipate?

The senate is at a disadvantage in any vote by sheer numbers. If you were the senate co-chair, how would you deal with that reality?

2.   In 2014, The *Washington Post* reported that a previously unheard of nine Senate and House committee chairs were retiring at the end of the session. The authors speculated that the reason was over the previous two decades power had been consolidated in leadership, diminishing the power of the committee chairs. In addition. In 1995, Speaker Newt Gingrich imposed six-year term limits on chairmen and empowered a steering committee of leadership appointees to pick chairs according to loyalty to leadership rather than seniority. The *Post* also noted that people were simply serving in Congress for a shorter period of time, choosing to leave for radio show jobs, think tanks, or other political offices,

> "there aren't enough lawmakers here who actually want to be here, who actually understand the long, slow march of history that Congress is. Ted Kennedy got it. Henry Waxman got it. Bob Dole got it. John McCain gets it. It's hard work, it's long and laborious, stuff doesn't happen fast, results are hard to come by, but each day/week/ month/year is the chance to move the needle a little bit in your ideological direction. That takes time and dedication."

Chris Cillizza, "Congressional Committee Chairs Have Lost Much of Their Prestige, Allure," *Washington Post*, April 6, 2014

3.   The term limits on House committee chairs really affected the House in 2015, when almost half of the committee chairmen had to hand the gavel over to someone new. This was called "a brain drain of historic proportions."

Although term limits remain popular in the Republican Caucus, some members argued that the rule "effectively sideline some of the party's most effective legislators." Proponents of term limits, however, argue they keep "committees vital with fresh ideas and preventing a small group of members from consolidating too much power." Daniel Newhauser, "Brain Drain: Self-Imposed Term Limits Shuffle Committees, House GOP Leadership," *CQ Roll Call*, Apr 22, 2014.

G. THE MEMBER'S OFFICE

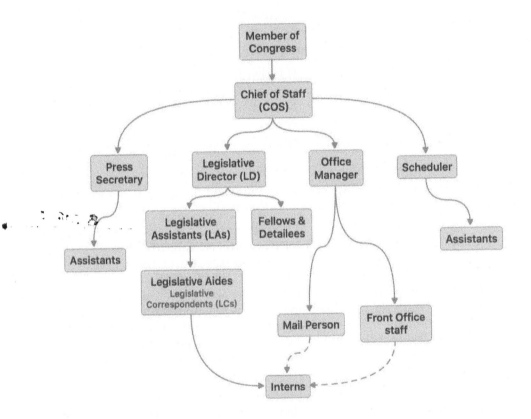

Members of Congress organize their offices according to their personal, legislative and communications needs. Still, most offices have a similar structure. Often Congressional offices are divided into three groups: policy, which researches, drafts, and communicates about legislation; communications, which responds to media requests and uses a range of methods to promote the work of the representative; and administration, which manages the office.

The **chief of staff** both advises the member on political matters and manages all aspects of the office's operation including staffing and budget decisions.

The **scheduler** manages requests for meetings with the member or other engagements where the member is expected to attend.

The **legislative director** (LD) guides the member on legislative priorities and strategy and helps both develop and promote the member's legislative agenda.

Legislative assistants (LA) research legislation and policy issues.

Legislative correspondents (LC) also research legislation and issues and draft responses to constituent questions and requests.

The **press secretary or communications director** develops and carries out the member's communication strategy. The director manages the press team and will often write the member's speeches and serve as the member's primary spokesperson.

Press assistants distribute press releases and try to increase the member's media coverage. Assistants will also compile media stories on the member, their district or important issues.

Staff assistants answer telephones, greet visitors, and do general jobs such as filing and mail.   STOP !

H. THE ROLE OF THE LEGISLATIVE LAWYER

In addition to a large number of lawyers serving in Congress and legislatures, there are thousands of lawyers employed by the 51 legislatures. They range from lawyers who advise members within their personal offices, the non-partisan lawyers who draft legislation in the House and Senate Counsel's Offices, and the lawyers who work developing both policy and legislative language for committees.

The House and Senate each have an Office of the Legislative Counsel that provides drafting services for committees and individual members. The Legislative Counsel and their assistants are fiercely non-partisan and often stay in their positions for lengthy periods—if not for entire careers. Although not mandatory, most bills get some level of review by legislative counsel. Sometimes the legislative counsel work closely with committee staff from policy development to final passage, and on other bills they may be asked to provide just technical assistance.

Until the early 20th Century members of Congress largely did their own drafting. In 1916, Columbia University's Legislative Drafting Research Fund provided Middleton Beaman to any Congressional committee that would accept his help. After the House Ways and Means Committee used him on several revenue bills, he became a fixture on

Capitol Hill until his retirement in 1949. In 1918, Congress funded a drafting office with two drafters, one appointed by the head of each chamber. They drafted bills and amendments for the committees, and for individual members if it did not interfere with committee work.

In 1970, during a reorganization of legislative operations, the office became two separate offices, one for each chamber.

For more information, see Tobias Dorsey, "Offices of the Legislative Counsel" § 2.16, *LEGISLATIVE DRAFTER'S DESKBOOK: A PRACTICAL GUIDE* (The Capitol.Net, 2006).

THE ART OF LEGISLATIVE LAWYERING AND THE SIX CIRCLES THEORY OF ADVOCACY
Chai Rachel Feldblum, 34 *McGeorge Law Review* 785 (2003)

The legislative lawyer is the "legal content person" and the "conduit" between the political players and the substantive legal players on any particular issue. The legislative lawyer must spend a significant amount of time learning the legal landscape of an issue, with a level of depth and sophistication parallel to those who litigate in the area or who produce academic writings in the area. The legislative lawyer must also be engaged directly with the political process, so that he or she will have a sophisticated understanding of the political pitfalls that may characterize any particular advocacy issue.

The legislative lawyer's substantive legal and policy knowledge, coupled with her understanding of political dynamics, forms the basis on which the legislative lawyer (in conjunction with the policy researcher) produces policy options and legislative proposals. The legislative lawyer's combined understanding of law and politics also shapes his or her ongoing negotiations with the various players, as the strategist coordinates the efforts that will lead to the legislation being ultimately successfully enacted into law (or a regulation ultimately successfully promulgated).

As with a lobbyist, a legislative lawyer's stock in trade is credibility. But his or her credibility must be established in two distinct arenas: that of substantive law and policy, and that of politics.

The legislative lawyer must be sufficiently skilled in legal analysis so as to understand the detailed and complex concerns of those who litigate or otherwise practice in the substantive legal arena under consideration for change. These substantive legal experts must feel the legislative lawyer is "good at law"—so that the legislative lawyer will be fully trusted to understand even complex legal analyses regarding existing law and proposed law.

At the same time, the legislative lawyer must establish her bona fides with the political establishment. The key players must feel that the legislative lawyer "gets the political scene"—so that the legislative lawyer will be fully trusted to understand even arcane and bizarre political concerns. For this to occur, the legislative lawyer must get to know the key political players in the particular endeavor, understand the particular political concerns at play, and be present at the range of meetings that are the mainstay of advocacy efforts.

The legislative lawyer also needs to be able to speak two languages well: law and English. The legislative lawyer should be able to engage in a complex legal discussion with the substantive legal experts. At the same time, the legislative lawyer must be able to translate those discussions into simple and useful English—that is, a format easily accessible to those whose most precious commodity is time and who are more interested in "bottom lines" than in discursive treatises.

. . .

Lawyers heavily populate the halls of federal, state and local legislatures and executive agencies today. Many lobbyists are lawyers, as are many legislators, staff people, and executive officials. But most of these lawyers do not spend a significant percentage of their time doing extensive legal research or writing long legal memos. Indeed, most of these individuals entered the legislative or executive arenas precisely because they were not so interested in legal text or precedent and more interested in policy, politics, and strategy. But legislatures and executive branches pass and implement laws that consist of detailed legal text. Thus, lawyers are seen as a "necessary evil." Lawyers who practice in an area of law under consideration are often brought in as "experts" who will provide advice on the text of a proposed law or regulation. But because these lawyers are individuals who have chosen to actually practice law, rather than engage in the political world, their engagement with the political world is often less than ideal. At best, these expert lawyers view the influence politics inevitably exerts on text as unfortunate and bizarre; at worst, they experience it as unconscionable or unacceptable. In many cases, the outcome for the legislative or regulatory language at issue is less than ideal.

. . .

A legislative lawyer, who is responsible for learning the law and the politics of an issue, can forestall such [legislative] impasses by facilitating informed conversations between the legal and political players.

. . .

The skills of a legislative lawyer are best understood by thinking about the chronological stages in which a legislative lawyer approaches his or her work. These stages are: assess the problem/issue; research the problem/issue; propose solutions and approaches; draft materials; and engage in oral presentations and negotiations.

1.   Assess the Problem/Issue

A legislative lawyer must first fully understand his client's desired policy goal. In a situation in which the legislative lawyer is hired to work directly for an organizational client (for example, in the same "government relations" office in which the lobbyists are hired—the optimal structural approach envisioned in the Six Circles Theory), this requires fully understanding what the organization's policy goals are.

The legislative lawyer must then be able to identify, and accurately assess, both the political landscape and the legal landscape that will govern his client's desired policy outcome. For a lobbyist, understanding both a policy goal, and grasping the politics surrounding the goal, is easily achievable. The entire role of the lobbyist is built around explaining a policy goal to a decision-maker and persuading the decision-maker of the merits of that outcome. One of the reasons lawyers become lobbyists is that they are interested in the policy analysis and human interaction required by that line of work. By contrast, a legislative lawyer who is interested in and steeped in the legal details of an issue may need to make an extra effort to fully understand both the policy goal and the politics surrounding the issue. Nevertheless, an understanding and assessment of both policy and politics is key to the foundation of good legislative lawyering work. It is that understanding, and that intuitive application of politics to law, that sets the legislative lawyer apart from lawyers who operate purely in the legal arena.

. . .

2.   Research the Problem/Issue

The second stage of work for the legislative lawyer is to research the issue. The foremost skill a legislative lawyer brings to this task is a sophisticated, refined, and sharpened ability to read text. By "text," I mean the actual words in a statute or regulation, or in a pending bill or regulation. By "read," I mean the ability to correctly ascertain what those words mean (or could mean).

It is difficult to overestimate the importance of the skill of "reading text." In the policy world, few people engage in a close, meticulous reading of all the relevant text. This is often because they lack time, and sometimes, because they lack interest or capacity. In any event, it is the legislative lawyer's almost obsessive focus on text that sets him or her apart from other players in the political arena.

"Obsessive" is not an inaccurate word to use in describing the necessary skill of reading text. Most relevant text is buried in surroundings of less relevant text. Laws are often amended over the years, resulting in odd placements of sections and provisions and in convoluted sentences. New bills often amend existing laws, so that the language of the bill cannot be understood without careful reference to and study of the existing law.

During the research stage, the legislative lawyer must meticulously find and understand every piece of text relevant to the policy goal being sought. No phrase is too small to be glossed over; no cross-reference too minor to escape unexamined. Opening clauses such as "subject to subsection (a)" or "except as provided in subsection (b)" are red flags for a legislative lawyer; they never escape further exploration.

Of course, such meticulous attention to text has always been the hallmark of a good lawyer—regardless of the field or arena in which the lawyer practices. What the legislative lawyer does, however, is bring this meticulous attention to, enjoyment of, and ability to read text into the political world, where most individuals usually have the time to read only executive summaries and bullet points. While the legislative lawyer must be able to translate his or her sophisticated understanding of text into usable documents and proposals (see skill number four below), it is when the legislative lawyer allocates time to read text and research law that the principal contributions of the legislative lawyer can begin to emerge.

To make a contribution, a legislative lawyer must read the relevant text with a keen understanding of the political dynamics surrounding the pending legislation or regulation. All lawyers engage in research with an eye to both law and politics. But the politics are different depending on the surroundings. Litigation lawyers deal with the politics of the judicial system, their clients, and their opposition. Organizational and transactional lawyers deal with the politics of the organization, community, or whatever entity they are dealing with. Legislative lawyers, by contrast, deal with the politics of the legislative branch, the executive branch, and the range of advocacy stakeholders interested in an issue.

It is usually not possible to absorb a sophisticated understanding of the politics of a situation simply by hearing a description of the relevant political dynamics. This is a situation in which "location, location, location" is the all-important component. It is only by sitting through (sometimes interminable) meetings with coalition partners, legislative staff people, and agency officials that a legislative lawyer can begin to absorb completely the political concerns and needs of the various stakeholders. Having done so, the legislative lawyer can then take into account those concerns when engaging in an interpretation of existing text or of new proposed legislative or regulatory text.

. . .

Operating in this system is a matter of temperament and skill. A legislative lawyer must be able to research and write under pressure, continue to perform well even when an issue has been raised for the sixth time, and maintain at least a façade of calm during all proceedings.

3.   Propose Solutions and Approaches to the Problem/Issue

After researching an issue or problem, a legislative lawyer must be able to propose approaches and solutions to the issue. The building blocks for this skill set are the same ones noted above: an ability to read text and an ability to gauge political realities. But this stage of work also requires creativity, assertiveness, and perception. (Flashes of brilliance are, of course, always welcomed by clients at this stage.)

A broad range of activities and documents come under the heading of "propose solutions and approaches." At bottom, however, they all revolve around proposing different legislative and administrative options for achieving a client's policy goals. These may include recommending support, opposition, or modification of a bill; recommending that a client focus on one particular program rather than another; or recommending that a client argue the law it needs has already been passed and the relevant agency need only issue appropriate implementing regulations.

In any of these activities, the legislative lawyer and the policy researcher will discern the range of possible solutions by engaging equally with players in the traditional legal, academic, and think-tank worlds, and with players in the political world. The goal of both the legislative lawyer and the policy researcher is to fully comprehend the positions of each player; to gain the trust of each of the players based on such comprehension, and to help the players figure out a solution that meets everyone's needs to the greatest extent possible.

. . .

At other times, the work involved in proposing solutions or approaches will require extensive negotiation and, perhaps, some subtle manipulation of text. For example, imagine several litigation lawyers have recommended the use of a certain phrase in a bill, but staff people for the key sponsors of the bill have resisted use of that phrase because of fear of adverse political ramifications. (This is the scenario I described above in which an impasse is often reached.) The legislative lawyer must first assess the issue—she must identify her client's policy goal and interests, the political dynamics affecting the bill, and the relevant legal provisions. During the research stage, the legislative lawyer must learn the relevant text in all its minute detail, must find and study all the relevant case law, must identify and talk with litigators in the area as well as any other sources who may be useful (e.g., in academia or in policy think tanks), and-through briefings and discussions with the strategist-must identify and understand any additional layers of relevant political reality.

. . .

4.   Draft Materials

The first two stages of legislative lawyering work—assessing and researching a problem or an issue—are essential for the legislative lawyer to devise creative and helpful solutions and approaches. The remaining two stages are essential for the legislative lawyer to "deliver" on that solution or approach. No matter how brilliant a legislative lawyer may be in her comprehension and creativity during the first three stages of work, if she cannot explain to others what she has learned and cannot help persuade the relevant players to come together in a consensus, she has not "delivered" as a legislative lawyer.

An essential mechanism through which one explains one's ideas and approaches is written materials. Learning to write for an advocacy effort is perhaps one of the hardest skills for lawyers (and law students) to learn. Lawyers have a tendency to set forth a great deal of information, cover all possible alternatives, and use terms hardly ever heard in ordinary conversation. While this is appropriate, and indeed, imperative in some settings, it can be deadly in an advocacy setting. Thus, the challenge for a legislative lawyer is to know a great deal of information, but to convey—in clear and simple written form—only that information which the audience targeted for the document or communication needs to know.

. . .

A legislative lawyer must be competent to write all the documents necessary for an advocacy effort—from the most simple to the most complex. Once a legislative lawyer is part of an advocacy effort, the solution to various political/ legal problems may depend on subtle and creative uses of text. In such cases, it is important that all documents used in the advocacy effort correctly reflect both the legal and political goals in play. This includes everything from detailed background papers to simple one-pagers of bullet points.

. . .

5.   Oral Presentation and Negotiation

Written communications are essential to conveying one's ideas, but nothing substitutes for in-person oral exchanges. Consensus is usually reached through a series of oral exchanges and negotiations. Thus, the ability to communicate and negotiate effectively is the final skill set of the legislative lawyer.

The oral communications of a legislative lawyer can be divided into two categories: explanatory and persuasive. Examples of explanatory communications are explanations to a client or a coalition of how a proposed bill changes existing law or why existing law must be rectified by legislation. Examples of persuasive communications are persuading a coalition that a proposed deal is a good one (despite the fact that it appears to give up a provision the coalition previously thought was essential), or persuading a staff person that a proposed legal provision does meet all the political concerns of her boss, or convincing an agency official that an existing legal provision would already achieve a particular policy goal if the agency simply issued appropriate implementing regulations.

When a legislative lawyer is engaged in an explanatory communication, he must be able to convey the relevant information clearly and concisely. Time is the most precious commodity in the legislative arena; attention spans of listeners are often short. As in writing, a legislative lawyer must know a great deal of information, but must be able to convey only what the listener absolutely needs to know about the issue at that point. In addition, if the legislative lawyer is to be an effective "conduit" between the legal/ academic world and the political world, he must be able to explain complicated legal concepts in simple English to those in the political world and be able to explain tangled political realities in simple English to those in the legal/academic world.

. . .

Negotiations represent a more complicated game of oral soccer. The strategist must first identify and engage the right players for the advocacy team to advance the client's goal. She must also identify the players for the other team and set up the game. The legislative lawyer and the policy researcher, working in concert with the strategist, then begin to move the ball among the players, helping to choreograph an effective game play. This requires building consensus within the advocacy team first and then moving forward to engage the opposing team.

. . .

As a description of the five skill sets of a legislative lawyer indicates, a good legislative lawyer brings both convenience and creativity to the legislative process. On the convenience front, the legislative lawyer quickly becomes the "go-to" person whenever a legislator, legislator's staff, or coalition person has a question about the legal content of an issue in an advocacy effort. Similarly, academic researchers and litigation lawyers benefit from having a clearly designated individual to whom they can convey their wisdom and who they can be assured will understand and appreciate their contributions.

There is also significant convenience in having the individual who knows the detailed text and substantive content of the advocacy effort be available and present for the range of meetings that make up the advocacy effort. Litigation lawyers who become involved in an advocacy effort, in addition to their usual legal activities, are essentially trying to do two jobs. Unless such lawyers take a leave from their other legal work, they will not always be available for meetings. The timing of the legislative process is erratic; an essential consultation and/or decision-making meeting can arise at a moment's notice. The convenience in having a legislative lawyer who is competent to make decisions about the wording of legislation or legislative history, and who is available for meetings, cannot be overestimated.

Finally, there is the convenience in having someone who knows both law and politics be involved in both the written and oral components of advocacy. Nothing the legislative lawyer writes should ever need to be rewritten to make it accessible to the target audience. Options presented by a legislative lawyer should never need to be reformulated to accommodate political realities. The explanation a legislative lawyer provides to a staff person should never need to be rephrased by a lobbyist in order to be useful for the staff person.

At times, a legislative lawyer will actually be able to come up with a creative solution to a legal problem (and sometimes a political problem) that neither the strategist/lobbyists nor the expert lawyers/academics would have arrived at by themselves. It is difficult to be creative without accumulating data and knowledge. By extension, if one can accumulate legal, policy, and political data with equal sophistication and comprehension, one can be more creative in devising new legal and policy solutions that will accommodate political realities.

CHAPTER 3

LEGISLATIVE STAFF ETHICS

■ ■ ■

Ethical issues as they apply to legislative staff, and lawyers in particular, are rarely examined. This is unfortunate, because like any area of legal practice, attorneys working for a legislature face a multitude of potential ethical issues. In many ways, the typical sources of guidance like the ABA Rules, are written with lawyers representing clients in court or institutions in mind. When the Rules refer to "government lawyers" they mean lawyers working for the President, governor or an executive agency. A legislature, however, is a different animal from courts or the executive branch. Just trying to determine who your client is when working for a legislature can be a very difficult problem and causes a multitude of ethical problems. Do lawyers working for a legislator owe a duty to a higher power than the legislator they directly report to? Should there be formal rules for legislative lawyers? Would rules such as these put lawyers at a disadvantage within a legislative context? Are formal ethics rules unnecessary because political considerations regulate legislative lawyers, along with other employees, well enough? Non-legal staff also face ethical difficulties and should be aware of the professional responsibility considerations that may affect how legislative lawyers perform their jobs.

American Bar Association Model Rules of Professional Conduct

Rule 3.9:   Advocate In Non-adjudicative Proceedings

A lawyer representing a client before a legislative body or administrative agency in a non-adjudicative proceeding shall disclose that the appearance is in a representative capacity and shall conform to the provisions of Rules 3.3(a) through (c), 3.4(a) through (c), and 3.5.

Comment on Rule 3.9

Rule 3.9   Comment

[1] In representation before bodies such as legislatures, municipal councils, and executive and administrative agencies acting in a rule-making or policy-making capacity, lawyers present facts, formulate issues and advance argument in the matters under consideration. The decision-making body, like a court, should be able to rely on the integrity of the submissions made to it. A lawyer appearing before such a body must deal

with it honestly and in conformity with applicable rules of procedure. See Rules 3.3(a) through (c), 3.4(a) through (c) and 3.5. [2] Lawyers have no exclusive right to appear before non adjudicative bodies, as they do before a court. The requirements of this Rule therefore may subject lawyers to regulations inapplicable to advocates who are not lawyers. However, legislatures and administrative agencies have a right to expect lawyers to deal with them as they deal with courts. [3] This Rule only applies when a lawyer represents a client in connection with an official hearing or meeting of a governmental agency or a legislative body to which the lawyer or the lawyer's client is presenting evidence or argument. It does not apply to representation of a client in a negotiation or other bilateral transaction with a governmental agency or in connection with an application for a license or other privilege or the client's compliance with generally applicable reporting requirements, such as the filing of income-tax returns. Nor does it apply to the representation of a client in connection with an investigation or examination of the client's affairs conducted by government investigators or examiners. Representation in such matters is governed by Rules 4.1 through 4.4.

Rule 3.3:   Candor Toward The Tribunal

(a)   A lawyer shall not knowingly:

(1)   make a false statement of fact or law to a tribunal or fail to correct a false statement of material fact or law previously made to the tribunal by the lawyer;

(2)   fail to disclose to the tribunal legal authority in the controlling jurisdiction known to the lawyer to be directly adverse to the position of the client and not disclosed by opposing counsel; or

(3)   offer evidence that the lawyer knows to be false. If a lawyer, the lawyer's client, or a witness called by the lawyer, has offered material evidence and the lawyer comes to know of its falsity, the lawyer shall take reasonable remedial measures, including, if necessary, disclosure to the tribunal. A lawyer may refuse to offer evidence, other than the testimony of a defendant in a criminal matter, that the lawyer reasonably believes is false. (b) A lawyer who represents a client in an adjudicative proceeding and who knows that a person intends to engage, is engaging or has engaged in criminal or fraudulent conduct related to the proceeding shall take reasonable remedial measures, including, if necessary, disclosure to the tribunal. . . .

(c)   The duties stated in paragraphs (a) and (b) continue to the conclusion of the proceeding, and apply even if compliance requires disclosure of information otherwise protected by Rule 1.6.

(d) In an ex parte proceeding, a lawyer shall inform the tribunal of all material facts known to the lawyer that will enable the tribunal to make an informed decision, whether or not the facts are adverse.

Rule 3.4:   Fairness To Opposing Party And Counsel

A lawyer shall not:

(a) unlawfully obstruct another party's access to evidence or unlawfully alter, destroy or conceal a document or other material having potential evidentiary value. A lawyer shall not counsel or assist another person to do any such act;

(b) falsify evidence, counsel or assist a witness to testify falsely, or offer an inducement to a witness that is prohibited by law; (c) knowingly disobey an obligation under the rules of a tribunal except for an open refusal based on an assertion that no valid obligation exists;

Rule 3.5:   Impartiality And Decorum Of The Tribunal

A lawyer shall not:

(a) seek to influence a judge, juror, prospective juror or other official by means prohibited by law;

(b) communicate ex parte with such a person during the proceeding unless authorized to do so by law or court order; (c) communicate with a juror or prospective juror after discharge of the jury if:

(1) the communication is prohibited by law or court order;

(2) the juror has made known to the lawyer a desire not to communicate; or

(3) the communication involves misrepresentation, coercion, duress or harassment; or (d) engage in conduct intended to disrupt a tribunal.

A. ETHICS & THE LEGISLATIVE LAWYER

THE ETHICS AND POLITICS OF LEGISLATIVE DRAFTING
David A. Marcello, 70 *Tulane Law Review* 2437 (1996)

In Part III, the Model Rules deal with the lawyer's role as advocate. Although taking as their dominant model the lawyer engaged in litigation, these rules do not apply exclusively to adjudicative proceedings. Rule 3.9 deals explicitly with the lawyer acting as "Advocate in Nonadjudicative Proceedings" and expressly requires compliance with Rules 3.3(a) through (c), 3.4(a) through (c), and 3.5.

. . .

The lawyer's personal duties of candor go further than most lawyers might assume without a careful reading of the Model Rules. Most might understand that a lawyer may not present false evidence or make a false statement of material fact or law to a legislative committee, but do most lawyers appreciate that the prohibition on false statements of material fact or law applies not only in communications with a tribunal, but also in communications with a third party? Do most counsel representing clients before a legislative committee understand their ethical obligation "to disclose to the tribunal legal authority in the controlling jurisdiction known to the lawyer to be directly adverse to the position of the client and not disclosed by opposing counsel"?

As a further buttress against deceitful conduct by an attorney, the Model Rules enjoin the lawyer not to assist a client "in conduct that the lawyer knows is criminal or fraudulent." Because most lawyers understand the impropriety of assisting criminal conduct, the key word may be "fraudulent." The Model Rules give a definition: " 'Fraud' or 'Fraudulent' denotes conduct having a purpose to deceive and not merely negligent misrepresentation or failure to apprise another of relevant information." The lawyer's duty not to assist a client in fraudulent conduct "applies whether or not the defrauded party is a party to the transaction." Rule 1.16 reinforces the duty by requiring a lawyer to decline or withdraw from representation when a client demands conduct from the lawyer that would "result in violation of the rules of professional conduct or other law." Thus, the ethical lawyer may be required both to disclose confidential information and to withdraw from representation of a client because of fraudulent conduct.

A hypothetical drawn from Louisiana experience may help to give some vitality to these ethical precepts. My friend was once called upon in his capacity as legislative staff counsel to draft an amendment in committee while the matter was being debated. The committee adopted the amendment without ever seeing a copy, based entirely on the presentation by a legislator who held in his hands throughout the discussion a copy of an amendment that the legislator had prepared. Following the favorable vote, the legislator presented my friend with the actual document he had held in his hands throughout the discussion; the amendment my friend had drafted based on that discussion was quite different. The legislator said, "This is the amendment." My friend replied, "Do you want me to tell them what this says, as opposed to what they voted for?" The legislator backed down but was not happy about it. My friend, who is a lawyer, had to play hardball in order to stay on the right side of legal ethics. Clearly, if he had gone along with the legislator, he would have been guilty of violating the duty against fraudulent conduct as well as the duty requiring candor toward a tribunal.

There are important practical differences between working for the executive branch of government and working for the legislature. Employees in the executive branch of government accept direction from a single leader who sets the policy of the administration. Those who work for the legislature, on the other hand, must deal with multiple factions and cannot generally afford to be perceived as the captive of any one of them. It may be easier in that context to maintain independence and integrity, because it is both ethically appropriate and politically prudent.

Legislative drafting personnel need to know that the ethical transgressions of subordinates can in certain circumstances be charged to their superiors. Rule 5.1(c) subjects a supervising attorney to disciplinary liability for a subordinate's violation of the rules of professional conduct where the supervisor either orders or knows of and ratifies the subordinate's unprofessional conduct. The comment to Rule 5.1 explicitly applies the rule to "lawyers having supervisory authority in the law department of an enterprise or government agency." Conversely, a directive from above is no excuse for a subordinate engaging in unethical conduct: "A lawyer is bound by the rules of professional conduct notwithstanding that the lawyer acted at the direction of another person." Legislative drafting personnel, whether supervisors or subordinates, must be wary of conduct—their own or someone else's—that skirts the limits of propriety.

NOTES & QUESTIONS

1. The District of Columbia Rules of Professional Conduct states,

   Rule 1.6—Confidentiality of Information (a) Except when permitted under paragraph (c), (d), or (e), a lawyer shall not knowingly: (1) reveal a confidence or secret of the lawyer's client;

   (2) use a confidence or secret of the lawyer's client to the disadvantage of the client; (3) use a confidence or secret of the lawyer's client for the advantage of the lawyer or of a third person.

   (b) "Confidence" refers to information protected by the attorney-client privilege under applicable law, and "secret" refers to other information gained in the professional relationship that the client has requested be held inviolate, or the disclosure of which would be embarrassing, or would be likely to be detrimental, to the client.

   . . .

   (j) For purposes of this rule, a lawyer who serves as a member of the D.C. Bar Practice Management Service Committee, formerly known as the Lawyer Practice Assistance Committee [1], or a staff assistant, mentor, monitor or other consultant for that committee, shall be deemed to have a lawyer-client relationship with respect to any lawyer-counselee being counseled under programs conducted by or on behalf of the committee. Communications between the counselor and the lawyer being counseled under the auspices of the committee, or made in the course of and associated with such counseling, shall be treated as a confidence or secret within the terms of paragraph (b). Such information may be disclosed only to the extent permitted by this rule. However, during the period in which the lawyer-counselee is subject to a probationary or monitoring order of the Court of Appeals or the Board on Professional Responsibility in a disciplinary case instituted pursuant to Rule XI of the Rules of the Court of Appeals Governing the Bar, such information shall be subject to disclosure in accordance with the order. (k) The client of the government lawyer is the agency that employs the lawyer unless expressly provided to the contrary by appropriate law, regulation, or order.

Comment

The term "agency" in paragraph (j) includes, *inter alia,* executive and independent departments and agencies, special commissions, committees of the legislature, agencies of the legislative branch such as the Government Accountability Office, and the courts to the extent that they employ lawyers (*e.g.,* staff counsel) to counsel them. The employing agency has been designated the client under this rule to provide a commonly understood and easily determinable point for identifying the government client.

ETHICAL OBLIGATIONS OF CONGRESSIONAL LAWYERS

Michael L. Stern, 63 *New York University Annual Survey of American Law* 191 (2007)

What are the ethical obligations of congressional lawyers? Despite the significant number of lawyers elected to Congress and employed by members, committees, and other congressional offices and agencies, this question has received relatively little attention. Those who have discussed the issue seem largely to have assumed that congressional lawyers are not subject to any formal ethical rules, beyond those applicable to all congressional staffers.

Many congressional lawyers perform functions largely indistinguishable from those performed by their non-lawyer colleagues. Though many of these activities—including conducting routine oversight of executive agencies, drafting proposed legislation, and negotiating the language of bills within Congress and with the executive branch—may be better performed by someone with a legal background, they nonetheless can be and often are performed by non-lawyers. This may lead to the conclusion—or to the tacit assumption—that congressional lawyers are not practicing law and need not concern themselves with the professional rules of ethics.

This, however, does not seem to be the view of the District of Columbia Bar, which has indicated that the congressional practice of law should be governed by its Rules of Professional Conduct. Thus, Rule 1.6 of the D.C.

your "client" is the agency 303 304

Rules of Professional Conduct, which restricts a lawyer's ability to reveal or use a client's confidence or secret, provides that "[t]he client of a government lawyer is the agency that employs the lawyer unless expressly provided to the contrary by appropriate law, regulation, or order." The comments to the rule explain that the term "agency" includes "committees of the legislature [and] agencies of the legislative branch such as the General Accounting Office."

Moreover, in 1977, a Legal Ethics Committee of the D.C. Bar, interpreting the Code of Professional Responsibility (the predecessor to the Rules of Professional Conduct), advised that the ethics rules applied to lawyers acting as attorneys to congressional committees.[5] The panel, while noting that the "Code is directed to the conduct of attorneys in its usual manifestation and is not specifically oriented toward the conduct of attorneys acting as counsel for congressional committees," nonetheless concluded that the disciplinary rules prohibited a committee counsel from requiring a witness to appear at televised hearings when the committee had been notified in advance that the witness would refuse to answer questions based upon the constitutional right against self-incrimination.

Apart from this, there appears to be little guidance on the ethical obligations of congressional lawyers. Neither the House nor Senate Ethics Manual suggests that congressional ethics rules impose any special ethical obligations on congressional lawyers. With the exception of a reference to "professional standards and responsibilities" in the statute establishing the Senate Legal Counsel, Congress does not appear to have addressed how, if at all, professional ethics apply to its attorneys.

In short, congressional lawyers operate with very little in the way of formal guidance on their ethical responsibilities, and they do so in an often-frenzied atmosphere that leaves little time for reflection on such matters. While they may assume that their activities are largely beyond the reach of the professional ethics rules, this may prove to be a dangerous assumption. Absent some clarification of the rules applicable to the congressional practice of law, a future clash between the congressional culture and that of the professional bar organizations is likely.

To explore further the issues involved in attempting to apply professional ethics standards to congressional lawyers, I will consider two different types of lawyers: (1) those who serve on the staff of congressional committees; and (2) those who provide legal services to a variety of congressional offices. In so doing, I will draw upon my experience both as a committee counsel and as a lawyer for an institutional congressional legal office.

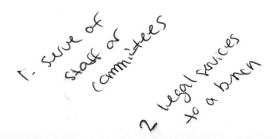

1 - serve on staff of committees

2 legal services to a branch

REPRESENTING REPRESENTATIVES: ETHICAL CONSIDERATIONS FOR THE LEGISLATURE'S ATTORNEYS

Robert J. Marchant, 6 *N.Y.U. Journal of Legislation & Policy* 439 (2003)

[handwritten margin note: 4 arguments why lawyer ethics need not apply]

The lack of scholarship concerning the professional responsibilities of legislative attorneys raises the question of whether the rules of professional ethics should apply to these attorneys. There are four primary arguments that can be made against the application of the rules of professional ethics to legislative attorneys. The first three arguments, which have received little attention from the courts and scholars, generally call for a complete exemption from the rules. The fourth argument, which has received a significant amount of scholarly debate, though not in the specific context of legislative attorneys, calls for an exemption only to the extent necessary to protect the public interest. Each of these arguments is seriously flawed.

A.   Legislative Attorneys are Not Practicing Law

[handwritten margin note: circled "1"]

The first argument against applying the rules of professional ethics to legislative attorneys is that legislative attorneys are not practicing law. This argument does not square with the facts. Although the specific test varies among jurisdictions, the practice of law generally includes preparing instruments by which legal rights are secured, giving legal advice and counsel, and rendering a service that requires the use of legal knowledge or skill. To varying degrees, legislative attorneys, and particularly legislative drafters and committee counsel, provide these services. In performing their jobs, legislative attorneys typically must ascertain and describe the current state of the law on a particular issue, the potential legal effect of a proposal, and any constitutional issues raised by the proposal. If the legislature is considering a proposal that may be unconstitutional, legislative attorneys typically explain options the legislature may consider in order to accomplish the intended effect in a more constitutionally defensible way. In addition, legislative attorneys who draft legislation arguably are preparing a legal instrument (typically, an introducible bill or amendment) that is primarily designed to affect the rights of certain persons under the law (persons who will be subject to the legislation upon enactment). Drafting legislation is akin to drafting a contract, except that legislation generally applies to all of society rather than only to the consenting parties. Finally, although there is no case discussing whether legislative attorneys are practicing law, at least one state bar association has publicly reprimanded a legislative attorney for practicing law while her license was suspended for failure to pay bar dues and failure to satisfy her continuing legal education requirements.

It is true that certain legislatures permit non-attorneys to draft legislation and to provide analysis of legislative proposals to legislators. This might indicate that legislative attorneys who perform similar tasks are not practicing law. However, legislative attorneys enrich the drafting or analysis services they provide by utilizing their legal training and expertise. For example, legislative attorneys may do extensive legal research to ascertain the scope of federal preemption in a particular area of the law or to determine how other states have addressed similar policy issues, or they may utilize their legal skills in interpreting and applying constitutional provisions or federal statutory requirements applicable to the states. Also, the fact that a non-attorney may provide the same services as an attorney does not necessarily prove that the attorney is not practicing law. An attorney who prepares an offer to purchase real estate on behalf of a client likely is practicing law, even though, in some states, a real estate agent who is not a licensed attorney may provide the same service.

B. Separation of Powers

The second argument against applying the rules of professional ethics to legislative attorneys is that the judicial branch is constitutionally prohibited from intruding into the lawmaking process, even to the extent reflected in the rules. According to this argument, the legislative and judicial powers are constitutionally vested in separate branches of government. Because legislative attorneys play an integral role in the operation of the legislative branch, the argument goes, it is unconstitutional for the judicial branch to dictate the manner in which legislative attorneys provide legal services to the legislature.

In the only case discussing this argument, In the Matter of Advisory Committee on Professional Ethics Opinion 621, the New Jersey Supreme Court emphasized that it had full authority to regulate the practice of attorneys who work for the legislature. The case involved a licensed attorney, Zublatt, who was offered a part-time position as an aide to a legislator. The New Jersey conflicts of interest statute prohibited such an employee from representing private clients before the board, agency, commission, or other part of government in which he or she was employed. Because much of Zublatt's income was derived from representing private clients before governmental agencies, he sought an opinion with regard to the meaning of the conflicts of interest statute from the legislative committee charged with advising legislative officers and employees about ethical standards. According to that committee, the statute prohibited Zublatt only from representing private parties before agencies of the legislative branch. However, Zublatt also sought an opinion from a committee that was under the jurisdiction of the state supreme court and that was charged with advising attorneys with regard to professional ethics. According to that committee, the rules of professional ethics prohibited Zublatt from representing private parties before any state agency in any branch of government, except when the state was not an adverse party. Zublatt and other interested parties then sought and obtained review from the New Jersey Supreme Court.

One argument put forth by various parties to the suit was that the judiciary lacked authority to regulate the activities of legislative aides who were lawyers, because the conflicts of interest statute vested the particular legislative committee with the exclusive authority to oversee the ethics of legislative officers and employees. This argument did not fare very well. As the court noted, "[B]y the conclusion of oral argument, it was clear that no one doubted the power of this Court in that regard." The court explained: [No] branch of government has the power to authorize, either explicitly or implicitly, conduct by attorneys that violates the ethical standards imposed by the judiciary . . . . We reject the contention that the establishment of ethical standards for a lawyer/government employee is uniquely a matter for the Legislature . . . . [When] the employee or officeholder is a lawyer, the Legislature's ethical mandate becomes a floor, not a ceiling. Ultimately, it is the Court that establishes the ethical standards to which an attorney is held, and neither the Legislature nor the Executive can diminish them.

Thus, the New Jersey Supreme Court affirmed an axiom of American legal practice: the judicial branch has inherent and exclusive authority to regulate the practice of law. Although this case dealt with the authority of the judiciary to regulate the activities of a legislative employee in his or her capacity as an attorney in private practice, the courts would likely support their own inherent and exclusive authority by, in effect, telling the legislature, "If you choose to hire attorneys, you get attorneys who are licensed and regulated by the judiciary." This conclusion seems to be undisputed with regard to attorneys for the executive branch, and there is no basis in the Constitution to treat the legislature's attorneys any differently. Attorneys currently play an integral role in the operation of the executive branch and, given the level of scholarship and discussion concerning the ethics of executive branch attorneys, it appears to be accepted commonly that the Constitution permits the court to regulate executive branch attorneys. In addition to the inherent and exclusive authority of the courts to regulate the practice of law, the minimal extent to which the rules of professional ethics would intrude into the legislative process is another reason why the separation of powers argument is unlikely to prevail. For example, the rule of professional ethics relating to conflicts of interest is potentially the most intrusive, because it may be construed to impede legislative attorneys from providing legal services to legislators on opposite sides of the same issue. However, the rule has this effect only if each legislator is viewed as the legislative attorney's client. This problem is avoided entirely if the institution of the legislature is viewed as the legislative attorney's client and the institution specifically authorizes its attorneys to provide services to competing legislators. Of course, it is possible to imagine a rule of professional ethics that arguably would violate the separation of legislative and judicial powers. Rules that required legislative attorneys to report to the court any criticism of the court system that was communicated in the scope of the attorneys' representation or that prohibited legislative attorneys from drafting any legislation that negatively affected judicial incumbents are obvious examples. The current rules of professional ethics, though, are not nearly so intrusive into the legislative process.

C.　Comity

The third argument against applying the rules of professional ethics to legislative attorneys acknowledges the judicial branch's inherent and exclusive authority to regulate attorneys, but posits that the judicial branch, if asked, would choose to exempt legislative attorneys as a matter of comity. It is certainly possible that the judicial branch would make this choice. Courts have shown a willingness, in certain cases, to share with the legislature the court's authority to regulate the practice of law. However, given the factors that likely would be important in a case involving the issue of comity, it is by no means certain that a court would choose to grant legislative attorneys such an exemption. Here again, the case of Opinion 621 is instructive. Although the court in that case expressly noted that it did not reach the issue of comity, the court evinced an openness to entertain the issue under the right set of facts.

The court explained:

While we assume that we may be more sensitive to the need for regulation of the bar in the public interest than are the Executive and the Legislature—since that is primarily our responsibility—we do not and should not assume that those branches are any less concerned with the preservation of public confidence in government. The Executive and the Legislature know, perhaps better than we, what appearances are likely to have an adverse effect . . . . While we recognize their commitment, we do not imply that we would accede . . . to the executive and legislative judgment about ethical prohibitions placed by the Act on lawyers serving as part-time legislative aides. However. . . . we believe that considerable deference should be given to their judgment.

Thus, under the court's analysis, one important factor in a case addressing the issue of comity likely would be whether the legislature, with due regard for the preservation of public confidence in government, has chosen to utilize its attorneys in a manner requiring an exemption from the rules of professional ethics. This factor, because it depends upon the actions of the particular legislature involved, requires a case-by-case analysis. Another important factor in the court's analysis would be the impact that an exemption from the rules of professional ethics would have upon the efficient operation of the other branches of government. This factor illustrates the significant difficulties the comity argument is likely to encounter. The important services provided by legislative attorneys argue against granting an exemption from the rules of professional ethics on the basis of comity. As noted above, ethical restraints on legislative attorneys are important not only for the institution of the legislature, but also for the democratic process itself. The courts may be unwilling to risk damaging the institution or the democratic process. Furthermore, the proposed legislative employment of the attorney in Opinion 621 would have involved many tasks that are not particularly legal in nature. It is reasonable to expect that the court would be more vigilant over the practices of legislative attorneys, who are hired primarily to provide legal services, and less deferential to the judgment of the legislative branch.

In addition, the rules of professional ethics were drafted, at some minimal level, with government attorneys in mind. This is another reason why the separation of powers and the comity arguments are unpersuasive. Although it is difficult to apply the rules to legislative attorneys, because the rules are primarily focused on the ethics of attorneys in private practice, the text of the various codes of professional conduct indicate that the courts believe they have the authority to regulate government attorneys and that they intend to do so.

B. WHO IS THE LEGISLATIVE LAWYER'S CLIENT?

Identifying their client is of supreme importance to the lawyer in matters of professional responsibility and ethics. To whom do you owe confidentiality? Who do you represent in a negotiation and how does that affect the tactics you use? Will there be a conflict of interest? To whom do you offer your advice and counsel, and is that assistance exclusive? A great deal of effort has gone into answering these questions for parts of the legal profession, especially those who work in the courthouse, but also lawyers who work for institutions and executive branch government lawyers. Legislative lawyers, however, have not received the same attention and guidance. Indeed, many of the ABA's model rules give little to no guidance to a legislative lawyer faced with an ethical dilemma. Even those who have served in similar positions in Congress have differing opinions as to who their client was and how to address certain ethical issues. Below are the opinions of three legislative counsel, two of whom served the Senate Judiciary Committee and one who served the Senate Foreign Relations Committee.

GOVERNMENT LAWYERING: THE ETHICS OF
REPRESENTING ELECTED REPRESENTATIVES

Kathleen Clark, 61 *Law and Contemporary Problems* 31 (1998)

Capitol Hill used to be referred to as "the last plantation." For the purposes of this symposium, however, I believe that it is more useful to think of Capitol Hill not in terms of the antebellum South but rather in terms of medieval Europe. Congress consists of a series of fiefdoms. To understand any particular lawyer's role in Congress, it is important to know which fiefdom the lawyer is part of, and who is its head.

. . .

When I tell people that I used to work at the Senate Judiciary Committee, most of them respond with the following question: "Did you work for the Committee itself, or for a particular Senator?" To the uninitiated, that may seem like a reasonable question, but it displays how little the questioner knows about the Committee. Those more familiar with its workings would know that, for the purposes of identifying the employer of a staff lawyer, there is essentially no such thing as "the Senate Judiciary Committee itself."

To explain this, it is perhaps best to start with a basic explanation of some of the different types of lawyers who work in the Senate. Some lawyers, such as the Senate Legal Counsel, who represents the Senate in court proceedings, work for the Senate as a whole. At first blush, this might seem like an impossibly difficult arrangement. Who, after all, can speak for the Senate as a whole? Fortunately, the statute that created the Office of Senate Legal Counsel also defines precisely when the Legal Counsel may act on behalf of the Senate, requiring a vote of the Senate as a whole, the Legal Counsel's bipartisan advisory committee, or the relevant committee.

. . .

Other lawyers make their services generally available to any Senator, in much the way that the Congressional Research Service makes its services available to all Members of Congress. For example, the Office of the Legislative Counsel provides technical advice on the drafting of legislation to "any committee of the Senate." Thus, before advising the chairman of the Senate Judiciary Committee to introduce a particular bill, I consulted a lawyer in the Office of Legislative Counsel to ensure that the bill was drafted properly and that it would be referred back to the Judiciary Committee. Legislative Counsel lawyers provide advice to Senators' staff, who may in some cases reject that advice. Some of their proposed revisions may be insufficiently sensitive to political issues. For example, they may propose the clarification of language that the Senator prefers to remain ambiguous. One finds in the Office of Legislative Counsel the kind of professionalism and attention to detail and consistency described by one commentator as necessary for careful legislative drafting. These lawyers seem to be both nonpartisan and nonpolitical. They seem to see themselves more as technicians than as political operators.

. . .

A third category of legislative lawyer works for a particular Senator. I refer to this third type as a "political lawyer" because she owes her loyalty and her job to an individual senator, and must be particularly sensitive to that Senator's political goals and interests. These lawyers can be further divided into two categories: those who work in the Senator's "personal office," and those who work as part of his "committee staff." Personal office staff tend to have responsibility for quite a wide range of issues, and therefore do not usually have the opportunity to develop expertise in a particular subject area. Many, although by no means all, Senate staffers are lawyers. Except for lawyers in the Office of the Senate Legal Counsel, there is no formal requirement that lawyers working in the Senate actually be licensed to practice law. In fact, the Chief Counsel of the Senate Judiciary Committee during the early 1990s had never taken a bar exam. Nevertheless, some Senate staff who are not lawyers engage in lawyer-like work, such as drafting legislation.

In general, committee staff are hired by an individual Senator to handle his work on a particular committee. The size of a Senator's committee staff depends on the Senator's seniority on the committee and on whether he is in the majority or the minority party. The longer the Senator's tenure on the committee, the larger his budget. Also, majority party Senators receive a larger budget than those of the minority party. Most committee staff tend to have less personal contact with the Senator, but have more of an opportunity to specialize in a particular substantive area. The Senate Judiciary Committee staff with whom I worked—like personal office staff—acted as though they owed loyalty to the particular Senator for whom they worked, rather than to "the Committee itself." In the case of the Senate Judiciary Committee, staffers describe their work not in terms of their immediate bosses, but in terms of their ultimate boss— the Senator for whom both they and their immediate bosses work.

. . .

If a legislative lawyer looked to the American Bar Association's Model Rules of Professional Conduct for guidance, she could be led very badly astray. For example, an official comment to Model Rule 1.13 states that a government lawyer's client "is generally the government as a whole," although in some circumstances the client may be a specific agency. Under this analysis, a lawyer working for the Senate Judiciary Committee could have several possible clients: the federal government "as a whole," the legislative branch of government, the Senate as an institution, or the Senate Judiciary Committee itself. As a matter of practice, however, none of these is the lawyer's actual client. Instead, the Judiciary Committee lawyer has as her client a specific Member of Congress to whom she owes her job and her professional loyalty.

The typical political lawyer on Capitol Hill does not see her role as the promotion of the public interest, except as her client/legislator defines for himself the public interest. There are limits to the kind of activities a political lawyer can engage in, just as there are limits to what any lawyer in private practice can do. It would be improper for a political lawyer to work on a legislator's purely personal legal problems, such as estate planning. Nor can the lawyer engage in the legislator's campaign work—at least not on government time—or assist a legislator in illegal activity. Beyond that, political lawyers act as though they have no particular obligation to the committee, to the legislative branch, to the Senate, to the United States, and certainly not to the public in general.

. . .

The Chairman's political lawyers would work on behalf of another Senator only at the direction of the Chairman himself. This particular Chairman was well-known for his cooperative relationships with other members of the Committee, even members from the opposing party. So when a minority member was facing a tough reelection battle and wanted to hold field hearings in several locations within his state, the Chairman authorized the hearings, and I attended the hearings as the Chairman's representative. (The minority-party Senator was the only member present at these hearings, and the full Committee did not pursue further action on this Senator's legislative proposal.)

Thus, in the legislative branch, the political lawyer's role is to promote the substantive agenda of the elected official, protect his political interests, and make him look good.

WHO'S THE CLIENT? LEGISLATIVE LAWYERING THROUGH THE REAR-VIEW MIRROR
Michael Glennon, 61 *Law and Contemporary Problems* 21 (1998)

I am invited to consider whom I regarded as my client when I was Legal Counsel to the Senate Foreign Relations Committee. Happily, I can answer succinctly: I do not know. Traditional notions of attorney-client relations do not really apply on Capitol Hill as they do in executive departments and agencies. There, a lawyer has one client—the President, or, depending upon its measure of independence, the agency. The legislative branch, on the other hand, comprises hundreds of potential clients—535 Members plus committees, subcommittees, and various legislative officers. Each of these entities pursues multiple, often conflicting, objectives. Rather than working for a particular body (a committee) or person (its chairman), committee counsel arguably work for the Senate as a whole—Members not on a committee, Members in minority, or Members concerned about matters on which the committee does not have a firm position. In a sense, committee counsel function almost as independent contractors, hopscotching about a political minefield in which the committee, or its chairman, or a Member seeks to vindicate views that are at odds with the views of the others, and using the counsel to help do it.

. . .

My thesis, therefore, is that committee counsel need seldom worry about high-minded attorney-client matters because the landscape does not lend itself to that way of thinking. While I recognize that the breadth of a counsel's discretion may vary from committee to committee, knowing how my peers operated leads me to be confident that my experience was not unique. And, lest one conclude that ethical discretion is unlimited and that no standards guide the committee counsel's conduct, I would suggest that some standards do indeed obtain. Those standards are similar to the traditional canons of legal ethics in some respects, and different in other respects. They are similar in the reason for their existence and in their content: They exist to encourage Members to seek expert counsel and in content are analogous to the canons of professional responsibility of legal ethics. They differ, however, in the way they are made, to whom they apply, and in the way they are enforced. They come from custom, not codification; they are applicable to all committee staff, not just lawyers; and they are enforced not with formal sanctions but through an informal process more akin to that used by dissatisfied customers of an inattentive tradesman— the cold shoulder. All of this will be developed with examples, but first, some background.

I was hired in 1977 by a personnel subcommittee consisting of the two top-ranking Senate Democrats on the Foreign Relations Committee (Sparkman and Church) and the two top-ranking Republicans (Javits and Case). . . .I worked for the majority, but continued to have the title of Legal Counsel to the full Committee. Like other staff members, my salary was paid by the full Senate; committees are its creation, and its pay structure reflects that. During this period, I also wore another hat, heading up an investigation of intelligence activities for the Subcommittee on International Operations.

. . .

I saw my policy preferences and the Committee's as virtually identical, and thus felt less restraint in exercising discretion that might otherwise be left to the client.

It is tempting to try to isolate distinct functions performed by committee counsel with a view to determining whether ethical principles varied from one function to the next, but the line between functions is too blurry to make the approach work. Formally, the principal functions that I performed were rendering legal advice to the Committee and its Members, on matters concerning international law, constitutional law, statutory law, and parliamentary procedure; negotiating on behalf of the Committee with representatives of the Executive Branch, other Senate committees, and the House members of conference committees; and carrying out oversight and investigative activities on behalf of the full Committee or one or more of its subcommittees.

. . .

In many activities, of course, I served the full Committee, and surely regarded the Committee as my client in every traditional sense. In, for example, drafting conditions to the Panama Canal Treaty, or writing the law-related portions of the committee report on that Treaty, or drafting amendments to the Taiwan Relations Act or its committee report, I saw my client as the full Committee and comported myself accordingly. In practical terms, this meant five things.

First, what I wrote reflected what I knew to be the collective views of the full Committee-not my own views or the staff director's, or the chairman's. To glean those views, I met with the Committee and listened as its members discussed legal issues, sometimes in response to questions that I put to them incident to the disposition of collateral policy issues. Second, what I wrote reflected what the Committee need necessarily and implicitly have assumed or decided in disposing of policy issues.

. . .

Third, confidentiality requirements applied. All Committee staff members were expected as a matter of course to hold confidential all matters discussed within closed meetings of the Committee. That requirement, it seemed to me, subsumed attorney-client norms that might otherwise have precluded the disclosure of information disclosed to me in confidence by a member of the Committee or its staff. That included the usual gossip and grapevine commentary, such as remarks made by Senators about other Senators.

It is in the realm of confidentiality expectations that the system's self-enforcing characteristics tend to be especially visible. I recall, in this regard, a lapse on my part that I can only describe as a product of frustration compounded by inattention. I had been asked by the chairman of a subcommittee to get to the bottom of a long-standing controversy. The State Department, it appeared, had enlisted the help of the CIA to smear a foreign journalist who was active in lobbying against a military junta friendly to the United States. The question was, "Who in the Department initiated the effort?" To find out, I deposed various Department officials. The journalist was a friend and supporter of the Chairman of the Subcommittee, so I kept the journalist generally informed as to how things were proceeding—which witnesses said what, basically—to see whether their testimony squared with his own recollection of events and what leads should be pursued. When troubling questions arose, I suggested to the Chairman that we needed to press harder and higher. No, he responded, it was time to back off; a friend of his (and mine) had just been appointed assistant secretary of state for that bureau, and, the chairman told me, he simply did not want to create problems for someone so new on the job. Meanwhile, the journalist was of course nonplussed by my sudden seeming indifference to his grievance and suggested in blunt terms that I get off my behind, put the gloves back on, and start swinging at the Department. I wanted to, of course, and I in effect told him so: "Look," I said, "it wasn't my decision. If you want action, talk to the Chairman." That, I soon realized, was a mistake. As I found out when the Chairman canceled our after-hours martinis, my job, he thought, was to be the fall guy, or at least to keep him from being the fall guy. And he was right: As a staffer, if not as a lawyer, my job was indeed to insulate him from the repercussions of his decision by keeping confidential even the fact that he had made it. When the Chairman makes a decision, a staff person-lawyer or not—should respect it; if that means keeping the fact of the decision confidential, so be it.

. . .

Finally, I thought that zealous representation of my client pertained especially to its institutional interests. Frequently, these interests escaped the note of Members unless specifically called to their attention. Frequently, these questions involved separation of powers disputes with a federal department or agency, or parliamentary "turf wars" with the House or with other Senate Committees. And, frequently, the willingness of the Committee to respond depended upon the play of personalities or politics— of which the staff is frequently unaware. For example, the House Committee, it seemed to me, was perennially jealous of the Senate's advice-and-consent prerogative, and forever interested in getting a cut of the action. I thought the Committee's lawyer ought to be cognizant of the House Committee's penchant for poaching. I drafted something I called the "Treaty Powers Resolution," and got Senators Clark, Church, Mondale, and Kennedy to co-sponsor it. Half the Committee opposed it, but it was reported because it had been included in a bill reported to the full committee by a subcommittee (Senator McGovern's) and a majority plus one was therefore required to strike it.

Similarly, the Committee was in constant jurisdictional conflicts with other Senate committees. Two stand out in my memory. The first was with a subcommittee of the Appropriations Committee, chaired by Senator Inouye. I pointed out that that Committee had encroached upon Foreign Relations' jurisdiction and suggested to Senator Hubert Humphrey, chairman of the relevant subcommittee, that he rise to a point of order on the Senate floor when the legislation came up. Humphrey responded: "Mike, if I took on Dan Inouye on the Senate floor on this, I'd come out looking like a piece of Swiss cheese." I had had no idea that Humphrey's power on the floor was dwarfed by Inouye's (or that Humphrey himself believed that it was).

The other incident involved a dispute that arose between the Committee and the CIA over Committee access to a certain set of classified documents. The Agency had simply refused to let us see them, on the ground that they had already been given to the Senate Select Committee on Intelligence. Remembering Humphrey's earlier response, and recalling that the Intelligence Committee was also chaired by Senator Inouye, I picked a Senator who I expected would have stronger institutional pride: Jacob Javits. Javits was smart, tough, and intensely devoted to the Committee. I went down to his hideaway office in the Capitol basement the morning before the Director of Central Intelligence, Stansfield Turner, was to testify before our Committee. I explained to Javits that, in establishing the Intelligence Committee, the Senate never intended to diminish Foreign Relations' jurisdiction. I was not disappointed, and I will never forget his response: "We'll kill him. We'll kill him." From what I was told by CIA people present with Turner at that meeting, Javits ripped the bark off of him. We got the documents.

. . .

So much for what matters where the application of the attorney-client relationship seemed clear. In many instances, it seemed unclear. Matters also became trickier when Senators on the other side of a dispute were effectively unrepresented by counsel. During the evacuation of Saigon in 1975, when a conference committee completed work on the "Vietnam Contingency Act," time was of the essence. One principle invariably honored by both Houses of Congress is—or at least was at the time—that the House that asks for the conference acts last on the conference report. The Senate had asked for a conference committee on this legislation. One member of the conference committee was the Senate majority leader, Mike Mansfield, who concluded, as is the majority leader's prerogative, to make the report—instantly—the Senate's pending business.5 In the process of discussing a few remaining legal matters with him, I pointed out that, in traditional parliamentary practice, the House, not the Senate, ought to act first on the conference report. My client, at the time, was, I suppose, the Senators who were members of the conference committee; most, but not all, would have supported what Mansfield did. So far as I could tell, I was the only person present who knew about the procedural irregularity that he was about to create. Was I obliged to tell others about it, who might have used this information to block it? I thought not; still, though, the meeting had been held in executive session and had involved classified reports from the besieged American embassy in Saigon and sensitive telephone conversations with the President, and if they were to be provided effective counsel—if they were to be provided any legal counsel—it would have been from me.

. . .

The traditional concept of "client" is simply of scant practical utility in the legislative process. Nor does it help much to categorize work by function and follow the thread back to the client. Lawyering functions overlap in legislative work, and the best way to understand who legislative lawyers serve is not to import an analytic framework (either the canons of professional responsibility or a functional analysis) from private practice, but to look at who those lawyers are, how their policy preferences compare to the legislators with whom they work, and what motivates the legislative lawyers to act as they do. In a free-wheeling, wide-open legislative context, the term "client" can be assigned to virtually any legislator or committee whose interests the lawyer is inclined to advance. The resulting rear-view mirror approach to lawyering creates an ethical regime that is largely indeterminate and may not comport with the tidy, not to say formalistic, traditional legal framework. Indeed, as I have tried to show, the ethical free-for-all poses problems for all staffers, not just legislative lawyers and committee counsel. But it is, I believe, the most accurate account of what goes on, and also the most honest.

LAWYERS IN CONGRESS
John C. Yoo, 61 *Law and Contemporary Problems* 1 (1998)

Whatever the reason, scholarly neglect of attorneys in Congress is unfortunate. The role of congressional lawyers is richer and more complex than the standard story about the executive branch lawyer's internal tug of war between politics and public service. Because of the unique institutional function of Congress in our political system, the functions and duties of the lawyers who serve in the legislature also are unique.

. . .

A . . . more common role of the congressional lawyer is his job in developing legislation. Because many important members of congressional staffs have law degrees, congressional lawyers often supervise the legislative process: the meetings with interest groups, the hearings, the committee mark-ups, the deals between legislators, the floor debates, the public and press relations, and the votes. To be sure, the staff lawyer's role usually does not extend in a significant way to the setting of legislative and political priorities and the initiation of legislation, which are within the domain of the Members of Congress, the Executive Branch, and non-governmental interest groups. Nonetheless, the lawyer's role in operating the procedures through which these proposals must pass raises interesting issues concerning the nature of the legislative process and the lawyer's role in that system.

. . .

Throughout this process, the congressional lawyer seeks to achieve certain procedural goals. The goals are not simply to distribute information that is favorable to the lawyer's side, but rather to see that certain elements of what might be called legislative procedural due process are followed:

(1) All hearings allow both the majority and minority to call witnesses;

(2) Witnesses receive the opportunity to make full statements for the record and to supplement the record with additional materials after the hearing;

(3) Senators of both parties receive equal time to ask questions and present their observations;

(4) The Executive Branch enjoys the right to testify on any issue;

(5) Both sides may include statements of virtually any length in the committee reports; and

(6) Senators may speak for an almost unlimited time during mark-up. These procedures, which are developed and observed by committee lawyers, ensure that both the majority and minority have an equal opportunity to make their arguments known.

Disseminating information by itself, however, serves little purpose. I would suggest that lawyers in Congress work to guarantee the free flow of information because it leads to greater deliberation about the merits of policy decisions. Presenting arguments in hearings and mark-ups forces the other side to respond to them. Contrary to the more pessimistic theories of legislation, no Senator likes to vote yes or no simply because he or she was told to do so by an interest group. During my tenure working for the Senate, no Senator in the Judiciary Committee rose and declared that he was voting for or against the property rights bill simply on the orders of the Sierra Club or of the Defenders of Property Rights. Instead, a legislator—regardless of his motivation for voting on a bill—wants an argument, a rationale, a justification for his vote, and the testing of these reasons leads to greater deliberation before the public on issues of policy. To be sure, the existence of procedures does not lead inevitably to the conclusion that Congress and its staff are working toward greater deliberation in policymaking. One could argue that legislative due process and the institutions that operate by it, such as committees, arose to ease problems that a public choice model of legislation might face. For example, if the legislature amounted to a bazaar with few, if any, procedures (other than the rule of the highest bidder), then the legislative process might devolve quickly into a political state of nature. Legislators might engage in extreme tactics—such as loading up every appropriations bill at the last minute with all manner of riders—because of a prisoner's dilemma problem. Procedures such as limiting the number of riders, or requiring bills to undergo the open process of hearing and committee mark-up, might arise after a series of tit-for-tat interactions by legislators.

Rules could create the context necessary to allow interest groups to purchase laws—by providing mechanisms for measuring political support, for guaranteeing that legislators will keep their promises, and for facilitating bargaining—that avoid a sort of tragedy of the legislative commons.

It might be thought that in pursuing either set of goals—greater deliberation or interest group politics—the congressional lawyer is not giving his full loyalty to his client (the Senator or committee that hired him), the Majority Leader that heads the Senate, or the political party that forms the network for the majority and sets its agenda. In regards to deliberation, because the congressional lawyer's ultimate client is Congress itself, Congress is best served when it acts in an open, considered manner rather than in a haphazard, ad hoc one. Not only may better public policy result, as neo-republicans like to think, but a deliberative process promotes the image of Congress in the public mind, thereby bolstering the legislature's power to impose its preferences upon the other branches. For a congressional lawyer, this goal is also in the best interests of the party, the leadership, and the Senator or committee; strengthening the political reputation of Congress enhances the means by which these various clients will seek to promote their agendas. With regard to public choice or institutionalist theories, the lawyer allows the process to function smoothly by making sure that rules are clear and are obeyed. Without these rules, the resulting uncertainty would undermine the bargaining or strategic interaction necessary for the passage of legislation.

It also might be thought that the congressional lawyer is playing a role that is in tension with democratic government. If the people want a policy, and they elect representatives to implement that policy, then lawyers delay and slow down progress toward that goal by imposing legislative due process procedures. Visiting the United States in the early nineteenth century, Alexis de Tocqueville observed that lawyers love order and formalities, which were "naturally strongly opposed to the revolutionary spirit and to the ill-considered passions of democracy." As a result, American lawyers, like the European nobility, "conceive a great distaste for the behavior of the multitude and secretly scorn the government of the people." The lawyer's procedural, formalist mindset buttresses the existing procedural hurdles for legislation, such as the Senate, the filibuster, the presidential veto, and judicial review, which themselves are counter majoritarian. Although the congressional lawyer may not knowingly play this role, his actions further enhance the mechanisms established by the framers to tame the legislature, which they feared "is every where extending the sphere of its activity, and drawing all power into its impetuous vortex." In this respect, the congressional lawyer acts as an unknowing agent of the separation of powers.

. . .

By training, lawyers understand the importance of neutral principles, of fair processes, and of rational arguments, and when working for Congress they inject these values into an institution that by its nature is designed to "exercise will instead of judgment." On a smaller scale, lawyers in Congress perform the same function that Alexis de Tocqueville observed that they play in American society as a whole, that of restraining ill-considered democracy. While they work to execute the will of Congress, congressional lawyers also act to temper that will, to ensure that it results from judgment as much as from passion.

ETHICAL OBLIGATIONS OF CONGRESSIONAL LAWYERS

Michael L. Stern, 63 *N.Y.U. Annual Survey of American Law* 191 (2007)

Attempting to apply existing professional ethics rules to committee lawyers creates a host of problems. First, the D.C. Bar's assertion that a committee counsel's client is the committee itself does not square with the understanding or conduct of most committee counsel. In many cases, committee lawyers are loyal solely to a single member, usually (but not always) the chairman or ranking member of the committee. For example, when I served as Deputy Staff Director for Investigations of the Senate Homeland Security and Governmental Affairs Committee ("HSGAC"), committee staff would typically identify themselves at meetings with outsiders by the name of the senator for whom they worked, rather than by the name of the committee or subcommittee that technically employed them. A staffer's loyalty was expected to be to the individual senator, not to the "committee."

Other committees operate in a more collegial fashion, with committee staff advising multiple members of the committee. A committee lawyer might work directly for a subcommittee chairman but be appointed by—and ultimately responsible to—the full committee chairman. In that case, the lawyer may view both members as his or her "clients." Some committee staffers—whether or not lawyers-may view themselves as owing duties to all committee members of their own party, though these duties would almost certainly be secondary to the duties owed to the chairman or member for whom the lawyer works directly. Moreover, except for those committees with unified, non-partisan staffs, it is very unlikely that a lawyer would view committee members not of his or her own political party in any sense as his or her "clients." On the contrary, majority committee staffers are more likely to view the minority committee members and staff as adversaries, and vice versa.

Take, for instance, the case of Manuel Miranda, who served as senior counsel on the majority staff of the Senate Judiciary Committee. Miranda was accused of improperly accessing, reading and disseminating documents of the minority party that were stored, unprotected, on a shared network. Miranda acknowledged accessing and reading some of the documents, but contended that the minority had been negligent in failing to protect the documents in "an obviously adversarial context." He further stated:

> I determined for myself that no unlawful, unauthorized hacking was involved in reading these unprotected documents. I knew that in law the duty falls on the other party to protect their [sic] documents. I also considered and studied the propriety or ethics of reading these documents. I knew that in legal ethics there is no absolute prohibition on reading *opposition documents* inadvertently disclosed and that these ethics are stricter than our situation in government service. . . . *I knew that I was not in a relation of confidence to the Senators or documents in question.*

Whatever one's views of Miranda's conduct, few on Capitol Hill would claim that the senators of the minority party were his "clients" or that he owed them a duty to promote their interests and protect their confidences. On the contrary, it was precisely because Miranda was not in a relationship of trust and confidence with these senators that many viewed his accessing the documents in question as improper.

The D.C. Bar's identification of a committee lawyer's client is not only inconsistent with the prevailing culture and norms on Capitol Hill, but it is also flawed as a legal matter. A congressional committee is, after all, merely the creature of the body that created it. Although committees are treated for some purposes as entities with independent legal existences, the House or Senate can, at any time, change the name, jurisdiction, and membership of any committee, or abolish it outright. Moreover, House committees, like the House itself, are not continuing entities, so each committee technically terminates at the end of each Congress and is succeeded by a new committee in the next Congress. Is a committee lawyer required to treat the new committee as a separate client for purposes of maintaining confidences and avoiding conflicts?

These are not just theoretical concerns. A number of years ago a counsel to a House committee raised a question as to whether he would violate attorney-client privilege or the applicable bar rules if he disclosed, to a successor committee, sensitive information he had received from a former committee member when the latter served on the prior committee. The House Office of General Counsel (OHC), where I served as senior counsel, analyzed the issue and concluded that the counsel could not invoke attorney-client privilege to withhold information from the House or its members. We concluded that the House is the equivalent of a "parent corporation" of any House committee and thus, assuming that the attorney-client privilege is applicable at all, the House itself retains the ultimate authority to decide whether or not to assert or waive that privilege.

Treating either the committee or an individual member as the counsel's client also raises a number of issues with regard to potential conflicts of interest. It is not unusual for a committee lawyer to move from one committee to another, or to move from working for one member to another. Under the D.C. Rules of Professional Conduct, treating either the member or the committee as the lawyer's client would seem to create difficult, if not insuperable, issues for the lawyer.

. . .

The explanation here may be that the congressional lawyer's true client is the legislative body itself. While he may owe loyalty-and his or her job—to a particular member or group of members, his or her professional ethical duty is to the institution as a whole. It is perfectly appropriate for him to be a zealous advocate of his principal's policy agenda, but in doing so he acts as any other congressional staffer would. It is when he advises a member to temper or re-frame policy objectives in light of legal considerations that affect the legislative body as a whole that he carries out a function that is uniquely that of the congressional lawyer.

REPRESENTING REPRESENTATIVES: ETHICAL CONSIDERATIONS FOR THE LEGISLATURE'S ATTORNEYS

Robert J. Marchant, 6 *N.Y.U. Journal of Legislation & Policy* 439 (2003)

Legislative attorneys have several potential clients: the public, the government as a whole, the institution of the legislature, the legislative service agency for which the legislative attorneys work, the committee to which the legislative attorneys provide services, or each individual legislator to whom the legislative attorneys provide services. A few of these options for identifying the client may be dealt with summarily. A legislative attorney does not represent the legislative service agency in which he or she works any more than an attorney in private practice represents his or her law firm. The legislative service agency, similar to a law firm, is designed to facilitate the provision of legal services to third parties by the attorneys who work there. In addition, for the reasons previously discussed, it is neither workable nor advisable for legislative attorneys to view their client as the public interest. Furthermore, because the pitfalls of authorizing legislative attorneys to represent the public interest also arise when the government as a whole is viewed as a legislative attorney's client, this Essay will not restate those arguments.

The options for viewing the institution of the legislature, a particular committee, or each individual legislator as the client are the most viable.

However, viewing each legislator as the client creates a key problem concerning conflicts of interest—a problem that can be avoided by viewing either the committee to which the legislative attorney provides services or the institution of the legislature as the client. In addition, viewing the institution of the legislature as the client best supports the institutional development of the legislature.

Viewing each legislator as the client of a legislative attorney is unworkable due to the multiple conflicts of interest that such a system would cause. It is common practice for legislative attorneys to provide legal services to legislators on competing sides of a particular issue as that issue wends its way through the legislative process. For example, a legislative attorney may draft a bill for a Democrat and then, after the bill is introduced, a Republican may ask the legislative attorney for help drafting amendments to change the bill, gut the bill of its efficacy, or even kill the bill. Similarly, a legislative attorney may help a committee chairperson who is a Republican formulate a bill, and then a Democratic committee member may ask the legislative attorney for a legal memorandum identifying all constitutional issues the bill creates. Providing services without regard to political affiliation is a defining characteristic of legislative attorneys. If each legislator is viewed as the legislative attorney's client, this practice would likely be prohibited under the rule against conflicts of interest. Although this rule would permit competing legislators to consent to such a conflict, the rule requires consent to be given after consultation.

These requirements are unworkable in the legislative process. Often, for example, there is a flurry of amendments that must be drafted and legal questions that must be answered while a bill is being debated on the floor. These drafting requests and legal questions routinely come from competing legislators. It is not operationally possible to require the particular house of the legislature to recess in order to allow the attorney to obtain consent for each such conflict from each legislator. Similarly, it would be awkward to require a legislative attorney to perform a conflicts check whenever he or she is asked a question at a committee hearing and to obtain consent during the hearing as each conflict arises.

It could be argued that this problem is avoided if each legislator provides a blanket consent to all such conflicts at the beginning of each legislative session. However, in addition to the obvious problems with obtaining informed consent in advance of any actual conflict, it is unclear what would happen to nonconsenting legislators. The legislature could choose to let non-consenting legislators draft their own legislation and could prohibit them from obtaining legal counsel from legislative attorneys, but that would place these legislators at a disadvantage vis-à-vis legislators who are permitted to use the services of legislative attorneys. Legislators arguably might be coerced into consenting to the conflict of interest in order to avoid this disadvantage. Alternatively, in order to treat all legislators fairly, and to avoid coercing a legislator's consent, the legislature may choose to provide each non-consenting legislator with a state-paid attorney, so that the legislator can obtain legal services commensurate with those provided to consenting legislators. However, because of the benefits of having one's own attorney (as opposed to sharing an attorney with a group of other legislators), in a short period of time most legislators would likely refuse to consent. The resulting cost to the taxpayers, combined with the loss of institutional standardization of the legislature's work, would not be justifiable.

Viewing the institution of the legislature or, if appropriate, a committee as a legislative attorney's client allows the legislature or the committee flexibility to structure the attorney-client relationship in the manner that avoids multiple conflicts of interest and best serves the legislative or committee process. In addition, this view of the client allows a legislature or committee to incorporate its own traditions into the attorney-client relationship. For example, if the institution of the legislature is the client, the legislature could adopt a rule declaring that the institution desires legislative attorneys to provide services to the institution by performing work for all legislators on a non-partisan basis. Under such a rule, there would be no conflict of interest between competing legislators. Similarly, the legislature could adopt a rule clarifying the confidentiality requirements applicable to legislative attorneys, including requirements with regard to maintaining confidentiality during conversations with legislators. Likewise, if a committee is the client, the committee could adopt a resolution declaring that the committee desires legislative attorneys to provide services to the committee by performing work for all committee members on a non-partisan basis.

Also, viewing the institution of the legislature as the client has the special benefit of best supporting the institutional capacity of the legislature. This view of the client acknowledges that the legislature exists as an entity with authority to govern its own affairs. Helping the legislature develop mechanisms for exercising that authority is consistent with efforts made during the last several decades to provide the legislature with the institutional capacity to develop and consider public policy. Also, consideration of the role legislative attorneys should play in the legislative process will encourage legislators to think carefully about and take responsibility for the legislature as an institution. In this way, a discussion of how to structure the manner in which legislative attorneys serve the institution of the legislature may help the legislature to avoid institutional decay.

There is an extensive body of scholarship with regard to the application of the entity client rule which legislatures could rely upon in structuring the roles of legislative attorneys. The legislature, like a corporation, is an entity, and legislative attorneys are in some ways akin to attorneys who work in a corporate legal department. The corporate model provides a useful framework which legislatures and legislative attorneys could use to construct a method of providing legal services to the legislature in a manner generally consistent with the private bar.

NOTES & QUESTIONS

Hypothetical 1:

You are the counsel for a legislative committee and have been engaged in negotiations over a Senate proposal on drug policy. The legal counsel for the Drug Enforcement Agency, who first hired you for your position in Congress and you have not only worked closely with her for 10 years but consider her a close friend, calls you to discuss the bill.

Your friend talks about data that her office had compiled about illegal drug usage that may be helpful to your negotiations. She also makes several suggestions about which provisions should and should not be included in the bill. She suggests that at least one provision is unconstitutional and that the House chair who has to sign off on the bill to get it to a vote in the House dislikes another provision so much that he will refuse to bring the bill to a vote if it contains the provision. Finally, she asks you what provisions your chair is likely to include in the bill.

When you suggest that information about the Senate bill is confidential, she says, "Come, on—we're all on the same side here!"

1. Can you maintain either a friendship or working relationship with this person after she left the legislature and took a position with the executive branch?

2. Can you ethically discuss aspects of this bill with her?

3. Would it be ethical to take information, such as the offered report from her?

4. Has your friend violated any sort of confidentiality by offering up information about what the House chair is likely to do?

5. If a government attorney (which you both are) has the government for a client according to the model rules, does that relieve you from any ethical considerations? Would this be a valid argument if your Chair is told you gave information to your friend?

6. If you do think you need permission before revealing information who should you go to avoid any ethical problems? Your direct staff supervisor? Your Committee chair? The full Committee? Someone from the majority leader's office?

Hypothetical 2:

You are the legal counsel for the Senate Judiciary Committee working for the chair. You were hired by the chair, sit in the same office space with her other staff and you consult with the chair on a daily basis about Committee business. In most every instance you see the chair as your client, and to whom you owe your loyalty and duty. In preparing for a hearing, the Committee's ranking member (the most senior committee member from the minority party) asks you for whatever information and briefing books that you have produced for the chair and the committee members from the majority party. The chair has told you not to give out this information because it includes data and evidence that undercut the chair's publicly stated position on the issue.

1. In a legislature it is sometimes difficult to tell when one is practicing law and when they are playing at politics. Politics is not just inherent to the legislative process, but is often essential for the process of deliberation, negotiation and compromise. As a lawyer, do you find the chair's request unethical?

2. Even though you may be closely aligned with the chair, do you feel you owe some loyalty to other members of the Committee?

3. If you feel the chair's request is unethical, what do you do?

Hypothetical 3:

You are the legal counsel for House Judiciary

Committee's Subcommittee on Crime and Homeland Security. You have been working closely with the chair on a very controversial and sensitive proposal on border security and immigration. Although your chair has been trying to include provisions that will make the bill popular with the rest of his political party's caucus, the House Speaker is one of the few members of the caucus opposed to a key provision. The Speaker's chief legal counsel calls you and asks you to provide a legal analysis against the provision and he needs the information immediately. You say you would need to talk to the Chair before giving that information. The chief counsel angrily reminds you that not only did the Speaker appoint your chair to his position, but that your monthly paycheck comes from the House of Representatives and not your chairman.

1. How do you react to this request?

2. Does it make a difference that the Speaker and your chair are at odds on this issue? Do you act differently if the Speaker was in favor of the provision? If she had not taken a position?

C. CAN THE LEGISLATIVE LAWYER BE A FREE AGENT?

WHO'S THE CLIENT? LEGISLATIVE LAWYERING THROUGH THE REAR-VIEW MIRROR
Michael Glennon, 61 *Law and Contemporary Problems* 21 (1998)

Often, counsel has discretion to pursue his own interests, even when those interests conflict with the expressed preferences of a member of the committee, though it normally is necessary under such circumstances to seek political cover by finding a sympathetic member of the committee to espouse those views. All this translates into opportunities for ideological entrepreneurship in which a committee counsel with a modicum of political savvy can, within certain parameters, advance his own philosophical interests.

. . .

In one sense, I always viewed the client as the Chairman. Sometimes, though, it appeared to me that the client was, in reality, the Senate. Still other times, the client appeared to be another Senator, sometimes not even a member of the Committee. I will elaborate.

I never undertook any activity at odds with what I knew to be the Chairman's position, or even with what I thought might be the Chairman's position. He, not I, was Chairman of the Committee, and I was there to act as his lawyer. Moreover, I regarded the Staff Director as acting in his stead, and treated his wishes as the wishes of the Chairman.

To be distinguished from situations where the Chairman had expressed specific views or desires were the many situations in which none were expressed, either explicitly or implicitly. Here, one's latitude was greater, though hardly unlimited. It was often possible, for example, to "shop" a bill, an amendment, or a speech until a receptive Senator was located. When, for example, Senator Church got into a public dispute with former CIA Director Richard Helms following Helms's conviction of lying to the Committee, I offered Church an op-ed piece, defending Church's view that the conviction was appropriate. He did not want to use it, apparently preferring to duck out of the fight. I then took the piece to Senator Clark, who sent it in to the New York Times, where it was published.

This sort of "Senator shopping" occurred all the time, and I was not the only member of the Committee staff who did it. Often, one would be aware of a particular Senator's interest in a specific topic, such as arms control, human rights, or nuclear proliferation, and an idea for an amendment on that topic—for a mark-up session or floor debate—was appropriately put to that Senator. That was, it seemed to me, squarely within the role of the staff, who were, after all, supposedly experts hired by the Committee to bring to its attention matters falling within their areas of expertise. The client, though, at least at that point, became more the individual Senator than the Committee.

Matters became trickier when the Senator fell within a Committee minority on the issue in question. One particular incident stands out in my memory. At issue was the so-called "extension" of the SALT I Interim Agreement in October, 1977. One group of Senators, a Committee majority, as it turned out, believed the Administration's action to be a circumvention of the Senate's prerogative of advice and consent to treaties. Some other Senators simply were not enthusiastic about arms control agreements with the Soviet Union. They hoped to trigger a major Senate debate on the question before the negotiations on SALT II were complete, and before the Administration had prepared for the debate (in part by educating Senators and staff on a fairly esoteric subject).

I thought their effort misguided from a legal as well as diplomatic standpoint. Constitutionally, the Administration had not entered into an agreement; it had merely announced a policy intention that was wholly within the President's exclusive power to articulate. Diplomatically, premature Senate action could have complicated seriously the ongoing SALT II negotiations, which were then entering a particularly delicate stage.

I tried to enlist Senators on and off the Committee to oppose a measure condemning the Administration's action. I got three—not enough to block the Committee from reporting the resolution, but enough to create parliamentary havoc on the Senate floor, if they could be persuaded to do that. They were. When the resolution reached the floor, I pointed out to one of their non-Committee allies that a point of order lay against the resolution (for certain technical reasons relating to the manner in which it had been hurriedly reported). The Senator made the point of order, it was sustained, and the measure was pulled from the Senate calendar. Regrouping, the measure's supporters called a time out (suggesting the absence of a quorum) and, when the Senate came back in session, announced that they had just met, in a corner of the Senate Chamber, had corrected the problem, and had just re-reported the bill, curing the parliamentary defect that had given rise to the point of order. I pointed out to our ally that the proponents' innovative solution had nevertheless presented another procedural problem (there was no committee report, necessitating that the measure lay over for a day). He therefore made another point of order. It was sustained, and the measure was again pulled from the Senate calendar, this time for good. The Congress then recessed for a holiday, and by the time it returned, the Administration had had enough time to line up allies on the House Foreign Affairs Committee to block the measure permanently.

Who was the client throughout this episode? If the client was the Committee, would not my action have been unethical, as an effort to thwart the will of its majority (and thus hardly "zealous representation" of the client)? On the other hand, had not the Committee itself made the judgment that every member of the Committee was entitled to the assistance of Committee staff, even if that member was the only member opposing the Committee's majority? For that matter, had not the Committee effectively made its staff available to the entire Senate (including our ally who rose to the points of order)? I had in the past—by request-written speeches for Senators who were not members of the Committee, though these were remarks made in support of legislation supported by the Committee's majority; but suppose they had opposed the Committee's position?

No rules governed these matters. I consulted with the Staff Director, who knew what I was doing; had he said stop, I surely would have. He did not. Perhaps some sort of waiver had thus occurred—if there existed an attorney-client relationship the requirements of which could be waived. I do not know. In the morass that is the legislative process, the formal canons of professional responsibility seem to be of little help. More pertinent, to borrow a phrase of Justice Jackson's, are the "contemporary political imponderables" of the specific situation. Sometimes it seems acceptable to act as a free agent, and other times it does not. You "know it when you see it," to paraphrase another Justice (Stewart)—but where and when the line is drawn, I am not sure. Another example illustrates the difficulty in applying the traditional canons.

NOTES & QUESTIONS

Hypothetical 1:

You are the legal counsel for the Senate Agriculture Committee, and you have just helped negotiate an omnibus farm bill in a conference committee with the House. To your great disappointment, the conferees voted to cut a school lunch program that you think is very valuable and useful for the health and well-being of disadvantaged children. You are so upset about this you draft an opinion article for your chair to submit to the country's largest newspaper demanding that the President veto the bill so that Congress will have to start again and include the lunch program. Although your chair agrees with your position and is also disappointed, he does not want to upset or embarrass his colleagues from the conference committee and tells you not to not to submit the article. That evening you are at a reception with another Senator (who is not on your committee) who is also upset that the school lunch program is being cut. You tell him about your opinion article that is ready for publication, and he asks if he could submit the article.

Is it unethical to provide the article to the Senator?

D. THE LEGISLATIVE LAWYER
& THE CONSTITUTION

LAWYERS IN CONGRESS

John C, Yoo, 61 *Law and Contemporary Problems* 1 (1998)

A significant aspect of the congressional attorney's job is as constitutional adviser to a Senator, a committee, or both. The unique institutional function of Congress in our republican system defines the contours of its lawyers' duties in the same manner that the function of the Executive Branch shapes the responsibilities of executive branch attorneys.

. . .

Congress' function as the lawmaking, rather than law-enforcing, branch requires attorneys in Congress to think more creatively about law. As is often the case, Congress must interpret the Constitution in areas that the Supreme Court has never and may never reach in the course of deciding cases or controversies. Fulfilling its constitutional duty as the voice of the people inevitably forces Congress to test the outer limits imposed on its powers by the Constitution. As James Madison wrote in The Federalist, the legislature is sufficiently numerous to feel all the passions which actuate a multitude; yet not so numerous as to be incapable of pursuing the objects of its passions, by means which reason prescribes; it is against the enterprising ambition of this department, that the people ought to indulge all their jealousy and exhaust all their precautions.

Attempting to remain faithful to the will of the people, Congress at times will articulate a vision of the Constitution that is at odds with that held by the Supreme Court. Perhaps the most notable example was the New Deal Congress' efforts to pass sweeping economic regulations in the face of hostile judicial precedent concerning the scope of the Commerce Clause. To be sure, the Supreme Court can and does strike down congressional efforts to reverse judicial decisions of constitutional law. Nonetheless, the same rationale that compelled Presidents Jefferson, Jackson, and Lincoln to challenge judicial supremacy applies with at least equal force to Congress: Congress is an equal coordinate branch and is entitled to interpret the Constitution in the course of fulfilling its own constitutional duty of legislating.

. . .

In assisting Congress in the performance of these functions, lawyers in Congress play an important role in advising members of the Senate and House. At a formalist level, because Congress does not bear the responsibility of executing the laws, congressional lawyers may not bear the same obligation to support the Constitution as that imposed on members of the other branches. Thus, any claim that Supreme Court decisions must be enforced because they are "law" might not apply to Congress with the same force as it does the Executive Branch. Unlike the Solicitor General, congressional lawyers do not hold any special relationship with another branch, such as the Supreme Court, that might override their loyalty to the members or institution of Congress. Although Article VI's Oath Clause includes senators and representatives, state legislators, and federal and state executive and judicial officers, it leaves out congressional officers and employees from the same duty to support the Constitution. Taken seriously, this selective omission suggests that the responsibility to uphold the Constitution belongs to the elected members of Congress, not their staffs. This reading, however, does not present a threat to constitutional government because members of Congress are the only ones who can exercise legislative power upon private individuals.

Even if one believed that congressional lawyers possess the same obligation to support the Constitution as that imposed on lawyers in the other branches of government, lawyers in Congress still may enjoy greater freedom to interpret the Constitution than their executive or judicial peers. If we view the committee counsel or legislative aide as the attorney, and the Member of the House, the Senator, or the committee as the client, then the proper job of the counsel or aide when confronted with a constitutional question is to explain the different approaches and arguments available. The client retains the ultimate authority to choose which actions to pursue and which legal arguments to adopt, and he or she cannot make that decision without being presented with the full range of constitutional arguments and options. . . . [U]nlike lawyers outside of the legislative branch, there is less need for quality control of congressional lawyers because any frivolous legal arguments they might make do not reach any court; they instead are filtered through Congress.

     . . .

The lawyer, however, plays a tempering role as well. At least in my experience, Senators take seriously the prospect that the Supreme Court may invalidate legislation they support. Aside from their desire to avoid unconstitutional decisions, they also want to avoid Supreme Court invalidation because of both the negative public attention as well as the delay such a legal challenge creates for legislative efforts to solve national problems. A congressional lawyer can advise a Senator to vote against a bill because it is flatly unconstitutional, or, even more usefully, he or she can counsel a Senator to modify or oppose a bill because it will be invalidated by the Supreme Court. In order to render predictions about the future actions of a coordinate branch of government, the congressional lawyer necessarily utilizes his technical knowledge of the legal and judicial system, as well as his political acumen, by developing a strategy that takes into account the likely actions and desires of other political actors.

The substantial political costs associated with Supreme Court intervention allow the lawyer to restrain unwise assertions of constitutional power or at least to persuade members of Congress to consider carefully certain courses of action. Of course, the lawyer must also balance this cautionary role with the lawyer's job to enable his client, who has the independent right to interpret the Constitution, to achieve his goals.

The congressional lawyer's role also might include providing Senators with political advice about the benefits and costs of relying upon different constitutional bases for action.

. . .

As an adviser, the lawyer in Congress performs a dual role in both recognizing the independent force of Congress' interpretive powers and tempering it. Congressional lawyers can moderate this power not by urging deference to the Supreme Court's opinions, but by demonstrating to Members of Congress the political benefits of operating within the Court's jurisprudence. The lawyers are able to do this, of course, because of the substantial prestige and respect that the Court has gained among the American public. However, as the Court expands the scope of its review farther into areas of social regulation over which the nation is deeply divided, it may weaken the congressional lawyer's ability to recommend cooperation by Congress and may provoke more congressional challenges to the Court.

NOTES & QUESTIONS

Hypothetical 1:

You are the counsel to the Judiciary Committee and your chair is intent on restricting antiabortion protestors from protesting outside health clinics that provide abortion. This is an important issue for your chair because her district includes several clinics and the patients have been complaining about how hard it is to enter the clinics, how loud the protests are, and that conflicts between protestors, patients and clinic staff at times have become violent. The lobbyist that represents the clinics has given your chair draft legislation. The provisions of the bill are extremely restrictive—to the point that protests would not be allowed anywhere near the clinics. Although there are no judicial rulings on point, courts have upheld reasonable restrictions on protests at health care facilities that only restricts as little speech as necessary to achieve the government's public safety goals. It is very likely that if this bill is made law that it will be struck down by a court. You mention this to the chair, but she says, "That's not my problem. My constituents want this version of the bill and that's what I'll try to give them. Just take their bill, put it in the right form, and file it."

1. Would it be ethical for you as lawyer, who has sworn to uphold the Constitution when you became a lawyer, to work on and submit a bill that is likely unconstitutional?

2. On the other hand, would it be ethical for you to refuse to follow your client's clear instructions?

3. What steps would you take in this instance?

4. If you knew that another committee or the other branch will fix the constitutionality problem, does that change your actions?

5. Would it be ethical to alert people in other parts of the legislature of your constitutional concerns?

E. THE LEGISLATIVE LAWYER & THE PUBLIC INTEREST

REPRESENTING REPRESENTATIVES: ETHICAL CONSIDERATIONS FOR THE LEGISLATURE'S ATTORNEYS

Robert J. Marchant, 6 *N.Y.U. Journal of Legislation & Policy* 439 (2003)

Although the public interest model has been referred to in numerous forums discussing the duties of government attorneys, it has been most forcefully outlined and defended by Professor Steven Berenson. Berenson argues that each government lawyer should determine the public interest to be served in the course of the lawyer's representation of the governmental client. In response to criticism of the public interest model, Berenson has suggested methods by which a government lawyer may make this determination. These methods include analyzing applicable judicial decisions, statutes, and constitutional provisions; contemplating the norms of legal culture; and consulting polling results and other tools used in the participatory model of bureaucracy, giving due regard to the interests of disadvantaged members of society. Presumably, once the public interest is identified, the ethical government lawyer must do no harm to the public interest and must refuse to assist a governmental client in harming the public interest.

It is almost always inappropriate for legislative attorneys to resort to these suggested methods of identifying the public interest and conform their activities accordingly. In the legislative context, such a model of practice would result in arbitrary decisions, made by persons who are not easily held accountable by the electorate, and that negatively affect the institution primarily charged with transforming the public interest into law.

. . .

[A]ssume that a committee chairperson requests that a legislative attorney analyze a memorandum prepared by a lobbyist. The memorandum points out that a bill being considered by the committee will result in a large reduction in tax liability for the industry the lobbyist represents. This result is not commonly known to members of the committee, including the author of the bill, and appears to have been unintended. The legislative attorney prepares a memorandum advising the chairperson of the accuracy of the lobbyist's analysis and asking the chairperson if she desires an amendment to the bill in order to close the unintended loophole. The chairperson requests, instead, that the legislative attorney return all information to the chairperson and keep the information confidential at the committee hearing unless a committee member asks the attorney directly for a similar legal opinion. Under the public interest model, the legislative attorney must decide whether honoring the chairperson's instructions would harm the public interest.

As discussed earlier, it is arguably in the public interest for committee chairpersons to obtain legal advice from non-partisan staff, especially when staff are asked to critique advice provided by lobbyists. The chairperson is unlikely to seek staff advice, though, if she fears that the staff attorney might disclose otherwise confidential information in order to protect the attorney's conception of the public interest. As a result, the legislative attorney reasonably might determine that, to protect the public interest, she will comply with the chairperson's request. On the other hand, the legislative attorney could just as reasonably believe that the public interest requires her to inform fully the legislature of the effects of the bill by distributing a memorandum explaining the loophole to all members of the committee or to all members of the legislature.

As these examples illustrate, the public interest model is inappropriate for legislative attorneys due to concerns about arbitrariness, lack of accountability, usurpation of legislative authority, separation of powers, and weakening of legislative institutions.

. . .

Of course, a legislative attorney should neither ignore precedent nor refrain from advising legislators on the current state of the law and the likelihood that a particular bill may be unconstitutional. As Berenson points out, governments hire lawyers for the purpose of obtaining this advice. But, contrary to Berenson's position, there is more involved here than a distinction analogous to that between putting forth frivolous claims and arguing for a good faith extension, modification, or reversal of existing law. History illustrates that legal precedents can be overruled and replaced. In fact, nothing in the Constitution prohibits the legislature from pursuing policies that blatantly violate legal precedents and that would clearly be frivolous to pursue in the courts. Presumably, it is better to facilitate free and open debate by drafting such legislation at the request of legislators than to prevent such legislation from being drafted at all. In addition, for the reasons noted earlier, it is better to have legislative attorneys drafting such legislation and advising the legislature of the constitutional issues and the costs involved in passing such legislation, than to have non-attorneys drafting the legislation and attorneys representing moneyed interests "advising" the legislature as to the constitutional issues.

. . .

If the public interest model of practice is applied, the effect likely will be a reduced role in the legislative process for legislative attorneys and an increased dependence by the legislature upon attorneys who are lobbyists and paid advocates. There are several reasons for this. As a general matter, it is a rare client who has no difficulty with being told "I won't do that for you." It is even less likely that a legislator will have no problem being told by a legislative attorney "I won't do that for you because I think you are going to harm the public interest." Legislatures, not legislative attorneys, are elected to represent the will of the public. A legislative attorney who refuses to conform to the client's desires, like any other lawyer, must be prepared eventually to have no client.

Legislators might also come to rely less on legislative attorneys due to political concerns and doubts about the professionalism of legislative attorneys. A legislative attorney might refuse to draft a politically popular bill or might disclose politically unpopular information. In either case, legislators likely would increasingly view legislative attorneys as politically dangerous and would hesitate to utilize their legal expertise. In addition, were some legislative attorneys to refuse, for personal ethical reasons, to act in a manner that other legislative attorneys did not find problematic, the legislature might begin to view at least some of its own lawyers as impediments to the legislative process. If the role of professional legal staff decreases, lobbyists who are members of the private bar and other attorneys who are paid to represent private interests will step in and satisfy the legislature's need for information.

F. LEGISLATIVE LAWYERS & THE EXECUTIVE BRANCH

WHO'S THE CLIENT? LEGISLATIVE LAWYERING THROUGH THE REAR-VIEW MIRROR
Michael Glennon, 61 *Law and Contemporary Problems* 21 (1998)

[C]onflicts of interest were ruled out. Representing the Committee meant not undertaking activities that would conflict. Of course, in the traditional sense that was easy: Mine was a full-time job, and I was hardly about to go out and sign up a client with conflicting interests. Nevertheless, I took the no-conflicts obligation seriously and interpreted it broadly. To me, its primary import lay in its implications for relations with the Executive Branch. I thought that the canon mandated an arms-length relationship unless the Committee explicitly enjoined cooperation. That meant, specifically, not accepting the "assistance" of the State Department, which was always available on almost every matter. When conference committees concluded their deliberations, for example, and the staff sat down to translate into proper legislative language the decisions that the conferees had made, State Department representatives constantly hovered about, often with language in hand to slip into the law. My view was that to accept their help would have been improper, though I am sad to say that that view was not shared on the House side.

The House Committee on Foreign Affairs worked hand-in-hand with State Department lawyers and shamelessly accepted their help. I often suggested that they do their own work, but House staff members would still disappear regularly into back rooms, only to emerge with freshly drafted provisions just off the typewriter of a State Department lawyer squirreled away out of sight. Perhaps it was my more recent exposure to academe, but I thought that collaboration unseemly, rather like slipping into a lavatory during an examination to trade answers. I accepted the Department's work only once, when I knew that it represented the Committee's intent; it was report language explaining an amendment they initiated to the Taiwan Relations Act, and their lawyer insisted that the provision was, after all, "their amendment." It was, but I still felt uneasy about accepting their words.

Similarly, I believed that a conflict of interest would have arisen had I sought, directly or indirectly, to move to a job in the Executive Branch from my position as the Committee's counsel. To make the friends necessary for such a move would have required pulling punches and seeking to curry favor downtown; that, it seemed to me, would inevitably have involved pulling back in the Committee's ongoing disputes with the Executive Branch. I was asked from time to time whether I was interested in a job with the Administration, and I always said no. I knew congressional staffers who were constantly angling for some job with the departments and agencies that they were supposed to be overseeing, and I never trusted them.

LAWYERS IN CONGRESS

John C, Yoo, 61 *Law and Contemporary Problems* 1 (1998)

The congressional lawyer's role as a check on the power of the institution he serves comes to the fore when Congress employs its powers of investigation and oversight. Congress' power to conduct such inquiries inheres in its power to study and pass legislation, and it has used this power from the very beginning of the Republic to investigate maladministration in the Executive Branch, to determine whether social conditions require new legislation, and to review the success of existing laws. Although the Reagan Administration ushered in the recent era of conflict between congressional investigatory powers and claims of executive privilege, such as the controversy over EPA Director Anne Burford or the hearings into the Iran-contra affair, the Clinton Administration has witnessed an intensified use of Congress' investigatory powers. Congress has undertaken numerous investigations involving allegations of misuse of official power, such as the hearings on Whitewater, on the firing of the White House Travel Office, on the misuse of FBI security files of Republican administration officials, and on the 1996 campaign finance scandals. As one would expect, lawyers populate these hearings and investigations, ranging from the criminal defense lawyers who advise witnesses to the special counsels who conduct the investigation to the lawyers who advise the Members of Congress who sit on the investigating committees.

Congress' constitutional power to conduct investigations and its auxiliary power to force witnesses to appear before it and produce evidence go formally unchecked. Congress may conduct investigations into any subject, so long as it is in furtherance of a valid legislative purpose. It may call any witness, seek any evidence related to its investigation, and hire an army of lawyers and staff to conduct the investigation. To force recalcitrant witnesses to testify, Congress may use its own power to impose civil contempt sanctions, which can involve the House or Senate issuing and executing an arrest warrant and imprisoning the witness. While Congress must observe the procedural guarantees of the Bill of Rights in conducting its investigations, it may be under no legal obligation to obey other protections not rooted in the Constitution. Since 1857, however, Congress has limited its own investigatory powers by passing a criminal contempt law that requires it to vote on whether to adopt a contempt resolution, and which then requires a contempt citation to be referred to a U.S. Attorney for prosecution. Because this procedure permits the President to order the U.S. Attorney not to pursue a prosecution or even to pardon a witness convicted of contempt, it allows for some separation of powers check on Congress' investigatory powers. Such restraints, however, might not apply to Congress' inherent, non-statutory power of contempt.

Despite its untrammeled powers of investigation, Congress generally recognizes several unwritten rules of restraint. In 1996, for example, the Judiciary Committee led the investigation into the Clinton Administration's alleged improper collection and handling of the FBI security files of members of previous Republican administrations. Before the Committee's hearings, staff lawyers sent letters to the White House and the Justice Department that were framed very much like discovery requests in federal civil litigation. Claims of privilege were accepted if a proper explanation was provided, documents were delivered in boxes at the last minute, Bates stamps and document indices were used. Committee staff conducted depositions at which the witness was permitted to bring counsel, invoke privileges, and refuse to answer questions. Staff lawyers recognized claims of attorney-client privilege, and they avoided areas involving the personal privacy of individuals (such as hiring records), even though Congress is under no obligation to observe discovery protections that are not rooted in the Constitution. Committee staff even recognized claims of executive privilege, despite Congress' independent authority, as suggested earlier, to interpret the Constitution. Staff did not force witnesses taking the Fifth Amendment to do so on television.

In following these unwritten rules, the congressional lawyer's restraining role is placed in the sharpest relief. Here, lawyers are acting to control perhaps Congress' most unrestrained power, which can operate free from any substantial check by the executive or judicial branches. As with the Committee's adoption of the federal discovery rules, these norms of behavior serve the purpose of supplying an off-the-shelf, widely understood system that allows attorneys to impose order upon the investigatory process. Lawyers need these rules, furthermore, precisely because the investigatory process itself has no inherent rules and, as such, is most vulnerable to abuse by Congress in the service of personal or wholly partisan agendas. As the only barrier standing between the individual and the broad power of Congress to conduct investigations, congressional lawyers are acting at their bravest; they cannot rely on Supreme Court decisions or other institutions to support their efforts to regulate congressional power.

G. THE LEGISLATIVE LAWYER & MORAL ISSUES

GOVERNMENT LAWYERING: THE ETHICS OF REPRESENTING ELECTED REPRESENTATIVES

Kathleen Clark, 61 *Law and Contemporary Problems* 31 (1998)

To what degree is a lawyer responsible for the actions that her client takes with the lawyer's assistance? If the action is illegal, the lawyer can be held legally responsible. Suppose, however, that the client's action is legally permissible but morally repugnant. In such a case, should the lawyer feel morally responsible or implicated because of her own participation in the client's wrongdoing?

The dominant ideology of the American legal profession seems to answer this question in the negative. Professor Stephen Pepper described this ideology as follows: Once a lawyer has entered into the professional relationship with a client, the notion is that conduct by the lawyer in service to the client is judged by a different moral standard than the same conduct by a layperson. . . As long as what lawyer and client do is lawful, it is the client who is morally accountable, not the lawyer.

. . .

The argument that a lawyer is "morally insulated" from responsibility for a client's wrongdoing is quite strong, and perhaps at its zenith, in the criminal defense context.

. . .

But is this "moral insulation" equally appropriate where the lawyer is assisting a client outside the adversary process in actions that will have effect in the future? When I worked on Capitol Hill, I felt torn by concern about the consequences of my actions, such as assisting in the negotiation of a conference report on an omnibus crime bill that would create more than fifty new death penalty provisions.

. . .

My role in this process was peripheral, and a filibuster prevented the bill from becoming law. After I left Capitol Hill, a later crime bill, which contained sixty death penalty provisions, was passed by the Congress and became law. Even an opponent of the death penalty might have been able to justify support for the legislation because it contained other laudable provisions.

Nonetheless, I am troubled by the death penalty, and was concerned about my own participation in expanding its availability. How would I feel years on when I learned of a criminal defendant who had been executed under these provisions? Would I feel implicated in that death?

Are such moral second-thoughts appropriate for a lawyer? From what I could discern, they are uncommon among the political lawyers on Capitol Hill. It may be that most political lawyers agree with the policy goals of legislators they represent, or that they believe their work generally furthers the public good even if it does some harm as well. Or it may be that they, perhaps like most lawyers, feel that they are "morally insulated" from the client's actions.

. . .

[P]olitical lawyers can take some solace in the reasoning of Professor Geoffrey Miller that they are mere advisers to elected officials. It is the elected officials who appropriately have the responsibility to determine which policy choice to make. Their legitimacy is derived not from the soundness of their reasoning but from their status as elected representatives.

On the other hand, where a political lawyer disagrees with the policy choice on moral grounds, should she defer her moral judgment to that of the elected official? Is the "moral insulation" approach adopted by so many lawyers in private practice appropriate for political lawyers? We need not look very far in the history of this century to see how government officials can cause massive harm. Not every policy disagreement constitutes a moral disagreement. Yet where it does, I am troubled by the notion that political lawyers should hide behind their deference to the elected representatives for whom they work.

. . .

[M]ost lawyers have yet to grapple significantly with their moral responsibility for the future consequences of their actions. This seems especially true for lawyers, such as those working on Capitol Hill, who function outside the adversary system and contribute to outcomes whose impact is largely prospective, rather than retrospective.

NOTES & QUESTIONS

Hypothetical 1:

You are a staff attorney working for the Senate Judiciary Committee. The chair announces that he wants to greatly expand the reach of death penalty statute to include several new crimes and circumstances. You believe that the current death penalty statute is deeply flawed because several people on death row have recently been exonerated by advances in DNA testing. There is little question that several people previously executed were innocent of the crimes. Believing that life is sacred, you have long been opposed to the death penalty. Furthermore, studies have shown that the death penalty is disproportionately applied to racial minorities and poor defendants. This data offends your sense of justice. When you express your point of view to the chief counsel and suggest that perhaps someone else on the staff could take the assignment, she replies, "Just do your job—draft an amendment that does what the chair wants and give it to me this week."

1. Given your strong moral objections, would you be able to draft the amendment?

2. Would it be ethical to simply refuse to draft the amendment?

3. Would your positions on these questions be different if you were the chief counsel rather than just a staff attorney?

4. If during your conversation with the chief counsel she reveals that the chair simply wants to add the amendment as a negotiating chip for the rest of the bill and that the provisions will be eliminated during the conference committee, does that change your answers?

H. SIMULATION: SENTENCING REFORM

Background: During his weekly radio address and blog posting, the President has called for drug sentencing reform. This came about shortly after recording star John Legend won the Academy Award for best song related to a film about the Civil Rights Movement of the 1960s. During his acceptance speech, watched by approximately 36.6 million people, he stated that the civil rights movement had to continue, because "More black men are in prison today than were in slavery at the time of the Civil War." This powerful message caused the President to call for a change to the primary driver of incarceration for African Americans during the past three decades—mandatory minimum federal prison sentences for a variety of drug crimes. The challenge which you are facing is to negotiate an amendment to the current drug statutes that best meets the interests of the all the parties most affected.

Mandatory minimum sentencing became popular in the 1980s to address the rampant drug problem of the time. Convinced that judges were not being tough enough on drug offenders, legislators across the country imposed mandatory minimum sentences for drug crimes. These sentences have disproportionately affected minorities, and especially the African American community.

The Players: The negotiations will take place between the following:

- **legal counsel(s) for the Senate Judiciary Committee:** You were hired by and report to the Chair of the Judiciary Committee, a liberal Democrat from California. You have been on the job for 10 months. For the past 10 years you have worked for the Justice Department—first as a prosecutor for the Miami U.S. Attorneys Office for 8 years and for the past 2 years in Office of Legal Policy at Justice Department Headquarters in DC. After a meeting with the Committee Chair last year, you were detailed to the Senate Judiciary Committee. Detailees have become more common in recent years—when Congressional leaders feel like they need more assistance on a particular topic, they will request personnel—sometimes by name—from the executive agency where they work. The agency continues to pay their salary, but the person works for the Congressional Committee for a set time—usually a year. This is what the Judiciary Chair did with you. She wanted the perspective of a prosecutor and someone who could "talk to the 'tough on crime' Republicans on the Committee." You have 2 months left on your detail, but the Chairman has given strong hints that she wants you to stay.

- **legal counsel(s) for the House Judiciary Committee:** Despite growing up poor in a rough neighborhood, you graduated *magna cum laude* from law school. You declined offers from Cravath, Ropes & Gray, and Squire, Patton, Boggs because you wanted to work in the public interest. When your member of Congress found out you were on the market, he hired you right away and for the last 4 years you have been working on the House Judiciary Committee staff, which he chairs. Your member of Congress represents a Virginia district with a sizable minority population. He is a fairly moderate Republican and possible future member of House leadership. The work you have done has been exciting, and you have come to admire your chair—even though you sometimes strongly disagree with him on policy.

- **commissioner(s) from the United States Sentencing Commission:** You have been a federal Judge since 2003 when President George W. Bush named you to be a district court judge in Orange County, California. In 2014, President Obama named you Chairman of the U.S. Sentencing Commission. Prior to being named a judge, you were a prosecutor and then a partner at a private firm specializing in white collar defense. You are known as a true believer in judicial discretion.

- **Deputy Assistant Attorney General(s) from the Justice Department:** You are the Principal Deputy Assistant Attorney General for the Office of Legal Policy at the Justice Department. Since graduating from Penn Law and obtaining a coveted spot in the Justice Department Honors Program, you have had several positions with DOJ. You were a prosecutor for the U.S. Attorney's Office in Washington DC, primarily prosecuting drug crimes. After a stint with the Civil Rights Division, you were detailed to the White House Counsel's Office immediately after this President took office. When the detail was up, you went back to DoJ and have now been in your position for 3 years.

- **lobbyist(s) for the National Black Church Initiative:** You are the chief Washington lobbyist for the National Black Church Initiative. Prior to taking this position, you were a lawyer for the Southern Poverty Law Center and then the NAACP and then changed careers to become a lobbyist. You prefer to take on clients with a strong sense of social justice. A few years ago, you became good friends with your neighbor in the hip NOMA neighborhood of Washington, the minister for a large Baptist church in the Southeast quadrant of Washington, and he hired you to represent the NBCI.

[Note: Each player will be given further "confidential instructions" that will be included in the teacher's manual.]

The Goal: Each player (or team) should decide on what they want to get out of this negotiation and what they need to do to obtain their goals. For the first part of the exercise, the representatives from the Sentencing Commission, Justice Department and NBCI should meet with the Judiciary Committee counsels and argue for their position and use whatever leverage they have to get them to adopt their organization's desired outcome. The counsels from the House and Senate Judiciary Committee will conduct a final negotiation and decide what the final bill will look like.

If they cannot come to an agreement, the law will continue on as written, and the President will be publicly frustrated at his efforts at sentencing reform.

Time: The players have 1.5 hours to come up with an agreement. For the first hour, the representatives from the Sentencing Commission, Justice Department and NBCI can strategize with each other or lobby the Judiciary Committee counsels. Players may meet with each other individually, or in groups of their own choosing. For the final 25 minutes, the Judiciary Committee counsels will meet and try to come to an agreement for changes—or continue the *status quo.*

Report: After the negotiation, each player must write a 1–2 page memorandum on the outcome. How did you do in the negotiation?

What ethical issues did you confront? How did you deal with them? Do you wish you could have done something differently? Were you bothered by the actions of any of the other players? Who do you think "won" the negotiation? Why?

Relevant Statutes

Penalties

Possession Offense	Mandatory Minimum Sentence (21 U.S.C. § 841)
Heroin (100 grams) Powder Cocaine (500 grams) Cocaine Base (crack) (28 grams) Marijuana (100 kilograms) Methamphetamine (5 grams)	5–40 years in prison, 20 years to life in prison if use leads to death or serious bodily injury.

Heroin (1 kilograms) Powder Cocaine (5 kilograms) Cocaine Base (crack) (280 grams) Marijuana (1,000 kilograms) Methamphetamine (50 grams)	10 years in prison up to life in prison, 20 years to life in prison if use leads to death or serious bodily injury.
With previous felony drug conviction	20 years in prison up to life in prison, life in prison if use leads to death or serious bodily injury.

Mandatory minimum sentences are created by stating the above sentence ranges and including the following statutory language:

> *Notwithstanding any other provision of law, the court shall not place on probation or suspend the sentence of any person sentenced under the provisions of this subparagraph which provide for a mandatory term of imprisonment if death or serious bodily injury results, nor shall a person so sentenced be eligible for parole during the term of such a sentence.*

21 U.S. Code § 860—Distribution or manufacturing in or near schools and colleges (a.k.a—school zones) (a) Penalty

Any person who violates section 841 (a)(1) of this title or section 856 of this title by distributing, possessing with intent to distribute, or manufacturing a controlled substance in or on, or within one thousand feet of, the real property comprising a public or private elementary, vocational, or secondary school or a public or private college, junior college, or university, or a playground, or housing facility owned by a public housing authority, or within 100 feet of a public or private youth center, public swimming pool, or video arcade facility, is (except as provided in subsection (b) of this section) subject to

(1) twice the maximum punishment authorized by section 841 (b) of this title; and at least twice any term of supervised release authorized by section 841 (b) of this title for a first offense. A fine up to twice that authorized by section 841 (b) of this title may be imposed in addition to any term of imprisonment authorized by this subsection. *Except to the extent a greater minimum sentence is otherwise provided by section 841 (b) of this title, a person shall be sentenced under this subsection to a term of imprisonment of not less than one year.* The mandatory minimum sentencing provisions of this paragraph shall not apply to offenses involving 5 grams or less of marihuana.

18 U.S. Code § 3553 (f) Limitation on Applicability of Statutory Minimums in Certain Cases (a.k.a.—"The Safety Valve")

Notwithstanding any other provision of law, in the case of an offense under section 401, 404, or 406 of the Controlled Substances Act (21 U.S.C. 841, 844, 846) or section 1010 or 1013 of the Controlled Substances Import and Export Act (21 U.S.C. 960, 963), the court shall impose a sentence pursuant to guidelines promulgated by the United States Sentencing Commission under section 994 of title 28 without regard to any statutory minimum sentence, if the court finds at sentencing, after the Government has been afforded the opportunity to make a recommendation, that—

(1)   the defendant does not have more than 1 criminal history point, as determined under the sentencing guidelines;

(2)   the defendant did not use violence or credible threats of violence or possess a firearm or other dangerous weapon (or induce another participant to do so) in connection with the offense;

(3)   the offense did not result in death or serious bodily injury to any person;

(4)   the defendant was not an organizer, leader, manager, or supervisor of others in the offense, as determined under the sentencing guidelines and was not engaged in a continuing criminal enterprise, as defined in section 408 of the Controlled Substances Act; and

(5)   not later than the time of the sentencing hearing, the defendant has truthfully provided to the Government all information and evidence the defendant has concerning the offense or offenses that were part of the same course of conduct or of a common scheme or plan, but the fact that the defendant has no relevant or useful other information to provide or that the Government is already aware of the information shall not preclude a determination by the court that the defendant has complied with this requirement.

CHAPTER 4

THE LEGISLATIVE PROCESS

■ ■ ■

A. IDEAS & POLICY DEVELOPMENT

ILTAM: DRAFTING EVIDENCE-BASED LEGISLATION FOR DEMOCRATIC SOCIAL CHANGE

Ann & Robert B. Seidman, 89 *Boston University Law Review* 435 (2009)

[Note: Professors Ann & Bob Seidman developed the Institutional Legislative Theory and Methodology (ILTAM) over the course of 30 years and used it to teach legislative drafting around the world.]

To describe a country, one should describe its institutions—its industries, banks, schools, hospitals, farms, factories, families, and a myriad more. To explain poverty, vulnerability, and the quality of governance, one should again look to a country's institutions. A country's inherited institutions define the relative poverty or wealth of different segments of its population. Essentially, institutions consist of repetitive patterns of social behaviors. Therefore, in order to change an institution one must change the social behaviors that comprise it.

. . .

Here we describe ILTAM as a guide to drafters seeking to design transformative evidence-based legislation likely to work. To that end, ILTAM prescribes a research report as an essential quality control for legislation. A well-constructed research report fulfills several functions. It provides the evidence a drafter needs to conceptualize, draft and justify a bill's detailed provisions. Publication of the research report should give legislators and stakeholders the evidence they require to assess whether that bill will likely work.

ILTAM's problem-solving methodology comprises four decision-making steps a drafter needs to conceptualize and develop a bill. With one important difference concerning Step 4, the same outline structures the research report's justification for the bill. This Part discusses those steps, essential for both designing the bill and outlining the research report.

Step 1:   *Describe (a) the Social Problem the Bill Targets, and (b) Whose and What Behaviors Comprise It*

In Step 1, ILTAM's methodology requires that the drafter provide evidence to describe the targeted social problem's surface appearance and whose and what behaviors constitute that problem. Frequently, the social problem appears on its surface as a pattern of inequitably distributed resources. A law cannot usefully command those resources to reallocate themselves. For that reason, the drafter must also describe whose and what behaviors constitute the social problem. In particular, to understand the problem fully the drafter must provide detailed evidence about those problematic behaviors, the relationships between them, and how each contributes to the targeted social problem. As indicated in the model of behavior in the face of the law, Figure 1 below, a law must take into account the problematic behaviors of two sets of social actors: (1) role occupants and (2) the implementing agencies. Role occupants consist of the actors whose behaviors the bill aims to change. The implementing agency has the task of taking steps to increase the probability that the primary role occupants conform their behaviors to the prescriptions addressed to them. The outcome of the fatal race, described in Part I, shouts that the drafter must design appropriate provisions to change the relevant problematic behaviors, not only of the primary role occupant, but also of the implementing agency, including its personnel. To evaluate the proposed bill effectively, the research report must provide the evidence necessary to describe the problematic behaviors of both the role occupant and the relevant implementing agency. Those behaviors constitute the social problem addressed.

Step 2:   *Explain the Behaviors that Comprise the Targeted Social Problem*

To change the problematic behaviors described in Step 1, the drafter must design a bill's detailed commands, prescriptions, and prohibitions so that they likely will induce both the role occupant and the implementing agency to behave as the bill prescribes. For the bill to work, its prescriptions must alter or eliminate the causes of the problematic behaviors. Therefore, Step 2 calls for explanations of each set of problematic behaviors described in Step 1. Step 2 requires the drafter to formulate explanatory hypotheses for the role occupants' problematic behaviors and provide evidence to warrant those explanations. The model of the law-making process shown in Figure 1 rests on the theoretical proposition that, in the face of a new law, an actor behaves by choosing within the constraints and resources of that actor's surround. To help the drafter formulate hypotheses as to the probable causes of behaviors in the face of a rule of law, the model guides the drafter in examining three broad categories of possible causes of each set of role occupants' problematic behaviors: (1) the actor's understanding of the relevant rule; (2) the actor's anticipation of the implementing agency's behavior; and (3) the non-legal constraints and resources of the actor's own environment. ILTAM further unpacks these three categories of possible explanations into seven subcategories:

1. the **Rule**, that is, the precise wording of the relevant existing cage of laws within which each actor behaves;

2. the actor's **Opportunity** to obey the law including factors in the actor's environment that facilitate the actor's obedience or disobedience of the Rule;

3. the actor's **Capacity** to obey the rule, that is, the actor's skills and resources that foster obedience or disobedience;

4. **Communication** of the law to the actor and the extent to which the actor learns about and understands the existing laws' prescriptions;

5. the actor's **Incentive** to obey or disobey the rule, in other words, the actor's interest in obeying or disobeying the existing law;

6. the **Process** by which the actor decides whether and how to obey the rule, and the input, feedback, and decision-making systems by which the actor chooses how to behave in the face of the rule; and

7. the actor's **Ideology** or his, her, or its values and attitudes as tradition and experience have shaped them.

[The Seidmans note that the first letters of these categories create the mnemonic "ROCCIPI," but the order of categories do not signify an order of importance.]

One way to characterize the above-described categories is in terms of subjectivity and objectivity. Two of the named causal factors, Incentives and Ideology, remain subjective because the actor's own perceptions influence them, while the relevant actor's objective circumstances define the other five factors. Broadly interpreted, these categories guide the drafter in formulating explanatory hypotheses, or educated guesses, as to all the possible causes of a set of actors' problematic behaviors. In turn, these explanatory hypotheses direct the drafter in capturing the evidence required to test their validity. By defining causal factors for the drafter to examine, ILTAM offer the drafter a guide for capturing the relevant evidence needed.

Step 3: Create a Legislative Solution

To translate a proposed policy into effectively implemented law, Step 3 requires the drafter to design the bill's detailed commands, permissions, and prohibitions. The drafter must design the bill's provisions to meet two overriding criteria. First, the commands, permissions, and prohibitions of the bill must logically prove likely to alter or eliminate the causes of the problematic behaviors described in Step 1 and explained in Step 2; otherwise, the bill will likely only poultice symptoms. Second, the solution adopted must prove more cost-effective than any logically-possible alternative. For Step 3, the drafter should list in the research report a menu of logically-possible alternative solutions, ensuring that each solution listed addresses one or more of the several causes of the problematic behaviors that were identified in Steps 1 and 2. In addition, the drafter should describe in detail the preferred solution embodied in the draft bill to demonstrate that it adequately addresses the social problem's causes. Third, and crucially, the research report should provide evidence to compare the social and the monetary costs and benefits of (a) the preferred solution, (b) the status quo, and (c) the nearest potential competitor solution. That analysis should demonstrate that the proposed bill's social and economic benefits outweigh its probable social and economic costs, including the government's prospective 'out-of-pocket' expenses. Furthermore, as part of the costs and benefits analysis, the research report should incorporate a social impact statement that describes the proposed legislation's likely consequences for those who usually have no seats in the halls of power, namely, the poor, disadvantaged minorities, women, and children.

Step 4:   Monitor and Evaluate

Thus far, the three steps described guide the drafter in both designing a bill and in structuring the accompanying research report. Here, we describe ILTAM's fourth and final step, which serves a rather different function. ILTAM emphasizes that decision-making about a bill does not conclude with its drafting or even its promulgation. In Step 4, ILTAM calls for monitoring and evaluating the implementation and social impact of every new law ex post to assess whether and how it works. Since the law-in-the-books and the law-in-action systematically differ, one would expect the evaluation to reveal that, in one or another particular way, the law did not work entirely as predicted. This result might reflect the drafter's failure to adequately ground the bill's detailed provisions on the relevant evidence or the reality that the prevailing circumstances—the world out there—have changed. If the resulting new problem proves sufficiently serious, given the resources and the political will to remedy it, the evaluation may lead to a new round of law-making. The reality just described underscores that law-making in today's rapidly changing world may require an ongoing process of drafting, implementing, monitoring, and redrafting.

With respect to designing the bill, Step 4 requires the drafter to ensure that, in the bill itself or elsewhere, the law provides for an adequate monitoring and evaluation mechanism. Further, this mechanism should specify criteria for gathering the evidence necessary to assess whether, after the bill has been in force a reasonable time, its provisions have effectively induced the implementing agency and the primary role occupant to behave as prescribed and whether those behaviors tend to ameliorate the targeted social problem. The monitoring and evaluating procedures must prove transparent and accountable. They must ensure that those affected, especially the poor and vulnerable, have opportunity to provide input and feedback of relevant evidence as to the law's impact on their lives. In short, this monitoring and evaluating process answers the question of whether the new law works as the research report predicted. Only after the drafter analyzes the law-in-action can improvements be made to ensure the law works. ILTAM underscores the advantages of requiring that drafters accompany important bills, including draft administrative regulations, with a research report. ILTAM's four-step problem-solving model provides drafters a guide for gathering and logically structuring the relevant evidence required to demonstrate—that is, predict—that the proposed bill will likely work. At the same time, the research report provides the facts that legislators, their constituents, and the general public need to assess the bill's detailed provisions' probable social impact. Effectively, in justifying the bill, a well-structured research report serves as a quality control for a new law. The research report not only aids drafters in the bill's design stage but also facilitates the participation of those most affected by the bill in its assessment stage and, if necessary, in improving the bill.

. . .

By requiring a systematic description and explanation of the empirical world ILTAM guides a drafter in discovering the relevant evidence required accurately to predict the behavior that a law will induce, and thus to justify it—that is, to persuade a rational skeptic that the law will likely work. Evidence-based drafting does not state an impossible dream. An evidence-based law will more likely induce its addressees to behave as prescribed and the resulting behaviors will more likely help to resolve the targeted social problem. By using existing facts to analyze the root causes of social problems when drafting bills, evidence-based legislation proves more likely to work. Committed to drafting evidence-based legislation, a drafter confronts vast fields of potentially relevant evidence. To winnow out the relevant from the irrelevant, ILTAM offers criteria of relevance that a drafter may use to determine which of the vast meadows of potential evidence will likely prove useful and which will not. These criteria rest, in the first place, on a recognition that a social problem consists of behaviors that together constitute a problematic institution.

NOTES & QUESTIONS

1. Where do policy ideas come from? Many different groups and individuals can contribute policy ideas or spur a legislator or committee to take up an issue:

- Constituents, through campaign meetings and promises, as well as case work;

- Media, reporting on "hot issues" or uncovering a problem;

- "Special Interests," which include corporations, non-profits, unions, farmers, etc.;

- The executive—governors and presidents usually have a policy agenda;

- Legislative leadership, also usually come to their position with a policy agenda;

- Individual members, can offer ideas and initiate the process through bill filing.

In a study of the legislative drafting process of the Senate Judiciary Committee, Professors Nourse and Schacter found that there was no single or "monolithic" drafting process. Ideas for new legislation came from many sources; "newspapers and court cases, lobbyists and the White House, Sunday-school teachers and law-review articles, to name a few." Victoria F. Nourse; Jane S. Schacter, "The Politics of Legislative Drafting: A Congressional Case Study," 77 *N.Y.U. L. Rev.* 575 (2002).

2. Why do some ideas languish for a long time, only to later gain wide-spread popularity? One explanation is the "Overton Window," a theory of change developed by Joe Overton in the mid-1990s. His insight was that different options within a policy area can be arranged in order from more free (less government intervention) to less free (more government intervention) to more). Along this spectrum, some group of adjacent policies are within a "window of political possibility," meaning legislators can support those without suffering at the polls. This window shifts, but the policies outside the window, are politically unacceptable at that time.

Overton believed that politicians rarely moved the window, but rather, react to and validate their options. Overton held that durable policy changes are those that are undergirded by strong social movements. The lawmakers who support policies outside the window fall into two categories: true leaders who can shift the window by themselves, or those who risk losing their office because they are out of step with the rest of society. See, Joseph Lehman, "A Brief Explanation of the Overton Window," http://www.mackinac.org/overton window#overton_window_container.

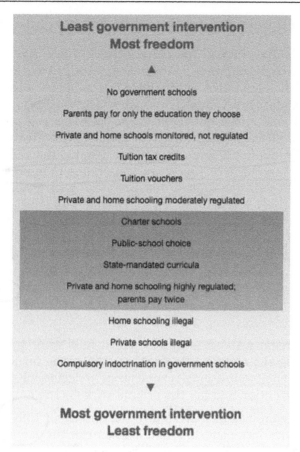

Least government intervention
Most freedom

▲

No government schools

Parents pay for only the education they choose

Private and home schools monitored, not regulated

Tuition tax credits

Tuition vouchers

Private and home schooling moderately regulated

Charter schools

Public-school choice

State-mandated curricula

Private and home schooling highly regulated;
parents pay twice

Home schooling illegal

Private schools illegal

Compulsory indoctrination in government schools

▼

Most government intervention
Least freedom

3.   An important aspect of the Seidmans' methodology is the production of a research report that acts as a quality control for the bill. The Seidmans' recognize that,

> a drafter cannot avoid making discretionary choices about the kinds of evidence required as to: (1) the nature and scope of the social problem, and whose and what behaviors constitute it; (2) which hypotheses as to the causes of those behaviors to put to empirical test; and (3) what alternative solutions to consider in the research report, and how to estimate and weigh those alternatives' socio-economic costs and benefits.

By offering a systematic review of the causes of the social problem and the rationale for the provisions included in a bill, the research report is meant to convince "the rational sceptic" that the new law will work as anticipated. If the rational skeptic/reader disagrees with the justifications or conclusions, they can overcome the bill with better facts and evidence, again with the goal of convincing an equally rational skeptic.

Stem Cell Case Study: Creating a Massachusetts Law

In early January 2004, Massachusetts state senator Cynthia Stone Creem met with her staff to decide what her legislative priorities would be for the rest of the legislative session. At this point the session was a year old, so the legislature's committees had heard testimony on the nearly 6,000 filed bills and either put them into a "study order," meaning the bill was unlikely to be considered further or was being actively worked on by one of the many standing committees that develop the substantive policy and legislative language, or the Ways and Means Committees that make sure the bills fit into the House and Senate's fiscal priorities. Now the legislature had only six months left of "formal sessions;" where the full chambers met to debate amend and pass bills. In July, the legislature would go into a six month "informal session;" with only periodic meetings to take up noncontroversial matters. The legislators use this time to run for reelection, since senators and representatives serve two-year terms. The final year of the session is also a good time to work on longer term projects that will be filed in January at the start of the new legislative session.

Senator Creem wanted to decide which bills were going to be office priorities during the often-hectic final months of the formal session. She also wanted to chart out a long-term course to decide what bills or policy areas needed attention and lay the groundwork for the next session.

Senator Creem was first elected to the Senate in 1998. A graduate of Boston University Law School, Cindy Creem ran the law firm started by her mother and father, Stone, Stone & Creem and practiced family law. Her senate district, comprised of nearly 100,000 people in the city of Newton and the towns of Brookline and Wellesley, is one of the most affluent and politically liberal districts in Massachusetts. When she joined the Senate, she was regarded as one of its most liberal members. By tradition, all senators in the majority Democratic caucus are either in leadership or chair a committee. For her first four years, Senator Creem chaired the Criminal Justice Committee. At the start of the current session, she was named the chair of the powerful Taxation Committee. This new committee presented the Senator and her staff with a steep learning curve; tax law is difficult to understand—never mind master—and everyone in the office was new to the subject. The Committee had over 600 bills to consider, including a massive 200 section corporate tax loophole closing bill proposed by Governor Romney. Senator Creem also remained busy with criminal justice issues such as opposing the death penalty and trying to reform mandatory minimum sentencing for drug offenses.

One bill on the staff's short list was related to stem cell research. A few weeks before, several scientists came to Senator Creem's office for assistance reforming a part of the state law that could potentially hamper their work. The scientists came to Senator Creem because she had previously filed a bill to inform expectant mothers of the possibility of banking the baby's cord blood to preserve the stem cells. When this bill was filed in 2000, such blood banking was a fairly new idea and was a fairly expensive venture, and the Public Health Committee had yet to take action on the bill. The scientists wanted something far more complicated: first, to change the language of an anti-abortion statute passed in the wake of *Roe v. Wade*; second, to remove the supervision of local prosecutors over research; and third, to provide state financial support to stem cell research. The scientists thought the changes would be simple to make. Senator Creem and her staff knew different.

Stem Cells

In the first years of the 21st century, scientists had only started to realize the potential of stem cells, which have ability to both divide without limit and to develop into any other types of human cell. Stem cells can be derived from a variety of sources. "Adult stem cells," which have been studied since the 1960s, can be found in a variety of places such as in teeth and the umbilical cord and have been used therapeutically. Recent techniques and understandings of cellular biology, however, allowed scientists to derive stem cells from fertilized human eggs. In 1998, University of Wisconsin's Dr. James Thompson isolated and studied "embryonic stem cells" for the first time. These stem cells are cultivated from human eggs that are fertilized *in vitro*, developed for 4 or 5 days, at which time a cell line can be derived. The fertilized egg never develops beyond the "blastocyst" stage; a ball of cells that contains the inner cell mass of undifferentiated stem cell that may eventually give rise to the embryo. The unusual properties of embryonic stem cells gave scientists insights into the beginnings of human life and development. Some researchers thought embryonic stem cells could be more versatile than adult stem cells and had the potential for breakthrough medical uses such as curing birth defects and cancer, and treating Parkinson's Disease, Alzheimer's Disease, heart disease and spinal cord injuries. In addition, by using the process of somatic cell nuclear transplantation, where the nucleus of an egg is replaced with the nucleus from a cell taken from the patient, scientists could create stem cells with the genetic code of the patient and assure the creation of genetic materials "designed" for the patient and without risk of rejection. Because the resulting egg is a clone of the donor's cell, this process is often called "therapeutic cloning."

Several Boston area scientists, led by Dr. Ann Kiessling, came to Senator Creem to make significant changes to the Massachusetts General Laws. Although stem cell research took place in Massachusetts, the scientists doing so operated in a legal grey area. A 1974 state statute, passed as a reaction to *Roe v. Wade*, prohibited experimentation on human fetuses, and allowed limited research after a cumbersome local government review process. Massachusetts General Law chapter 112 § 12J, stated:

> *Experimentation on human fetuses prohibited; medical procedures authorized; consent; approval; civil and criminal liability and proceedings; (a) I. No person shall use any live human fetus whether before or after expulsion from its mother's womb, for scientific, laboratory, research or other kind of experimentation. This section shall not prohibit procedures incident to the study of a human fetus while it is in its mother's womb, provided that in the best medical judgment of the physician, made at the time of the study, said procedures do not substantially jeopardize the life or health of the fetus, and provided said fetus is not the subject of a planned abortion. In any criminal proceeding a fetus shall be conclusively presumed not to be the subject of a planned abortion if the mother signed a written statement at the time of the study, that she was not planning an abortion.*
>
> . . .
>
> *IV. No person shall knowingly sell, transfer, distribute or give away any fetus for a use which is in violation of the provisions of this section. For purposes of this section, the word "fetus" shall include also an embryo or neonate.*
>
> *V.   Except as hereafter provided, whoever violates the provisions of this section shall be punished by imprisonment in a jail or house of correction for not less than one year nor more than two and one-half years or by imprisonment in the state prison for not more than five years and by the imposition of a fine of up to ten thousand dollars.*

A fetus could be studied only if the procedures would not jeopardize its life or health. The real roadblock to research was that the statute defined the term "fetus" in extraordinarily broad terms, covering every stage of development from embryo to "neonate," which is a live baby.

A scientist could avoid prosecution if an Institutional Review Board (IRB) certified that the proposed procedure did not jeopardize the life or health of a fetus and gave a reasonable basis for its decision. The IRB's decision was then reviewed by the locally elected prosecutor, the District Attorney of the county where the IRB operated. If the District Attorney had "reasonable grounds" to believe that the procedure would violate the statute, it was her responsibility to bring suit in the Superior Court and argue the proposed experiment was forbidden. Researchers or their institution could also bring suit in the Superior Court to establish the legality of its research. The state's Supreme Judicial Court could then review the court's written judgment. If the courts ruled an experiment violated the statute, the District Attorney was to give notice of the ruling to the researcher and the public in a newspaper of general circulation. The local researchers believed this statute was a potential roadblock to their work and a disincentive for researchers from other parts of the country to relocate to Massachusetts.

Meanwhile, other states, notably New Jersey and California, had recently passed statutes that would encourage stem cell research. This state action filled a perceived gap left by the federal government. In 1995, Congress added, and President Clinton ultimately signed, the Dickey-Wicker Amendment to the Federal budget. This amendment prohibited researchers or their institutions from using federal funds to research stem cells:

> SEC. 509. (a)None of the funds made available in this Act may be used for—(1) the creation of a human embryo or embryos for research purposes; or (2) research in which a human embryo or embryos are destroyed, discarded, or knowingly subjected to risk of injury or death greater than that allowed for research on fetuses in utero under 45 CFR 46.208(a)(2) and Section 498(b) of the Public Health Service Act [1](42 U.S.C. 289g(b)) (Title 42, Section 289g(b), United States Code).
>
> (b) For purposes of this section, the term "human embryo or embryos" includes any organism, not protected as a human subject under 45 CFR 46 (the Human Subject Protection regulations) . . . that is derived by fertilization, parthenogenesis, cloning, or any other means from one or more human gametes (sperm or egg) or human diploid cells (cells that have two sets of chromosomes, such as somatic cells).

The Dickey-Wicker Amendment was included in every budget between 1995 and 2004. In 2002, President George W. Bush allowed some research, but limited federal assistance to just the research on the then existing 22 stem cell lines. The federal restrictions caused institutions to impose many restrictions on researchers to protect against the loss of federal financial support. Some researchers would set up "kosher labs," that had no equipment purchased with federal funds, for just their stem cell work. Other scientists, like Dr. Kiessling, set up private foundations to fund stem cell research without reliance on federal dollars. Since the federal government effectively removed itself from stem cell research, some states saw an opportunity to attract researchers for the purpose of economic growth. Often, these came in the form of making large sums of state money available to researchers. California, for example, issued $1 billion in bonds to support stem cell research over 10 years. Other states quickly followed suit either offering tax incentives, bond issues, and general fund allocations dedicated to stem cell research.

Some lawmakers felt as though Massachusetts needed to "catch up" to these states before it lost out on research talent and the valuable biomedical industry. Scientific and medical research is a cornerstone of the Massachusetts economy. Massachusetts is home to a large community of scientific researchers based at its many colleges and universities. In turn, new companies are constantly being formed both to conduct research and development, and to market commercial applications of the scientific breakthroughs. Therefore, the bio-medical industry is seen as one of the primary engines for economic growth in Massachusetts. This industry is a highly competitive one, with researchers willing to move their labs or join institutions in other states that were welcoming to their research. Despite Massachusetts' traditional advantages, the old state law on research and a lack of plan to counter California's spending put the Bay State's biomedical industry at risk.

The Massachusetts Legislature

The Massachusetts Legislature consists of two branches, a Senate with 40 members, and the House of Representatives, which has 160 members. Senators and representatives are all elected for two-year terms in even number years. Although the Massachusetts Legislature is a full-time, "professional legislature," many members hold other jobs as lawyers, realtors, businessmen, administrators, or professors. Massachusetts legislators also tend to be more male and better educated than the population at large.

The Legislature has 26 standing joint committees, each with 17 members, 11 appointed by the House Speaker and 6 appointed by the Senate President. The committees are run jointly by a co-chair from each chamber. In the House, being a chairman is considered a leadership position, typically obtained after serving several sessions as a rank-and-file member with increasing responsibility. In the Senate, every Senator from the Democratic Caucus is given either a leadership position or a committee chairmanship immediately after election. This makes the House far more hierarchical with power concentrated in the Speaker's office and the Senate more egalitarian. Although the Senate President is still a very powerful office, nearly every member of the chamber has some measure of power and influence.

Senator Creem's staff noted that a stem cell bill had no natural "home" in a committee; there were four possible committees for the House and Senate Clerks to send the bill to: her old committee Criminal Justice (because it would revise a criminal statute), Science & Technology, Commerce & Labor, or Healthcare. This made it difficult to predict whether a committee chair hostile to stem cell legislation could control the bill's fate. Even if the bill made it out of committee, its fate would then be in the hands of the Senate President and Speaker of the House, who could decide whether to take up the bill before their chamber for a vote.

Robert E. Travaglini became Senate President in 2003. He earned a bachelor's degree from Boston State College in 1974, and spent 23 years as an elected official, first as a Boston City Councilor and for 15 year as a state senator. His political base is his home neighborhood of East Boston. "Eastie" is a tight-knit, predominantly Italian-American, working class, Catholic neighborhood. Speaker Thomas Finneran had been a member of the House since 1979. He is a graduate of Northeastern University and Boston College Law School. Representing a fairly racially diverse section of Dorchester, Finneran had long been considered one of the most fiscally and socially conservative Democrats in the House. In 1996, he defeated a more moderate Democrat to become Speaker by combining other conservative Democrats with the chamber's Republicans.

From afar, Massachusetts appears to be the most staunchly Democratic and liberal states in the nation. Massachusetts repeatedly sends liberal icons like Ted Kennedy and Elizabeth Warren to Congress, and the Massachusetts Legislature reflects this hegemony: in 2004 there were only 29 Republicans in the 200-seat legislature; 6 in the Senate and 23 in the House.

Despite this numerical superiority, there were significant ideological differences within the Democratic caucus. One branch of the party represents the liberals who place priority on certain issues such as the environment, civil rights and social equality. The other branch represents the more "blue collar" voter whose primary interests are in job security and related economic issues. Often times, the later are more conservative on social issues. Whereas the "liberals" tend to live in the suburbs, many more conservative Democrats are from ethnic neighborhoods in the various urban areas of Boston, Worcester, Springfield, Lowell, Fall River and New Bedford. These districts tend to be heavily Irish, Italian, Polish and French Canadian—all with high concentrations of Roman Catholics.

Senator Creem had already dealt with this cultural and religious divide amongst Democrats with the recent law creating "buffer zones" around reproductive health centers. This law balanced the right to free speech with the right to obtain reproductive medical care. Many "pro-life" Democrats vehemently opposed the bill. Still, Senate President Birmingham (D) and Governor Cellucci (R) supported the bill, and a large majority of the House pushed a very reluctant Speaker Finneran (D) to bring the measure to a vote. The Senate passed the bill 27–12 and the House voted 107–48 in favor of passage. Although clear majorities, had the governor vetoed the bill, the veto may have been sustained.

In 2004, 12 senators belonged to either the Knights of Columbus, a Catholic fraternal organization, or another ethnic organization which is traditionally aligned with the Catholic Church like the Sons of Italy or the Ancient Order of Hibernians. Likewise, 23 House members belonged to the Knights of Columbus and another 18 belonged to a traditionally Catholic ethnic organization. The Knights of Columbus are very clear where they stand on stem cell research. When selling members insurance, the K of C states:

> We guarantee not to invest in companies that deal in abortions, contraception, human cloning, embryonic stem cell research, for-profit health care that pays for any of the aforementioned, and pornography. The Knights of Columbus is unapologetically Catholic both professionally and fraternally. Our faith informs our work at every level, including the evaluation of each investment we make.

Therefore, the divide among Democrats would be an important consideration when taking up an issue such as stem cell research.

Even if a stem cell bill made it through the legislature, another significant hurdle could be Governor Mitt Romney. A graduate of Harvard Law and Business Schools, Mitt Romney was an extremely successful venture capitalist with the Boston firm Bain Capital. After a failed attempt to unseat Senator Edward Kennedy in 1994, he gained national attention for heading up the 2002 Winter Olympics in Salt Lake City. Shortly after the end of the Olympics, he returned to Massachusetts and was elected Governor in November 2002. Based on his statements during the campaign, many expected Governor Romney to continue the fiscally conservative but socially liberal policies of the three Republicans who preceded him in the Governor's Office. After winning election, however, Governor Romney started tacking to the right on social issues as rumors grew that he wanted to run for President.

The governor may return an enacted bill to the legislature with amendments, or he may veto a measure outright. A gubernatorial veto may be overridden by a vote of 2/3rds of each chamber. If Governor Romney opposed a stem cell bill, passage would therefore be far more complicated; legislators would have to craft a bill that could win a veto proof super-majority in each chamber.

Skills Exercise

Based on the Stem Cell Case Study reading, write a short memo (1–2 pages) as if you are the legal counsel to Senator Creem. What should she do with the scientist's request to file a more comprehensive bill? Is this issue worth her time and effort? Where would you look for more information? Who and what organizations will be your allies on this issue? Who will be your opponents? Please complete this before reading the next part of the case study.

B. BILL FILING

1. CONGRESS

Only members of Congress may introduce legislation, although occasionally a member introduces legislation by request of the president. Members and their staff typically consult with nonpartisan attorneys in each chamber's Office of Legislative Counsel for assistance in putting policy proposals into legislative language. Members may circulate the bill and ask others in the chamber—often via "Dear Colleague" letters—to sign on as original co-sponsors of a bill to demonstrate a solid base of support for the idea. In the House, a bill is introduced when it is dropped in the hopper (a wooden box on the House floor). In the Senate, the bill is submitted to clerks on the Senate floor. Upon introduction, the bill will receive a designation based on the chamber of introduction, for example, H.R. or H.J.Res. for House-originated bills or joint resolutions and S. or S.J.Res. for Senate-originated measures. It will also receive a number, which typically is the next number available in sequence during that two-year Congress.

In the House, bills then are referred by the speaker, on the advice of the nonpartisan parliamentarian, to all committees that have jurisdiction over the provisions in the bill, as determined by the chamber's standing rules and past referral decisions. Most bills fall under the jurisdiction of one committee. If multiple committees are involved and receive the bill, each committee may work only on the portion of the bill under its jurisdiction. One of those committees will be designated the primary committee of jurisdiction and will likely take the lead on any action that may occur.

In the Senate, bills are typically referred to committee in a similar process, but in almost all cases, the bill is referred to only the committee with jurisdiction over the issue that predominates in the bill. In a limited number of cases, a bill might not be referred to committee, but instead be placed directly on the Senate Calendar of Business through a series of procedural steps on the floor. See, https://www.congress.gov/legislative-process/introduction-and-referral-of-bills.

2. CALIFORNIA

If a person or group has an idea for legislation, they must persuade a legislator to author a bill. The legislator sends the idea and any bill language to the Legislative Counsel's Office, which creates the actual bill. The original legislator, and perhaps the sponsoring groups, will then review the bill. If the author is a senator, the bill is introduced at the Senate Desk; if an Assembly member, at the Assembly Desk, where it is assigned a number and read for the first time. See, https://www.senate.ca.gov/legislativeprocess.

C. THE COMMITTEE PROCESS

Committee Handbook for the New Mexico Legislature

The New Mexico Legislative Council Service (2012)

POWERS OF COMMITTEES

Committees Are Agents of House and Senate

(*Mason's Manual of Legislative Procedure* Section 615)

A committee is the agent of the legislative body that appoints it. The sole purpose of its existence is to carry out the will of the legislative body.

The senate or house cannot delegate its powers and responsibilities to one of its committees. Only when it adopts a report of one of its committees does that act of the committee become an act of the legislative body.

A committee can only recommend, and until its recommendations are adopted by the legislative body, the recommendations have no force.

A committee can make any recommendation it sees fit concerning legislation, or it can refrain from making any recommendation.

. . .

Subcommittees

(Mason's Section 650)

With the exception of the committee of the whole, any committee may appoint a subcommittee composed of members of that committee. The subcommittee has only the powers and duties conferred upon it by the parent committee. It reports only to the parent committee from which it was appointed. It cannot report to the legislative body.

The subcommittee is a convenient work device for committees having unusually heavy workloads. By distributing the hearing and discussion of bills among several subcommittees, the work of the committee may be made more efficient. The parent committee, nevertheless, must adopt or reject the subcommittee's recommendations before they become a part of the committee's recommendations to the legislative body.

. . .

HOW DO BILLS GET TO COMMITTEE?

When a bill is introduced in either house of the legislature, it is almost always sent to one or more standing committees of that house. This procedure of sending a bill to a committee is called "referral". If a bill is sent back to a committee after it has been reported out, the procedure is called "re-referral".

Methods differ in the two houses for determining where a bill will be sent. Senate rules state that the senator introducing the bill must attach a note to the bill indicating to which committee or committees it should be referred. If any member in the senate objects to this referral, the whole senate must decide the question. In the case of bills coming over from the house, the rules provide for the whole senate to make the referral. Actually, the referral is made by the senate leaders, usually acting through the majority leader (Senate Rules 11–14 and 11–14–1).

In the house, the speaker has the sole authority to refer bills to a committee or committees, whether or not they originated in the house (House Rule 11–14).

If the bill contains an appropriation or requires the expenditure of public money, the rules of both the house and senate provide that it be referred, in the case of the house, to the appropriations and finance 18 committee and, in the case of the senate, to the finance committee (House and Senate Rules 11–14–2).

If a bill is amended in a committee to provide for an appropriation or the expenditure of public money, or if the bill contains provisions that were overlooked at the time of its original referral, it is the responsibility of the committee to call this fact to the attention of its respective legislative body so that the bill may be referred to the proper finance committee.

Because most pieces of legislation deal with more than one issue area, bills, resolutions and memorials are frequently referred to two or more committees. In addition, a desire to balance committee workloads often results in referral of legislation to several committees. In those cases, the report of each committee of referral must be considered by the legislative body before the bill can be sent to a subsequent committee of referral. If the effect of the action of the legislative body on the report is to kill the bill, it is not sent to subsequent committees of referral.

. . .

COMMITTEE PROCEDURE

Procedure

There are no special rules of procedure for committees. The house rules require that the rules of order of the house govern the parliamentary procedure of the house special and standing committees, which means that when the rules are silent, the committee will be governed by *Mason's Manual of Legislative Procedure*. The senate has no correlative rule, but since it, too, has adopted Mason's, its committees should refer to that manual whenever in doubt about procedure (Senate Rule 24–2). There are cases, however, in which the rules of both houses should not be rigidly applied (Mason's Section 632).

. . .

Order of Business

The order of business is generally left up to the chair of the committee. With the exception of House Rule 9–10(e), which requires house committees to discuss bills in the order in which they are referred to committees (except when agreed upon by a majority of the committee), there are no official guidelines on how a committee shall proceed with its business.

One suggested procedure for getting the committee under way is:

1. the chair calls the committee to order;

2. the chair requests the secretary to call the roll;

3. upon the basis of the roll call, the chair makes a determination of a quorum;

4. the chair announces that the committee will proceed with the consideration of House (or Senate) Bill (or Resolution) _____;

5. the chair calls upon the sponsor to explain the bill, after which an opportunity is usually provided for members of the public to speak on the measures; and

6. the chair opens the floor for debate by the other members.

Manner of Considering Measures

If the committee desires, the procedure followed in the committee of the whole may be used and the legislation may be read section by section or paragraph by paragraph. In this case, opportunity for discussion and amendment must be permitted on each section before the committee proceeds to the reading of the next section. When this method is used, the question is not put on each section separately, but is reserved until discussion on the entire piece of legislation is completed, and then the question is put on the whole document as amended.

When a committee originates a measure, the above procedure should be followed.

In some cases, the committee may not wish to read each section of the bill. The chair may simply ask, "Is there any discussion on, or amendment to, Section 1?. . . Is there any discussion on, or amendment to, Section 2?". . . etc., until each section is covered, and the question is put on the whole bill (as amended, if there are any amendments).

Generally, in New Mexico, however, committees simply discuss legislation as a whole and not section by section.

HEARINGS IN THE HOUSE OF REPRESENTATIVES: A GUIDE FOR PREPARATION AND PROCEDURE

Richard C. Sachs, Thomas P. Carr (CRS, updated June 13, 2006)

Hearings are the primary information gathering technique committees use in policy making and oversight. Hearings may be held on issues in the absence of specific legislation, but many examine on particular legislative proposals. In either case, hearings serve a variety of purposes. Hearings inform Members, staff, and the public about measures and issues, and help assess the intensity of support for proposals. Hearings serve to monitor government programs and activities, and expose problems that Congress can later correct. Hearings give citizens an opportunity to participate in the policy process, and help build the public record for a measure or issue.

For a number of reasons, house committees act only on a minority of the measures introduced and referred to them. For instance, a committee often receives many proposals in each major policy area within its jurisdiction, but ultimately may choose to act on only a few measures in each such area, if any. Committees usually send a bill to an appropriate subcommittee for initial consideration, although committees do not uniformly require such referral. A committee may decide to send a bill to subcommittee for initial scrutiny because of the technical nature of the issue, the history of prior handling of the matter, or political factors, among other reasons. When a committee or a subcommittee considers a measure, it generally takes four actions. When a subcommittee initiates some of the four actions, the extent to which the full committee repeats some of these steps varies among committees and from issue to issue. The sequence of actions assumes the committee favors a measure, but at any time the committee may discontinue action.

First, a committee may seek agency comment by sending a copy of the measure to the executive departments or agencies having relevant policy expertise and soliciting their written evaluation of the proposal. The executive agency typically sends a copy of the measure to the Office of Management and Budget (OMB) for a determination as to consistency with the President's program.

Second, a committee may decide to hold one or more hearings. Further committee action without hearings is the exception, although hearings have been bypassed to move measures expeditiously through committee or because of action on a related bill in the previous Congress. The importance of this action has been noted by congressional scholar Walter J. Oleszek: "The decision to hold a hearing is often a critical point in the life of a bill. Measures brought to the floor without first undergoing the scrutiny of hearings will likely receive sharp criticism. . . . The importance of the committee stage is based on the assumption that the experts—the committee members—carefully scrutinize a proposal, and hearings provide a demonstrable record of that scrutiny." (Walter J. Oleszek, CONGRESSIONAL PROCEDURES AND THE POLICY PROCESS, 6th ed. (Washington: CQ Press, 2004), p. 93.)

Third, a committee will meet to "mark up," or recommend amendments to the legislation, based in part on information received at hearings. Markup is the critical stage where the committee decides how the language of the bill should appear when it is presented to the House for consideration. While a bill can be subsequently amended on the House floor, committees have the important prerogative of shaping legislation before consideration by the full chamber.

Fourth, the full committee will report the legislation to the floor; subcommittees must report to their parent committees. When a committee reports a measure, it is also required to issue a written report that typically describes and explains the measure's purposes and provisions and tells Members why the measure should be passed. The report also may summarize any relevant hearings that were held. This reporting requirement may be waived.

. . .

Committees hold legislative hearings on measures or policy issues that may become legislation. Sometimes a committee holds hearings on multiple measures before ultimately choosing one vehicle for further committee and chamber action. Most often the goal of a legislative hearing is the consideration of a measure for enactment into law. These hearings provide a forum where facts and opinions on legislation can be presented by witnesses with diverse backgrounds, including Members of Congress and other government officials, representatives of interest groups and academia, and from additional citizens affected by the proposal.

. . .

Preparation for Hearings Preliminary Issues

A committee considers a variety of issues in deciding whether to hold a hearing. A committee must define the information it needs, evaluate the policy matters or the political message it wishes to communicate, and then determine whether a hearing is the best method of achieving its goals. A hearing agenda is influenced by several factors, including timing of the hearing, the salience of issues to the nation, the importance of policies to interest groups, and matters of significance to the President, House leaders, and other Representatives. Programs under a committee's jurisdiction that need to be reauthorized generally receive committee scrutiny, as do instances of reported waste, fraud, or abuse.

Each committee receives dozens or even hundreds of proposals for possible examination and studies matters not embodied in specific legislation. In the context of this overall workload, a committee must decide whether holding a particular hearing is the best use of staff and funds. A committee also considers whether and how a hearing would fit into its overall schedule. It may be particularly difficult for committees with broad jurisdictions to justify the allocation of limited resources to a hearing, or even to find time in its crowded schedule.

In order to obtain approval for a hearing, committee staff often prepare a preliminary hearing memorandum for the chair that includes information such as the scope and purpose of the hearing, the expected outcome, possible witnesses, how many hearing days are planned, and perhaps the views of the minority party. Informal discussion with committee members and staff may suffice.

. . .

Choosing and Inviting Witnesses

Choosing witnesses is often one of the most important issues in planning a hearing. Committees pay careful attention to which viewpoints will be represented, who should testify, and the order and format for presenting witnesses.

In some cases a committee will strive to make sure that all reasonable points of view are represented, while in other cases witnesses expressing only particular points of view will be invited. House rules allow the minority party members of a committee to call witnesses of their choice on at least one day of a hearing, if a majority of these Members makes this request to the committee chair before completion of the hearing (House Rule XI, clause 2(j)(1)). In lieu of this formal option, the minority sometimes works informally with the majority to invite witnesses representing its views.

In order to testify, a witness must be invited by the committee. Before officially inviting a witness, committee staff identify and often interview prospective candidates. When suitable witnesses are found, the committee chair typically sends a formal letter of invitation. This letter generally gives the witness some basic information, including the purpose, subject, date, time, and place of the hearing. In addition to specifying the portion of a measure or issue the witness should address, the letter may contain a limitation on the length of the witness's oral testimony. The committee may send the witness additional information. This information may include a list of committee members, the committee's rules, the measure under consideration, and material from the media relating to the issue. Often a staff contact is indicated. Staff will sometimes meet with witnesses before a hearing to answer questions and to review procedure.

Advance Written Testimony

A letter of invitation also may request that the witness send the committee biographical information and an advance copy of written testimony. House rules require each witness (insofar as is practicable) to file with the committee an advance copy of written testimony, and then to limit oral remarks to a brief summary of his or her statement (House Rule XI, clause 2(g)(4)).

. . .

Format and Order of Witness Testimony

Committees determine the form at and order of presenting witnesses. According to one traditional format, a witness summarizes his or her written statement and then takes questions from committee members before a second witness testifies. Committees have used different formats recently, and it has become common to present witnesses with diverging viewpoints as a panel. The usual practice in this case is for all witnesses on the panel to make statements, then for committee members to pose questions to the panel. Some observers believe that this format produces a more stimulating debate and more effectively elicits pertinent information. Committees have experimented with several other formats for gathering information, which may not always be considered formal hearings. For instance, committees have held seminars consisting of briefings by experts with informal opportunities for asking questions, and roundtable discussions where committee members and staff have a free-flowing dialogue with knowledgeable outsiders.

. . .

Briefing Books

Committees often ask staff to prepare summary and background material for use by their members before and during a hearing. This information is sometimes assembled into briefing books or folders to present issues in a systematic, uniform way. Briefing books might include a variety of items, including a description of the subject, scope, and purpose of the hearing. For legislative hearings, a copy and explanation of each measure under consideration, and a comparison of all measures to be discussed, are useful. Background material might include relevant statutes and regulations, court decisions, press articles, agency reports, academic studies, and a chronology of major events. In order to assist members with witnesses, the books might contain a list of witnesses in their order of appearance, a copy or summary of written testimony, and biographical information. Briefing material might also include questions or talking points for committee members to use in opening statements and in examining witnesses.

Before a hearing, committee staff sometimes brief members and other staff. Staff may conduct oral briefings in addition to, or in lieu of, preparing briefing books. These sessions provide an opportunity to discuss matters of particular interest to individual committee members.

Publicity and Media Considerations

A committee's goal in holding a hearing often is not narrowly limited to collecting information for policy development. The goal may include publicizing an issue or problem to focus attention on it. Public exposure of a problem at an oversight or investigative hearing can be a particularly effective technique. Public officials often seem responsive to correcting program deficiencies when an issue has been broadly publicized. Hearings also are used to build support for a proposal among the public generally or certain sectors thereof. Members and witnesses make arguments that form part of the public record in support of future committee action, such as reporting a measure.

House rules influence how a committee plans for media coverage and other publicity matters. For example, House rules require that hearings be open to the public, as well as to radio, television, and still photography coverage, unless a committee votes to close a hearing (House Rule XI, clause 2(g)(2)(A)). Hearings may be closed only for limited and specific reasons—for example, to deal with information that could compromise national security. . . . Detailed provisions of House rules dealing with broadcasting committee hearings point up the importance to Congress of television coverage (House Rule XI, clause 4).

. . .

Closing a Hearing

The vast majority of committee hearings are open to the public, as required under House rules; but House rules permit committees to close a hearing for specific reasons, and outline the procedure for doing so (House Rule XI, clauses 2(g)(2) and 2(k)(5)). A hearing may be closed to the public "because disclosure of testimony, evidence, or other matters to be considered would endanger the national security, would compromise sensitive law enforcement information, or would violate any law or rule of the House of Representatives." In order to close all or part of a hearing, a committee must vote by roll call in open session and with a majority present. When a quorum is present for taking testimony, however, a committee may vote to close a hearing (1) because the anticipated testimony at an investigative hearing "may tend to defame, degrade, or incriminate any person,"; or (2) solely to discuss whether there is reason to continue the hearing in closed session.

House rules permit most committees to close a hearing on a specific day and on one subsequent day of hearings. The Committees on

Appropriations, Armed Services, and Intelligence, however, may vote to close their hearings for five additional, consecutive days of hearings.

. . .

Oral Testimony of Witnesses

Under House rules, each committee requires witnesses to limit their oral testimony to a brief summary of their argument, insofar as is practicable (House Rule XI, clause 2(g)(4)). In the interest of time, and because written testimony generally is available to the committee in advance, it is usually not necessary or desirable for a witness to read his or her entire written statement. On some committees the chair has the discretion to determine how long a witness may speak. On the Committee on Agriculture, witnesses may be limited to brief summaries of their statements within the time allotted to them, at the discretion of the chair. Other committees have adopted rules stipulating how long a witness may speak, typically for five minutes.

. . .

Five-Minute Rule for Questioning Witnesses

The question and answer period which follows a witness's opening statement presents an opportunity for a committee to build a public record and to obtain information to support future committee actions. Committee staff sometimes prepare questions or talking points for committee leaders and other members. In some cases, the expected line of questioning is discussed in advance with witnesses.

House rules generally accord committee members five minutes to question each witness until every member has had this opportunity (House Rule XI, clause 2(j)(2)). In practice, many committees allow an extension of time by unanimous consent, and a few committees, such as Veterans' Affairs, specify this in their rules. After the first round of questioning under the five-minute rule, committees can determine how to dispose of any additional time. Some committees' rules specify a procedure for using additional time. For example, the rules of the House Committee on International Relations provide for a second round of questioning under the five-minute rule, while rules of the Committee on Agriculture allow the chair to limit the time for further questioning.

. . .

Post-Hearing Activities

After examining the last witness, the committee chair closes the hearing. The chair may summarize what has been learned about the issue, and comment on the future committee schedule or expected action. After a day of hearings, staff may be asked to prepare a summary of testimony. The summary may be distributed to committee members and the press and become part of any published hearing. Follow-up questions can be prepared and submitted to witnesses for written replies to clear up points not resolved during the hearing. If the hearing is investigative, the committee can prepare and issue its report. If the hearing is legislative, the committee may proceed to mark up and report a measure to the House. Finally, committees attend to administrative details following a hearing, such as restoring the hearing room to its original condition and sending thank-you letters to witnesses.

NOTES & QUESTIONS

1.   The Legislative Reorganization Act of 1946 requires the Library of Congress to bind each committee's printed hearings at the end of each Congressional session. Since 2000, most committees have made written testimony and/or hearing transcripts available online. (See, https://guides.loc. gov/finding-government-documents/congressional-committee-reports.)

2.   The process for preparing Senate hearings is very similar to the House process described above. For a checklist see, Valerie Heitshusen, "Senate Committee Hearings: Preparation," *Congressional Research Service*, December 4, 2017 (7–5700 www.crs.gov 98–489).

3.   The Committee Handbook for the New Mexico Legislature suggests the following procedure for committee hearings:

There is no fixed procedure for the conduct of a hearing. Each committee may use any method it finds to be workable and fair.

One procedure is outlined below and may be used as a guide.

A.   Call to order and announcements: The chair calls the committee to order and, after determining that a quorum is present, announces the name of the committee (in case any person is mistakenly appearing before the wrong committee) and introduces the committee members and the numbers and subjects of the legislation being heard that day. The chair may also announce the procedure to be followed by the committee in hearing witnesses.

B.   Roster of appearance: Any person who desires to appear before the committee on a measure being heard that day is asked to give the committee secretary the person's name and the name of the organization or group the person represents and to state whether the person wishes to speak for or against the measure.

C.   Sponsor's presentation: The chair then asks the sponsor of the measure to explain it. After the sponsor's general review, the sponsor may be allowed to have one or more witnesses supplement the explanation.

D.   Appearance of witnesses: Following the explanation by the sponsor and witnesses, each person who has given the person's name to the secretary is called upon in alternate order of those for and those against the bill. The chair may also call for testimony by others in the room who wish to be heard. The committee, in advance of the hearing, may place a time limit on the presentation of each witness. If a large delegation is present, all of whom are testifying in essentially the same vein, the chair, in the interest of time, may request the group to designate one or two spokespersons, and the chair may announce that the committee take notice of the size of the delegation.

E.   Questions by the committee: After the sponsor and each person appearing as a witness have made their presentations, the chair gives committee members the opportunity to ask questions of them.

D. DRAFTING AND RE-DRAFTING BY COMMITTEE

Much of the drafting process takes place at the committee stage. The initial bill may have been a policy idea written out in very broad or general terms. The hearing process allows the committee a chance to educate itself about an issue and gather evidence that will inform or justify the provisions of a redrafted bill. In their article above, Professor Ann & Bob Seidman give a methodology for a single person to develop policy and fully draft a bill. In this case study, Professors Nourse and Schacter offer a case study showing the drafting process as it exists in Congress. They focus on the work of the Senate Judiciary Committee, and the contributions of drafters in several positions: committee staffers, senators, lobbyists, and committee staff from the Office of Legislative Counsel.

Prof. Nourse and Prof. Schacter interviewed sixteen counsels working either for the full Judiciary Committee or one of its six subcommittees. The respondents were politically balanced; eight worked for Republican senators, and eight worked for Democratic senators. They also spoke to two lawyers from the Senate's Office of the Legislative Counsel who had experience working with the Judiciary Committee.

THE POLITICS OF LEGISLATIVE DRAFTING:
A CONGRESSIONAL CASE STUDY

Victoria F. Nourse; Jane S. Schacter, 77 *N.Y.U. Law Review* 575 (2002)

A.   Complexity and Variability in Legislative Drafting

The first strong theme to emerge from our interviews is that respondents repeatedly-and emphatically-rejected the notion of a monolithic drafting process and described in some detail the ways in which the drafting process can vary. This diversity begins at the very inception of a bill. Respondents told us, for example, that ideas for new legislation came from a broad array of sources—newspapers and court cases, lobbyists and the White House, Sunday-school teachers and law-review articles, to name a few. More pertinent for our purposes, the drafting process itself can look very different in different contexts, and our interviews made clear the rich array of contexts in which drafting takes place.

. . .

1. Multiple Drafters

To gain a better understanding of the drafting process, we asked staffers about the role of various potential participants in the drafting process. We specifically asked about staffers themselves, senators, professional drafters from the Legislative Counsel's office, and lobbyists. Because we did not observe any drafting ourselves, what we report, of course, can reflect only the staffers' perceptions of the roles these parties play. In pressing this line of inquiry, we had in mind that the Supreme Court, for example, routinely has referred to legislators as the drafters of federal law. Sometimes the Court refers simply to "Congress" as the drafter, but frequently the justices specify "legislators" as drafters. It may well be that the justices do not actually believe this to be true; they may be invoking a fiction or using a simple proxy for a process they know to be more complex. Nevertheless, Supreme Court opinions typically place the legislator in the role of drafter.

Staffers

Perhaps unsurprisingly, our staff respondents saw themselves as centrally involved in bill drafting efforts. They also richly described the role of others in drafting but consistently described staffers as having principal responsibility for producing bill drafts. The precise nature of their roles in drafting varied widely according to the bill. Some of this variability, of course, flows from the diversity of subject-matter areas under the Judiciary Committee's jurisdiction. When asked to describe their most recent drafting effort, for example, respondents covered a lot of substantive territory, including gun control, juvenile crime, bankruptcy, intellectual property, victims' rights, Y2K liability, employment discrimination, antitrust law, and more. Subject-matter area, in turn, influenced staffers' roles relative to other players. For instance, in the crime area, staffers saw themselves as more important because of a relative lack of lobbying interests, while in areas like intellectual property, there was a consensus that lobbyists had a significant role.

Senators

Most staffers indicated that, as a general rule, senators themselves did not write the text of legislation: "[My senator] does not draft. He is an idea guy."

"Senators are generalists. Very few senators write their own language."

. . .

All in all, only a minority of staffers reported that their respective senators engaged in any substantial drafting of language for a bill. Three staffers said that their senators did draft at least some language on amendments or bills. But even these staffers tended to characterize drafting by a senator as unusual. Two of these three staffers said that involvement with words was not typical for their particular senators or for most senators. Overall, eleven of twelve responding staffers said that senators, as a general rule, do not draft text as an original matter. Respondents expressed little concern about the relative lack of involvement by senators in drafting text. Some of their explanations suggest it is a question of time and the vast range of issues on which senators must legislate: "Senators have no time to actually write language. [My senator's] schedule is amazingly dense."

. . .

Although staffers placed themselves at the center of the drafting process, they also insisted that they sought to implement the policies of their senators, not to impose their own views. They saw themselves as faithful agents in the drafting process. As one put it: "It's a member's power, not the staffer's." Another considered it "laughable" to believe that staffers routinely act outside the parameters of their bosses' positions on legislative matters. Some staffers emphasized that senators reviewed staff work carefully and that staffers had strong incentives—including keeping their jobs—to ensure that their drafting efforts did not diverge from their bosses' positions and remained loyal to their senators' missions.

Lobbyists

Every staffer we interviewed told us that lobbyists regularly were involved in drafting bills. Staffers seemed to use a broad concept of lobbyist, one that included any group-profit or nonprofit-that had an interest in influencing legislation and either had information relevant to the issue or potentially would be affected by the legislation. Thus, the term "lobbyist" sometimes included administrative agencies, the White House, the Justice Department, or even federal judges, as well as church groups, universities, and homeless shelters. When a bill touched on a substantive area in the committee's jurisdiction that was heavily lobbied, staffers indicated that it was highly likely that lobbyists would offer up draft language, be asked to do so by staff, or receive from staff proposed language for the lobbyists' comments. Intellectual property, bankruptcy, and "hot button" issues like gun control, abortion, and pornography were areas in which staffers indicated there was extensive lobbyist involvement. Lobbyists were active even in areas that lacked strong financial interests, for example, matters affecting children's interests. The only area in which we heard that paid lobbyists had a limited role was standard criminal law issues, where there is no real lobby but where the Department of Justice is a regular player. We address in some detail, in Section II.D below, the dynamics of lobbyist involvement in drafting. But for purposes of understanding the complexity of the drafting processes as seen by respondents, it is sufficient at this point simply to note the rather significant role of outside interests in the drafting process.

Legislative Counsel

The Legislative Counsel's office is specifically constituted to assist the Senate in drafting legislation. In our interviews, we discussed Legislative Counsel's role in the drafting process with both staffers and with two Legislative Counsel attorneys with extensive experience with the Judiciary Committee. Unlike the practice in some states, no law or rule requires that Senate legislation be drafted by Legislative Counsel attorneys. Legislative Counsel attorneys told us that, because of the non-mandatory nature of their role, their involvement in writing any particular bill is "strictly up to the client" (i.e., the senator or the committee). Legislative Counsel attorneys, therefore, "live on [their] reputation and good relationships."

i.   *Legislative Counsel from the Perspective of Committee Staffers*

Every respondent said that Legislative Counsel attorneys had some role in the drafting process. Respondents differed, however, in how they described the nature and importance of that role. Many staffers told us that the role of the Legislative Counsel's office varied from bill to bill. On some occasions, the staffer would send a memo describing what the proposed legislation would do and then would receive back a first draft from the Legislative Counsel's office. More typically, however, a staffer would prepare a first draft and then forward it to Legislative Counsel attorneys for what was repeatedly characterized as "stylistic" or "technical" input:

> "[The Legislative Counsel's attorneys] make sure [the bill] gets in the right section of the Code, clarify language, [make] sure it's clear what's being amended, 'get it right.'" "Legislative Counsel does things like check cross-references, check subsection references, etc."

> "I use Legislative Counsel to format, not so much for substantive purposes." "Legislative Counsel gets involved in almost all cases. They put [drafts of the statute] in the proper form. You need Legislative Counsel input to be sure about the form, conventions of drafting, etc."

Comments by some staffers suggested an inverse relationship between how long a staffer had been on the job and the use of Legislative Counsel attorneys. As one put it, "especially because many staffers have not been here that long," the Legislative Counsel's office "has an important role." One staffer explained that he works with the Legislative Counsel's office, but that its role for him has changed as he has become more experienced:

> Early on, [Legislative Counsel] would draft the bill. Now, I do the first draft and give it to them to tighten and polish. They will take

out extra words, see certain aspects of the big picture for drafting when [I am] lost in the details of one subsection, etc.

. . .

ii.   *Legislative Counsel from the Perspective of Legislative Counsel Attorneys*

Legislative Counsel attorneys reported that they receive work from the Judiciary Committee in a variety of ways. This can range from receiving the most amorphous "specs" for a bill (e.g., "We want to make the tax code more fair") to reviewing a comprehensive first draft of a bill written by someone other than a Legislative Counsel attorney. When Legislative Counsel attorneys receive bills written by others, it is usually a staffer, a lobbyist, or an administrator who has drafted the bill.

Legislative Counsel attorneys see their principal objective as to produce a clear, well sequenced statute. Legislative Counsel's style favors certain elements, such as setting out general rules and exceptions, making liberal use of definitions, including an effective date, and providing coordination rules. When called upon to improve a bill drafted by someone else, Legislative Counsel attorneys say that they frequently encounter problems like a lack of definitions, inconsistent usage of statutory terms, poor organization, or ambiguity in identifying the statutory actors or statutory exceptions.

Despite the considerable variability in the sources and content of assignments given to the Legislative Counsel's office, one near constant is that the request for assistance comes from committee staffers rather than senators themselves. Legislative Counsel attorneys strongly assert their nonpartisan nature and emphasize that they stand in an attorney-client relationship with senators and staffers. "We are lawyers first," one told us. Because of this attorney-client relationship, Legislative Counsel attorneys do not communicate with any outside groups, except in the presence of a staffer. Legislative Counsel attorneys sometimes do observe the role of lobbyists or others in the drafting process, but only in the presence of staffers. More often, their knowledge of the role played by any outside group is both limited and filtered through staffers.

2.   Multiple Drafting Processes

The picture of the drafting process that emerged from our interviews is one of striking variability. There was widespread agreement among staffers that different drafting processes are engaged for different kinds of bills. Sometimes more than one process is applied to the same bill, and the use of one drafting process at a later time (for example, drafting on the floor or in conference) can wipe out the results of an earlier process. We describe below several versions of the drafting process that emerged in our interviews.

The Extended Drafting Process

The most thorough drafting process that staffers told us about was described by one in these terms: We [the staffers] will come up with an idea, make a list of points to cover. Legislative Counsel will then draft or revise the draft written by staff. We might consult with the [full committee] staff before sending it to Legislative Counsel or other offices to reach some kind of consensus. We might vet language with lobbyists whose clients would be affected by the bill or would be concerned about the bill. [The] final layer [might involve a] check with the [presidential] administration.

This general outline suggests that thorough, time-consuming drafting of this sort is staff driven and that the process involves more negotiation and consultation than exacting word choice. This description was consistent with several stories we heard about various pieces of major legislation. In describing work on drafting a large bankruptcy bill, for example, one staffer said: We began with [staff] meetings asking [about] the goal of the [party] caucus. We met with consumer groups, credit card companies, and banks, looking at what would be feasible. After a first draft [by the staff], we sent it to Legislative Counsel and then vetted it with groups and others in the Senate.

. . .

Consensus Drafting

In a variant of this extended process, staffers told us that some bills were drafted jointly by staffers working for several senators. Language would be negotiated jointly in order to achieve consensus in a committee markup. Sometimes, staff of members who supported and opposed a bill would meet before the markup, and a bill would be hammered out by the principal interests in a "committee substitute."

. . .

Staffers noted, however, sharp limits on this kind of consensus-oriented drafting process. On some issues there was no room for compromise. Abortion and pornography were cited by one staffer as the kind of "edgy" partisan issues as to which accommodation was unlikely. In other cases, compromise did not represent consensus-driven decision making but, instead, was forced by powerful decision makers on the committee when, for example, a member "needed" to have a bill for reelection purposes and the committee chair was willing to push the issue.

NOTES & QUESTIONS

Professors Nourse & Schacter propose several process reforms based on their research. These include: an expanded role for the Legislative Counsel's office to increase the extent to which rules of construction and other judicial principles are made part of the drafting process. OLC could "increase congressional awareness of potential interpretive outcomes and more systematically enable drafters to make drafting choices in light of these potential outcomes." As an alternative OLC could prepare drafting guides or checklists for the use of committee staffers.

Committee Handbook for the New Mexico Legislature

The New Mexico Legislative Council Service (2012)

COMMITTEE REPORTS

Contents

A committee report may contain only that which is agreed upon by a majority of the committee and which has been acted upon in a meeting with a quorum present.

The report must include all amendments to the measure approved by the committee and its recommendation of the action that should be taken on the measure (Mason's Sections 663 and 664).

Preparation

It is the duty of the committee secretary to prepare the committee report; however, on occasion, it may be prepared by a member of the committee or, upon request of the committee, by the legislative council service.

Authentication

Committee reports are authenticated by the chair of the committee by the chair's signature in the space provided on the report form (Mason's Section 665).

Improper Committee Reports Committee reports that are not considered at a regular meeting of the committee are improper reports. The presiding officer may refuse to accept any report on a bill or other measure when the presiding officer has knowledge that it was improperly acted upon.

Legislation not properly reported from a committee is not entitled to a place upon the legislative calendar and will be referred back to the committee (Mason's Section 675).

Minority Reports

The report of the majority on a committee is the report of the committee. It should not be referred to as the "majority report".

If a minority report is submitted, it has only the status of an expression of views of those persons on the committee submitting the report and may not be acted upon in the legislative body except upon the adoption of a motion to substitute it for the report of the committee.

NOTES & QUESTIONS

1.   This is the table of contents for a 2019 report on a bill to reauthorize the September 11th Victim Compensation Fund of 2001:

Mr. Nadler, from the Committee on the Judiciary, submitted the following

REPORT
[To accompany H.R. 1327]
[Including cost estimate of the Congressional Budget Office]

The Committee on the Judiciary, to whom was referred the bill (H.R. 1327) to extend authorization for the September 11th Victim Compensation Fund of 2001 through fiscal year 2090, and for other purposes, having considered the same, report favorably thereon without amendment and recommend that the bill do pass.

CONTENTS

2.   When searching for legislative intent, Judge Robert Katzmann notes in one decision that "committee reports are among 'the most authoritative and reliable materials of legislative history.'" *United States v. Gayle*, 342 F.3d 89, 94 (2nd Cir. 2003)(quoting, *Disabled in Action of Metro. N.Y. v. Hammons*, 202 F.3d 110, 124 (2nd Cir. 2000). On the other hand, Justice Antonin Scalia rejected using such legislative history, stating "We are a Government of laws, not of committee reports." *Blanchard v. Bergeron*, 489 U.S. 87, 98–99 (1989)(Scalia, J., concurring in part and concurring in the judgment).

3.   Given the weight a judge may give to a committee report, what information should be included?

4.   Some states do not have lengthy committee reports but may have a "committee statement" that gives important information about the committee stage of a bill but is often far shorter than the committee reports produced by Congress. For example, a Nebraska committee considered a bill to protect the freedom of expression for student journalists. When the bill went to the full legislature, the committee statement was two and a half pages and included:

- The hearing date;
- The committee;
- The bill introducer;
- A one-line statement of what the bills seeks to do;
- The roll call vote for the final committee action;
- Who gave oral testimony both for and against;
- Who submitted written testimony and who they represent;
- A summary of purpose and/or changes. In this case, the summary was, "LB 88 seeks to establish protections for student journalists at both the high school and postsecondary level. The bill provides protections from discipline for exercising free speech and press rights. Student media advisors are protected from dismissal or retaliated against for protecting the student or refusing to infringe on protected content." And
- A section-by section summary.

Finally, the committee statement is signed by the chair. See, https://nebraska legislature.gov/FloorDocs/107/PDF/CS/LB88.pdf.

What value will this shorter type of statement be to courts? Agencies? The public? Other legislators? The Governor?

Stem Cell Case Study: Part II

Senator Jack Hart (D-South Boston), the Senate chair of the Economic Development and Emerging Technologies Committee ("Committee"), had to prepare for an important caucus. The stem cell bill reported from the Committee a few hours before would be the focus of that day's formal session. It certainly had been a busy three months for Sen. Hart since he was surprised by Senate President Travaglini's appointment to chair the new Committee. Now he had to chart how the Senate would deal with an ever more complicated bill that was completely redrafted by the House Committee chair.

The caucus typically takes place a few hours before a formal session is set to begin to discuss the business of the day, to hear candid and unfiltered opinions about the bills before the Senate, to work out potential amendments and to generally ensure a smooth, although vigorous, debate.

Most weeks the Democrats would meet in the Senate President's large and ornate ceremonial office and have lunch. The Republicans met in the Minority Leader's office down the hall. The only staff present at the Democratic caucus would be the Senate Counsel and perhaps the President's chief of staff.

Given the importance of the bill, the Republicans had been invited to meet with the Democrats and Senator Hart was expected to lead the discussion. What had the Committee learned during the process? What concerns were raised and which of them were valid?

Why did the House Committee members redraft the bill the way they did? Did those changes still allow for the policy the original sponsors, including the Senate President, preferred? Could a bill be crafted that would be veto proof? What details still needed to be worked out?

Just a few minutes before, Jack's staff had finished summarizing the House's committee redraft of the bill and analyzing what scientific research it allowed and restricted. Now Jack headed over to the Senate President's office to meet with his colleagues.

The Previous Session

Based on her meetings with the stem cell scientists, Senator Creem had her staff draft and file a bill that would remove the legal barriers and hindrances on stem cell research and take positive steps to encourage such research. The bill, "An Act Relative to Stem Cell Research," was relatively simple:

- A findings and purposes section stating that embryonic research could relieve human suffering from disease and injury and acknowledging the important contributions currently being made by Massachusetts scientists;

- Definitions for the terms "donated to medicine," "embryo," "financial inducement," and "uterus;"

- A statement that the policy of Massachusetts would be to foster research in regenerative medicine;

- Requiring human embryonic research be approved by an institutional review board;

- Criminal penalties for anyone who transferred an embryo donated to medicine into a uterus, and on human cloning;

- Excluding embryos donated to science from the existing prohibitions on experimenting with fetuses; and

- A grant program to encourage stem cell research.

The bill was held in committee for several months without action. Still, when an economic stimulus package was "fast-tracked" during the end of the session, Senator Creem convinced her Senate colleagues to include the bill language in the omnibus bill. The stem cell provisions, however, were cut out of the final bill by the House of Representatives and the conference committee. Many laid the blame for removing the stem cell language on Speaker Thomas Finneran, who opposed stem cell research. Ironically, later that year Speaker Finneran left the House to become the President of the Massachusetts Biotechnology Council. That cleared the way for Sal DiMasi, a more socially liberal representative and Finneran's Majority leader, to become Speaker. Salvatore F. DiMasi represented the Third Suffolk District in the House since 1979. His core constituency was the neighborhood where he was born and lived in his entire life, the North End of Boston, the heart of Boston's Italian community. Speaker DiMasi graduated from Boston College with a degree in accounting and earned his law degree from Suffolk University Law School in 1971. During his legislative career, Speaker DiMasi served as the chair of several committees: Banks and Banking, Criminal Justice, and Judiciary. A social liberal, he supported health care reform and gay marriage, and opposed casino gambling. Speaker DiMasi supported stem cell research, and the change in House leadership made a stem cell research bill a real possibility during the 2005–2006 session.

The 2005 Legislature

Besides the election of Sal DiMasi as Speaker, another important event for the 2005 session was Senate President Travaglini's health. President Travaglini battled and overcame cancer during the final half of 2004. This led him to become much more interested in the possibility of new biotechnology leading to the cures for diseases like the one he had survived.

Senate President Travaglini made stem cell research a priority of the legislative session in his first address to the Senate, Travaglini discussed his cancer diagnosis and the prospects of embryonic stem cells to cure cancer patients. During the speech, he announced that he was working with two Harvard scientists, Dr. Kevin Eggen and Dr. Douglas Melton and would file a new bill in a few weeks. Senator Creem and her staff were thrilled; her issue would now be leading the Senate agenda.

On February 9, 2005, President Travaglini filed his version of the bill. Sen. Travaglini stated, "This bill serves as a first step in bolstering this area of research and specifically removes any doubt about state support and clears the path for future expansion in this cutting-edge field." As seen in the appendix, the Travaglini bill was very similar to the Creem bill. President Travaglini's bill:

- had a slightly different title;
- forbade selling embryos that were donated for research; and

- eliminated Sen. Creem's proposed grant program to encourage stem cell research.

After meeting with the Senate President, Senator Creem decided to set aside her own bills and signed on as a co-sponsor of the Senate President's bill; the Senate President's bill would be the vehicle for any such legislation and, as a practical matter, it was better to try influence and strengthen the Senate President's bill rather than continue to promote her bill. In exchange for her support, the Senate President promised that she would be involved in the bill throughout the legislative process. Senator Creem understood that the bill would need significant changes and would require complicated bill drafting. Below is a portion of an internal memorandum to Senator Creem.

Memorandum

To: Sen. Creem

From: Josh & Richard

Date: February 2, 2005

Re: Stem Cell Research

. . .

We believe that the language of our bill should be different to be more precise and more consistent with recent scientific advances. This is especially true when it comes to defining what an embryo is for the purposes of allowing or forbidding certain types of research, properly defining the types of stem cells that may be legally researched, and the inclusion of a time limit for embryos before they are too advanced to be ethically studied.

1.   What is an embryo?

This is the primary question that is debated at length by scientists and ethicists. Unfortunately, the definition of "embryo" has been transformed in recent years due to the need for more understandable terms related to infertility clinics. The general problem is exacerbated by statutes such as the one in Massachusetts where embryo is defined so broadly that there is no difference between an embryo and a fetus.

. . .

Whereas scientists once called everything an embryo until it became a fetus, they have now identified numerous different earlier stages of development. Most significant was the identification of a fertilized egg as a "zygote," which exists for 2–3 weeks before becoming an "embryo." The end of the zygotic stage is marked by the development of the "primitive streak."

. . .

Although research seemingly clarifies the issue, the use of lay terms has obscured the true nature of embryos. In recent decades, people have created a multitude of fertilized eggs for the purposes of in vitro fertilization. When a fertilized, and developing, egg was placed into the mother's womb, the doctor would often call it an "embryo" even though it did not have the primal streak, because it was a more accessible term than "zygote." This has significantly increased the confusion.

Additionally, the ability to artificially "activate eggs through the process of parthenogenesis causes further confusion by giving rise to eggs with the capability to cultivate cells, but without the possibility of growing into a fetus that may not be considered embryos at all.

Ultimately, the international standard for ethical research is 14 days. As a practical matter, this is the crucial period for research and zygotes older than 14 days do not offer the same interest for scientists.

. . . .

3.   Recommended Changes to the Creem Bill

- *We should make the following changes to our bill:*

- *Break out definitions of three types of stem cells, currently included within the definition of "embryo."*

- *Add definition of "ovasome" and include within permissible areas of research (i.e., within definition of "donated to medicine".)*

- *Section 12EE(b) ought to include the term "parthenogenesis" within permissible clinical applications."*

. . .

Opposition

Opponents to stem cell research began organizing as soon as President Travaglini made his support for the issue known. In January, anti-abortion activists gathered at historic Faneuil Hall to mark the anniversary of *Roe v. Wade,* and to rally against abortion and other threats to life issues such as stem cell research. Catholic Archbishop Sean P. O'Malley urged the group to fight laws that go against their faith. Raymond Flynn, a former Democratic Boston Mayor and ambassador to the Vatican, targeted elected officials even more bluntly. Flynn stated that being a good American and a Catholic are more important than the Democratic Party's future. Flynn stated, "Ask the candidates, 'Will you vote pro-life?' If they say no, say 'Well you don't have my vote." During the next few weeks, key legislators, including powerful Democratic committee chairs, such as Rep. Philip Travis (D-Rehoboth), argued that stem cell research opened the door to human cloning, Rep. Travis stated, "I'll do everything I can to defeat this in the House. This is absolutely wrong." The executive director for

Massachusetts Citizens for Life, Marie Sturgis, stated, "We are concerned that this puts human life in the hands of biotech firms and scientists. This is an attack on the integrity and dignity of the human being. Senator Travaglini was at one time an embryo as we all were. An embryo is a human being."

Although not as strident as some, this bill drew the "concern" of Governor Romney. On February 10th, Governor Romney sent a letter to Senator Travaglini, which congratulated the Senate President for bringing focus to the area of stem cell research but advocated a more restrictive law based on ethical concerns. Romney's letter:

1. touted the great promise of adult stem cell lines;

2. argued for research on existing embryonic stem cell lines, "consistent with President Bush's federal policy;

3. stated that Massachusetts should allow research on stem cells taken from "surplus embryos created as part of an in vitro fertilization process if they would otherwise be discarded," provided there was no compensation for embryos and parents of embryos have rights over what would be done with them.

4. establish an "Ethics and Compliance Commission" to regulate clinical practices and

5. prohibit "all human cloning and the creation of new human embryos for the purposes of research."

Romney concluded his letter by stating that Massachusetts institutions were already "cloning human embryos" for "benevolent motives." Still, he believed "cloning human embryos for research or reproduction crosses the boundary of ethics." "Lofty goals do not justify the creation of life for experimentation and destruction." Governor Romney later told the *New York Times* that some practices at Harvard and other institutions in Massachusetts doing research probably go too far ethically.

The Economic Development Committee

Another notable change during the 2005 session was the reorganization of the Legislature's committee structure to focus on subjects that had not received enough attention in recent years, including the creation of the Economic Development and Emerging Technologies Committee (hereinafter "Committee"). Some committees, such as the Judiciary and Taxation Committees, can become overwhelmed by hundreds of bills. Another problem is that overlapping jurisdictions often led to "turf wars" between committees.

By rule, the Committee was given sole power over "biotechnology" and "stem cell research medical technology." In addition, to start the session, the Committee had one bill to consider: the Travaglini stem cell bill. Who would lead the new committee? President Travaglini named Senator Jack Hart and Speaker DiMasi appointed Rep. Dan Bosley.

Senator Jack Hart's political base was the politically super-charged neighborhood of South Boston. South Boston and neighboring Dorchester at the time were politically dominated by white, working class and ethnically Irish voters. The people of this district have traditionally identified so closely with the Catholic Church that they would routinely identify themselves by Catholic parish (Senator Hart is from Gate of Heaven Parish), rather than neighborhood. This district is also home to several labor union headquarters, including: Ironworkers Local 7; Pipefitters Local 537; and International Brotherhood of Electricians Local 103. Senator Hart's core voters tended to be economically liberal but conservative on social issues. Jack graduated from the Jesuit run Boston College High School, Tufts University and Harvard's Kennedy School of Government. He served in the Massachusetts House from 1997–2002 when he joined the Senate, making him the most powerful elected official in South Boston. Senator Hart supported pro-life positions throughout his political career, and during his initial stem cell press conference, he emphasized the economic development aspect of the bill, "We want to send a signal that we are looking to have the opportunity to be open for business." Still, Senator Hart was open to learning the science behind the bill. For example, when President Travaglini, Senator Creem, Senator Hart, and a few staff members met to discuss the need for stem cell legislation, when Senator Hart learned more about somatic cell nuclear transplant, and that parthenotes could not develop into human beings, he seemed to become more comfortable justifying his pro-life positions with his support of the bill.

Rep. Daniel Bosley grew up in Western Massachusetts in the small city of North Adams. Situated in mostly rural Berkshire County, North Adams was an economically depressed urban area that has never recovered from the loss of its manufacturing base in the 1970s. Rep. Bosley graduated with honors from North Adams State College, and while serving in the Massachusetts Legislature earned a Master's in Public Affairs from the University of Massachusetts. First elected to the House in 1987, Rep. Bosley was known for his quick wit and ability to master complicated policy issues. He rose through the House ranks and in 1997, he became the chairman of the Commerce & Labor Committee. He was a natural to take this new chair.

The Committee Hearing

The Economic Development and Emerging Technologies Committee held a public hearing on Senator Travaglini's bill just 10 days after the bill was filed. The Committee invited a wide range of witnesses including academics, business leaders, hospital officials and researchers. As is true of all Massachusetts bills, the public could not only attend the hearing, but could testify. As a result, committee hearings on controversial proposals sometimes last for 8–10 hours. Hundreds of experts, advocates and opponents of the bill attended the hearing.

Senator Hart opened the hearing by stating that both the Senate President and the Speaker were "intent on introducing the bill to the floor in the near future." Sen. Hart also stated that the issue was a complex one that deserved a full vetting by all interested parties. Given the complexity of the subject, the committee waived the typical time limitations on testimony—3–4 minutes, which help keep hearings relatively short and to prevent repetition.

Early in the hearing, Chairman Bosley admitted struggling with the question, "when does human life begin?" Bosley said that the committee is trying to "split that moral hair." That question set the tone for the hearing with a variety of witnesses testifying about the bill's moral and ethical implications.

Senator Travaglini testified that researchers need to be able to create small groups of stem cells to expedite development of life-saving tissues and cures for illnesses. He said, "Opponents carelessly attack this type of research as 'cloning new embryos.' To be clear, somatic cell nuclear transfer does not involve the creation of fertilized eggs, nor does it involve the cloning of human beings."

Glenn Mangurian, a Hingham man who suffered a spinal cord injury in 2001 said, "I have a very simple message for you, and that is one of hope. Hope is the foundation of our society. Medical research offers hope to many and fear to a few."

Patricia Payne, a 14-year sufferer of Parkinson's Disease opposed research on human embryos said, "My suffering is not the real issue here. The real issue is what we are being asked to do in order to relieve my suffering. The end does not justify the means."

Catholic priest Tad Pacholczyk, a trained scientist and director of education for the National Catholic Bioethics Center, testified, "The decision to make human life simply to destroy it is a little short of barbarism. Once sperm meets the outer coat of an egg, it sets in motion a new cascade of events that will lead to an adult human being under the proper circumstances. They have great potential. They have the potential to become taxpayers. They have the potential to become voters. And we have a responsibility to safeguard those embryos."

Dr. Marjorie Clay, an ethicist at the University of Massachusetts Medical School testified that the issues had been clouded by the misuse of the word "embryo." Dr. Clay stated that fertilized eggs should not be considered embryos because they cannot reach their full potential of becoming human without a host such as a uterus or laboratory conditions that simulate a uterus. Dr. Clay said that it took 24 hours for an egg to become fertilized, and not precisely at the moment of conception. Therefore, the cells made available for research in Senator Travaglini's bill should be considered "preembryonic."

Dr. Ann Kiessling, a stem cell researcher and professor at the Harvard Medical School, addressed the confusion about human eggs and embryos. She testified, "Nature does not regard every egg, or every fertilized egg, as a new life. Eggs naturally fertilized by sperm must send signals to the mother at the right time, or they are quickly discarded by the uterus to make way for a new fertilized egg." She stated that most fertilized eggs fail to become embryos because they are defective, and other eggs can naturally 'activate' without fertilization. Spontaneously activated eggs, or 'parthenotes,' are not "lives," but could be "valuable therapeutic tools." She concluded that, "nature has already provided highly accurate milestones for judging when an egg has become an embryo, there is no reason to overturn nature's definition."

Cynthia Fisher, representing the Massachusetts Biotechnology Council, urged the Committee to act quickly so Massachusetts would not lose its leverage in the medical and life sciences field, "The train has left the station. Other states are truly committed. We are lagging behind as we stand here today."

Senator Mark Montigny (D-New Bedford), a supporter of the bill, but an outspoken critic of the pharmaceutical industry, stated: "This [bill] should be driven solely by scientists and we should be thorough in our deliberations. I absolutely do not trust the industry to self police. We need to put medicine and research first, not economic development and job creation."

At the end of the hearing, the Committee heard from Catholic Priest Thomas DiLorenzo, who was conducting daily protests in front of Senator Travaglini's house in East Boston. Father DiLorenzo pounded the table and warned lawmakers that embryonic stem cell research was contrary to "God's will." He stated that his daily protests let the "neighborhood know that our senator is for the exploitation of human life."

The Debate Continues

During the next few weeks, the State House took on the look of a college campus, with all manner of symposia, lectures, briefings and presentations to educate members and staff about the science and ethical issues of stem cell research. On March 1st, for example, Massachusetts Citizens For Life held a three-hour symposium to offer the "facts" about stem cell research from "leading experts in the field."

On March 6th, the *Boston Globe* published an op-ed column by Governor Romney entitled, "The problem with the stem cell bill:"

A fundamental principle of an ethical society is that no life should be exploited for the benefit of another. A just legal code recognizes the inherent value of every life. This is where our founders began: every human being has inalienable rights, the first among them is life. . .

Supporters of the bill are correct that the state law regulating embryonic research is ambiguous and in need of revising. A proposal designed to give the law clarity, however, should not be vague on the matter of human cloning. This is the problem with the bill.

Despite the comforting assurances of its supporters, it would not ban human cloning. On the contrary, the bill would countenance the cloning of embryos for research, and it may invite even worse abuses down the road.

The bill's sponsors promise us they have 'crafted strong ethical safeguards,' resting their case on the distinction between cloning for human reproduction and cloning for research. Research cloning involves the creation of a human embryo for purposes of experimentation, with the intent to destroy it. Reproductive cloning would continue the process by implanting this embryo into a uterus.

However, the process of cloning only occurs once, with the creation of the embryo—a unique genetic entity with the full complement of chromosomes. Once cloning occurs, a human life is set in motion.

Calling this process 'somatic cell nuclear transfer,' or conveniently dismissing the embryo as a mere 'clump of cells' cannot disguise the reality of what occurs: A genetically complete human embryo is brought into being. It is manipulated and experimented upon like so much research material. And then that emerging life is destroyed and discarded. Imagine row after row of laboratory racks, filled with growing human embryos: a 'Brave New World'. . . .

In the days leading up to the Committee issuing its report and Senate's debate on the bill, Governor Romney launched a state-wide radio ad campaign urging its defeat. The Governor said,

"Cloning would mean creating new human life, new embryos, just for experimentation. . .If like me you support stem cell research, but you oppose cloning human embryos, please tell your legislator. Help me oppose the radical cloning bill now on Beacon Hill."

The conservative Family Research Council sponsored Dr. William Hurlburt, a researcher and ethicist who sat on President Bush's Council on Bioethics, to present Senate staffers with a PowerPoint presentation about the bill's flaws, "that would have been suited to a college lecture hall." Dr. Hurlburt argued that the medical community needed clear prohibitions to prevent unethical research. He also advocated for research to take place on genetically modified human materials that could not develop into embryos, thus removing the moral problem of destroying life for the benefit of research.

Meanwhile, U.S. Senator Edward Kennedy endorsed the Travaglini bill at an event in Boston. Kennedy criticized the bill's opponents, including Governor Romney, who would criminalize research that holds great hope for patients, "We should do all we can to support the search for medical breakthroughs that will keep Massachusetts on the cutting edge of science, not put up unwarranted barriers to new progress and new cures."

Legislators also had an opportunity to gauge the opinions of the electorate. A poll conducted by the Civil Society Institute from March 7–9, 2005 showed that voters strongly supported embryonic stem cell research 70%–21%, and that the margin of support increased to 82%–15% with a minimal explanation of what embryonic stem cell research involved. Only 18% of respondents had heard of the controversial process of somatic cell nuclear transplant (SCNT), but after a minimal explanation, voters supported the process 80%–13% with 7% saying they were not sure. Interestingly, once the word "cloning" was used support fell significantly. Although SCNT is the method by which a cell is therapeutically cloned, pollsters found that when asked if they support "cloning that doesn't result in human birth but is designed to develop stem cells for medical research," voters approved 62%–30% with 8% saying they were not sure. Not surprisingly, voters disapproved cloning when specifically designed to result in a human birth 84%–10% with 6% not sure. Overall, the voters favored the proposed Massachusetts stem cell legislation 81%–15%. The poll also showed that the bill was supported by 62% of self-described "conservatives" and 76% of all Catholics polled.

The Egg Donation Issue

Another ethical issue suddenly emerged during this time. On February 25, 2005, Judy Norsigian, the executive director of Our Bodies Ourselves and a prominent activist on women's issues, published an opinion column in the *Boston Globe* questioning the ethics of encouraging women to donate or sell their eggs to researchers. She argued that far more thought had to be given to the effects on egg donors:

> *Omitted from the polarized debate is any discussion of the thousands of women who will need to undergo egg extraction procedures for such [somatic cell nuclear transfer] embryo cloning.*

A primary concern is the substantial risks to women's health posed by the extraction procedure and the inability to obtain true informed consent from egg donors given the current lack of adequate safety data. . .

[F]ormer chief medical officer at the Food and Drug Administration, Dr. Suzanne Parisian, [says]"many of the drugs used during these procedures have not been adequately studied for long term safety, nor do some of these drugs have FDA approval for these specific indications. This is not widely understood and has led to significant misunderstanding about the risks involved for women who donate eggs," whether for reproductive purposes or for research cloning.

Ms. Norsigian highlighted that the drugs used to stimulate egg production had been shown to cause ovarian hyper-stimulation syndrome in 3–8% of patients, and in some cases can progress rapidly to a life-threatening condition days after completion of egg collection. Another drug used in the IVF process, Lupron, has been shown to cause depression, memory loss, liver disease orders, bone loss, and sever muscle, joint, and bone pain. Ms. Norsigian called on drug companies to release all safety data for drugs used in egg extraction. Finally, whereas the risks of participating in IVF procedures are significant, the reward is a child. The cost-benefit calculus for research related egg donation is, perhaps impossible to obtain.

Ms. Norsigian's argument resonated with several legislators, especially the women legislators, who expressed fears that legalizing and encouraging embryonic research would create a demand for human eggs and potentially lead to the exploitation of poor women, who might be willing to risk their health for the money they could obtain by selling their eggs. The fear for several legislators—especially those who represented poor or minority constituencies; was that researchers would look to their constituents to get the genetic material for their experiments despite the health risks. Unlike IVF donation, where the eggs from "desirable" donors brought a premium, it would not matter who made the donation for stem cell research. Therefore, poor or minority women would be paid far less for their eggs and undergo a procedure that could have great health repercussions, all without truly informed consent.

The Economic Development Committee Report

On March 28, 2005, the Economic Development Committee released its version of the bill. The Committee significantly redrafted the Travaglini bill before reporting that the new language "ought to pass" to the chamber where the bill originated, in this case the Senate. Key changes are highlighted in the appendix below. The fact that the Travaglini bill was so significantly amended demonstrates a truth about the joint committee system in the Massachusetts Legislature—the House of Representatives has the votes to control any joint committee they desire. Because House members outnumber Senate members 11–6 on the Economic Development Committee, there is greater discipline on behalf of House members, and the fact that such a complicated bill causes rank and file members to look to the chairman from their branch to give them advice on how to vote, all led the House members to vote as a block and release a bill that was more restrictive and provided greater state oversight of the scientific community than Senator Travaglini and other Senate leaders wanted.

First, the Committee changed the title to "An Act Relative To Biotechnology."

Next, the Committee took greater pains to define the concept of an "embryo." This language defined an "embryo" broadly—anything from a single cell to eight weeks of development. An embryo, therefore, exists from the moment that the single-cell egg is activated, most typically when it comes into contact with sperm. After 8 weeks—or 56 days—most scientists consider the entity to be a "fetus," and therefore, given even greater legal protections.

The Committee would allow scientific research on an "extracorporal embryo;" those embryos created outside of the body through somatic cell nuclear transplant or fertilized during IVF and donated to research by the embryo's "parents." Research on parthenotes or an egg fertilized in a lab was not allowed. The Committee also took steps to protect "discarded" IVF embryos and the rights of the "parents" by adopting the Governor's position that the donation of "embryos" could only be made after "informed consent." The most relevant changes in the Committee bill were the definitions for "Donated To Research," "Informed Consent," "Valuable Consideration," and the newly added Section 3.

The bill was silent on the issue of compensating women for their eggs, which was still being actively debated and discussed by legislators and staff alike.

The Committee's bill also provided far more regulation and oversight of the research community than the Creem or Travaglini bills. Whereas those bills relied exclusively on institutional review boards or ethics committees to approve or disapprove proposed research, this version created several layers of oversight:

- Institutional review boards were to sign off on any research, but had to, "consider the ethical and medical implications of the proposed research." Furthermore, if an IRB authorized research that was not authorized by this legislation, the institution could be held liable and fined up to $100,000.

- The bill created an advisory council to recommend changes to relevant laws and regulations to "promote scientific inquiry and protect human subjects." The Council would have 15 members appointed evenly between the Governor, Senate President and Speaker.

The Department of Public Health would provide "administrative support" as requested.

The bill also addressed the original problem, MGL. Ch 112 § 12J, by empowering the Attorney General, rather than the local district attorney, to approve biomedical research.

Perhaps most significantly, the bill empowered the Department of Public Health to regulate stem cell research. Under Massachusetts law, an agency cannot promulgate regulations without legislative authorization. This provision effectively invited an agency controlled by Governor Romney to regulate the industry as the Governor saw fit. Further, the Committee bill required the state regulations to be consistent with the existing very restrictive federal regulations.

Finally, there were several other provisions that served to curtail certain aspects of scientific research, including:

- A whistleblower provision that would shield employees who disclosed activities that they believed to be in violation of the law;

- Provisions that hospital employees, including physicians and nurses, could not be required to collect umbilical cord or placental blood if said collection conflicts with their bona fide religious practices and beliefs; and

- significant criminal penalties including: a 5-year prison sentence and $100,000 fine for people who engaged in disallowed embryonic research; a 10-year sentence and $1 million fine for engaging in human reproductive cloning; and a 5-year sentence and a potential $100,000 fine for persons who improperly obtains human embryos, gametes, or cadaveric fetal tissue for research purposes, or who creates an embryo with the purposes of donating the embryo for research.

When the bill came for a vote by the Committee, four senators, including Sen. Hart, reserved their right not to vote on the committee's version of the bill. Senators Hart, Karen Spilka (D-Ashland), Mark Montigny (D-New Bedford) and Richard Tisei (R-Wakefield) said that although they supported stem cell research, they had concerns about the Committee's version of the bill. Interestingly, most of the Committee members saw the Committee bill for the first time that morning. Rep. Barry Finegold (D-Andover) attempted to postpone the committee's vote for a week, but the committee rejected his motion.

Skills Exercise

Based on the Stem Cell Case Study reading, write a short memo (1–2 pages) as if you are the legal counsel to the Economic Development & Emerging Technology Committee to Committee Chair Hart. What should the Senate do at this point in the process? Give an outline of what provisions should be included in a Senate redraft.

[Note: Please do this exercise before reading later parts of the case study.]

Related Documents

SENATE, No. 25

Mr. Travaglini, a petition (accompanied by bill, Senate, No. 25) of Robert E. Travaglini, Cynthia Stone Creem, Harriette L. Chandler and other members of the General Court for legislation to promote stem cell research. Economic Development and Emerging Technologies.

The Commonwealth of Massachusetts

"

In the Year Two Thousand and Five.

"

AN ACT PROMOTING STEM CELL RESEARCH

Be it enacted by the Senate and House of Representatives in General Court assembled, and by the authority of the same, as follows:

SECTION 1.

Chapter 112 of the General Laws is hereby amended by inserting after section 12CC the following 2 sections:—

Section 12DD.   The general court finds and declares that:

(a) human embryonic stem cell research, and other research in regenerative medicine present a significant chance of yielding fundamental biological knowledge from which may emanate therapies

to relieve, on a large scale, human suffering from disease and injury; and

(b) the extraordinary biomedical scientists situated in Massachusetts within institutions of higher education, research institutes, hospitals and biotechnology and pharmaceutical companies possess the capability of contributing significantly to the welfare of mankind by performing outstanding research in this field.

Section 12EE. (a) For the purposes of this section and section 12DD, the following words shall have the following meanings unless the context clearly requires otherwise:

"Donated to medicine", an embryo(s) originating from an in vitro process or human embryonic germ cells, when, for purposes of biomedical research or medical care or treatment, the persons contributing genetic material do so in the absence of financial inducement and after fulfillment of the requirements of applicable federal and state laws concerning informed consent.

"Embryo", includes any human embryo whether formed by fertilization, somatic cell nuclear transfer, ~~or~~ parthenogenesis, or other means.

"Financial inducement", any valuable consideration, excluding (i) reimbursement for reasonable costs incurred in consideration, excluding: connection with a donation; and (ii) reasonable compensation to a donor from whom an oocyte or somatic cell is recovered for the time, burden and risk of such recovery and the preparation for it. Whether costs or compensation are reasonable shall be determined by a duly appointed Institutional Review Board, provided the determination is made with due diligence and in good faith.

"In vitro", a process conducted outside the human body in an artificial environment, such as in vitro fertilization or somatic cell nuclear transfer.

"Uterus", a uterus or fallopian tube.

(b) It shall be the policy of the commonwealth to foster research and therapies in regenerative medicine, including, in particular, that research and clinical applications involving the derivation and use of human embryonic stem cells, human embryonic germ cells, placental and umbilical cord cells and any human adult stem cells, including research and clinical applications involving somatic cell nuclear transplantation, shall be permitted.

(c)(i) No person shall use an human embryo donated to medicine in scientific research or other kind of experimentation or study without the prior written approval of a duly appointed Institutional Review Board or other duly appointed ethics committee setting forth the approval of the Board or ethics committee for the research, experimentation or study. The written approval shall contain a detailed description of the research, experimentation or study by attachment of a protocol or other writing and shall be maintained as a permanent record by the Board, ethics committee, or ~~by~~ the hospital or other entity for which the Board or ethics committee acts.

(ii) No person shall knowingly sell any embryo donated to medicine for valuable consideration. For purposes of this subsection "valuable consideration" excludes reasonable payments associated with storage, quality control, preservation, processing or transportation of such embryos donated to medicine.

(d) An embryo donated to medicine, pursuant to this section, shall not be transferred to a uterus.

(e) Human reproductive cloning is hereby prohibited.

(f) A person who violates subsections (d) or (e) shall be punished by imprisonment **in** the state prison for not more than 5 years, or in a jail or house of correction for not less than 1 year nor more than 2 ½ years or, or by a fine of not more than $25,000, or by both such fine and imprisonment.

SECTION 2. Subsection (a) I of section 12J of said chapter 112, as appearing in the 2002 Official Edition, is hereby amended by adding the following paragraph:—

For the purposes of this section, fetus shall include a neonate and an embryo, but shall exclude an embryo donated to medicine pursuant to section 12EE.

SECTION 3. Subsection (a) IV of said section 12J of said chapter 112, as so appearing, is hereby amended by striking out the second sentence.

———

Economic Development and Emerging Technologies
Committee Redraft of S. 25 [Selected provisions]

AN ACT RELATIVE TO BIOTECHNOLOGY

Chapter 111J

REGULATION OF THE BIOTECHNOLOGY INDUSTRY IN THE COMMONWEALTH

Section 1.

As used in this chapter the following words shall have the following meanings:— . . .

"Blastocyst", a preimplantation embryo consisting of cells that are organized into an inner and outer cell layer surrounding a fluid filled cavity. The cells of the inner layer, from which embryonic stem cells are derived, consist

of undifferentiated cells that have the potential to become any type of cell in the human body.

. . .

"Donated to Research", when, in the absence of remuneration, and after fulfillment of the requirements of applicable federal and state law concerning informed consent, the person or persons from whose cells the embryo has originated or will originate gives the embryo or cells to another person with the limitations that the recipient(s) shall use the extant or resultant embryo in biomedical research, and shall not transfer the embryo to a uterus or nurture the embryo beyond fourteen days development.

. . .

"Embryo", an organism of the species homo-sapiens from the single cell stage to eight weeks development whether formed by fertilization, somatic cell nuclear transfer, parthenogenesis, or other means.

"Extracorporeal embryo", an embryo formed and maintained outside of the human body.

. . .

"Informed Consent", the written consent of the donor or patient obtained in accordance with the "donated for research" requirements and of 45 CFR 46.116 and 45 CFR 46.117, as may be amended from time to time;

. . .

"Somatic Cell Nuclear Transfer", the technique in which the nucleus of an oocyte is replaced with the nucleus of a somatic cell and stimulated to divide until it reaches the blastocyst stage from which stem cells can be derived.

. . .

"Valuable Consideration", includes any interest, profit or benefit of value, but shall not include reasonable payment for the removal, processing, disposal, preservation, quality control, storage, transplantation, or implantation of gametes, embryonic or cadeveric fetal tissue. . . . .

Section 2.

(a) Research involving the derivation and use of human embryonic stem cells, including somatic cell nuclear transfer, human adult stem cells from any source, umbilical cord stem cells, and placental cells shall be

permitted. Said research shall only be conducted upon the written approval of a duly authorized Institutional Review Board. The written approval of the Institutional Review Board shall include a detailed description of the research, experimentation or study to be conducted and a detailed description of the research or a copy of the protocol all of which shall be maintained as a permanent record by such Board or by the hospital or institution for which the Board acts. In addition to the approval process described above, the Institutional Review Board shall consider the ethical and medical implications of the proposed research.

. . .

Section 3.   A physician or other health care provider who treats a patient with in vitro fertilization therapy shall provide the patient with timely information sufficient to allow that patient to make an informed and voluntary choice regarding the disposition of any extracorporeal embryos or gametes remaining following said treatment.

A patient to whom information is provided pursuant to paragraph 1 of this section shall be presented with the option of storing, donating to another person for reproduction, donating for research purposes, or otherwise disposing of any unused extracorporeal embryos or gametes. A person who elects to donate any extracorporeal embryos or gametes remaining after receiving in vitro fertilization therapy shall provide informed consent for said donation.

"Section 9. The department, with the advice of the biomedical research advisory council, shall enforce the provisions of this chapter and shall adopt regulations, which shall be consistent with any existing federal regulations relative to biomedical research, relating to the administration and enforcement of this chapter." . . . .

SECTION 3.   Subsection (a) I of section 12J of Chapter 112 of the General Laws, as appearing in the 2002 Official Edition, is hereby amended by adding at the end thereof the following:—For the purposes of this section, fetus shall include a neonate and an embryo, but shall exclude a donated extracorporeal embryo created by somatic cell nuclear transfer pursuant to section 2 of chapter 111J or an extracorporeal embryo donated for research pursuant to section 3 of chapter 111J.

Sources:

- Amy Lambiaso, "Senate Leaders File Bill To Promote Stem Cell Research," *State House News Service* February 9, 2005.

- Associated Press, "Massachusetts Governor Expresses Concerns Over Stem Cell Research" *Boston Herald*, February 10, 2005.

- Amy Lambiaso, "Stem Cell Push Turns Out Crowd, Sparks Debate Over Health, Life, Jobs," *State House News Service*, February 16, 2005.

- Judy Norsigian, "Risks to Women in Embryo Cloning," *Boston Globe*, February 25, 2005.

- Mitt Romney, "The Problem With the Stem Cell Bill," *Boston Globe*, March 6, 2005.

- Scott S. Greenberger, "Romney's Ads Blast Stem Cell Measure," *Boston Globe*, March 30, 2005.

E. FLOOR DEBATE & AMENDMENT

Traditionally, the Senate floor debates are set by the majority leader, who since the early part of the 20th century, has been privileged to be recognized and speak first each day. Often scheduling, amendments, and how the debate will proceed is worked out in advance by the majority and minority leaders. Once debate begins, nearly every motion is approved by unanimous consent.

In contrast, the House is controlled by many rules and precedents that make up the parliamentary procedure allowing the chamber to act on bills and resolutions. The procedure used depends on how long members want to debate and how extensively the legislation must be amended. The House considers most legislation with limited debate and no floor amendments. On more complex or controversial bills, the Rules Committee recommends procedures for debate. Many major bills are first considered in the Committee of the Whole, which has more flexible rules, before being passed by a simple majority vote of the House.

Legislative Process In Minnesota

Minnesota Senate Counsel, Research, and Fiscal Analysis Office (2016)

II. Second Reading

A. When a bill has completed consideration in committee and is ready for debate on the floor, it is given its "second reading." The second reading consists of the Secretary of the Senate or Chief Clerk of the House reading aloud the number of the Senate or House file.

III. Senate General Orders and Calendar

A. Senate General Orders

1. To assist the members and the public in knowing what bills will be coming up for debate and in what order, the Secretary of the Senate prepares "a list of all bills, resolutions, reports of committees, and other proceedings of the Senate that are referred to the Committee of the Whole." This list is called "General Orders." The General Orders list must show each bill's file number, its title, authors, and its procedural history so far in the body. Senate Rule 22.1.

2. Considered in Order

a. The bills are listed in the order in which they were given their Second Reading. b. "Items on General Orders may be taken up in the order in which they are numbered, as ordered by the Chair of the Committee on Rules and Administration, or as otherwise ordered by a majority of the committee." Senate Rule 22.2.

3. One-Day Lie-Over

a. To insure that everyone has an opportunity to read the bills before they are debated, each bill must lie over for a day after it appears on General Orders and before it is debated in the Committee of the Whole.

b. "General Orders, together with all bills required to be included on it, must be electronically available or printed at least one calendar day before being considered in Committee of the Whole." Senate Rule 22.3.

B. Committee of the Whole

1. Bills taken up on General Orders are considered in the Committee of the Whole, which is the whole Senate meeting as a committee, unless the bill is considered on the Consent Calendar or as a Special Order. Senate Rule 23.1.

2. The President may appoint another member to preside over each meeting of the Committee of the Whole. Senate Rule 23.2.

3. Unlimited Debate

a. The limits on the number of times a member may speak on a question are relaxed.

b. "[A] member may speak more than twice on the same subject and a call for the previous question may not be made." Senate Rule 23.3.

4. Traditionally, one of the primary purposes of the Committee of the Whole was to avoid roll-call votes before final passage.

. . .

C. Senate Calendar

1.   A List of Bills That Have Passed the Committee of the Whole

a.   When a bill has completed consideration in the Committee of the Whole, a new engrossment of any amendments is prepared and it is placed on a second list, printed on paper colored yellow on the Senate's Web site, called the "Calendar."

b.   "The Secretary shall make a Calendar of all bills, resolutions and other matters approved by the Committee of the Whole for final action. The Secretary shall place them on the Calendar in the order in which they have been acted upon in Committee of the Whole." Senate Rule 24.1.

2.   Bills on the Calendar Must lie over for a day before they are voted on for final passage.

3.   "The Calendar must be electronically available or printed at least one calendar day before the matters on it are considered." Senate Rule 24.2.

4.   There is little debate on bills on the Calendar, since that was done in the Committee of the Whole, and amendments are not in order.

5.   The bill is given its "Third Reading" by the Secretary of the Senate reading its title aloud.

6.   It is placed on final passage. Final passage requires a majority of the whole body on a roll-call vote. IV. House General Register and Calendar for the Day A.

    . . .

VII. Voting

    A.   Roll Call

    1.   Final Passage

    a.   The Constitution requires a roll-call vote on final passage.

    b.   "No law shall be passed unless voted for by a majority of all the members elected to each house of the legislature, and the vote entered in the journal of each house." Minn. Const. art. IV, § 22.

    2.   Demanding a Roll Call

    a.   In the Senate, any member may demand a roll-call on any question at any time before the start of voting on a question. The roll call must be entered in the Journal, unless the Senate is taking a roll call vote using the electrical voting system. Senate Rule 40.3.

    b.   In the House, it takes 15 members to demand a roll-call vote on any other question. House Rule 2.03.

    B.   Voice Vote

    1.   Voice votes are used for all questions on which a roll call is not required or demanded.

2. The electronic voting board makes taking a roll-call vote a relatively speedy matter, but it still takes time. So, some votes are still taken as voice votes, with the presiding officer announcing the result.

C. Division

1. If the call is close, any member may question it by demanding a division.

2. "The President shall declare the result of the vote. If a member questions the result of a vote, the President shall order a division." Senate Rule 40.1

3. A division is taken by asking members to stand at their desk to be counted. A count is taken for both "yes" and "no" votes.

VIII. Amendments

A. The primary voting activity on the floor is on amendments. An amendment may be offered by any member, but there are a few procedural requirements it must meet.

B. In Writing

1. Any member may demand that an amendment be in writing. Senate Rule 27.1. Oral amendments are rarely offered unless they are very short or simple.

C. Approved by the Engrossing Secretary

1. In the Senate, every amendment must be approved as to form before it may be offered. This approval is given by the Engrossing Secretary, who makes sure that the amendment is drawn to the latest engrossment of the bill and that, if adopted, it can be properly engrossed into it. In other words, that the amendment will "fit" into the bill.

D. Copies for All Members Made by the Desk

1. A paper copy must be available for member who requests it.

2. Making copies for the Senate or House takes time. When many amendments are being proposed in rapid succession, it can take extra time to get an amendment approved by the Engrossing Secretary and then have copies made.

E. Germaneness in the Senate

1. An amendment must be "germane." Under Senate Rule 35.2, an amendment is not germane if it relates to a substantially different subject or accomplishes a substantially different purpose.

a. The first test is whether the amendment relates to a substantially different subject. This test is relatively flexible. For example, if a bill relates to dogs, one might argue that an amendment adding a section relating to cats is not germane and therefore out of order. But the sponsor of 16 the amendment could make the counter argument that the subject of the bill is really domestic animals, and that the amendment relating to cats is germane and therefore in order.

b.　The second test for germaneness under Rule 35 is whether the amendment is intended to accomplish a "substantially different purpose" than that of the bill to which it is proposed. This test is harder to meet. It not only protects against the development of garbage bills or Christmas-tree bills on a variety of subjects, it also protects an author from unfriendly amendments that would cause the bill to stray too far from the path the author has kept it on up to this point in the process.

. . .

IX.　Debate

A.　Maintaining Order and Decorum

1.　Both the Senate and the House have rules in place to help maintain order and decorum during debate and allow for a respectful exchange of ideas.

2.　In the Senate

a.　A Senator must not speak until recognized by the President. Senate Rule 36.1.

b.　Senators must only speak to the question under debate. Members must also avoid personality. Senate Rule 36.2.

c.　"When a member is speaking, no one may stand between the member speaking and the President." Senate Rule 36.6.

d.　"All remarks during debate shall be addressed to the President." Senate Rule 36.8.

e.　"When a member is called to order, the member shall be silent until it is determined whether or not the member is in order. If a member is called to order for words spoken in debate, the words excepted to must be taken down in writing by the Secretary immediately." Senate Rule 36.10.

THE LEGISLATIVE PROCESS ON THE HOUSE FLOOR: AN INTRODUCTION

Dr. Stanley Bach & Christopher M. Davis,
Congressional Research Service, 95–563 (2019)

A complicated body of rules, precedents, and practices governs the legislative process on the floor of the House of Representatives. The official manual of House rules is more than 1,000 pages long and is supplemented by 30 volumes of precedents, with more volumes to be published in coming years. Yet there are two reasons why gaining a fundamental understanding of the House's legislative procedures is not as difficult as the sheer number and size of these documents might suggest.

First, the ways in which the House applies its rules are largely predictable, at least in comparison with the Senate. Some rules are certainly more complex and more difficult to interpret than others, but the House tends to follow similar procedures under similar circumstances. Even the ways in which the House frequently waives, supplants, or supplements its standing rules with special, temporary procedures generally fall into a limited number of recognizable patterns.

Second, underlying most of the rules that Representatives may invoke and the procedures the House may follow is a fundamentally important premise—that a majority of Members should ultimately be able to work their will on the floor. Although House rules generally recognize the importance of permitting any minority—partisan or bipartisan—to present its views and sometimes propose its alternatives, the rules do not enable that minority to filibuster or use other parliamentary devices to prevent the majority from prevailing without undue delay. This principle provides an underlying coherence to the various specific procedures discussed in this report.

The Nature of the Rules

Article I of the Constitution imposes a few restrictions on House (and Senate) procedures—for example, requirements affecting quorums and roll-call votes—but otherwise the Constitution authorizes each house of Congress to determine for itself the "Rules of its Proceedings" (Article 1, Section 5).

This liberal grant of authority has several important implications. First, the House can amend its rules unilaterally; it need not consult with either the Senate or the President. Second, the House is free to suspend, waive, or ignore its rules whenever it chooses to do so. By and large, the Speaker or whatever Representative is presiding usually does not enforce the rules at his or her own initiative. Instead, Members must protect their own rights by affirmatively making points of order whenever they believe the rules are about to be violated. In addition, House rules include several formal procedures for waiving or suspending certain other rules, and almost any rule can be waived by unanimous consent. Thus, the requirements and restrictions discussed in this report generally apply only if the House chooses to enforce them.

Limits on Debate

If for no other reason than the size of its membership, the House has found it necessary to limit the opportunities for each Representative to participate in floor deliberations. Whenever a Member is recognized to speak on the floor, there is always a time limit on his or her right to debate.

The rules of the House never permit a Representative to hold the floor for more than one hour. Under some parliamentary circumstances, there are more stringent limits, with Members being allowed to speak for no more than 5 minutes, 20 minutes, or 30 minutes.

Furthermore, House rules sometimes impose a limit on how long the entire membership of the House may debate a motion or measure. Most bills and resolutions, for instance, are considered under a set of procedures called "suspension of the rules" (discussed later in this report) that limits all debate on a measure to a maximum of 40 minutes. Under other conditions, when there is no such time limit imposed by the rules, the House (and to some extent, the Committee of the Whole as well) can impose one by simple majority vote. These debate limitations and debate-limiting devices generally prevent a minority of the House from thwarting the will of the majority.

House rules also limit debate in other important respects. First, all debate on the floor must be germane to whatever legislative business the House is conducting. Representatives may speak on other subjects only in one-minute speeches most often made at the beginning of each day's session, special order speeches occurring after the House has completed its legislative business for the day, and during morning hour debates that are scheduled on certain days of the week. Second, all debate on the floor must be consistent with certain rules of courtesy and decorum. For example, a Member should not question or criticize the motives of a colleague.

The Calendars and the Order of Business

When a House committee reports a public bill or resolution that had been referred to it, the measure is placed on the House Calendar or the Union Calendar. In general, tax, authorization, and appropriations bills are placed on the Union Calendar; all others go to the House Calendar. In effect, the calendars are catalogues of measures that have been approved, with or without proposed amendments, by one or more House committees and are now available for consideration on the floor. Placement on a calendar does not guarantee that a measure will receive floor consideration at a specified time or at all. Because it would be impractical or undesirable for the House to take up measures in the chronological order in which they are reported and placed on one of the calendars, there must be some procedures for deciding the order in which measures are to be brought from the calendars to the House floor—in other words, procedures for determining the order of business.

Clause 1 of Rule XIV lists the daily order of business on the floor, beginning with the opening prayer, the approval of the Journal (the official record of House proceedings required by the Constitution), and the Pledge of Allegiance. Apart from these routine matters, however, the House never follows the order of business laid out in this rule. Instead, certain measures and actions are privileged, meaning they may interrupt the regular order of business. In practice, all the legislative business that the House conducts comes to the floor by interrupting the order of business under Rule XIV, either by unanimous consent or under the provisions of another House rule. Every bill and resolution that cannot be considered by unanimous consent must become privileged business if it is going to reach the floor at all.

In the House Under the Hour Rule

One of the ironies of the legislative process on the House floor is that the House does relatively little business under the basic rules of the House. Instead, most of the debate and votes on amendments to major bills occur in Committee of the Whole (discussed below). This is largely because of the rule that generally governs debate in the House itself.

The rule controlling debate during meetings of the House (as opposed to meetings of the Committee of the Whole) is clause 2 of Rule XVII, which states in part that a "Member, Delegate, or Resident Commissioner may not occupy more than one hour in debate on a question in the House." In theory, this rule permits each Representative to speak for as much as an hour on each bill, on each amendment to each bill, and on each of the countless debatable motions that Members could offer. Thus, there could be more than four hundred hours of debate on each such question, a situation that would make it virtually impossible for the House to function effectively.

In practice, however, this "hour rule" usually means that each measure considered "in the House" is debated by all Members for no more than a total of only one hour before the House votes on passing it. The reason for this dramatic difference between the rule in theory and the rule in practice lies in the consequences of a parliamentary motion to order what is called the "previous question."

When a bill or resolution is called up for consideration in the House—and, therefore, under the hour rule—the Speaker recognizes the majority floor manager to control the first hour of debate. The majority floor manager is usually the chair of the committee or subcommittee with jurisdiction over the measure and most often supports its passage without amendment. This Member will yield part of his or her time to other Members and may allocate control of half of the hour to the minority floor manager (usually the ranking minority member of the committee or subcommittee). However, the majority floor manager almost always yields to other Representatives "for purposes of debate only." Thus, no other Member may propose an amendment or make any motion during that hour.

During the first hour of debate, or at its conclusion, the majority floor manager invariably "moves the previous question." This nondebatable motion asks the House if it is ready to vote on passing the bill. If a majority votes for the motion, no more debate on the bill is in order, nor can any amendments to it be offered; after disposing of the motion, the House usually votes immediately on whether to pass the bill. If the House defeats the previous question, however, opponents of the bill would then be recognized to control the second hour of debate, and might use that time to try to amend the measure. Because of this, it is unusual for the House not to vote for the previous question—the House disposes of most measures considered in the House, under the hour rule, after no more than one hour of debate and with no opportunity for amendment from the floor.

These are not very flexible and accommodating procedural ground rules for the House to follow in considering most legislation. Debate on a bill is usually limited to one hour, and only one or two Members control this time. Before an amendment to the bill can even be considered, the House must first vote against a motion to order the previous question. For these reasons, most major bills are not considered in the House under the hour rule. In current practice, the most common type of legislation considered under the hour rule in the House are procedural resolutions reported by the House Committee on Rules that are commonly referred to as "special rules" (discussed below).

In Committee of the Whole and the House

Much of the legislative process on the floor occurs not "in the House" but in a committee of the House known as the Committee of the Whole (formally, the Committee of the Whole House on the State of the Union). Every Representative is a member of the Committee of the Whole, and it is in this committee, meeting in the House chamber, that many major bills are debated and amended before being passed or defeated by the House itself. Most bills are first referred to, considered in, and reported by a standing legislative committee of the House before coming to the floor. In much the same way, once bills do reach the floor, many of them then are referred to a second committee, the Committee of the Whole, for further debate and for the consideration of amendments.

. . .

General Debate

There are two distinct stages to consideration in Committee of the Whole. First, there is a period for general debate, which is routinely limited to an hour. Each of the floor managers usually controls half the time, yielding parts of it to other Members who want to participate in the debate. During general debate, the two floor managers and other Members discuss the bill, the conditions prompting the committee to recommend it, and the merits of its provisions. Members may describe and explain the reasons for the amendments that they intend to offer, but no amendments can actually be proposed at this time. During or after general debate, the majority floor manager may move that the committee "rise"—in other words, that the committee transform itself back into the House. When the House agrees to this motion, it may resolve into Committee of the Whole again at another time to resume consideration of the bill. Alternatively, the Committee of the Whole may proceed immediately from general debate to the next stage of consideration: the amending process.

Amending Process

The Committee of the Whole may consider a bill for amendment section by section or, in the case of appropriations measures, paragraph by paragraph. Amendments to each section or of the bill are in order after the part they would amend has been read or designated and before the next section is read or designated. Alternatively, the bill may be open to amendment at any point, usually by unanimous consent. The first amendments considered to each part of the bill are those (if any) recommended by the committee that reported it. Thereafter, members of the committee are usually recognized before other Representatives to offer their own amendments. All amendments must be germane to the text they would amend. Germaneness is a subject matter standard more stringent than one of relevancy and reflects a complex set of criteria that have developed by precedent over the years. The length of general debate on a bill is determined either by unanimous consent or, more frequently, by adoption of a procedural resolution reported by the Committee on Rules that typically affects various aspects of the procedures for considering that bill. These resolutions are discussed in the section of this report titled "Under a Special Rule Reported by the Committee on Rules."

The Committee of the Whole votes only on amendments; it does not vote directly on the bill as a whole. And like the standing committees of the House, the Committee of the Whole does not actually amend the bill; it only votes to recommend amendments to the House. The motion to order the previous question may not be made in Committee of the Whole, so, under a purely open amendment process, Members may offer whatever germane amendments they wish. After voting on the last amendment to the last portion of the bill, the committee rises and reports the bill back to the House with whatever amendments it has agreed to. Purely open amendment processes have been rare in recent Congresses; the amendment process is far more frequently structured by the terms of a special rule reported by the Rules Committee and adopted by the House. . . .

. . .

Final Passage

When the committee finally rises and reports the bill back to the House, the House proceeds to vote on the amendments the committee has adopted. It usually approves all these amendments by one voice vote, though Members can demand separate votes on any or all of them as a matter of right. After a formal and routine stage called "third reading and engrossment" (when only the title of the bill is read), there is then an opportunity for a Member, virtually always from the minority party, to offer a motion to recommit the bill to committee. If the House agrees to a "simple" or "straight" motion to recommit, which only proposes to return the bill to committee, the bill is taken from the floor and returned to committee. Although the committee technically has the power to re-report the bill, in practice, the adoption of a straight motion to recommit is often characterized as effectively "killing" the measure. "Straight" motions to recommit are rare.

. . .

Under a Special Rule Reported by the Committee on Rules

Clause 1(m) of Rule X authorizes the Rules Committee to report resolutions affecting the order of business. Such a resolution—called a "rule" or "special rule"—usually proposes to make a bill in order for floor consideration so that it can be debated, amended, and passed or defeated by a simple majority vote. In effect, each special rule recommends to the House that it take from the Union or House Calendar a measure that is not otherwise privileged business and bring it to the floor out of its order on that calendar. Typically, such a resolution begins by providing that, at any time after its adoption, the Speaker may declare the House resolved into Committee of the Whole for the consideration of that bill. Because the special rule is itself privileged, under clause 5(a) of Rule XIII, the House can debate and vote on it promptly. If the House accepts the Rules Committee's recommendation, it proceeds to consider the bill itself.

One fundamental purpose of most special rules, therefore, is to make another bill or resolution privileged so that it may interrupt the regular order of business. Their other fundamental purpose is to set special procedural ground rules for considering that measure; these ground rules may either supplement or supplant the standing rules of the House. For example, the special rule typically sets the length of time for general debate in Committee of the Whole and specifies which Members are to control that time. In addition, the special rule normally includes provisions that expedite final House action on the bill after the amending process in Committee of the Whole has been completed. Special rules may also waive points of order that Members could otherwise make against consideration of the bill, against one of its provisions, or against an amendment to be offered to it.

The most controversial provisions of special rules affect the amendments that Members can offer to the bill that the resolution makes in order. As noted above, an "open rule" permits Representatives to propose any amendment that meets the normal requirements of House rules and precedents—for example, the requirement that each amendment must be germane. A "modified open rule" permits amendments to be offered that otherwise comply with House rules but imposes a time limit on the consideration of amendments or requires them to be preprinted in the Congressional Record. At the other extreme, a "closed rule" prohibits all amendments except perhaps for committee amendments and pro forma amendments ("to strike the last word") offered only for purposes of debate. A "structured" rule, which is the most common type of rule, permits only certain specific amendments to be considered on the floor. These provisions are very important because they can prevent Representatives from offering amendments as alternatives to provisions of the bill, thereby limiting the policy choices that the House can make. Open rules have been rare in recent Congresses.

However, like other committees, the Rules Committee only makes recommendations to the House. As noted above, Members debate each of its procedural resolutions in the House under the hour rule and then vote to adopt or reject it. If the House votes against ordering the previous question on a special rule, a Member could offer an amendment to it, proposing to change the conditions under which the bill itself is to be considered. Because the adoption of a special rule is often viewed as a "party loyalty" vote, however, such a development is exceedingly rare. All the same, it is important to remember that while the Rules Committee is instrumental in helping the majority party leadership formulate its order of business and in setting appropriate ground rules for considering each bill, the House retains ultimate control over what it does, when, and how.

NOTES & QUESTIONS

1.   The House rules may be found in the House manual, published each Congress and titled *Constitution, Jefferson's Manual and Rules of the House of Representatives*. The House's procedures are summarized in *House Practice: A Guide to the Rules, Precedents and Procedures of the House*, by Charles W. Johnson, John V. Sullivan, and Thomas J. Wickham Jr., (2017).

2.   Established in 1789, the Committee on Rules is among the oldest standing committees in the House. Sometimes called "The Speaker's Committee" because it is the principal way the Speaker maintains control of the House floor. Due to the vast power the Rules Committee has over the business of the House, membership is heavily weighted in favor of the majority party. Currently, there are 9 majority members and 4 minority members. In addition to writing the special rules for the consideration of legislation discussed above, the Rules Committee also considers original jurisdiction measures; typically changes to the standing rules of the House. So long as the Committee has the support of a majority of the House, there is little it cannot do during debate, including: deeming a bill passed and self-executing amendments rewriting all or some of a bill. See, https://rules.house.gov/about.

3.   The process for the Rules Committee to report a special rule is as follows:

- The committee of jurisdiction sends a letter requesting a hearing by the Rules Committee;

- The Committee holds a hearing where House members from the committee of jurisdiction or who wish to offer amendments appear as witnesses;

- The Committee, in consultation with the majority leadership and the substantive committee chairs, determines the type of rule to be granted, including the amount of general debate, the amendment process, and waivers to be granted, if any;

- The special rule is reported and filed from the floor while the House is in session;

- The special rule is considered and debated in the House. After a one-day layover, special rules may be considered on the House floor at any time. The rule is debated under the hour rule managed by a Committee majority party member, and by custom, one-half the time is yielded to a minority member of the Committee.

4.   Special Rules can be written in many ways, but fall into some general categories:

- Open Rules—permit the offering of any amendment that otherwise complies with House rules, and allows debate under the 5-minute rule;

- Modified-Open Rules—places some restrictions on offering amendments, either through a pre-printing requirement or an overall time limit on consideration of amendments;

- Structured Rules—specify that only certain amendments may be considered and specify the time for debate;

- Closed Rules—effectively eliminate the opportunity to consider amendments, other than those reported by the committee reporting the bill.

5.   Here is the floor rule for the Climate Action Now Act (H.R. 9, 2019):

COMMITTEE ACTION:

REPORTED BY A RECORD VOTE OF 7–4 on Monday, April 29, 2019.

FLOOR ACTION ON H. RES. 329:

Agreed to by record vote of 226–188, after agreeing to the previous question by record vote of 228–191, on Wednesday, May 1, 2019.

MANAGERS: McGovern/Lesko

1.   Structured rule for H.R. 9.

2.   Provides 90 minutes of general debate on the bill with 60 minutes equally divided and controlled by the chair and ranking minority member of the Committee on Foreign Affairs and 30 minutes equally divided and controlled by the chair and ranking minority member of the Committee on Energy and Commerce.

3.   Waives all points of order against consideration of the bill.

4.   Provides that the bill shall be considered as read.

5.   Waives all points of order against provisions in the bill.

6.   Makes in order only those amendments printed in the Rules Committee report. Each such amendment may be offered only in the order printed in the report, may be offered only by a Member designated in the report, shall be considered as read, shall be debatable for the time specified in the report equally divided and controlled by the proponent and an opponent, shall not be subject to amendment, and shall not be subject to a demand for division of the question.

7.   Waives all points of order against the amendments printed in the report.

8.   Provides one motion to recommit with or without instructions.

Stem Cell Case Study: Part III

The Senate

The same day that the Economic Development Committee released its version of the bill, the Senate met in a caucus, and when the chamber came into session, substituted a new version of the bill, Senate Number 2028, which looked a lot like an expanded version of the original Travaglini bill.

First, the Senate renamed the bill, "An Act related to the Promotion of the Biotechnology Industry in the Commonwealth."

Second, like the Committee, the Senate adopted a new chapter of the General Laws to encourage and regulate research. This version of the bill, although more complex than the original Travaglini-Creem bill, still attempted to be as open to research as possible. Interestingly, this version omits any definition of "embryo", although the concept of an embryo is referenced many times. As seen in the appendix, the essential definitions are "pre-implantation embryo" and "parthenotes:" the two types of biological entities exempted from the prohibition from research in GL ch. 112 sec. 12J.

Third, informed consent continued to be a subject for debate in the Senate. The Senate originally defined "Informed consent" as:

> **"Informed consent", consent for the donation of embryos or other participation in research pursuant to this chapter, which complies with requirements of a duly appointed institutional review board.**

On the floor, four women senators filed an amendment that was ultimately adopted that strengthened the informed consent provisions:

The definition of "informed consent" was expanded and tied to the federal standards of consent:

> **"Informed consent", consent for the donation of embryos, consent for participation in in-vitro fertilization, or consent for any other process where an egg is extracted from a woman, or other participation in research pursuant to this chapter, which complies with requirements of a duly appointed institutional review board, and which follows the procedures stipulated in 45CFR Part 46.116 and 117.**

The documentation of research approved by an IRB also had to include information pertaining to informed consent issues.

Fourth, the amount of information given to patients was expanded dramatically. The Senate version brought to the floor mirrored the language drafted by the Committee.

The Senate, however rejected an amendment offered by Senator Richard Moore that was meant to prevent "the victimization of women" by forbidding research on human embryonic stem cells until the Department of Public Health had a chance to promulgate the appropriate regulations:

Amendment Number 6.

Amendment to Senate Bill No. 2028

Mr. Moore moves to amend the bill, Senate No. 2028, in section 1, in proposed section 3(a) of chapter 111L of the General Laws, by adding the following 2 sentences:

"In order to prevent the victimization of women in the acquisition or potential acquisition of human eggs for research purposes, no research or clinical applications involving the derivation and use of human embryonic stem cells or human embryonic germ cells shall be permitted before the promulgation of regulations by the Massachusetts department of public health that ensure that the highest ethical standards are in place for governing such research and prior approval by the department before any such research is initiated and that penalties have been adopted for violations of

said standards. For the purpose of this section, the term "highest ethical standards" shall mean standards that prohibit the creation and destruction of human life for the purpose of research and shall prevent the victimization of women in the acquisition of human eggs for research."

This amendment was rejected.

The Senate also addressed the oversight issue. Many senators were concerned that the Committee handed too much regulatory power to the Romney controlled Department of Public Health. The Senate's bill responded with a more limited oversight program.

The Senate resisted specifying that institutional review boards "consider the ethical and medical implications of the proposed research." Likewise, there was no penalty to an institution whose IRB authorized research not allowed by the legislation as opposed the Committee's $100,000 fine. In an attempt to make obtaining permission easier, the Senate added a section that established a public IRB through the University of Massachusetts within 120 days of the passage of the stem cell law. The public IRB was meant to be open to any institution conducting research under this chapter and was meant to make institutional review easily available to small—under 50 employees—institutions.

The Senate did, however, adopt the Committee's idea of an advisory council. Still, its purpose and composition would be different. Rather than making recommendations to the General Court regarding changes to the law or the regulations "necessary to promote scientific inquiry and protect human subjects" the Senate's charge to the advisory board was broad and open:

Section 4 (a) For the purposes of reporting to the governor, president of the senate, and speaker of the house of representatives on the status of human embryonic stem cell research and proposing modifications to the regulation of such research, there shall be a Massachusetts stem cell research advisory board.

Although Senator Hart wanted some form of oversight, he and Senate supporters did not want the Administration to put up roadblocks to research. Sen. Hart pointed out that many members of the biotech industry objected to the House version of oversight, because it would create too many impediments.

Unlike the Committee's 15-member board appointed evenly by the Governor and the leaders of the Senate and House, the Senate version would have only 7 members, all of whom had to have a background in biological research fields or in medical ethics. The Senate President and House Speaker would each have 3 appointments, and the Governor would get just one appointee. On the Senate floor, Senator Hart successfully introduced an amendment that expanded the advisory board to 8 members by adding a second Romney representative, the Commissioner of Public Health.

Like the Committee version, the advisory board would receive "administrative support" from the Department of Public Health. The Senate, however, gave the Board far greater information about research activity in that stem cell researchers would be required to file annual reports with the board.

Where the Committee replaced District Attorney review of research with the Attorney General, the Senate chose to delete any prosecutorial review.

Finally, instead of allowing the Department of Public Health to regulate stem cell research, the Senate version required that the DPH to license stem cell researchers who wished to employ somatic cell nuclear transfer. On the floor, this licensing process was expanded to anyone who wished to conduct human embryonic stem cell research. See, Appendix A Section 6(a). Still, the Senate as a whole clearly was concerned about the ability of the DPH to hold up the licensing process. Therefore, a new paragraph was added by amendment that stated an institution that complied with the clauses above (the fee and documentation) "shall not have their license unreasonably delayed, and provided that if the department took longer than 30 days to issue the license, the institution would be considered licensed."

The Senate also adopted a few of the limiting provisions endorsed by the Committee such as the whistleblower provision and protection for hospital employees who had religious objections to this type of research. The Senate also adopted criminal penalties for persons who: conduct research without the approval of an IRB, or purchases or sells a pre-implantation embryo for "valuable consideration," would be punished as recommended by the Committee, with imprisonment for up to 5 years and a fine of up to $100,000. The Senate also adopted the Committee's recommendation for the level of punishment of those who attempt human reproductive cloning: imprisonment for up to 10 and a fine of up to $1 million.

Senate Minority Leader Brian Lees offered the Committee version of the bill as an amendment. This was voted down overwhelmingly.

The Senate

Senator Creem spoke on the Senate bill. Her speech touches on the anticipated economic benefits, but focuses more on the therapeutic promise of stem cells:

Mr. President: Over the last several weeks, we have all learned more about cellular biology than any of us thought possible. In fact, one scientist from Harvard expressed to me how impressed she was with how hard legislators had worked in an effort to get this bill "right." And Mr. President—I believe that is what we have—a bill that clarifies current law, sends an unmistakable message to the scientific community that stem cell research is welcome in Massachusetts and puts into place several extremely important protections.

Some have claimed that we are rushing to support research because it will lead to economic development. It is true that the biotechnology and medical fields are increasingly important sectors of our economy. It is also true that other countries and states are spending millions of dollars to lure scientists and businesses away from Massachusetts. Unless we act immediately and decisively, Massachusetts may be left sitting on the sidelines wondering what could have been while other states pioneer this promising field of research. By encouraging stem cell research, we may in fact attract thousands of jobs and billions of dollars in future investment.

But to make that the focus cheapens what we are trying to do today. The true value of stem cell research is that it could very well alleviate the suffering of untold millions of people around the world. We are on the doorstep of having scientists utilize stem cells to develop organs, recreate nerve tissue, reconstitute cells and cure—not treat—but cure diseases. When my grandchildren are my age dreadful conditions such as diabetes, Parkinson's disease, Lou Gehrig's disease and MS may be a distant memory.

Mr. President—that goal—that this vote may lead to a better, healthier and longer life for people around the globe, is one of the noblest reasons ever offered in this chamber to support a piece of legislation.

I read recently that this bill is moving too quickly and has not had enough input from women. First, I filed legislation like this several years ago and I had hopes that it would become law last year. I have also worked closely with several women on this issue including Dr. Ann Kiessling from Harvard Medical School—a woman who literally wrote the book on stem cell research.

To be fair, men have been consulted too: Doctors Scadden and Melton from Harvard have been instrumental in this effort, and I would also like to thank Sanjay Gupta, a graduate student at the BU School of Public Health, who has spent the semester as an intern in my office and has helped me understand these complicated issues.

This bill is well thought out and accomplished what the scientific community needs.

This bill will encourage the study of all forms of stem cells—adult stem cells, embryonic stem cells, those cells taken from umbilical cord blood and those cells that are developed from eggs that have not even been fertilized.

This bill does not devote a dime of state money to stem cell research—I hope that we will address that issue in the near future. What this bill does, however, is a much more important first step. Under a poorly written statute, scientists currently must ask for permission to conduct their research from a district attorney who may have done worse in high school science than I did.

In fact, when Dr. William Hurlbut, a member of the President's Council on Bioethics, spoke here at the State House, he showed a slide of a human embryo that was drawn by Leonardo DaVinci. Under current law, DaVinci could have been prosecuted for creating that image unless he had the permission of a local prosecutor.

Even our district attorneys admit that this is a useless review process and does nothing but create obstacles to research and sends the wrong message to the scientific community.

Let me be clear—this research is already being done in Massachusetts. We are removing obstacles, but even more importantly we are sending a message that Massachusetts embraces legitimate scientific inquiry and that we are not going to retreat into a new dark ages.

The simple change in this bill should not have generated much controversy at all—but it has because there is so much confusion surrounding stem cell research. A lot of the confusion comes on the issue of cloning. Unfortunately, some people—either out of ignorance—or to spread fear—have stated that this bill legalizes and endorses the cloning of people. This type of fear mongering must be stopped. This bill imposes an absolute and unambiguous ban on human reproductive cloning. Any mad scientist that attempts to clone a person—or to implant a manipulated or altered embryo into a womb will be punished with fines as high as $1 million and a prison sentence of up to ten years. But those sentences are simply a precaution—every scientist, researcher and medical official that we have heard from over the last several months has said that no one in the legitimate scientific community is attempting to clone people. They themselves consider it to be immoral, unethical and would never be approved by the peer review boards that sign off on scientific research.

This bill does, however, specifically allow for the somatic cell nuclear transplantation, sometimes called therapeutic cloning. This amazing process allows scientists to create stem cells with the genetic make-up of the patient so that it may be used to treat and cure them of their ailments without the risk of rejection. This process is not the same as reproductive cloning, and as people realize the distinction, they are overwhelmingly in favor of not just allowing this research to continue, but to encourage it.

Finally, this bill provides for continuing oversight with the creation of a Stem Cell Research Advisory Board, which I believe will ensure that research is being conducted in accordance with legal and ethical guidelines.

Other versions of the bill—in my opinion—takes a step backward. They replace the District Attorney with a political oversight board that is controlled by a Governor—who—at least this week—opposes what many scientists view as the most promising form of stem cell research. They would also restrict research to that which is allowable under federal law. Mr. President, this is a time to advance scientific inquiry—not repeat the mistakes of the federal government.

The Governor's proposal takes an even greater leap backwards. He has gone so far as to propose new criminal penalties for those scientists who utilize somatic cell nuclear transplantation. That Governor Romney would actually lock up those scientists whose life work is to cure diabetes and Parkinson's Disease is abominable.

Mr. President, the laws need to be clarified to remove unnecessary political obstacles to legitimate research—to let scientists around the world know that our labs are welcoming environments for their work—and to ensure that research is done in an ethical manner.

Mr. President, I congratulate you and Senator Hart for your hard work on this legislation and I hope that my colleagues join me in supporting this thoughtful and well-crafted bill.

Members of the biotechnology community stated they preferred the Senate's version. Stephen Mulloney, government relations director for the Massachusetts Biotechnology Council stated, "Here at MBC we're very favorably inclined to support the Senate provision. What the legislators are trying to do and the committee struggled mightily with it, is to strike a balance between appropriate oversight and academic freedom. The Senate bill does a better job."

The House

Rep. Bosley called the Senate's substitution of a new bill "unfortunate" and said that he was concerned about giving regulatory authority to a completely independent board. He stated that because the members of the advisory board are appointed by the Senate President and Speaker, "They don't report to anyone, they have no penalties, so it doesn't matter what they do. They license and give written permission to research institutions to do work. That is not advisory in nature and therefore they can't appoint the boards."

After the House received the Senate's bill, House leadership replaced the Senate language with a modified version of the Committee version of the bill. Still, opponents of stem cell research attempted to prevent the bill from being debated. First, there was a motion to postpone debate until mid-May in the hopes that President Bush's Council on Bioethics would issue a white paper on ethical questions related to stem cell research. This effort to postpone debate was defeated by a vote of 24–126. Next, there was a motion to refer the bill to the Joint Committee on Public Health, which was defeated by a vote of 25–126.

One of these amendments, offered by Rep. Loscocco, and meant to alter the bill's provisions concerning therapeutic cloning, prompted the following exchange on the House floor:

Rep. Loscocco said the bill is the most important thing we will decide in our term. It truly is a defining moment. We are deciding whether the protection of all human life is our goal. Let's skip the phone debate. Regardless of the semantics of what constitutes human cloning, this bill promotes the creation of human life with the sole purpose of destroying it. We have to justify whether to social good justifies that. The term pre-embryo does not exist in the science books. Indeed, the science on this is compelling. Place two embryos before the best scientists, one from fertilization and one from SCNT, there are no differences. They are identical human life. All of us started out as a bunch of cells. Implantation is one step in the process, as is birth, aging and death. Whether before or after 13 days, the resulting embryo is human life. Let's be honest to ourselves. Let's have a forthright and lively debate on the real issue—is it appropriate to create human life for the purpose of destroying it even if the goals are noble. Why should we vote to limit the destruction to 14 days, based on the artificial timeline? Why? Because it makes us feel better. It makes us feel harmless. We arbitrarily limit what we call life. We are only fooling ourselves. Do the ends justify the means, or don't they? I have heard much discussion about women's health issues. At 30 days, a female embryo has all the eggs that women will have for her entire life. At about 30 to 45 days, cell differentiation occurs and organs begin to form. Organs are there for the taking. If we want them, why not commit embryonic development to 45 or 60 days. At 45 days, it's no different than five days. It's either human life in process or it isn't. In Roe vs. Wade, the Supreme Court weighed competing interests. The bill before us purposefully allows life to be created. That alone makes the debate different. We can set the boundaries, not the court. Science wants no boundaries. It will do what can be done. Our job as legislators will be to establish boundaries. Our authorization will begin a whole new chapter of history with large-scale creation of human life. Millions and millions of embryos created, some with diseases in nicely landscaped buildings. They will be simple commodities waiting to be harvested. Why are we rushing on something of such great importance? The bill takes altered nuclear transfer, proposed by a world-renowned Stanford professor, it would alter the cell of a nucleus before cloning takes place. Therefore human life is never created. If we say the human embryo is a Ferrari, but all we need is the engine, then why create the Ferrari and not just the engine? Altered nuclear transfer is very real. A council would have to review it and report back to us by Jan. 31, 2006. It would say that embryonic stem cell research would be acceptable, but not creating human life. There have been no cures using embryonic stem cells and thousands of cures using adult cells. That's not to say we don't need embryonic stem cells. The demand for results will inevitably mean we will be asked to extend the 14 days to greater and greater lengths. It can not and will not be the magic number if you allow the bright line to be passed today. We will inevitably end up with fetal farms—so much cattle to be harvested. Do you want to be remembered as pragmatic or principled? Will you be comfortable looking in the mirror or realize to your horror that it's too late? Let's be brave in defining the debate.

Rep. Bosley said I agree it's a serious debate. We have to look at issues we didn't think we would when we were campaigning for office. I ran for office because my district lost manufacturing jobs. I never thought I would have to make decisions on the ethics of what is an embryo. We vote on a lot of things we didn't think we would. Times change. Science changes. He is right to say we should be intellectually honest. He is not right that he assigns his moral views upon myself or anyone else. I have done a lot of studying of this issue. I would like to take a few points. He says we will be at 30 days, 45 days. We worked hard not to decide what life is. We decided if this was acceptable. We didn't have the science ten or 20 years ago. This forces us into making decisions on the floor. I am very comfortable with the 14 days. After that, you are probably dealing with adult stem cells. Embryonic stem cells are probably occurring at about day 5 or 6. Sometimes cells or embryos develop more slowly. It's an important piece. I disagree with the gentleman that you are going to kill something to cure something. In the first 14 days, you are dealing with a series of cells. It is not true that every embryo becomes a human being. I feel comfortable in the first 14 days that we are not destroying life to create life. If the chance to unlock cures to diseases that are out there, ethically we have the responsibility to do as much as we can do. We can't use adult stem cells for Juvenile Diabetes. Most medical ethicists have more problems with what Dr. Hurlbut is trying to do than with embryonic stem cell research. He genetically corrupts an egg. That is more ethically unacceptable. What Dr. Hurlbut is suggesting has never been done. We are giving people a false hope that there is some way out of this ethical choice we have to make individually. I think we should allow embryonic stem cell research and SCMT. Let's not give false hope.

. . .

Rep. Loscocco said I would like to question the comments of Rep. Bosley. Dr. Hurlbut came to the State House at his own expense and explained this in great detail. Many members were not here. A human being is the combination of the sperm and the egg. If you modify the sperm or egg at the beginning, it's never an embryo. The gentleman from North Adams says he is comfortable with the 14 days. Many of us do have moral objections to that. Why are we rushing that? Why not get something that is clearly not a human embryo? SCNT is no less speculative than altered nuclear transfer. It is comparable but would not yield a human embryo. Why do we automatically have to go down the most controversial path? Rep. Loscocco requested a roll call and there was support.

ON ENGROSSMENT: Question came on engrossing the bill, as amended throughout the day.

Rep. Bosley said this is the kind of day I look forward to in the House. We get up here and debate issues. It is substantive and educational. We exchange ideas in a manner people expect us to. This has been a tremendous debate. In this country, there are 400,000 embryos in in-vitro clinics. I hope we can use those to unlock cures to diseases like diabetes, Alzheimer's Parkinson's. Researchers are unanimous about the potential that exists to cure those diseases, which afflict 80 million to 100 million people in the US. Hearing stores about people you know—when people do that it puts a human face on those diseases. That is important for us to remember. There is a lot of talk about this in the newspapers, in ads. This goes into a new area of science. We tried to provide for the forward movement by allowing embryonic stem cell research and SCMT and at the same time putting in thoughtful restrictions. This is been a long day but a very historic day. I hope the bill is engrossed.

Rep. Peterson said I too want to commend the members for the thoughtful debate on this important issue. I too want to see cures come for debilitating diseases. I support stem cell research. I do have a problem with SCNT. Scientists, researchers all want to go to that very edge of the boundary that they can dream and think about and use to create cures and breakthroughs. I comment them for that. But as we have gone through history, every time we move that line, draw that boundary, one of the first things we look at is that line ethical? This bill goes to the very edge of what they only at this point believe holds promise. It still is at the point at this time of conjecture and in my mind creating life to harvest something out of that and destroy it. I don't believe we need to go to that point today. In a couple of weeks there will be a white paper talking about alternatives. We would be able to create and harvest stem cells needed to further the research. I for one am not ready to go to that point when in a year or a few short months we will have the information to maybe have the ability to take the ethical question out of this debate. It's a very difficult issue. We have had a long debate. I have the utmost respect for all of you when you make this vote today. I don't believe we need to draw that line to the very outer boundary. I urge the members not to engross the bill.

Rep. Bosley requested a roll call and there was support. Time was 7:51 pm.

Rep. Toomey said though I am in favor of many aspects of this, I will vote against it because it will almost certainly lead to taking advantage of economically disadvantaged women. There is an assumption that this will cure multiple diseases. Possibilities are nothing more than speculative. Experimentation is limited due to the unpredictability of these cells. Countries that have made the decision, there has been little success. There is a proven track record of alternative sources of stem cells from bone marrow and cord blood.

Rep. Toomey continued: Rather than rush into the problematic practice of embryonic stem cell research, we should focus on effective treatments. The Women's Caucus is concerned about imperiling economically disadvantaged women. Drugs may have no FDA approval and have serious side effects. There is little doubt where they will look for willing donors. There won't be enough willing donors for research and the desperate and destitute will be targeted. We have seen how nebulous the term informed consent can be. Informed consent sounds wonderful but has very little meaning in the outside world. Who will be there for the 18-year-old mother being offered money to sell her eggs to put food on the table? Will companies really let informed consent stand in the way of their progress? Human embryonic cloning and exploitation of donors are not getting appropriate attention. Diabetes is in my family. I have been a willing participant in a diabetes prevention program. We all hope a cure is found. Stem cells are promising, but we must approach cautiously.

Rep. Parente said I am feeling in the pink today (light applause). I spent 25 years on Beacon Hill. Sometimes I fear that a couple of people I worked with in the past were really damaged embryos. I am going to be a comedian when I leave. During the abortion debate, the discussion was is it a blob or a baby. The discussion was when is the best time to kill it. You can see how we progressed from earlier debates. I remember standing here as a freshman—I remember World War II. A paper was written for the New England Journal of Medicine. What the author predicted is coming true. That day I said gee, this might be the slippery slope. We may be talking someday about euthanasia. A gentleman screamed Mr. Speaker you stop her from saying that. How dare she mention that word? Isn't it funny? I am still here looking back. Now there is assisted suicide and living wills. Didn't Mass General try to override the health care proxy just a few weeks ago? One reason why embryonic stem cell research has slowed down is they say the embryonic stem cell is uncontrollable. It runs amuck like a two-year-old. They can't control it yet. I worked in cancer research in the early 50s as a medical librarian typing up records. They were rather detailed. I learned a lot. I learned what causes the cells to keep dividing. I really didn't want to make it seem I was against our Speaker who is supporting this. In spite of my being in pink condition, he was gracious to me. I have had a long-time interest in the subject of right to life, which is now called right to die. I was hoping language was not in the final version and it is. They expect you won't understand the terminology and you can slip in things. When I read the literature I had to keep my computer on and my thesaurus handy. I happened to catch Dr. Kass discussing stem cells and he said the people who would make this decision—us— were not the experts. Yet we are expected to make a decision on such a weighty subject. He was not willing to create life only to destroy it. It's said it's not going to be life until they implant it somewhere or in a petri dish. It's said there are 400,000 embryos available. Explain to me what is the difference between creating this embryo for purposes of regeneration and the in-vitro fertilization. Aren't they both life? Where are we going with all of this and why don't we perfect what we are already working on? I told a nice colleague of mine today, we are creating life and we are going to kill it. And she said, yes think of all the good we are doing for someone else. I said can I have your heart? She said yes when I die. I said no, I want it now. I am not voting to be ornery. You are invited to my pink office. I wonder if some of you will be here 25 years from now. I know your hearts are in the right places. Concepts are great but it's the operationalization of that concept that I worry about. It's what's in the statute and what the scientists want. We had a debate on living wills years ago. I was against that but for the health care proxy. Ted Koppel had a nationwide hookup on who lives and who dies and who decides. I said who is going to make these decisions? Who cares about how we are dying? Insurance companies will tell us who lives and who dies. That is what I am afraid of. When you don't call it life until a certain point, that allows fooling around.

Rep. Harkins said the decision on this is very easy for me. It's not predicated as much on the scientific as the personal side. I have a four-year-old grandson named Charlie. A stroke paralyzed him at one. The arteries to the brain are malformed. That is what caused the stroke. It is one of the diseases that may be addressed by this bill. Charlie's parents have put him into an early intervention program. I looked over their IEP. Their goals for Charlie were so humble. They say we know Charlie Is not going to go to Harvard, but we would like him to have friends. He can't answer them so children walk away from him. He is working to say two or three sentences.

Rep. Harkins continued: I don't know if this research is going to help Charlie but I know it will give hope to my son and his wife. I don't want someone to have to take care of Charlie. I want Charlie to be made whole. There are millions of children like him. They need hope and their parents need hope. No matter how you vote, I hope 159 of your will think about being Charlie's friend.

After nearly 6½ hours of debate, the House engrossed the bill by a vote of 117–37. Although the majority was comfortably more than needed to override a gubernatorial veto, everyone involved was aware that this margin was possible because the House version of the bill was so limited. The restrictions on research were far greater than what the Senate was willing to put in place and the oversight was far more onerous. Now both chambers had produced their versions of the bill with two divergent visions of what stem cell research would be permitted. Now the hard work of coming to a conclusion—as so often is the case on controversial and complicated bills; was left to a conference committee.

Sources:

- Cyndi Roy, "Senate Advances Stem Cell Bill, Differences Emerge Between Branches," *State House News Service*, March 28, 2005.

- Debate reporting by the *State House News Service*, March 31, 2005. The Massachusetts Legislature does not make an official transcript of floor debate, but the *State House News* gives a very acurate account of the debate.

NOTES & QUESTIONS

1. One of the theoretical benefits of a joint committee system is that issues and bill language can be worked out at the committee level, with the "expert" legislators from each branch working together and from the same set of information attained during the hearing process. In addition, it is much easier to amend the bill in committee as opposed to the formal amendment

process that takes place on the floor of either chamber. That did not really happen in this case—why?

2.   Professors Nourse and Schacter point out the difficulty of drafting legislation "on the floor" as policy changes and alterations are being made combined with tight deadlines. They write:

> In the Senate, where there are virtually no rules, it is possible that senators will choose to construct a bill during debate. Indeed, at least a part of every major bill is so constructed in the form of "managers' amendments," which are typically provisions deemed acceptable to both political parties and included in one omnibus attachment. If this is where a bill is drafted, then the normal processes of drafting change. As one staffer put it, "There is no chance to do legal research here. . . . There is no 'adult supervision.' We do a quick read and correct it on the fly."

This situation creates "ugly" and "haphazard" bill language that does not get public scrutiny. Provisions could be "slipped-in" for the political benefit of one member, or provisions might be at odds with one another. One staffer stated, "Sometimes no one is focusing on the text. Thank God for a bicameral legislature. Things can happen quickly, in the dark, in the long bills where no one has seen it. On the other hand, it is the worst process except for the alternatives." See, Victoria F. Nourse, Jane S. Schacter, "The Politics of Legislative Drafting: A Congressional Case Study," 77 *N.Y.U. L. Rev.* 575 (2002).

3.   How would you characterize the speeches made on the bill? Who were the intended audiences?

4.   In a "colloquy," two or more members will exchange information—or put certain information on the record—through a series of questions and answers. Often these exchanges are planned out in advance for the purpose of creating a legislative history. See, William S. Moorhead, "A Congressman Looks at the Planned Colloquy and Its Effect in the Interpretation of Statutes," 45 *A.B.A. J.* 1314 (1959). Judge Mikva wrote, "that is the material that judges later will solemnly pore over, under the guise of 'studying the legislative history.'" See, Abner J. Mikva, "A Reply to Judge Starr's Observations," 1987 *Duke LJ.* 380, 384 (1987). This can be problematic, because, as Judge Mikva points out, there is no way to distinguish a real debate on an issue and a planned colloquy when reading the *Congressional Record*. See, Abner J. Mikva, "Reading and Writing Statutes," 28 *Tex. L. Rev.* 181, 185 (1986).

5.   Sometimes, judges will use floor speeches to discredit or lessen the evidentiary power of other sources of legislative history. An infamous example is then Judge Scalia's concurring opinion in *Hirschey v. FERC*, 777 F.2d 1, 7 n.1 (D.C. Cir. 1985) (Scalia, J., concurring). Scalia quoted a colloquy from the Senate debate where Senators Armstrong and Dole discussed the committee report on the relevant legislation. During the exchange, Senator Dole admitted to having not read the report, to which Sen. Armstrong stated,

[F]or any jurist, administrator, bureaucrat . . . or others who might chance upon the written record of this proceeding, let me just make the point that this is not the law, it was not voted on, it is not subject to amendment, and we should discipline ourselves to the task of expressing congressional intent in the statute. *Hirschey v. FERC,* (citing 128 *Cong. Rec.* 88659 (daily ed. July 19, 1982)).

6.   Should all floor speeches be given the same weight when interpreting a statute? Perhaps one can only make sense of floor speeches with a deep knowledge of the individual legislator's role in creating the bill. In that case, should you read Sen Creem and Rep. Bosley's remarks on stem cell research differently from Rep. Loscocco?

F. CONFERENCE COMMITTEES

RESOLVING LEGISLATIVE DIFFERENCES IN CONGRESS: CONFERENCE COMMITTEES AND AMENDMENTS BETWEEN THE HOUSES

Elizabeth Rybicki, Congressional Research Service, August 3, 2015

Introduction

The process of resolving the legislative differences that arise between the House of Representatives and the Senate is one of the most critical stages of the legislative process. It is also potentially one of the most complicated. Each chamber continues to be governed by its own rules, precedents, and practices, but at this stage, each house also must take into account the preferences and, to some extent, the procedures of the other. This report summarizes the procedures the two houses of Congress use most frequently to resolve their legislative differences. It is based upon an interpretation of the rules and published precedents of the House and Senate and an analysis of the application of these rules and precedents in recent practice.

. . .

The Need for Resolution

Before Congress can submit a bill or joint resolution to the President for his approval or disapproval, the Senate and the House of Representatives must agree on each and every provision of that measure. It is not enough for both houses to pass versions of the same measure that are comparable in purpose but that differ in certain technical or even minor details; the House and Senate must agree on identical legislative language. Nor is it enough for the two chambers to approve separate bills with exactly the same text; the House and Senate both must pass the same bill. In sum, both chambers of Congress must pass precisely the same measure in precisely the same form before it can become law.

Each of these requirements—agreement on the identity of the measure (e.g., H.R. 1 or S. 1) and agreement on the text of that measure—is considered in turn in the following sections of this report.

Selection of the Measure

Because both chambers must pass the same measure before it can become law, at some point during the legislative process the House must act on a Senate bill or the Senate must act on a House bill. Congress usually meets this requirement without difficulty or controversy. In some cases, however, selecting the measure may require some parliamentary ingenuity and can have policy and political consequences.

After either house debates and passes a measure, it sends (or "messages") that bill to the other chamber. If the second house passes the first house's bill without any amendments, the legislative process is completed: Both houses have passed the same measure in the same form. If the second house passes the bill with one or more amendments, both chambers have acted on the same measure; now they must resolve the differences between their respective versions of the text if the measure is to become law. In most cases, either the House or the Senate can be the first chamber to act. However, the Constitution requires that all revenue measures originate in the House, and the House traditionally has insisted that this prerogative extends to appropriations as well as tax measures. Thus, the House normally acts first on such a measure, and, consequently, it is a House-numbered bill or joint resolution that Congress ultimately presents to the President for enacting appropriations or tax laws. In some cases, the proponents of a measure may decide that one house or the other should act first. For example, a bill's supporters may first press for floor action in the chamber where they think the measure enjoys greater support. They may hope that success in one house may generate political momentum that will help the measure overcome the greater opposition they expect in the second chamber. Alternatively, one house may defer floor action on a bill unless and until it is passed by the other, where the measure is expected to encounter stiff opposition. The House leadership, for example, may decide that it is pointless for the House to invest considerable time, and for Representatives to cast possibly unnecessary and politically difficult votes, on a controversial bill until after an expected Senate filibuster on a comparable Senate bill has been avoided or overcome.

. . .

Two Methods of Resolution

Once the House and Senate have passed different versions of the same measure, there are basically two methods they can use to resolve the differences between their versions.

One method involves a conference committee—a panel of Members representing each house that attempts to negotiate a version acceptable to both chambers. Historically, Congress has sent most major bills to conference committees. The other method makes a conference committee unnecessary by relying instead on amendments between the houses— Senate amendments to the House position, House amendments to the Senate position, or both. The two houses shuttle the measure back and forth between them, each chamber proposing an alternative to the position of the other or insisting on its own position, in the hope that both houses eventually will agree on the same position. The essential nature of each method can be described relatively simply. However, potential variations abound. Occasionally, some combination of the two methods may be used. For example, the House and Senate may begin the process of resolving their differences by amending each other's amendments. Then they may decide to go to conference if the first method is not totally, or even partially, successful. Alternatively, the two houses may decide immediately to create a conference committee, but that conference committee might resolve only some of the differences between their two versions. If so, the two chambers may accept whatever agreements the conferees have reached and then attempt to deal with the remaining disagreements through an exchange of amendments between the houses.

. . .

The Informal Alternative to Conference

If the House and Senate versions of a measure are submitted to conference, the conference committee must meet formally and, if it resolves some or all of the differences between the houses, prepare both a conference report and a joint explanatory statement. To avoid these and other requirements, the two chambers may use the process of sending amendments between the houses as an informal alternative that achieves much the same purpose and result as would a conference committee. The purpose of a conference committee is to negotiate a settlement of the legislative differences between the two chambers. But these negotiations do not have to take place in the official setting of a conference committee meeting. They also can occur through informal discussions among the most interested Representatives and Senators and their staffs. If such informal discussions are successful, their results can be embodied in an amendment between the houses.

As the second house nears or reaches completion of floor action on a measure, the staffs of the respective House and Senate committees are likely to be comparing the two versions of the bill and seeking grounds for settling whatever differences exist. After initial staff discussions, the House and Senate committee leaders themselves may become involved. If these informal and unofficial conversations appear productive, they may continue until a tentative agreement is reached, even though no conference committee has yet been created. If the tentative agreement proves acceptable to other interested Representatives and Senators, a conference committee may be unnecessary.

Instead, when the bill with the second house's amendments has been returned to the first chamber, the majority floor manager may, under the appropriate rules or practices of that house, call up the bill and propose that the House or Senate (as the case may be) concur in the second chamber's amendments with some amendments. He or she then describes the differences between the House and Senate versions of the measure and explains that the proposed amendments represent a compromise that is agreeable to the interested Members of both houses. The floor managers may express their confidence that, if the first house accepts the amendments, the other chamber also will accept them. If the first house does agree to the amendments, the second chamber then considers and agrees to them as well, under its procedures for considering amendments of the "other body." In this way, the differences between the House and Senate are resolved through the kind of negotiations for which conference committees are created, but without resort to a formal conference committee.

The Stage of Disagreement

Since the purpose of conference committees is to resolve legislative disagreements between the House and Senate, it follows that there can be no conference committee until there is disagreement—until the House and Senate formally state their disagreement to each other's positions. A chamber reaches this stage either by formally insisting on its own position or buy disagreeing to the position of the other house, and so informing the other house. Once the House or Senate reaches the stage of disagreement, it cannot then agree to (concur in) a position of the other chamber, or agree with an amendment, without first receding from its disagreement.

The stage of disagreement is an important threshold. Before this threshold is reached, the two chambers presumably are still in the process of reaching agreement. Thus, amendments between the houses, as an alternative to conference, are couched in terms of one chamber concurring in the other's amendments, or concurring in the other's amendments with amendments.

. . .

Arranging for a Conference

If the differences between the House and the Senate cannot be resolved through the exchange of amendments between the houses, two possibilities remain. First, stalemate can lead to the death of the legislation if both chambers remain adamant. Second, the two houses can agree to create a conference committee to discuss their differences and seek a mutually satisfactory resolution. Historically, major bills have been sent to conference, either after an unsuccessful attempt to resolve the differences through amendments between the houses or, more often, without such an attempt having even been made.

. . .

Selection of Conferees

After either house requests or agrees to a conference, it usually proceeds immediately to select conferees (or managers, as they may also be called). The selection of conferees can be critically important, because it is this group—sometimes a small group—of Representatives and Senators who usually determine the final form and content of major legislation.

In the House, clause 11 of Rule I authorizes the Speaker to appoint all members of conference committees and gives him certain guidelines to follow:

> The Speaker shall appoint all select, joint, and conference committees ordered by the House. At any time after an original appointment, the Speaker may remove Members, Delegates, or the Resident Commissioner from, or appoint additional Members, Delegates, or the Resident Commissioner to, a select or conference committee. In appointing Members, Delegates, or the Resident Commissioner to conference committees, the Speaker shall appoint no less than a majority who generally supported the House position as determined by the Speaker, shall name Members who are primarily responsible for the legislation, and shall, to the fullest extent feasible, include the principal proponents of the major provisions of the bill or resolution passed or adopted by the House.

These guidelines carry weight as admonitions but they necessarily give the Speaker considerable discretion, and his or her exercise of this discretion cannot be challenged on the floor through a point of order.

In the Senate, the presiding officer is almost always authorized by unanimous consent to appoint "the managers on the part of the Senate." The Senate could also grant this authority to the presiding officer by agreeing to a motion arranging for a conference (Rule XXVIII, paragraph 2). Before the formal announcement of conferees in each chamber, a process of consultation takes place that vests great influence with the chairman and the ranking minority member of the committee (and sometimes the subcommittee) that had considered the bill originally. These Representatives and Senators almost always serve as conferees. Furthermore, they usually play an influential, and often a controlling, role in deciding the number of conferees from their respective chambers, the party ratio among these conferees, and which of their committee colleagues shall be appointed to the conference committee. In the House, the Speaker often accepts without change the list developed by the House committee leaders; the presiding officer in the Senate always does so.

. . .

Instructing Conferees

After the House or Senate decides to go to conference (either by requesting the conference or agreeing to a request from the other house), its conferees usually are appointed immediately. Between these two steps, however, both houses have an opportunity (although usually only a momentary opportunity) to move to instruct the conferees. For example, the managers may be instructed to insist on the position of their house on a certain matter, or even to recede to the position of the other house.

Instructions are not binding in either house. They are only admonitions, or advisory expressions of position or preference. No point of order lies in either the House or the Senate against a conference report on the ground that conferees did not adhere to the instructions they received.

. . .

Because conference committees are created to resolve disagreements between the House and Senate, the authority of House conferees is limited to the matters in disagreement between the two houses. House conferees have no authority to change matters that are not in disagreement—that is, either matters that appear in the House and Senate versions of the measure in identical form, or matters that were not submitted to the conference in either the House or the Senate version. Furthermore, as House conferees consider each matter in disagreement, their authority is limited by the scope of the differences between the House and Senate positions on that matter. The House's managers may agree on the House position, the Senate position, or some middle ground. But they may not include a provision in a conference report that does not fall within the range of options defined by the House position at one extreme and the Senate position at the other.

. . .

Also, if one house proposes to amend some existing law and the other chamber does not, the scope of the differences over this matter generally is bounded by the proposed amendments, on the one hand, and the pertinent provisions of existing law, on the other. Thus, the House conferees may agree on the proposed amendments or on alternatives that are closer to existing law.

. . .

Notwithstanding this specificity, determining whether a conference substitute includes some new "matter" is far more difficult than determining whether the conferees' agreement on an appropriation for a program falls within the scope of the differences between the funding levels originally proposed by the House and Senate.

. . .

Historically, the Senate has interpreted its rules and precedents affecting the content of conference reports in ways that grant conferees considerable latitude in reaching agreements with the House. . . . Under current practice, the Senate takes a commonsense approach to deciding whether new matter is sufficiently relevant to constitute "a germane modification of subjects in disagreement."

. . .

Conference Procedures and Reports

Rules of procedure guide and constrain the legislative activities of both the House and Senate. So it is striking that there are almost no rules governing procedure in conference. The members of each conference committee can select their own chairmen. They also can decide for themselves whether they wish to adopt any formal rules governing such matters as debate, quorums, proxy voting, or amendments, but usually they do not. The only rules imposed by the two houses governing conference committee meetings concern approval of the conference report and the openness of meetings to all conferees and to the public. A majority of the House managers and a majority of the Senate managers must approve and sign the conference report. Decisions are never made by a vote among all the conferees combined. All votes take place within the House delegation and within the Senate delegation. This is why there is no requirement or necessity for the two houses to appoint the same number of conferees; five Senate conferees, for example, enjoy the same formal collective power in conference as 25 House conferees.

Until the mid-1970s, conference meetings were almost always closed to the public; now they are open unless a specific decision is made to close part or all of a meeting.

. . .

Floor Consideration of Conference Reports

A conference report may be presented or filed at almost any time the House or Senate is in session, but not when the Senate is in executive session or when the House has resolved into Committee of the Whole.

. . .

Conference reports may not be amended on the floor of either house. Conferees are appointed to negotiate over the differences between the versions of the same bill that the two houses have passed; the delegations return to their respective chambers with identical recommendations in the form of a report that proposes a package settlement of all these differences. The House and Senate may accept or reject the settlement, but they may not amend it directly. If conference reports were amendable, the process of resolving bicameral differences would be far more tortuous and possibly interminable.

NOTES & QUESTIONS

1.   Courts traditionally consider conference committee reports as authoritative indicators of legislative intent. *In re Party City Securities Litigation*, 147 F. Supp. 2d 282 (D.N.J. 2001); *Bay View, Inc. v. U.S.*, 278 F.3d 1259, 32 Envtl. L. Rep. 20360 (Fed. Cir. 2001); *In re Silicon Graphics Inc. Securities Litigation*, 183 F.3d 970, Fed. Sec. L. Rep. (CCH) P 90610, 44 Fed. R. Serv. 3d 1311 (9th Cir. 1999), as amended, (Aug. 4, 1999).

2.   In Louisiana, a conference committee is composed of three members from each house. By House rule, the House appointees includes the member who authored or handled the legislation, the chairman of the committee that handled the legislation, and one member appointed by the speaker. The Senate members of a conference committee consist of "three Senators appointed by the President." Unlike standing committees, the rules do not require conference committees to meet and take action in open, public meetings. The typical procedure in Louisiana is a "round-robin" whereby a proposed conference committee report is prepared and circulated among the six members in private, who assent by signing the report or disagree by refusing to sign the report.

Although the purpose of the conference committee is to resolve differences between the houses, in Louisiana, and in other jurisdictions, conferees have the same power as standing committees to propose changes to legislation; both changes to the bill language that is in disagreement and to text that is not in disagreement. Conferees may add new text or even propose text that has been previously considered and rejected in one of the chambers. The floor vote on adoption or rejection of the conference committee report is an "all or nothing" vote. See, P. Raymond Lamonica, Jerry G. Jones, "Conference committees and the Conference Committee Report § 3:18," LOUISIANA LEGISLATIVE LAW AND PROCEDURE HANDBOOK (2017).

3.   Lamonica and Jones worry that Louisiana conference committees may violate certain constitutional principles,

> When combined with their smaller membership, limited time for action, "all or nothing" votes on the report and (especially) with their more private nature, the present conference committee procedure in Louisiana raises a significant question regarding constitutional notice in the legislative process. One purpose of constitutional legislative process requirements discussed previously is to facilitate informed deliberation and voting by members, including those

without the benefit of participating in the committee process on a particular bill. Another purpose, equally important, is to provide notice to the public of matters under consideration and the opportunity for public scrutiny and reasonable comment. No Louisiana cases presently have addressed whether the current conference committee procedure conflicts with constitutional and controlling statutory requirements regarding procedures and public scrutiny of the legislative process. P. Raymond Lamonica, Jerry G. Jones, "Conference committees and the Conference Committee Report § 3:18," LOUISIANA LEGISLATIVE LAW AND PROCEDURE HANDBOOK (2017).

Are these concerns valid? How could they be resolved?

4.   Professor Seth Grossman claims that Congress is "in an era of conference committee ascendancy." Whereas conference committees once functioned as agents of the House and Senate, recently they have become too powerful and independent with great control over lawmaking. He argues that conference committees add provisions that were not passed by either house, remove provisions that should be non-conferencable, and insert legislation independent of the bills sent to them. Since conference committees are all-or-nothing affairs, conference committees often add unpopular measures to "must-pass" legislation. Even though a majority of legislators would have voted against the unpopular elements of the conference report, they often feel obligated to vote for the broader conference report. Since conference committee reports are nearly always enacted by Congress, power has dramatically shifted toward conference committees—and the congressional leadership who appoint and control them. See, Seth Grossman, "Tricameral Legislating: Statutory Interpretation in an Era of Conference Committee Ascendancy," *N.Y.U. J. of Legis. & Pub. Pol'y* (2006).

Part of this power shift has come from a manipulation of the House and Senate Rules. First, Prof. Grossman argues that conferences are not transparent. After a *pro forma* opening session, conference committees then typically go behind closed doors to make a compromise and committee report. Second, Prof. Grossman accuses the House majority leadership of undermining the rules that prevent consideration of conference reports until three days after they are published in the Congressional Record. The rule is meant to give House members sufficient time to review the conference reports, especially where a bill differs greatly from what the House passed. The speaker and Rules Committee, however, can undermine these rules by preventing points of order during consideration of the conference committee report.

Who benefits from this change? Prof. Grossman argues that this shift in power to conference committees benefits special interests. Because a small subset of the conference committee (often along with the majority party leadership) controls the process, combined with the secrecy of proceedings, conferences "can easily be exploited to advance the causes of special interests." Grossman states that, "provisions favoring special interest groups, many of which members of Congress would hesitate to associate themselves with publicly, are added to conference reports." To illustrate, Grossman points to a provision giving $50 billion in tax breaks to tobacco companies, which only took 47 words, inserted on page 322 of an 809-page tax bill. Many members of Congress had no idea that the bill included the highly controversial provision and were outraged when they later discovered that they had unintentionally voted for it when they approved the omnibus tax bill.

Grossman argues that the power of conference committees requires a new approach by courts when interpreting statutes. In fact, he proposes a new rule of statutory construction:

"When a congressional statute is the result of a House-Senate conference committee, a court should narrowly construe any provision of the enacted measure which was not included in the versions passed by each chamber individually."

Prof. Grossman asserts that this canon will limit the effects of the rent-seeking measures, encourage Congress to re-embrace traditional lawmaking procedures, and restore the balance of power among conference committees, the House, and the Senate.

5.   Is Prof. Grossman's proposed canon of construction wise? Will it have the desired effect? How else could Congress deal with the transparency issues? How could it prevent special interests from manipulating the process?

6.   Drafting during a conference committee also presents problems. In their study of drafting for the Senate Judiciary Committee Professors Nourse and Schacter observed:

Several staffers identified, as another venue for drafting, the House-Senate conferences that legislators use to reconcile differences in bills that are passed by both bodies. Like drafting on the floor, drafting in conference was described by staffers with a significant measure of concern. Several staffers thought that pressures of time, and the political imperative to get a bill "done," bred ambiguity. Indeed, one staffer emphasized that while it was well and good to draft a bill clearly, there was no guarantee that the clear language would be passed by the House or make it through conference. Staffers noted that in House-Senate conferences: "They can do behind closed doors what can't be done on the floor." "[T]here are deals cut with four people in the room, deals on the floor are dropped, nobody knows what's in the bill. There is a big incentive for people to be in conference because it is a big site of action. You can draft carefully and then it gets dropped in conference, and they put in something from the House that you never saw."

"You work hard, and someone in the House will want to put their fingerprints on something and will mess it up at the end."

Victoria F. Nourse, Jane S. Schacter, "The Politics of Legislative Drafting: A Congressional Case Study," 77 *N.Y.U. L. Rev.* 575 (2002).

Stem Cell Case Study: Part IV

At this point in the process, the Senate had enacted a much more developed version of the Travaglini-Creem Bill, and the House had enacted the bill that Chairman Bosley and the House staff drafted for the Economic Development and Emerging Technologies Committee Report. Given the differences between the bills, there was little question the Stem Cell issue would go to a conference committee.

A conference committee is particularly advantageous for the Senate in Massachusetts. At the Joint Committee stage the representatives outnumber senators 11–6, in a conference committee there are equal numbers of House and Senate members. Conferences also give greater weight to minority party members in that one minority party member from each chamber must be appointed to the conference. This gives them a 33% stake in the conference as opposed to the 17.6% stake minority members have on joint committees. Still, each member appointed to a conference committee must have voted in favor of their chamber's version of the bill, so the conferees typically negotiate as a unit regardless of party. To issue a report, two members of each delegation must agree to the language of the compromise bill. In Massachusetts, the conferees typically vote to make the deliberations closed to the everyone except the conferees, their staff and leadership. Still, some conferences—even on major bills—have been kept open to the press and public.

To negotiate on behalf of the House Speaker DiMasi appointed Rep. Bosley, Rep. Lida Harkins (D-Needham) and Rep. Bradford Hill (R-Ipswich). Senate President Travaglini appointed Sen. Hart, Sen. Creem and Sen. Tarr (R-Gloucester). Given the importance of this issue, the Senate President, Speaker and their staffs were intimately involved in the negotiations.

Assignments:

1.   Your chair (either Sen. Hart or Rep. Bosley) has asked you to be his point staff person during the conference. He wants your opinion on the following issues:

- Should the conference be open or closed?

- Do the conferees need to hear from anyone else or any other organizations before issuing its report?

- What provisions do you anticipate the other chamber's negotiators will be most insistent upon?

- What provisions are most important to your chamber?

- What is your negotiating strategy during this exercise?

2. Below is what conferees call a "crosswalk." It summarizes the House and Senate provisions on each item within the bill. During the conference, the committee fills in the final column with the agreed to policy or language. Remember, no single item is negotiated in a vacuum—compromise often comes from negotiating with all of the provisions in play.

Provision	Senate Version	House Version	Conference
Title	An Act related to the Promotion of the Biotechnology Industry in the Commonwealth	An Act Relative to Biotechnology	
Key definitions	"Pre-implantation embryo", any in vitro human embryo whether formed by fertilization, somatic cell nuclear transfer or other means, which has not experienced more than 14 days of development; provided, that such lengths of time does not include any interval in which such development has been suspended, such as through freezing. "Parthenogenesis," the development of an egg without fertilization. "Somatic Cell Nuclear Transfer", replacement of	"Embryo", an organism of the species homo-sapiens from the single cell stage to eight weeks development whether formed by fertilization, somatic cell nuclear transfer, parthenogenesis, or other means. "Extracorporeal embryo", an embryo formed and maintained outside of the human body. "Somatic Cell Nuclear Transfer", the technique in which the nucleus of an oocyte is replaced with the nucleus of a somatic cell and stimulated to	

	the nucleus of an oocyte egg with the nucleus from any other non-reproductive human cell.	divide until it reaches the blastocyst stage from which stem cells can be derived.	
Informed consent definition	"Informed consent", consent for the donation of embryos, consent for participation in in-vitro fertilization, or consent for any other process where an egg is extracted from a woman, or other participation in research pursuant to this chapter, which complies with requirements of a duly appointed institutional review board, and which follows the procedures stipulated in 45CFR Part 46.116 and 117.	"Informed Consent", the written consent of the donor or patient obtained in accordance with the "donated for research" requirements and of 45 CFR 46.116 and 45 CFR 46.117, as may be amended from time to time;	
Human material eligible for research	Pre-implementation embryo or parthenote.	a donated extracorporeal embryo either created by somatic cell nuclear transfer or donated for research.	

Institutional review boards (IRB)	IRB must give annual written approval for the derivation of stem cells from a pre-implantation embryo. Requires University of Massachusetts to establish a public IRB within 120 days to facilitate research approval.	IRB must give annual written approval for the derivation of stem cells from a pre-implantation embryo. IRBs required to also "consider ethical and medical implications of the proposed research" Institutions may be fined $100,000 if its IRB authorizes research not allowed by statute.	
Prosecutorial review of research	None	Attorney General	
Stem cell advisory board	8 members: 3 appointed by each the Senate President and House Speaker; 1 appointed by the Governor; Commissioner of Public Health. Stem cell researchers must make annual reports to Board on research. Board to report to the Governor,	15 members: 5 appointed by each the Governor, Senate President and House Speaker. Board to make recommendations to DPH and Legislature for statutory & regulatory changes "necessary to promote scientific	

	Senate President and House Speaker "on the status of human embryonic stem cell research and proposing modifications to the regulation of such research." Administrative support from Department of Public Health.	inquiry and protect human subjects." Administrative support from Department of Public Health.	
Department of Public Health (DPH)	DPH to only license researchers conducting human embryonic stem cell research, but researchers in compliance with the statute shall not have a license "unreasonably delayed."	Full regulatory power Regulations must be consistent with existing federal regulations relative to biomedical research.	
Criminal Penalties (Research violations)	Persons who conduct research without the approval of an IRB, or purchases or sells a pre-implantation embryo for "valuable consideration," to be punished with imprisonment for up to 5 years and a fine of up to $100,000.	Persons who conduct research without the approval of an IRB, or purchases or sells a pre-implantation embryo for "valuable consideration," to be punished with imprisonment for up to 5 years and a fine of up to $100,000.	

Criminal Penalties (Human cloning)	Persons who attempt human reproductive cloning to be punished with imprisonment for up to 10 and a fine of up to $1 million.	Persons who attempt human reproductive cloning to be punished with imprisonment for up to 10 and a fine of up to $1 million.	

G. THE LEGISLATURE & THE EXECUTIVE

The veto power makes the president or the governor an extraordinarily important player in the legislative process. Far from becoming involved only after the House and the Senate present an enacted bill to him, executives can be active participants in the development of bills.

If any Bill shall not be returned by the President within ten Days (Sundays excepted) after it shall have been presented to him, the Same shall be a Law.

U.S. CONST., Art. I Section 7

No bill or resolve of the senate or house of representatives shall become a law, and have force as such, until it shall have been laid before the governor for his revisal; and if he, upon such revision, approve thereof, he shall signify his approbation by signing the same. But if he have any objection to the passing of such bill or resolve, he shall return the same, together with his objections thereto, in writing, to the senate or house of representatives, in whichsoever the same shall have originated; who shall enter the objections sent down by the governor, at large, on their records, and proceed to reconsider the said bill or resolve. But if after such reconsideration, two thirds of the said senate or house of representatives, shall, notwithstanding the said objections, agree to pass the same, it shall, together with the objections, be sent to the other branch of the legislature, where it shall also be reconsidered, and if approved by two thirds of the members present, shall have the force of a law: but in all such cases, the votes of both houses shall be determined by yeas and nays; and the names of the persons voting for, or against, the said bill or resolve, shall be entered upon the public records of the commonwealth.

MASSACHUSETTS CONST., Part II, Chapter 1, Article 2.

Each Bill Passed By The Legislature Shall Be Presented To The Governor. It Becomes A Statute If It Is Signed By The Governor. The Governor May Veto It By Returning It With Any Objections To The House Of Origin, Which Shall Enter The Objections In The Journal

And Proceed To Reconsider It. If Each House Then Passes The Bill By Roll Call Vote Entered In The Journal, Two-Thirds Of The Membership Concurring, It Becomes A Statute.

CALIFORNIA CONST., Article IV Sec 10 (A).

THE DIRECTOR

EXECUTIVE OFFICE OF THE PRESIDENT OFFICE OF MANAGEMENT AND BUDGET WASHINGTON, D.C. 20503

February 28, 2017

M-17-19

MEMORANDUM FOR THE HEADS OF DEPARTMENTS AND AGENCIES

FROM: Mick Mulvaney Director

SUBJECT: Legislative Coordination and Clearance

This memorandum and the attachment provide an overview of the Executive branch's formal legislative coordination and clearance process. Please share this with policy officials in your agency.

Adherence to the requirements of the clearance process serves the needs of the President by ensuring that agency legislative proposals and recommendations, as well as testimony, are consistent with his policies and programs. We request that agency legislative proposals, letters, and testimony discussing or involving legislation be submitted to the Office of Management and Budget (OMB) as far in advance of a needed clearance as feasible.

OMB runs a clearance process on these items, which requires sufficient time to review and coordinate with all relevant agencies, and offices in the Executive Office of the President.

OMB Circular No. A-19 details the requirements and procedures for legislative coordination and clearance. The attachment summarizes the major elements and the essential purposes of the clearance process.

We will be working with you to ensure the timely transmittal to Congress of legislative proposals necessary to support the President's legislative agenda and the Fiscal Year 2018 Budget. As decisions are made on these matters, we will be in contact about details related to the drafting, review, and clearance of these proposals.

Thank you for your cooperation.

Attachment:

THE LEGISLATIVE CLEARANCE FUNCTION

This paper summarizes the major elements of the legislative clearance function that the Office of Management and Budget (OMB), working with other offices in the Executive Office of the President (EOP) and with the agencies, carries out on behalf of the President.

Background

The President's legislative responsibilities are founded in his constitutional duties and powers. In executing his executive duties, the President generally outlines legislative recommendations through the Inaugural address, State of the Union address, Budget, Economic Report, and other communications. The compilation of these recommendations constitutes the President's Program. In supporting the President's Program, agencies within the Administration: (1) submit to the Congress legislative proposals needed to carry out the President's Program; (2) convey the Administration's views on legislation that the Congress has under consideration; and (3) recommend approval or disapproval of bills passed by the Congress.

OMB's legislative clearance function allows for all affected agencies to engage and reconcile differences on legislative proposals and communications that are cleared and transmitted to the Congress. The primary goals of the clearance process are to ensure that: (1) agencies' legislative communications with Congress are consistent with the President's policies and objectives; and (2) the Administration "speaks with one voice" regarding legislation. During clearance, OMB circulates items to affected agencies and EOP offices for their review, and ensures that all issues are resolved before providing final clearance to the transmitting agency.

1. PRESIDENTIAL VETOES

Article I, section 7 of the Constitution grants the President the authority to veto legislation passed by Congress. There are two types of vetoes: the "regular veto" and the "pocket veto."

The regular veto is a qualified negative veto. The President returns the unsigned legislation to the originating house of Congress, typically with a memorandum of disapproval or a "veto message." Congress can override the President's decision if it musters the necessary two-thirds vote of each house. President George Washington issued the first regular veto on April 5, 1792. The first successful congressional override occurred in 1845.

The pocket veto is an absolute veto that cannot be overridden. The veto becomes effective when the President fails to sign a bill after Congress has adjourned and is unable to override the veto. The authority of the pocket veto is derived from the Constitution's Article I, section 7, "the Congress by their adjournment prevent its return, in which case, it shall not be law." President James Madison first used the pocket veto in 1812. Congress and the President have clashed over the term "adjournment." The President has attempted to use the pocket veto during intra- and inter-session adjournments and Congress has denied this use of the veto.

Presidential attitudes about vetoes have changed significantly over the years. George Washington vetoed only bills that he thought unconstitutional; so, the first six presidents combined vetoed just 10 bills. Andrew Jackson began vetoing bills he did not like and vetoed 12 bills. Congress and President John Tyler had a lengthy battle between over vetoes. After Tyler vetoed four bills in 1842, Representative John Quincy Adams, declared on the House floor that Tyler's vetoes put Congress and the executive branch "in a state of civil war." A committee chaired by Adams investigated Tyler's abuse of the veto and recommended both impeaching Tyler and passing a constitutional amendment to restrict the President's power to stop legislation. Congress ultimately did neither and Tyler vetoed six more bills before leaving office. The all-time leader in vetoes was Franklin D. Roosevelt who vetoed 635 pieces of legislation during his 12 years as President. Since Ronald Reagan vetoed 78 bills during the 1980s, his successors have used the veto power more sparingly with only 10 vetoes during the Trump Administration. From Washington to Trump, presidents have vetoed a total of 2,584 bills.

Congress rarely overrides a veto. Through the Trump Administration, only 112 bills (4.3%) became law over the president's objection. In fact, Congress did not override a veto until the last day of the 1845 session when John Tyler's veto of a bill related to revenue cutters and steamers (precursor to the Coast Guard) became law. The number of times Congress overrides a veto can indicate the relative strength or popularity of the president. Franklin Pierce and Andrew Johnson both had over half of their vetoes suffer overrides. In contrast, Franklin Roosevelt only saw nine of his 635 vetoes (1.4%) undone by Congress.

Modern Presidential Vetoes

Years	President	Regular Vetoes	Pocket Vetoes	Total Vetoes	Vetoes Overridden
1933–1945	Franklin D. Roosevelt	372	263	635	9
1945–1953	Harry S. Truman	180	70	250	12
1953–1961	Dwight D. Eisenhower	73	108	181	2

Modern Presidential Vetoes

Years	President	Regular Vetoes	Pocket Vetoes	Total Vetoes	Vetoes Overridden
1961–1963	John F. Kennedy	12	9	21	. . . . .
1963–1969	Lyndon B. Johnson	16	14	30	. . . .
1969–1974	Richard M. Nixon	26	17	43	7
1974–1977	Gerald R. Ford	48	18	66	12
1977–1981	James Earl Carter	13	18	31	2
1981–1989	Ronald Reagan	39	39	78	9
1989–1993	George H. W. Bush	29	15	44	1
1993–2001	William J. Clinton	36	1	37	2
2001–2009	George W. Bush	12	. . . . .	12	4
2009–2017	Barack H. Obama	12	. . . . .	12	1
2017–2021	Donald J. Trump	10	. . . . .	10	1
Total		1518	1066	2584	112

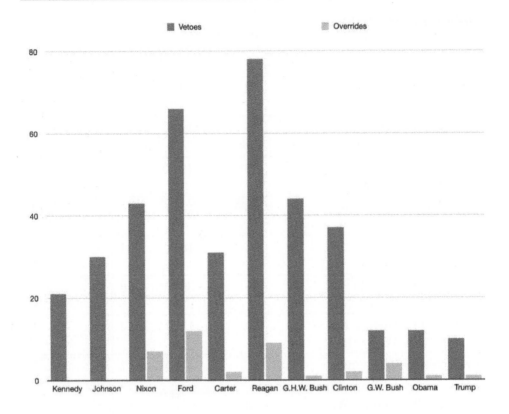

OMB CIRCULAR NO. A-19
Revised September 20, 1979

TO THE HEADS OF EXECUTIVE DEPARTMENTS AND ESTABLISHMENTS SUBJECT: Legislative coordination and clearance

1. Purpose. This Circular outlines procedures for the coordination and clearance by the Office of Management and Budget (OMB) of agency recommendations on proposed, pending, and enrolled legislation. It also includes instructions on the timing and preparation of agency legislative programs.

. . .

10. Enrolled Bills. Under the Constitution, the President has 10 days (including holidays but excluding Sundays) to act on enrolled bills after they are presented to him. To assure that the President has the maximum possible time for consideration of enrolled bills, agencies shall give them top priority.

a. Initial OMB action. OMB will obtain facsimiles of enrolled bills from the Government Printing Office and immediately forward one facsimile to each interested agency, requesting the agency's views and its recommendation for Presidential action.

b.　Agency action. Each agency receiving such a request shall immediately prepare a letter presenting its views and deliver it in duplicate to OMB not later than two days (including holidays but excluding Sundays) after receipt of the facsimile. OMB may set different deadlines as dictated by circumstances. Agencies shall deliver these letters by special messenger to OMB.

c.　Preparation of enrolled bill letters.

(1)　Agencies' letters on enrolled bills are transmitted to the President and should be written so as to assist the President in reaching a decision. Each letter should, therefore, be complete in itself and should not, as a general rule, incorporate earlier reports by reference.

(2)　Agencies' letters on enrolled bills are privileged communications, and agencies shall be guided accordingly in determining their content.

(3)　Because of the definitive nature of Presidential action on enrolled bills, agency letters shall be signed by a Presidential appointee.

(4)　Agencies' letters shall contain:

(a)　an analysis of the significant features of the bill including changes from existing law. OMB staff will advise the agencies on which one should write the detailed analysis of the bill where more than one agency is substantially affected;

(b)　a comparison of the bill with the Administration proposals, if any, on the same subject;

(c)　comments, criticisms, analyses of benefits and shortcomings, or special considerations that will assist the President in reaching a decision;

(d)　identification of any factors that make it necessary or desirable for the President to act by a particular date;

(e)　an estimate of the first-year and recurring costs or savings and the relationship of the estimates to those previously incorporated in the President's budgetary program;

(f)　an estimate of the additional number of personnel required to implement the bill; and

(g)　a specific recommendation for approval or disapproval by the President.

(5) Agencies recommending disapproval shall submit with their letters a proposed veto message or memorandum of disapproval, in quadruplicate, prepared on legal-size paper and double-spaced. Such messages or memoranda should be finished products in form and substance that can be used by the President without further revision.

(6) Agencies may wish to recommend issuance of a signing statement by the President. Agencies so recommending shall submit with their letters a draft of such statement, in the same form and quantity as required for a proposed veto message. In some cases, OMB may request an agency to prepare a draft signing statement.

(7) Agencies' letters on private bills shall cite, where appropriate, precedents that support the action they recommend or that need to be distinguished from the action recommended.

d.   Subsequent OMB action. OMB will transmit agencies' letters to the President, together with a covering memorandum, not later than the fifth day following receipt of the enrolled bill at the White House.

Two Approaches to Vetoes—California & Massachusetts

California

In California gubernatorial vetoes are rarely challenged by the legislature:

"An old Sacramento adage uses baseball imagery to explain the power of California's chief executive at the end of the legislative process: 'The governor bats last.' "

Of course, California's Constitution allows the legislature to override a veto by a supermajority. Depression-era Gov. James Rolph saw 11 vetoes overridden in a single day in 1933. more recently during Gov. Jerry Brown's second term at the end of 1979 and into 1980, the Legislature overrode his veto four times, which the LA Times called a "historic string of defeats," and characterized the Governor's veto to be "as awesome to legislators and lobbyists these days as a popgun." Governor Brown at the time was exploring a presidential run and was perceived as being uninterested in the job.

Since then, however, overrides have become so rare that the veto is seen as "sacrosanct." In a 2017 book California State Library historian Alex Vassar stated that a vote to override is "seen as a significant insult to the governor and major disruption to the balance of power relationship between the three branches."

This is true even when there is broad bipartisan support for a bill. In 2015, Governor Brown vetoed a bill that would allow terminally ill patients to use experimental drugs in spite of a 76–2 vote of the Assembly and by 40 to 0 in the Senate. Rather than override, legislators promised to file amended legislation.

Gov. Brown left office in January 2019 after five terms as governor spanning almost 50 years. Some wonder if his departure will mark a shift in the balance of power in Sacramento. Since 1990, term limits significantly limited the length of legislative careers. In 2012, voters loosened term limit restrictions to allow a total term of service to be 12 years. This change may either give lawmakers either more experience in the Capitol than the new governor, or legislators may expect to serve long after the next governor is out of office. Either way, legislators may be more willing to vote to override in the future.

See: John Myers, "Once California's governor vetoes a bill, lawmakers almost never challenge the decision" *LA Times*, September 30, 2018. (http://www.latimes.com/politics/la-pol-ca-road-map-governor-veto-override-california-legislature-20180930-story.html).

Massachusetts

Stem Cell Case Study: Part V

After the Legislature passed a stem cell bill, it was far different from the bill first filed by Senator Creem. It had gone from a single page bill to one that was far more complicated and went into greater detail. Once the bill was presented to the governor for his approbation, Mitt Romney had his best opportunity to affect the language of the bill. So far, he had merely used his "bully pulpit" to try and shape public opinion about the language that the legislature was considering. He had not, however, tried to lobby legislators to use specific language or to amend how the bill was structured and phrased. After enactment, however, the Massachusetts Constitution allows the Governor to return bills along with a message laying out his objections and alternative measures or language that would be necessary for executive approval. This process gives the Governor an important formal role in the drafting process beyond simply approving or vetoing a bill. Often, it is this Constitutional power that allows a Governor to engage in negotiations with legislators from the very beginning of the legislative process. Governor Romney did not exercise this leverage in this instance and largely removed himself from the drafting of the bill. This may be for several reasons:

1.   He planned to veto any measure that allowed human embryonic research to burnish his national conservative credentials;

2.   He understood that the legislative leaders were anticipating a veto and therefore was already constructing a bill that had veto-proof support;

3.   Any effort on details would not be necessary since he hoped to thwart its implementation after passage.

On May 12, however, the Governor returned the bill to the Senate with his proposed amendments. Below is the Governor's message to the Legislature:

SENATE, No. 2052

May 12, 2005

To the Honorable Senate and House of Representatives:

Pursuant to Article LVI of the Constitution of the Commonwealth, as amended by Article XC, Section 3 of the Amendments to the Constitution of the Commonwealth, I am returning to you for amendment Senate Bill No. 2039, "An Act Enhancing Regenerative Medicine In The Commonwealth."

I support stem cell research, and like many people I am optimistic about the potential for medical advances that can be obtained through this science. I also support changes to the law that would allow research on stem cells taken from surplus embryos created as part of an in vitro fertilization process if the embryos would otherwise be discarded. I commend the Legislature for its attention to these important issues.

However, like other powers gained through modern science, the power to conduct this research must be bounded by our respect for human life. I am therefore proposing changes to the bill that will allow stem cell research to proceed without crossing ethical boundaries.

I will address each of these amendments in turn, providing specific corrective language in each case:

1.   When Human Life Begins. The bill changes the Commonwealth's long-standing definition of the point at which human life begins, a highly significant change that may not have been known to all of the members voting on this legislation. Since 1974, Massachusetts law has defined "Unborn child" as "the individual human life in existence and developing from fertilization until birth." See M.G.L. c. 112, § 12K. Section 8 of the bill would fundamentally change this definition and declares that human life now begins upon "implantation of the embryo in the uterus."

The definition of when life begins is a matter of profound moral and ethical consequence. It implicates a much broader array of issues than the relatively discrete question of whether stem cell research should be permitted.

The bill's proposed change to this definition is misguided on at least two levels. First, it is completely unnecessary to alter the Commonwealth's definition of the beginning of life in order to accomplish the objectives of the bill.

In addition, the selection of implantation as the start of life ignores the very real possibility of scientific advancements allowing embryos to grow for days, weeks, or even months before implantation, if implantation indeed remains necessary at all.

Accordingly, I propose that the bill be amended as follows:

By striking section 8 of the bill, thereby restoring the original definition of "Unborn child."

* * * *

2.   *Human Embryo Farming*. *Section 8(b) of the proposed Chapter 111L permits "human embryo farming" in the laboratory: the large-scale growing of human embryos by the fertilization of eggs with sperm cells.*

Section 8(b) states: "No person shall knowingly create an embryo by the method of fertilization with the sole intent of donating the embryo for research. Nothing in this section shall prohibit the creation of a pre-implantation embryo by somatic cell nuclear transfer, parthenogenesis or other asexual means for research purposes." (emphasis added).

This language does not expressly prevent scientific laboratories and researchers from creating human embryos through the fertilization of eggs with sperm cells for their own purposes, so long as they do not "donate" the embryos to anyone else. Therefore, under the legislation, a laboratory could obtain donated eggs and donated sperm to create a virtually unlimited supply of human embryos for experimentation.

The creation of embryos by therapeutic cloning, in the rare instances where this procedure has been attempted, has proven exceedingly difficult. In fact, it has never been successfully accomplished in the United States. By contrast, the creation of embryos through fertilization has been accomplished routinely for years at in vitro fertilization clinics. For this reason, this legislation does not simply open the door to cloned embryos; rather, it sanctions the mass production of human embryos by conventional fertilization. The opening left by Section 8(b) is ripe for abuse and must be closed.

Accordingly, I propose that the bill be amended as follows:

By inserting, in Section 1 of the bill, after the first sentence of section 8(b) in chapter 111L, the following sentence:—

No person shall knowingly create an embryo by the method of fertilization with the sole intent of using said embryo for research.

* * * *

3. The Exploitation of Women. The high demand for eggs for researchers either to farm human embryos for experimentation or to produce human embryo clones, could unintentionally foster the exploitation of women. Many will be poor women who will choose to donate their eggs in exchange for compensation.

The procedure to obtain eggs uses powerful drugs to suppress and stimulate the ovaries. This procedure has resulted in hospitalization, and even death in some cases. While many women are willing to accept these risks during in vitro fertilization to produce a baby, it is far from clear whether these risks would be willingly borne by women donating eggs for research purposes if not for financial remuneration.

Therefore, in addition to the requirement set out in the legislation that women be made aware of the risks associated with donating eggs for research purposes, the bill should strictly limit any compensation to the donor to reimbursement of out-of-pocket costs actually paid by the donor, for such items as transportation and medical services. Compensation for the donor's time, discomfort, and/or inconvenience should be prohibited.

Accordingly, I propose that the bill be amended as follows:

By inserting, in Section 1 of the bill, in the definition of "Valuable Consideration" in section 2 of chapter 111L, the following sentence:—

As applied to consideration to be paid to egg donors, "valuable consideration" is any interest, profit or benefit of value, except for reimbursement of out-of-pocket expenses actually paid by the donor in connection with the egg donation. Nothing in this definition shall be construed to limit consideration for eggs made available for reproductive purposes.

* * * *

4. Human Embryo Cloning. Like other powers gained through modern science, the power to clone life presents a challenge not only of intelligence and resourcefulness, but also of character and conscience. As the discoveries of modern science create tremendous new hope, they must also be consistent with appropriate ethical boundaries that preserve the respect for human life.

This bill allows the cloning of genetically complete human embryos solely for the purpose of experimentation. Human cloning for any purpose— whether for research (so-called "therapeutic cloning") or reproduction (so- called "reproductive cloning")—is ethically wrong. Once cloning occurs, a human life is set in motion. It is a complete genetic entity with a full complement of human chromosomes.

Accordingly, I propose that the bill be amended as follows:

By inserting, in Section 1 of the bill, the following additional section in chapter 111L:—

Section 11. Notwithstanding any general or special law to the contrary, including any provision of this chapter to the contrary, human cloning, by any means, including somatic cell nuclear transfer, is hereby prohibited in the Commonwealth. No person shall knowingly attempt, engage in, or directly or indirectly assist in, human cloning for any purpose. No person shall knowingly purchase, sell, transfer, or otherwise obtain human embryonic, gametic or cadaveric fetal tissue for the purpose of human cloning.

A person who violates the provisions of this section shall be punished by imprisonment in a jail or house of correction for not less than five years nor more than ten years or by imprisonment in the state prison for not more than ten years and by a fine of up to one million dollars. In addition, to such penalty, a person who knowingly violates the provision of this section and derives a financial profit from such violations shall be ordered to pay all such profits to the commonwealth as damages.

* * * *

I urge your favorable consideration of my proposed amendments.

Respectfully submitted,
Mitt Romney
Governor

On May 19th, the Senate again debated the stem cell issue. In an attempt to support the Republican Governor, Senate Minority Leader Brian Lees offered four amendments, three of which were rejected on a voice vote and one which had a role a role call and was defeated by a vote of 34–4.

Later that day, the House considered Governor Romney's amendments. First, the House concurred with the Senate amendment. The House then took up each of the Governor's amendments independently of each other. The first amendment was rejected 46–109. The second amendment was rejected 48–107. The third amendment was rejected 42– 113. The fourth amendment was rejected 43–112.

Each branch re-enacted the bill and sent it back to the Governor. Governor Romney, unable to propose further amendments, finally vetoed the bill on May 27, 2005. His message stated:

To the Honorable Senate and House of Representatives:

Pursuant to Part the Second, Chapter I, Section I, Article II of the <u>Constitution</u> *of the Commonwealth, I am returning unsigned Senate Bill No. 2039, "An Act Enhancing Regenerative Medicine in The Commonwealth."*

I cannot in good conscience allow this bill to become law. As a Commonwealth, we are bound together as a people united for the common good. The common good at stake in this debate is the preservation of the dignity of human life, and the laying of the groundwork for the advancements in the treatment of disease. Sadly, we have sacrificed the former in our hasty pursuit of the latter.

Like many people, I believe we should encourage medical discovery and seek out new cures, and there are many features of this bill that I support for those reasons. Research on adult and umbilical stem cells, as well as on surplus embryos created as part of an in vitro fertilization process if adoption is not an option, I believe all fall within appropriate ethical boundaries. However, it is wrong to allow science to take an assembly line approach to the production of human embryos, the creation of which will be rooted in experimentation and destruction.

I proposed amendments to the bill by letter dated May 12, 2005 that would have allowed stem cell research to proceed within acceptable ethical boundaries. These changes would have maintained the Commonwealth's longstanding definition that life begins at conception; strengthened protections to prevent the exploitation of women; prohibited "embryo farming," or the large scale cultivation of human embryos for research through conventional fertilization; and banned the cloning of new human embryos solely for the purpose of experimentation.

These changes were not adopted and I therefore return Senate Bill No. 2039 unsigned.

Respectfully submitted,

MITT ROMNEY,

Governor.

A few days later, on May 31st, the Senate easily overrode the Governor's veto by a vote of 35–2. The vote was closer in the House: 112–42, but still enough to override the Governor's veto and make the bill law.

NOTES & QUESTIONS

1.   Gerry Brown's vetoes were almost never questioned once he was reelected to the governorship in 2011, yet Gov. Romney's vetoes were constantly threatened by the Democratic super-majority in the Massachusetts legislature. Like Gov. Brown in 1979, Gov. Romney was looking toward a presidential run. How much does perceived weakness or disinterestedness play into veto overrides?

2.   Could Gov. Romney have done more to affect the stem cell law? How?

2.   SIGNING STATEMENTS

THE PRESIDENTIAL SIGNING STATEMENTS CONTROVERSY

Ronald A. Cass & Peter L. Strauss, 16 *William and Mary Bill of Rights Journal* 11 (2007)

Presidential signing statements have come out of obscurity and into the headlines. Along with salutary attention to an interesting issue, the new public visibility of signing statements has generated much overblown commentary. The desire to make these little-known documents interesting to the public-and to score points in the inevitable political battles over any practice engaged in by a sitting President-has produced a lot of discussion that misleads the public and has tended to obscure the significant issues surrounding the use of signing statements. Reflection may help put the discussion in a more useful perspective.

I.   Signing Statement Basics, Constitutionality, and Interpretive Weight

A.   The Basics of Signing Statements

Presidential signing statements are formal documents issued by the President, after wide consultation within the executive branch, when he signs an enacted bill into law. They state the President's understanding of the legislation he is signing and also may give instructions to the executive branch regarding how the new law's provisions are to be treated. That is a positive development. While such views have been formulated throughout our history, only since Ronald Reagan's presidency have signing statements become readily available public documents. It is always useful for the citizenry (and Congress) to know how the executive branch understands the laws Congress enacts.

President Reagan's motivations for raising the visibility of presidential signing statements doubtless included increasing presidential influence within government and influencing the outcome of judicial proceedings when controversies about interpretation arose. Yet his use of signing statements was also understandable as a reaction to the increasing tendency of Congress, generally in the control of Democrats at the time, to present him with extremely complex bodies of legislation (notably, omnibus budget measures) that no President could reasonably be expected to veto even though they included occasional objectionable components among their hundreds of separate provisions.

Many of the provisions that have been addressed in signing statements from Reagan on reflect congressional initiatives that all Presidents find troubling. The recent GAO Report, for example, studied the signing statements accompanying eleven appropriations acts for Fiscal Year 2006. Of 167 provisions (out of several thousand) singled out for mention in these statements, 107 involved apparent requirements for congressional pre-approval of executive actions inconsistent with the Supreme Court's decision in *INS v. Chadha. Chadha*, of course, was decided early in the Reagan administration, and Congress's disregard of its teachings has been notorious; it is probably no coincidence that the increase in the use of presidential signing statements dates from this time.

One can identify three separate legal questions about the use of signing statements. The first and simplest is whether they are constitutional. The second would be what, if any, legal force such statements have when issued, in the courts or within the President's administration. Finally, and related to the second, is whether any of the particular uses of signing statements, on their individual merits, embody inappropriate views of presidential power or otherwise give rise to rule-of-law concerns. We have not the slightest doubt, on the first question, that signing statements are constitutional. The second and third questions are harder.

B.   The Constitutionality of Signing Statements

Although the Constitution says nothing about signing statements, it also is silent regarding the reports regularly written by congressional committees. The President takes an oath to support the Constitution and the laws of the United States and has clear authority to explain how he views the legislation he is signing or deciding not to sign, just as congressional committees have authority to explain their views on the legislation they send forward. His obligation to "take Care that the Laws be faithfully executed" clearly extends to the Constitution he has sworn to uphold as well as to statutes, and thus gives him authority to advise agencies how they may avoid constitutional issues lurking in the details of complex and generally desirable measures. Surely Congress, by burying objectionable detail in such a measure, as is increasingly its practice, cannot defeat this responsibility. Claims that signing statements, as such, violate the Constitution and transgress constitutional separation of powers are either silly or radically overbroad.

C.   The Legal Force of Signing Statements

This question has three related aspects: first, whether a view of statutory meaning expressed in a signing statement has evidentiary weight for an interpreter of the statute; second, whether, because this view comes from the President, it has the same kind of force for an interpreting court as is associated with certain agency interpretations under the decision in *Chevron U.S.A., Inc. v. Natural Resources Defense Council, Inc.*; and, third, whether the view expressed in a signing statement is binding on agency interpreters. The arguments in favor of these statements having legal, not merely evidentiary, force distinguish presidential signing statements interpreting law from the issues surrounding the use of legislative history. The prospect that signing statements could have such effects may also help explain concerns expressed by the ABA and other signing statement critics.

1. Evidence of Meaning

Viewed simply as evidence possibly bearing on statutory interpretation, the question respecting presidential signing statements' effect on judicial interpretation is largely the same as with congressional contributions to legislative history. The best evidence of what a law means almost always is the words used in the law itself. But the size, complexity, and mixed parentage of laws today sometimes produce text that, read literally, is difficult to credit as what could have been reasonably understood by those who enacted it. The words enacted into law, in other words, are either difficult to decipher without additional information or are seemingly at odds with what a reasonable, neutral observer would conclude was the meaning understood by those who enacted the law. At times, the law is ambiguous and the legislative history clears up a point. At other times, the law is clear enough and the legislative history is designed to revise the understanding in ways that never would have commanded majority support in the legislature-which is why lobbyists work so hard to have favorable language that could not make it into the law inserted into the history.

Presidential signing statements offer the same benefits and the same problems. They can assist in understanding a law, or they can state a view that, while capturing the President's view of good law, could never have commanded majority support in the legislature. Like legislative history, and unlike a veto override vote, there is no clear way of testing the congruence of the President's view with the congressional majority. Unlike much legislative history, the signing statement at least is likely to state the clear view of one essential player in the enactment of law.

Courts have developed principles of construction to sort through what weight to give text and history in particular contexts. These do not provide great clarity as to what courts, or even individual judges, will do in any given case. Nor is any set of general rules likely to be able to resolve the difficult issues respecting actual interpretation of law-that is why the canons of construction have been so effectively ridiculed for many years by Karl Llewellyn and many more. The point is not that there is a simple answer to the weight to be given presidential signing statements. The current practice of courts sensibly accords different weight to presidential signing statements in different circumstances. The recent GAO Report, for example, finds judges especially cautious where the President's stated view has obvious partisan overtones. The essential point respecting the evidentiary weight to be accorded presidential signing statements by courts charged with construction of the law is that the analysis presents problems quite similar to those associated with congressional legislative history.

2.   The *Chevron* Issue

Courts have said that when statutory language is ambiguous, and has been reasonably interpreted by an administrative agency charged to administer the statute, the courts must accept that interpretation rather than engage in their own independent analysis. Later decisions have qualified this principle as limited to interpretations that emerge from public procedures or other contexts in which Congress has clearly envisioned the responsible agency exercising such authority. But the exact contours of that limitation are anything but precise.

Given the current state of play on judicial deference to the executive branch's interpretations of law, one can imagine the government arguing that a signing statement announcing the President's reasonable interpretation of an ambiguous provision is entitled to the same treatment as an agency's. Yet such statements are not products of public procedures such as are used in agency notice-and-comment rulemaking. Thus, they would seem to fall outside the ambit of interpretations that the courts have recently identified as meriting strong judicial deference.

While this issue has yet to be presented, one Supreme Court decision from last year, upholding the Oregon assisted-suicide statute in the face of a similar kind of interpretation made by then-Attorney General John Ashcroft, suggests that the Court would not give the same deference to presidential signing statements as to interpretations contained in agency legislative rules. But three Justices dissented from that holding, and Justice Alito, who in other contexts has voted to uphold strong executive claims, did not participate. For one of us, the Court's 5–4 split during the current term in *Massachusetts v. EPA* was similar, giving no deference to, and indeed showing a degree of disdain for, an agency's interpretation despite statutory text committing the decision to the judgment of the agency administrator. We both agree that observers concerned about strong executive authority will be inclined to oppose Chevron use of signing statements.

3.   Intra-Executive Branch Instructions

Signing statements can be used within an administration to help resolve disputable questions of interpretation. There are many different executive officials who might have a hand in the implementation, and therefore the interpretation, of statutory instructions. A signing statement provides the President's direction on which interpretive turn to take. The question is how far the President can go in giving legally binding directions to other executive branch officers.

One increasingly prevalent view is that officials in cabinet departments and other governmental bodies are obliged to accept the President's interpretation of law in carrying out their duties, because as chief executive, he is entitled to give executive branch officials instructions of this sort. The President must appoint the most important governmental officials, is the person in whom executive authority is entrusted by the Constitution, and (for those holding this view) must also have unconstrained authority to remove executive officers who do not carry out their duties to the President's satisfaction. Because the Constitution vests the national government's executive authority in the President, everyone else in the executive branch derives executive authority from him. In short, according to this view, the President's interpretation governs within the administration because he is the boss. Under this view, cabinet officials and other executive officials are obliged to regard presidential interpretations stated in signing statements as legally binding upon them.

The opposing view is that although the Constitution does make the President chief executive, nonetheless (outside the military and foreign relations contexts) its text repeatedly imagines that legal responsibility for law administration will be placed in the hands of others. When Congress enacts statutes conferring regulatory authority, it generally confers that authority on an agency head, not on the President. In this view, his duties with respect to ordinary domestic administration are those of an overseer, not decider. Congress has more power to structure the instruments of government-it can, for example, limit the President's removal authority over regulatory officials to those who have given him "cause" for removal. Even where it has not done this, so that the President can remove from office anyone whose administration displeases him (as is the case for cabinet secretaries, for example), an administrator who sees the legal responsibility for particular decisions as his own, not the President's, may find it easier to resist presidential "instructions." And removal may carry a high political cost. Not only does the President invite conflict over his interpretation of the law-and possibly congressional efforts to revise the law in ways not congenial to the President-but the President also will have to get congressional approval of the successor he appoints.

People holding this view note the many historical struggles between Presidents and their appointees as evidence that there is at least an understood political cost to the assertion of strong presidential power over some officials and particularly over their interpretations of law. These commentators fear that if high officials believe that they have a legal obligation to let the President decide disputed points within their statutory responsibilities, the result will be a concentration of enormous power in one place and that the President may often be successful in exercising that power confidentially and without public process. This they see as the road to presidential tyranny. In this view, when statutes confer regulatory authority on agencies, not on the President, actual interpretation is the business of the agencies and outside the President's authority directly to determine.

Remarkably, the question just how strong is the character of our unitary executive remains contested after more than two hundred years. And that contest intimately connects with some aspects of the current signing statement controversy. The view that our Constitution creates a strong, unitary executive entails presidential control over interpretation of law. The confluence of Presidents' increased use of signing statements and the increasing attention to the strong unitary executive view thus helps explain the recent concern about signing statements-which then are not simply statements about the President's views but more directly instructions to subordinates about what to do.

Resolving the legal weight of signing statements turns in part on construction of the same constitutional material that is contested in disputes over the degree to which executive authority is unitary. But note that this is a dispute about the constitutional meaning of the presidency and not about signing statements as such; the same issues would attach to any presidential control efforts, whenever and however made. That they are made publicly, and at the very initial stages of law administration, which is in the nature of signing statements, is not in itself a source of concern; if anything, these two characteristics are of benefit to the country and to the Congress. The real questions concern the view of constitutional authority they may assert.

II. If the President Believes a Statute Is Unconstitutional, Must He Veto It?

Signing statements often raise questions about the constitutionality of the legislative elements they address, and a frequent criticism is that such doubts require not a statement (with accompanying declarations that the provisions are not to be enforced or respected) but a veto. The question here is what the President properly may do when he believes a statutory provision is contrary to constitutional command. This is a question of congruence with rule of law precepts, rather than with any express or implied constitutional limitation on the President. But it is a serious question in its own right.

One pole of the controversy is marked by the simple, sweeping assertion that the President should never sign legislation if he believes it has provisions that are unconstitutional. This is the analytical twin to the sweeping assertion of signing statements' unconstitutionality. It is similarly bold, broad, and wrong. Presidents, just as much as judges, are responsible for upholding the Constitution; they take an oath to do so. They have independent constitutional authority for asserting views of constitutional meaning. And, just like every other officer with similar constitutional authority, they are responsible for doing what best advances their view of constitutional command.

In a world of large, complex laws-some running to hundreds of pages-no official is tied to a simple, two-choice model of possible actions. Legislators need not vote against a large, complex law because they believe one of its provisions to be unconstitutional. They may support the law and trust that the problematic provision will not be enforced or will be struck down in court in an appropriate case. Judges, similarly, are not always required to invalidate in its entirety legislation that has one or two unconstitutional provisions. So, too, a President is not limited to either vetoing legislation that has one or two provisions he believes to be unconstitutional or signing it without objection. The President-like any individual legislator-might well decide that, on balance, a law is beneficial, even if he believes that one or more provisions violate constitutional strictures. The practical political reality is that Congress, ignoring common precepts like "single subject" rules, frequently deploys statutory complexity as a weapon against the veto; indeed, appropriations measures are often so prolix that no member of Congress is likely to know all that they contain, and individual members have been able to perpetuate a good deal of statutory mischief by manipulating this reality. And the Supreme Court, in Clinton v. City of New York, struck down a law that might have provided a realistic alternative means for dealing with these legislative abuses by giving the President line-item veto authority over certain spending provisions.

In our view, then, no President is bound simply to go along with every aspect of every statute he may sign into law. In taking care that the laws "be faithfully executed," the President is not obliged to assure the enforcement of elements of the laws that are contrary to constitutional command. Subject to reservations that the executive branch may not simply ignore whole statutory schemes of which it disapproves, decisions by the President and other executive branch officials respecting law enforcement generally warrant extraordinary deference by other branches. In this context especially, they should be expected to place constitutional command over legislative command. It is hardly surprising if the President is particularly concerned to protect the constitutional powers of the presidency and seeks to tailor executive branch implementation of laws accordingly. Our disagreements, really, are about what those powers are, not the instrument by which the President chooses to voice them.

So, for example, if Congress includes a legislative veto provision in a complex law-as it has done numerous times since the Supreme Court ruled such provisos unconstitutional in *INS v. Chadha*—the President might properly choose to sign the legislation, but also properly choose not to respect the unconstitutional legislative veto provision. In those circumstances, a signing statement indicating the President's view that the provision is unconstitutional advances rule of law interests. It puts others on notice of his intentions with respect to the law, accords with respectable views of constitutionality, and comports with institutional interests of the executive branch. All of those elements advance the predictability and legitimacy of the law. This has generally been the pattern of presidential uses of signing statements. The two of us have our disagreements about the views of the Constitution and executive authority these statements may express, but the objection, so far as there is one, is to the message, not the medium.

III. Occasionally, Signing Statements Are Misused

In our judgment, one use of presidential signing statements, in and of itself, undermines the rule of law. If the law put before the President is one that at its core would command conduct that the President believes to be unconstitutional, the President sends a clear message by vetoing the law-he is willing to stand on principle and reject legislation that is fundamentally not in line with his view of the Constitution. If the President signs such a law while suggesting that its core provisions are unconstitutional, he reduces the clarity and predictability of the law.

The line between the proper and improper uses of the veto versus signing statements obviously can be argued. There is no bright line dividing the good from the bad. None of the signing statements associated with the complex appropriations statutes recently studied by the GAO was bad, however; their very complexity and the all-or-nothing choice Congress gave President Bush about the veto made his use of signing statements to identify trouble spots acceptable whether or not we would agree (we do not) that all of the spots that he identified were properly called troublesome. But there are relatively clear examples of misuse of signing statements-uses that reduce the clarity and consistency of the law-from presidencies of the left and of the right.

Consider, for example, President Bill Clinton's signing of the Social Security Independence and Program Improvements Act of 1994, which made the Social Security Administration (SSA) an independent agency. Although the law made other changes, a central provision, widely noted in contemporaneous accounts, made the agency independent of the President. It gave the agency's single administrator a six-year term of office-longer than a presidential term-and provided that the administrator could be removed only for cause. President Clinton did not veto the law, but his signing statement indicated that he viewed this change as an unconstitutional encroachment on the power of the presidency.

Similarly, President George W. Bush chose to sign the Detainee Treatment Act of 2005, sponsored by Senators McCain and Graham among others, despite his clear disagreement with the law's core provisions. The Act recommits the United States to observance of the Geneva Conventions and other laws respecting torture and the humane treatment of prisoners. In signing the bill into law, President Bush expressed concern that it intruded on constitutionally preserved presidential authority and reserved the choice to refuse enforcement of key portions of the law. His objection was not to an incidental aspect of otherwise desirable legislation but went to the very heart of what Congress had done.

In both cases, the Presidents' decisions to sign the laws while condemning central provisions sent decidedly mixed messages, seeming to give with one hand and take back almost as much with the other. In the second case, this concern is compounded by the probabilities that presidential actions inconsistent with the statute will be taken out of public view and that judicial review of those actions is unlikely. A President convinced that the six-year term of the SSA Administrator was unconstitutional could anticipate both publicity and a judicial test of his view. But both actions are hard to defend as preferable to vetoes of legislation the President believes violates the Constitution at its core. Had they not had recourse to a signing statement publicly expressing their strong disagreement with the law, it is hard to imagine that the Presidents would have signed these bills.

Such uses of signing statements constitute the limited set that can properly be addressed under the heading of "misuse." We underscore, in light of other pronouncements about signing statements (and particularly pronouncements about the ABA's resolution on signing statements), that the misuse label properly attaches only to a small subset of presidential signing statements-and that it is important to avoid tarring other presidential signing statements with an overly broad brush.

Conclusion

After all is said and done, the presidential signing statement clearly should be understood to be an appropriate, often helpful-and certainly constitutional-tool of presidential participation in the process of enacting and enforcing our laws. Although a smaller set of signing statements accompany actions that are not consistent with rule of law values, and others express interpretations of questionable validity, the signing statement itself is implicated as a problematic device only when it lowers the cost of the offending conduct. This occurs when the President signs a law that he believes, in its core provisions, so fundamentally violates the

Constitution that he cannot with a straight face declare its constitutional merits outweigh its flaws.

The problem is not that the President says too much too often about the laws he signs, but instead that he reduces the clarity and predictability of the law if he signs legislation that he is declaring wrong at its core-and wrong in ways that, as an independent constitutional actor, he has an obligation to confront. Ultimately, it is the very fact of his independent constitutional authority that makes a subset of signing statements problematic-not because the President oversteps his bounds in saying so much but because he falls short of his obligation to the Constitution to veto laws that he believes stand primarily as vehicles for violating our most fundamental legal charter.

NOTES & QUESTIONS

1.   Prof. Christopher Bryant points out that 2006 "was the year of the presidential signing statement." This was because George W. Bush signed a defense appropriations bill into law but issued a signing statement declaring that the McCain Amendment, which prohibited "cruel, inhuman, or degrading treatment" of any persons in U.S. custody, would be construed "in a manner consistent with the constitutional authority of the President to supervise the unitary executive branch and as Commander in Chief . . . [in order to] protect[ ] the American people from further terrorist attacks." In effect, this statement reserved the President's right to authorize torture in situations concerning national security.

The American Bar Association's (ABA) appointed a task force to review and report on the use of signing statements. The task force characterized the use of signing statements as a threat to the rule of law and, in part, recommended creating a federal cause of action allowing a court to make a declaratory judgment on the legal validity of future presidential signing statements.

Prof. Bryant, however, argues, that a court-based solution would be "ill-advised and counter-productive." He argues Congress is in a stronger position to force the president to comply with the law and Constitution than the courts. Congress is clearly empowered to force the president to "take Care that the Laws be faithfully executed" through exposing wrongdoing, withholding appropriations, refusing to confirm appointees, taking adverse action on the president's agenda, failing to reauthorize executive agencies and programs, and ultimately through impeachment.

Courts, on the other hand, have less political legitimacy to challenge a presidential policy and usually cannot publicly defend their judgments in the media. Prof. Bryant argues that the ABA's proposal to ask the judiciary to review presidential signing statements, "would place an enormous weight on a slender reed." Worse, the existence of a judicial mechanism could supplant or stifle Congressional action and exacerbate Congress's tendency to neglect oversight of the executive. Christopher Bryant, "Presidential Signing Statements and Congressional Oversight," 16 *Wm. & Mary Bill Rts. J.* 169 (2007).

2.   Are signing statements a threat to the rule of law as the ABA declared? How should Congress deal with signing statements?

CHAPTER 5

CONSTITUTIONAL REQUIREMENTS
& CONSIDERATIONS

■ ■ ■

When legislatures at any level are considering legislation, they must conform to the constitutional provisions that require a certain procedure and may restrict the form of a bill. Some constitutions, such as the Massachusetts and the United States Constitutions place very few restrictions on the legislature or Congress other than that money bills must originate in the House of Representatives. In contrast, other states have adopted a variety of restrictions on legislative procedure, each to deal with perceived defects in the legislative system—corrupt practices, hidden agendas, and hastily crafted laws. The most common of these are original purpose clauses, single subject rules and clear title requirements. Many states also require bills to be considered for minimum amount of time, typically three days, in each chamber before final passage. Other states have even more restrictions on their legislatures. For example, the Nebraska Constitution requires that the legislature operate with the doors open and all votes be taken "viva voce," that is "in the living voice." The first section of this chapter will take common constitutional provisions and explore what they mean and how various states apply them.

One effect of these constitutional provisions is that statutes can be challenged in court as unconstitutional if the legislature does not follow the various provisions. An otherwise valid statute can be struck down for a "technicality." This creates an issue for courts—what evidence will the court consider when reviewing such challenges. The U.S. Supreme Court and several state supreme courts have adopted the "Enrolled Bill Rule," where the court will only strike down a statute if the constitutional violation is apparent within the enrolled bill. Over the years courts have created several other rules that allow greater evidentiary latitude. Some states now operate under the "Extrinsic Evidence Rule," that allows courts to review any evidence of a constitutional violation. Section II will discuss the Enrolled Bill Rule and its alternatives.

Finally, when legislatures consider new legislation, they are often faced with substantive constitutional issues. Since the issues are new and the law is developing, legislators are often faced with difficult issues that may pit public safety against individual rights or even various rights in conflict with each other. There may or may not be any judicial guidance for the legislature to rely upon, and a statute may be enforced for years before the provisions are challenged in court and are either upheld or struck down. How do legislators interpret their constitution and consider substantive constitutional problems?

A. PROCEDURAL REQUIREMENTS

STATE CONSTITUTIONS AND LEGISLATIVE PROCESS: THE ROAD NOT TAKEN

Michael E. Libonati, 89 *Boston University Law Review* 863 (2009)

The entrenchment in state constitutions of rules of legislative practice and procedure is among the most striking features of the evolution of state legislatures. The purpose of these regulatory provisions is more easily understood in light of their history. In early state constitutions, the legislature is typically afforded broad autonomy. Consider the following examples: "The Senate shall . . . determine its own rules of proceedings," and "The House of Representatives shall . . . settle the rules and orders of proceeding in their own house." Despite the promise of autonomy suggested by such language, the incorporation of rules of parliamentary law into state constitutions began early. The constitutional history of Pennsylvania illustrates this tendency. The earliest Pennsylvania Constitution, the "radical" constitution of 1776, contains several provisions designed to assure openness, deliberation, and accountability in governance by the unicameral legislature: a two-thirds quorum requirement for doing business; a provision calling for open sessions; weekly printing of votes and proceedings during session including recording "the yeas and nays on any question, vote or resolution where any two members require it"; and a provision requiring a formal enacting clause for all laws.

The distrust of the legislature, seen by Jacksonian democrats as an engine for churning out special privileges for interest groups, produced a wave of constitution-making in half of the states between 1844 and 1853. These reformers created "a blueprint for the due process of deliberative, democratically accountable government." These process reforms continued through the period 1861–1880, during which more than forty states revised old or created new constitutions. Professor G. Alan Tarr summarized these developments:

> In 1835 Alexis de Tocqueville observed that "the legislature of each state is faced by no power capable of resisting it." But beginning in the 1830s, state constitution-makers sought to impose limits on these supreme legislatures. Initially, their restrictions focused on the process of legislation. Some state constitutions required extraordinary majorities to adopt certain types of legislation, under the assumption that it would be more

difficult to marshal such majorities for dubious endeavors. . . . Other provisions required that the amendment or revision of laws not proceed by mere reference to their titles, that statutes be phrased in plain language, that taxing and spending measures be enacted only by recorded vote, and—most importantly—that no special laws be enacted where a general law was possible. By the end of the nineteenth century, most state constitutions included several of these procedural requirements.

The 1873 Pennsylvania Constitutional Convention, where the primary focus was legislative reform, illustrates Tarr's observations. That Convention created an interrelated set of provisions implementing a broad vision of deliberative democracy applicable to each phase of the lawmaking process from drafting legislation to final passage.

Most state constitutions do not follow the federal model, which has little to say about lawmaking procedures. Instead, like Pennsylvania's modern constitution, they incorporate most of the procedural norms that emerged during the nineteenth century. At the drafting phase, each bill must contain a title that "clearly expresses" the subject matter of the body of the proposed law. In addition to the title's notice function, each bill, except appropriations, is restricted to "one subject" in order to forestall "log-rolling" and to focus the legislature's attention on discrete policy issues. The rule that bills amending or cross-referencing existing laws must include the amended or referenced legislation in their text also furthers values of notice and clarity. Particular rules apply to drafting appropriations measures to ensure notice and bar log-rolling. An additional safeguard promoting clarity stems from the void-for-vagueness doctrine rooted in the due process clause of state and federal constitutions.

Constitutional rules of procedure were designed to promote accountability and enhance participation and deliberation. In the Pennsylvania constitutional model, the state house is directly accountable for originating revenue bills. The committee system is recognized and strengthened by the requirement that all bills be referred to a committee and printed. To prevent surprise and foster public notice, no bill can be altered or amended on its passage through either chambers as to change its original purpose, and every bill must be read at length and printed before the final vote.

Principles of accountability and majority rule are embedded in the requirements that a majority of the elected members of each chamber cast a recorded vote on every bill, that the presiding officer of each chamber authenticate by signature the fact that the measure was approved, and that the fact of signing must be entered in the journal.

One can, of course, view these procedural constraints as entrenching the path-dependent result of yesterday's controversies. A case can be made for the proposition that most of these provisions are failed efforts at legislative reform, unworthy of contemporary attention. In many states, judges have refused to enforce all but a few of these procedural constraints. This is because "a substantial number" of state courts adhere to the "enrolled bill rule" which prevents any evidence outside the text of the enrolled bill itself from being introduced as evidence showing constitutional violations of rules governing the process of enactment. Thus, rules concerning drafting such as the single subject and clear title rules are reviewable because a violation can be determined from the text of the enactment. But violations of majority vote, referral to committee, printing and reading, limited session, and similar procedural rules are not reviewable in a jurisdiction adhering to the enrolled bill rule. Even without the enrolled bill rule, a state court can refuse to enforce procedural rules by holding that judicial intervention violates separation of powers doctrine.

NOTES & QUESTIONS

1.   Although Professor Libonati points out that legislative process rules are often not enforced by courts, some courts have forcefully argued that constitutional provisions must be enforced. When deciding whether a statute was illegitimate because the legislature had not used the precise enacting clause wording found in the Tennessee Constitution the Tennessee Supreme Court wrote:

> Constitutions are expressions of the sovereign will of the people, the fountain of all power and authority. The several departments of the government are created and vested with their authority by them, and they must exercise it within the limits and in the manner which they direct. The provisions of these solemn instruments are not advisory, or mere suggestions of what would be fit and proper, but commands which must be obeyed. Presumably they are all mandatory. Certainly no provision will be construed otherwise, unless the intention that it shall be unmistakably and conclusively appears upon its face. The supremacy and permanency of republics depend upon the maintenance of the fundamental law, in its integrity, as written in Constitutions adopted by the people; and it is the solemn duty of all those temporarily vested with power, in all departments of the state, to do this. The necessities of a particular case will not justify a departure from the organic law. It is by such insidious process and gradual encroachment that constitutional limitations and government by the people are weakened and eventually destroyed. It has been well said:

>> "One step taken by the Legislature or judiciary in enlarging the powers of government opens the door for another, which will be sure to follow, and so the process goes on until all respect for the fundamental law is lost, and the powers of government are just what those in authority please to make or call them."

State v. Burrow, 11 Cates 376 (Tenn. 1907).

1. WHERE TO BEGIN? ENACTING CLAUSES

"The enacting clause of all bills shall be 'The People of the State of New York, represented in Senate and Assembly, do enact as follows,' and no law shall be enacted except by bill." NEW YORK CONSTITUTION Art. III § 13

"The legislative authority of this state shall be vested in a general assembly, which shall consist of a senate and house of representatives; and the style of every law shall be, 'Be it enacted by the General Assembly of the State of Iowa.'" IOWA CONSTITUTION Art. III § 1.

"The style of the laws shall be: The People of the State of Michigan enact." MICHIGAN CONSTITUTION Art. IV § 23.

STATE V. BURROW
Supreme Court of Tennessee
11 Cates 376 (1907)

Written laws, in all times and all countries, whether the edicts of absolute monarchs, decrees of King and Council, or the enactments of representative bodies, have almost invariably, in some form, expressed upon their face the authority by which they were promulgated or enacted. The propriety of an enacting clause in conformity to this ancient usage was recognized by the several states of the Union after the American Revolution, when they came to adopt Constitutions for their government, and without exception, so far as we can ascertain, express provision was made for the form to be used by the legislative department of the state in enacting laws. This was done in this state when it adopted a Constitution in 1796, and the same provision then made is to be found in our present Constitution, adopted in 1870. The purpose of provisions of this character is that all statutes may bear upon their faces a declaration of the sovereign authority by which they are enacted and declared to be the law, and to promote and preserve uniformity in legislation. Such clauses also import a command of obedience and clothe the statute with a certain dignity, believed in all times to command respect and aid in the enforcement of laws. These are the sole purposes of an enacting clause. It is not of the essence of the law, adds nothing to its meaning, and furnishes no aid in its construction. It is a form, but one that is necessary to be used in legislation.

JOINER V. STATE

Supreme Court of Georgia
223 Ga. 367 (1967)

UNDERCOFLER, JUSTICE.

Appellee filed a motion to dismiss the appeal in this case because the transcript of evidence was not filed within the time prescribed by law and no proper application for an extension of time was made.

. . .

[The trial court] Held:

The Appellate Practice Act of 1965 (Ga.L.1965, pp. 18, 21, 26) as amended requires the transcript of evidence to be filed within 30 days after the filing of the notice of appeal (Code Ann. s 6–806) or an application must be made within that period for an extension of time for such filing (Code Ann. s 6–804). This court has repeatedly held that the provisions of this Act are mandatory and unless complied with the appeal must be dismissed.

On March 30, 1967 the Governor approved what is termed the 'Appellate Practice Act of 1965 Amended. No. 114 (House Bill No. 157).' Section 3 thereof states, in part, 'An appeal shall not be dismissed nor consideration thereof refused because of failure of the court reporter to file the transcript of evidence and proceedings within the time allowed by law or order of court, unless it affirmatively appears from the record that such failure was caused by the appellant.' This purported amendment contains no enacting clause and the question arises whether this omission invalidates this purported amendment so that the Appellate Practice Act of 1965 as previously amended remains unchanged by it.

A study of this question reveals that, 'All written laws, in all times and in all countries, whether in the form of decrees issued by absolute monarchs, or statutes enacted by king and council, or by a representative body, have, as a rule, expressed upon their face the authority by which they were promulgated or enacted. The almost unbroken custom of centuries has been to preface laws with a statement in some form declaring the enacting authority.' It is interesting to note that the use of an enacting clause first appeared in the Acts of Parliament in 1433 and from the year 1445 it has continued to be a regular part of English statutes. 'The enacting clause is that portion of a statute which gives it jurisdictional identity and constitutional authenticity. The form is almost completely standardized beginning with, 'Be it enacted by,' and concluding with an identification of the legislative body from which the act emanates. The constitutions of forty-four (now 46) states specify the form of the enacting clause. Only the constitutions of Delaware, Georgia, Pennsylvania, and Virginia, as well as the Constitution of the United States, are silent on the point. * * * (and)

Congress, by statute (Act of Feb. 25, 1871, c. 71, 16 Stat. 431, 1 U.S.C.A. s 21) has provided a specific form of enacting clause.'

'The purpose of an enacting clause is to establish the act; to give it permanence, uniformity and certainty; to afford evidence of its legislative, statutory nature, and to secure uniformity of identification, and thus prevent inadvertence, possible mistake, and fraud.' Although though it might be argued that an enacting clause is a mere matter of form, a relic of antiquity, and serves no useful purpose, we think it is essential for the reasons just cited. Traditionally, the General Assembly of Georgia has used an enacting clause.

The necessity for an acting clause in an Act of the General Assembly has never been decided directly by this court but in *Walden v. Town of Whigham*, the court refused to give effect to a purported charter amendment of that town because the amendatory measure contained no enacting clause whatever and consisted merely of the caption of the act and a repealing clause. This case was later distinguished in *Fowler v. Stone* because the Act there involved was held to contain an enacting clause.

Accordingly, we hold that the 'Appellate Practice Act of 1965 Amended. No. 114 (House Bill No. 157).' is a nullity and of no force and effect as law.

NOTES & QUESTIONS

1.   In *State v. Burrow*, 11 Cates 376 (Tenn. 1907), the Tennessee Supreme Court examined a statute that did not precisely comply with the state's Constitution. Whereas the Constitution states, "The style of the laws of this state shall be, 'Be it enacted by the General Assembly of the state of Tennessee,'" the enacting clause of the disputed statute omitted the words "the state of." The court held,

> The only difference claimed by the petitioner to be in them is the omission in the latter of the words "the state of." We do not think that this constitutes an appreciable difference, but that they are, in fact and in law, the same—that they are absolutely synonymous.

> The sovereign authority they import is the same. They clothe the act with the same dignity, and are equally efficient to promote uniformity in legislation.

> It is impossible to point out in the form given in the Constitution any element of governmental authority, or shade of human thought, which is not contained in the enacting clause of the statute. No one can read the latter without being impressed with the fact that the statute purports to be enacted by the General Assembly of the state of Tennessee.

. . .

Can it, then, be said that the apparent omission of the three words, "the state of," which the human mind involuntarily and with absolute certainty supplies in reading the enacting clause of the statute, when all the purposes of the constitutional provision are accomplished, can have the effect to vitiate a law otherwise duly enacted by the General Assembly and approved by the Governor of the state? We think not. To hold that it did would be to sacrifice substance to the myth of noncompliance with a form in a matter where every purpose of the framers of the organic law had been fully effectuated. Such an absurd result was not intended and cannot be allowed. . . .

2.   In contrast, in *Mertz v. States*, 318 Ark. 390 (1994), the Arkansas Supreme Court held a proposed local ordinance violated the state constitution's enactment clause provision. Proponents argued that even though the ordinance did not include the constitutionally mandated language, but the petition was "in substantial compliance" with the constitution and a circuit judge found the petition's language was sufficient to inform potential voters of the source of the legislative authority being exercised. The Court found the constitutional requirements clear and without leeway.

3.   Should form be elevated to such a level that an otherwise valid statute becomes unconstitutional?

2.   ANTI-LOGROLLING PROVISIONS: ORIGINAL PURPOSE, SINGLE SUBJECT AND CLEAR TITLE

Many state constitutions include so-called anti-logrolling provisions. The Oxford English dictionary traces the use of the term "logrolling" back to the 1820s and defines it as, "The practice of exchanging favors, especially in politics by reciprocal voting for each other's proposed legislation." See, https://www.lexico.com/definition/logrolling. The most common anti-logrolling provisions are rules concerning protecting a bill's original purpose, requiring bills contain a single subject, and bills have a clear title. These provisions are generally found in constitutions written or re-written during the second half of the 19th century and early part of the 20th century and reflect a suspicion of the legislative process. While often discussed together, each of the requirements have different purposes, with different tests for compliance.

Original purpose provisions limit a legislature's ability to change a bill. Although these provisions generally allow amendments during the legislative process, the original purpose rule prevents a bill being changed to such a degree that legislators do not realize what they are voting into law. In theory, the rule protects the legislative process because legislators (and the public) can monitor the progress of a bill by title alone because the purpose of a bill will not change dramatically during the process. This rule also protects the rules governing the introduction of bills since new bills cannot come to a vote in the form of an amendment.

The single subject and clear title rules are often closely associated with each other, but with different legal requirements. The perception is that logrolling is easier in omnibus bills with many, often unrelated, provisions. Single subject requirements force legislators to vote on distinct measures based on the merits. By limiting the scope of bills, legislators can better understand and discuss the issues presented. Without such a rule, several measures, none of which have majority support—in other words classic logrolling—can become law. The single subject rule also protects the executive's role in the process by not forcing the governor to make an all or nothing choice on a complex bill. Clear titles have two purposes: to give notice to legislators and the public as to what provisions the bill contains, and prevent legislators from inserting unrelated matters into a bill. Both purposes theoretically safeguards openness and honesty in the legislative process. See, Martha J. Dragich, "State Constitutional Restrictions on Legislative Procedure: Rethinking the Analysis of Original Purpose, Single Subject, and Clear Title Challenges," 38 *Harv. J. on Legis.* 103 (2001).

PENNSYLVANIANS AGAINST GAMBLING EXPANSION FUND V. COMMONWEALTH

Supreme Court of Pennsylvania
583 Pa. 275 (2005)

CHIEF JUSTICE CAPPY.

In this matter, we are asked to resolve, inter alia, numerous facial constitutional challenges to the regularity of the procedures employed by the General Assembly in enacting Act 2004–71, The Pennsylvania Race Horse Development and Gaming Act (the "Gaming Act" or the "Act").

. . .

At the outset, it is important to make clear that we are neither passing on the wisdom of the substantive provisions of this Act nor on whether gaming in general is in the best interests of the citizens of our Commonwealth. These decisions are for the General Assembly. We are only considering the discrete legal issues that have been raised for our review primarily regarding the constitutionality of the procedure by which the General Assembly passed this piece of legislation.

The Complaint, as well as the brief of Petitioners, sets forth the material facts regarding House Bill 2330 of 2004 ("HB 2330") and the process by which that bill became the Gaming Act. Specifically, HB 2330 was introduced on February 3, 2004. It was titled "An Act Providing for the Duties of the Pennsylvania State Police Regarding Criminal History Background Reports for Persons Participating in Harness or Horse Racing." At this point in time, the bill dealt exclusively with the Pennsylvania State Police providing support to the State Harness and Horse Racing Commissions by performing criminal history checks and the verification of fingerprints of applicants for licensure under the Race Horse Industry Reform Act of 1981. It was one page in length. (H.B. 2330 Printer's No. 3251).

Thereafter, the bill went through three considerations in the House and two considerations in the Senate. In the last consideration in the Senate on Thursday, HB 2330 was again reported out of the Law and Justice Committee in the Senate. On July 1, 2004, the bill was presented to the Senate for a third and final consideration. In the Senate, Senator Tomlinson offered Amendment No. A3055 which amended HB 2330. HB 2330 was given a new printer number, Printer's No. 4272 (SLJ No. 45). After a number of unsuccessful attempts to amend the bill further, the bill was passed back to the House for acceptance or rejection. The bill was passed at approximately 2:00 a.m. on Friday July 2, 2004 (which was still considered the July 1, 2004 legislative session for purpose of computing legislative days). On July 2, 2004, HB 2330 was sent to the House with a Senate message and was referred to the House Rules Committee. On Saturday July 3, 2004, HB 2330 was reported out of the House Rules Committee, submitted to a vote in the House on a committed basis, was passed, and was signed in the House. On Sunday July 4, 2004, the bill was signed in the Senate. Governor Edward Rendell signed the bill into law on Monday, July 5, 2004, as Act 71 of 2004.

July 1, 2004, the content of the bill was amended. Additionally, the bill's title was changed to express the multiple amendments made to the bill. These amendments were extensive, increasing the length of the bill from one page to 145 pages which included seven chapters and 86 sections. The bill as amended included the creation of the Pennsylvania Gaming Control Board ("Gaming Control Board" or "Board"), the issuance of gambling licenses authorizing the creation of a variety of slot machine casinos, the generation and distribution of revenues from the licenses, the creation of numerous funds including the Gaming Fund, the Pennsylvania Horse Race Fund, the Gambling and Economic Development and Tourism Fund, the Property Tax Relief Fund as well as a Compulsive and Problem Gambling Treatment Fund. Additionally, the amended bill contained a chapter regarding administration and enforcement and provided for exclusive jurisdiction in our Court regarding disputes over the issuance of licenses and challenges to the Gaming Act.

On Saturday, July 3, 2004, the bill as amended was submitted to the House for a vote on a committed basis; the amended bill was passed and was signed in the House. The next day, on Sunday, July 4, 2004, the bill was signed in the Senate. On Monday, July 5, 2004, Governor Edward Rendell signed the bill into law as Act 71 of 2004.

Approximately five months later, on December 10, 2004, Petitioners filed their Complaint in which they alleged that the Gaming Act is unconstitutional since it was passed in violation of Article III, Sections 1, 3, 4, 6, and 10 of the Pennsylvania Constitution and is an unconstitutional delegation of power to the Gaming Control Board. Certain Respondents filed preliminary objections in the nature of a demurrer contending that the enactment of the Gaming Act did not violate our Constitution. The Gaming Control Board filed an answer to the Complaint, as well as an application for summary relief pursuant to Pennsylvania Rule of Appellate Procedure 1532(b), in essence, raising the same issues as were raised by the other Respondents in their preliminary objections.

. . .

Article III can be viewed as a constellation of constitutional requirements that govern various aspects of the legislative enactment procedure. Each of these provisions was born in a time in which Pennsylvanians were experiencing rapid growth economically and " 'wrenching' social change." An enormous growth in the corporate form of business organization led to significant concentrations of wealth and the corruption of numerous legislators. Corruption took the form of special laws legislation, logrolling, and arbitrary favoritism and was met with a demand for reform. The Constitutional Convention of 1872–73 was convened to reform corrupt legislative behavior, and to this end, the result was the constitutional strictures contained in Article III. Thus, while these changes to the Constitution originated during a unique time of fear of tyrannical corporate power and legislative corruption, these mandates retain their value even today by placing certain constitutional limitations on the legislative process.

Section I (A)

Specifically, Article III, § 3 of our Pennsylvania Constitution sets forth dual mandates for the General Assembly which prohibit the passing of a bill that contains more than one subject and requires that the subject be clearly expressed in its title. The focus of Petitioners' primary challenge is Section 3's single subject requirement.

> No bill shall be passed containing more than one subject, which shall be clearly expressed in its title, except a general appropriation bill or a bill codifying or compiling the law or a part thereof.

Petitioners merge their arguments regarding single subject and clearly expressed title. This is not necessarily surprising, as in *City of Philadelphia*, our Court indicated that these twin requirements are interrelated in that they both proscribe introducing measures into bills without providing reasonable notice of the same. Although interrelated, and Petitioners address these two aspects of Article III, Section 3 together in their brief, we will parse the arguments and consider the twin directives separately.

With respect to the single subject requirement, Petitioners argue that, in interpreting Article III, Section 3, in *City of Philadelphia*, our Court set forth the relevant standard to be utilized in determining whether the process by which a piece of legislation has been enacted withstands constitutional challenge. In sum, Petitioners maintain that the amendments to a bill must be "germane" to the bill's subject. Whether the subject matter is viewed as the Commonwealth's "Racehorse Industry" or "Pennsylvania Horse Racing Industry Development and Other Gaming," Petitioners assert that the germaneness test is not met and that by changing the bill to encompass more than one subject, the General Assembly violated Article III, Section 3.

Respondents counter that the Gaming Act does not violate Article III, Section 3 because the amendment made to HB 2330 was germane to the general subject of the bill. Respondents offer that amendments to bills are permissible when the amendments are germane to and do not wholly change the general subject of the bill. Indeed, Respondent's state that it is expected that legislation will be transformed during the enactment process. According to Respondents, courts have traditionally taken a broad view of the overall subject of a bill. Unlike the legislation at issue in City of Philadelphia, in which the vast subject of "municipalities" was rejected as overly broad for constitutional purposes, here, all provisions of the Gaming Act relate to the single subject of regulating gaming.

. . .

In broad terms, Article III's aim was to "place restraints on the legislative process and encourage an open, deliberative, and accountable government." More specifically, Section 3 was designed to curb the practice of inserting into a single bill a number of distinct and independent subjects of legislation and purposefully hiding the real purpose of the bill. Related thereto, the single subject requirement prohibits the attachment of riders that could not become law as is, to popular legislation that would pass. An additional benefit of the Section 3 requirements is that there will be a greater probability that a bill containing a single topic will be more likely to receive a considered review than a multi-subject piece of legislation. As we indicated in *City of Philadelphia*, the single subject requirement proscribed the inclusion of provisions into legislation with-out allowing for "fair notice to the public and to legislators of the existence of the same." Thus, reasonable notice is the key stone of Article III, Section 3.

While recognizing the importance of Section 3, we acknowledged that bills are frequently subject to amendments as they proceed through the legislative process and not every supplementation of new material is violative of the Constitution. Thus, "where the provisions added during the legislative process assist in carrying out a bill's main objective or are otherwise 'germane' to the bill's subject as reflected in its title," the requirements of Article III, Section 3 are met. Id. Article III, Section 3 must have, however, some limits on germaneness, for otherwise virtually all legislation—no matter how diverse in substance—would meet the single-subject requirement, rendering the strictures of Section 3 nugatory. As stated by our *Court in Payne v. School Dist. of Coudersport Borough* (1895), "no two subjects are so wide apart that they may not be brought into a common focus, if the point of view be carried back far enough." Thus, defining the constitutionally-valid topic too broadly would render the safeguards of Section 3 inert. Conversely, the requirements of Section 3 must not become a license for the judiciary to "exercise a pedantic tyranny" over the efforts of the Legislature.

In light of this tension, as well as the purpose of Article III, Section 3, our focus in *City of Philadelphia* fell upon whether there was a single unifying subject to which all of the provisions of the act are germane. While acknowledging that exercising deference by hypothesizing a reasonably broad topic was appropriate, to some degree, in determining whether the bill passed constitutional muster, the vast subject of "municipalities" stretched the concept of a single topic beyond the breaking point. Indeed, it was not apparent how the diverse subject-matter had a logical or legislative nexus to each other. Finding that, as virtually all of local government is a municipality, the proposed subject was simply too broad to qualify for single subject status for purposes of Article III, Section 3.8 Thus, we struck the statute as constitutionally infirm.

In contrast to *City of Philadelphia*, in the matter *sub judice*, there is a single unifying subject—the regulation of gaming. The single topic of gaming does not encompass the limitless number of subjects which could be encompassed under the heading of "municipalities." Specifically, HB 2330 sets forth the legislative intent of regulating gaming, creates the Gaming Control Board, establishes policies and procedures for gaming licenses for the installation and operation of slot machines, enacts provisions to assist Pennsylvania's horse racing industry through other gaming, and provides for administration and enforcement of the gaming law, including measures to insure the integrity of the operation of slot machines.

. . .

Section II

In addition to the single subject requirement, Article III, § 3, as noted above, also mandates that the subject of the bill must be clearly expressed in its title:

> No bill shall be passed containing more than one subject, which shall be clearly expressed in its title, except a general appropriation bill or a bill codifying or compiling the law or a part thereof. PA. CONST. art. III, § 3.

Petitioners first submit that the title of the one-page bill must be referred to in determining whether the current title is constitutionally defective. Petitioners then compare the title of HB 2330 as originally drafted with the new title as amended by the Senate. Combining concepts relating to clear expression of title with single subject and the overarching concept of germaneness, Petitioners assert that the "obliteration of the title and purpose of the 1-page act is fatal to the constitutionality of the amendment and re-moves any possibility that the amendment is germane to the purpose and subject of the 1-page act." Similarly, Petitioners maintain that "the change in titles, conclusively shows that § 1 and § 3 of Article III forbidding amendments which change a bill's purpose and deal with more than one subject have been violated."

Respondents argue that Article III, Section 3 requires that the title of a law indicate its contents so that the members of the General Assembly can vote on the legislation with circumspection. In sum, Respondent's agree that Article III, Section 3 prohibits a title from being deceptive. Respondents offer that as long as the title of the law indicates its contents, the bill satisfies its constitutional requirement of placing members of the General Assembly on notice so that they can vote on the legislation with consideration of its circumstances and consequences. Thus, according to Respondents, a violation of Article III, Section 3 occurs "only when (1) the legislators were actually deceived as to the act's contents at the time of passage; or (2) that the title on its face is such that no reasonable person would have been on notice as to the act's contents."

Applying this standard, Respondents maintain that there is no evidence that the title of HB 2330 was deceptive. There is no assertion that legislators actually were deceived as to the contents of HB 2330. Furthermore, the final title put reasonable persons on notice as to the contents of the Gaming Act. Thus, there was no constitutional violation of Article III, Section 3's clear title requirement.

As originally introduced, HB 2330 was entitled:

AN ACT PROVIDING FOR THE DUTIES OF THE PENNSYLVANIA STATE POLICE REGARDING CRIMINAL HISTORY BACKGROUND REPORTS FOR PERSONS PARTICIPATING IN HARNESS OR HORSE RACING

The Senate amended the title of the bill prior to passage and in doing so, as pointed out by Petitioners, incorporated no part of the original title:

AMENDING TITLE 4 (AMUSEMENTS) OF THE PENNSYLVANIA CONSOLIDATED STATUTES, AUTHORIZING CERTAIN RACETRACK AND OTHER GAMING; PROVIDING FOR REGULATION OF GAMING LICENSEES, ESTABLISHING AND PROVIDING FOR THE POWERS AND DUTIES OF THE PENNSYLVANIA GAMING CONTROL DEPARTMENT OF REVENUE, THE DEPARTMENT OF HEALTH, THE

OFFICE OF ATTORNEY GENERAL, THE PENNSYLVANIA STATE POLICE, AND THE PENNSYLVANIA LIQUOR CONTROL BOARD; ESTABLISHING THE STATE GAMING FUND, THE PENNSYLVANIA RACE HORSE DEVELOPMENT FUND, THE PENNSYLVANIA GAMING ECONOMIC DEVELOPMENT AND TOURISM FUND, THE COMPULSIVE PROBLEM GAMBLING TREATMENT FUND AND THE PROPERTY TAX RELIEF FUND; PROVIDING FOR ENFORCEMENT; IMPOSING PENALTIES; MAKING APPROPRIATIONS; AND MAKING RELATED REPEALS.

As noted above, Article III, Section 3, mandates that the single subject contained in a bill must be "clearly expressed in its title" In *Scudder v. Smith* (1938), we emphasized that the purpose of the clear title requirement was to "put the members of the Assembly and others interested on notice, by the title of the measure submitted, so they might vote on it with circumspection." "In essence, Article III, Section 3 prohibits legislative draftsmen from proposing acts with titles calculated to mislead and deceive [and] assures against the practice of the intentional masking of acts with misleading or 'omnibus' titles."

Our case law interpreting this constitutional provision also makes clear, however, that it is only reasonable notice that is required. We have held that while the Constitution requires that the title of the bill be clear, it "does not require a title to be an index or synopsis of an act's contents." Indeed, to require the title to catalogue every provision of a bill might not only make the title unworkably long, but might foster the very problems that the requirement was meant to prevent.

Based upon the purpose behind the clear expression of title requirement, as well as the practical realization that a title does not need to express each and every subtopic contained in the bill, we set forth the burden one must meet in order to sustain a constitutional challenge to the expression of title. "[O]ne who seeks to declare a title unconstitutional under this provision must demonstrate either (1) that the legislators and the public were actually deceived as to the act's contents at the time of passage, or (2) that the title on its face is such that no reasonable person would have been on notice as to the act's contents." Stated another way, a title will be held to be constitutional if it puts a reasonable person on notice of the general subject matter of the act.

Looking at the title of the Gaming Act, and comparing the substance of the Act to its title, we believe that Petitioners have failed as a matter of law to show that the title is violative of Article III, Section 3. There is no allegation that any legislator actually was deceived as to the contents of HB 2330. Furthermore, the title passes constitutional muster as it clearly puts a reasonable person on notice of the general subject matter of the Act. Specifically, the Act covers a variety of subtopics regarding the subject of gaming: the Gaming Control Board; Licensees; Revenues, including the establishment of a number of funds; administration and enforcement of the provisions of the Act; making appropriations, and repealing certain acts and parts of acts. Each of these primary subtopics is set forth in the title by clear expression.

Therefore, with the strong presumption regarding the constitutionality of legislation and considering the constitutionality of the Act with all doubts being resolved in favor of a finding of constitutionality, we hold that as a matter of law, the title of the Gaming Act puts reasonable persons on notice of the subject matter contained therein, and therefore, does not run afoul of the clear expression of title requirement found in Article III, Section 3 of our Constitution.

Section III

Next, Petitioners contend that the Gaming Act violates the "change in original purpose" prohibition of Article III, Section 1 of our Constitution. Specifically, Petitioners offer that case law suggests that Article III, Section 1 is aimed at deterring confusion, misconduct, and deception. Both the original title and the amended title are deceptive, according to Petitioners, and the deception is evidenced by the "means by which this bill was hastily pushed through both the Houses of the General Assembly." Related thereto, Petitioners assert that the House "was disenfranchised to the extent that virtually the entire bill could only be amended if the House rules were first suspended by a two-thirds majority vote of all members— a fact which resulted in the House being unable to amend this bill in any manner." In sum, Petitioners argue that it is "the 'ramrod' element of this bill [that] provides the confusion and deception element."

Suggesting that there is a lack of case law on Article III, Section 1, Petitioners point to case law from other jurisdictions in which legislation was found to be unconstitutional when an amendment to a bill changed its original purpose. Thus, because the General Assembly made numerous changes to the original bill that dealt with fingerprinting at racetracks, and according to Petitioners, changed the specific original purpose of the bill, it is violative of Article III, Section 1.

Respondents answer that the Gaming Act does not violate Article III, Section 1 because the original purpose of HB 2330 remained the same from inception to passage—to regulate gaming. While the bill was amended materially and expanded to contain additional topics, they all were related to the broad and original purpose of regulating gaming. Respondents maintain that our Court has been hesitant to strike legislation due to an alleged change in purpose. Recognizing that the legislative process often requires material changes to legislation during its passage, Respondents contend that our Court has held that an Article III, Section 1 challenge will be rejected if "the bill in final form, with a title that clearly stated its contents, was presented to each house for its consideration and adoption." The Gaming Act, according to Respondents, clearly passes this test, and even if the initial and finally passed versions of the bill are compared, the purpose, at its origin and final passage, were both to regulate gaming.

Article III, Section 1 provides that in passage through the legislative bodies, a bill shall not be altered or amended to change its original purpose: No law shall be passed except by bill, and no bill shall be so altered or amended, on its passage through either House, as to change its original purpose. PA. CONST. art III, § 1.

Contrary to Petitioners' assertions, our Court has spoken to the meaning of Article III, Section 1 and offered an analysis to be engaged in when considering a constitutional challenge based on this provision in *Consumer Party v. Commonwealth*. In that decision, the Court was faced with an attack on legislation that, as originally introduced, proposed changes to county codes relating to county officials of counties of the third through eighth classes. After submission to a committee, the legislation was amended significantly to contain substantially different provisions relating to the salaries and compensation of certain Commonwealth officials.

A unanimous Court, while stressing the mandatory nature of Article III, Section 1, set a very high bar for finding a violation of this provision. Our Court recognized the practical realities of passing legislation and narrowly focused the inquiry. It reached its decision that Article III, Section 1 was not violated, not by comparing the original purpose to the purpose at final passage, but by considering only the bill at final passage. Consistent with this concentration, our Court inquired as to whether the legislation put the members of the General Assembly and others interested on notice so that they could "act with circumspection." As stated by the Court, "here the bill in final form with a title that clearly stated its contents, was presented to each house for its consideration and adoption. Under these circumstances, there is no basis for sustaining a challenge under Article III, Section 1."

The Court went on to address the challengers' contention, like that argued by Petitioners *sub judice*, that the procedure utilized deprived other interested parties of notice and prevented members of the Legislature from voting with circumspection. The Court rejected this argument, focusing solely on the alleged deceptive nature of the final legislation:

> As noted the title and content of the legislation in final form were in no way deceptive. We will not assume that the majority of members in each house voting in favor of this legislation did not fully understand this piece of legislation. Implicitly, appellants are seeking to extend the language of Article III, section 1 to provide for a sufficient time frame during consideration of the

measure in its ultimate form for communication between the constituency and the legislator before a vote is taken. There is nothing in the language of Article III, section 1 that would support such an interpretation.

Thus, the Court strictly limited its review in a challenge brought pursuant to Article III, Section 1 by viewing the title of the legislation and its content in final form. Ultimately, the Court found that the legislation did not violate Article III, Section 1.

This limited construct employed by the Court in *Consumer Party*, however, has not always been strictly and faithfully followed by our lower courts. Indeed, the Commonwealth Court has considered a challenge under Article III, Section 1 by comparing the initial and finally passed versions of a piece of legislation. Furthermore, scholarship has criticized the narrow approach taken in *Consumer Party*.

Upon closer inspection of our now close to twenty-year-old decision, we find that the analysis offered in *Consumer Party* resembles the analysis set forth for reviewing challenges under Article III, Section 3 and fails to give full significance to the language employed in the constitutional provision itself—"change its original purpose." This verbiage certainly suggests a comparative analysis, that is, some form of comparison between an "original" purpose and a final purpose to determine whether an unconstitutional alteration or amendment has occurred so as to change the original purpose of the bill. It also suggests an aim broader than just ensuring that the title and contents of the final bill are not deceptive, but also includes a desire for some degree of continuity in object or intention. Accordingly, we believe that the language adopted by the conventioneers, as well as their purpose in adopting Article III, Section 1 counsel towards, and are best served by, an analytical construct that involves comparison between the original purpose and the final purpose of the bill, as well as consideration of whether the final bill and title are deceptive.

Thus, we now hold that a court entertaining a challenge to legislation under Article III, Section 1 must conduct a two-part inquiry. First, the court will consider the original purpose of the legislation and compare it to the final purpose and determine whether there has been an alteration or amendment so as to change the original purpose. Second, a court will consider, whether in its final form, the title and contents of the bill are deceptive.

Regarding the determination of the original purpose of the legislation, we recognize the realities of the legislative process which can involve significant changes to legislation in the hopes of consensus, and the "expectation" that legislation will be transformed during the enactment process. Furthermore, our Court is loathe to substitute our judgment for that of the legislative branch under the pretense of determining whether an unconstitutional change in purpose of a piece of legislation has occurred during the course of its enactment. For these reasons, we believe that the original purpose must be viewed in reasonably broad terms.

Consistent with our suggestion in *City of Philadelphia*, it is helpful for a reviewing court to hypothesize, based upon the text of the statute, as to a reasonably broad original purpose. Given this approach of considering a reasonably broad original purpose, the General Assembly is given full opportunity to amend and even expand a bill, and not run afoul of the constitutional prohibition on an alteration or amendment that changes its original purpose. The original purpose is then compared to the final purpose and a determination is made as to whether an unconstitutional alteration or amendment, on its passage through either house, has taken place so as to change its original purpose.

Regarding the second prong of this analysis, it will be for the court to determine whether in its final form, the title and contents of the bill are deceptive. If the legislation passes both the purpose comparison and deception inquiries, it will pass constitutional muster.

Applying this construct to the facts of the case, we first consider the original purpose of the bill, and do so in reasonably broad terms; we then compare the original purpose to the final purpose to determine if the purpose has changed. As introduced, HB 2330 provided the State Police with the power and duty to perform criminal background checks on, and identify through conducting fingerprinting, those applicants seeking a license from the State Horse Racing and State Harness Racing Commissions. Considering the original purpose in reasonably broad terms, we believe that here, and in this instance akin to our finding above regarding a single unifying subject, the original purpose of the bill was to regulate gaming. As finally passed, although significantly amended and expanded, we find that the primary objective of the legislation was to regulate gaming. Based on the above, we conclude that the bill was not altered or amended to change its original purpose.

As to the second prong of the analysis, we consider whether the title and the content of the bill in final form were deceptive. Consistent with our finding above regarding the sufficiency of the title, we find that the final title was not deceptive. It placed reasonable persons on notice of the subject of the bill. Furthermore, we find that while amendments to HB 2330 were substantive and came at the end of the consideration cycle, the contents of the bill were not deceptive.

Thus, recognizing that a statute must be upheld unless it clearly, palpably, and plainly violates the Constitution, we hold, as a matter of law, that the process by which HB 2330 became law did not violate Article III, Section 1's prohibition on alteration of amendment so as to change the original purpose of the bill.

NOTES & QUESTIONS

1.   Did the Pennsylvania Court's test undermine the constitutional protections?

2.   The Missouri Supreme Court recently considered whether its legislature followed the state constitution's single subject, title and original purpose provisions. In *Missouri Coalition For The Environment v. Missouri*, 593 S.W.3d 534 (Mo. 2020) a special interest tried to invalidate a statute regulating land purchases by state agencies. Although the Missouri constitutional provisions are very similar to Pennsylvania, the standards and effects on legislation are different.

On the single subject provision, the Missouri Court stated, "the test for whether a bill addresses a single subject is *not* how the provisions relate to each other, but whether the provisions are germane to the general subject of the bill. The provisions of the bill will be found germane to a single subject if 'all provisions of the bill fairly relate to the same subject, have a natural connection therewith or are incidents or means to accomplish its purpose.'" To make a determination, the Court looks at the title of the bill, and if the bill's original purpose is "properly expressed" in the enacted bill title, the title determines the bill's subject. In this case, the title "An act to repeal section 34.030, RSMo, and to enact in lieu thereof one new section relating to state purchases of land" revealed the single subject of the bill was "state purchases of land." The Court found that every bill provision was germane to state land purchases and has a "natural connection with and [is] incidental to accomplishing [a] single purpose." A person reading this title, therefore, would not be misled about the bill's subject.

The Court found that the clear-title requirement applied to the enacted bill, not the original. Further, the title is clear if it indicates generally the subject of the bill, "The title cannot be so broad as to obscure the contents or render the single-subject requirement meaningless. Neither can a title be so narrow or underinclusive that it describes certain particulars or details of the act rather than its broader subject with the result that some provisions of the act do not conform to the restrictions listed in its title." The Court had previously approved the title "relating to health services" since the title was "sufficiently specific to describe the subject of the bill without becoming too detailed."

Original purpose is "the general purpose of the bill," and while the details can change, if the purpose of the originally introduced bill is the same as the final version, the Constitutional provision is satisfied. The original purpose is determined through the provisions of the bill and does not have to be found in the title or anywhere else. This is especially true since the title can change during the process. Further, the purpose should not be confused with a "bad or secret motive" on behalf of the legislature to pass a bill. As a result, the Court acknowledged that it rarely invalidates legislation due to an original purpose challenge.

3.   Professor Libonati argues that state constitutional procedural constraints entrench "the path-dependent result of yesterday's controversies" and many are "failed efforts at legislative reform." Often, judges refuse to enforce the provisions due to "enrolled bill rule" limits on the evidence a court may consider that would prove a constitutional violation concerning the process of enactment. While single subject and clear title rule violations can be proven through the text of the enactment, violations of majority vote, referral to committee, printing and reading, and limited session violations are not reviewable in an enrolled bill jurisdiction. Other courts may refuse to enforce legislative procedural rules due to the separation of powers doctrine. See, Libonati, "State Constitutions and Legislative Process: The Road Not Taken," *89 B.U. L. Rev.* 863 (2009). The enrolled bill doctrine is examined at length below.

In fact, state courts uphold legislation against procedural challenges "more often than not." For example, from the 1970s until 2000, the Minnesota Supreme Court decided only five single subject/clear title cases and upheld the statute in all of the cases. In contrast, in *People v. Cervantes*, the Illinois Supreme Court struck down the entire Safe Neighborhoods Law for violation of the single subject restriction—five years after the statute went into effect. The Illinois Legislature passed this Act on neighborhood safety problems such as gangs, drugs, and guns, but included provisions on the Women, Infants, and Children (WIC) nutrition program, and the licensing of secure residential youth care facilities. The Illinois Supreme Court found no logical connection between those provisions and the rest of the Act. The Court declared the entire act unconstitutional leading to the dismissal of the defendant's gunrunning charge and led to prosecutors dropping many other firearms charges. Given political changes to the Illinois Legislature over five years, it could not reenact the gun control provisions of the original Safe Neighborhoods Law. See, Martha J. Dragich, "State Constitutional Restrictions on Legislative Procedure: Rethinking the Analysis of Original Purpose, Single Subject, and Clear Title Challenges," 38 *Harv. J. on Legis.* 103 (2001).

Should courts be more aggressive in these cases? What are the advantages and disadvantages of each approach?

4.   Is logrolling even a bad thing? In "Single Subject Rules and the Legislative Process," 67 *U. of Pitt. L. Rev.* 803 (2006), Professor Michael D. Gilbert argues that it benefits the legislators and courts should be more accepting of the practice.

If logrolling were always detrimental, then a flat ban on it would be sensible. If logrolling were always beneficial, then a ban would be misplaced. In reality, logrolling is probably in between. Sometimes it helps, and sometimes it hurts. This would not present a problem if courts had perfect information and judicial review was costless. Judges could distinguish between beneficial and harmful logrolls and only strike down the latter. Time spent on filtering logrolls would not be socially costly. Of course, these conditions do not hold. An act that looks harmful may be integral to the subsequent passage of an act that generates substantial social returns. Striking down the first act could scuttle the deal. Alternatively, legislation that seems sound could, due to shifts in the many variables that affect public policy, yield social losses. Indeed, the very terms beneficial and harmful imply a metric for sorting good laws from bad ones. But is that metric based on utility maximization, satisfaction of preferences, equity, efficiency, or something else? And over what timeframe would the metric be calculated? Because of these intractable information problems, there is no reason to suppose that courts can accurately distinguish between beneficial and detrimental logrolls. Thus, there is no reason to suppose that case-by-case judicial review will produce a social benefit.

The key, then, is to adopt a presumption about logrolling that minimizes overall social costs. If, on average, logrolling produces a social benefit, broadly defined, then courts should presume that every instance of logrolling is allowable, since they cannot tell which logrolls produce a benefit and which do not. If, on average, logrolling causes harm, and if the benefits of judicial review outweigh the costs, then logrolling should be banned, and courts should review legislation and strike down logrolled bills.

I argue that courts should adopt a presumption in favor of logrolling. They should assume that logrolling on the whole is socially beneficial, and therefore individual logrolled bills are constitutionally sound.

3.   MOVING TOO QUICK? THE THREE-DAY RULE

YOUNGSTOWN CITY SCHOOL DISTRICT
BOARD OF EDUCATION V. OHIO

Supreme Court of Ohio
161 Ohio St. 3d 24 (2020)

O'CONNOR, C.J.

In this appeal, we are asked to determine whether 2015 Am.Sub.H.B. No. 70 ("H.B. 70") or the process by which it was enacted violates the Ohio Constitution. For the reasons explained below, we hold that the bill does not usurp the power of city school boards, as alleged, in violation of Article VI, Section 3 of the Ohio Constitution and that it received sufficient consideration for purposes of Article II, Section 15(C). Thus, we affirm the judgment of the Tenth District Court of Appeals.

I.   FACTS AND PROCEDURAL BACKGROUND

On February 18, 2015, H.B. 70 was introduced in the Ohio House of Representatives. As introduced, the bill's purpose was to enact new sections within R.C. Chapter 3302 to authorize school districts and community schools to create community learning centers at schools where academic performance is low. The bill defined a "community learning center" as a "school * * * that participates in a coordinated, community-based effort with community partners to provide comprehensive educational, developmental, family, and health services to students, families, and community members during school hours and hours in which school is not in session." H.B. 70, Section 1. The bill as introduced was ten pages long.

That day, February 18, the House considered H.B. 70 for the first time. On February 25, 2015, the House considered the bill a second time and referred it to the House Education Committee. On May 19, 2015, the House considered the bill a third time and then passed it.

The bill was introduced in the Senate and considered for the first time on May 20, 2015. On May 27, 2015, the Senate considered the bill a second time and referred it to the Senate Education Committee.

On June 24, 2015, the Senate Education Committee reported the bill back to the Senate with two amendments. One amendment expanded the definition of facilities that were eligible to become community learning centers, and the other modified the structure of academic-distress commissions under existing law. When it was reported out of committee, the bill had increased from 10 to 77 pages. A significant portion of the amended bill consisted of revisions to the existing law on academic-distress commissions, including the requirement . . . that for any district that has received an overall grade of "F" on its state report card for three consecutive years . . . a commission must appoint a chief executive officer who has "complete operational, managerial, and instructional control" over the district. The final bill still provided for the creation of community learning centers—the original focus of H.B. No. 70.

The entire Senate considered H.B. 70 for the third time later that day. The Senate adopted two additional but substantially shorter amendments on the Senate floor. One amendment set forth a residency requirement for at least one of the members of an academic-distress commission. The second amendment clarified that a chief executive officer for a school district appointed by an academic-distress commission would serve at the pleasure of the commission. After adopting the amendments, the Senate passed the bill.

The House received the Senate's version of the bill on the same day that the Senate passed it. The House voted to concur in the Senate's amendments to the bill. Governor Kasich then signed the bill into law, and the legislation became effective October 15, 2015. H.B. 70 remained 77 pages in its final form.

        . . .

The Youngstown School Board sought this court's discretionary review, and we accepted the following propositions of law for review:

> The Ohio Constitution's Three Reading Rule is a mandatory provision. A bill allowing school boards and communities to jointly provide supportive services to schools that is transformed overnight into an amended bill imposing the installation of unelected CEOs imbued with complete operational, managerial, and instructional control of school districts must comply with the Three Reading Rule.

> Am. Sub. HB 70, which radically amended R.C. 3302.10 to include the appointment of an unelected chief executive officer who is vested with complete operational, managerial, and instructional control of a school district, usurps the powers of elected boards of education in violation of Ohio Constitution Article VI, Section 3.

II. ANALYSIS

We must determine whether H.B. 70 or the process by which it was enacted violates the Ohio Constitution. This case is readily resolved by application of existing standards.

A. The Three-Consideration Rule

The first proposition requires us to consider the three-consideration clause of the Ohio Constitution, which states:

> Every bill shall be considered by each house on three different days, unless two-thirds of the members elected to the house in which it is pending suspend this requirement, and every individual consideration of a bill or action suspending the requirement shall be recorded in the journal of the respective house.

Article II, Section 15(C), Ohio Constitution. We have held that "where it can be proven that the bill in question was not considered the required three times, the consequent enactment is void and without legal effect." *Hoover v. Franklin Cty. Bd. of Commrs. (1985)*. However, the bill need not contain exactly the same language in each of the three readings to be valid. "[A]mendments which do not vitally alter the substance of a bill do not trigger a requirement for three considerations anew of such amended bill. But, '[w]hen the subject or proposition of the bill is thereby wholly changed, it would seem to be proper to read the amended bill three times, and on different days * * *.' "

We later characterized a vitally altered bill as one "departing entirely from a consistent theme." *State ex rel. Ohio AFL-CIO v. Voinovich (1994)*. However, we recognized that we "would be setting dangerous and impracticable precedent" by identifying a bright line distinguishing bills that are heavily amended from those that are vitally altered. Instead, we explained that a court's key consideration should be whether the bill maintained a common purpose both before and after its amendment.

In *Voinovich*, we concluded that a bill retained its common purpose, despite heavy amending, when the bill began as a 4-page-long biennial appropriation for the Bureau of Workers' Compensation but eventually passed with 20 pages of amendments that replaced the five-member Industrial Commission with a three-member one and changed various substantive and procedural laws relating to workers' compensation. We held that these amendments could be distinguished from the ones in *Hoover*, a case in which we had held that a bill was vitally altered because it had been introduced to enact provisions related to criminal nonsupport but was amended to enact provisions related to the financing, acquisition, and construction of nonprofit hospital and healthcare facilities.

In this case, the parties do not contest that each chamber considered H.B. 70 on three different days, and no party argues that there was a vote to suspend the three-consideration requirement. The Youngstown School Board contends that the three considerations of the bill by each chamber do not pass constitutional muster, because the bill that the House considered on all three occasions and that the Senate considered on the first two occasions was materially different than the bill that the Senate considered on the third occasion and that the House ultimately passed. The state counters that the bill that was originally introduced had the same common purpose as the bill that was eventually passed: improving education in underperforming school districts.

We agree with the state. The versions of H.B. 70 as introduced and as enacted had a common purpose of seeking to improve underperforming schools, even though there are differences in the tools through which each version pursued that goal. Despite the introduced and enacted bills' differences, they are more similar to the bills at issue in *Voinovich*, in which we found no vital alterations, than to the ones in *Hoover*, in which the bill had been vitally altered. Specifically, when first introduced, the bills in *Voinovich* and the present case started out with a relatively minor proposed change. In *Voinovich*, the proposed bill was to appropriate funding for the Bureau of Workers' Compensation, and in this case, the proposed bill introduced community learning centers as a tool to improve underperforming schools. Both bills then underwent substantial changes. In *Voinovich*, the enacted bill changed procedures for the adjudication of workers' compensation claims, and in this case, the enacted bill changes the process for outside intervention in an effort to improve underperforming schools. However, in both *Voinovich* and the present case, the themes of the bills as introduced and as enacted were consistent. Furthermore, in this case, the text of the bill as introduced remained in the enacted bill. The changes were therefore not in theme or even in purpose but simply in the method chosen to pursue the General Assembly's goals. That stands in stark contrast with the bills at issue in Hoover, in which the themes and purposes of the bill as introduced and as enacted were entirely different and none of the original text remained in the final wording.

We are sympathetic to the Youngstown School Board's argument that the process here was different than in *Voinovich*. In *Voinovich*, we recognized that although the bill was heavily amended between readings, "both houses deliberated * * * for several months. Hearings were held" and the governor announced that "he would veto any appropriations bill that did not also substantially reform the underlying workers' compensation system." By contrast, here, the evidence establishes that the Senate Education Committee reported out a heavily amended H.B. 70 on June 24 and the House and Senate passed that amended version on the same day. However, the three-consideration rule does not require any specific level of deliberation or debate as long as the bill is not vitally altered, and this court has explained that it will not put itself "in the position of directly policing every detail of the legislative amendment process when bills are passed containing a consistent theme."

Similarly, the three-consideration rule does not allow this court to consider the legislative proceedings leading to an amendment. A substantial portion of the first dissenting opinion is devoted to recounting the "clandestine" process that led to the enactment of H.B. 70, but the law, including our precedent, limits our review of the bill. It is not our role to police how the amended language came into existence. . . .

DONNELLY, J., dissenting.

Article II, Section 15(C) of the Ohio Constitution declares that "[e]very bill shall be considered by each house on three different days * * *." Today, a majority of the court discards the three-consideration rule set forth in the Constitution and accepts in its place the far less bothersome rule of one-and-done. In an egregious display of constitutional grade inflation, the majority gives passing marks to an act that was not considered three times by either house.

Indeed, this is more like a tale of two bills. One bill, as introduced in the Ohio House of Representatives, authorized local school districts to establish community learning centers as an additional local resource. That bill received due consideration by both houses of the legislature. The other bill, offered at the 11th hour, provided for a state takeover process aimed at underperforming public schools throughout Ohio. Those material alterations, which were bootstrapped to the original bill, were considered once by the Senate on June 24, 2015, and, through political muscle and partisan control, were thereafter passed by the Senate and concurred to by the House that same day. By any fair measure, the amendments added by the Senate at the 11th hour did not receive the requisite three considerations in either house.

In my view, the enactment of Am.Sub.H.B. No. 70 woefully fails to meet the letter or the spirit of the three-consideration rule. Yet, regrettably, in its willful disregard of the facts and superficial treatment of precedent, a majority of the court hands out a passing grade. Because I believe that facts and precedent dictate that the 2015 enactment of Am.Sub.H.B. No. 70 is unconstitutional, I vehemently dissent.

. . .

As articulated by Justice Douglas in his concurring opinion in *Hoover*, "the purpose of the 'three reading' rule is to prevent hasty action and to lessen the danger of ill-advised amendment at the last moment. The rule provides time for more publicity and greater discussion and affords each legislator an opportunity to study the proposed legislation, communicate with his or her constituents, note the comments of the press and become sensitive to public opinion."

. . .

[T]he only amendment to H.B. No. 70 occurred just prior to its third consideration in the Senate, when the 10-page community-learning-centers bill ballooned by operation of Am.Sub.H.B. No. 70 into a 77-page academic-distress-commission state-takeover bill. The Senate then considered and immediately passed the bill, sending it that same day to the House, where it was rushed to a vote and passed on party lines over strenuous objections, all within a span of approximately 12 hours.

There were no hearings on the amendment. There was no public debate on the amendment. Far from stimulating open discussion about his plans, the governor and the staff of the Department of Education operated in complete secrecy in order to conceal the state-written takeover plan. There was no announcement to the press. The legislators had no opportunity to study the proposed legislation, much less communicate with their constituents to determine their reactions to the proposed amendment. This is precisely the kind of "hasty action" taken "at the last moment," that the three-consideration rule should guard against.

I am sorely distressed that this court has missed the opportunity to uphold fundamental principles of the Ohio Constitution—principles that must not be swept aside in a rush to pass hasty legislation. The wise framers of the Constitution carefully fashioned checks and balances that are a cornerstone to our democratic system and that provide for good governance. The intent of the framers of the Constitution should guide this court.

Here, the history of the Constitution shows that the language was amended in 1973 to change the requirement from "[e]very bill shall be fully and distinctly read on three different days * * *" to "[e]very bill shall be considered by each house on three different days * * *." They rejected proposals to eliminate the three-reading rule from the Constitution and leave it to legislative rule. The drafters understood the three-consideration rule to be a safeguard against hasty action and the courts are the means to enforce that safeguard.

. . .

Today's decision sets a new low for constitutional compliance with Article II, Section 15(C) of the Ohio Constitution. For all the talk about academic distress, it is sadly our constitutional form of government that is in distress by this decision. The state legislature could honor our Constitution simply by applying its legislative requirements as they are written. It failed. Likewise, this court could honor our Constitution simply by applying its terms as they are written. It too has failed. I cannot and will not join in this travesty of justice. I dissent.

NOTES & QUESTIONS

1.   Do you think the House was surprised by the extensive amendment the Senate added? Would more time have made a difference?

2.   Recall the fact pattern in *Pennsylvanians Against Gambling*, where the legislature radically changed a bill over the course of Fourth of July weekend. The petitioners claimed the Senate amended bill was so fundamentally different from the original House bill that had five readings was effectively a different bill. Therefore, the final bill was not considered on three separate occasions by each house. The Court rejected this argument, "[A]n amended bill need not be referred to committee and considered on those separate days if the amendments are germane to, and do not wholly change, the general subject of the bill."

3.   The California Constitution mandates an even longer period of consideration for bills—31 days, unless 3/4ths of the legislators in that chamber agree to a shorter period. In addition, bills may not be passed without publishing the final language, including all amendments, on the internet for at least 72 hours. See, CALIFORNIA CONST. Art. IV § 8.

4.   WHO CONTROLS THE PURSE? THE ORIGINATION CLAUSE AND MONEY BILLS

"All Bills for raising Revenue shall originate in the House of Representatives; but the Senate may propose or concur with Amendments as on other Bills."—U.S. CONST. Art. I § 7

OPINION OF THE JUSTICES TO THE HOUSE OF REPRESENTATIVES

Supreme Judicial Court of Massachusetts
471 Mass. 1201 (2015)

To the Honorable the House of Representatives of the Commonwealth of Massachusetts:

The undersigned Justices of the Supreme Judicial Court respectfully submit this response to the questions set forth in an order adopted by the House of Representatives on May 22, 2015 and transmitted to us on that date. The order poses five questions concerning the State budget legislation for fiscal year 2016. All of the questions involve Part II, c. 1, § 3, art. 7, of the Massachusetts Constitution, which we will refer to as the origination article. They ask, among other things, whether certain provisions in the House budget bill rendered it a "money bill" within the meaning of the origination article, and whether the Senate improperly "originated" a money bill in violation of this article.

As explained below, we are of the view that the House bill was a money bill, and that the Senate did not improperly originate a money bill.

[Note: In March 2015, the Governor filed his recommended budget for fiscal year 2016, which included a provision delaying the application of a certain tax deduction for one year. When the House passed its budget (House No. 3401), it included both the tax deduction delay (§ 48), and an expanded land tax credit (§ 76). The Senate passed its own budget (Senate No. 3), which included the delayed deduction provision, as well as provisions that expanded the earned income tax credit and increased the personal exemption (§ 31D) and to increase the excise tax on some flavored tobacco products (§ 34A). As typical, the two versions of the budget went to a conference committee. At that stage the House voted to ask if the Senate's amendments violated the origination clause.]

By its order dated May 22, 2015, the House has posed the following five questions to us:

"1. Does an amendment to an existing session law postponing the effective date of a previously enacted tax expenditure, as set forth in section 48 of House No. 3401, render House No. 3401 a 'money bill' pursuant to Part II, c. 1, § 3, art. 7, of the Constitution of the Commonwealth?

"2. Does an amendment to an existing General Law increasing the expenditure of tax credits as set forth in section 76 of House No. 3401, render House No. 3401 a 'money bill' pursuant to Part II, c. 1, § 3, art. 7, of the Constitution of the Commonwealth?

"3. If the answers to question 1 and question 2 are in the negative, would it be violative of Part II, c. 1, § 3, art. 7, of the Constitution of the Commonwealth for the Senate to 'transfer money or property from the people to the State' by initiating the repeal of the current statutory mechanism requiring the tax rate on personal income be set at 5% upon satisfaction of certain fiscal requirements and replacing that reduction mechanism with a permanently fixed tax rate on personal income of 5.15% as set forth in section 31D of Senate No. 3?

"4. If the answers to question 1 and question 2 are in the negative, would it be violative of Part II, c. 1, § 3, art. 7, of the Constitution of the Commonwealth for the Senate to 'transfer money or property from the people to the State' by initiating a new tax on certain tobacco products as set forth in section 34A of Senate No. 3?

"5. If the answer to question 1 or question 2 is in the affirmative, does the substitution by the Senate of the text of Senate No. 3 for the text of House No. 3401 result in the Senate originating a money bill in violation of Part II, c. 1, § 3, art. 7, of the Constitution of the Commonwealth?"

The House order expresses grave doubt as to whether its budget bill, House No. 3401, as engrossed and transmitted to the Senate, was a "money bill" for purposes of the origination article; as to whether the Senate had the authority to insert its tax-related provisions into the bill that originated in the House; and as to the constitutionality of the Part B income tax provision and the flavored cigar excise provision in the Senate bill if enacted into law.

. . .

Questions 1 and 2. The first and second questions submitted to us ask whether the delayed FAS 109 deduction provision and the conservation land credit provision, respectively, render House No. 3401 a "money bill." For the reasons we describe, we conclude that House No. 3401 is, indeed, a money bill.

The origination article has provided since the inception of our Constitution that "[a]ll money bills shall originate in the house of representatives; but the senate may propose or concur with amendments, as on other bills." This provision grew out of the ancient English tradition regarding taxation, that "all grants in Parliament of subsidies to the King must begin in the House of Commons" and not in the unelected House of Lords. Comparable provisions have been adopted by approximately twenty States. The United States Constitution, too, contains an "origination clause," art. I, § 7, cl. 1, of the United States Constitution, which was modeled on our own. Although the Federal courts' decisions interpreting the Federal origination clause do not bind us, we have given careful consideration to those decisions when construing our own origination article, given that the two provisions are similarly worded and were adopted almost contemporaneously.

The Justices of this court have discussed the meaning of the term "money bill" on three prior occasions. In our earliest reported advisory opinions, the Justices stated that an examination of valuation reports prepared by the towns and plantations of the Commonwealth was not a money bill and, therefore, not subject to the origination article. One century later, the Justices opined that the origination article does not apply to "bills that appropriate money from the Treasury of the Commonwealth to particular uses of the government, or bestow it upon individuals or corporations," rather, it is "limited to bills that transfer money or property from the people to the State."

The Justices analyzed the scope of the origination article most recently in 1958, providing an advisory opinion to the Senate concerning a bill designed to permit the Commonwealth to maintain railroad passenger services on a segment of the former Old Colony lines. The funding for costs entailed by that bill was to be raised by local property taxes and by assessments on certain cities and towns. The Justices noted that the Federal origination clause "has not been understood to extend to bills for other purposes which incidentally create revenue." Reasoning that "[s]uch taxes as are imposed locally [by the bill] to reimburse the Commonwealth for expenditures made by it are purely incidental to the main objects of the bill," the Justices concluded that the origination article did not apply.

With this background in mind, we come to the view that House No. 3401 is a money bill subject to the origination article. For one, the delayed FAS 109 deduction provision effectively increases the amount of tax revenue that the Commonwealth will realize from certain corporations in fiscal year 2016, by making those corporations ineligible for a tax deduction in that year. By dint of this provision, House No. 3401 is a money bill within the narrow meaning that the Justices have ascribed to this term in the past: it "transfer[s] money or property from the people to the State."

The conservation land credit provision also affects the amount of tax money that will be transferred from the people to the Commonwealth. That provision reduces the Commonwealth's expected tax revenue, by raising the maximum tax credit that may be claimed by taxpayers donating certain land to conservation agencies. The question thus arises whether a bill concerning the "transfer [of] money or property from the people to the State" is a money bill even where it causes the amount of revenue being transferred to the State to be less than it would have been under the preexisting legislative scheme. We note that the United States Supreme Court has not addressed this issue under the Federal origination clause. The majority of United States Circuit Courts of Appeals have held that "all legislation relating to taxes (and not just bills raising taxes) must be initiated in the House." Given that the delayed FAS 109 deduction provision increases the Commonwealth's anticipated tax revenue for the upcoming fiscal year and thereby renders House No. 3401 a money bill, we do not express a view on this issue under our own origination article.

As previously mentioned, a bill devoted to another purpose or purposes that "incidentally create[s] revenue" is not a money bill. For two reasons, we do not view House No. 3401 as such a bill. First, the types of bills that we and the United States Supreme Court have situated in this category of bills have been devoted to specific, well-defined programs and goals. House No. 3401, by contrast, serves a multitude of purposes. As the House's version of the "general appropriation bill," required annually by art. 63, § 3, of the Amendments to the Massachusetts Constitution, House No. 3401 contains three detailed sections concerned with the Commonwealth's appropriations for the upcoming year; but it also features more than one hundred outside sections, devoted to topics ranging from the registration of "home infusion pharmacies" to the timeframe for certain proceedings before the Sex Offender Registry Board. A bill designed to implement so broad an array of legislative goals cannot soundly be said to have one or more "main objects" to which revenue creation is incidental.

Second, we would not consider House No. 3401 to be a bill that creates revenue "incidentally" even if we were to assume that the bill's single most prominent purpose is, as its title suggests, to "mak[e] appropriations." General appropriation bills are required by our constitution to be "based upon the budget" recommended by the Governor. The Governor's budget must "contain a statement of all proposed expenditures of the commonwealth for the fiscal year . . . and of all taxes, revenues, loans and other means by which such expenditures shall be defrayed." That is to say, the universe of appropriations brought together in a general appropriation bill—those necessary to conduct the general business of the Commonwealth in the coming year—is by nature intertwined with measures designed to ensure that the necessary funds are available in the Commonwealth's coffers. In this sense, the revenue provisions at issue here in the general appropriation bill for fiscal year 2016 are not "incidental" to a particular purpose (except in the sense that all tax legislation is intended to support the Commonwealth's expenditures); rather, these provisions "raise[ ] revenue to support Government generally." *United States v. Munoz-Flores*, 495 U.S. at 398.

Our response to questions 1 and 2 is therefore that House No. 3401 is a "money bill" by virtue of the delayed FAS 109 deduction provision, irrespective of whether the conservation land credit provision also would render the bill a money bill.

Questions 3 and 4. Given that questions 3 and 4 are contingent on negative answers to both questions 1 and 2, and we have not given negative answers to those questions, we need not answer questions 3 and 4.

Question 5. We read the final question essentially as follows. Even if House No. 3401 is a money bill—as we have said, supra, that it is—did the manner in which the Senate adopted Senate No. 3 amount to "origination" of a new money bill, in violation of the origination article? We conclude that it did not; namely, that Senate No. 3 remains a money bill that originated, as required, in the House of Representatives.

This final question assumes, as do we, that Senate No. 3 made comprehensive revisions to House No. 3401. In our view, these revisions did not amount to the origination of a new bill. The origination article provides that, when a money bill has originated in the House, "the senate may propose or concur with amendments, as on other bills." An examination of the journals of the House and the Senate reveals that it is commonplace for one branch of the Legislature to "amend" a bill passed in the other branch by "striking out all after the enacting clause and inserting in place thereof" a different text. The same practice is prevalent in other jurisdictions. The Senate's power to propose amendments to money bills "as on other bills" thus encompasses even far-reaching alterations.

The Federal courts have so held in interpreting the phrase (identical to that in our origination article), "the senate may propose or concur with amendments as on other bills." *Garcia v. San Antonio Metro. Transit Auth.*, 469 U.S. 528 (1985), concerned a law that, as introduced in the United States House of Representatives, would have created an inheritance tax; the United States Senate amended the bill by enacting a corporate tax instead. The United States Supreme Court rejected an origination clause challenge to the law, stating that

"[t]he bill having properly originated in the House, we perceive no reason in the constitutional provision relied upon why it may not be amended in the Senate in the manner which it was in this case. The amendment was germane to the subject-matter of the bill, and not beyond the power of the Senate to propose."

. . .

Our answer to question 5 is that the manner in which Senate No. 3 was passed did not amount to the Senate originating a money bill in violation of the origination article.

NOTES & QUESTIONS

1.   The MASSACHUSETTS LEGISLATIVE DRAFTING GUIDE (2010 ed.) stated that, money bills are "those that affect state tax revenue, either an increase or decrease, for general purposes. Bills that appropriate money do not meet this definition.

2.   The Massachusetts Constitution authorizes the Governor, the Executive Council, and each branch of the Legislature to call on the Justices

for "opinions . . . upon important questions of law, and upon solemn occasions." See, MA CONST. Part II, c. 3, art. 2. (as amended by Art. 85). Would it be useful for the U.S. Constitution to have a similar provision?

3.   See, Medina, "The Origination Clause in the American Constitution: A Comparative Survey," 23 *Tulsa L.J.* 165, 166 (1987).

UNITED STATES V. MUNOZ-FLORES
Supreme Court of the United States
495 U.S. 385 (1990)

JUSTICE MARSHALL delivered the opinion of the Court.

This case raises the question whether 18 U.S.C. § 3013, which requires courts to impose a monetary "special assessment" on any person convicted of a federal misdemeanor, was passed in violation of the Origination Clause of the Constitution. That Clause mandates that "[a]ll Bills for raising Revenue shall originate in the House of Representatives." U.S. Const., Art. I, § 7, cl. 1.

. . .

The United States seeks to differentiate an Origination Clause claim from other constitutional challenges in two ways. The Government first argues that the House has the power to protect its institutional interests by refusing to pass a bill if it believes that the Origination Clause has been violated. Second, the Government maintains that the courts should not review Origination Clause challenges because compliance with that provision does not significantly affect individual rights.

. . .

Even if we were to assume that the House does have more powerful incentives to refuse to pass legislation that violates the Origination Clause, that assumption would not justify the Government's conclusion that the Judiciary has no role to play in Origination Clause challenges. In many cases involving claimed separation of powers violations, the branch whose power has allegedly been appropriated has both the incentive to protect its prerogatives and institutional mechanisms to help it do so. Nevertheless, the Court adjudicates those separation-of-powers claims, often without suggesting that they might raise political questions. In short, the fact that one institution of Government has mechanisms available to guard against incursions into its power by other governmental institutions does not require that the Judiciary remove itself from the controversy by labeling the issue a political question.

. . .

What the Court has said of the allocation of powers among branches is no less true of such allocations within the Legislative Branch. See, e.g.,

Chadha, 462 U.S., at 948–951, (bicameral National Legislature essential to protect liberty); The Federalist No. 63 (defending bicameral Congress on ground that each House will keep the other in check). The Constitution allocates different powers and responsibilities to the House and Senate. The authors of the Constitution divided such functions between the two Houses based in part on their perceptions of the differing characteristics of the entities. See The Federalist No. 58 (defending the decision to give the origination power to the House on the ground that the Chamber that is more accountable to the people should have the primary role in raising revenue); The Federalist No. 64 (justifying advice and consent function of the Senate on the ground that representatives with longer terms would better serve complex national goals). At base, though, the Framers' purpose was to protect individual rights. As James Madison said in defense of that Clause: "This power over the purse may, in fact, be regarded as the most complete and effectual weapon with which any constitution can arm the immediate representatives of the people, for obtaining a redress of every grievance, and for carrying into effect every just and salutary measure." The Federalist No. 58, p. 359. Provisions for the separation of powers within the Legislative Branch are thus not different in kind from provisions concerning relations between the branches; both sets of provisions safeguard liberty.

. . .

B

. . . In the case of "Bills for raising Revenue," § 7 requires that they originate in the House before they can be properly passed by the two Houses and presented to the President. The Origination Clause is no less a requirement than the rest of the section because "it does not specify what consequences follow from an improper origination," . . . . None of the Constitution's commands explicitly sets out a remedy for its violation. Nevertheless, the principle that the courts will strike down a law when Congress has passed it in violation of such a command has been well settled for almost two centuries. That principle applies whether or not the constitutional provision expressly describes the effects that follow from its violation.

Even were we to accept JUSTICE STEVENS' contrary view—that § 7 provides that a bill becomes a "law" even if it is improperly originated—we would not agree with his conclusion that no remedy is available for a violation of the Origination Clause. Rather, the logical consequence of his view is that the Origination Clause would most appropriately be treated as a constitutional requirement separate from the provisions of § 7 that govern when a bill becomes a "law." Of course, saying that a bill becomes a "law" within the meaning of the second Clause does not answer the question whether that "law" is constitutional. To survive this Court's scrutiny, the "law" must comply with all relevant constitutional limits. A law passed in violation of the Origination Clause would thus be no more immune from judicial scrutiny because it was passed by both Houses and signed by the President than would be a law passed in violation of the First Amendment.

. . .

JUSTICE STEVENS, with whom JUSTICE O'CONNOR joins, concurring in the judgment.

In my opinion, a bill that originated unconstitutionally may nevertheless become an enforceable law if passed by both Houses of Congress and signed by the President. I therefore believe that it is not necessary to decide whether 18 U.S.C. § 3013 was passed in violation of the Origination Clause.

. . .

My reading of the text of § 7 is supported by examination of the Constitution's purposes. I agree with the Court that the purpose of the Origination Clause is to give the most " 'immediate representatives of the people' "—Members of the House, directly elected and subject to ouster every two years—an "effectual weapon" for securing the interests of their constituents. For four reasons, I believe that examination of this purpose supports the view that the binding force of an otherwise lawfully enacted bill is not vitiated by an Origination Clause violation.

First, the House is in an excellent position to defend its origination power. A bill that originates in the Senate, whether or not it raises revenue, cannot become law without the assent of the House. The House is free to rely upon the Origination Clause to justify its position in a debate with the Senate, regardless of whether constitutional concerns alone drive the House's position. The Senate may expect that an improperly originated bill will confront a coalition in the House, composed of those who oppose the bill on substantive grounds and those who would favor it on substantive grounds but regard the procedural error as too important to ignore. Taxes rarely go unnoticed at the ballot box, and there is every reason to anticipate that Representatives subject to reelection every two years will jealously guard their power over revenue-raising measures.

Second, the House has greater freedom than does the Judiciary to construe the Origination Clause wisely. The House may, for example, choose to interpret "Bills for raising Revenue" by invoking a test that turns largely upon the substantive economic impact of the measure on society as a whole, or may determine the House of origination by identifying the legislators who were most responsible for the content of the final version of the bill. If employed by the House, rather than the Judiciary, inquiries so searching obviously create no tension between enforcement of the

Origination Clause and the democratic principle of the legislative process—a principle which the Clause itself is designed to serve. The House may also examine evidence, including informal private disclosures, unavailable (or incomprehensible) to the Judiciary.

Third, the House is better able than this Court to judge the prejudice resulting from an Origination Clause violation, and so better able than this Court to judge what corrective action, if any, should be taken. The nature of such a power may be comprehended by analogy to our own recognition that a constitutional defect in courtroom procedure does not necessarily vitiate the outcome of that procedure. I see no reason to believe that a defect in statehouse procedure cannot also be harmless: A tax originated in the Senate may nevertheless reflect the views of the people as interpreted by the House, whether because of a coincidence in the judgment of the two branches or because the House directly influenced the Senate's labor. The House's assent to an improperly originated bill is unlikely to be given if its Members believe that the procedural defect harmed the bill's substance. Yet, it would be difficult to imagine how this Court could reasonably assess the prejudice resulting from any particular Origination Clause violation. On my interpretation of § 7, the Constitution confides this responsibility to the House of Representatives instead. One consequence of this interpretation is that an expansive construction of the Clause by the House need not impose spurious formalities, since spurious violations may be ignored.

Fourth, the violation complained of by respondent is unlike those constitutional problems which we have in the past recognized as appropriate for judicial supervision. This case is not one involving the constitutionality of statutes alleged to effect prospective alterations in the constitutional distribution of power. No defect in the representative process threatens to impede a democratic solution to the problem at issue. No claim is made that this statute deals with subjects outside the sweep of congressional power, or that the statute abrogates the substantive and procedural guarantees of the Bill of Rights. Nor, finally, does respondent contend that the Constitution has been violated because action has been taken in derogation of structural bulwarks designed either to safeguard groups specially in need of judicial protection, or to tame the majoritarian tendencies of American politics more generally. Indeed, this case presents perhaps the weakest imaginable justification for judicial invalidation of a statute: Respondent contends that the judiciary must intervene in order to protect a power of the most majoritarian body in the Federal Government, even though that body has an absolute veto over any effort to usurp that power. The democratic structure of the Constitution ensures that the majority rarely if ever needs such help from the Judiciary.

5. CAN THE LEGISLATURE DO THAT? ANTI-DELEGATION

WEST PHILADELPHIA ACHIEVEMENT CHARTER ELEMENTARY SCHOOL V. SCHOOL DISTRICT OF PHILADELPHIA

Supreme Court of Pennsylvania
635 Pa. 127 (2016)

CHIEF JUSTICE SAYLOR.

In this matter we address whether legislation designed to help the Philadelphia School District recover from financial hardship violates the non-delegation rule.

[Note: Pennsylvania has assisted public schools experiencing financial distress since 1959. Starting in 1998, the School Act allowed the Secretary of Education to declare a school district distressed and appoint a chief executive officer ("CEO") to oversee the school, suspend or revoke charters, and suspend both state regulations and School Act requirements. In 2001, the legislature amended the Act to provide that after a declaration of distress, a five-member School Reform Commission ("SRC"), mostly appointed by the Governor, would have sweeping powers to oversee a school district, including the power to suspend charters, regulations and School Act provisions. In December 2001, the Secretary declared the Philadelphia School District distressed, suspending the Philadelphia School Board's powers and appointing a SRC to govern the district. A charter school sought to renew its charter and the SRC conditioned renewal on meeting student performance targets, even though the school was not in corrective action status as required by law. The SRC also required the school to enroll no more than 400 students even though state law did not impose enrollment caps on charter schools.]

In the Complaint, the Charter School challenged the constitutionality of Section 696(i)(3), arguing that it "gives the SRC unlimited discretion and power to suspend provisions of the School Code without establishing standards or restraints on the use of that power." Complaint at 25. The Charter School asserted that this power is in violation of the non-delegation precept of Article II, Section 1 of the state Constitution. The school maintained that, while the Legislature may delegate authority to execute or administer laws, it must establish standards and limit such delegation so that the administrative agency tasked with executing the laws conducts itself in compliance with legislative purposes. Thus, the Charter School expressed that a delegation of legislative authority is constitutional only if the General Assembly sets forth the policies guiding the delegation and surrounds it with definite standards and limitations. According to the Charter School, Section 696(i)(3) of the Distress Law lacks the limitations and standards necessary to render it a constitutionally-permissible delegation of legislative authority.

. . .

Article II, Section 1 of the Pennsylvania Constitution states that "[t]he legislative power of this Commonwealth shall be vested in a General Assembly, which shall consist of a Senate and a House of Representatives." PA. CONST. art. II, § 1. The non-delegation rule has been described as a "natural corollary" to this text. [S]ee also *W. Mifflin Area Sch. Dist. v. Zahorchak*, 607 Pa. 153, 158 n. 5, 4 A.3d 1042, 1045 n. 5 (2010) (noting that Section 1 "has been interpreted to . . . require [ ] that the basic policy choices involved in legislative power actually be made by the Legislature." The precept, which has its origins in the separation-of-powers doctrine, is of early lineage, see *Wayman v. Southard*, 23 U.S. (10 Wheat.) 1, 43, 6 L.Ed. 253 (1825) (Marshall, C.J.), and was expressed by political theorists who influenced the framers of the Constitution. See, e.g., John Locke, SECOND TREATISE OF GOVERNMENT § 141 (1690) (observing that legislative power "consists of the power to make laws, not to make legislators," and indicating, moreover, that the legislature is not free to transfer its lawmaking powers to any other body because such power was delegated to the legislature by the people); cf. 1 William Blackstone, COMMENTARIES ON THE LAWS OF ENGLAND (1753) (remarking that a member of the House of Commons could not delegate his vote to a proxy "as he himself is but a proxy for a multitude of other people"). See generally Baron De Montesquieu, THE SPIRIT OF THE LAWS XI:6 (1748) (suggesting that political liberty requires a separation of legislative, executive, and judicial powers), quoted in THE FEDERALIST No. 47 (James Madison).

This Court has considered multiple categories of non-delegation challenges. One such category involves statutes in which the General Assembly enacts a law but leaves its effectiveness to be determined by another person or entity via the ascertainment of some material fact or state of affairs. For example, in *Locke's Appeal*, 72 Pa. (22 Smith) 491 (1873), the Court approved a local-option law by which the electors of a municipality could vote to either allow or prohibit the sale of alcohol within the district. The Court explained that the Legislature passed the law, which included such provisions as penalties for violating any ban on the sale of alcohol, but left its effectiveness to be determined by ascertainment of a fact, namely, the majority vote of the district's electors. Thus, *Locke's Appeal* upheld the challenged statute.

Another category of cases in which delegation has been challenged involves the legislative establishment of primary objectives or standards and the entrustment to another entity to "fill up the details under the general [legislative] provisions[.]" So long as adequately-defined standards and methodologies are provided by the Legislature, the administrative action involved may be as narrow as the grant or denial of a license, or as broad as the setting and adjustment of minimum and maximum wholesale and retail prices of a commodity to ensure fairness to producers and consumers and to regulate the supply of that commodity.

The enactment under review contains aspects of both of these classifications. It assigns to an executive branch official the duty to ascertain facts preliminary to a determination that a school district of the first class is in distress. That part of the law is uncontroversial. The contested issue is whether the Legislature provided adequate standards to channel the SRC's discretion in choosing which portions of the School Code to suspend pursuant to Section 696(i)(3) in order to remediate such distress.

Initially, we agree with Respondents that via the Distress Law, as amended in 1998 and 2001, the Legislature sought to empower the SRC to take actions which it might deem necessary or convenient to alleviate the School District's ongoing financial crisis. While this is a salutary goal, the means chosen to effectuate it were extremely broad: the Legislature gave the SRC what amounts to carte blanche powers to suspend virtually any combination of provisions of the School Code—a statute covering a broad range of topics. This Court's decisions addressing the non-delegation rule have never deemed such an unconstrained grant of authority to be constitutionally valid. To the extent Respondents couch the legislative intention to remediate the School District's financial distress as a standard, moreover, we find this to be more aptly described as the legislative objective. Indeed, neither Section 696(i)(3) nor the Distress Law generally imposes any discernible standards or restraints in relation to the selection of School Code provisions for suspension. Those high-level determinations are left entirely to the SRC's discretion, and it is not apparent that any mechanism exists to either channel or test the SRC's exercise of such discretion.

The SRC's actions in the present case demonstrate the point: the SRC suspended a number of significant aspects of the Charter School Law and, in effect, rewrote some of that law in the form of its Charter Schools Policy. One aspect of the Charter School Law that the SRC suspended sets forth the bases for nonrenewal or termination of a charter and allows a charter school which suffers an adverse decision to obtain a hearing and administrative review before the State Charter School Appeal Board. This suspension undermines the concept that the SRC's decision making is, realistically, subject to standards set forth by the Legislature. Furthermore, that the Charter Schools Policy is essentially a legislative document is illustrated by, inter alia, its addition of eight new criteria for nonrenewal or revocation of a charter above and beyond those decided on by the Legislature in Section 1729–A of the Charter School Law.

The Distress Law also lacks any mechanism to limit the SRC's actions so as to "protect[ ] against administrative arbitrariness and caprice." This is a substantial deficiency because this Court has generally viewed the inclusion of such limitations as a necessary condition to satisfy the non-delegation rule.

In *Tosto v. Pa. Nursing Home Loan Agency* (1975), for example, the Court considered a non-delegation challenge to the Nursing Home Loan Agency Law—a statute designed to provide financing for nursing home capital improvements undertaken to accommodate the health and safety needs of a nursing home's residents. *Tosto* rejected the constitutional attack because the law provided "detailed guidelines for certain important agency decisions," as well as "numerous procedural guidelines for protection against administrative arbitrariness[.]" These requirements included a legislative mandate that the agency establish neutral criteria for use in determining priority among applicants and develop standardized forms for loan applications. The Court concluded that the use of such "criteria and forms is an important safeguard against the arbitrariness of ad hoc decision making."

. . .

[T]he Distress Law does not merely empower the SRC to grant or deny charters. It permits the SRC to govern many substantive aspects of the delivery of public education in Philadelphia—including the operation of charter schools—through the suspension of virtually any combination of School Code provisions and associated regulations. In this regard, Petitioner argues, persuasively in our view, that:

> The power to suspend the requirements of the Public School Code is an extremely broad power and is especially broad in the context of this case. The Public School Code is a significant body of law that is subdivided into more than 60 articles and hundreds of statutes, with far-reaching effects on the creation, operation, finances, and legal rights of students, teachers, and taxpayers. The Code concerns widely divergent topics such as public bidding requirements, school construction, reimbursements between the Commonwealth and school districts, [and] rules for the auditing of school finances. . . . Pursuant to the statutes that make up the various parts of the Code, the State Board of Education has promulgated a vast set of regulations embodied in Title 22 of the Pennsylvania Code, which itself outlines an extremely complex regulatory scheme governing the manner in which public education is delivered in Pennsylvania. . . . [T]he SRC could potentially suspend every single requirement contained in the Charter School Law. It could, for example, suspend the provisions governing the funding formula for charter schools contained in

Section 17–1725–A and do away with the School District's obligation to pay charter schools at all.

The Distress Law gives the SRC these broad powers pursuant to a generalized legislative objective of mitigating the School District's adverse financial circumstances. For the reasons given above, we do not view such objective as supplying either a constitutionally adequate guiding standard or an effective channeling mechanism relative to the SRC's discretionary suspension powers.

. . .

In summary, we hold that Section 696(i)(3) of the School Code, 24 P.S. § 6–696(i)(3), is unconstitutional as it violates the non-delegation rule of Article II, Section 1. Accordingly Respondents' actions taken pursuant to that provision are null and void, and Respondents are permanently enjoined from taking further action under the authority it confers.

JUSTICE BAER, dissenting.

I respectfully dissent from the majority's holding that Section 6–696(i)(3) of the Distress Law, 24 P.S. § 6–696(i)(3), which grants the School Reform Commission ("SRC") the power to suspend provisions of the Public School Code, constitutes an unlawful delegation of legislative authority in violation of Article II, Section 1 of the Pennsylvania Constitution.1 In my view, Section 6–696(i)(3) does not delegate legislative power, but rather delegates the authority to suspend legislation that affects the economic stability of a school district in financial distress, which is constitutionally permissible pursuant to Article I, Section 12.2 Accordingly, I would reject the constitutional challenge raised by the West Philadelphia Achievement Charter School ("Charter School") and deny the Charter School's request for injunctive relief.

. . .

My analysis begins with an examination of what constitutes legislative power. Legislative power has been defined as the power "to make, alter, or repeal laws." Accordingly, "[i]t is axiomatic that the Legislature cannot constitutionally delegate the power to make law to any other branch of government or to any other body or authority."

The legislature may, however, constitutionally delegate to another body the authority to execute and administer a law so long as the General Assembly makes the basic policy choices and provides adequate standards and guidelines to allow the other body to carry out those legislative policies. Significantly, in reviewing the adequacy of guiding standards incorporated in a law, this Court looks to the law as a whole, considering its purpose and scope, the subject matters covered therein, the duties prescribed and the broad or narrow powers granted. the general assembly is not required "to provide a detailed how-to manual within each and every legislative act" in order to supply adequate standards, and all details of administration need not be precisely or separately enumerated in the statute.

. . .

While there is superficial appeal to the Charter School's contention that the suspension power is so broad that it effectively enables the SRC to "legislate," a close examination of the challenged provision and the statutory scheme of which it is a part reveals that the SRC is empowered only to suspend those provisions of the Public School Code that result in financial distress to the school district for the limited period during which the economic crisis of the school district continues. Because Section 6–696(i)(3) does not authorize the SRC to legislate by making, altering, or repealing the law, it is not an unconstitutional delegation of legislative power.

By enacting Section 6–696(i)(3) and the Distress Law as a whole, the General Assembly has made the basic policy determination to preserve the failing school district by identifying and remediating sources of financial distress "notwithstanding any other law to the contrary." The SRC does not hold the power over basic policy choices inherent in the Public School Code, but may only exercise its discretion to suspend those provisions that preserve the school district by remediating identified types of financial distress.

I do not believe the Legislature afforded the SRC carte blanche powers to suspend any combination of the School Code provisions. The standards guiding the SRC's exercise of discretion in determining which provisions of the Public School Code to suspend appear both in Section 6–696(i)(3) itself, which enumerates several provisions that may not be suspended, as well as in the Distress Law as a whole, which, as noted, makes clear that remediation efforts are aimed at resolving the financial distress of the school district. A suspension of a provision of the Public School Code that is immaterial to the contemplated advancement of financial stability is simply unauthorized. Although the suspension power granted to the SRC is somewhat broad, it is necessarily so, as the breadth of the standard is driven by the breadth of the problem, and the problem here is unquestionably great. Because the General Assembly can neither predict all causes of refractory distress within such a complex system nor statutorily prescribe precisely how to remedy the effects in all instances, the grant of broad authority is required to effectuate the purposes of the legislation.

Additionally, the Distress Law contains procedures to protect against arbitrary or ad hoc decision-making by the SRC. The Distress Law requires the SRC to submit annually a report to the Governor and the Education Committees of both the House of Representatives and the Senate regarding progress made toward improvements in fiscal and academic performance.

The General Assembly therefore brings to bear a multi-branch review of both the performance of the SRC in abating distress and, ultimately, whether financial distress continues to exist at all. By requiring the SRC to report annually to the Commonwealth's chief executive and the legislative committees, the Distress Law holds the SRC accountable to perform in accordance with the remedial purposes of the Distress Law. Finally, the Distress Law authorizes the Governor to remove a member of the SRC prior to expiration of the term of office upon proof by clear and convincing evidence of malfeasance or misfeasance. In my view, the improper exercise of an enumerated power, such as the suspension power, could constitute grounds for removal of SRC members.

In conclusion, I acknowledge that the General Assembly's grant of suspension power to the SRC has vast implications on all charter schools, as well as other individuals and entities involved in public education in the Philadelphia School District. The enormity of the power conveyed and the dramatic effects resulting from exercise of that authority, however, do not render Section 6–696(i)(3) unconstitutional under the anti-delegation clause where the General Assembly made the requisite basic policy decisions inherent in the legislation and afforded adequate guidance to the SRC in exercising the suspension authority. It cannot be ignored that a party challenging a legislative enactment bears the heavy burden of demonstrating that the statute clearly, palpably, and plainly violates the constitution. In my opinion, the Charter School has simply failed to satisfy that burden here.

NOTES & QUESTIONS

What is the future of the non-delegation doctrine as the administrative state grows?

B. THE ENROLLED BILL RULE

English and American common law cases held that an enrolled bill was conclusive evidence of valid enactment and no other evidence was admissible. This doctrine holds that an enrolled bill, signed by the presiding officers of the House of Representatives and the Senate as conclusive evidence of the text passed by both houses of Congress. This rule limits a court's ability to inquire as to whether the legislature followed constitutional requirements when passing a piece of legislation. The separation of powers doctrine requires that courts must presume a legislative act is valid. The legislature is a coordinate branch of government requiring respect and legislation is entitled to even greater respect. Courts, therefore, should resist reviewing the work of an equal branch of government. Courts have also justified the doctrine as a matter of convenience. Legislatures would be too burdened by preserving its records to validate a bill's enactment. Further, the evidence produced during the legislative process, including legislative journals, may be unreliable, and should not be used to contradict the enrolled bill.

MARSHALL FIELD & CO. V. CLARK

Supreme Court of the United States
143 U.S. 649 (1892)

MR. JUSTICE HARLAN delivered the opinion of the court.

[Note: A department store argued that the tariffs on goods it imported were unconstitutional because the statute violated the Origination and Presentment Clauses. Appellants argued that the congressional records of proceedings found in the journal and committee reports, showed that a particular section was not in the bill enrolled by the House speaker and Senate president through their signatures and approved by the president, meaning the bill was not passed by Congress.]

The argument, in behalf of the appellants, is that a bill, signed by the speaker of the house of representatives and by the president of the senate, presented to and approved by the president of the United States, and delivered by the latter to the secretary of state, as an act passed by congress, does not become a law of the United States if it had not in fact been passed by congress. In view of the express requirements of the constitution, the correctness of this general principle cannot be doubted. There is no authority in the presiding officers of the house of representatives and the senate to attest by their signatures, not in the president to approve, nor in the secretary of state to receive and cause to be published, as a legislative act, any bill not passed by congress.

But this concession of the correctness of the general principle for which the appellants contend does not determine the precise question before the court; for it remains to inquire as to the nature of the evidence upon which a court may act when the issue is made as to whether a bill, originating in the house of representatives or the senate, and asserted to have become a law, was or was not passed by congress. This question is now presented for the first time in this court. It has received, as its importance required that it should receive, the most deliberate consideration. We recognize, on one hand, the duty of this court, from the performance of which it may not shrink, to give full effect to the provisions of the constitution relating to the enactment of laws that are to operate wherever the authority and jurisdiction of the United States extend. On the other hand, we cannot be unmindful of the consequences that must result if this court should feel obliged, in fidelity to the constitution, to declare that an enrolled bill, on which depend public and private interests of vast magnitude, and which has been authenticated by the signatures of the presiding officers of the two houses of congress, and by the approval of the president, and been deposited in the public archives, as an act of congress, was not in fact passed by the house of representatives and the senate, and therefore did not become a law.

The clause of the constitution upon which the appellants rest their contention that the act in question was never passed by congress is the one declaring that 'each house shall keep a journal of its proceedings, and from time to time publish the same, except such parts as may in their judgment require secrecy; and the yeas and nays of the members of either house on any question shall, at the desire of one-fifth of those present, be entered on the journal.' Article 1, § 5. It was assumed in argument that the object of this clause was to make the journal the best, if not conclusive, evidence upon the issue as to whether a bill was, in fact, passed by the two houses of congress. But the words used do not require such interpretation. On the contrary, as Mr. Justice Story has well said, 'the object of the whole clause is to insure publicity to the proceedings of the legislature, and a correspondent responsibility of the members to their respective constituents. And it is founded in sound policy and deep political foresight. Intrigue and cabal are thus deprived of some of their main resources, by plotting and devising measures in secrecy. The public mind is enlightened by an attentive examination of the public measures; patriotism and integrity and wisdom obtain their due reward; and votes are ascertained, not by vague conjecture, but by positive facts. * * * So long as known and open responsibility is valuable as a check or an incentive among the representatives of a free people, so long a journal of their proceedings and their votes, published in the face of the world, will continue to enjoy public favor and be demanded by public opinion.' 2 Story, Const. §§ 840, 841.

In regard to certain matters, the constitution expressly requires that they shall be entered on the journal. To what extent the validity of legislative action may be affected by the failure to have those matters entered on the journal we need not inquire. No such question is presented for determination. But it is clear that, in respect to the particular mode in which, or with what fullness, shall be kept the proceedings of either house relating to matters not expressly required to be entered on the journals; whether bills, orders, resolutions, reports, and amendments shall be entered at large on the journal, or only referred to and designated by their titles or by numbers,—these and like matters were left to the discretion of the respective houses of congress. Nor does any clause of that instrument, either expressly or by necessary implication, prescribe the mode in which the fact of the original passage of a bill by the house of representatives and the senate shall be authenticated, or preclude congress from adopting any mode to that end which its wisdom suggests. Although the constitution does not expressly require bills that have passed congress to be attested by the signatures of the presiding officers of the two houses, usage, the orderly conduct of legislative proceedings, and the rules under which the two bodies have acted since the organization of the government, require that mode of authentication.

The signing by the speaker of the house of representatives, and by the president of the senate, in open session, of an enrolled bill, is an official attestation by the two houses of such bill as one that has passed congress. It is a declaration by the two houses, through their presiding officers, to the president, that a bill, thus attested, has received, in due form, the sanction of the legislative branch of the government, and that it is delivered to him in obedience to the constitutional requirement that all bills which pass congress shall be presented to him. And when a bill, thus attested, receives his approval, and is deposited in the public archives, its authentication as a bill that has passed congress should be deemed complete and unimpeachable. As the president has no authority to approve a bill not passed by congress, an enrolled act in the custody of the secretary of state, and having the official attestations of the speaker of the house of representatives, of the president of the senate, and of the president of the United States, carries on its face a solemn assurance by the legislative and executive departments of the government, charged, respectively, with the duty of enacting and executing the laws, that it was passed by congress. The respect due to coequal and independent departments requires the judicial department to act upon that assurance, and to accept, as having passed congress, all bills authenticated in the manner stated; leaving the courts to determine, when the question properly arises, whether the act so authenticated, is in conformity with the constitution.

It is admitted that an enrolled act, thus authenticated, is sufficient evidence of itself—nothing to the contrary appearing upon its face—that it passed congress. But the contention is that it cannot be regarded as a law of the United States if the journal of either house fails to show that it passed in the precise form in which it was signed by the presiding officers of the two houses, and approved by the president. It is said that, under any other view, it becomes possible for the speaker of the house of representatives and the president of the senate to impose upon the people as a law a bill that was never passed by congress. But this possibility is too remote to be seriously considered in the present inquiry. It suggests a deliberate conspiracy to which the presiding officers, the committees on enrolled bills, and the clerks of the two houses must necessarily be parties, all acting with a common purpose to defeat an expression of the popular will in the mode prescribed by the constitution. Judicial action, based upon such a suggestion, is forbidden by the respect due to a co-ordinate branch of the government. The evils that may result from the recognition of the principle that an enrolled act, in the custody of the secretary of state, attested by the signatures of the presiding officers of the two houses of congress, and the approval of the president, is conclusive evidence that it was passed by congress, according to the forms of the constitution, would be far less than those that would certainly result from a rule making the validity of congressional enactments depend upon the manner in which the journals of the respective houses are kept by the subordinate officers charged with the duty of keeping them.

. . .

We are of opinion, for the reasons stated, that it is not competent for the appellants to show, from the journals of either house, from the reports of committees, or from other documents printed by authority of congress, that the enrolled bill, designated 'H. R. 9416,' as finally passed, contained a section that does not appear in the enrolled act in the custody of the state department.

NOTES & QUESTIONS

1.   Many states have moved away from the enrolled bill rule and adopted other standards—often revolving around the information contained in the legislative journals:

Modified Enrolled Bill Rule: Some states generally accept the enrolled bill rule but make exceptions for information contained in the constitutionally required journal entries. Since specific acts must be recorded in the journal, the constitutional framers intended the journals to serve as proof that those acts were performed, and, therefore, this evidence is reliable.

Pure Journal Entry Rule: Legislative journals offer proof of a bill's legitimate passage by the legislature following the provisions of the constitution. If the journal does not show the legislature complying with constitutional requirements, that is conclusive evidence the requirement was not fulfilled. For instance, if the constitution requires a vote, but the journal does not contain a vote tally, that may be sufficient to invalidate a bill.

Affirmative Contradiction Rule: Since the lack of a journal entry is ambiguous, some courts have adopted a rule where the legislative journals are conclusive, but a law is invalid only where the journal affirmatively shows the required procedures were not followed. However, a legislature could defeat this rule by omitting key information from the journal and calling it a "mistake."

Mixed Rule: Under this rule, if the constitution requires a journal entry of a legislative action, the lack of an entry is *prima facie* evidence the law is invalid. If the constitution does not affirmatively require the act be recorded in the journal, the courts will presume that the act happened unless the journal shows id did not.

For greater analysis of each rule see, David Sandler, "Forget What You Learned in Civics Class: The 'Enrolled Bill Rule' and Why It's Time to Overrule Field v. Clark," 41 *Colum. J.L. &Soc. Probs.* 213 (2007).

THE ASSOCIATION OF TEXAS PROFESSIONAL
EDUCATORS V. KIRBY

Supreme Court of Texas
788 S.W.2d 827 (1990)

RAY, JUSTICE.

This is a direct appeal from a trial court judgment denying a temporary injunction in a suit challenging the constitutionality of House Bill 2566 (H.B. 2566), Seventy-First Legislature. The trial court expressly held that the "enrolled bill rule" precluded inquiry into the constitutional defects alleged by plaintiffs, even though the legislative journals and stipulated facts showed conclusively that the bill signed by the Governor had not been passed by the legislature. We hold that when the official legislative journals, testimony by the presiding officers of both houses, and stipulations of the attorney general acting in his official capacity conclusively show clerical error in the enrolled bill, an exception to the enrolled bill rule applies. We therefore reverse the judgment of the trial court and remand this cause for further proceedings.

The Association of Texas Professional Educators and Carolyn Little (collectively, the "Teachers") sued W.N. Kirby as State Commissioner of Education to enjoin the enforcement of H.B. 2566, an act amending certain provisions of the Texas Education Code relating to the teacher career ladder system. The Teachers alleged H.B. 2566 was unconstitutional because the bill as passed by the House of Representatives and the Senate was not the bill signed by the presiding officer of each house, as required by Tex. Const. art. 3, § 38; nor was the bill as passed by both houses presented to the Governor for his approval as required by Tex. Const. art. 4, § 14. . . . The temporary injunction portion of the suit was tried on stipulated facts. The factual stipulations included certified copies of the relevant portions of the legislative journals for H.B. 2566. There is nothing in the legislative records or the trial court record in any way casting any doubt as to the stipulated facts.

The House and Senate versions of H.B. 2566 differed, and the bill accordingly went to conference committee. The conference committee report produced the version of the bill that was presented to and adopted by the Senate. In particular, section 23 of the conference committee version of the bill provided:

This Act takes effect September 1, 1989, except that Section 5 takes effect September 1, 1990.

After the conference committee report was signed but before the bill was enrolled, someone crossed out the number "5" by hand in section 23 of the bill and wrote the number "7" above the crossed-out number. The Senate voted to approve the conference committee report before the clerical change. It is uncertain whether this editorial change occurred before or after the House voted on the conference committee report. The change is not dated, signed, or initialed. The enrolled bill was definitely not the version passed by the Senate.

The clerical change of the "5" to the "7" was carried forward in the enrolling process. In particular, the clerical change was included in the enrolled bill as signed by the Lieutenant Governor, Speaker of the House, and Governor. Thus the enrolled version of the bill, certified to have been as passed by the presiding officers of each house of the legislature, contained this section 23:

This Act takes effect September 1, 1989, except that Section 7 takes effect September 1, 1990.

After the Governor had signed the enrolled bill, the presiding officers and respective education committee chairpersons of each house discovered the "editorial change made in the process of enrolling the bill." They jointly wrote Commissioner Kirby urging him to enforce the Act as if the clerical error had not occurred, in order to make the Act internally consistent and to effect legislative intent.

After receiving the letter, Commissioner Kirby requested a formal opinion from the Attorney General. The Attorney General issued an opinion that the Act had to be enforced as signed by the Governor because of the enrolled bill rule, and suggesting ways to reconcile the internal inconsistencies in the bill.

The enrolled bill rule provides that the "enrolled statute," as authenticated by the presiding officers of each house, signed by the governor (or certified passed over gubernatorial veto), and deposited in the secretary of state's office, is precisely the same as and a "conclusive record" of the statute that was enacted by the legislators. Under the strict enrolled bill rule, the House and Senate Journals are not more reliable records of what occurred than the enrolled bill, and no extrinsic evidence may be considered to contradict the enrolled version of the bill.

When this court last wrote concerning the enrolled bill rule, we approved a court of civil appeals opinion stating that the "statement of the rule is too broad," but that the dignity of the long-standing cases adopting it required its application to the facts of that case. With the present case we are presented with facts for which the blind application of the rule is too broad.

The enrolled bill rule is contrary to modern legal thinking, which does not favor conclusive presumptions that may produce results which do not accord with fact. While the variety of state constitutional provisions and procedures make generalization difficult, the present tendency favors giving the enrolled version only prima facie presumptive validity, and a majority of states recognize exceptions to the enrolled bill rule.

We agree with decisions from our sister states that an exception to the enrolled bill rule must exist to avoid elevating clerical error over constitutional law. Some of the analysis from the decisions of other states is instructive in formulating the exception we will recognize. Pennsylvania courts have stated that when the attorney general acting in his official capacity stipulates to the legislative facts concerning a bill, and the certified legislative records show there is no dispute that such are the facts, then the court has a duty to determine if the bill was constitutionally enacted. *Consumer Party of Pennsylvania v. Commonwealth* (PA, 1986). In Illinois when the attorney general's concession in the briefs is that the legislators themselves and all legislative records concede that the bill that passed both houses was not the bill signed by the governor and certified as the enrolled version, the court must take action to declare the law was not constitutionally enacted. *Yarger v. Board of Regents* (Ill. 1983). In Kansas the exception to the enrolled bill rule applies when the legislative journals "show affirmatively, clearly, conclusively and beyond all doubt that the bill as enrolled was not the bill passed." *Harris v. Shanahan* (Ks. 1963). To hold otherwise would raise form over substance, fiction over fact, and amount to government by clerical error. The Missouri Supreme Court has held the enrolled version of the bill is not constitutionally enacted when it is "inadvertently modified en route. No clerical employee has the authority to make any addition, deletion or modification in a bill as passed by both houses." *State ex rel. Ashcroft v. Blunt* (Mo.1985). We therefore recognize as a narrow exception to the enrolled bill rule that when the official legislative journals, undisputed testimony by the presiding officers of both houses, and stipulations by the attorney general acting in his official capacity conclusively show the enrolled bill signed by the governor was not the bill passed by the legislature, the law is not constitutionally enacted. When the official legislative journals, presiding officers and attorney general all concur that the enrolled bill is not the bill passed by the legislature, the exception applies as a matter of law.

NOTES & QUESTIONS

1. *Marshall Field & Co. v. Clark* has not been reversed by the Supreme Court, so the enrolled billed doctrine is still consistently applied in the federal system and in several states. In fact, some state supreme courts have recently reaffirmed their adherence to the doctrine: See, e.g., *Wash. State Grange v. Locke*, 105 P.3d 9, 22–23 (Wash. 2005); *Birmingham-Jefferson Civic Ctr. Auth. v. City of Birmingham*, 912 So. 2d 204, 219–21 (Ala. 2005); *Med. Soc'y of S.C. v. Med. Univ. of S.C.*, 513 S.E.2d 352, 356–57 (S.C. 1999). Commentators point out that the principal contemporary justification for EBD continues to be the respect due to a coequal branch and separation-of-powers arguments, which are "as powerful today as when *Marshall Field* was decided." See, Brief for the Respondent in Opposition at 6, 12–14, *Public Citizen v. U.S. Dist. Court for Dist. of Columbia*, 552 U.S. 1076 (2007) (No. 07–141); see also, *OneSimpleLoan*

v. U.S., 496 F.3d 197, 208 (2007) ("[T]he separation-of-powers concerns at the forefront of *Marshall Field* . . . are surely undiminished by the passage of time . . . ."). "Mutual regard between the coordinate branches and the interest of certainty" were also the two grounds Justice Scalia relied upon in his concurrence in *United States v. Munoz-Flores.* Ittai Bar-Siman-Tov, "Legislative Supremacy In The United States?: Rethinking The 'Enrolled Bill' Doctrine," 97 *Georgetown L.J.* 323 (2009).

2.   Professor Ittai Bar-Siman-Tov argues that the "factual and doctrinal developments since *Marshall Field* was decided in 1892 significantly erode its soundness." He argues that the EBD prevents judicial review of the legislative process, which "requires special attention," if not what Professor Louis Henkin calls "strict and skeptical scrutiny." Louis Henkin, "Is There a "Political Question" Doctrine?," 85 *Yale L.J.* 597, 600 (1976). Professor Bar-Siman-Tov argues that poor legislative record keeping justifies the EBD, which is not the case in most jurisdictions that now use modern and electronic record keeping systems. Citing, *D & W Auto Supply v. Dep't of Revenue*, 602 S.W.2d 420, 423 (Ky. 1980). In addition, the existence of audio and video recordings make legislative actions easier to prove.

The enrollment process is also significantly different now than it was at the time of *Marshal Field*. Whereas Congress used to pass far fewer bills, and a committee on enrollment reviewed bills before the presiding officers signed the legislation, modern practice gives far more power to the clerk of the House and the secretary of the Senate. Prof. Bar-Siman-Tov argues, "the signatures of the presiding officers on the enrolled bill "soon meant little more than that the bill had been checked by persons in whom they had confidence . . . .' " The legislative officers, therefore, play just a symbolic role in authenticating bills. Prof. Bar-Siman-Tov argues the enrolled bill doctrine is an impermissible delegation of both judicial and lawmaking powers to the legislative officers of Congress who then have the exclusive ability to determine the validity of legislation. Ittai Bar-Siman-Tov, "Legislative Supremacy In The United States?: Rethinking The 'Enrolled Bill' Doctrine," 97 *Georgetown L. J.* 323 (2009).

3.   Should courts have the power to examine and pass judgment on the activities of the legislature? One commentator suggests that, "judicial review of legislative procedures is not significantly distinguishable from the judiciary's active oversight of the executive." The courts routinely review whether administrative agencies properly followed the Administrative Procedure Act ("APA") rulemaking procedures. If an agency failed to follow required procedures, courts vacate the regulation. It is not entirely clear why the Court should not require similar diligence in the passage of statutes. See, David Sandler, "Forget What You Learned In Civics Class: The 'Enrolled Bill Rule' And Why It's Time To Overrule *Field v. Clark*," 41 *Colum. J.L. & Soc. Probs.* 213 (2007).

4.   Although many states have abandoned the enrolled bill rule, other states, such as Illinois, have moved toward the rule. The Illinois Supreme

Court discusses the Rule in *Geja's Cafe v. Metropolitan Pier and Exposition Authority*, 153 Ill.2d 239 (1992):

> Plaintiffs next argue that we should overturn the tax because the General Assembly did not comply with constitutionally required procedures when it passed the Act. Specifically, the General Assembly did not comply with the three-readings requirement of article IV, section 8(d), of the Illinois Constitution.
>
> . . .
>
> Two things are clear to the members of this court. The first is that, contrary to plaintiffs' assertion, the enrolled bill doctrine was clearly anticipated by the Framers of the Constitution. As noted in *Benjamin v. Devon Bank* (1977), the Committee on the Legislature of the constitutional convention explained that the purpose of the enrolled bill doctrine is to avoid judicial nullification of statutes on purely procedural grounds:
>
> " 'Presently Illinois has the "journal entry" rule as distinguished from an "enrolled bill" rule. It is proposed that Illinois adopt the "enrolled bill" rule.
>
> The "journal entry" rule means that a piece of legislation can be challenged in the courts by pointing to a defect in its passage as reflected in the journal. Under this rule, a statute duly [sic] passed by the General Assembly and signed by the Governor may be attacked in the courts, not necessarily on its merits, but on some procedural error or technicality found in the legislative process. The "journal entry" rule, as a result, leads to complex litigation over procedures and technicalities.
>
> The "enrolled bill" rule would provide that when the presiding officers of the two houses sign a bill, their signatures become conclusive proof that all constitutional procedures have been properly followed. The "enrolled bill" rule would not permit a challenge to a bill on procedural or technical grounds regarding the manner of passage if the bill showed on its face that it was properly passed. Signatures by the presiding officers would, of course, constitute proof that proper procedures were followed.' " *Benjamin*, quoting, 6 *Record of Proceedings, Sixth Illinois Constitutional Convention* 1386–87.
>
> The second thing that is apparent to this court is that the General Assembly has shown remarkably poor self-discipline in policing itself. Indeed, both parties agree that ignoring the three-readings requirement has become a procedural regularity. This is quite a different situation than that envisioned by the Framers, who enacted the enrolled bill doctrine on the assumption that the General Assembly would police itself and judicial review would not be needed because violations of the constitutionally required procedures would be rare. "[W]e determined, in accordance with many other states that

have adopted the enrolled bill rule and have found no difficulties, that * * * if they were to commit any fraud or chicanery, the legislature would certainly take care of them." 4 PROCEEDINGS 2881.

Plaintiffs urge us to abandon the enrolled bill doctrine because history has proven that there is no other way to enforce the constitutionally mandated three-readings requirement. While plaintiffs make a persuasive argument, we decline their invitation. We do so because, for today at least, we feel that the doctrine of separation of powers is more compelling. However, we defer to the legislature hesitantly, because we do not wish to understate the importance of complying with the Constitution when passing bills. If the General Assembly continues its poor record of policing itself, we reserve the right to revisit this issue on another day to decide the continued propriety of ignoring this constitutional violation.

LEGISLATIVE SUPREMACY IN THE UNITED STATES?: RETHINKING THE "ENROLLED BILL" DOCTRINE
Ittai Bar-Siman-Tov, 97 *Georgetown Law Journal* 323 (2009)

Separation of powers, due respect for the legislature, and other prudential concerns (such as the interest of certainty and stability of the law) are important and legitimate considerations. However, these considerations should not lead to complete non-enforcement of the Constitution's lawmaking provisions and to turning the legislative process into a sphere of unfettered legislative omnipotence. Instead, these concerns counsel self-restraint and caution in exercising judicial review of the legislative process, which can be effectively achieved by other judicial means.

The Field Court seemed to assume that "[e]very other view subordinates the legislature, and disregards that coequal position in our system of the three departments of government," and "would certainly result" in the "evils" EBD aims to avoid. Consequently, it favored these prudential considerations over judicial "fidelity to the Constitution." However, there are, in fact, alternatives to EBD that represent a better balance between these competing considerations. These alternatives enable enforcement of the Constitution while being mindful of the respect due to the legislature and of other prudential and institutional considerations. Instead of carving an unjustified exception to Marbury and to the most fundamental principles of American constitutionalism, they provide flexibility for prudence and greater attention to the legitimacy of judicial action in the circumstances of every case. Rather than providing a complete taxonomy of the alternatives to EBD, this Part will only briefly mention some examples from the wide range of possible alternatives.

Most discussions about alternatives to EBD tend to focus on alternative evidentiary rules. Indeed, the different evidentiary rules in the states provide a wide spectrum of alternatives that range from limited and defined exceptions to EBD to its complete rejection, and from rules that allow only a specific type of evidence (such as legislative journals) to the "extrinsic evidence rule," which permits consideration of any authoritative source of information. Even courts that follow the "extrinsic evidence rule" can adequately take into account the "comparative probative value" argument and other considerations underlying EBD by according the enrolled bill a prima facie presumption of validity and establishing a heavy burden of proof. Kentucky, for example, requires "clear, satisfactory and convincing evidence" in order to overcome the prima facie presumption that an enrolled bill is valid, and New Jersey follows a similar rule.

The possible alternatives to EBD are not limited, however, to the evidentiary question. The prudential concerns underlying EBD can also be addressed by other means that range from the justiciability stage to the remedial stage. One example in the justiciability stage is standing. Some scholars have already argued, in the context of criticizing the political question doctrine, that "interests ... such as judicial respect for the processes of the coordinate branches ... can be protected adequately by thoughtful adherence to the principles of standing." "Thoughtful adherence" to standing requirements can also address other concerns expressed by supporters of EBD, such as excessive litigation and misuse of judicial review of the legislative process by "an undeserving but resourceful litigant," especially when this litigant is a legislator seeking a "judicial windfall" after losing in the legislature. The current federal standing requirements, especially where legislators are concerned, seem to be demanding enough to alleviate these concerns.

Another option in the justiciability stage is limiting the timing of judicial review. New Jersey, for example, adopted a mechanism for judicial review that allows the Governor or any two or more citizens of the state to challenge legislation on procedural grounds, and permits courts to go well beyond the enrolled bill to examine journals, testimonies, and other evidence. Instead of EBD and standing, New Jersey adopted other limitations, such as limiting procedural challenges to one year after the law has been filed with the Secretary of State.] This limitation is aimed at alleviating Field's concerns about certainty and stability of the law and reliance interests. Timing limitations can also alleviate concerns about excessive judicial intervention in the legislative process by limiting judicial review to the post-enactment stage. Such timing limitations can be supplemented by the usual ripeness and mootness rules.

The remedial stage also provides ample means to address prudential considerations. As Professor Henkin argued in another context, such considerations can be adequately addressed through the courts' broad powers of equitable discretion to withhold relief for "want of equity." There are several remedial tools that can effectively address, for example, Field's fear from "the consequences that must result if this court should feel obliged . . . to declare that an enrolled bill, on which depend public and private interests of vast magnitude . . . did not become a law." One example is the doctrine of "relative voidability," which instead of treating any unconstitutional law as null and void, allows judicial discretion in choosing the remedy according to the essence (or degree) of the unconstitutionality and to the circumstances of the case. In the context of judicial review of the legislative process, courts that follow this doctrine examine considerations such as the severity of the defect in the legislative process, whether the statute would have been passed had it not been for the defect, the degree of reliance on the statute, the extent of the reasonable expectations that it created, and the consequences that will arise from declaring it void.

Other remedial tools that can address the concerns underlying EBD include severability (that is, the judicial power to strike down only parts of the statute when the valid and invalid portions are severable from each other); the court's authority to grant its decisions only prospective application; or to give suspended declarations of invalidity. The latter is particularly fitting for judicial review of the legislative process that is in its nature a remand to the legislature, which can reenact the same statute, provided the proper procedure is followed. The Manitoba Language Rights case provides one of the most striking examples. In this case, the Supreme Court of Canada found that the province of Manitoba had for almost a century violated the constitutional manner-and-form requirement to enact and promulgate its laws in both English and French. The Court was well aware of the consequences of invalidating over ninety years of law in Manitoba, but did not shirk from its duty to enforce the constitution. Instead, the Court gave the unconstitutional laws temporary effect and used the remedy of a suspended declaration of invalidity, thereby allowing the legislature sufficient time to translate, reenact, print and publish all its laws in both languages.

Finally, prudence and self-restraint can also be incorporated in judgments on the merits. For example, courts can limit their review according to the severity of the defect in the legislative process. As the following examples illustrate, courts that exercise judicial review of the legislative process employ different formulations for the same idea that not every violation and flaw in the enactment process will justify judicial intervention, and that judicial review would be limited only to severe defects. New Jersey courts, for example, emphasized that they will set aside legislation only when "the unconstitutionality of what has been done is manifest" and will therefore not set aside legislation for "immaterial trivialities." Similarly, according to the German Constitutional Court's case law, "only a legally evident error in the legislative procedure leads to the nullity of the legal provisions in question." The Spanish Constitutional Court also held that only a flaw in the legislative process that "substantively impede[s] the crystallization of the House's will" will lead to the invalidation of the law, and the Israeli Supreme Court will intervene only when a "defect that goes to the heart of the process" occurred in the legislative process.

Courts may also limit the grounds for judicial review of the legislative process according to the status of the norm violated in the enactment process (for example, limiting their review to violations of constitutional requirements, as opposed to violations of lawmaking requirements in statutes and internal rules, or distinguishing between mandatory and directory provisions in the Constitution).

All these are means that courts in the states or in other countries successfully employ to address the same concerns underlying Field. New Jersey is an excellent example for the effectiveness of alternatives to EBD in addressing Field's prudential concerns. New Jersey adopted its mechanism for judicial review of the legislative process in 1873. From 1873 to 2005, there were apparently only sixteen reported procedural challenges, and only four of them were successful. According to Professor Grant, the "reason for so few petitions" and the success of this mechanism in New Jersey is the heavy burden of proof the courts employed and their general "judicious self-restraint." Moreover, evidence from several other states also seems to suggest that even without the constraint of EBD, state courts generally exercise self-restraint and only rarely invalidate legislation based on defects in the lawmaking process. Similarly, while recognizing their authority to review the legislative process in the late 1980s, to this day Israeli courts did not strike down even a single statute based on defects in its enactment process. The reason for this telling fact is that "the court has created and built around itself reservations, restraints and constraints, when it is asked to exercise a power of review over the [legislature]." These examples suggest that the concerns underlying EBD can be adequately addressed by other means.

Admittedly, some of these alternatives will be more easily applicable to the federal system than others. This Article does not necessarily recommend wholesale adoption of all the alternatives described above, nor does it prescribe a specific solution. The aim is merely to demonstrate that there is a wide range of possible means that are significantly less costly (at least in the sense of infidelity to the Constitution) and apparently no less effective in addressing the justifications for EBD. This in itself also suggests that it is becoming increasingly hard for EBD to meet Justice Cardozo's challenge and "justify [its] existence as means adapted to an end."

NOTES & QUESTIONS

1.   The philosophical opposite of the enrolled bill rule is the **extrinsic evidence rule**, which holds that an enrolled bill is presumed valid, but permits attack by "clear, satisfactory, and convincing" evidence establishing that the constitutional requirements which the court deems mandatory have not been met. In *Pennsylvanians Against Gambling*, 575 Pa. 542 (PA 2003) the Court stated, "Therefore, relief will be granted to Petitioners only where it is warranted solely from the face of the title and content of the bill as enrolled, together with the judicially noticeable legislative history."

The downside to this type of probative evidence rule is that creates a balancing test; one that may be better at regarding what actually happened but is more uncertain and does not guarantee the correct result. Further, depending on the circumstances, different factfinders might come to different conclusions. Another consideration is that a probative evidence rule may increase time and financial costs on litigants and the courts to conduct a thorough review of legislative documents. Lengthy hearings could replace a simple disposition under the enrolled bill rule. Still, courts have sorted through legislative histories in other contexts. Prof. Sandler argues that these drawbacks are "minimal."

Further, the impacts of a probative evidence rule invalidating legislation could be minimized through high standards of proof such as a "clear and convincing evidence" test or a constitutional abuse of discretion review that recognizes that "[t]here is some point at which evidence, though it exists, becomes so slight and so thoroughly outweighed by contrary evidence, that it would be an abuse of discretion to base a decision upon it." Second, if the error is harmless or minor, or Congress has amended a statute, thus ratifying the original defective statute, there would be no need to invalidate the legislation. Prof. Sandler also suggests that courts could stay a decision to invalidate legislation to give Congress a chance to fix the defect, greatly reducing the impact of finding a statute unconstitutional.

Prof. Sandler states, "It is highly unlikely, though not inconceivable, that Congress will seek to address this issue itself" since some states have passed legislation requiring that courts consider extrinsic evidence. Still, Congress has little incentive to abandon the enrolled bill rule and allow greater judicial review of its work. Therefore, he suggests the Supreme Court should take the next opportunity to adopt the extrinsic evidence rule.

See, David Sandler, "Forget What You Learned in Civics Class: The 'Enrolled Bill Rule' and Why It's Time to Overrule *Field v. Clark*," 41 *Colum. J. L. & Soc. Probs.* 213 (2007).

C. SUBSTANTIVE CONSTITUTIONAL LAW

In addition to a constitution's provisions that relate to the lawmaking process, the legislature must also consider other constitutional restrictions on its power. It is the responsibility of legislators to consider whether legislation protects—or at the very least does not violate—the substantive constitutional rights of the people. Too often this is thought of as the exclusive province of the judiciary. Still, a legislature is often dealing with new problems and crafting novel solutions without the benefit of judicial precedents to guide them. In addition, at the federal level Congress cannot ask the Supreme Court for an advisory opinion on legislative provisions that may be a close call. It would seem natural that a legislature writing a law for future and general application will consider constitutional issues differently than a judge who is considering a specific case in controversy. Deciding where rights begin and end—and balancing different rights—in a legislative context may often involve judicial precedents and academic theories. It may also be intensely practical. When the Colorado Legislature was considering restricting protests around reproductive health clinics, legislators had to consider the free speech rights of the protestors as well as the privacy and safety of clinic patients. Within set areas around clinic doors, protestors could not come within eight feet of another person without permission. The Supreme Court later found these restrictions constitutional. See, *Hill v. Colorado*, 530 U.S. 703 (2000). What the Court did not consider is how the legislature settled on eight feet; how was that determined to be the right distance to protect everyone rights? The legislators drafting the bill stood with their arms out and touched fingertips. They measured the distance between them and decided it should be just a little more than that—eight feet. A legislature's role as a constitutional interpreter and protector has not been explored often. This section's case study allows the reader to put themselves in the shoes of Virginia legislators faced with the hot button issue of gun control.

LEGISLATIVE CONSTITUTIONAL INTERPRETATION
Neal Kumar Katyal, 50 *Duke Law Journal* 1335 (2001)

This is an Essay about "the how" of constitutional interpretation. Much attention has been devoted to the question of how the Constitution is interpreted in courts. Rather little attention has been devoted to the question of how the Constitution is interpreted elsewhere in the government. The Constitution tells us that Congress, the President, and state legislators and courts must adhere to its terms, but it does not tell us how much interpretive power each actor should have, nor does it prescribe rules for each actor to use when interpreting the text. I argue that constitutional interpretation by Congress is, and should be, quite different from constitutional interpretation by courts. In so doing, I combine insights from political scientists about the ways Congress operates with insights from constitutionalists who fear open-ended interpretation.

Congressional interpretation is a recurring problem in constitutional law. In the last four years, momentous events have forced us to rethink how Congress should approach the task. In 1997, the Supreme Court struck down the Religious Freedom Restoration Act (RFRA) on the ground that Congress could not expand constitutional rights through ordinary legislation. The next year, Congress was required to make a judgment about the meaning of the phrase "high Crimes and Misdemeanors" in President Clinton's impeachment trial. Last year, the Supreme Court declared unconstitutional a statute that excused law enforcement officials from providing the four warnings specified in *Miranda v. Arizona*. A separate decision announced the belief that only the Court has the power to define the meaning of the Fourteenth Amendment. More recently, in the wake of the 2000 presidential election, a wide debate ensued about the contours of the right to vote, Congress's role in counting electoral votes, and the meanings of the Twelfth and Fourteenth Amendments. Each of these events challenges us to consider whether Congress should use the techniques of constitutional interpretation that are so familiar to courts.

My conclusion is that because of its unique institutional features, Congress should interpret the text in ways the courts should not. For example, I suggest that Congress should take popular values and beliefs into account when formulating constitutional principles. I also suggest that the virtues and vices of adhering to precedent are somewhat different for legislative precedent than for judicial *stare decisis*. The structural variances between the courts and Congress can be analyzed profitably to develop a theory of interbranch interpretation that takes advantage of the comparative strengths of each branch. The institutional differences between the branches can be a source of richness, rather than a constitutional weakness.

Legislative constitutional interpretation provides one avenue for reconciling what have generally been thought to be two incompatible goals: a living Constitution and a democratic government. The question addressed in this part is how to create a theory of constitutional interpretation that permits endurance but is attentive to the countermajoritarian difficulty. I shall argue that Congress, not the Court, is often best situated to make the judgments necessary to create a Constitution of relevance to Americans today. In the face of contestability over text, history, and structure, if a constitutional question raises an issue of popular values or broad factual assessments, Congress may be better than the Court at making this determination. Especially when text, history, and structure are ambiguous, Congress's interpretations as a politically accountable actor will be useful.

A.   A Proposal

The fear of countermajoritarianism has led many to insist on strict construction of the Constitution's text. This fear has strong implications for the way Article III courts should conduct their interpretation, but it does not necessarily apply to situations where politically accountable actors are doing the interpreting. Public accountability imparts a subtle elasticity to congressional interpretation, and this feature makes it desirable for Congress to interpret the Constitution in ways that courts should not.

The key, and often overlooked, structural distinction between courts and Congress is that the latter is well-situated to understand the views of the people. Members of Congress are up for reelection every two or six years. Because they attend constituent "meet-and-greets," fundraisers, and a host of other political functions, members of Congress are able to infuse their judgments with the views of those they represent. Our Constitution presumes that the government's key decisions will be made by the people, and its legitimacy is grounded in the consent of the governed. Democratic participation is not only an inherent good; it also provides a mechanism to police transgressions by elected officials. When lawmakers interpret the Constitution in unwarranted ways, they can be voted out of office. On the Court, by contrast, life tenure and salary guarantees insulate the Justices from reprisal. The Justices mingle with a tiny number of people and have little incentive to understand life beyond the cloister where they work. The countermajoritarian difficulty surfaces in Court decisions because the Justices have little competence at discerning popular views and no accountability for the judgments they render. For those worried about the vigor of popular rule in America, there is much to fear from judicial interpretation. Therefore, judges should labor under special interpretive guidelines precisely because they lack the accountability of members of Congress.

This theory of interpretation emphasizes that courts are poorly suited to reading shifts in popular will. They are removed from the people, unelected, and have little incentive to understand popular mores—features highlighted by strict constructionists. Congress, on the other hand, frequently makes determinations as to shifts in popular opinion, beliefs, and ideals. Because of Congress's structural superiority in these tasks, it should take a larger role in interpreting those clauses of the Constitution that are meant to evolve over time.

This is not the proper time and place to get into a debate over what those clauses may be. Suffice it to say that if any clauses should be subject to a living and evolving interpretation, it is almost always preferable that the legislature be the branch making these choices. For example, it is commonplace for liberals and conservatives alike to recognize that the Eighth Amendment's Cruel and Unusual Punishments Clause has a meaning that grows with time to reflect " 'the evolving standards of decency that mark the progress of a maturing society.' " Indeed, the Court often states that the meaning of "due process" depends on contemporary values. For example, in the recent *Lewis* case the Court decreed that "the threshold question" in a due process challenge to executive action was whether the conduct was "so outrageous[ ] that it may fairly be said to shock the contemporary conscience." Such words can be read as invitations for legislative interpretation of the Constitution—not simply instructions to courts, which, after all, are comparatively ill-suited to make such broad-based and final societal determinations.

. . .

In addition to the advantages derived from institutional competence, there are also accountability advantages to this course of action. This is the lesson contained in a key letter from James Madison to Spencer Roane. Madison criticized the Supreme Court for misinterpreting the Founders' views on nationalization. Madison believed that Congress should make its own constitutional judgments against nationalization due to its accountability. Congress could "abstain from the exercise" of such powers if it were convinced that the Court was wrong. If members of Congress made the wrong choice, "their Constituents . . . can certainly under the forms of the Constitution effectuate a compliance with their deliberate judgment and settled determination." Madison recognized the possibility of dual tracks of constitutional interpretation, the possibility that both actors—courts and Congress—would analyze constitutional questions and abstain from decision if necessary. To Madison, accountability served to deter unpopular constitutional interpretations and to remove from power those who author them.

. . .

There is a more obvious point to be made about *stare decisis*, which is that Congress, and not the Court, might be in a better position to decide whether social expectations have indeed crystallized around a given constitutional interpretation. The signals that reveal such crystallization are best read by Congress, not the Court.

NOTES & QUESTIONS

1.   In THE DEMOCRATIC CONSTITUTION 238–39 (2004) Neal Devins and Louis Fisher argue that the judiciary does not have "the final word on constitutional questions," but those issues are resolved by "coordinate construction" among the branches. Further, each of the branches bring different institutional capabilities to the process. See also Larry D. Kramer, THE PEOPLE THEMSELVES: POPULAR CONSTITUTIONALISM AND JUDICIAL REVIEW 248 (2004).

2.   In TAKING THE CONSTITUTION AWAY FROM THE COURTS 187 (1999) Prof. Mark Tushnet argued for a "populist constitutional law" that took control of constitutional law away from the courts and to define constitutional rights defined by politics oriented to the principles of the Declaration of Independence.

3. Further reading:

- Neal Kumar Katyal, "Legislative Constitutional Interpretation," 50 *Duke L.J.* 1335, 1359–78 (2001);

- Jeremy Waldron, "The Core Case Against Judicial Review," 115 *Yale L.J.* 1346 (2006) (If a society has "good working democratic institutions" legislatures can protect rights as well as judicial review);

- Keith E. Whittington, "Extrajudicial Constitutional Interpretation: Three Objections and Responses," 80 *N.C. L. Rev.* 773, 846 (2002) ("the judiciary's most useful role may be in framing constitutional disputes for extrajudicial resolution and in enforcing the principled decisions reached elsewhere rather than in autonomously and authoritatively defining constitutional meaning").

Case Study: Gun Control in Virginia

The gun control debate in Virginia became supercharged after several high-profile shootings. On May 31, 2019, a gunman killed 12 people in a mass shooting at the Virginia Beach Municipal Center. The previous week, 9-year-old Markiya Simone Dickson was shot and killed in a South Richmond park. These incidents fueled the national effort on gun control kicked off by the 2018 killing of 17 people at a high school in Parkland, Florida. Virginia had already experienced another mass shooting in 2007 at Virginia Tech when a gunman with two semi-automatic pistols shot and killed 32 people and wounded 17 others. The Virginia Tech shooting was the deadliest school shooting in the history of the United States to that date.

These events encouraged many of the victims of gun violence and their families to become gun safety advocates. Virginia, however, also has a long tradition of hunting and gun ownership, with approximately 45% of Virginians owning a firearm.

To understand this issue, one must remember that gun ownership, and gun regulation, in Virginia is far older than the 2nd Amendment.

In 1619, the Virginia House of Burgesses met for five days and enacted America's first formal gun law in America, which prohibited colonists from transferring guns to Native Americans. The penalty for this crime was death. In 1680 the Assembly passed a law restricting slaves from carrying weapons. In 1791, Virginia ratified the Bill of Rights, including the right to keep and bear arms. In 1950 Virginia passed the Uniform Machine Gun Law Act, which required all machine guns be registered with the State Police within 24 hours of purchase. In 1979 possessing a firearm in an elementary, middle or high school building with intent to use it in a threatening manner became a Class 6 felony. Although Virginia passed a "one gun a month law," it was repealed in 2012 because opponents of the law claimed it was no longer necessary.

According to Prof. Robert J. Spitzer, despite the long history of firearms use and regulation by states, the gun control debate is "typically framed as a fierce, zero-sum struggle" pitting advocates of stronger gun laws against supporters of gun rights. Therefore, most people involved in this debate sees a victory for one side as a loss for the other. Still, many gun owners, including NRA members, favored universal background checks and keeping firearms away from the mentally ill.

The shootings in Virginia Beach led Governor Ralph Northam to call a special session to consider gun safety measures. The Governor and his Democrat allies focused their efforts on 8 measures which they believed had the strongest public support. Each of these bills would spur on a statewide debate on the right to bear arms as protected by the Virginia and United States Constitutions. Unfortunately for the Virginia Assembly, the courts have only recently started defining the contours of the 2nd Amendment leaving legislators to define the limits of the right through legislation.

Courts and the Second Amendment

Gun rights advocates threatened to sue to protect their right to bear arms. Legislators, therefore, had an incentive to draft laws that would stand up to judicial scrutiny. Unfortunately, courts have not given much guidance on what the 2nd Amendment means.

The Second Amendment to the U.S. Constitution reads:

A well regulated Militia, being necessary to the security of a free State, the right of the people to keep and bear Arms, shall not be infringed.

U.S. Supreme Court 2nd Amendment cases are, at best, sparse. The first time the Court applied the Amendment to an Act of Congress came in *United States v. Miller*, 307 U.S. 174 (1939), which was a challenge to the National Firearms Act of 1934 (NFA). The Roosevelt Administration originally sought a law where most private ownership of firearms would be eliminated. Ultimately, Congress passed the NFA, which required persons possessing certain firearms, including machine guns and short-barreled rifles, register the weapon with the Federal government and pay a $200 tax at both the time of registration if the weapon was transferred. The federal District Court found the Act violated the Second Amendment and the case went to the Supreme Court. In a short, confusing opinion that is cited by activists on both sides of the gun debate, Justice McReynolds, held the NFA did not violate the 2nd Amendment. He reasoned a short-barreled shotgun was not related to "a well regulated militia."

The next case came 69 years later in District of *Columbia v. Heller*, 554 U.S. 570 (2008). The Court examined the Firearms Control Regulations Act of 1975 and a local District of Columbia law that restricted residents from owning handguns, (except those registered prior to 1975) and those possessed by active and retired law enforcement officers.

The law also required that all firearms including rifles and shotguns be kept "unloaded and disassembled or bound by a trigger lock." In a 5–4 decision authored by Justice Scalia, the Court ruled that the Second Amendment protects an individual's right to keep and bear arms for traditionally lawful purposes such as self-defense within the home, and that the Act violated the litigants' right to bear arms. Heller held that "whatever else [the Second Amendment] leaves to future evaluation, it surely elevates above all other interests the right of law-abiding, responsible citizens to use arms in defense of hearth and home." The Court also recognized that the right was limited in scope and subject to some regulation. One specific limitation was the 2nd Amendment protected only weapons "typically possessed by law-abiding citizens for lawful purposes." The Court also said some regulations are "presumptively lawful,"

> [N]othing in our opinion should be taken to cast doubt on longstanding prohibitions on the possession of firearms by felons and the mentally ill, or laws forbidding the carrying of firearms in sensitive places such as schools and government buildings, or laws imposing conditions and qualifications on the commercial sale of arms.

In *McDonald v. Chicago*, 561 U.S. 742 (2010), the Supreme Court found that the right of an individual to "keep and bear arms," as protected by the 2nd Amendment, is incorporated by the Fourteenth Amendment and is enforceable against the states.

The Fourth Circuit Court of Appeals, which includes Virginia, has traditionally taken a narrow interpretation of the 2nd Amendment. However, in *U.S. v. Chester*, 628 F.3d 673 (4th Cir. 2010), the 4th Circuit took the approach required by Justice Scalia's Heller decision, and did an extensive historical analysis of the scope of the right to determine if a person convicted of a domestic abuse misdemeanor could be denied a firearm license. The court did not find a historical basis for denying gun rights to people convicted of a misdemeanor and so vacated the lower court's ruling.

It is not surprising that the Federal amendment looks like its Virginia counterpart, given that Virginian James Madison drafted the Bill of Rights. The Virginia version reads:

> That a well regulated militia, composed of the body of the people, trained to arms, is the proper, natural, and safe defense of a free state, therefore, the right of the people to keep and bear arms shall

not be infringed; that standing armies, in time of peace, should be avoided as dangerous to liberty; and that in all cases the military should be under strict subordination to, and governed by, the civil power. Virginia Const. Art. I § 13.

In *DiGiacinto v. Rector and Visitors of George Mason University*, 281 Va. 127 (2011), the Virginia Supreme Court considered whether a George Mason University regulation prohibiting the possession of weapons on its campus, violates the Constitution of Virginia or the United States Constitution. The plaintiff was not a student or employee of GMU, but utilized the university's resources, including its libraries, and wanted to exercise his right to carry a firearm into the GMU buildings. This was a case of first impression on the right to bear arms provision of the Virginia Constitution. The plaintiff contended the Virginia provision offered greater protections than the 2nd Amendment. The Court, however, held that the protection of the right to bear arms expressed in Article I, § 13 of the Constitution of Virginia is co-extensive with the rights provided by the Second Amendment of the United States Constitution, concerning the issues presented in this case.

Relying heavily on *Heller* and *McDonald*, the Court held that the right to keep and bear arms is not "a right to keep and carry any weapon whatsoever in any manner whatsoever and for whatever purpose," and that longstanding regulatory measures such as "laws forbidding the carrying of firearms in sensitive places such as schools and government buildings, or laws imposing conditions and qualifications on the commercial sale of arms," were valid.(quoting Heller, 554 U.S. at 625–28). The University was a "sensitive place" and could Constitutionally restrict firearm possession on campus.

Gov. Northam's Special Session

In the wake of the Virginia Beach shootings, Gov. Northam called a special General Assembly session on July 9 to consider and hopefully pass a slate of gun safety measures. He said, "We continue to lose too many lives to senseless and preventable acts of gun violence, but we have the power to make meaningful change. Now is the time to act—Virginians deserve votes and laws, not thoughts and prayers. I urge the members of the General Assembly to engage in a thorough, meaningful discussion about these proposed bills and to allow every member to cast their votes on the floor."

Gov. Northam proposed eight bills (For detailed summaries, see Appendix A):

- Requiring background checks on all firearms transfers. The bill mandates that any person selling, renting, trading, or transferring a firearm must first obtain the results of a background check before completing the transaction. This would close the so called "gun show loophole," where private sales at gun shows do not have to perform background checks like gun dealers.

- Banning dangerous weapons including assault weapons, high-capacity magazines, bump stocks and silencers.

- Allowing a person only one handgun purchase within a 30-day period.

- Requiring that lost and stolen firearms be reported to law enforcement within 24 hours.

- Creating an Extreme Risk Protective Order, allowing law enforcement and the courts to temporarily take a firearm from persons who exhibit dangerous behavior or presents an immediate threat to themselves or others.

- Prohibiting all individuals subject to final protective orders from possessing firearms.

- Enhancing the punishment for allowing access to loaded unsecured firearm by a child from a Class 3 Misdemeanor to a Class 6 felony. The bill also raises the age of the child from 14 to 18.

- Enabling localities to enact any firearms ordinances that are stricter than state law for regulating firearms in municipal buildings, libraries and at permitted events.

Polling found broad support for stronger gun safety measures. In February 2018 poll by Wason Center for Public Policy at Christopher Newport University of registered voters found:

84% supported background checks for private gun sales, including 76% of Republicans. Nearly 65% support a ban on "assault-style" weapons, including 49% of Republicans. 54% of those polled said controlling who buys a firearm was more important that protecting gun rights.

A 2019 Washington Post-Schar School poll found that 75% of Virginia respondents called gun policy a "very important" issue.

When the special session began, however, the Republican controlled House and Senate ended the session after 90 minutes and adjourned until Nov. 18. Afterwards, House Speaker Kirk Cox told reporters that the Governor's efforts were "an election-year stunt." Speaker Cox joined Senate President pro tempore Stephen D. Newman (R-Bedford), saying that Republicans proposed their own "common sense" legislation such as increasing mandatory minimums for people who use guns in violent crimes and to restrict gun rights for released convicted felons.

Del. C. Todd Gilbert (R-Woodstock) said, "I hope we will find ways to work together, and that can happen if Democrats don't try to throw red meat to their base while talking in brochure platitudes. As we go through this process, the key question that I hope all legislators will ask is whether what we have in place already is being enforced to the fullest extent of the law and whether what is being proposed will actually capture criminal acts."

Many gun rights activists, however, were most concerned about proposed bans and confiscate AR-15s and other assault-style weapons. Since their introduction in the 1960s, approximately 8 million AR-style rifles have been produced and sold. The weapons are particularly popular because they are considered easy to use and modifiy with different scopes, stocks and rails. One of the most popular brands of "standard capacity" AR magazines is the Magpul PMAG M3 They're reasonably priced, easy to find, and generally quite reliable. The most commonly purchased magazine holds 30-rounds, but Magpul also sells 10, 20, and 40-round versions of the PMAG, and a 60-round drum variation. The 10- and 20-round magazines are especially useful for shooting from prone or other positions where a longer magazine might get in the way.

Speaking about an assault weapons bill that did not have an explicit grandfather clause, Sen. Amanda Chase, (R-Chesterfield), said that the Democrats have "already filed some extreme legislation that will hurt law-abiding citizens."

The bill sponsor, Sen. Adam P. Ebbin (D-Alexandria) said, "No one is coming for assault weapons that people already own. We are about public safety, and Sen. Richard Saslaw (D-Springfield) and I agree that our bill will forbid the future sale of these weapons, and that it is simply not practical to consider collecting anybody's weapons."

Sen. Chase, who recently left the Senate Republican Caucus but retains her party affiliation, says she intends to introduce legislation to ban gun-free zones, even though she knows that "nothing will pass." Indeed, nothing did pass; the Republican majority referred the various bills to the Virginia Crime Commission for study:

Virginia General Assembly

AUTHORIZED BY THE VIRGINIA HOUSE REPUBLICAN CAUCUS AND THE VIRGINIA SENATE REPUBLICAN CAUCUS

July 9, 2019

Dear Senator Obenshain and Delegate Bell:

As you know, the General Assembly convened today for a Special Session called by Governor Northam in response to the tragedy that occurred in Virginia Beach earlier this year. We continue to pray for the victims, their families, and the Virginia Beach community. Like you, we are committed to keeping our streets, neighborhoods, counties, and cities free from all forms of violence—including gun violence. The General Assembly has consistently taken steps to make the Commonwealth safer, and the results speak for themselves. Our Commonwealth is one of the safest states in the nation. Our firearm mortality rate is below the national average. We have the fourth lowest violent crime rate in the country. And as Governor Northam proudly pointed out in a January press release, Virginia also has the lowest recidivism rate in the country. We have achieved this because of our brave men and women in law enforcement, a strong criminal justice system, and by enacting sound, evidenced-based public policy through thoughtful legislative dialogue. Following the 2007 murders at Virginia Tech, then-Governor Tim Kaine convened a blue-ribbon commission that produced dozens of recommendations on mental and behavioral health. We took similar action after the tragedy in Parkland, Florida. The bipartisan Select Committee on School Safety produced meaningful legislation to address systemic weaknesses and keep our kids safer. We believe we should once again take a thoughtful and deliberative approach. To that end, we respectfully direct the Virginia State Crime Commission undertake a systematic review of the events that occurred in Virginia Beach and proposed legislative changes to Virginia's laws concerning firearms and public safety. The investigation into these events is ongoing. The Virginia Beach City Council recently authorized an independent investigation into the tragedy that hopefully will provide much needed insight. The Crime Commission should carefully review any findings that are available because of the independent investigation as part of its effort. We have asked the committees of the House and Senate to refer all legislation introduced during the Special Session to the Crime Commission for review. Any additional legislation filed by members of the General Assembly before July 19 should also be included. We ask the Chairman of the Crime Commission, in consultation with the Executive Committee, to schedule a meeting no later than August 23, 2019, to begin its work, and to make its final report to the General Assembly after November 12, 2019. The Crime Commission is a widely-respected, bipartisan panel known for its substantive work on matters of public policy. We are confident that, under your leadership, the Crime Commission will be able to better understand what steps Virginia might take to keep our communities safe without the distraction of partisan politics. We thank you for your service to the Commonwealth and your work on this important issue.

Respectfully yours,

M. Kirkland "Kirk" Cox   Thomas K. Norment, Jr.
Speaker   Majority Leader, Senate of Virginia

Over the course of the two-day hearing, the Commission heard testimony from law enforcement, gun safety activists, researchers, public policy experts, and citizens.

During the Commission hearing gun safety proponents argued that in the previous year gun violence's involved in more than 1,000 deaths in Virginia. Gun safety advocate Leanne Fox said, "We know there are solutions for gun violence. It's our legislator's jobs to write laws that keep us safe and respect the second amendment, and they're not doing that."

Andy Goddard, whose son was shot and wounded during the Virginia Tech shooting, said Virginia lawmakers have too often used a reactive approach to gun violence, "Whether we want to call it an epidemic or not, more than 1,000 people dying [per year] where I was born would have been a total epidemic."

Lori Haas testified, "When almost three Virginians are killed every day, that is an epidemic, that is a crisis, and we are not doing our jobs if we are not responding."

Gun rights supporters, however, claimed that a rush to limit second amendment rights would result in bad public policy that criminals would not listen to in the first place. Chris Kopacki, the Virginia Director of the NRA, argued that the state needed to better enforce existing laws before creating new ineffective laws. Jay McDaniels, who open carried a firearm to the Commission hearing, stated, "These laws are never going to be effective because criminals don't follow them. Stop infringing on my rights, and do your job to protect my rights." President of the Virginia Citizen's Defense League, Phillip Van Cleave said, "One way to stop drunk drivers from killing sober drivers would be to forbid sober drivers from driving on the road at any time. If that sounds stupid and backwards, welcome to the world of gun control."

One of the experts who testified before the Crime Commission was The Heritage Foundation's Amy Swearer, a senior legal policy analyst in the Meese Center for Legal and Judicial Studies. Swearer argued Virginia adopt only narrow measures to control gun violence, such as the red flag laws, as opposed to "extreme or broad restrictions on Second Amendment rights." Swearer testified by claiming the U.S. is not facing a gun violence crisis:

Americans are safer today from violent crime—including firearm-related crime—than we have been at any point during my lifetime. We are, in fact, in the midst of a decade of historically low rates of violent crime. Even though the number of guns in this country has increased by about 50 percent since the early 1990s, the rate of homicide and gun-related homicide has fallen by about 50 percent.

Swearer argued that focusing on untreated mental health conditions would be meaningful way to address gun-related violence without "broadly infringing on the Second Amendment rights of all lawful gun owners."

In response to Swearer's comments the chair of a legislative committee studying mental health issues Sen. Creigh Deeds (D-Bath County) said that "people with mental illnesses are more likely to be the victims of gun violence rather than the perpetrators." In 2013, Sen. Deed's son Gus, who had been diagnosed with bipolar disorder, committed suicide with a gun after stabbing Deeds multiple times. It should be noted that Sen. Deeds had also been a hunter and member of the NRA since the age of 10 years. Sen. Deeds was quoted as hoping that Republican and Democratic legislators could have a "mature conversation . . . and really do something substantive for the people of Virginia" that might save as a model for other states.

Most of the discussion at the Commission hearing centered on fortifying the state's background check system, "red flag" extreme risk protective orders, and limiting the number of "gun-free zones."

After the hearings, the Democratic members of the Crime Commission released a statement saying the testimony showed the public support policies like universal background checks, extreme risk orders, and banning high-capacity magazines. They also claimed the testimony could have been given during a regular committee hearing during the special session, which would have allowed the legislators to take votes on the bills. Instead, the Republican leadership deferred to the Crime Commission was a strategy to "neutralize the conversation."

Republican leaders, however, called the testimony a "thoughtful and deliberate study" that would lead to meaningful action when the General Assembly reconvened after the November elections. House Majority Leader Todd Gilbert (R-Shenandoah) released a statement: "We have learned over the last two days that the best path to keeping people safe is enforcing existing law, holding criminals accountable, strengthening our mental health systems, and using targeted intervention strategies that divert people from lives of violence."

The Crime Commission later released its report:

2019 Crime Commission Report

MASS KILLINGS AND GUN VIOLENCE STUDY SUMMARY

Following the Special Session called by the Governor, Senate Majority Leader Thomas K. Norment, Jr., and Speaker M. Kirkland Cox sent a letter to the Crime Commission on July 9, 2019, requesting "a systematic review of the events that occurred in Virginia Beach and proposed legislative changes to Virginia's laws concerning firearms and public safety."

As a result of this letter request, Crime Commission staff was asked to examine these matters and provide a report to the General Assembly. Staff determined that inconclusive evidence exists to develop recommendations. While staff researched a wide variety of policies and many other matters related to gun violence, the overall findings from the research were often insufficient, mixed, contradictory, or based on limited methodology. The absence of recommendations should not be interpreted as a finding that no changes to Virginia's laws are necessary. Any changes to these laws are policy decisions which can only be made by the General Assembly. A large amount of information was collected and numerous policy considerations were identified in relation to gun violence and the proposed changes to Virginia's laws. As such, staff is available to provide technical assistance to members of the General Assembly.

SYSTEMATIC REVIEW OF THE EVENTS THAT OCCURRED IN VIRGINIA BEACH

A systematic review of the events that occurred in Virginia Beach on May 31, 2019, was not able to be completed. On September 24, 2019, staff attended a public meeting where the Virginia Beach City Council was updated on the status of the investigations. However, two separate law enforcement investigations by the Virginia Beach Police Department and the Federal Bureau of Investigation will likely take several more months to complete. Additionally, the security risk management firm (Hillard Heintze) retained by the City of Virginia Beach to conduct an independent investigation is planning to present its report to the Virginia Beach City Council on November 13, 2019.

WRITTEN COMMENTS

The Crime Commission accepted a total of 4,145 written comments relating to gun violence between July 19, 2019 and September 30, 2019, which consisted of 3,297 emails and 848 letters or post cards. All of these written comments were reviewed by staff and emailed to Crime Commission members.

. . .

During the first month, staff focused efforts on reviewing legislation introduced during the Special Session and planning for the August Crime Commission meetings. Staff conducted a cursory review of 78 bills and grouped the legislation into categories based upon their subject matter. Additionally, staff began a literature review of gun violence in an effort to identify specific topics for discussion at the August meetings. Staff spent an extraordinary amount of time coordinating the logistics of these meetings. On August 19, 2019, Crime Commission members heard detailed presentations from federal and state agencies and reports from leading academic researchers. On August 20, 2019, members heard testimony from bill patrons, organizations, interest groups, and comments from members of the general public. After the August meetings, staff examined the following policies, as well as many other matters related to gun violence, based upon information presented at those meetings and legislation introduced during the Special Session:

1. Assault Rifle/Firearm Accessory Restrictions (e.g., magazine capacity, suppressors)

2. Background Checks for Private Firearm Sales and Transfers

3. Child Access Prevention/Safe Storage of Firearms

4. Crisis Response Plans for Victim Services

5. Domestic and Intimate Partner Violence

6. Enhanced Penalties/Mandatory Minimum Sentences

7. Local Authority to Regulate Firearms

8. Restoration of One Handgun Per Month Purchase Limit

9. Reporting of Lost and Stolen Firearms

10. Substantial Risk Orders ("Red Flag" Laws)

11. Suicide Prevention

Staff sought to ascertain the intended outcome of any proposed changes, determine the effectiveness of such changes, and identify any unintended consequences if such changes were implemented. It was determined that inconclusive evidence exists to develop recommendations due to the following factors:

• Limited availability of studies on particular policies;

• Difficulty isolating the impact of individual policies;

• Nature of the evidence from research findings being insufficient, mixed, or contradictory;

• Methodologies of studies being limited;

• Bias associated with particular studies; and,

• Unavailable or limited data.

The absence of recommendations should not be interpreted as meaning that no changes to Virginia's laws are necessary, but rather that any changes are policy decisions which can only be made by the General Assembly

2019 Election

On November 5th, all 140 seats in the General Assembly were up for election. Democrats won enough seats to take control of both the House and the Senate for the first time in over 20 years. After the election, Democrats would have 55-to-45 House majority and a 21-to-19 majority in the Senate.

Many observers gave partial credit for the electoral victories to campaign donations from gun-safety advocacy groups and increasing public support for gun safety policies. The money from gun safety advocates was particularly significant; Everytown for Gun Safety, which was co-founded by former New York City Mayor Michael Bloomberg spent over $1.5 million on the Virginia elections. In contrast, the NRA spent only $350,269. The way the Republicans handled the previous session also became a campaign issue. Legislators from both parties had filed more than 70 gun related bills, but none were sent to the Governor. The special legislative session may have reinforced the perception that the Legislature would not address the issue without a change.

On election night, Gov. Northam, released a statement that the results indicated Virginia voters "want us to finally pass common-sense gun safety legislation, so no one has to fear being hurt or killed while at school, at work, or at their place of worship." The next day, Gov. Northam told his Cabinet he would pursue gun-safety measures in the next legislative session, including: background checks on all firearm sales; banning assault weapons, high-capacity magazines, bump stocks and silencers; reinstating Virginia's one-gun-a-month law; and a "red flag" law that would allow law enforcement officers and courts to temporarily remove a gun from the possession of someone they have determined to be a risk to themselves or others.

Sanctuary Cities

One of the byproducts of the Democratic victories at the polls and Governor Northam's gun safety agenda was the rise of "2nd Amendment Sanctuaries." The movement is styled after the cities that declared themselves "undocumented immigrant sanctuaries," an effort to protect residents from stricter federal immigration laws and enforcement by the Trump administration.

Shortly after the election, gun-rights activists started lobbying local and county governments, mostly in rural areas of the state, to approve 2nd Amendment sanctuary resolutions. The county supervisors responsible for the resolutions said the measures were a message to legislators and the Governor that their communities opposed restrictions on guns. A supervisor in New Kent claimed the masses had spoken and his county would not support the proposed restrictions.

Several county sheriffs have also backed the sanctuary resolutions. King William Sheriff Jeff Walton said he is in support of the county's resolution because he is a constitutional officer. "I took an oath to uphold the Constitution," Walton said. "I plan to do that." Erich Pratt, of the Guns Owners of America, said, "When a state starts denying the constitutionally protected rights of its citizens, then it is completely legitimate for officials at lower levels to step in and protect citizens."

A legal adviser to the Virginia Beach Sheriff's Office, however, was concerned that the sanctuary resolutions would cause a crisis for local police departments, who take an oath to enforce Virginia state laws that are now in direct conflict with ordinance passes by their local governing body. The Virginia Beach City Council later passed a weaker resolution expressing its strong support for the gun rights of law-abiding citizens but stopped short of declaring a sanctuary.

The Virginia Association of Chiefs of Police and Foundation took a more cautious tone, and actually indicated that its members of about 275 police chiefs and deputy chiefs supported universal background checks.

These sanctuary designations may be of limited legal effect. Virginia is a "Dillon Rule" state, which means localities are subject to a narrow interpretation of local authority and can only take actions as allowed by the state government. The U.S. Supreme Court has upheld the Dillon Rule in Tabler v. Fairfax County (1980) and its use by most states. Therefore, the state can prevent local governments from creating or enforcing rules that conflict with state law. Even if the Dillon Rule were not a factor, state law would probably preempt local ordinances anyway.

Sanctuary proponents respond that the resolutions don't violate the Dillon Rule because there is no new local law, but a pledge by local officials to not use public funds to enforce any new state gun laws.

Still, Del. Mike Mullin, (D-Newport News), called the movement "political theater," saying, "The voters have spoken and they want common-sense gun control." Gov. Northam warned counties that state law enforcement officers are obliged to enforce state laws. Kris Brown, the president of the Brady Campaign to Prevent Gun Violence, called the sanctuary movement a dangerous marketing campaign" and a "political gimmick" intended to make people believe constitutionally valid gun laws infringed on peoples' Second Amendment rights.

Still, local police officers and county sheriffs exercise wide discretion in enforcing the law, and state police alone could not enforce any unpopular gun laws. George Mason Law Professor Robert Leider suggested that if an assault weapon ban were to pass, police might be less rigorous in enforcing gun laws due to political blowback from gun owners.

Other cities and counties around the country, even in states not considering gun legislation, followed Virginia's lead and declared themselves "sanctuaries." By early 2020, more than 200 counties nationwide had declared themselves Second Amendment sanctuaries in two months. By the time the Assembly reconvened in 2020, 150 Virginia localities, including 91 out of 95 counties, adopted sanctuary resolutions.

People were also confused about the true legal meaning of the sanctuaries. In fact, some people were under the impression that the sanctuary declarations swept away all gun laws. A Tazewell County administrator heard from a couple who were denied licenses to sell guns and now want to sell them. The owners of Rudy's Computer & Pawn Shop in Bluefield, asked officials if the resolution would make the store "exempt from State penalties for handling a transfer of any so called 'banned' weapons."

Virginia legislators, however, were aware that the significance of the Sanctuary Movement would depend largely on how far the Legislature would go in passing gun legislation.

The Demonstration

On January 17th, President Trump joined the debate by Twitter, "Your 2nd Amendment is under very serious attack in the Great Commonwealth of Virginia. That's what happens when you vote for Democrats, they will take your guns away. Republicans will win Virginia in 2020. Thank you Dems!"

On January 20th, 22,000 gun rights protestors descended on Richmond to protest against the Governor's firearms proposals. The rally was organized by a grassroots gun-rights group, the Virginia Citizens Defense League, which holds a yearly, typically a low-key, rally in Richmond with a few hundred gun activists. Due to the national attention given to Virginia, busloads of activities came from around Virginia and several other states to join the rally.

Gov. Northam was concerned about violent fringe groups joining in on the protests, "Over the past few days, the news has confirmed that this rally is attracting extreme individuals and groups—including national hate, neo-Nazi, and white supremacist groups—who are threatening violence and looking to advance a violent agenda." Partially related to this, Gov. Northam declared a state of emergency and banned firearms from the Capitol grounds, which upset gun rights activists even more. Although the rally's organizers sued, the State Supreme Court upheld the ban.

Rather than turning violent, the crowd was characterized as "festive," with chanting and signs denouncing Gov. Northam. The rally remained peaceful, and police only arrested one person—a woman who covered her face with a bandanna and would not remove it despite getting two warnings by police.

The protests further galvanized the gun rights activists. Del. Gilbert stated, "I think that should be a wake up call to Democrats that maybe they're about to go too far. To set us up where we're gonna completely ignore the way that rural Virginians choose to live and protect their families, I just think sets up for really bad outcomes on so many levels in the future."

The Session

Less than a week after the gun rights demonstrations in Richmond, the Assembly started its session and began considering Gov. Northam's eight bill gun safety package:

- Universal background checks on all firearms sales and transactions;

- Ban on assault weapons, high-capacity magazines, bump stocks and silencers;

- Allowing one handgun purchase within a 30-day period;

- Requiring reports of lost and stolen firearms;

- Creation of an extreme risk protective order, or "Red Flag" Law;

- Prohibition persons with protective orders from possessing firearms;

- Penalties or allowing access to loaded, unsecured firearm to a child;

- Allow localities to regulate firearms in municipal buildings, libraries and at permitted events.

The local CBS television station predicted the upcoming legislative session would be "the greatest gun law fight in a generation." Robert D. Holsworth, a political analyst at Virginia Commonwealth University said the upcoming General Assembly session would "generate global coverage," and that the 2019 election "represents a sea change in the politics of gun control [and] in Virginia politics as well—the biggest change in a generation."

The 40 members of the Senate tend to be older, more tenured and less racially diverse than the House, and in recent years have taken less liberal positions than the House in many areas, including labor and immigration. The day before the General Assembly began its new session on January 8, the Democrats caucused behind closed doors. Four senators from rural districts, Chap Petersen (D-Fairfax City), R. Creigh Deeds (D-Bath), John S. Edwards (D-Roanoke), and Lynwood W. Lewis Jr. (D-Accomack) informed the caucus that they wouldn't support all eight the Governor's gun bills. The most troubling bill for this group was the assault weapons ban.

Explaining his position, Sen. Petersen said, "You can't discount people that were raised and grew up in this state and have their own traditions. You can't just suddenly kick them to the curb." Sens. Deeds and Edwards said the legislation's definition of "assault firearm" was imprecise. Sen. Surovell also said he was concerned by a provision that forced owners to give up large-capacity magazines without compensation, which he considered an unconstitutional "taking" of property.

All of the firearms bills for the new session would be sent to the Senate Judiciary Committee for review and a vote to advance the bill to the full Senate. The Judiciary Committee membership was:

Democrats	Republicans
John S. Edwards (chair)	Thomas K. Norment, Jr.
Richard L. Saslaw	Mark D. Obenshain
L. Louise Lucas	Ryan T. McDougle
R. Creigh Deeds	Richard H. Stuart
Scott A. Sourovell	William M. Stanley, Jr.
Jennifer L. McClellan	A. Benton Chafin, Jr.
Jennifer B. Boysko	
J. Chapman Petersen	
Joseph D. Morrissey	

The major question for the new session was, how would the Virginia Legislature define the right to bear arms? How far can the state regulate gun ownership and use? And what does that right prevent the Legislature from doing? If you were in the position the 40 state senators found themselves in, where would you draw the line? What is the basis for those decisions?

Appendix A: Governor Northam's Firearms Package as Filed

Background Checks

HB 2 Firearm transfers; criminal history record information checks, penalty.

Introduced by: Kenneth R. Plum

SUMMARY AS INTRODUCED:

Firearm transfers; criminal history record information checks; penalty. Requires a background check for any firearm transfer and directs the Department of State Police (the Department) to establish a process for transferors to obtain such a check from licensed firearms dealers. A transferor who sells a firearm to another person without obtaining the required background check is guilty of a Class 6 felony. The bill also provides that a transferee who receives a firearm from another person without obtaining the required background check is guilty of a Class 1 misdemeanor. The bill exempts transfers (i) between immediate family members; (ii) that occur by operation of law; (iii) by the executor or administrator of an estate or by the trustee of a testamentary trust; (iv) at firearms shows in accordance with law; (v) that are part of a buy-back or give-back program; (vi) of antique firearms; (vii) that occur at a shooting range, shooting gallery, or any other area designed for the purpose of target shooting, for use during target practice, a firearms safety or training course or class, a shooting competition, or any similar lawful activity; or (viii) that are temporary transfers that (a) occur within the continuous presence of the owner of the firearm or (b) are necessary to prevent imminent death or great bodily harm. The bill removes the provision that makes background checks of prospective purchasers or transferees at firearms shows voluntary. The bill also provides that the Department shall have three business days to complete a criminal history record information check before a firearm may be transferred. The bill establishes an appropriation for the fiscal impact of the bill and authorizes the Director of the Department of Planning and Budget to allocate such appropriation among the agencies and programs impacted by the bill.

Assault Weapons

SB 16 Assault firearms and certain firearm magazines; prohibiting sale, transport, etc., penalties.

Introduced by: Richard L. Saslaw

SUMMARY AS INTRODUCED:

Prohibiting sale, transport, etc., of assault firearms and certain firearm magazines; penalties. Expands the definition of "assault firearm" and prohibits any person from importing, selling, transferring, manufacturing, purchasing, possessing, or transporting an assault firearm. A violation is a Class 6 felony. The bill prohibits a dealer from selling, renting, trading, or transferring from his inventory an assault firearm to any person. The bill also prohibits a person from carrying a shotgun with a magazine that will hold more than seven rounds of the longest ammunition for which it is chambered in a public place; under existing law, this prohibition applies only in certain localities. The bill makes it a Class 1 misdemeanor to import, sell, barter, or transfer any firearm magazine designed to hold more than 10 rounds of ammunition.

HB 961 Assault firearms, certain firearm magazines, etc.; prohibiting sale, transport, etc., penalties.

Introduced by: Mark H. Levine

SUMMARY AS INTRODUCED:

Prohibiting sale, transport, etc., of assault firearms, certain firearm magazines, silencers, and trigger activators; penalties. Expands the definition of "assault firearm" and prohibits any person from importing, selling, transferring, manufacturing, purchasing, possessing, or transporting an assault firearm. A violation is a Class 6 felony. The bill prohibits a dealer from selling, renting, trading, or transferring from his inventory an assault firearm to any person. The bill also prohibits a person from carrying a shotgun with a magazine that will hold more than seven rounds of the longest ammunition for which it is chambered in a public place; under existing law, this prohibition applies only in certain localities. The bill makes it a Class 6 felony to import, sell, transfer, manufacture, purchase, possess, or transport large-capacity firearm magazines, silencers, and trigger activators, all defined in the bill. Any person who legally owns an assault firearm, large-capacity firearm magazine, silencer, or trigger activator on July 1, 2020, may retain possession until January 1, 2021. During that time, such person shall (i) render the assault firearm, large-capacity firearm magazine, silencer, or trigger activator inoperable; (ii) remove the assault firearm, large-capacity firearm magazine, silencer, or trigger activator from the Commonwealth; (iii) transfer the assault firearm, large-capacity firearm magazine (defined as over 12 rounds), silencer, or trigger activator to a person outside the Commonwealth who is not prohibited from possessing it; or (iv) surrender the assault firearm, large-capacity firearm magazine, silencer, or trigger activator to a state or local law-enforcement agency.

The bill further states that any person who legally owns an assault firearm on July 1, 2020, may retain possession of such assault firearm after January 1, 2021, if such person has obtained a permit from the Department of State Police to possess an assault firearm in accordance with procedures established in the bill. A person issued such permit may possess an assault firearm only under the following conditions: (a) while in his home or on his property or while on the property of another who has provided prior permission, provided that the person has the landowner's written permission on his person while on such property; (b) while at a shooting range, shooting gallery, or other area designated for the purpose of target shooting or the target range of a public or private club or organization whose members have organized for the purpose of practicing shooting targets or competing in target shooting matches; (c) while engaged in lawful hunting; or (d) while surrendering the assault firearm to a state or local law-enforcement agency. A person issued such permit may also transport an assault firearm between any of those locations, provided that such assault firearm is unloaded and secured within a closed container while being transported. The bill also provides that failure to display the permit and a photo identification upon demand by a law-enforcement officer shall be punishable by a $25 civil penalty, which shall be paid into the state treasury. The bill also requires the Department of State Police to enter the name and description of a person issued a permit in the Virginia Criminal Information Network (VCIN) so that the permit's existence and current status will be made known to the law-enforcement personnel accessing VCIN for investigative purposes.

"One Gun A Month"

SB 69 Handguns; limitation on purchases, penalty.

Introduced by: Mamie E. Locke

SUMMARY AS INTRODUCED:

Purchase of handguns; limitation on handgun purchases; penalty. Prohibits any person who is not a licensed firearms dealer from purchasing more than one handgun in a 30-day period and establishes such an offense as a Class 1 misdemeanor. The bill exempts from this provision (i) persons who have been issued a certificate by the Department of State Police under certain circumstances and with an enhanced background check, (ii) law-enforcement agencies and officers, (iii) state and local correctional facilities, (iv) licensed private security companies, (v) persons who hold a valid Virginia concealed handgun permit, (vi) persons whose handgun has been stolen or irretrievably lost or who are trading in a handgun, (vii) purchases of handguns in a private sale, and (viii) purchases of antique firearms.

Lost or Stolen Firearms

HB 9 Firearms; reporting those lost or stolen, civil penalty.

Introduced by: Jeffrey M. Bourne

SUMMARY AS INTRODUCED:

Reporting lost or stolen firearms; civil penalty. Requires that, if a firearm is lost or stolen from a person who lawfully possessed it, such person shall report the loss or theft of the firearm to any local law-enforcement agency or the Department of State Police within 24 hours after such person discovers the loss or theft or is informed by a person with personal knowledge of the loss or theft. The bill requires the relevant law-enforcement agency to enter the report information into the National Crime Information Center. A violation is punishable by a civil penalty of not more than $250. The bill provides that a person who, in good faith, reports the loss or theft is immune from criminal or civil liability for acts or omissions that result from the loss or theft. The immunity does not apply to a person who knowingly gives a false report. The bill does not apply to the loss or theft of an antique firearm.

"Red Flag" Law

SB 240 Firearms; removal from persons posing substantial risk of injury to himself, etc., penalties.

Introduced by: George L. Barker | all patrons . . . notes | add to my profiles | history

SUMMARY AS INTRODUCED:

Firearms; removal from persons posing substantial risk; penalties. Creates a procedure by which any attorney for the Commonwealth or any law-enforcement officer may apply to a general district court, circuit court, or juvenile and domestic relations district court judge or magistrate for an emergency substantial risk order to prohibit a person who poses a substantial risk of injury to himself or others from purchasing, possessing, or transporting a firearm. If an emergency substantial risk order is issued, a judge or magistrate may issue a search warrant to remove firearms from such person. An emergency substantial risk order shall expire on the fourteenth day following issuance of the order. The bill requires a court hearing in the circuit court for the jurisdiction where the order was issued within 14 days from issuance of an emergency substantial risk order to determine whether a substantial risk order should be issued. Seized firearms shall be retained by a law-enforcement agency for the duration of an emergency substantial risk order or a substantial risk order or, for a substantial risk order and with court approval, may be transferred to a third party 21 years of age or older chosen by the person from whom they were seized. The bill allows the complainant of the original warrant to file a motion for a hearing to extend the substantial risk order prior to its expiration. The court may extend the substantial risk order for a period not longer than 180 days. The bill provides that persons who are subject to a substantial risk order, until such order has been dissolved by a court, are guilty of a Class 1 misdemeanor for purchasing, possessing, or transporting a firearm; are disqualified from having a concealed handgun permit; and may not be employed by a licensed firearms dealer. The bill also provides that a person who transfers a firearm to a person he knows has been served with a warrant or who is the subject of a substantial risk order is guilty of a Class 4 felony. The bill creates a computerized substantial risk order registry for the entry of orders issued pursuant to provisions in the bill.

Restrictions on Persons with Protective Orders

HB 1004 Protective orders; possession of firearms, surrender or transfer of firearms, penalty.

Introduced by: Michael P. Mullin

SUMMARY AS INTRODUCED:

Protective orders; possession of firearms; surrender or transfer of firearms; penalty. Prohibits any person subject to a permanent protective order (i.e., a protective order with a maximum duration of two years) from knowingly possessing a firearm while the order is in effect, provided that for a period of 24 hours after being served with a protective order such person may continue to possess such firearm for the purposes of selling or transferring it to any person who is not otherwise prohibited by law from possessing such firearm. A violation of this provision is a Class 6 felony. The bill also provides that a court shall order a person subject to a permanent protective order to (i) within 24 hours, surrender any firearm possessed by such person to a designated local law-enforcement agency or sell or transfer any firearm possessed by such person to a dealer or to any person who is not otherwise prohibited by law from possessing such firearm and (ii) certify in writing that such person does not possess any firearms or that all firearms possessed by such person have been surrendered, sold, or transferred and file such certification with the clerk of the court that entered the protective order within 48 hours after being served with a protective order. The bill provides that any person who fails to certify in writing in accordance with this section that all firearms possessed by such person have been surrendered, sold, or transferred or that such person does not possess any firearms is guilty of a Class 1 misdemeanor. The bill provides procedures for designating a local law-enforcement agency to receive and store firearms, as well as a process to return such surrendered firearms. The bill also makes it a Class 4 felony for any person to sell, barter, give, or furnish any firearm to any person he knows is prohibited from possessing or transporting a firearm who is the subject to a permanent protective order.

Minors Access to Firearms

HB 1083 Minors; allowing access to firearms, Class 1 misdemeanor.

Introduced by: C.E. Cliff Hayes, Jr.

SUMMARY AS INTRODUCED:

Allowing access to firearms by minors; penalty. Provides that any person who recklessly leaves a loaded, unsecured firearm in such a manner as to endanger the life or limb of any person under the age of 18 is guilty of a Class 6 felony. Current law provides that any person who recklessly leaves a loaded, unsecured firearm in such a manner as to endanger the life or limb of any child under the age of 14 is guilty of a Class 3 misdemeanor.

Local Control of Firearms

HB 421 Firearms, ammunition, etc.; control by localities by governing possession, etc., within locality.

Introduced by: Marcia S. "Cia" Price (Same as SB. 35, introduced by: Scott A. Surovell)

SUMMARY AS INTRODUCED:

Control of firearms by localities. Grants localities authority to adopt or enforce an ordinance, resolution, or motion governing the possession, carrying, storage, or transporting of firearms, ammunition, or components or combination thereof in the locality. Various provisions limiting such authority are repealed. Provisions limiting the authority of localities and state governmental entities to bring lawsuits against certain firearms manufacturers and others are also repealed.

The bill also provides an exception to the requirement that an ordinance enacted regarding the disposition of certain firearms acquired by localities must provide that any firearm received be offered for sale by public auction or sealed bids to a person licensed as a dealer. The bill allows such ordinance to provide that if the individual surrendering the firearm requests in writing that the firearm be destroyed, then such firearm will be destroyed by the locality.

Appendix B
Virginia Criminal Penalties

CLASS	FELONY	MISDEMEANOR
One	life/death	up to 12 months
Two	20 years to life	up to 6 months
Three	5 years to 20 years	fine only
Four	2 to 10 years	fine only
Five	1 to 10 years	
Six	1 to 5 years	
Special	penalty varies	penalty varies

CHAPTER 6

BILL DRAFTING

■ ■ ■

Bill drafting is a collaborative effort. Often legislators will claim to be the author of a bill, but this is just a well understood shorthand that they were willing to put their name on a legislative proposal that, depending on the stage in the legislative process, may have had a few—or many—people contribute to the drafted language. Although some legislators draft bills, or at least are heavily involved in the drafting, this is rare. More often bill language comes from staff, special interests, agency personnel, and the legislature's professional drafting office. The language may change dramatically in committee, on the House or Senate floors, or in conference committee. It is extraordinarily rare for a bill to be unchanged from filing to the presidential or gubernatorial desk.

How does someone become an accomplished drafter? Some of the skills can be learned in the classroom. Since 1964, the University of London has offered a short four-week class on legislative drafting that has trained thousands of legal practitioners. Since 2004, The University's Sir William Dale Center has offered an advanced legal degree in Drafting Legislation, Regulation, and Policy. At Boston University School of Law many students have participated in the semester-long Legislative Policy and Drafting Clinic since the 1970s. This clinic has evolved over time, but students are assigned a project from a Massachusetts legislator where they research the social problem, formulate a policy, and draft a bill.

Traditionally, however, training in legislative drafting has been a learn-by-doing apprenticeship with a drafting office or a sink or swim learning curve working for a legislator. The U.S. House Office of Legislative Counsel (HOLC), which is a professional and non-partisan drafting office serving the House, pairs new attorneys with senior drafters for up to two years to work on many bills, learn the craft, and develop their drafting skills. See, Sandra Strokoff, "How Our Laws Are Made: A Ghost Writer's View" (Ms. Strokoff served as the House Legislative Counsel) (https://budgetcounsel.files.wordpress.com/2017/12/holc-article.pdf). Many offices also produce drafting manuals and guidelines to bring greater clarity and uniformity to legislative language.

There are many reasons why legislative language contains errors, defects and loopholes. The legislative process is constantly changing and amending legislative language and the drafter is almost always under time constraints, demands by policy makers to use imprecise language to either leave flexibility to courts and agencies, avoid controversy or gain votes. Sometimes there simply is not enough time to double check the language for consistency and errors.

The greatest challenge for the drafter, however, is often just using imperfect tools like words to clearly communicate the will of the legislature. James Madison recognized this when defending the proposed Constitution in The Federalist No. 37:

> "All new laws, though penned with the greatest technical skill, and passed on the fullest and most mature deliberation, are considered as more or less obscure and equivocal, until their meaning be liquidated and ascertained by a series of particular discussions and adjudications. Besides the obscurity arising from the complexity of objects, and the imperfection of the human faculties, the medium through which the conceptions of men are conveyed to each other adds a fresh embarrassment. The use of words is to express ideas. Perspicuity, therefore, requires not only that the ideas should be distinctly formed, but that they should be expressed by words distinctly and exclusively appropriate to them. But no language is so copious as to supply words and phrases for every complex idea, or so correct as not to include many equivocally denoting different ideas. Hence it must happen that however accurately objects may be discriminated in themselves, and however accurately the discrimination may be considered, the definition of them may be rendered inaccurate by the inaccuracy of the terms in which it is delivered. And this unavoidable inaccuracy must be greater or less, according to the complexity and novelty of the objects defined. When the Almighty himself condescends to address mankind in their own language, his meaning, luminous as it must be, is rendered dim and doubtful by the cloudy medium through which it is communicated."

Hopefully, this chapter will assist the aspiring drafter to choose not only the correct words but also the correct forms and structures for legislative language.

A. WHO DRAFTS LEGISLATION?

Legislative Scrutiny in the United States: Dynamic, Whole-Stream Scrutiny

Sean J. Kealy, 9 *Theory & Practice of Legislation* 227 (2021)

Drafting in the United States Congress

Legislative drafting in the United States is a complex process. Unlike the centralized Great Britain model, or the European model where executive agencies draft bills, the American legislative process has many participants. While the President and executive agencies present bills to Congress each year, the executive branch is not the primary bill drafter. Members of Congress file the vast majority of bills based upon news reports, requests from constituent groups, lobbyists, etc. Who is drafting or amending bill language depends greatly on where a bill is in the legislative process. This polylithic process includes the professional drafters of the House and Senate Offices of Legislative Counsel, the lawyers and policy staff of the various Congressional committees, the agencies impacted by particular legislation, and outside advocacy groups representing special interests. This section will discuss the contributions of each of these actors.

The House and Senate Offices of Legislative Counsel

The U.S. Senate and House of Representatives each have an Office of the Legislative Counsel, which provides drafting services to its members and committees. While a valuable resource, the offices' services are not required; bills may be drafted without their assistance or simply reviewed for proper form.

Until the early 20th century, legislators generally drafted their own bills. In 1916, a Columbia University fund meant to encourage better legislative drafting hired Middleton Beaman to provide drafting assistance to any committee that would accept his assistance. After he drafted several revenue bills for the House Ways & Means Committee, he became "indispensable," and served as Legislative Counsel for another 33 years until 1949. In 1918, Congress appropriated funds for a "Legislative Drafting Service," directed by two drafters, one appointed by the Speaker of the House and the other by the President of the Senate. The drafting service mainly assisted committees, but could also assist individual members if there was time.

With a major Congressional reorganization in 1970, the Office became two distinct offices. The mandate of the new House Office of Legislative Counsel (HOLC) is to: advise House conference committees during negotiations and preparing reports; advise the committees on draft legislation when requested; assist members managing floor debate; and draft legislation and provide drafting advice to House members. The

Senate Office of Legislative Counsel (SOLC) continues under its original mandate, "The Office of the Legislative Counsel shall aid in drafting public bills and resolutions or amendments thereto on the request of any committee of the Senate."

The Offices typically hire recent law graduates who want to be career drafters. The legislative counsels and their assistants are appointed on a nonpartisan basis and actively promote a culture free from partisan bias. The Offices train new attorneys through a version of the apprenticeship method where senior staff supervise and mentor junior members. The Office attorneys also maintain strict attorney-client relationships and cannot divulge information about their work for a member without express permission. HOLC and SOLC have grown dramatically since 1970 with over three times as many attorneys working today. The larger staffs allows the Offices's attorneys to specialize allowing the drafters to develop a better understanding of the relevant statutes and judicial decisions. The increased staff also allows drafters to work as teams on important bills.

Although the use of the legislative counsel's offices is optional, they have become an integral part of the Congressional process. Client requests for drafting services range from an e-mail with an outline of desired policy, to a well-developed bill written by committee staff or an outside actor such as a lobbyist or agency. The assigned Office attorney will typically then meet with the requesting staff to determine the member's objectives and scope of the proposal before drafting. How the Offices are employed sometimes depends on the experience and needs of the client.

B. Committees

Committees are the workhorses of any legislature; the place where bills are researched, written and re-written. The members, and especially senators, tend not be involved in the details of legislative language unless the bill is particularly politically important or controversial. Still, the members take the lead in setting the policy. In contrast, committee staff, and particularly the committee's attorneys view themselves as central to bill development; either drafting themselves or coordinating language from special interests or agencies. When outside entities provide language, the staff will typically amend the language to reflect the requirements of other interested groups, the policy preferences of the committee members, and, in particular, the desired policy of the chair.

The committee lawyers operate at the intersection of law, policy and politics, analyzing and manipulating legal text according to political dynamics. This type of lawyer must be versed in both the legal aspects and the political realities of an issue to produce creative policy options, draft legislative language, and negotiate a final product within difficult time constraints. Experienced committee attorneys can "elevate the field of legislation" by producing bills that are "better written, more tightly organized, and less ambiguous."

C. Lobbyists & Special Interests

Lobbyists and special interests are intimately involved in the legislative process, including bill drafting. When a bill touches upon their area of interest, lobbyists may either draft bill language, or committee staff may ask for their input on existing bill language.

Lobbyist input not only has a strong influence on legislative language, but is often welcomed by the members and staff due to their subject matter expertise. This is especially true when time is tight and information and resources are needed quickly. Even with the larger staffs of the modern Congress, there still is not enough capacity to identify and work through every potential issue raised by proposed legislation. Lobbyists, focused on limited issues for distinct clients affected by a proposal can often provide a different and valuable perspective. Lobbyists can also clearly articulate policy goals and provide detailed bill analysis including potential problems and unforeseen results. The lobbyists often also clearly articulate policy goals allowing drafters to produce clearer statutory language.

Congressional staff, while willing to accept the drafting assistance; or even entire drafts from lobbyists, generally do not take them at face value. Often they send these contributions to the Legislative Counsel to refine the language and highlight potential issues. Still, lobbyists are viewed as a net positive and an important component to bringing expertise to statutory drafting.

D. Agencies

Another key actor for both legislative drafting and scrutiny is the administrative agency. The Constitution authorizes the president to submit legislative proposals to Congress. Most often, these proposals, and the related bill language, are generated by the various agencies. Agencies also routinely draft legislative proposals both at the request of Congress and on their own initiative.

Agency proposals typically come from the agency's program level, which is tasked with implementing the law, and are most aware of how the law could or should be changed. Many agencies have its own office of legislative counsel that will draft legislative language based on the policy idea. Proposed bills are then sent to the department's office of legislative affairs" to circulate the language with various agency actors for their clearance or approval. This process frequently results in more edits and substantive changes. After submitting the language to the Office of Management and Budget for Presidential clearance, the legislative affairs office will transmit the language to Congress. Agencies also frequently monitor proposed legislation on its area of expertise from all sources.

The Office of Management and Budget (OMB) reviews and clears agency legislation for the President. This process assists agencies plan its legislative objectives, coordinate their legislative program with its annual budget proposal, and assists OMB and the Executive Office of the President develop the President's legislative program and budget. The OMB clearance process involves soliciting input and approval from every agency that may have an interest in the legislation and the OMB ultimately resolves any interagency disputes on policy or language. Once OMB clears the language, the proposing agency can submit the bill to Congress.

Given agency expertise and the expectation that the agency will implement the prosed law, Congress and agency personnel will have many—typically collaborative—contacts during the legislative process. Congress frequently asks agencies to either draft bills or review proposals generated by a member, committee, or special interest. This assistance to Congress is generally offered regardless of the member's political party or disagreement with the bill's policy. Agencies are also involved at several key subsequent legislative steps, including: committee mark-up sessions, floor debates, and during conference committee negotiations.

Agency drafters generally follow the same drafting conventions as the Congressional Offices of Legislative Counsel try to present "finished products" to Congress. The quality of agency generated bills differs depending on the agency, but some have recently invested in their legislative drafting capacity by hiring current and former HOLC and SOLC staff.

B. CREATING RULES

Every legal rule in a statute should have an identified actor and what the legislature requires, permits, or forbids that actor to do, and what qualifiers limit the rule. If the rules are not clear about who must do what the courts, agencies and role occupants will struggle to interpret the law.

The rules will be far clearer if the drafter writes:

- in the active voice,
- keeps the subject close to verb and verb close to direct object, and
- uses parallel sentence structure.

ILTAM: DRAFTING EVIDENCE-BASED LEGISLATION FOR DEMOCRATIC SOCIAL CHANGE

Ann & Robert Seidman, 89 *Boston University Law Review*, 435, 452–453 (2009).

As indicated in the model of behavior in the face of the law, Figure 1 below, a law must take into account the problematic behaviors of two sets of social actors: (1) role occupants and (2) the implementing agencies. Role occupants consist of the actors whose behaviors the bill aims to change. The implementing agency has the task of taking steps to increase the probability that the primary role occupants conform their behaviors to the prescriptions addressed to them. . . .

MODEL: THE LAW-MAKING PROCESS

The drafter needs a comprehensive understanding of what are the targeted role occupants, which agency will enforce the law, and the best tools to induce the role occupants to follow the law. In every instance, the drafter must understand and work within the resources available and constraints on the agencies and role occupants.

NOTES & QUESTIONS

There are three types of rules found in legislation: commands, discretion, and stipulation.

Commands require an actor to do—or not do—something. The drafter must also think through what will compel an actor to comply—effective statutes will include a penalty if the actor fails to follow the command.

Rules of discretion allow an actor to do something that is otherwise prohibited. For instance, if you go to the beach and the sign says, "Dogs are allowed on the beach from 7 p.m. until sunset," The general rule is a command that dogs are not permitted on the beach, with a rule of discretion that they can be there for about an hour in the evening during the summer months. There is, however, no requirement that you bring your dog to the beach at that time.

Rules of stipulation create a legal status or relationship such as creating an agency or commission or defining the requirements to become a registered nurse. Very often rules of stipulation link together other rules.

Toby Dorsey suggests using an "If-Then Model" to think through the rules needed to achieve a desired policy. This method focuses the drafter on the consequences of certain behavior:

> Here's how the If-Then model works in practice. The following sentences are in a form typically used for rules of law:
>
>> The Secretary shall do X.
>>
>> The Secretary may do Y.
>>
>> The Secretary shall not do Z.
>>
>> The If-Then model suggests they can be written as:
>>
>> If the Secretary does not do X, then [consequence 1].
>>
>> If the Secretary does Y, then [consequence 2].
>>
>> If the Secretary does Z, then [consequence 3].

Tobias A. Dorsey, "If-Then Model § 4.32," LEGISLATIVE DRAFTER'S DESKBOOK (TheCapitol.Net, 2006).

Mr. Dorsey also points out that the actor in any rule should be a legally accountable person, including natural persons and fictional extensions of people such as government agencies, corporations, and other legal entities.

"If the actor is not a legally accountable person, the action loses meaning and the law seems unjust or absurd. Consider a rule that a dog may not walk on the grass, or that a school bust must stop at railroad crossings. The dog and the bus can't read, and can't conform their conduct to, the rule. Are they to be punished? What purpose would that serve? The client probably means to target the owner of the dog and the driver of the bus, but perhaps they client means to target someone else, such as the keeper of the grass or the crossing guard." Tobias A. Dorsey, "Actor-Action Model § 4.31," LEGISLATIVE DRAFTER'S DESKBOOK (TheCapitol.Net, 2006).

Tennessee Legislative Drafting Guide
Office of Legal Services, Tennessee General Assembly (2018)

(e) LEGAL ACTION VERBS

In stating the legislative objective, the drafter must pay particular attention to the verb forms the drafter uses to establish the duty, right, power, entitlement, or disentitlement. There has been much change in how legal action verbs have been used over the years. The trend has been to discourage the routine use of "shall" and substitute words that have a more specific meaning attached to them. Because there has been change, the drafter will find that much of the existing law will not reflect the modern trend away from the routine use of "shall." Therefore, when amending existing law, the drafter should exercise discretion on the appropriate action verb to use, keeping in mind the multiple considerations when updating archaic and outdated language as discussed in subsection (e) of Chapter 3. The following chart may be helpful when determining the drafter's needs.

Shall	Has a duty to, Has to
Must	Is required to (to achieve an end)
Shall Not	Is prohibited
May	Is permitted to, Has a right to, Has discretion to, Is authorized to [+ verb]

Is Entitled To Has a right to [+ noun]

Will	Expresses a policy or a future contingency in the manner of normal English
Can	Is legally or physically capable
Cannot	Is legally or physically incapable

(1)　The goal of the drafter should be to reduce the use of "shall" by using it only to impose a duty on a person or body or to mandate action by a person or body. That is, the drafter should only use "shall" to say a person or a body "has a duty to" do something or "has to" do something.

CORRECT: The commissioner shall adopt rules.

INCORRECT: The commissioner must adopt rules.

(2)　"Shall" should not be used in sentences that require an action to achieve an end. "Must" rather than "shall" is the proper action verb to use when the action is only required to achieve an end.

(3)　Avoid using "shall" to confer a right. If "shall be" can be replaced with "is" or "are," make the replacement.

CORRECT: To be eligible for parole, a prisoner must demonstrate...

INCORRECT: To be eligible for parole, a prisoner shall demonstrate...

CORRECT: The director is entitled to compensation of twelve thousand dollars ($12,000) a year.

CORRECT: Compensation for the director is twelve thousand dollars ($12,000) a year.

INCORRECT: The director shall receive compensation of twelve thousand dollars ($12,000) a year.

(4) Do not use "shall" to state what the law is or how it applies in the future. A common problem in legislative drafting is that the word "shall" is often used to indicate a legal result rather than a command. This is known as a "false imperative."

(5) When using "shall" to mandate an action in which the outcome is in the discretion of the actor, include alternative actions the actor may take.

CORRECT: Nine (9) members shall be appointed to the board.

INCORRECT: The board shall be composed of nine (9) members as follows:

CORRECT: The commissioner shall approve or deny an application within thirty (30) days.

INCORRECT: The commissioner shall approve an application within thirty (30) days.

(6) Use "must" rather than "shall" to express requirements, that is, statements about what people or things must be rather than what they must do. "Must" is usually correct in passive sentences imposing requirements.

(7) "May" means "is permitted to," "is authorized to," "is entitled to" or "has power to." "May" authorizes or permits rather than commands.

(8) If the drafter finds that "shall" or "may" could both be used, redraft the sentence to avoid the use of either legal action verb.

CORRECT: Professions must be licensed by the state.

INCORRECT: Professions shall be licensed by the state.

CORRECT: The appointee qualifies for office by taking the official oath and filing the required bond.

INCORRECT: The appointee shall qualify for office by taking the official oath and filing the required bond.

INCORRECT: The appointee may qualify for office by taking the official oath and filing the required bond.

DRAFTING LEGISLATION

U.S. House Office of Legislative Counsel
https://legcounsel.house.gov/holc-guide-legislative-drafting#VII

VII. Three important conventions

A.   The terms "means" and "includes"

The basic distinction between these two terms is that "means" is exclusive while "includes" is not. If a definition says that "the term 'X' means A, B, and C", then X means only A, B, and C and cannot also mean D or E. If a definition says that "the term 'X' includes A, B, and C", then X must include A, B, and C, but it may also include D or E, or both. Thus, the phrase "includes, but is not limited to" is redundant. In fact, using it in some places out of an abundance of caution could cause a limitation to be read into places where it is not used.

B.   The terms "shall" and "may"

The term "shall" means that an action is required; the term "may" means that it is permitted but not required. While this might seem obvious, a common misconception concerns the phrase "may not", which is mandatory and is the preferred language for denying a right, power, or privilege (e.g., "The Secretary may not accept an application after April 1, 2011."). "Shall not" perhaps sounds stronger and is usually construed to have the same meaning, but it is subject to some (rather arcane) interpretations that are best avoided.

C.   Use of the singular preferred

In general, provisions should be drafted in the singular to avoid the ambiguity that plural constructions can create. Take, for example, this provision: "Drivers may not run red lights.". It is ambiguous as to whether there is any violation unless multiple drivers run multiple red lights. This problem can be avoided by rewriting the provision as follows: "A driver may not run a red light.".

Section 1 of title 1, United States Code, provides that in determining the meaning of any statute, unless the context indicates otherwise, singular terms include the plural and plural terms include the singular. In the simple example above, this rule of construction would eliminate any ambiguity by instructing that the reader substitute "driver" for "drivers" and "red light" for "red lights". But it is preferable for a provision to be clear on its face, and the rule of construction also works in the other direction to foreclose any argument (however tenuous) that the redrafted provision applies to only one driver.

C. "AND/OR"

Iowa Bill Drafting Guide And Style Manual
Iowa Legislative Services Agency (2017)

Use of "and/or". The general consensus of opinion in cases in many jurisdictions over the nation is contrary to the use of the expression "and/or". This is true in Iowa. In general the term "and" means to add something to what has already been said; "or" means in the alternative. The word "and" is a conjunctive and the word "or" a disjunctive. Use of the terms together is contradictory. The writer should be able to determine which term is correct. In most cases the word "or" is proper to convey the thought of "one, or the other, or any of them". The word "and" is proper to convey the thought of both, or "all of them". If emphasis is needed the use of terms such as "any of the following", "all of the following", "either of the following", "or both", and similar modes of expression should be sufficient. The expression "and/or" has been attacked by numerous authorities.

One authority notes it is "a device for the encouragement of mental laziness"; another authority states "It is a bastard sired by Indolence (he by Ignorance) out of Dubiety.".

The drafter of legislation in Iowa should avoid the use of the expression "and/or".

D. WORDS

"Broadly speaking, the short words are the best, and the old words when short are best of all."—Winston S. Churchill

PLAIN ENGLISH IN MICHIGAN STATUTES AND RULES STATUTES
Carol Cousineau & Roger Peters, Michigan Bar Journal,
79 Mich. B.J. 40 (January, 2000)
Reprinted with the permission of the Michigan State Bar

I was reminded again of the importance of each word we use in drafting legislation and how closely the changes we make are analyzed by a recent article in "Benchmarks," the District Court Judge's Association newsletter. In the article, the author discusses a recent statutory amendment changing "shall have" to "has" and argues that the change in tense affects the applicability of the provision. I cannot speak to the Legislature's intent regarding this specific issue, but as part of our continuing effort to use plain language principles, we often make this type of change in drafting amendatory bills. The fact that this was raised as an issue illustrates that, even when editing using plain language principles, we need to consider how each word we change may affect the meaning of the law, sometimes in unforeseen ways.

We, the Legal Division of the Legislative Service Bureau, are a nonpartisan staff within the Legislature consisting of 22 attorneys and 18 support staff who provide bill drafting and related legal services to members of the Michigan Senate and House of Representatives. The support staff includes four editors/proofreaders who review documents for accuracy as well as sentence construction, grammar, and spelling. Unlike some states that have a revisor of statutes to correct errors in and improve the clarity of statutes after they are passed, the Legal Division has the responsibility of determining the form and style of the statutes as we go through the process of creating or amending statutes.

The Legal Division also drafts Joint Resolutions that propose amendments to the State Constitution of 1963. Because of the nature and historical significance of this document, we rarely edit existing provisions of the Constitution.

We do, however, use plain language principles in proposed new language as we do in the statutes.

Through the years, we became more aware of the plain language movement through various publications and seminars by such experts as Reed Dickerson and Bryan Garner. As a result of our exposure to these ideas, it is now the Legal Division's policy to use plain language principles in drafting new statutory language and, if possible, to edit old statutory language as we amend it. Because most of the Legislature's bills propose amendments to current law, the improvement of archaic and unclear language is being accomplished incrementally. It is, however, a lengthy, on-going process that will continue for many years to come.

As part of our efforts to make the Michigan statutes more readable and understandable, we recently modernized the format of bills for introduction in the Senate and House of Representatives. We also conformed our citations to the more commonly used style provided in the Michigan Uniform System of Citation, effective February 10, 1987, and The Bluebook: A Uniform System of Citations (Cambridge: The Harvard Law Review Association, 16th ed, 1996).

The style used in the titles of amendatory bills changed from this:

A bill to amend sections 520 and 522 of Act No. 281 of the Public Acts of 1967, entitled "Income tax act of 1967," section 520 as amended by Act No. 245 of the Public Acts of 1995 and section 522 as amended by Act No. 55 of the Public Acts of 1996, being sections 206.520 and 206.522 of the Michigan Compiled Laws.

To this:

A bill to amend 1967 PA 281, entitled "Income tax act of 1967," by amending sections 520 and 522 (MCL 206.520 and 206.522), section 520 as amended by 1995 PA 245 and section 522 as amended by 1996 PA 55.

In editing existing statutes, we are constantly aware of the potential ramifications of our changes. Since the courts may occasionally look at grammatical construction in interpreting the law, we select our words with great care. We try to follow basic plain language principles and use the present tense, use the active rather than the passive voice, avoid archaic words and phrases, avoid the subjunctive mood, eliminate false imperative, avoid using the same word for different things, trim verbose prose, and eliminate redundancies.

All of these changes are not always possible, though, for several reasons. Political considerations, such as a prior agreement on specific language by interested groups, may prevent editing. Interstate compacts are not edited by agreement. Portions of certain laws, such as worker's compensation and labor relations statutes, have been judicially construed or are written to conform to federal law and are carefully edited, if at all. An attorney general opinion or administrative rule may already provide an interpretation of existing language that is necessary to preserve. Additionally, amendments are often added on the Senate or House floor that have not been seen or written by any of our attorneys and that may not conform to the plain language style.

The following is an example of the editing we did, in addition to some substantive changes required, to an older statute (MCL 211.62) in a House Bill of this legislative session:

From this:

Sec. 62. It shall be the duty of the county clerk, on the filing of the said petition, to at once present the same to the circuit judge of the county in which said delinquent tax lands are situated, and it shall be the duty of said circuit judge to make an order in the form herein prescribed, which order, when so made and signed by the circuit judge, shall be countersigned by the county clerk as register in chancery, and recorded by him in the proper books of his office, and thereupon it shall be the duty of said county clerk to immediately make a true copy of said order, and transmit the same to the auditor general. Said order shall be substantially in the following form: . . .

To this:

Sec. 62. If a petition is filed, the county clerk shall present the petition to the circuit court of the county in which the delinquent tax property is located and the circuit court shall enter an order as prescribed in this section. The county clerk shall countersign the order, record the order in the proper books of his or her office, and transmit a true copy of the order to the state treasurer. The order shall be substantially in the following form: . . .

In creating new statutes, the task of adhering to plain language principles is generally easier. Our attorneys often start from scratch and strive to use those principles in the original draft.

The work product of each of our attorneys is checked by another attorney for issue-spotting, as well as for plain language principles. We also occasionally receive drafts of new acts from new outside sources. Unfortunately, outside authors are sometimes offended that we do not just accept these drafts without changes. We must, however, make all bills conform to our drafting style, including plain language principles, wherever possible.

The Legal Division is very proud that several of our attorneys have received Clarity Awards for new acts they have written. We are also very proud of the fact that we are slowly but surely making the Michigan Compiled Laws some of the most easily readable state statutes in the country through a continuous editing process using plain language principles.

NOTES & QUESTIONS

1.   Legislative drafters should strive to be clear. Long time drafter Toby Dorsey suggests five elements of clarity: be simple, he ordinary, be brief, be consistent, and be readable. At times these elements work together; simplicity often comes when one is both consistent and brief. On the other hand, they can also be at odds. A complex sentence redrafted as several simple sentences sacrifices brevity. Ultimately, how to draft a stature comes down to the drafter's good judgement. Tobias Dorsey, *LEGISLATIVE DRAFTERS DESKBOOK* (TheCapitol.Net, 2006).

2.   Although clarity is a significant virtue for the legislative drafter, it is not always achievable. The legislative process dynamic is often to blame, including time constraints and the occasional need to be deliberately ambiguous.

In their case study on Congressional drafting, Professors Nourse and Schacter interview several staff members. Congressional staffers report that there is often insufficient time to achieve textual clarity, with time related pressure leading to "errors, inertia, [and] not understanding completely the potential . . . pitfalls of a law." This is especially true when the bill is on the floor or in a conference committee. This problem is compounded if the staffer working on language is inexperienced.

Deliberate ambiguity often happens when the legislators cannot agree on a particular point of a bill. The ambiguous language is often the result of a compromise or to push a problem into the future—or into another forum such as a court. Often, ambiguous language allows the legislation to move forward. As one staff member stated, "This is not a law school process, it is a political process. Sometimes one cannot allow the perfect to be the enemy of the good." See, Nourse and Schacter, "The Politics of Legislative Drafting: A Congressional Case Study," 77 *N.Y.U. L. Rev.* 575 (2002).

3.   What other reasons can you think of that lead to a willful lack of clarity? Recall the Stem Cell Case Study in Chapter 4; the Senate wanted to use the term "embryo" without defining what exactly that was. This was in large part due to the understanding that science was quickly redefining when the embryonic stage began and ended. Too much clarity may have undermined the law in a few years. Another reason for ambiguity is to give the responsibility to the implementing agency when drafting regulations. There are good reasons for this: the agency is typically much more expert on that subject than the legislature; changing circumstances may require adjustments and regulations can be changed after than laws; and the agency may need the flexibility to use different solutions to a problem in different places.

Massachusetts Legislative Research and Drafting Manual
Counsel to the Senate & Counsel to the House of Representatives (2010)

B. Simple Language

Do not say:	Say:
absolutely null and void and of no effect	Void
Accorded	Given
adequate number of	enough
adjudged, ordered, and decreed	adjudged
admit of	allow
among and between	among (if more than 2 involved); between (if two or more but treated individually)
Approximately	about
at the place where	where
by means of	by
cause it to be done	done
constitute and appoint	appoint
do and perform	do
does not operate to	does not
during such time as	while
during the course of	during

endeavor (as a verb)	try
enter into a contract with	contract with
evidence, documentary and otherwise	evidence
Evince	show
except that	but
for the reason that	because
Forthwith	immediately
Frequently	often
full and adequate (or, full and complete)	full
Herein	in the act (or section, or item)
Heretofore	before this. . . .takes effect
in accordance with	under
in the event that	if
in the interest of	for
is authorized and directed	shall
is authorized to	may
is directed	shall
is entitled (in the sense of has the name)	is called
it is the duty	shall
it shall be lawful to	may
law passed	enacted
occasion (as a verb)	cause
or, in the alternative	or
party of the first part	(the party's name)
per annum	per year
per centum	per cent
prosecute its business	carry on its business
provision of law	law
pursuant to	under
Render	give
said, same, such	the, this, that, these, those
shall be deemed to be	is or shall be

subsequent to	after
successfully completes or passes	completes or passes
suffer (in the sense of permit)	permit
to the effect that	that
until such time as	until
with the object of changing (or other gerund)	to change (comparative infinitive)

Tennessee Legislative Drafting Guide

Office of Legal Services, Tennessee General Assembly (2018)

(e)   ARCHAIC AND OUTDATED LANGUAGE

(1)   There are terms that were once used by drafters that may now be considered outdated and possibly offensive. The following is a list of terms that should give a drafter pause prior to usage:

• insane	• crippled	• idiot
• defective person	• feeble-minded	• handicapped person
• senile	• retarded	• handicap
• mental defect	• retardation	• physical defect

(2)   The form and style guidelines contained in this guide should always be followed when drafting new code provisions, including avoiding the use of outdated language. However, when amending current law, updating outdated terms may not be the best approach due to considerations such as prior judicial constraints, model language, or the complexity of the language.

Finding the Right Word

The great poet Emily Dickinson may have learned her love of words from her father Edward, who was a lawyer and represented the town of Amherst in the Massachusetts House of Representatives, the Massachusetts Senate and in the U.S. Congress. When writing her poems, Dickinson often suggested alternative words and phrases—variants— above the line. It is often striking how the variants change the meaning of a line, stanza, or entire poem.

He fought like those Who've nought to lose—

+He gave himself
Bestowed Himself to Balls

As One who for a further Life

Had not a further Use—

Invited Death—with bold attempt—

           +shy
But Death was Coy of Him

As Other Men, were Coy of Death.

To Him—to live—was Doom—

His Comrades, shifted like the Flakes

When Gusts reverse the Snow—

           +remained
But He—was left alive Because

         +Urgency
        +Vehemence
Of Greediness to die—

NOTES & QUESTIONS

1.   Often finding the right word is the hardest part of legislative drafting, even with all of the options available in the English language. Unfortunately, we cannot include variants, but must pick the word and hope the various people reading the statute will get the intended meaning.

2.   If the right word does not exist, how can the drafter take advantage of definitions within a statute?

E. PUNCTUATION

Careful punctuation is essential to legislative drafting. A favorite punctuation joke is to consider the effect of forgetting the comma in the phrase "Let's eat, grandma."

Massachusetts Legislative Research and Drafting Manual
Counsel to the Senate & Counsel to the House of Representatives (2010)

5.   Punctuation.

a.   Punctuate carefully. Changing a comma can change the entire meaning of a sentence.

b.   Ordinarily, do not use a comma before "and" or "or" to separate the last of a conjunctive series of three or more words, phrases or clauses in a sentence. Example: "men, women and children."

c.   Use a colon to introduce a list of items.

d.   Try to avoid using parentheses except in the designating of section divisions. Example: "subsection (a)".

e.   Do not use brackets as punctuation.

f.   Use quotation marks when defining a word or phrase. Example: In this section, "cost of construction" shall mean. . . .

g.   Use commas for clarity, especially to set off an introductory phrase or clause, or to separate independent clauses.

Example: "The committee shall have several responsibilities, including, but not limited to, analyzing cases and recommending possible reforms."

Basic Considerations In Drafting Legislation (Connecticut)
Connecticut Legislative Commissioners' Office (2015)

Punctuation and Quotation Marks

Punctuation marks that follow quotation marks are placed outside the quotation marks, not inside, unless part of the quoted material itself.

Example:

For the purposes of this section, "insurance-support organization" does not include "consumer reporting agency".

Example:

Such acknowledgment may be transmitted by facsimile or by e-mail and shall read as follows: "I am aware of my right to choose the licensed repair shop where the damage to the motor vehicle will be repaired.".

The statutes do not use a final comma in a series; however, if the series is enumerated, use a final comma.

Example:

Apples, pears and oranges (NOT: Apples, pears, and oranges).

Example:

(1) apples, (2) pears, and (3) oranges.

NOTES & QUESTIONS

Punctuation can have a dramatic impact on a statute's meaning. Sir Roger Casement started working for Irish independence from Great Britain in 1905. During World War I, Casement attempted to forge an alliance with Germany to obtain weapons and training so Irish rebels could revolt against England. He met with a German diplomat in New York City and travelled to Germany to recruit an Irish brigade composed of captured soldiers being held as prisoners of war. Although this effort was unsuccessful, the Germans attempted to send rifles, machine guns, and ammunition. The British Navy, however, intercepted the weapons before the ship got the cargo to Ireland. The British authorities arrested Casement when he returned to Ireland and charged him with high treason, sabotage and espionage against the Crown. The trial was highly publicized, but the prosecution had trouble proving its case because the Treason Act of 1351 seemed to require the treasonous activities to have happened on English, or perhaps British, soil. The crucial language applied to persons being "adherent to the king's enemies in his realm, aiding and giving them comfort in the realm or elsewhere." The prosecution argued that the words "or elsewhere" applied to both parts of that sentence, so Casement's activities in Germany constituted treason. The defense argued this interpretation required a comma before the words "or elsewhere." The court decided that a comma should be read in the unpunctuated original Norman-French text, to expand the applicability of the law. Casement would later write that he was to be "hanged on a comma." In 1916, Casement was put to death at the age of 51. One commentator wrote that this case "is a sad example of the power of punctuation when interpreting a statute." See, Frank McNally, "Comma chameleon: An Irishman's Diary about the sometimes fatal effects of punctuation: A comma and Roger Casement's fate," *The Irish Times*, Jan 28, 2015.

F. SENTENCES

Utah Legislative Drafting Manual
Utah State Legislature (2014)

v. Structure of a Legislative Sentence

As with most writing, the core of a statutory unit is the sentence. A good guideline is to limit a sentence to a single idea or thought.

A. In General

An experienced legislative drafter suggests that in crafting a legislative sentence it is important to:

- identify the action, actor, and consequences before putting pen to paper;

- not be formulaic in how you arrange the elements of a sentence, use your judgment;

- keep the actor near the action, and if the action has an object, keep the object near the action;

- use a sentence that is generally short or medium in length, e.g., 20–25 words;

- convey one major point with a sentence and avoid a sentence that is compound or has complex clauses;

- if there are several or complex qualifiers, state the rule first and then the qualifiers in more than one sentence;

- draft a sentence in a manner that emphasizes the concept that is most important; and

- arrange words with care.

B. Agreement (Subject/verb and pronoun/antecedent)

A basic, but at times forgotten, rule of drafting is the creation of agreement between subject and verb and between pronoun and antecedent. A pronoun like a noun has four basic properties, *i.e.*, number, person, gender, and case, and must agree with its antecedent in number, person, and gender.

Example:

Do not say: If the division determines an application is incomplete, they shall . . .

Say: If the division determines an application is incomplete, it shall . . .

Massachusetts Legislative Research and Drafting Manual
Counsel to the Senate & Counsel to the House of Representatives (2010)

C. Sentence Structure

1. Parallel Structure.

Use of correct parallel structure aids comprehension. For example, do not say "A copy may be obtained by mail or if a person appears personally." Instead, say "A person may obtain a copy by mail or by appearing personally."

2.   Subject.

Unless it is clear from the context, use as the subject of each sentence the person or entity to whom a power, right or privilege is granted or upon whom a duty, obligation, or prohibition is imposed.

3.   Verbs.

a.   Use the present tense and the indicative mood.

b.   Do not use the passive voice.

c.   The singular is sometimes simpler and clearer than the plural. For example, "A possibility of reverter is subject to limitations in the document that creates it." is preferable to "Possibilities of reverter are subject to limitations in the documents that create them." Use the plural, however, if its use is the least awkward solution, especially to avoid gender-specific pronouns.

4.   Finite Verbs.

If possible, use finite verbs instead of their corresponding participles, infinitives, gerunds or other noun or adjective forms. Do not say "give consideration to;" say "consider." Do not say "is applicable;" say "applies."

5.   Use of Infinitives.

Avoid split infinitives. They often undermine the clarity of the law. If qualifying words separate infinitive phrases repeat "to" in each phrase; if no qualifying words intervene, do not repeat "to."

6.   Modifiers.

If a modifier is intended to affect all terms in a series, the terms should be linked together with the conjunctive "and" or the disjunctive "or." If a modifier is intended to affect only one term, the modifier should be placed immediately before or after the term and the other terms in the series should be set off with commas or semicolons.

7.   Provisos.

Provisos (which usually begin "provided, however, that") are acceptable, especially in line items of appropriation bills, however because they can unnecessarily complicate a sentence structure, try to avoid them. Instead, depending on context, begin the new clause with "but" or "if" or simply start a new sentence.

G. BILL STYLE AND STRUCTURE

1. BILL STYLE

LEGISLATIVE SCRUTINY IN THE UNITED STATES: DYNAMIC, WHOLE-STREAM SCRUTINY

Sean J. Kealy, 9 *Theory & Practice of Legislation* 227 (2021)

A significant reform to Congressional drafting was the development of the House Office of Legislative Counsel's *Manual on Drafting Style*. Given the complex nature of the Congressional process, there is great advantage to having uniform standards for drafting legislation. Drafting conventions not only promote consistency and clarity, but also democratic values. Until very recently, however, Congress employed many drafting styles. Over the past 30 years, the Manual has had a tremendous impact on the uniformity and quality of bill drafting.

The U.S. Congress did not have a drafting style manual until 1989 when the House Legislative Counsel, Ward M. Hussey wrote *Style Manual; Drafting Suggestions for the Trained Drafter*. In 1995 the House Office of Legislative Counsel revised the *Style Manual* and issued the *House Legislative Counsel's Manual on Drafting Style (Manual)*, which continues to be the primary drafting manual on Capitol Hill. The *Manual* reflected Mr. Hussey's belief in the need for uniformity in drafting Federal laws and had a "broad impact on Federal Legislation."

Written in easily understood and entertaining prose, the *Manual* argues that a uniform style is a tool for attorneys to "reduce chaos to order," and "gives clearly defined, steady, and predictable guidance for the structure and expression of legislation." The *Manual* also implores drafters to use clear, punchy language and short simple sentences, that are readable and understandable. Further, drafting uniformity would help prevent giving aid to "those who are looking for grounds to misinterpret the language or to criticize the process or product involved." Mr. Hussey adapted a form of "revenue style" drafting used in tax bills, which he called "office style." The goal of this effort was that "in time, all Federal law will be in the office style."

Today, the Offices of Legislative Counsel use office style as extensively as possible, but sometimes a project's circumstances or the preferences of the committee staff will cause deviations in style. As the Manual states, "the diversity of individuals drafting makes a consensus on a precise guide respecting structure and style an impossibility."

How successful has Mr. Hussey's experiment been in the intervening 30 years? Given how big and complex Congress is, it has been highly successful. Most bills are now drafted in office style. Still there are some exceptions: appropriations bills are still drafted in its traditional "appropriations style;" positive law titles of the U.S. Code are amended in U.S. Code style; and old laws are often amended consistent with the statute's existing style. In addition, there are some differences between the office style as used by the House and the Senate. Still, the development and wide use office style has marked a major step forward for improved legislative quality.

In addition to the *Manual*, the House Office of Legislative Counsel also offers some shorter, but very useful, tools to facilitate communication and collaboration between its attorneys and their Congressional clients. These include a web page entitled "Drafting Legislation" and an eleven-page document entitled "Introduction to Legislative Drafting." These guides include basic information on the various forms of legislation considered by Congress; basic units of bill organization; a general template for structuring content; and advice on using particular provisions such as purposes and findings provisions, appropriations provisions, and effective date provisions.

NOTES & QUESTIONS

1.   The *House Legislative Counsel's Manual on Drafting Style*, by Ward M. Hussey & Ira B. Forstater, may be found at: https://legcounsel.house.gov/sites/legcounsel.house.gov/files/documents/draftstyle.pdf.   "Drafting Legislation," may be accessed at: https://legcounsel.house.gov/holc-guide-legislative-drafting); and "Introduction to Legislative Drafting," may be accessed at: https://legcounsel.house.gov/sites/legcounsel.house.gov/files/documents/intro_to_drafting.pdf. There are several other excellent guides on legislative drafting including:

- Arthur Rynearson, *Legislative Drafting Step-By-Step* (International Law Institute & Carolina Academic Press, 2013);

- Tobias Dorsey, *LEGISLATIVE DRAFTER'S DESKBOOK* (The Capitol.Net, 2006);

- Lawrence E. Filson and Sandra L. Strokoff, *THE LEGISLATIVE DRAFTER'S DESK REFERENCE*, 2nd. ed. (Washington, D.C.: CQ Press, 2008).

2.   Tobias Dorsey gives examples, and highlights the differences of, appropriations style, traditional style, revenue style, modified revenue style ("office style") and Code style. Tobias Dorsey, "Appendix 8.10," *LEGISLATIVE DRAFTER'S DESKBOOK* (The Capitol.Net, 2006). The House and Senate Offices of Legislative Counsel now use software that can format bills into office style, appropriations style, or U.S. Code style.

3.   When Congress revises a statute in its original drafting style the drafter is using the "Roman Rule," that is, when in Rome, do as the Romans do. Should drafters scrap the Roman Rule and take the opportunity to rewrite

the amended statute in the modern office or U.S. Code styles? What problems may arise from that change?

4.   Many states also have a drafting manual to guide drafters in that jurisdiction. The National Council of State Legislatures posts links to available manuals at: https://www.ncsl.org/legislators-staff/legislative-staff/research-editorial-legal-and-committee-staff/bill-drafting-manuals.aspx.

2.   BILL ORGANIZATION

LEGISLATIVE DRAFTING STEP-BY-STEP
Arthur J. Rynearson (Carolina Academic Press, 2013)

Organization of a "Simple Bill"

SECTION 1. SHORT TITLE.

SEC. 2. CONGRESSIONAL FINDINGS.

SEC. 3. PURPOSE.

SEC. 4. DEFINITIONS.

SEC. 5. [GENERAL AUTHORITY]

> (a)   [General Rule].—
>
> (b)   [Exception].—

SEC. 6. [LIMITATIONS]

> (a)   [Prohibition] [or] [Restriction].—
>
> (b)   [Exception]
>
> (c)   [Waiver]

SEC. 7. [ADMINISTRATIVE PROVISIONS].

> (a)   [Reporting Requirements]
>
> (b)   [Special audits] [?]
>
> (c)   [Powers] [?]

SEC. 8. SENSE OF CONGRESS.

SEC. 9. AUTHORIZATION OF APPROPRIATIONS.

SEC. 10.EFFECTIVE DATE [?] or TERMINATION DATE [?]

I

110TH CONGRESS
1ST SESSION

H. R. 1254

To amend title 44, United States Code, to require information on contributors to Presidential library fundraising organizations.

IN THE HOUSE OF REPRESENTATIVES

MARCH 1, 2007

Mr. WAXMAN (for himself, Mr. DUNCAN, Mr. CLAY, Mr. PLATTS, and Mr. EMANUEL) introduced the following bill; which was referred to the Committee on Oversight and Government Reform

---

A BILL

To amend title 44, United States Code, to require information on contributors to Presidential library fundraising organizations.

1   *Be it enacted by the Senate and House of Representa-*

2 *tives of the United States of America in Congress assembled,*

3 **SECTION 1. SHORT TITLE.**

4   This Act may be cited as the "Presidential Library

5 Donation Reform Act of 2007".

6 **SEC. 2. PRESIDENTIAL LIBRARIES.**

7   (a) IN GENERAL.—Section 2112 of title 44, United

8 States Code, is amended by adding at the end the fol-

9 lowing new subsection:

3. INTRODUCTORY PROVISIONS

a. Titles

Minnesota Revisor's Manual
The Minnesota Office of the Revisor of Statutes (2013)

2.5 TITLE

(a) Generally.

A title is required by the Minnesota Constitution and the joint legislative rules. In view of these provisions, the title of a bill:

- must express the one subject of the bill;

- must express, in general terms, the purpose of the bill;

- should include certain phrases required by legislative custom;

- must list the provisions of coded and uncoded law that are being added, amended, or repealed in the bill; and

- should be clear and brief.

(b) Legal considerations.

(1) Constitution. The Minnesota Constitution provides in article IV, section 17, that "No law shall embrace more than one subject, which shall be expressed in its title." It is often referred to as the "single subject" or "one subject" rule. . . .

(2) Joint Rule 2.01.

Joint Rule 2.01 states: "The title of each bill shall clearly state its subject and briefly state its purpose."

The joint rule provides direction to drafters on how the single subject rule is to be implemented. The one subject of the bill must be clearly stated in the title. Drafters attempt to satisfy this requirement by using a general subject or topic descriptor. The joint rule also adds the additional requirement that the title to the bill briefly state its purpose. See the discussion in paragraph (d).

Joint Rule 2.01 also states: "When a bill amends or repeals an existing act, the title shall refer to the chapter, section or subdivision." See the discussion in paragraph (c), clause (5), for the form of these references.

(c) Form.

The format of a bill's title has several parts divided by layout or punctuation.

Fig. 1

A bill for an act

Relating to natural resources; regulating state parks; prohibiting littering; providing criminal penalties; amending Minnesota Statutes 20_,section 85.20, by adding a subdivision.

Massachusetts Legislative Research and Drafting Manual
Counsel to the Senate & Counsel to the House of Representatives (2010)

Title.

Use a short, descriptive title for every bill, to help the House and Senate Clerk refer the bill to the proper joint committee.

Examples:

An Act regulating firearms.

An Act establishing the department of social services.

Traditionally, the infinitive form is not used. For example, do not say "An Act to regulate firearms," but say "An Act regulating firearms."

NOTES & QUESTIONS

1.　Recall from Chapter 5 on constitutional requirements that very often a bill's title must title be descriptive of the contents of the bill. Some legislatures feel this is satisfied by fairly short titles such as the one from Minnesota above. Other states, such as Pennsylvania have adopted much more detailed titles, such as the one for the statute at issue in *Pennsylvanian's Against Gambling Expansion Fund v. Commonwealth*:

AMENDING TITLE 4 (AMUSEMENTS) OF THE PENNSYLVANIA CONSOLIDATED STATUTES, AUTHORIZING CERTAIN RACETRACK AND OTHER GAMING; PROVIDING FOR REGULATION OF GAMING LICENSEES, ESTABLISHING AND PROVIDING FOR THE POWERS AND DUTIES OF THE PENNSYLVANIA GAMING CONTROL DEPARTMENT OF REVENUE, THE DEPARTMENT OF HEALTH, THE OFFICE OF ATTORNEY GENERAL, THE PENNSYLVANIA STATE POLICE, AND THE PENNSYLVANIA LIQUOR CONTROL BOARD; ESTABLISHING THE STATE GAMING FUND, THE PENNSYLVANIA RACE HORSE DEVELOPMENT FUND, THE PENNSYLVANIA GAMING ECONOMIC DEVELOPMENT AND TOURISM FUND, THE COMPULSIVE PROBLEM GAMBLING TREATMENT FUND AND THE PROPERTY TAX RELIEF FUND; PROVIDING FOR ENFORCEMENT; IMPOSING PENALTIES; MAKING APPROPRIATIONS; AND MAKING RELATED REPEALS.

2.   Some states and the Congress make provisions for a short title as well as the official title. The short title becomes a "nickname" people can use to refer to the bill, and later the law. Tobias Dorsey points out that the federal level the short title is almost purely a political function, and the drafter should avoid playing a role in the process. See, Tobias Dorsey, "Short Title 7.61," *LEGISLATIVE DRAFTER'S DESKBOOK* (The Capitol.Net, 2006).

b.   Enacting Clauses

Texas Legislative Council Drafting Manual
Texas Legislative Council (2020)

SEC. 3.04.   ENACTING CLAUSE. The enacting clause is required by Section 29, Article III, Texas Constitution, and is indispensable. The enacting clause must be in exactly the following words:

BE IT ENACTED BY THE LEGISLATURE OF THE STATE OF TEXAS:

A document without an enacting clause is not a bill, and under house precedents it may not be amended for the purpose of inserting an enacting clause and may not be referred to committee.

NOTES & QUESTIONS

Without an enacting clause, the legislative document is not a bill, but a resolve or a memorial that will not have the same legal effect as a bill if passed.

4.   SUBSTANTIVE PROVISIONS

a.   Findings & Purposes Provisions

Arizona Legislative Bill Drafting Manual
Arizona Legislative Council (2019)*

Arizona Legislative Council

4.18 LEGISLATIVE INTENT; FINDINGS SECTIONS

General rule

Generally, a bill should not include an intent section (also called a "purpose" or "legislative findings" section). There are several reasons for this:

* Redundancy. Because each draft should include all provisions that are necessary to carry out legislative intent in the substantive text of the draft, a statement of intent, purpose

---

*   Selections reprinted with permission from Arthur J. Rynearson, Legislative Drafting Step-By-Step (Durham: Carolina Academic Press, 2013), 112–113.

or findings that mirrors the substantive text is redundant and thus unnecessary.

- Conflict. A statement of intent, purpose or findings that is initially drafted to be in harmony with substantive provisions of a bill may become irrelevant to or in direct conflict with the provisions as subsequently amended. If the statement is not also amended or repealed at the time of the subsequent statutory amendment, the unchanged original statement may confuse the status of the law.

- Misuse of undefined terms. A statement of intent, purpose or findings that purports to state the goal of the proposed legislation may do so by using undefined terms that differ from the terms used in substantive provisions of the bill. The undefined terms may be used later by a court to interpret the act's substantive language either more broadly or more narrowly than was intended. See, e.g., *Friends of Mammoth v. Board of Super. of Mono County*, . . . in which the court construed the undefined term "project" by using a broad legislative intent statement, achieving a result that appears to be significantly at odds with the act's substantive language.

- Unforeseen effects. A statement of intent, purpose or findings may include provisions that directly or indirectly grant rights, prohibit actions or are otherwise substantive in nature, having unforeseen effects on other seemingly unrelated laws.

- Judicial and administrative misuse of argumentative language. A statement of intent, purpose or findings may contain language intended to promote the merits of a bill. If the language is construed by a court in the context of rights or privileges accorded in the substantive provisions of the act, the court's interpretation may yield a result that may not have been intended. See, e.g., *Matter of D.E.R.*, . . . in which the court interpreted a phrase within a legislative intent statement that included sweeping language about protecting individuals to mean that a developmentally disabled individual is entitled to be protectively placed in an environment that requires funding by the county over and above federal, state and county matching monies. . . .

<u>Exceptions</u>

An intent clause may be useful under the following circumstances:

- <u>Recodification</u>. If a bill only recodifies existing law without making any substantive changes, a statement of legislative intent may clarify this fact.

- <u>Constitutionality</u>. If there is reasonable probability that a provision of a bill may be declared unconstitutional, a statement of legislative intent may indicate compliance with constitutional requirements that is not otherwise apparent. Also, a statement of legislative purpose or intent may counter an allegation of unreasonableness or arbitrariness by indicating a rational basis for action by the legislature. See 1A *Sutherland Statutory Construction* §§ 20:3 to 20:5 (7th ed. 2009).

NOTES & QUESTIONS

1.   Many jurisdictions discourage using findings and purposes sections. The House Office of Legislative Counsel's *Guide to Legislative Drafting* states these provisions are "generally unnecessary" since they are often redundant of the operative text of the bill. Findings and purposes may also conflict with the bill provisions, possibly causing problematic interpretations. Still, a statement of purpose may be useful to clarify the intent "of a particularly complex provision" or to establish Congress's power to regulate a certain activity, such as a case of interstate commerce.

2.   The Stem Cell Case Study in Chapter 4 highlighted that the Massachusetts Senate insisted the final bill include a findings and purposes section:

Section 1. The general court finds and declares that:

(a)   human embryonic stem cell research and other research in the life sciences and regenerative medicine present a significant chance of yielding fundamental biological knowledge from which may emanate therapies to relieve, on a large scale, human suffering from disease and injury;

(b) the extraordinary biomedical scientists working within institutions of higher education, research institutes, hospitals, biotechnology companies and pharmaceutical companies can contribute significantly to the welfare of mankind by performing outstanding research in these fields; and

(c)   it shall be the policy of the commonwealth to actively foster research and therapies in the life sciences and regenerative medicine by permitting research and clinical applications involving the derivation and use of human embryonic stem cells, including research and clinical applications involving somatic cell nuclear transfer, placental and umbilical cord cells and human adult stem cells and other mechanisms to create embryonic stem cells which are consistent with this chapter. It shall further be the policy of the commonwealth to prohibit human reproductive cloning.

Why was this statement necessary?

b. Definitions

Definitions have a variety of uses: to avoid repetition, to use a word differently from its ordinary meaning, or to specify a particular technical usage of a word. If, however, the ordinary or dictionary meaning of a word is enough, there is no need for a definition. This is a powerful tool in the drafter's toolbox—far from the "plain meaning" ideal, if a word does not exist, the drafter can create it; likewise, if a word's common meaning needs to be stretched beyond recognition, that is also possible.

WAGGING, NOT BARKING: STATUTORY DEFINITIONS
Jeanne Frazier Price, 60 *Cleveland State Law Review* 999 (2013)

More than 25,000 definitions nestle quietly within the fifty-one titles of the United States Code. The variety of those definitions defies expectations. The meanings of nouns, verbs, adjectives, adverbs and even prepositional phrases are described, sometimes by lengthy and nearly impossibly complicated texts and at other times by one- or two-word synonyms. Single words are defined, as are compound words and simple and complex phrases.

Although practitioners and academics routinely interact with statutory definitions, there has been little discussion of the functions served by those definitions or of their utility. We seem to accept the existence and even the necessity of statutory definition with little introspection; we have not closely examined the consequences, either expected or unintended, of definitions and their impact, conscious or not, on a reader's understanding of a text.

. . .

If statutory definitions do in fact serve important legislative functions and affect the balance of power between legislators and interpreters, we ought to know more about them. Examining the statutory definition in depth may lead to more nuanced and mindful drafting of definitions and to better informed interpretations. By understanding what definitions accomplish-or purport to accomplish-and how they affect cognition, we may be in a better position to determine when definitions are appropriately included in legislation and how best to formulate those definitional texts. We may also find that defining terms-or defining terms in particular ways-may not always serve clarity, consistency, or comprehensibility; in some situations, no definition may be the better plan.

. . . .

IV. Purposes of Definition

The statutory definition may—intentionally or not—narrow the lens of meaning or expand it; the best definitions may simply and succinctly restate meaning in a way that suggests to the reader a particular sense out of many possible ones. But definition inevitably-sometimes subtly, sometimes radically-changes meaning even as it tries to accurately reflect it. If a single word "invites" meaning, rather than fixes it, then more words may either bewitch a reader, offering too rich a combination of implications, or starve him, taking away the staples of meaning on which he normally depends. The more we talk about meaning, the more we change it. So, why define? What legislative ends are achieved by the statutory definition? And, are those ends furthered by particular types or techniques of definition?

A. Creating a Model

If law structures and orders a community, an arrangement of legislation like the U.S. Code might represent a model for the organization and operation of the community that it governs. In imposing order on a diverse, complicated, and messy reality and, at the same time, anticipating how things will change, statutes are often framed in what Judge Posner has called "a highly specific language." That highly specialized language establishes standards to which the governed are expected to conform. To textually establish a structure for governance, Manuel Atienza, Ruiz Manero, and others have suggested that two vehicles are required: "norms of conduct and definitions or conceptual rules." Definitions, "allow the identification of norms by elucidating the sense in which expressions are used." Falling within a statutory definition results in becoming subject to normative rules. The interpretation of text is in many ways private; but legislation can be successful and legitimate only to the extent that meaning is public and shared. Legislation assumes that the governed can both understand the import of statutory text and appropriately conform its behavior to that text. If the "use of language assumes a competence in the audience that the utterance does not convey," we can appreciate why definitions have come to be the rule, rather than the exception, in legislation. In a perfect world, definitions could establish that competence among the audience and fill the gap between the specialized language used by those who govern and the ordinary language employed by the governed. Technical language employs specialized vocabularies; unfamiliar terms are used and familiar words are used in unusual ways. In the absence of definition, legislators either assume that meaning is shared among readers or are intentionally ambiguous or vague, preferring to leave to courts and other interpreters the hard work of determining the precise application of a statutory term. By assigning a name to an object or abstraction, the legislature instructs its audience that the defined term—functioning almost as a sign—stands for what the definition either describes or dictates. The legitimacy of the definition, or the degree to which the audience accepts what the legislature says, may have something to do with both the type of term defined and the techniques used to define it. By defining terms, statutes create categories into which behaviors, entities, individuals, and actions-both present and future-are somehow made to fit. Rules enumerated in legislation apply only to the extent that the associated definitions are somehow satisfied. With respect to prescriptive definitions, the conditions set forth in the definition must be met and, with respect to descriptive ones, the instance to which the normative provisions apply must somehow sufficiently resemble the prototypical category member. If the entirety of the U.S. Code is in some sense a model of the real world, then definitions serve as building blocks in constructing that model.

B.   Controlling the Future

When it defines, the legislature requires that words used in the statute be understood in particular ways. When terms are defined prescriptively, the power of the reader to interpret the word or phrase is even more severely restricted. To define is to limit, and by setting forth the meaning of a term, legislative drafters may set limits beyond which interpreters cannot venture.

Legislation enacted in 2010 established a complex regulatory structure designed to administer health care benefits and insurance. Venturing into uncharted waters, Congress incorporated more than four-hundred definitions into the text of the Patient Protection and Affordable Care Act. Among those definitions is one for "qualified health plan," which sets forth terms and conditions that any health plan wishing to be treated as such is required to meet. The definition is prescriptive; if any one of its conditions is not satisfied, the health plan is not entitled to whatever benefits are available to qualified health plans. When the legislation was drafted, Congress was less than omniscient with respect to the future landscape of federally mandated health insurance. But, by establishing that only those health plans in compliance with specific and detailed conditions would qualify for certain treatment, Congress sought to ensure that at least certain aspects of the health care regime comported with legislative expectations. Interpreters would theoretically be powerless to designate other instances of health plans falling outside statutory parameters as "qualified health plans."

Even definitions with descriptive features allow legislatures to exercise some control over readers, and to erect boundaries outside of which interpretation ought not to stray. So, "motor vehicles," defined in sections

30B and 30D of the Internal Revenue Code, are vehicles that are "manufactured primarily for use on public streets, roads, and highways (not including a vehicle operated exclusively on a rail or rails) and which [have] at least 4 wheels." At least for purposes of the Internal Revenue Code, a motorcycle can never be classified as a motor vehicle. Other descriptive definitions explicitly exclude instances from the definition's scope. An "existing major fuel-burning installation" is, according to the statutory definition, one that is (unsurprisingly) not a new major fuel-burning installation; the definition goes on to exclude from the definition of "existing major fuel-burning installation" two categories of installations that would otherwise qualify. Again, under no (foreseeable) circumstances could interpretation of the statute confer "major fuel-burning installation" status on those two types of facilities.

Like any category into which some events and objects must fall and others be excluded, a definition ranks and relates the experiences and events to which it may apply in comparison to each other. As items are either included or excluded from a category, they are deemed either similar or distinct. Absent definition, categories established by statutory text still exist, but their boundaries are more likely to expand and contract in reaction to both developments in the area and unforeseen applications of the statutory text. Definitions impede—if not completely forestall—normal evolutions in word meaning, at least in a statutory context. If, in ordinary discourse and usage, the meaning of a word is always a work in progress, then the role of the definition is to finish the job. From the perspective of a legislative drafter who wishes to ensure a particular understanding of statutory text-a and limit the alternatives available to interpreters-"the deader the better," at least with respect to word meaning. The choice of definitional techniques-whether descriptive or prescriptive, connotative or denotative-may signal the extent to which drafters-intentionally or not-have effectively either closed the meaning of the term, admitting no unexpected interlopers, or left meaning open, acknowledging the impossibility of anticipating all circumstances.

Definition may also allow drafters to close loopholes and prevent "willful misinterpretation." By making clear that particular instances fall outside of the statutory definition, drafters recognize that the text of the definition itself might admit instances not intended to be included, and that interpreters might successfully pervert statutory language to accomplish outcomes contrary to the legislative purpose. By explicitly removing those instances from the definition's compass, drafters try to ensure the intended interpretation.

Schauer distinguishes between the "long-term mobility of language [and] its short-term plasticity." The fact of definition addresses the mobility of word meaning over time, while the choice of definitional techniques signals, at least to some extent, the willingness or reluctance of the legislature to live with at least some malleability in the definition's application.

C. Being Precise and Increasing Certainty

If definitions control future interpretations of the statute, they may also clarify current application of the statute and promote predictability. To the extent that the meaning of terms used in statutes is expressed precisely, those individuals governed by a statute may be better able to comply with its dictates and conform behavior to the standards enumerated. Precisely defining terms used in statutes might narrow the margin of uncertainty in application, and reduce the number of hard cases.

Sometimes, precisely establishing the limits of a term's scope makes perfect sense. The word "child" is defined repeatedly in the U.S. Code. Depending on the context in which it appears, "child" may or may not include individuals who are more than eighteen years of age, who can support themselves, who are married, who are not related by blood to a parent, who are not yet born, or who have died. Each particular statutory definition of the word narrows the lens of meaning in the context of what it is about a child that is important in the statutory context.

But for every precisely worded definition that clarifies a term's application, another equally precisely defined term complicates an understanding of what instances are covered by the term's reach. The definition of "food" in 7 U.S.C. § 2012 is a long and complicated one; it excludes all "hot foods" except those that fall within any of six clauses. The structure of the definition is such that it, first, incorporates an ordinary understanding of "food," and then, (i) excludes certain categories of what we would think of as food (i.e., hot food); (ii) enumerates exceptions to those excluded categories (thereby bringing more instances of "food" into the fold); and, finally, (iii) adds new categories of normally non-food items (like equipment used to procure food) to the definition's scope. In a definition that is more than six hundred words long, clarity and comprehension may have been sacrificed in an effort to be precise.

"Consumer product" is defined in Title 42 of the U.S. Code in the context of energy conservation programs. In section 6291, "consumer product" is associated with a definition that, first, excludes an item that we would ordinarily think of as a consumer product (automobile); second, limits the term's compass to objects that consume energy or, in a small number of cases, water (thereby eliminating large classes of objects that we ordinarily understand to be consumer products); and, third, eliminates the requirement that the particular object is actually used by a consumer. In the case of "food" and "consumer product," it is hard to see how precision in definition increases clarity. The definitions may, indeed, serve certainty, but at significant cost in terms of understandability.

If the intent behind definition is to reduce, if not eliminate, indeterminacy and vagueness, it is an effort whose success is undermined by everyday language use. The more precise the definition of a common or ordinary term, the more baggage accompanies it throughout its statutory life. But that baggage-cumbersome and unwieldy-is very different from the cloud of meaning that customarily surrounds a word or phrase used in ordinary discourse.

D.   Promoting Readability and Efficiency in Drafting

Most legislative drafting manuals justify the use of definitions by suggesting that including definitions in the text of a statute results in an economy of expression and improvements in readability. The rationale is that by assigning a name to a complex set of conditions or attributes, drafters are able to state statutory provisions more succinctly and clearly. And, as a result, the statutory message is more easily received and understood. Moreover, use of the definition ensures—at least in theory—that terms are used consistently throughout what may be a lengthy text.

If legislation is expressed in a technical language, its vocabulary is likely to consist of terms of art that either have no meaning in ordinary English or have several different meanings. Those terms of art are often shorthand expressions of complicated concepts whose application is confined to a particular discipline; "one of the primary utility features of a technical language is that it enables those of us who speak it to say more in a more comprehensible, thorough and exact way, using less time and fewer words than ... ordinary English." The logic of defined terms is evident in some of the especially convoluted and apparently meaningless terms defined in the U.S. Code. Phrases like " 'Rita GO Zone," "Wilma GO Zone," "Price-Anderson Incident," and "means-tested Federal benefit program" stand in the place of textual descriptions of what those terms represent.[106] Assigning a name to all of the instances or phenomena subsumed in the definition allows the statute's normative provisions to be more efficiently articulated and ensures that there are no discrepancies or contradictions among the statute's possibly many references to the phenomenon or group of objects.

While the legislature may very well intend that those otherwise meaningless terms be understood consistently across a statute, it is more of a stretch to suggest that legislators who define common terms intend a similarly consistent interpretation. A reader wonders if legislators remember the definitions of common terms set forth in one part of a statute as they draft other sections that occur much later in the text.

Literature suggests that "lexical chunks"-content rich phrases or groupings of words-are more easily learned and better incorporated into a cognitive model, at least by children, than individual words. Perhaps frequently repeated terms that refer back to a statutory definition will trigger responses that are appropriate, as gauged by the normative provisions of statutory text.

E. Leveling the Playing Field

Some definitions succinctly, and without elaboration, clarify the ways in which words or phrases are used in statutes. These statements, far from assigning a definitive meaning to a particular word or phrase, instead, put drafters and readers alike on notice, and create a context in which the statute can be situated. They are almost not definitions in a classic sense, yet they are designated as such by statute. So, in the context of Head Start programs, "health" is defined as follows:

> the term "health," when used to refer to services or care provided to enrolled children, their parents, or their siblings, shall be interpreted to refer to both physical and mental health.

The definition evidences the intent of the legislation that-at least with respect to either mental or physical health-there should be no question about the scope of the term as used in the statute. Similarly, the definitions section of the Copyright Act includes this short definition (if we can call it that) of "device, machine or process:" "A 'device', 'machine', or 'process' is one now known or later developed."

To the extent that the sense of a term is quickly and simply clarified, we expect readers to share at least some of the same responses to the word or phrase. With compatible, albeit inexact, understandings of meaning created by quasi-definition, there is at least a context established so that individual comprehension can take place on the same plane. The definition sets forth ground rules-easy to remember and articulate-that apply throughout a reading of the statute. The definition establishes a shared cognitive space that ensures that drafters and readers share some assumptions and understandings, inexact though they may be.

If definitions sometimes efficiently clarify by inclusion, they may equally well exclude certain possible interpretations. The definition of "database" in the Federal Agency Data Mining Reporting Act does not tell us what it necessarily is; the definition only informs us as to what it is not: "[t]he term 'database' does not include telephone directories, news reporting, information publicly available to any member of the public without payment of a fee, or databases of judicial and administrative opinions or other legal research sources." 112 In 5 U.S.C. § 8342, "child" is deemed to include natural or adopted children, but not stepchildren. And, in 5 U.S.C. § 8421, the only definition of "service" is a statement to the effect that "the term 'service' does not include military service." If a term is capable of attracting different meanings, one purpose of definition is to ensure that the appropriate sense is the one attached to the word in the statute.

. . . .

VI. Conclusion

When the temptation to define strikes, resistance should follow. Defining without a valid and well-identified purpose risks complicating the statute and creating the potential for unforeseen questions unrelated to the statute's purpose. The legislative drafter should carefully consider what the definition is intended to accomplish and how best to further those purposes.

If the statute is part of a complex scheme designed to order a sphere of activity, where individuals-depending on their attributes and actions-are entitled to be treated in particular ways, then assigning a name to those groups of actors might be useful. If the drafter wants to ensure that particular instances are certainly and forever entitled to particular treatment, no matter how the interpreter chooses to read the text, then a definition can clarify an instance's status. For purposes of modeling behaviors, a performative definition may fit the bill-if an instance falls or purposefully comes within the scope of a definition, the named thing is treated appropriately.

The drafter may see no other way to make her meaning and communication plain other than by definition. She may be unsure whether a particular term will be understood by her audience as she intends it to be. Or she may wish to forestall anticipated misinterpretation. A definition can provide information and direction on how a particular term is to be understood.

In relegating particular instances to a specified treatment, the definition functions as a performative. In clarifying the sense of words in text, the definition's predominant role is to enable successful communication. In either case, the benefits of precisely defining a word or phrase that is already easily associated with a well-accepted meaning are dubious. Articulating definitions of well-understood and unambiguous terms may in fact be detrimental to both communicative and performative goals. If the definition is performative in nature-if qualifying under it invests an individual or activity with rights or obligations-the point is to put the audience on notice. Defining words already having well-established meaning and then asking them to perform speech act functions demands too much of them. And, the audience may be frustrated as it is expected to invest common terms of ordinary meaning with special powers.

If, on the other hand, the purpose of the definition is to strengthen or clarify a legislative communication, defining a well-understood word risks not only unintentionally changing its meaning, but fixing it in time. If the drafter intends a word of ordinary meaning to have that ordinary meaning in the statute, why define it at all? Why diminish the nuances and complexities of meaning? If the drafters wish to change a word's ordinary meaning through definition, to either expand or restrict its compass, it may be better to use an invented or descriptive term instead.

Definition may be advisable, however, to clarify the intended meaning of ambiguous or unsettled terms or to establish groups of individuals or activities entitled to particular treatment. No matter what purposes it serves, however, the definition ought to be simple and succinct in its statement. Long and convoluted definitions seldom promote clarity or certainty, and they surely make a legislative text more difficult to read, as repeated reference to the definition's details is required throughout the reading of the statute.

No matter what she seeks to accomplish in defining a term, the legislative drafter would do well to realize that definition is a process that is always incomplete. Word meaning inevitably changes and unforeseen situations occur that are not addressed by definitions purportedly covering all circumstances. Better to take into account the indeterminacy of word meaning in drafting a definition than to attempt to completely and finally memorialize the meaning of a term.

Regardless of the goal, the drafter ought not to confuse clarity, certainty, and precision. The last does not always lead to the first or the second. While the definition ought to be clear in its import-the reader should be able to understand what instances are generally covered or what sense of the word is intended-it need not be absolutely certain. The definition may leave open the question of whether some outliers are encompassed within it. Or, it may, with certainty, include or exclude particularly hard cases. But it need not do so by precisely and interminably enumerating all of the characteristics of every qualifying or disqualified instance. To try to do so would be both expensive, from a drafting perspective, and futile.

NOTES & QUESTIONS

1.   Professor Price writes, "When the temptation to define strikes, resistance should follow." On the other hand, the House and Senate Offices of Legal Counsel in recent years have encouraged the inclusion of more definitions. Legislative Counsel must often probe what a member of Congress or their staff mean by a word with different possible meanings and use that information to craft definitions. In 1973, Congress passed 1,086 pages of public laws and defined only 285 terms. In 2009, Congress defined 1,435 terms in 3,496 pages of public laws. See, Jarrod Shobe, "Intertemporal Statutory Interpretation and the Evolution of Legislative Drafting," 114 *Colum. L. Rev.* 807, 829–830 (2014). Should definitions be encouraged or resisted?

2.   Federal Appeals Court Judge Robert Katzmann drew on many sources to interpret ambiguous words:

In my experience, the judge's work in interpreting statutes takes place not on the lofty plane of grand, unified theory, but on the ground of practical, common sense inquiry. In approaching the interpretive task, a judge can use several tools, including: text, statutory structure, history, word usage in other relevant statutes, common law usages, agency interpretations, dictionary definitions, technical and scientific usages, lay usages, canons, common practices, and purpose. The judge pulls from the interpretive toolbox those instruments that can help extract what the statute means in light of congressional purposes. The toolbox can help the judge, for example, appreciate the institutional context that may serve as a guide to understanding a statute's meaning. See, Robert Katzmann, *Judging Statutes* (Oxford Univ. Press 2014); Ron Collins, Ask the author: Chief Judge Katzmann on statutory interpretation, *SCOTUSblog* (Oct. 27, 2014, 8:00 AM), https://www.scotusblog.com/2014/10/ask-the-author-chief-judge-katzmann-on-statutory-interpretation/.

3.   If a term is not defined then practitioners, courts, and agencies will often look for the common understanding—or ordinary meaning—of the word. By using a word as it would be naturally understood, courts can better apply statutes as the legislature meant and both policy makers and the governed can have a common understanding of statutory language. What materials do courts use to determine the ordinary meaning? Often judges will refer to dictionaries, but then have to choose between multiple meanings in the same dictionary or across different dictionaries. Sometime courts refer to literature such as *Moby Dick* or the *Bible*, or even the works of Dr. Seuss. Judges may cite a word's usage in other parts of the law, including judicial decisions or other governmental materials. Some critics, however, argue that the "ordinary meaning" standard just allows a judge to read their own policy preferences into a statute. See, Valerie C. Brannon, "Statutory Interpretation: Theories, Tools, and Trends," *Congressional Research Service* (April 5, 2018) (https://www.everycrsreport.com/reports/R45153.html#_Toc510711650). Is the ordinary meaning the best way to read and interpret statutes? What method would be preferable?

4.   The limits of "ordinary meaning" were clear when Nebraska passed a "safe-haven" law, where parents could abandon an unwanted child at a hospital without questions or penalty. One version of the Webster's New Collegiate Dictionary contains six different definitions for the word "child." The Nebraska Legislature likely meant "child" to mean definition 1: "an unborn or recently born person;" or perhaps definition 2: "a young person esp. between infancy and youth." Many other people, however, seemingly understood the meaning of "child" to be the broad definition 4: "a son or daughter of human parents." After the law passed people left 35 children between the ages of 10 and17 at state hospitals before the Legislature amended the law by limiting the scope of "child" to 30 days of age. See, Erik Eckholm, "Nebraska Revises Child Safe Haven Law," *New York Times*, Nov. 21, 2008 (https://www.nytimes.com/2008/11/22/us/22nebraska.html).

5. In addition to definitions, the House and Senate Offices of Legislative Counsel also encourage including exceptions to prevent a bill from being unintentionally broad. For example, when some members of Congress wanted to penalize anyone who imported dog- or cat-fur products legislative counsel asked how the law would be applied if the person was living or vacationing abroad with a dog or cat and that pet died? Bringing the pet back to the U.S. to be buried or preserved through taxidermy could expose them to legal penalties. As a result, the U.S. Code now includes the exception:

> "This subsection shall not apply to the importation, exportation, or transportation, for noncommercial purposes, of a personal pet that is deceased, including a pet preserved through taxidermy."

See, Jarrod Shobe, "Intertemporal Statutory Interpretation and the Evolution of Legislative Drafting," 114 *Colum. L. Rev.* 807, 830–831 (2014).

c. Drafting for Agencies

The administrative state has grown dramatically with Congress entrusting more discretion and power to the agencies that implement the laws. Agency personnel can become a tremendous resource to a legislature through their expertise, institutional memory, and faithful execution of the law. However, like any institution, agencies can also develop a culture, particular ideology, biases and unique processes. By nature, institutional behavior is very difficult to change or redirect. When new people come into the organization they learn the "way things are done" and the institution perpetuates itself. At times, agencies with a strong culture can frustrate lawmakers: agency personnel may want to concentrate on familiar issues, not the new issues of concern to legislators. Also, administrators may be so focused on their own issues that they do not see how their activities affect other parts of the government. Another problem is a strong sense of inertia—if the agency has always done something, why change?

Drafting legislation always requires a careful consideration of the agencies involved. The legislators must consider what different agencies do—and not do—well. Often legislators and their staff learn about the strengths and weaknesses of individual agencies by working with them over time.

Strengths	Weaknesses
efficiency: agencies can divide labor among its personnel, allowing it to quickly and efficiently handle even complicated tasks	**inefficiency:** The division of labor that can make agencies efficient, can also make these organizations difficult to navigate and "bureaucratic"

expertise: by focusing on one set of related issues and employing experts in a particular field to gather and analyze data, agencies may be one of the most reliable sources of information;	**narrow focus:** by focusing on one area, the agency may not understand what other parts of the government are doing or how the agency fits into the government as a whole;
flexibility: typically, agencies can change regulations and move resources faster than the legislature can pass a new law. Therefore, they can proactively address changing situations. Agencies can also use different methods to achieve similar goals in different locations	**inertia:** agencies with strong cultures may resist innovation or new ways of dealing with problems.
perspective: institutions can exist for generations and agencies are typically very good at keeping records of what circumstances led to a new law or why it was interpreted as it was. This institutional memory can be extremely valuable to lawmakers.	**agency capture:** agencies too close to special interests can become an advocate, rather than a regulator, of industry. Captured agencies may operate according to the wishes of special interests rather than the legislature.

Drafting a statute with an agency in mind is very fact and circumstances specific:

- What agency or agencies will be implementing this law?
- What do those agencies do well?
- Are there any concerns about those agencies?
- Will the agency resist what the legislature wants to do, requiring specific statutory commands?
- Does the agency need flexibility to address the problem?
- Can existing agencies properly implement the law?
- Should there be a new agency?

Many times, it is tempting to create a new agency, but this carries its own advantages and disadvantages:

New Agency Advantages	New Agency Disadvantages
Enthusiastic officials	More expensive
Create a new ideology/culture	Longer time to implement law
Avoid existing patterns of behavior	Create possibility of "turf wars"

Minnesota Revisor's Manual
The Minnesota Office of the Revisor of Statutes (2013)

3.7 ORGANIZATION OF STATE GOVERNMENT

(a) General considerations.

A bill creating a new agency, board, commission, or department to administer a new program or regulate an occupational group should be drafted with the following general considerations in mind:

- The drafter must provide for all necessary features of a well-functioning operation.

- The drafter must determine if identical or similar programs or functions already exist in other agencies. Similar or identical programs or functions may exist in the statutory authority for other agencies. The drafter must provide the necessary repeals, amendments, or distinctions to coordinate the old and new agencies. Minnesota Statutes, section 15.039, governs the transfer of powers among agencies unless stated otherwise.

- The drafter must be familiar with the statutory elements common to all agencies. Among the common elements are provisions for naming the agency, administrative rulemaking, budgeting, and employment and compensation of employees. The drafter must ensure that the agency will fit within these common provisions or that suitable exceptions to them are stated.

- The drafter should set an effective date that leaves enough time for the new agency to be set up. Effective dates are important for transfers of duties between agencies as well.

- The drafter should easily be able to locate earlier bills to use as models, as this type of legislation is frequently introduced, if not finally enacted.

(b) Basic provisions for creating a new agency.

A drafter should consider providing the following information in any bill that creates a new agency:

- Indicate whether the agency is a state agency and whether it is within the executive, legislative, or judicial branch, or independent. Indicate whether the agency is part of an existing agency. Name the agency according to the nomenclature established by Minnesota Statutes, section 15.012. Consider whether it should be added to the list of departments of state in Minnesota Statutes, section 15.01.

- Specify who controls the agency, whether a single person, a multiple-person board or commission, or some combination.

- Specify the qualifications of either the person or the members of the board or commission that controls the agency.

- Specify the manner of election, selection, and termination of the person or the members of the board or commission that controls the agency. Consult Minnesota Statutes, sections 15.0575 to 15.06 and 15.066 for statutory restrictions. If the drafter intends Minnesota Statutes, chapter 15, to apply to the new agency, the applicable sections should be specified. If these statutory sections are not going to apply to the new agency, the drafter should include the following phrase: "Notwithstanding section 15.0575 (or whichever section) . . . ." General provisions relating to advisory task forces are in Minnesota Statutes, sections 15.014 and 15.059.

- In addition to Minnesota Statutes, chapter 15, consider whether any aspects of Minnesota Statutes, chapters 14, 16A, 16B, 16C, 43A, and 179A, should apply. If a state agency is created, these chapters generally apply unless a statement is made to the contrary.

- State the duties or responsibilities of the agency.

- State the powers of the agency. A drafter should ensure that there is some relationship between the powers granted and the duties stated elsewhere in the bill. For example, if the agency is established to study a problem, the drafter should consider whether the agency should have the power to issue subpoenas.

- If several compartmentalized functions will exist within the agency, the drafter may wish to consider whether separate divisions within the agency should be specified by law.

- If the agency will produce revenue in some fashion by charging fees or by selling a product, the drafter should specify the manner in which the fees or prices are determined and the receipts are distributed. The alternatives available include a statutory appropriation of money received for the agency's use, or, more usually, a requirement that all money received by the agency be deposited in the state's general fund.

- If the agency is permitted to employ staff, specify the status of agency employees. Are they in the classified or unclassified service, or do they have a special status? See Minnesota Statutes, chapter 43A.

- Provide for administrative rulemaking. See section 3.9 for further analysis of the considerations involved when drafting a bill that grants rulemaking authority to an agency.

- If the agency will be heavily involved with regulating the activities of individuals, it may be best to set out the outlines of its procedures or the limitations on its authority. These matters should not be left solely to administrative rulemaking. Bills establishing licensing boards should be consistent with Minnesota Statutes, sections 116J.69 to 116J.71, and chapter 214.

- If the agency deals in an area that grants a new right or regulates or prohibits an activity of individuals, the drafter should specify those substantive rights or prohibitions.

- State the relationship, as appropriate, to the governor, the legislature, or the Supreme Court, as the ultimate supervisor.

- State any sanctions or penalties either for persons dealing with the agency or for agency officers or employees.

- Indicate any temporary provisions, such as initial terms of office or temporary powers.

- Set out any necessary appropriations of state funds to set up or operate the agency.

- Consider the name to be given the new agency. Is there any agency with a similar name or performing a similar function? Consider a naming convention that will distinguish between the two agencies.

d. Organization

Delaware Legislative Drafting Manual
Legislative Council's Division of Research (2019)

E.   Body of the Bill.

Although the body of a bill is one of its required parts, it is made up of a series of optional parts. Each optional part is usually designated as a bill "Section," with a capital "s." Bill Sections (Section 1, Section 2, Section 3, etc.) divide a bill and should never be confused with Code sections (§ 1201, § 1202, § 1203, etc.), which divide a chapter of the Code. The body of the bill must always contain at least one bill Section, which must be labeled as "Section 1."

In dividing the body of a bill into Sections, use care in crafting clear, logical divisions. And, if amending the Code, include only those portions of the Code that belong within the division created by the Section. For example, if the intent is to create a new chapter of the Code, the bill should have one Section, which should include only those new Code sections intended to be part of the new chapter. However, if the intent is to amend multiple Code sections within an existing chapter, the drafter may create one Section and include all of the Code sections to be changed within an existing chapter, or the drafter may create one Section for each individual Code section to be changed within the existing chapter. The latter is preferred and, in choosing this method, take care not to allow additional Code sections to be added to a Section in the drafting process before introduction or by an amendment. When crafting the prefatory language for a Section, cite to the Code section, rather than a subsection or paragraph, even if planning to amend just one subsection or paragraph. The body of the bill carries constitutional implications with it as well. The single subject rule, discussed previously in subsection B, regarding Bill Titles, requires that the body of the bill be germane to the subject of the legislation to which the bill title refers. Thus, the scope of the body of a bill may not be beyond the scope of the title of the bill, which is why the phrase "relating to" is so useful in a bill title.

HOUSE OFFICE OF LEGISLATIVE COUNSEL: GUIDE TO LEGISLATIVE DRAFTING

(https://legcounsel.house.gov/holc-guide-legislative-drafting#IV)

General template for structuring content

Our Office generally tries to organize the content of a bill, and provisions within a bill, according to the template below. We do not always follow this template, but it is often our starting point when we think about how to put together a draft.

General rule: State the main message.

Exceptions: Describe the persons or things to which the main message does not apply.

Special rules: Describe the persons or things to which the main message applies in a different way or for which there is a different message.

Transitional rules.

Other provisions.

Definitions.

Effective date (if appropriate).

"Authorization of appropriations" provisions (if appropriate).

LEGISLATIVE DRAFTING STEP-BY-STEP
Arthur J. Rynearson (2013)

Part II: Organizing a Section

Introduction

Sections are the building blocks of legislation, with each section performing a particular function. The exact content of a section, however, is not preordained. While the United States Code requires each section to "contain, as nearly as may be, a single proposition of enactment", the vagueness of the standard permits the drafter after a wide latitude of interpretation. Although performing only one function, a typical section sets forth more than one duty, delegation, entitlement, or internal rule, and each distinct legal effect must be kept separate within this section in order to promote readability. Proper section organization does exactly that.

Subdividing a Section

Subsets or Itemizations.—A section may be subdivided by either of the following two methods, or any combination of the two:

    (1) By Whole Sentences.—In its entirety, forming neat subsets of whole sentences.

    (2) By Grammatical Clauses.—In fragments, by itemizing the section's grammatical clauses.

Nomenclature of the Subdivisions of a Section.—A section is subdivided in descending order using alternating alphabetical and numerical designations, as follows:

Subsections: (a), (b), (c), etc.

Paragraphs: (1), (2), (3), etc.

    Subparagraphs: (A), (B), (C), etc.

        Clauses: (i), (ii), (iii), etc.

            Subclauses: (I), (II), (III), etc.

The designation system in United States legislation is an arbitrary system that is useful only if applied consistently. Alternative systems may easily be imagined but the in system described above has near universal acceptance in United States federal legislative drafting. Treaty texts and the legislation of many parliamentary democracies, however, use different systems.

"Noah's Ark Principle".—For each level of subdivision, there must be at least two items, meaning that if the drafter wishes for a subsection (a), then the drafter must at least provide for subsection (b), and so forth down the hierarchy of subdivisions. The failure to designate at least a second item in a level of hierarchy means that subdivision at that level is not possible and that the expression should remain with the next higher level of the hierarchy. This is basic principle of subdivision seems to elude many novice drafters who insist on stranding a single subsection, paragraph, subparagraph, or clause without a partner. For this reason the author refers to the concept as the "Noah's Ark Principle" of section organization in an attempt to shame the drafter into compliance, but of course Noah would object as there may be more than two items at anyone level!

NOTES & QUESTIONS

1.   The structure of a bill, of course, varies from jurisdiction to jurisdiction—and sometimes between chambers within the same legislature. The operative sections, however, should be organized in a manner that is useful to the reader. The Massachusetts Drafting Manual states, "Avoid an organization that requires an understanding of a later section in order to understand an earlier section. Group together all sections dealing with a common subject matter."

2.   Into the 20th Century, many statutes were blocks of text, rather than being divided into subsections, paragraphs and subparagraphs. How does using subdivisions promote greater clarity and understanding?

3.   How much harder would it be to understand this federal statute penalizing the possession of a firearm during a drug crime (118 U.S. Code § 924(c)) if the drafter did not subdivide the language?

    A.   Except to the extent that a greater minimum sentence is otherwise provided by this subsection or by any other provision of law, any person who, during and in relation to any crime of violence or drug trafficking crime (including a crime of violence or drug trafficking crime that provides for an enhanced punishment if committed by the use of a deadly or dangerous weapon or device) for which the person may be prosecuted in a court of the United States, uses or carries a firearm, or who, in furtherance of any such crime, possesses a firearm, shall, in addition to the punishment provided for such crime of violence or drug trafficking crime—

        i.   be sentenced to a term of imprisonment of not less than 5 years;

        ii.   if the firearm is brandished, be sentenced to a term of imprisonment of not less than 7 years; and

      iii. *if the firearm is discharged, be sentenced to a term of imprisonment of not less than 10 years.*

    B. *If the firearm possessed by a person convicted of a violation of this subsection—*

      i. *is a short-barreled rifle, short-barreled shotgun, or semiautomatic assault weapon, the person shall be sentenced to a term of imprisonment of not less than 10 years; or*

      ii. *is a machine gun or a destructive device, or is equipped with a firearm silencer or firearm muffler, the person shall be sentenced to a term of imprisonment of not less than 30 years.*

    C. *In the case of a second or subsequent conviction under this subsection, the person shall—*

      i. *be sentenced to a term of imprisonment of not less than 25 years; and*

      ii. *if the firearm involved is a machine gun or a destructive device, or is equipped with a firearm silencer or firearm muffler, be sentenced to imprisonment for life.*

    4. Notice the use of "and" and "or" as connectors in the above statute.

e. Prefatory Language

Basic Considerations In Drafting Legislation (Connecticut)
Connecticut Legislative Commissioners' Office (2015)

PREFATORY LANGUAGE

The prefatory language of a bill tells the reader whether the bill is creating new law or amending existing law (see section following for Effective Dates).

If new, the prefatory language will be simply the word "new" in capital letters and in parentheses, followed by the effective date of the section.

   Example:

   Section 1.   (NEW) (*Effective October 1, 2015*) The dinosaur footprint of Eubrontes is the state fossil.

   Sec. 2.   (NEW) (*Effective October 1, 2015*) Each person who excavates a site designated a prehistoric site shall. . . .

If the bill is not creating an entirely new law but is instead changing (amending) an existing statute, the drafter uses standard prefatory language to inform the reader what statute is being changed (but note that the existing law is not really "repealed", merely amended).

Example:

Sec. 8. Subsection (a) of section 51–165 of the general statutes is repealed and the following is substituted in lieu thereof (*Effective October 1, 2015*):

In even-year sessions, the drafter might be amending a statute that was newly enacted or amended in the preceding year. In such a case, the drafter cites in the prefatory language the section of the even-year supplement to the General Statutes.

Example:

Sec. 5. Section 54–86*l* of the 2014 supplement to the general statutes is repealed and the following is substituted in lieu thereof (*Effective October 1, 2015*):

<u>Note:</u> *The entire General Statutes are republished biennially, near the start of each odd-year session. Near the start of each even-year session, a supplement to the General Statutes is published. The supplement only includes new statutes enacted during the preceding odd-year session or previously existing statutes that were amended during the preceding odd-year session.*

To find out if a statute has been amended in the preceding odd-year session, look in the reference table of General Statutes Amended or Repealed or in the even-year supplement to the General Statutes for that year.

Occasionally, there are statutes with double sections, i.e., existing statutes with amendments that will go into effect in the future. Such occurrences are rare and beyond the scope of this document; if the drafter is faced with such a circumstance, the LCO may be contacted for guidance.

Minnesota Revisor's Manual
The Minnesota Office of the Revisor of Statutes (2013)

(2) Introductory phrase. The introductory phrase is the phrase that tells the reader what law is being amended or repealed, or where the law is to be coded. An introductory phrase appears on lines 11.1, 11.5, and 11.9 of Figure 5:

Fig. 5

11.1	Section 1. Minnesota Statutes 20.., section 15A.082, is amended to read:
11.2	**15A.082 COMPENSATION COUNCIL.**
11.3	Subdivision 1. **Creation.** A compensation council is created to assist the
11.4	legislature in each even-numbered year. . . .
11.5	Sec. 2. [293.21] REFUND OF TAX ERRONEOUSLY COLLECTED.
11.6	The commissioner of revenue shall refund any tax erroneously paid or
11.7	collected and shall reimburse the general fund for the expenses of implementing
11.8	this chapter.
11.9	Sec. 3. REPEALER.
11.10	Minnesota Statutes 20.., section xxx.xx, is repealed.

The text of the section, whether or not it is divided into subdivisions, always begins on a new indented line after the section headnote. If the section contains subdivisions, the text begins immediately after the subdivision headnote.

6. PENALTIES

KENTUCKY BILL DRAFTING MANUAL
Kentucky Legislative Research Commission (2011)*

Sec. 210. Penalties

Frequently, the sponsor of a statute wants sanctions imposed for its violation. Normally, these are criminal sanctions. In this case it is necessary to use particular care in writing the elements of the crime. If the elements of the Sec. 210 16 crime are not clearly and simply stated, a court may be able to declare the statute unconstitutional due to vagueness. Thus, the format of the Penal Code (KRS Chapters 500 to 534) is frequently used. This is a strict outline format with the penalty as the last section.

If the drafter is adding a section to the Penal Code, he or she must utilize the Penal Code format and penalty structure. The penalty structure of the Penal Code is: capital offense, Class A felony, Class B felony, Class C felony, Class D felony, Class A misdemeanor, Class B misdemeanor, and violation. Capital offenses and felonies result in the death penalty or imprisonment in the penitentiary as possible penalties. Misdemeanors

---

*   Selections reprinted with permission from Arthur J. Rynearson, Legislative Drafting Step-By-Step (Durham: Carolina Academic Press, 2013), 112–113.

result in jail time, fines, or both. Violations result in fines only. The drafter should check the Penal Code for the specifics of each of these penalties.

If the drafter is creating a criminal offense elsewhere in the statutes, the Penal Code penalty structure or the Penal Code format is not controlling. In many chapters, the Penal Code format is used for the offense, while the penalty is found at the end of the chapter in a ".990" section.

Traditional penalties result in fines or imprisonment. In most cases, if the imprisonment is to be served in the penitentiary, the offense is a felony. If the imprisonment is to be served in the county jail, the offense is a misdemeanor. In Kentucky the practice has been that offenses with more than a year of imprisonment are felonies and those with sentences of up to one year are misdemeanors. There is no distinction in the amount of a fine between misdemeanors and felonies.

With regard to imprisonment, various qualifying terms may be used. Maximum sentences are always specified; sometimes minimum sentences are specified. Other terms include permitting the sentences to be served on weekends or other times convenient to the defendant. Sometimes statutes prohibit probating part of the sentence or increase the penalty for repeated offenses. Sometimes the first or second offense might be a misdemeanor and subsequent offenses felonies.

Fines provide a virtually unlimited source of variation. The most commonly used provisions are minimum and maximum fines, but others, such as requiring the fine to be double or triple the amount of gain from the commission of the Sec. 210 offense, requiring the fine to be double or triple the damage caused, or making each day a separate offense for fine purposes, are also relatively common. Daily fines are particularly common in regulatory offenses where many defendants are wealthy and can afford to pay minor fines as a cost of doing business.

Additional monetary penalties, other than fines, are sometimes imposed. Court costs, restitution to victims (either in the amount stolen or in the amount of damage), making the defendant pay the costs of prosecution, requiring payment of a service fee to be divided among state agencies, and similar items have been required under state or federal law.

Various nonmonetary penalties have been imposed over the years and sometimes prove effective. Typical nonmonetary penalties include: seizure and forfeiture of property used to commit a crime; seizure and forfeiture of the proceeds of crime; seizure and forfeiture of things purchased with proceeds of the crime; revocation, suspension, or denial of licenses (motor vehicle operators, professional, occupational, etc.); forfeiture of public office; prohibition against holding public office; prohibition against engaging in certain professions or activities; required education, reeducation, or repassing of tests; required medical or psychological treatment (drug treatment for certain drivers, etc.); and prohibitions against engaging in certain types of business.

The type and range of penalty are virtually unlimited; however, several considerations emerge. The penalty must not be cruel or unusual. This constitutional prohibition generally refers to physical cruelty and torture. A more practical consideration is that the penalty chosen, or the combination of penalties chosen, should be designed to protect the public, deter criminal activity, and neither be so lenient or so strict as to be disproportionate. Penalties that are too lenient do not discourage criminal activity and may, in fact, enhance certain types of violations, particularly where the defendants can afford to pay a fine or to weather the penalty easily. In this case the fine or other penalty may become a permit fee for violation of the law. If the penalty is too strict or is felt to be disproportionate to the crime, the public, through jurors or judges, will not impose the penalty or will seek ways to get around its imposition through suspending the sentences or similar tactics. In this case, police and prosecutors quickly learn that the penalty will not be enforced, and enforcement may slacken.

In creating penalties that fit a crime, the drafter should look at the crime and look at the most frequent violators or potential violators of the law, and then consider what penalty would most likely deter the crime or constitute an adequate public sanction for its commission. Large fines, seizure of assets and property, and repayment of costs of prosecution may deter criminal activity by corporations or affluent defendants but have little meaning to those without financial resources. Imprisonment has an effect on anyone who might be incarcerated, and it can be utilized without regard to financial resources as a deterrent. Suspension or revocation of licenses has been found effective against professional misconduct in some cases.

Drafters need to think about the costs of imposing certain types of penalties, particularly incarceration. Imprisonment in the penitentiary creates a long-term cost for the state; imprisonment in a county jail creates a cost for county government. Thus, other programs are being used either in lieu of incarceration or as an adjunct thereto. For example, there are work-release programs for misdemeanants requiring inmates to pay all or part of the costs of incarceration; home incarceration programs requiring the defendants to stay in their homes with approved monitoring devices (which the defendants pay for); intensive probation; and community service.

Whichever penalty or combination of penalties is chosen, careful consideration of all of the above factors combined with careful drafting is necessary, as criminal statutes are more narrowly construed by the courts and are construed in favor of the defendant.

Texas Legislative Council Drafting Manual
Texas Legislative Council (2020)

(c)   Civil penalties. A civil penalty is an enforcement mechanism by which a wrongdoer is made civilly liable to the state or a political subdivision for an amount of money. Although the penalty resembles a fine, the fact that it is civil rather than criminal obviates the strict burden of proof required to establish criminal responsibility. The state or political subdivision files a civil action against the wrongdoer and need only show by a preponderance of the evidence that the prohibited conduct was committed.

Because the remedy is civil, the attorney general, instead of the local prosecuting attorney, may be authorized to prosecute the action on behalf of the state. Although Section 21, Article V, Texas Constitution, might seem to make representation of the state in a state trial court the prerogative of county and district attorneys, courts have approved laws providing for representation by the attorney general in legislatively created causes of action.

Because the civil penalty has many attributes of criminal punishment without the corresponding procedural protections, some persons have questioned the propriety of the remedy. In spite of this, the civil penalty is well established in Texas law, its popularity largely due, no doubt, to the features that some find objectionable. A civil penalty is typically provided for as follows:

Sec. 35.034. CIVIL PENALTY. (a) A license holder who fails to file the report required by Section 35.033 within the time specified by that section is liable to the state for a civil penalty of $1,000 for each day the failure continues.

(b)   The attorney general may sue to collect the penalty.

(f)   Administrative penalties. An administrative penalty is an enforcement device similar in some respects to a civil penalty. In fact, some persons characterize the administrative penalty as a type of civil penalty, although others consider it to be a separate type of penalty. The administrative penalty is similar to the civil penalty discussed earlier in that it resembles a fine and in that the prohibited conduct must be proved only by a preponderance of the evidence instead of by the stricter burden of proof that applies to criminal cases.

The major differences between an administrative penalty and the civil penalty discussed earlier relate to the entity that assesses the penalty and to the assessment procedure. A court assesses a civil penalty, while an administrative agency assesses an administrative penalty. Two examples of an administrative penalty are provided below.

7. REPEALING CLAUSES

Florida Guidelines For Drafting Legislation
Florida House Bill Drafting Service (2014)

REPEALS

Section 6 of Article XII of the Florida Constitution provides in part that:

> All laws . . . shall remain in force until they expire by their terms or are repealed.

Some bills consist of nothing more than a statement which repeals present law. In drafting bills which contain amended or created text, it is sometimes necessary to also repeal existing statutes. The drafter must be particularly careful not to overlook current law which, if left on the books, would be in direct conflict with the new law. Do not create new provisions and then rely on repeal by implication. A repealing section should be set forth which makes specific reference to the conflicting or superseded statutes. This serves to prevent much confusion and difficulty later in interpreting and applying the new law.

Does the repealed language have to be set forth in the bill?

When repealing a section of the statutes in its entirety, it is not necessary to set forth the text of the section and hyphen through it. Cite the section to be repealed, indicating that it is repealed, as in the following example:

Section 28.   <u>Section 198.0919, Florida Statutes, is repealed.</u>

Since no text is set forth to indicate the substance of what is being repealed, an accurate title provision must be included in the title of the bill to give the reader sufficient notice of the effect of the repeal.

With respect to instances in which there is a desire to repeal a subdivision of a section (subsection, paragraph, etc.), it is recommended that such subdivision be set forth in the bill, hyphenated, and characterized as "amended" rather than "repealed."

What about using a "general repealer" clause?

A provision sometimes found in older bills is the so-called "general repealer" which goes something like this: "All laws in conflict with this act are hereby repealed." <u>Sutherland's Statutory Construction</u> makes the following comment about a general repealer clause:

> An express general repealing clause to the effect that all inconsistent enactments are repealed, is in legal contemplation a nullity.

We strongly recommend that the general repealer not be used since it adds nothing to good drafting technique and may cause confusion.

H. TECHNICAL PROVISIONS

1. SEVERABILITY CLAUSES

Minnesota Revisor's Manual

The Minnesota Office of the Revisor of Statutes (2013)

2.17 SEVERABILITY OR NONSEVERABILITY CLAUSE (a) Generally. A severability clause is a provision that keeps the remaining provisions of a statute in force if any portion of that statute is declared void or unconstitutional by a court. (b) Legal considerations. Minnesota Statutes, section 645.20, establishes a statutory presumption that all laws are severable. A court may sever an unconstitutional void provision from a law and leave the remaining valid provisions, unless the law includes an explicit nonseverability clause. In addition, the court could either find that the legislature would not have enacted the valid provisions without the void one, or that the remaining valid provisions, standing alone, are incomplete and incapable of being executed in accordance with legislative intent. (c) Form. When used in a bill with more than one section, the severability or nonseverability clause should be in a separate section immediately following the enacting clause or near the end of the bill immediately preceding the repealer section and effective date section, if any. When written as part of a single section, the severability or nonseverability clause should be the first or last subdivision. Chapter 2: Bill Drafting 41 (d) Examples. Examples of a severability provision and a nonseverability provision follow in Figures 31 and 32:

Fig. 31

11.13	Sec. ... **SEVERABILITY.**
11.14	If any provision of this act is found to be unconstitutional and void, the remaining
11.15	provisions of this act are valid.

Fig. 32

11.13	Sec. ... **NONSEVERABILITY.**
11.14	If any provision of this act is found to be unconstitutional and void, the remaining
11.15	provisions of this act are void.

(e) Drafting advice. If it is intended that the provisions of a bill not be severable, the drafter should specify that they are not. On the issue of whether or not the legislature would have enacted the valid provisions without the void ones, the drafter can clarify the issue for the court by including an explicit severability or nonseverability provision that clearly expresses the legislature's intent. However, an explicit severability clause may not prevent a court from finding that the remaining provisions are incomplete and incapable of being executed in accordance with legislative intent.

NOTES & QUESTIONS

Some states have statutes providing for blanket severability. Massachusetts has such a statute, Mass. G.L. c. 4, § 6(11), and its drafting manual cautions that "use of severability clauses in some acts but not others may create a negative implication that severability is not intended in acts where the language does not appear." See, *Massachusetts General Court Legislative Research and Drafting Manual* (2010).

2. SUNSET CLAUSES

Delaware Legislative Drafting Manual
Legislative Council's Division of Research (2019)

L.   Sunset Clause; Contingent Sunset Clause.

A "sunset clause" provision is an expiration provision used to provide a time or circumstance upon which the power or effectiveness of an act, provision, or specific agency expires. As such, a sunset clause can be a useful political device to temporarily raise revenues or enact a program allowing for review by a later General Assembly to determine if the revenues or program are still needed.

Example of a Sunset Clause:
This Act expires 3 years after its enactment into law, unless otherwise provided by a subsequent act of the General Assembly.

The following is an example of how the Code Revisors add language to the Code online, based on how a bill is drafted, to indicate that a law has a sunset date.

Example:
As drafted in the bill: (c) The Trust Fund terminates on July 1, 2024, unless terminated sooner or extended by the General Assembly.
As appears in Code online: § 7012. Delaware Manufactured Home Relocation Trust Fund. [Terminates effective July 1, 2024]

A variation on a sunset clause is a provision which speaks only to a certain point in time, or which is applicable only for a certain window in time that may occur in the future. In essence, such a variant creates a hidden sunset clause, as once the time period passes, the rest of the provision is no longer operative.

> **Examples of Hidden Sunset Clauses:**
> A person who purchases a dog or cat between January 1, 2006 and April 1, 2008 shall pay $15 for a license for the dog or cat.
>
> The Department shall collect annual fees, payable annually or in quarterly installments, during calendar years 2012, 2013, and 2014 from each source that is required to register with the Department as set forth in subsection (a) of this section.

If a client chooses to employ such a mechanism, advise the client that the language, and any associated with it, will not be operative beyond the established time period and will require a new bill to amend or remove the hidden sunset date. If possible, avoid drafting a hidden sunset date as it can last in the Code for decades after the class of people or the time period to which it refers have come and gone.

If the time period or limitation involves only a few people or if the time period itself will be limited in nature, do not include it within that portion of the bill intended for inclusion within the Code. Instead, place it in a separate Section at the end of the bill.

Just as there are contingent effective dates, there may be contingent sunset dates. To create a contingent sunset date, review this section as well as the Contingent Effective Date provisions of Section J of this chapter.

> **Example of a Contingent Sunset Date:**
> If the Government of New Castle County conducts a general reassessment of all real estate within New Castle County, the deletion of the existing version of § 2601(a)(3) of Title 14 and the insertion of the new version of § 2601(a)(3) of Title 14 by this Act expires upon the Secretary of the Board of Education of the New Castle County Vocational Technical School District notifying the Registrar of Regulations of the reassessment for computing New Castle County property taxes operative retroactive to the date of reassessment. The Registrar of Regulations shall publish notice of the date of fulfillment of this contingency in the monthly Register of Regulations.

. . .

When drafting a bill to extend or remove a sunset date provision, be mindful of the sunset date. Introduce the legislation well in advance of the sunset date. Bills have sunsetted waiting for the Governor to sign amendments to the sunset date. If a sunset date in legislation passed by a supermajority vote needs to be extended or removed, the legislation doing so must be passed by the same supermajority vote.

3. SAVINGS & TRANSITIONAL CLAUSES

Texas Legislative Council Drafting Manual
Texas Legislative Council (2020)

SEC. 3.12.   SAVING AND TRANSITION PROVISIONS.

(a) Introduction. Saving and transition provisions help to minimize the disruption and inequities that often attend the taking effect of legislation.

A saving provision "saves" from the application of a law certain conduct or legal relationships that occurred before or existed on the effective date of the law. One example is the "grandfather clause," which is discussed in Subsection (h) of this section. Another type, commonly used when a criminal statute is amended or repealed, provides for the continued application of the former law to conduct occurring before the effective date of the repeal or amendment. Section 311.031, Government Code, is a general saving clause applicable to those codes to which the Code Construction Act applies.

Transition provisions provide for the orderly implementation of legislation, helping to avoid the shock that can result from an abrupt change in the law. The most common transition provision is the effective date section, which provides for orderly implementation of a statute by delaying its effective date or by providing staggered effective dates for various provisions. Section 3.14 of this manual specifically addresses delayed and staggered effective dates.

A legislator making a drafting request is usually much more concerned about the substance of the requested bill than about saving or transition problems, and it is the drafter's responsibility to attempt to foresee any problems of this type that might arise and to ensure that they are dealt with appropriately. Foreseeing these problems requires a combination of legal and practical analysis, imagination, and common sense. The task begins with the question: What are the undesirable consequences that might occur if this law were enacted with no saving or transition provisions? If the proposed law is covered by the Code Construction Act, the drafter must consider whether the general saving provisions of that act take care of the problems adequately. If that act does not apply or does not adequately resolve the problem, the drafter must fashion whatever provisions are necessary, consistent with the objectives and desires of the legislative client.

(d) Occupational licensing. If a new occupational licensing act prescribes substantial educational or similar requirements for obtaining a license, the legislature occasionally will choose to include a "grandfather clause" (see Subsection (h) of this section) exempting from all or some of the requirements those persons who already have substantial experience in the occupation. For example:

SECTION 14.   A person who has engaged in the practice of cake decorating in this state for at least three years 1 It is common in transition and applicability sections to refer to "the effective date of this Act." A drafter must be careful in using that phrase in bills that have provisions that take effect at different times (see Section 3.14(h) of this manual), as the potential for ambiguity (which "effective date" is meant?) exists. An alternative is to use, in a transition or applicability section, the specific effective date of the bill or provision. The danger this approach poses is that an amendment to the bill might change the effective date without addressing the date in the transition or applicability section. 43 3 preceding the effective date of this Act is entitled to obtain a license under Section 2754.101, Occupations Code, as added by this Act, without fulfilling the educational requirements prescribed by Section 2754.103, Occupations Code, as added by this Act, if the person has the other qualifications required by Section 2754.102, Occupations Code, as added by this Act, and if, before January 1, 2022, the person:

(1) submits an application as required by Section 2754.104, Occupations Code, as added by this Act;

(2) passes the examination required by Section 2754.105, Occupations Code, as added by this Act; and

(3) pays the required license fee. The effective date prescribed for a new licensing law can also serve a transition purpose. See Section 3.14(k) of this manual.

(h) The "grandfather clause."

"Grandfather clause" has come to refer to a provision in a licensing statute that automatically grants a license or similar prerogative to those established in an occupation or business before its regulation.

Normally, these clauses function by exempting an applicant from a licensing examination on the justification that "those already practicing their profession were lawfully and satisfactorily performing their services on the date the regulatory act became effective . . . ."

Like the regulatory statutes of which they are a part, grandfather clauses are subject to the constitutional considerations of equal protection and due process. Texas courts have found that a clause meets the requirements of equal protection if it is "neither capricious nor arbitrary" in its policy

4. EFFECTIVE DATE PROVISIONS

Arizona Legislative Bill Drafting Manual
Arizona Legislative Council (2019)

4.10 EFFECTIVE DATE AND TIME OF ENACTMENTS

General effective date

As stated in article IV, part 1, § 1 (3), Constitution of Arizona, the general effective date of enactments is the ninety-first day after the date on which the session of the legislature enacting them is adjourned *sine die*. For example, if the legislature adjourned *sine die* on May 15, the general effective date would be August 14 the instant after midnight (i.e., 12:01 a.m.). State v. Soloman, 117 Ariz. 228, 571 P.2d 1024 (1977). Exceptions to the general effective date are as follows:

- A bill that has a specific delayed effective date.

- A bill that is conditionally enacted. (See § 4.4.)

- An emergency measure that is passed by a "supermajority" vote of the legislature. (Article IV, part 1, § 1(3), Constitution of Arizona.)

- A supplemental appropriation. (See § 5.5.)

- An act increasing state revenues through new or increased taxes or assessments ("Prop. 108"). (Article IX, § 22, Constitution of Arizona.) (See § 4.15.)

Note: If a law goes into effect during a legislative session because it contained an emergency clause or met "Prop. 108" requirements, the drafter must conform other applicable bills and amendments that are still being considered during the same session to that now-current law.

. . .

Emergency clauses

If the sponsor of a bill wants the bill to become immediately effective on the signature of the governor, the drafter should add an emergency clause, the wording of which is:

Sec. ___. Emergency This act is an emergency measure that is necessary to preserve the public peace, health or safety and is operative immediately as provided by law.

A bill containing an emergency clause must receive a two-thirds vote in each house of the legislature in order for the emergency clause to be effective. If the bill is adopted by less than a two-thirds vote, it is considered enacted without the emergency clause and, therefore, becomes effective on the general effective date.

Note: An emergency measure cannot be given an effective date, applicable to the entire bill or sections of the bill, other than the date on which the governor signs the bill.

. . .

Retroactivity of statutes

Section 1–244, A.R.S., requires that the retroactivity of a statute be "expressly declared." However, a statute may have retroactive effect if it is merely procedural and the statute does not affect or impair vested rights. Bouldin v. Turek, 125 Ariz. 77, 607 P.2d 954 (1979). To expressly declare that an act or a statute applies retroactively, the drafter should add a section toward the end of the bill similar to the following:

Sec. __. Retroactivity This act (or, section 42–6102, Arizona Revised Statutes, as added (or amended) by this act,) applies retroactively to from and after June 30, 2019.

. . .

Delayed effective date

The following is an example of a delayed effective date:

Sec. __. Effective date Section 23–113, Arizona Revised Statutes, as added by this act, sections 23–527 and 23–528, Arizona Revised Statutes, as amended by this act and the repeal of section 23–554, Arizona Revised Statutes, by this act are effective from and after December 31, 2020.

Note: If amending a previously enacted section that has a delayed effective date, the drafter must make sure that the new changes do not become effective before the underlying section by including a delayed effective date section like the one in the above example.

NOTES & QUESTIONS

1.   Federal laws take effect on its date of enactment. In contrast, the 90-day delay before a new law takes effect is fairly common among the states. What are the public policy considerations for this delay?

2.   Delaying the effective date is often necessary for provisions setting up a new agency or program. An essential question for the drafter is: how much time will the new entity need to organize, hire staff, create regulations, etc.?

3. Laws applied retroactively can be problematic. Statutes that affect individual rights retroactively may be unconstitutional. Even if the retroactive law is constitutional, such as a change to tax laws, that is almost always deeply unpopular because taxpayers have not had a chance to plan for the newly imposed tax bill.

I. SKILLS EXERCISES

Exercise 1: The chair of the Natural Resources and Agriculture Committee asks you to redraft this old statute on livestock feed. She says it is confusing and hopelessly out of date.

> A person who sells, or offers or exposes to sale, as a feeding stuff, an article which contains an ingredient that is deleterious to livestock or has in his possession such an article, packaged and prepared, as a feeding stuff commits an offense punishable by up to five years in prison unless he proves that he did not know, and with reasonable care could not have known, that the article contained a deleterious ingredient and, if he obtained the article from another person, on demand by or on behalf of the prosecutor he gave all the information in his power about the person from whom he obtained it and as to any mark applied to the article when he obtained it: Provided that proceedings for an offense under this section shall not be instituted unless the article has been sampled by an inspector in the prescribed manner on the premises on which it was sold or exposed or offered for sale or on which it was prepared for sale or consignment and the sample has been analyzed in accordance with this Act.

- What policy questions would you like the chair to clarify during the redrafting process?

- What words could or should be replaced? How would you decide whether to keep a particular word?

- How could this section be better organized?

Exercise 2: Since 1904, Massachusetts penalized the simple possession of marijuana with a criminal penalty of up to a year in prison, a fine of up to $1,000, or both fine and imprisonment. Mass. Gen. Law ch. 94C § 34. In 2008, the voters passed an initiative petition that made possession of one ounce of marijuana subject to just a civil penalty. When recreational marijuana became legal for adults in 2016, the Legislature amended the 2008 law to apply only to offenders between the ages of 18 and 21.

Chapter 94C § 32L.

Notwithstanding any general or special law to the contrary, possession of 2 ounces or less of marihuana shall only be a civil offense, subjecting an offender who is 18 to 21 years of age, inclusive, to a civil penalty of one hundred dollars and forfeiture of the marihuana, but not to any other form of criminal or civil punishment or disqualification. An offender under the age of eighteen shall be subject to the same forfeiture and civil penalty provisions, provided he or she completes a drug awareness program which meets the criteria set forth in Section 32M of this Chapter. The parents or legal guardian of any offender under the age of eighteen shall be notified in accordance with Section 32N of this Chapter of the offense and the availability of a drug awareness program and community service option. If an offender under the age of eighteen fails within one year of the offense to complete both a drug awareness program and the required community service, the civil penalty may be increased pursuant to Section 32N of this Chapter to one thousand dollars and the offender and his or her parents shall be jointly and severally liable to pay that amount.

Except as specifically provided in section 24I of chapter 90, chapter 94G and chapter 387 of the acts of 2008, neither the Commonwealth nor any of its political subdivisions or their respective agencies, authorities or instrumentalities may impose any form of penalty, sanction or disqualification on an offender for possessing 2 ounces or less of marihuana. By way of illustration rather than limitation, possession of 2 ounces or less of marihuana shall not provide a basis to deny an offender student financial aid, public housing or any form of public financial assistance including unemployment benefits, to deny the right to operate a motor vehicle or to disqualify an offender from serving as a foster parent or adoptive parent. Information concerning the offense of possession of 2 ounces or less of marihuana shall not be deemed "criminal offender record information," "evaluative information," or "intelligence information" as those terms are defined in Section 167 of Chapter 6 of the General Laws and shall not be recorded in the Criminal Offender Record Information system.

As used herein, "possession of 2 ounces or less of marihuana" includes possession of 2 ounces or less of marihuana or tetrahydrocannabinol and having cannabinoids or cannabinoid metabolites in the urine, blood, saliva, sweat, hair, fingernails, toe nails or other tissue or fluid of the human body. Nothing contained herein shall be construed to repeal or modify existing laws, ordinances or bylaws, regulations, personnel practices or policies concerning the operation of motor vehicles or other actions taken while under the influence of marihuana or tetrahydrocannabinol, laws concerning the unlawful possession of prescription forms of marihuana or tetrahydrocannabinol such as Marinol, possession of more than 2 ounces of marihuana or tetrahydrocannabinol, or selling, manufacturing or trafficking in marihuana or tetrahydrocannabinol. Nothing contained herein shall prohibit a political subdivision of the Commonwealth from enacting ordinances or bylaws regulating or prohibiting the consumption of marihuana or tetrahydrocannabinol in public places and providing for additional penalties for the public use of marihuana or tetrahydrocannabinol.

- How would you redraft this statute?

Exercise 3: The chair of the Criminal Justice Committee wants to establish a witness protection program to allow prosecutors help witnesses that are being threatened leading up to trial. The Ways and Means Committee will allocate $2 million over the next three years for witness protection, but the question remains who will be in charge of the money and decide when a prosecuting office can access the money and how much they will get.

There are several possibilities: The Secretary of Public Safety who is appointed by the Governor, the elected Attorney General, the ten elected county district attorneys, the trial court system, or the State Police. All of these offices want to see greater witness protection, but there are problems with each: secretary is not a prosecuting office and does not want to step on the toes of the Attorney General or district attorneys. The Attorney General does not want to have to turn down a request from a district attorney. The district attorneys from smaller counties are worried the money could be mostly devoted to the two largest counties. these had a strong desire to take on the program, yet all had particular strengths to contribute to the program. The trial court worries about judicial officials becoming involved in ongoing cases in this way. The State and local police say they don't have the resources for any new responsibilities.

The chair wants to both combine the strengths of the offices, avoid "turf wars," and begin operations immediately after the bill is signed into law. Draft a recommended solution.

CHAPTER 7

LOBBYISTS & ADVOCACY

■ ■ ■

"Suppose you go to Washington and try to get at your government. You will always find that while you are politely listened to, the men really consulted are the men who have the biggest stake— the big bankers, the big manufacturers, the big masters of commerce. . . .The government of the United States at present is the foster child of special interests."—Woodrow Wilson, *THE NEW FREEDOM* (1916)

"I am in this race to tell the corporate lobbyists that their days of setting the agenda in Washington are over. I have done more than any other candidate in this race to take on lobbyists—and won. They have not funded my campaign, they will not run my White House, and they will not drown out the voices of the American people when I am president."—Sen. Barack Obama, Speech in Des Moines, IA (2007)

"I have lobbyists that can produce anything for me. They're great."—Donald J. Trump, announcing his Presidential candidacy (June 16, 2015)

There is no school to become a lobbyist, and typically no professional requirements before working in the field. Due to the perceived influence behind closed doors and scandals like the one surrounding Jack Abramoff, lobbying is an easy target for derision. Regardless of what the public thinks about lobbyists, they are not just important to the legislative process, but essential. Further, lobbying is a Constitutionally protected activity. While the profession can be—and needs to be—regulated, it can never be eliminated because, at its core, lobbying is protected by the First Amendment right to petition, freedom of association, and freedom of speech.

Justice Brennan famously observed that there is "a profound national commitment to the principle that debate on public issues should be uninhibited, robust and wide-open."

Lobbying is a popular job for former legislators and staff members when they get tired of being paid government wages. In addition, many of the skills essential to practicing law are extremely valuable in the lobbying world; no wonder so many lobbyists have law degrees.

There is, however, no one type of lobbyist or style of lobbying. Who gets hired to advocate for an entity or interest depends largely on who the client is and what they need to accomplish. This chapter will explore how lobbyists influence the legislative system and how lobbyists are regulated.

A. LOBBYING: HISTORY & BACKGROUND

"LOBBYISTS"

Senator Robert C. Byrd, THE SENATE, 1789–1989 (vol. 2) pp. 491–508

Mr. President, in 1869, a newspaper correspondent published this vivid description of a monster in the Capitol building: "Winding in and out through the long, devious basement passage, crawling through the corridors, trailing its slimy length from gallery to committee room, at last it lies stretched at full length on the floor of Congress-this dazzling reptile, this huge, scaly serpent of the lobby." What was this awful creature? It was intended as the embodiment of lobbyists, who were proliferating in the years after the Civil War and who, many believed, were corrupting the Congress. Even today, the media tend to portray legislative lobbyists as some form of monster. And yet, we realize that lobbyists play an important and essential role in the legislative process. Today, in my continuing series of addresses on the history of the Senate, I shall attempt to penetrate some of the myths and mysteries surrounding lobbyists over the past two hundred years.

. . .

Lobbyists have been at work from the earliest days of the Congress. William Hull was hired by the Virginia veterans of the Continental army to lobby for additional compensation for their war services. In 1792, Hull wrote to other veterans' groups, recommending that they have their "agent or agents" cooperate with him during the next session to pass a compensation bill. In 1795, a Philadelphia newspaper described the way lobbyists waited outside Congress Hall to "give a hint to a Member, teaze or advise as may best suit."

. . .

Complementing the freewheeling attitude which many government officials in those days took towards the relationship between public office and private enterprise was the reality of living and working in the Washington of the early nineteenth century. The embryonic capital bore no resemblance to the cosmopolitan centers of Philadelphia and New York, let alone the great European capitals. The city was dusty and malaria-ridden in the summer, damp and cold in the winter. Social and cultural amenities were few. Many senators left their families at home and took rooms in the boardinghouses that surrounded the Capitol Building. It was an atmosphere in which the so-called "social lobby" could thrive, and thrive it did. Clubs, brothels, and "gambling dens" became natural habitats of the lobbyists, since these institutions were occasionally visited by members of Congress, who, far from home, came seeking good food, drink, and agreeable company.

The excesses of ante-bellum lobbying reached their height in the early 1850's when Samuel Colt sought passage of a bill to extend his patent for seven years. A congressional investigation later disclosed that, in addition to staging lavish entertainments for wavering senators, "more than one" of Colt's agents "have at different times presented pistols to certain members," including "a handsome Colt pistol, as a present," to a representative's "little son, only eleven or twelve years of age."

{Bribe

. . .

By the 1850's, railroad construction, largely underwritten by federal land grants and other subsidies, further increased the presence of lobbyists in Congress.

. . .

Businesses hired lobbyists to gain a sympathetic hearing for their legislative aims.

Because a single lobbyist often did not possess wide enough contacts, they were forced to hire several different agents. [Railroad owner] Collis Huntington estimated that his rival railroad operator, Tom Scott, had hired two hundred lobbyists for the congressional session of 1876–1877. The cost of so many agents was enormous, and the results were far from certain. Tom Scott, for instance, did not win congressional support for his railroad. Businessmen felt caught in a bind; not always certain that a lobbyist possessed the influence he claimed, an entrepreneur, nevertheless, feared that not hiring him might cause lucrative government support to slip away. The correspondence of leading businessmen is filled with complaints about lobbying costs, including hotel accommodations, entertainment, cigars, and champagne. According to Professor Rothman, railroad passes were freely distributed in the effort to win supporters. Again, Huntington complained: "When in Washington, I had to give out many passes, mostly at the request of Senators and Members of Congress, and since Congress adjourned I think we have averaged six letters per day from Senators and Members of Congress asking for passes over the road. . . . This giving free passes is all wrong." Sometimes it also meant direct payments to members of Congress. Collis Huntington argued, "We must take care of our friends."

Periodically, lobbying scandals broke into the press and caught public attention. The Credit Mobilier scandal of 1872 revealed that a member of the House, Representative Oakes Ames, had distributed railroad stocks to senators and representatives in return for their support for railroad legislation.

. . .

Some of the lobbying techniques of the Gilded Age were not unlike those of today, with speeches supplied, analyses prepared, opposition arguments suggested, personal contacts with key members, appearances-before committees, and grassroots campaigns generated by lobbyists. Time and circumstance have conspired to render other scenes from the Gilded Age unfamiliar to the current observer. Gone are the elegant parlors of society matrons where senators and representatives were lavishly entertained by winsome female lobbyists.

. . .

By contrast, Margaret Susan Thompson's THE "SPIDER WEB", CONGRESS AND LOBBYING IN THE AGE OF GRANT argued that lobbyists became the scapegoats for other congressional ills, and that, even during the Gilded Age, lobbyists performed beneficial services. She wrote that Congress was unprepared for the vast economic changes occurring in the nation and needed all the help it could get. As the predominant branch of government, Congress had overextended itself. Henry Adams asserted that "Congress is inefficient, and shows itself more and more incompetent, as at present constituted, to wield the enormous powers that are forced upon it." Turnover of membership was high; levels of parliamentary expertise were correspondingly low. Neither house had formal floor leadership. There was practically no staff, either for committees or for individual members.

At the same time, pressures on the federal government were steadily increasing. The more crowded the congressional agenda became-with issues of finance, industry, internal improvements, and international relations-the more interests demanded to be heard. This is the nub of what political scientists call "pluralistic democracy." Although we often hear a hue and cry about "special interests," everyone, in a sense, belongs to a multitude of these interests: we are defined by our gender, race, age, ethnicity, religion, economic status, educational background, and ideological bent. Some groups are better funded or better organized than others: corporate interests, organized labor, New Right political action committees. Some groups, especially the very young, the very old, the very poor, are the least organized and the least able to make their needs heard. Nevertheless, they all have a "special interest" in congressional actions. Members of Congress, of course, attempt to represent all of the various interests within their constituencies, but they must establish some priorities. Lobbyists attempt to shape those priorities by reminding them of the needs of specific groups.

. . .

As lobbying became perceived as dangerous and a corrupting influence, Congress responded with a variety of reforms. The first effort to regulate lobbyists took place in 1876 when the House required all lobbyists to register with the clerk of the House.

. . .

Progressive presidents like Theodore Roosevelt and Woodrow Wilson took advantage of these popular images of lobbyists and business corruption as leverage for their reform legislation. In seeking public support for lower tariff rates, President Wilson trained his fire on the lobby with this sharply worded attack: "Washington has seldom seen so numerous, so industrious, or so insidious a body. The newspapers are being filled with paid advertisements calculated to mislead the judgment of public men not only, but also the public opinion of the country itself. There is every evidence that money without limit is being spent to sustain this lobby, and to create an appearance of a pressure of public opinion antagonistic to some of the chief items of the tariff bill. . . . It is thoroughly worth the while of the people of this country to take knowledge of this matter. Only public opinion can check and destroy it."

. . .

Slowly but surely, lobbying reforms were enacted. Democrats and progressive Republicans prevailed on the Senate Judiciary Committee to investigate lobbying activities in 1913, and each senator publicly revealed any personal finances that might benefit from a change in the tariff. In 1919, Congress prohibited any lobbying effort with appropriated funds. This move was designed to prevent agency officials from conducting public relations campaigns, such as stimulating letters and telegrams, in order to influence the passage of legislation.

By the 1920's, Washington lobbying had begun to develop many of the features we associate with it today. Lobbying broadened its scope beyond financial and commercial interests, and the free-lance lobbyist was supplanted by collective action in the form of membership associations, which had been growing and developing since the beginning of the century. In addition, lobbying techniques began to change. For example, the telephone, telegraph, and radio intensified the development of grassroots lobbying.

. . .

In 1930, a subcommittee of the Senate Judiciary Committee continued investigating lobbying practices. . . .[Senator Hugo Black] had been advocating that lobbyists publicly register their names, objectives, salaries, and monthly expenses. Then, in the spring of 1935, lobbyists for public utility companies led a particularly furious assault on the Wheeler-Rayburn bill that was designed to break up public utility holding companies. The mountain of letters and telegrams that covered Capitol Hill bore all the evidence of an orchestrated campaign, inspiring Black to launch an investigation.

The hearings made headlines when Senator Black called in Western Union officials, who testified that the 816 telegrams one representative received were all dictated and paid for by a lobbyist for the Associated Gas and Electric Company. Evidence of large payments for propaganda activities was also uncovered. In a radio address, Black told listeners that Americans had a constitutional right to petition, but that no "sordid or powerful group" had a right to present its views "behind a mask concealing the identity of that group." He denounced the "high powered, deceptive, telegram-fixing, letter-framing, Washington-visiting" utility company lobby, and argued that funds for such activities came from citizens' utility bills. "Just contemplate," said Senator Black, "what a good time people are having on your money in Washington!"

As a result of his efforts, the Public Utilities Holding Company Act was amended to provide for registration of all company agents. Black also introduced legislation for registration of all lobbyists, which passed the Senate and House in different versions. Although efforts to reconcile the two bills failed, Congress was willing to regulate lobbying on an industry-by-industry basis, adding registration provisions to the Merchant Marine Act of 1936 and the Foreign Agents Registration Act of 1938. At the same time, many states enacted lobbying disclosure laws.

Immediately after World War II, the Joint Committee on the Organization of Congress studied ways to make Congress more efficient. . . .At the joint committee's recommendation, Congress adopted the Federal Regulation of Lobbying Act, which became Title III of the Legislative Reorganization Act of 1946. This act defined a lobbyist as any person "who by himself, or through any agent or employee or other persons in any manner whatsoever, directly or indirectly, solicits, collects, or receives money or any other thing of value to be used principally . . . to influence, directly or indirectly, the passage or defeat of any legislation by the Congress of the United States." Anyone meeting this description was required to register name, address, salary, and expenses with the secretary of the Senate and the clerk of the House, and to file quarterly reports on funds received or spent, "to whom and for what purpose" those funds were paid, "the names of newspapers and magazines in which the lobbyist 'caused to be published' articles or editorials," and the proposed legislation the lobbyist was employed to support or oppose. Lobbyists were also required to keep detailed accounts of all contributions of five hundred dollars or more made to members of Congress. Criminal penalties were assigned for any violation of this act.

In 1954, the Supreme Court upheld these lobbying registration requirements in the case of *U.S. v. Harriss*. The Court defined the legislation narrowly, however, finding that it did not apply to groups or individuals who spent their own money to lobby Congress directly. It also exempted groups whose principal purpose was something other than lobbying.

. . .

Calls to strengthen the lobbying law were heard in the wake of the Watergate scandal and the activities of Korean lobbyist Tongsun Park. In 1976, the Senate drafted and passed more specific definitions of lobbyists and lobbying practices, but intensive lobbying pressures-principally arguing that the new requirements would violate the free speech rights of lobbyists-kept the measure from passing the House. During the 1980's, the Senate Governmental Affairs Committee continued to hold hearings on lobbying registration and to consider new approaches to this old issue. In the Ninety-ninth Congress, the committee produced an excellent report, containing a discussion of the history of lobbying. I recommend the report, CONGRESS AND PRESSURE GROUPS: LOBBYING IN A MODERN DEMOCRACY, to all those interested in the subject.

Today's lobbying is more diverse than ever before, with an organized lobby formed, seemingly, around virtually every aspect of American social and economic life. No longer do the lobbying groups come solely from Washington's great law firms and associations. Public relations companies, consulting groups, and specialized accounting, medical, and insurance firms have joined their ranks. All these, and others, engage in a multitude of activities, from raising money for election campaigns to conducting technical studies, with the ultimate goal of influencing the course of legislation and government policy.

Modern technology has made it possible for far-flung group members to stay in almost constant contact with their lobbying representatives in Washington. The explosion in the electronic media and the televising of House and Senate debates have resulted in better-informed interest groups, who, in turn, more readily communicate their message to their members, legislators, and other targets. Congressional offices are frequently flooded with telegrams, telephone calls, letters and postcards (sometimes preprinted), as a "grassroots" campaign moves into full swing, mobilized by one or another interest group on a given issue. Among the most effective interest groups today in bringing such organized pressure to bear upon legislators are the labor unions, the banking interests, the gun lobby, the pro-Israel lobby, anti-abortion and freedom-of-choice groups, civil rights organizations, environmentalists, and consumer interests.

The past fifteen years have witnessed a political phenomenon: the development and proliferation of political action committees (PACs). These

Political action committees (margin annotation)

PACs are formed by special interest groups for the purpose of funneling contributions to the political campaigns of members of Congress and other office seekers, and they constitute a subtle but sophisticated form of lobbying. Spiraling campaign costs in this electronic age have made members of Congress increasingly dependent upon PAC contributions. Incumbents and challengers alike, unless they are inordinately wealthy, besiege scores of PACs in every election for money to finance their ravenous advertising and other political expenditures.

. . .

It should be clear from my remarks that Congress has always had, and always will have, lobbyists and lobbying. We could not adequately consider our work load without them. We listen to representatives from the broadest number of groups: large and small; single-issue and multi-purposed; citizens groups; corporate and labor representatives; the public spirited and the privately inspired. They all have a service to fulfill. At the same time, the history of this institution demonstrates the need for eternal vigilance to ensure that lobbyists do not abuse their role, that lobbying is carried on publicly with full publicity, and that the interests of all citizens are heard without giving special ear to the best organized and most lavishly funded.

NOTES & QUESTIONS

1.   Lobbying is really petitioning government and speaking to public officials through surrogates, much as a defendant speaks to the prosecutor, judge, and jury through an attorney.

Dean Nicholas Allard, a prominent lobbyist in Washington DC and former Dean and President of Brooklyn Law School, asked in an article,

"Why should I have to hire a lobbyist to talk with my government?" It is a legitimate threshold question. After all, it is our government, which is supposed to be working for us. Well consider, for example, that you had a medical issue that, God forbid, required surgery. Would you operate on yourself? No, of course not. You would want the best, most experienced specialist that you could find. The same can be said if you have an interest in a significant public policy issue. It's not always brain surgery, but you take my point. Lawyers have a saying: Anyone who represents themselves in court has a fool for a lawyer and an idiot for a client. Similarly, the arenas where our laws are written and policies made and implemented are even more difficult venues to make your case than in a court room. Professionals, expert advocates, are needed in both settings. Nicholas W. Allard, "The Seven Deadly Virtues of Lobbyists: What Lawyer Lobbyists Really Do," 13 *Election L.J.* 210, 211–19 (2014)

2.   Who uses lobbyists and how effective are they? A 2009 study, "Who Wins in Washington," surveyed more than 300 lobbyists and government officials on a random sample of nearly 100 issues.

Of the 1,244 lobbyists by the type of organization that they represent, citizen groups (organizations representing an issue or cause without any direct connection to a business or profession) make up about 26%. Trade associations and business associations like the Chamber of Commerce represented 21%. Individual businesses lobbying on their own behalf made up 14%. Eleven percent were professional associations (such as the American Medical Association). Formal coalitions specific to an issue made up 7%. Unions made up 6%. Think tanks and foundations represented 6% of the total. The remaining categories were: governmental associations (such as the National Governors Association) 3%; nonprofit institutions (such as hospitals and universities) 3%; and all other (including churches, individual experts, and international NGOs) 3%. See, Baumgartner et al., *Lobbying & Policy Change* (2009) 9–13.

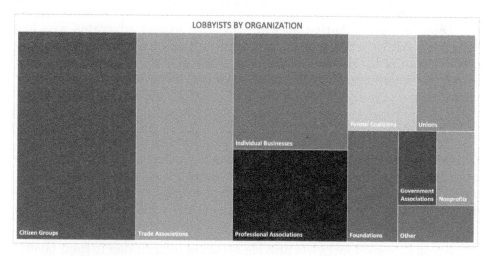

3.   Forty percent of federal lobbyists represent business interests compared to just 14% for citizen groups. Although citizen groups spend less on lobbying and lobby on fewer issues than businesses, policy makers often see them bringing greater public legitimacy. The study found that with fewer resources citizens groups are often spread thin and become involved in more issues than business interests sometimes creating a "David and Goliath" situation. For instance, on environmental issues the American Petroleum Institute has about 270 staff and an annual budget of $42 million. Still, citizens groups often coordinate efforts with other groups to affect policy and they may have powerful allies among elected officials. See, Baumgartner et al., *Lobbying & Policy Change* (2009) 9–13.

4.   Organizations seldom act in isolation from one another, often forming loose confederations on an issue and giving small organizations greater influence. Coalitions can be either traditional allies who naturally come

together on several issues or traditional adversaries that form an ad hoc coalition on a specific issue. The word "coalition" has become one of the buzzwords of contemporary lobbying, and coalition building has become one of the major tasks of contemporary lobbyists. "Whenever you can put a coalition together, you do it," counsels one Colorado lobbyist. The more groups on one's side and the fewer on the other, the more effective the effort. Alan Rosenthal, *The Third House: Lobbyists and Lobbying in the States* (Second. Ed.) 147–148, 153–166.

5.   What groups represent you in Washington DC or in your state capital?

B. WHAT DO LOBBYISTS DO?

THE SEVEN DEADLY VIRTUES OF LOBBYISTS: WHAT LAWYER LOBBYISTS REALLY DO
Nicholas W. Allard, 13 *Election Law Journal* 210 (2014)

Lobbyists are adaptive, forward-thinking expert advocates who are vital to a healthy, self-correcting representative democracy. Good lobbyists achieve results by building consensus. They give voice to and empower those who seek to petition the government. . . . They have "seven deadly virtues":

. . .

The first thing lobbyists do is provide information to the government to inform its decisions. . . . While no one can deny that our federal and state governments have their fair share of experts in every field imaginable, often times the information simply does not reach the decision makers. . . . Lobbyists bring information to those decision makers, and an informed decision is certainly preferred to simple guesswork. . . .

Second . . . good lobbyists provide accurate information to their clients about how the government works, what to expect, what is realistic. . . . Navigating the maddeningly confusing maze of government bureaucracy and frequently encountering intransigence and delay severely constrains each citizen's ability to exercise their constitutional rights; lobbyists act as guides that inform and manage the expectations of their clients. . . .

Third, lobbyists help keep the system honest by holding other interests and lobbyists accountable—it's an adversarial process. It is commonly accepted that competition breeds excellence and it is the lobbyist who competitively advocates for the ideas and interests of its clients. When the system works, and the rules are followed, the best ideas win out. . . .

Fourth, lobbyists help keep the system honest by holding the government accountable. Government officials often do not like this—they would rather not have this thorn in their side—just like the press is often regarded as an annoyance, a necessary evil. Both the right to petition, and freedom of the press are protected in the First Amendment as important checks on government power. . . .

Fifth, professional lobbyists comply with rules. Crooks and amateurs do not do this. People who make their living lobbying must comply to continue practicing and their clients insist on compliance. Ironically, in my experience, the bigger the corporate client, the more the company is interested in compliance. . . .

Sixth, lobbyists make sure others follow the rules—they are whistle blowers about noncompliance by other lobbyists. . . .

Seventh, lobbyists provide civility and help discordant, partisan dug-in interests come together and find solutions. . . . When there are partisan quarrels in Congress and in the government, lobbyists can be back-channel messengers, come up with solutions, talk to people, reduce flaring temperatures, and figure out how to overcome an impasse.

NOTES & QUESTIONS

1.   Professor William K. Muir drew upon his experiences working for the California Legislature during the 1970s to write *Legislature: California's School for Politics* (1982). He not only echoed Dean Allard's assessment of lobbyists as essential providers of information, but compared them to the faculty in a very exclusive school:

> "If the legislators were the "scholars," who were the teachers? The outside faculty were the lobbyists. As one Democratic assemblyman put it, "When there is legislation involving complicated matters which I don't fully understand, I call in proponents and opponents (separately, mind you), and in five minutes they describe very succinctly what legislation does. I get the pros and cons very quickly. I can learn things which would have taken five hours of research if I had to assign staff to find out from scratch."
>
> . . .
>
> "As a teacher, the lobbyist also framed the intellectual issues, pointed out subtleties in a situation, and implied a conclusion. All the teaching was done in an adversary context. To teach "the pros and cons" from their vantage point there were lobbyist for nearly everybody—the old and the young, the wealthy and the poverty-stricken, the boss and the worker, the farmer and the rancher, the sailor and the mountaineer, the citizen and the immigrant." William K. Muir, *Legislature: California's School for Politics* 18–23 (1982).

2.   Clive S. Thomas and Ronald J. Hrebenard categorized lobbyists into five groups and estimated the proportion of each group operating in state capitals.

contract	25%
in-house	33%
government & legislative liaison	25%–30%
citizen or volunteer	10%
private individual/self-appointed	1%–2%

See, Ronald J. Hrebenard, Clive S. Thomas, "Trends in Interest Group Politics in the States, *Book of the States 2003* (Council of State Governments, 2003).

3. Contract lobbyists may work independently or in a lobbying firm and take on a number of clients ranging from under ten to dozens of clients. They are "guns for hire," are not dependent on any one client, and may lobby on a multitude of issues. In the past, these lobbyists were commonly defined by their ability to access (and influence) legislators through entertainment and political contributions. That style is on the decline with lobbyists relying more on providing information and analysis.

In-house lobbyists work for a specific organization such as a company, trade or professional association, or a union. These lobbyists are closely identified with the organization they represent and work to promote the reputation of the organization. They will monitor the legislature for bills of interest to the organization, testify on its behalf, and meet with policy makers, often with other officers, lawyers or experts from the organization.

Governmental lobbyists represent associations for a variety of government actors such as local governments, police chiefs, school districts, a municipality, or county. The style of their lobbying tends to be informational and not overtly political.

Alan Rosenthal also identified a category of "cause lobbyists" who represent citizen groups, nonprofits and other single-issue groups working in the public interest. The clients typically do not have a commercial interests but are arguing for a particular philosophical and ideological position, for example, The League of Women Voters, The Sierra Club, the Catholic Church, the California Children's Lobby, Mothers Against Drunk Driving, and so on. Rosenthal says these lobbyists tend to be true believers, are less likely to seek compromise and are less concerned than contract or in-house lobbyists about building relationships with legislators. In contrast to the contract "hired guns," these lobbyists avoid becoming insiders for fear of being co-opted by the system and often prefer to lobby through the media or grass roots campaigns.

See, Alan Rosenthal, *The Third House: Lobbyists and Lobbying in the States* (CQ Press, 2000) 18–20, 38–40.

4. In their classic work *The Legislative Process in the United States* (Random House 1977), Professors Malcolm Jewell and Samuel Patterson identified five distinct lobbyist role orientations:

"The Contact Man": The classic lobbyist who makes crucial contacts with legislators by walking the legislative halls, visiting legislators, and establishing relationships with staff and legislators. These lobbyists are gregarious, likes to talk about legislative process, and is detail oriented. They achieve their client's goals through personal influence and personal contact with legislators. This type of lobbyist was relatively rare at the federal level by the 1970s, and probably even more so now. At the state level, where access to legislators is easier, contact lobbyists are still common.

"The Campaign Organizer": These lobbyists organize grass-roots support for their client's legislative program. The organizer makes contacts with leaders in their client's areas of interest and regularly communicates with the rank-and-file members of the client's organization. The organizer tries to convince legislators many of their constituents support the organization's position through grass roots events at the capitol, generating media coverage, and letter writing campaigns.

"The Informant": The informant conveys information to legislators without necessarily advocating a particular position or program. The preferred way to influence policy is to testify to committees on bills within their area of expertise or simply provide information to legislators.

"The Watchdog": This lobbyist closely watches the legislature's activities for developments that might affect their clients. When relevant legislation is filed or starts to move through the process, they alert their clients so they can start trying to influence the decision makers.

"The Strategist": Jewell & Patterson called the strategist a "lobbyist's lobbyist" who develops a legislative strategy that is often executed by other lobbyists.

5.　　In LOBBYING ON A SHOESTRING, activist turned professional lobbyist Judith Meredith offers two rules of the game: (1) Elected and appointed officials make different decisions when watched by the affected constituents; and (2) lobbying is simply getting the right information to the right people at the right time.

One of the most difficult aspects of lobbying is "the ask." Meredith states that the ultimate goal of communicating with a legislator is getting a commitment to act.

"Asking a legislator for support is one thing; getting a commitment for it is something else. Although you may be reluctant to ask for a commitment in your first attempts, do try. But be prepared for a noncommittal response. . . .

"You can accept this in the first contact. But it some point, you'll have to count how many firm supporters you have; then it's time to press for a commitment.

"Even professional lobbyists disagree on how to elicit this commitment. Some take a hard line: "We have to ask you to say yes or no right now." Others are friendlier: "I hope you can be with us." Different legislators respond to different approaches depending on their personalities, how much they know or care about the issue addressed by the bill, and the strength of the support and in opposition in the district. Generally, legislators hate to make commitments on bills—at all. If they are unfamiliar with the issue and haven't yet heard from the opposition, they are likely to resist even harder. Don't fight them; just keep feeding them information about the bill and keep building up the local support for it. Judith C. Meredith, LOBBYING ON A SHOESTRING (Massachusetts Continuing Legal Education, 2000).

AM I. . .LOBBYING?

New York State Joint Commission on Public Ethics, January 2019
www.jcope.ny.gov

What is lobbying?

Lobbying is an attempt to influence a specific list of governmental decisions or actions. *"Lobbying"* and *"Lobbying Activities"* are collectively defined in the Lobbying Act, and include any attempt to influence:

- the passage or defeat of legislation;

- the adoption, modification or rescission of an executive order;

- the adoption, modification or rescission of a state agency regulation; or

- a decision related to a governmental procurement.

Lobbying can occur at the State or local level. Anyone who engages in such activity is a "Lobbyist" under the law. However, not all Lobbying must be reported. (See below).

A Client is the person or organization on whose behalf and at whose request Lobbying Activity is conducted. A Client can either retain an outside Lobbyist to assist it in its Lobbying efforts, or it can utilize one or more individuals within the Client's own organization to Lobby on its behalf. In the latter case, the organization would be both a Lobbyist and a Client.

Every year millions of dollars are spent on Lobbying in New York. Clients retain or employ Lobbyists to influence government policies on topics ranging from energy and natural resources, to education, healthcare, labor issues, veteran affairs, transportation and other issues affecting special interests and members of the public.

When must Lobbying be reported?

For Lobbying to be reportable, two things must occur: (1) a Lobbyist has engaged in Lobbying Activity; and (2) such Lobbyist incurs, expends or

1. You have to have lobbied

2. You must be $ more than 5k a year

receives (or reasonably anticipates incurring, expending or receiving) more than $5,000 in compensation and expenses related to Lobbying Activities in a calendar year.

The $5,000 threshold must be computed cumulatively across all Lobbying Activities. In other words, if a Lobbyist has or reasonably anticipates having compensation and expenses adding up to more than $5,000 across all Lobbying Activities (including all Clients), then the Lobbyist must file reports disclosing such activity. Similarly, any Client that spends more than $5,000 on lobbying in a calendar year must file reports disclosing such activity.

Direct vs. Grassroots Lobbying

Lobbying can occur in two forms: Direct Lobbying or Grassroots Lobbying. Direct Lobbying involves direct contact between a Lobbyist and the government official the Lobbyist is seeking to influence. Face-to-face meetings, telephone calls, distribution of written materials, e-mails, and social media interactions all fall under the umbrella of Direct Lobbying.

Grassroots Lobbying is indirect and involves soliciting another to make direct communication with a Public Official. It often occurs through advertisements, rallies, receptions, social media or grassroots communications. For more information about Direct and Grassroots Lobbying, see the Commission's regulations at 19 NYCRR Parts 943.6 and 943.7.

Grassroots Lobbying

Grassroots Lobbying is essentially an attempt to advance a position by generating support and action from the public.

In order for a communication to be considered Grassroots Lobbying, it must take a clear position on a specific "government action" and urge the public or a segment of the public to contact a Public Official in support of that position.

For more information about Grassroots Lobbying, see 19 NYCRR Part 943 of the Commission's regulations and Advisory Opinion 16-01 at www. jcope.ny.gov.

Procurement Lobbying = contract or purchase

Procurement Lobbying is an attempt to influence a government contract or purchasing decision. The procurement in question must be for more than $15,000 for the Lobbying to be considered reportable under the Lobbying Act.

A State or local government agency will often issue a Request for Proposal ("RFP") describing what commodity it seeks to purchase. Vendors respond to the RFP by submitting a bid for consideration. Once a State entity posts an RFP, Lobbying Activity is restricted until the State or local agency has selected a vendor.

What are some restrictions on Lobbyists, Clients, and Lobbying?

Gifts to Public Officials Lobbyists and Clients of Lobbyists are prohibited from giving gifts to Public Officials.

Public Officials generally include the four statewide elected officials (Governor, Lieutenant Governor, Comptroller and Attorney General), members and employees of the Legislature, and officers and employees of State agencies, boards, departments, and commissions. Officers and employees of local municipalities with a population of over 5,000 also qualify as Public Officials under the Lobbying rules. For a more detailed definition of "Public Official," see 19 NYCRR Part 934.2(q) of the Commission's regulations.

Generally, a gift is anything valued at more than $15; however, some items so valued may not be gifts. For a list of exclusions and other rules, see the Commission's regulations at 19 NYCRR Parts 933 and 934. The gift restrictions are in place to avoid creating the appearance that a gift is being offered to either influence the Public Official or to reward them for performing their public duties.

NOTES & QUESTIONS

Alan Rosenthal identified a shift away from direct lobbying to grassroots mobilization, which he defined as "the identification, recruitment, and mobilization of constituent-based political strength capable of influencing political decisions. Of course, grass roots lobbying requires: resources to develop a field operation; a cause that motivates people to get involved; and a large affiliation base. Unions have always utilized grass roots lobbying, but now certain businesses have joined in. For instance, Anheuser-Busch can organize a huge number of people: over 24,000 employees concentrated in nine states; 750 wholesalers that operate in every state and employ over 30,000 people; 500,000 retail stores selling their products; and hundreds of suppliers including farmers and manufacturers of cans, bottles and cardboard. Mobilizing this group takes time—maybe as much as 3–4 weeks, so even such a big corporation has limited time to react to a legislative proposal. See, Alan Rosenthal, *The Third House: Lobbyists and Lobbying in the United States* (CQ Press, 2000); 147–148, 153–166.

1. SOCIAL MEDIA & LOBBYING

One of the fastest changing aspects of lobbying is the use of the internet and social media. According to a 2016 survey of Washington lobbyists, lawyers, association executives and think tank leaders, 38% said they expect organizations to increasingly use social media to influence policymakers. Another 21% expected organizations to increase their digital capabilities. Only 17% said they expect organizations to increase traditional lobbying activities. The *Washington Post* reported that several lobbying firms had been "scrambling to launch and expand their public affairs, public relations and digital communications divisions." See, Catherine Ho, "K Street Says Social Media Are Growing Faster Than Traditional Lobbying As Way To Influence Washington," *Washington Post*, November 3, 2016.

In response, states have had to adjust lobbying laws and regulations to keep pace.

Official Compilation of Codes, Rules and Regulations of the State of New York
Title 19 NYCRR Part 943 (2018)

943.3   Definitions.

(v)   Social Media means any mobile or internet-based platform designed to enable and facilitate communication and sharing of information among multiple users.

(w)   Social Media Campaign means an organized and/or coordinated series of Lobbying Activities carried out using one or more Social Media platforms.

943.6   Direct Lobbying

All definitions in section 943.3 are in effect unless otherwise noted below.

(a)   Definitions.

(1)   *Direct Contact*

(i)   Means any communication or interaction directed to a Public Official, including, but not limited to:

(a)   Verbal communications;

(b)   Written communications;

(c)   Electronic communications, including electronic mail, Social Media communications, and Internet communications;

(d)   Attendance at a meeting with a Public Official; or

(e)   Presence on a phone call with a Public Official, when the Official is aware of such presence;

(ii)   Direct Contact with a Public Official also includes direct contact with the members of the Public Official's staff.

(iii) Direct Contact does not include any communication that is directed to a group of which a Public Official is incidentally a member, or is intended for the public. For example, the following generally will not constitute Direct Contact:

(a) An opinion piece published in a newspaper;

(b) A statement made to a reporter that is published or broadcast 20 by a media outlet;

(c) A blog post;

(d) Attendance at a speech or public meeting;

(e) A speech to a group or at a public meeting; or

(f) Any of the communications listed in subsection 943.6(c)(5)(ii).

. . . .

(c) Direct Lobbying through Social Media

(1) A Social Media communication that Attempts to Influence an action enumerated in section 1–c(c)(i)–(x) of the Lobbying Act constitutes Direct Contact for purposes of Direct Lobbying if such communication:

(i) Is directly sent to a Social Media account known to be owned or controlled by a Public Official; or

(ii) Creates a direct electronic link to any Social Media account known to be owned or controlled by a Public Official.

(2) Direct Contact with a Public Official through a Social Media communication also includes contact that is targeted and directed to members of the Public Official's staff through a Social Media communication and done with the knowledge that such persons are members of the Public Official's staff.

(3) *Individual Lobbyist—When to Include*

(i) An employee of an organization engaged in Direct Lobbying via Social Media is required to be identified as an Individual Lobbyist of the organization if:

(a) the individual makes Direct Contact with a Public Official in the course of the individual's employment; and

(b) such Contact is not a part of a coordinated, mass Social Media Campaign engaged in by the organization.

For example, if an organization has drafted a post on its Facebook page and 24 requires its employees to share the post and tag a Public Official as part of a Social Media Campaign conducted by the organization, such employees need not be identified as Individual Lobbyists of the organization.

. . .

(5) Examples

(i) Any of the following could be Direct Lobbying through Social Media:

(a) A direct message sent to a Public Official through Social Media (e.g., through Facebook Messenger, Twitter Direct Message);

(b) A post on a Public Official's Social Media page;

(c) A post on a person's own Social Media page that tags a Public Official, when the post is done in the course of such person's employment; or

(d) A tweet tagging a Public Official, when posted by a person in the course of such person's employment.

(ii) The following, standing alone, would not constitute Direct Lobbying through Social Media:

(a) A post that references, but does not tag, a Public Official, even if the Public Official is among the person's or organization's friends or followers;

(b) A post on a person's own Social Media page that takes a clear position on an action enumerated in section 1–c(c)(i)–(x) of the Lobbying Act that does not tag a Public Official, even if the Public Official is among the person's friends or followers; or

(c) A tweet that references, but does not tag, a Public Official, even if the Public Official is among the poster's followers.

NOTES & QUESTIONS

1. Are these definitions and restrictions overly broad? Not broad enough?

2. Who benefits from using social media to lobby?

2. MONEY & LOBBYING

"We had a hierarchy in my office in Congress. If you're a lobbyist who never gave us money, I didn't talk to you. If you're a lobbyist who gave us money, I might talk to you." Former U.S. Representative Mick Mulvaney (R-SC) to a meeting of the American Bankers Association in 2018.

Money and lobbying are synonymous. Every year lobbyists donate—and arrange for their clients to donate—to elected officials. Some lobbyists can direct many thousands, if not millions, of dollars to candidates. What effect does this have money have on the legislative system?

Buckley v. Valeo, 424 U.S. 1 (1976) was a landmark decision on money and politics through a challenge to key provisions of the Federal Election Campaign Act of 1971, as amended in 1974. The Act limited political contributions to $1000 per candidate with an overall limitation of $25,000 per contributor; an overall ceiling on campaign spending by candidates and convention spending by political parties; and created disclosure requirements for contributions and expenditures to a newly established Federal Election Commission. The statute also provided public funding for qualified candidates and political parties. These reforms were the result of the Watergate Scandal and the increasing costs of elections; the $400 million spent in 1972 for the presidential nomination and election campaigns was almost 300% more than was spent during the 1952 campaign. The Act was meant to strengthen public confidence in the political process. In the underlaying appellate decision, the DC Circuit heard arguments that "the need to seek contributions is a democratic check on candidates." Senator Joe Biden (D-DE), however, argued that candidates felt pressure to avoid speaking on issues for fear of losing campaign donations and Senator Russell Long (D-LA) stated, "(W)hen you are talking in terms of large campaign contributions ... the distinction between a campaign contribution and a bribe is almost a hair's line difference."

The Supreme Court held that restrictions on individual contributions to political campaigns did not violate the First Amendment and that the FECA protected the political system from dishonest practices. However, restrictions of campaign expenditures, the limitation on candidates using their own money, and the limitations on total campaign spending all violated the First Amendment because they all reduce the quantity of speech without a compelling government need. This case is the basis for the notion that spending money equals speech.

CITIZENS UNITED V. FEDERAL ELECTION COMM'N
Supreme Court of the United States
558 U.S. 310 (2010)

JUSTICE KENNEDY delivered the opinion of the Court.

Citizens United is a nonprofit corporation. . . . In January 2008, Citizens United released a film entitled *Hillary: The Movie*. We refer to the film as *Hillary*. It is a 90-minute documentary about then-Senator Hillary Clinton, who was a candidate in the Democratic Party's 2008 Presidential primary elections. *Hillary* mentions Senator Clinton by name and depicts interviews with political commentators and other persons, most of them quite critical of Senator Clinton. *Hillary* was released in theaters and on DVD, but Citizens United wanted to increase distribution by making it available through video-on-demand.

. . .

In December 2007, a cable company offered, for a payment of $1.2 million, to make *Hillary* available on a video-on-demand channel called "Elections '08." . . .

To implement the proposal, Citizens United was prepared to pay for the video-on-demand; and to promote the film, it produced two 10-second ads and one 30-second ad for *Hillary*. Each ad includes a short (and, in our view, pejorative) statement about Senator Clinton, followed by the name of the movie and the movie's Website address. Citizens United desired to promote the video-on-demand offering by running advertisements on broadcast and cable television.

B

Before the Bipartisan Campaign Reform Act of 2002 (BCRA), federal law prohibited—and still does prohibit—corporations and unions from using general treasury funds to make direct contributions to candidates or independent expenditures that expressly advocate the election or defeat of a candidate, through any form of media, in connection with certain qualified federal elections. An electioneering communication is defined as "any broadcast, cable, or satellite communication" that "refers to a clearly identified candidate for Federal office" and is made within 30 days of a primary or 60 days of a general election. The Federal Election Commission's (FEC) regulations further define an electioneering communication as a communication that is "publicly distributed." "In the case of a candidate for nomination for President . . . publicly distributed means" that the communication "[c]an be received by 50,000 or more persons in a State where a primary election . . . is being held within 30 days." Corporations and unions are barred from using their general treasury funds for express advocacy or electioneering communications. They may establish, however, a "separate segregated fund" (known as a political action committee, or PAC) for these purposes. The moneys received by the segregated fund are limited to donations from stockholders and employees of the corporation or, in the case of unions, members of the union.

. . .

The law before us is an outright ban, backed by criminal sanctions. Section 441b makes it a felony for all corporations—including nonprofit advocacy corporations—either to expressly advocate the election or defeat of candidates or to broadcast electioneering communications within 30 days of a primary election and 60 days of a general election. Thus, the following acts would all be felonies under § 441b: The Sierra Club runs an ad, within the crucial phase of 60 days before the general election, that exhorts the public to disapprove of a Congressman who favors logging in national forests; the National Rifle Association publishes a book urging the public to vote for the challenger because the incumbent U. S. Senator supports a handgun ban; and the American Civil Liberties Union creates a Web site telling the public to vote for a Presidential candidate in light of that candidate's defense of free speech. These prohibitions are classic examples of censorship.

Section 441b is a ban on corporate speech notwithstanding the fact that a PAC created by a corporation can still speak. A PAC is a separate association from the corporation. So the PAC exemption from § 441b's expenditure ban, § 441b(b)(2), does not allow corporations to speak. Even if a PAC could somehow allow a corporation to speak—and it does not—the option to form PACs does not alleviate the First Amendment problems with § 441b. PACs are burdensome alternatives; they are expensive to administer and subject to extensive regulations. For example, every PAC must appoint a treasurer, forward donations to the treasurer promptly, keep detailed records of the identities of the persons making donations, preserve receipts for three years, and file an organization statement and report changes to this information within 10 days.

. . .

PACs have to comply with these regulations just to speak. This might explain why fewer than 2,000 of the millions of corporations in this country have PACs. . . . . PACs, furthermore, must exist before they can speak. Given the onerous restrictions, a corporation may not be able to establish a PAC in time to make its views known regarding candidates and issues in a current campaign.

Section 441b's prohibition on corporate independent expenditures is thus a ban on speech. As a "restriction on the amount of money a person or group can spend on political communication during a campaign," that statute "necessarily reduces the quantity of expression by restricting the number of issues discussed, the depth of their exploration, and the size of the audience reached." *Buckley v. Valeo*. Were the Court to uphold these restrictions, the Government could repress speech by silencing certain voices at any of the various points in the speech process. If § 441b applied to individuals, no one would believe that it is merely a time, place, or manner restriction on speech. Its purpose and effect are to silence entities whose voices the Government deems to be suspect.

Speech is an essential mechanism of democracy, for it is the means to hold officials accountable to the people. The right of citizens to inquire, to hear, to speak, and to use information to reach consensus is a precondition to enlightened self-government and a necessary means to protect it. The First Amendment " 'has its fullest and most urgent application' to speech uttered during a campaign for political office."

For these reasons, political speech must prevail against laws that would suppress it, whether by design or inadvertence. Laws that burden political speech are "subject to strict scrutiny," which requires the Government to prove that the restriction "furthers a compelling interest and is narrowly tailored to achieve that interest."

. . .

Premised on mistrust of governmental power, the First Amendment stands against attempts to disfavor certain subjects or viewpoints. Prohibited, too, are restrictions distinguishing among different speakers, allowing speech by some but not others. As instruments to censor, these categories are interrelated: Speech restrictions based on the identity of the speaker are all too often simply a means to control content.

Quite apart from the purpose or effect of regulating content, moreover, the Government may commit a constitutional wrong when by law it identifies certain preferred speakers. By taking the right to speak from some and giving it to others, the Government deprives the disadvantaged person or class of the right to use speech to strive to establish worth, standing, and respect for the speaker's voice. The Government may not by these means deprive the public of the right and privilege to determine for itself what speech and speakers are worthy of consideration. The First Amendment protects speech and speaker, and the ideas that flow from each.

. . .

We find no basis for the proposition that, in the context of political speech, the Government may impose restrictions on certain disfavored speakers. Both history and logic lead us to this conclusion.

The Court has recognized that First Amendment protection extends to corporations.

This protection has been extended by explicit holdings to the context of political speech. Under the rationale of these precedents, political speech does not lose First Amendment protection "simply because its source is a corporation." *Pacific Gas & Elec. Co. v. Public Util. Comm'n of Cal.*, 475 U. S. 1, 8 (1986)("The identity of the speaker is not decisive in determining whether speech is protected. Corporations and other associations, like individuals, contribute to the 'discussion, debate, and the dissemination of information and ideas' that the First Amendment seeks to foster"). The Court has thus rejected the argument that political speech of corporations or other associations should be treated differently under the First Amendment simply because such associations are not "natural persons."

. . .

[*First National Bank of Boston v.*] *Bellotti*, 435 U.S. 765 (1978), reaffirmed the First Amendment principle that the Government cannot restrict political speech based on the speaker's corporate identity. Bellotti could not have been clearer when it struck down a state-law prohibition on corporate independent expenditures related to referenda issues:

"We thus find no support in the First ... Amendment, or in the decisions of this Court, for the proposition that speech that otherwise would be within the protection of the First Amendment loses that protection simply because its source is a corporation that cannot prove, to the satisfaction of a court, a material effect on its business or property. . . . [That proposition] amounts to an impermissible legislative prohibition of speech based on the identity of the interests that spokesmen may represent in public debate over controversial issues and a requirement that the speaker have a sufficiently great interest in the subject to justify communication.

. . .

Media corporations are now exempt from § 441b's ban on corporate expenditures. Yet media corporations accumulate wealth with the help of the corporate form, the largest media corporations have "immense aggregations of wealth," and the views expressed by media corporations often "have little or no correlation to the public's support" for those views. Thus, under the Government's reasoning, wealthy media corporations could have their voices diminished to put them on par with other media entities. There is no precedent for permitting this under the First Amendment.

The media exemption discloses further difficulties with the law now under consideration. There is no precedent supporting laws that attempt to distinguish between corporations which are deemed to be exempt as media corporations and those which are not. "We have consistently rejected the proposition that the institutional press has any constitutional privilege beyond that of other speakers." With the advent of the Internet and the decline of print and broadcast media, moreover, the line between the media and others who wish to comment on political and social issues becomes far more blurred.

. . .

The law's exception for media corporations is, on its own terms, all but an admission of the invalidity of the anti-distortion rationale. And the exemption results in a further, separate reason for finding this law invalid: Again by its own terms, the law exempts some corporations but covers others, even though both have the need or the motive to communicate their views. The exemption applies to media corporations owned or controlled by corporations that have diverse and substantial investments and participate in endeavors other than news. So even assuming the most doubtful proposition that a news organization has a right to speak when others do not, the exemption would allow a conglomerate that owns both a media business and an unrelated business to influence or control the media in order to advance its overall business interest. At the same time, some other corporation, with an identical business interest but no media outlet in its ownership structure, would be forbidden to speak or inform the public about the same issue. This differential treatment cannot be squared with the First Amendment.

There is simply no support for the view that the First Amendment, as originally understood, would permit the suppression of political speech by media corporations. The Framers may not have anticipated modern business and media corporations. Yet television networks and major newspapers owned by media corporations have become the most important means of mass communication in modern times. The First Amendment was certainly not understood to condone the suppression of political speech in society's most salient media. It was understood as a response to the repression of speech and the press that had existed in England and the heavy taxes on the press that were imposed in the colonies. The great debates between the Federalists and the Anti-Federalists over our founding document were published and expressed in the most important means of mass communication of that era—newspapers owned by individuals. At the founding, speech was open, comprehensive, and vital to society's definition of itself; there were no limits on the sources of speech and knowledge. The Framers may have been unaware of certain types of speakers or forms of communication, but that does not mean that those speakers and media are entitled to less First Amendment protection than those types of speakers and media that provided the means of communicating political ideas when the Bill of Rights was adopted.

. . .

Even if § 441b's expenditure ban were constitutional, wealthy corporations could still lobby elected officials, although smaller corporations may not have the resources to do so. And wealthy individuals and unincorporated associations can spend unlimited amounts on independent expenditures. Yet certain disfavored associations of citizens— those that have taken on the corporate form—are penalized for engaging in the same political speech.

When Government seeks to use its full power, including the criminal law, to command where a person may get his or her information or what distrusted source he or she may not hear, it uses censorship to control thought. This is unlawful. The First Amendment confirms the freedom to think for ourselves.

THE THIRD HOUSE: LOBBYISTS AND LOBBYING IN THE STATES

Alan Rosenthal (2010, Second. Ed.); 136–137

What Does Money Buy?

Public interest groups and the press have no doubt that money talks and that legislators listen. Admitting that well-heeled groups have a constitutional right to lobby the legislature, the executive director of New Jersey Common Cause articulated a widely held view: "What distorts it is the volume with which the special interests speak, and the amplifier is campaign contributions." Along these lines, environmental and consumer groups complain specifically about the monetary advantages of business. Many critics of the campaign-finance system in the states argue the contributions tend to buy particular votes, even if they do not buy particular legislators. There is little evidence to support such contentions, even though those groups and organizations that make the biggest contributions are also likely to wield substantial influence. The influence, however, may have preceded the money rather than derived from it.

Considerable research has been conducted on the impact of campaign contributions at the congressional level. Most of the studies have tried to relate money to roll call votes, with very mixed results. A few have found a relationship; others have found a weak relationship, with party, ideology, and constituency more important; and still others have found little or no relationship whatsoever. But studies that focus on floor votes fail to take into account many key actions that take place elsewhere, or more subtle ones, which are difficult to discern and impossible to quantify. A few congressional studies, though, have gone further. One examined contributions to members of the House Ways and Means Committee and found indirect influence. Money tended to "facilitate access and amplify lobbying messages," rather than serve as a direct exchange for favors. Another study, which also looked at the politics of committee decision making, concluded that the participation of members was more important than their votes, especially in the case of representatives who were sympathetic anyway. Money mainly bought the marginal time, energy, and legislative resources the committee participation required.

There is widespread agreement among lobbyist that campaign contributions facilitate access. But nearly every constituent has, or can have, access. "Access," in this sense means more than the dictionary definition of "admission," "approach," or "entrance." It means, to some extent, preferential treatment. If legislators have a pile of telephone (or e-mail) messages awaiting them at the end of the day, they will likely put at the top of the pile—along with other priority messages—those from the angels who back them. If legislators are overwhelmed during the end-of-the-session crunch, their big contributors have a somewhat better chance than others are reaching them.

It is unlikely that campaign contributions buy votes and such, except perhaps in very isolated cases. Most contributions tend to follow, rather than precede, the vote. That is to say, people and PACs alike mostly give to candidates and parties with whom they have a policy affinity. They may not be soulmates, but they share general views, such as Republican share with business and Democrats share with labor. Contributions, however, may affect not the vote, but other aspects of legislators' behavior. Steady financial support may impel legislators to take leadership roles on an issue that a group endorses. Or, if legislators oppose a measure backed by one of their core contributors, they may vote against it but not lead the charge to defeat it. John Vasconcellos, a veteran member of the California assembly, described the softening effects of money: "When you know that the next day you've got to ask for thousand dollars or five thousand dollars for your campaign from some group, it is more difficult to explicitly 'anti' their position. You may speak against them, but you speak more softly rather than rant and rave." If a legislator speaks out forcefully, he may persuade several colleagues and bring over some votes that otherwise might have supported the measure. If a campaign contribution can help prevent that, it would have served the contributor's purpose.

NOTES & QUESTIONS

1.　In 2014, CNN Money reported on the companies that spent the most lobbying federal lawmakers. CNN reported that most businesses are lobbying for the long-term benefits. Given how slowly the federal government moves, lobbying dollars spent one year may not show any impact until much further down the road. Here is CNN's list of the most active publicly traded companies from 2009—2014 by money spent on lobbying:

1.	General Electric:	$134 million
2.	AT&T:	$91.2 million
3.	Boeing Co.:	$90.3 million
4.	Northrop Grumman:	$87.9 million
5.	Comcast Corp.:	$86.4 million
6.	Verizon:	$86.4 million
7.	FedExCorp.:	$85.7 million
8.	Exxon Mobil:	$85 million
9.	Lockheed Martin:	$78.8 million
10.	Pfizer:	$77.8 million

What do these companies get for the money? General Electric's lobbying was likely related to taxes. In 2010, GE paid zero taxes to the IRS by reporting a $408 million loss in America despite a $10.8 billion profit internationally. In 2011, Comcast convinced the government to approve its $30 billion acquisition of NBC Universal. In 2014, Comcast was again seeking federal antitrust approval for its $45 billion takeover of rival Time Warner Cable. Comcast's effort was unsuccessful, later withdrawing the bid due to the threat of a federal anti-trust lawsuit. Major defense contractors such as Northrop Grumman, Boeing and Lockheed Martin combined to spend almost $280 million during this period when as budget cuts threatened military spending. CNN pointed out that Google is the new power player, spending almost $16 million in 2013, compared to just $4 million back in 2009. During that time, Google fought with the Federal Trade Commission over net neutrality and the NSA over surveillance of its customers' email. See, Jesse Soloman, "Top 10 Companies Lobbying Washington," *CNN Money*, October 1, 2014.

By 2020 the companies spending the most on federal lobbying were Facebook and Amazon. Facebook, with antitrust lawsuits hanging over the company and CEO Mark Zuckerberg being summoned to Washington for Congressional hearings, spent nearly $20 million in 2020—18% more than in 2019. Amazon, which is expanding its business as a government contractor, spent about $18 million in 2020, a one-year increase of 11%. See, Ryan Tracy, Chad Day and Anthony DeBarros, "Facebook and Amazon Boosted Lobbying Spending in 2020," *Wall Street Journal*, Jan. 24, 2021.

GAINING ACCESS: A STATE LOBBYING CASE STUDY
Trevor D. Dryer, 23 *Journal of Law & Politics* 283, 309–19 (2007)

[Note: In 2000, California voters passed Proposition 34 that limited individual campaign contributions per election to: $3,000 for state legislature; $5,000 for statewide elective office; and $20,000 for governor. The law also limits contributions to political parties and committees to support or defeat candidates. The law also prohibits lobbyists' contributions to officials they lobby. The findings and purposes section stated in part that these campaign finance limitations would "reduce the influence of large contributors with an interest in matters before state government by prohibiting lobbyist contributions."]

In this case study, California lobbyists are interviewed about how they gain access and how money and term limits affect their ability to influence legislators.

Diversity in Gaining Access

Lobbyists reported that they gain access to decision makers in a variety of ways largely dependent on two factors: whether the lobbyist works for a for-profit lobbying firm or non-profit institution and what "type" of legislator is being lobbied. Interviewees believed that money plays a larger role in for-profit firms gaining access, whereas non-profit institutions rely more on the reputation and prestige of their institution. Additionally, the legislature is not a monolith: it is composed of individuals with particular personalities and values. I was told repeatedly that there is no single way to "gain access," but that certain things tend to matter: donations made by a client; the identity of the client itself; a lobbyist's reputation or knowledge on a certain subject matter; the knowledge of the legislator on a particular subject matter. Beyond making a lot of sense, this observation suggests that reducing the flow of money from lobbyists to legislators may alter the methods lobbyists use to gain access, but likely will not diminish their influence.

Lobbyists' Individual Contributions

The first theme to emerge from my research was that the lobbyists I interviewed overwhelmingly believed that Proposition 34's campaign contribution ban has virtually no effect on the practice of lobbying. Lobbyists repeatedly and consistently remarked that the era of personally making campaign contributions had already largely ended. Even before Prop. 34's ban on political contributions took effect, none of the individuals interviewed reported making personal campaign contributions while they were working as lobbyists even though they were legally allowed to do so. One lobbyist observed, "The notion of [influencing legislators by means of] personal contributions has never suffused the California lobbying experience. Maybe some lobbyists gave some personal money, but usually small amounts ... and mostly to local people." The general consensus among those interviewed was that making political contributions is disadvantageous for two reasons: it is bad for business and it can hurt one's reputation. As one lobbyist put it, "Once you start making contributions to your best friends, other guys find out about it and are on to you. Then are you going to clam up or start giving money to everyone? It doesn't take much thought to see that it will cause you embarrassment and make you a person to avoid around the capitol." If a Californian lobbyist begins handing out donations, she will soon have to give equal contributions to all 80 members of the assembly and all 40 members of the senate to avoid playing favorites: assuming a donation of a thousand dollars each, this can quickly add up to a large chunk of the lobbyist's salary. Lobbyists worried that if they were not evenhanded in their contributions, they would alienate some members and hurt their ability to obtain meetings or to communicate their clients' positions on various bills. Given that a lobbyist's main job is to influence legislation on behalf of her clients, such a loss of legislative access could prove disastrous for business. In fact, several respondents said that it was an unofficial policy at their firm that lobbyists would never make personal contributions to candidates for elective office. It seems that the only exception is for close personal friends running for local office; in this case, some lobbyists seemed willing to make small donations, typically in the range of a couple hundred dollars. The interviewees reported that this was the practice long before Proposition 34's passage; therefore, the bill did little to alter behavior.

Beyond the potential for alienating legislators, interviewees remarked that making political contributions could lead to public embarrassment. A tenacious reporter could easily look up the political contributions made by a lobbyist to various members and construe those donations as a quasi-bribe. The negative publicity resulting from an unflattering article would be more than just embarrassing: such press would be likely to induce clients to move to other lobbying firms. Indeed, the fear of journalistic attack seems to be responsible for the end of direct-giving by lobbyists to legislators: according to the lobbyists I interviewed, the end of direct-giving coincided with the passage of disclosure laws in the mid-1970s. Once lobbyists were required to report their donations and campaigns to disclose their received contributions, reporters or interested citizens could with a little effort ascertain how much a lobbyist was giving and to whom. Many lobbyists soon thought it better to make indirect contributions, which would be more difficult to track through disclosure reports. This remains the practice today. Examination of disclosure forms filed with the Secretary of State back up these assertions. The vast majority of lobbyists I interviewed did not make political contributions in the legislative session leading up to the passage of Proposition 34 (or at least contributions that they reported), nor have they made contributions since. Only a couple of these lobbyists made any contributions (again, one of them was a former member of the legislature). Those who did contribute did so in small amounts (often to local candidates) and continued to contribute even after the ban went into effect. All of my interviews and all of the forms I saw suggested that the passage of Proposition 34 simply regulated a practice already largely out of favor.

There is Still Money in Politics

That lobbyists are prohibited from personally contributing money to campaigns does not mean that they do not play a large and significant role in the money game. Lobbyists at private firms reported that members have come to expect that lobbying firms will help them raise money, typically by holding large fundraisers where they get their clients to write checks up to the limit for personal and PAC contributions. These client fundraisers (during which a candidate can raise as much as $20,000 on a single evening) aren't tracked by disclosure documents. Thus, it is virtually impossible for interested citizens to link up the names of the actual donors (which are publicly reported) with the names of the lobbyists who organized the events and advised them to contribute (these names are nowhere reported). As one individual working for a private firm remarked, "The firm is on the hook for giving a lot of money and getting their clients to max out to the various members they work with. The firm holds fundraisers for a whole host of folks. . . .[Members of the legislature] listen to the people who not only explain things to them, but also people who hold fundraisers and help them stay in office." Another person felt that lately members are becoming bolder in their requests for cash. He reported that frequently members even call lobbying firms asking them to hold fundraisers. This seems at odds with the claims of many lobbyists about the danger of making personal contributions. If lobbying firms held a fundraiser for one member of the legislature, wouldn't they feel compelled to hold them for every member? Why not just refuse to hold fundraisers altogether? When pressed on this issue, interviewees did not have a particularly good answer. Most interviewees reported that their firms did not hold fundraisers for all members of the legislature, rather they picked members to support who could best help further their clients' interests (e.g., members in key leadership positions or on committees with jurisdiction over the areas in which their clients worked). Additionally, they often held fundraisers with a specific group of clients—biotech clients, for example—for a particular member of the legislature. They would hold a fundraiser for a different member with other clients. How they picked which members to support is outside the scope of this paper, but would be an interesting topic for future research. Typically lobbyists report that they stay one step removed from the actual exchange of money. When asked about how they fundraise, the lobbyists I spoke to answered that they primarily organize fundraisers and invite clients or otherwise advise clients how to donate. Lobbyists may also develop a contribution strategy for their executives or PACs to get money to key allies in the legislature. Lobbyists felt that members of the legislature know that they have this sort of fundraising power and will often be more willing to meet with lobbyists who also are instrumental in helping them raise large quantities of money. Every lobbyist interviewed believed that these large fundraisers are what members care about, not the individual checks lobbyists may or may not make to their campaigns.

Lobbyists Gain Access in Multiple Ways

Not surprisingly, lobbyists reported gaining access to legislators in a variety of ways. During the course of interviews, I was struck by how well lobbyists knew members of the legislature and what it would take to get a meeting with them. In questioning lobbyists about how they gain access, most responded by first breaking legislators into various categories such as "good" and "bad" or "those interested in policy" versus "those who aren't" or members who are "well informed" versus those who are "along for the ride." It appeared that respondents had roughly characterized members of the legislature and then decided how to best approach them based on this characterization. One lobbyist summed it up well. "Members will talk to people depending on a multiple factors. . . . Well-motivated members will meet with articulate people regardless of financial considerations. . . . There are some others that are there for a ride and money is a big deal. [A donation] doesn't directly influence their vote, but it helps gain access. Money [is also typically] transferred to them in the form of independent expenditures." After creating categories, lobbyists then typically described the slightly different approaches they would take to gain access to a decision maker in the group.

1.   "Policy Wonks"

Virtually all respondents identified a group of legislators who were genuinely concerned with creating good public policy and would expend the time and energy necessary to fully inform themselves on the issue and make carefully reasoned decisions. I have labeled this group "policy wonks." Most all of the people I interviewed remarked that the vast majority of the members of the current legislature fall into this category. These members want to fully understand the history of bills, as well as the implications and potential benefits and drawbacks of the piece of legislation. Because term limits can prevent individual members from developing expertise and can lead to larger staff turnover (further exacerbating the problem), lobbyists reported that many of these members turn to them to help for advice and background on the issue. Respondents believed with near unanimity that if a lobbyist developed a reputation in a certain area, he or she could easily gain access to "policy wonks" to discuss bills in their area of expertise. Many respondents remarked that a lobbyists' reputation for telling the truth and doing reliable research was what allowed them to continue to enjoy significant access; those who became sloppy or used too much blatant "spin" often lost their reputation in the capitol and were less effective in gaining access through this route. A couple of lobbyists related that it is not uncommon in Sacramento for legislators to proactively call lobbyists and ask for briefings on certain bills. When further questioned about this practice, most of the lobbyists believed that legislators who proactively solicited briefings were likely calling several lobbyists to solicit a spectrum of opinions on the issue. "They [the members] know you're representing a viewpoint, but you can give them information that they don't have at the tip of their fingertips." Beyond just data, the lobbyists provide analysis to "policy wonks," helping members understand the potential political pitfalls from voting a certain way or how a bill will affect various constituent groups. It appeared from the interviews that legislators the lobbyists placed into the "policy wonk" category liked to gather information from a variety of sources and viewed knowledgeable lobbyists as a very convenient way to obtain information, even if it meant that lobbyists would present their client's viewpoint. Because legislators are aware that the information is based on lobbyists' perceptions, it is unclear whether members called a particular lobbyist because of his perceived expertise or because he represented clients whose interests aligned with the agenda of the legislator. The lobbyists I interviewed could have been overestimating their ability to persuade legislators of the soundness of a client's position, conveniently forgetting the number of times a legislator called them for advice and then voted the other way.

2.   "Money Types"   *Donate to get "in"*

Lobbyists described another category of members of the legislature as "money types" or individuals who were "along for the ride" and cared more about being re-elected than about the policy they were setting. For these individuals, lobbyists felt contributions play a significant role. A majority of lobbyists I interviewed remarked that this group was a small minority of individuals in Sacramento, though some noted that they believe all of the members were concerned with fundraising to varying degrees. Still, for those identified as "money types", the concern for fundraising is extreme: "Everything is judged by money," one lobbyist remarked, "access, bill passage—everything." If you coordinated client donations or a large fundraiser for these legislators, you would be able to arrange meetings and otherwise gain access without any problem. "Without arranging donations, it's difficult." From the interviews, it was apparent that there are a significant minority of legislators who give preferential treatment to large donors and are much more willing to meet with individuals who help to keep them in office. This process often starts even before a candidate runs in his or her first primary. Candidates commonly make appointments with lobbying firms before they declare their candidacy in the hope of convincing lobbyists to recommend to their clients that they make contributions. This is also good for the lobbyist. As one lobbyist explained, "If your client makes contributions, there is a credit that is attached to that that leads to a greater willingness to meet with the lobbyist or instructions to staff to give appointments." Lobbyists believed that the process continues once the member is in office; this commonly held opinion has even greater force when one examines the timing of the fundraisers. One individual explained that the legislature has a carefully timed calendar of key legislative dates that is publicly released. For example, bills have to be out of the originating committee by a certain date in April and out of the Finance Committee in June and through the first house shortly thereafter (unless it is a two year bill). Interviewees reported that members often hold key fundraisers in the days leading up to each calendar deadline, which gives lobbyists an opportunity to get face time (for a price) with the member before key votes to pass or kill legislation. While not vote trading per se, this partly explains the pressure on lobbyists and lobbying firms to hold big fundraisers and advise their clients where they should strategically place their money. While this may sound like almost a quid pro quo arrangement, several lobbyists described it in more benign terms. Legislators aren't in the business of trading money for access; it is simply "human nature" that a person is more likely to meet with someone she knows and with whom she has had prior positive interactions. By helping raise needed cash, a lobbyist develops a positive personal relationship with the legislator: this relationship makes it more likely that she will agree to meet with the lobbyist in the future. This relationship and access does not guarantee that the legislator will vote how the lobbyist wants: it simply ensures that the lobbyist's position is heard and considered. As one lobbyist put it, "If you had a fundraiser, [legislators] meet the people who have paid to come. So, the next day when [legislators] have to return calls, they'll return calls of the people they've met. It's not buying votes, but they'll listen to people they know." This sort of comment helps to explain why lobbying firms hold fundraisers frequently. During these fundraisers, they can introduce their own lobbyists to new members of the legislature and also link up these members with various clients. The fundraiser thus serves as a form of networking that lobbyists believe greatly facilitates future meetings with legislators—they not only met the legislator and developed a relationship, they also helped the legislator raise needed funds. While this sounds intuitively true, it is impossible to discern from these perceptions whether legislators are taking meetings with lobbyists because they are an acquaintance or because they know that the individual was (at least partly) responsible for filling their campaign coffers. Indeed, the legislator herself may not be able to precisely elucidate the influence of each factor in her decision to give a meeting.

3.   Non-Profits and Prestige

While not a different category of legislators, the lobbyists' description of gaining access would be incomplete without a word about their non-profit colleagues. Prominent non-profit organizations, whether public interest groups or educational institutions, appeared to gain access to legislators in a very different way than their for-profit counterparts. In the course of this study I spoke with three lobbyists who had spent part of their career working for non-profit institutions. Lobbyists remarked that because 501(c)(3) organizations are prohibited from making political expenditures, the money game plays a much smaller role in their lobbying activities. While some organizations have set up separate segregated funds (PACs), I was surprised to learn that lobbyists perceive PAC donations from these groups as having very little influence on their gaining access to decision makers. Lobbyists believed that access was granted or denied based on the prestige of the non-profit organization or the political/social message their organization conveys to the public. For example, a conservative legislator will not likely accept PAC donations from or take meetings with "liberal" groups such as the ACLU or NARAL even if they needed the money; the political fallout and damage to future fundraising would not be worth the risk. Conversely, legislators who want to promote a certain political agenda or assure their constituents of their positions on particular issues may take the donation as sign of aligning themselves with the organization's cause. Similarly, lobbyists felt that educational institutions use their status and prestige to gain access without having to play the money game. "The money game doesn't get played there," remarked one former educational institution lobbyist, "we [got] access from our expertise, name and reputation." Lobbyists reported that legislators liked being "affiliated" with educational institutions and always seemed to relish the opportunity to work with them on issues. Additionally, respondents felt that educational institutions have a general reputation for existing above the political fray, which makes them attractive sources of information. One individual observed, "[Educational institutions] have a reputation for being an honest broker [sic], which means that [they] don't have to curry favor with legislators to gain access." This makes intuitive sense. Educational institutions can bring their significant expertise to bear on an issue, while also providing a degree of credibility to a bill or situation. Especially in areas where the bill involves an area of science or public policy in which the institution has expertise, the endorsement of an educational institution provides a large degree of legitimacy. Several lobbyists believed that this legitimacy coupled with the prestige of doing business with universities plays a significant role in allowing educational lobbyists to gain easy access to members on their name alone.

NOTES & QUESTIONS

1. In 1990, California voters passed Proposition 140, which imposed term limits of three two-year terms for Assemblymen and two four-year terms for Senators. Proponents wanted to bring back the concept of "citizen legislators," and some hoped that term limits would lessen the influence of special interests. Professor Dryer's case study found "near unanimity" among lobbyists that term limits increased the influence of lobbyists in the California Legislature. Lobbyists became the "institutional memory" of the Legislature and relatively inexperienced legislators increasingly relied on their expertise. Another factor is that term limited members choose to run for other offices, thus requiring more reliance on lobbyists to raise money. One lobbyist opined that the "money game . . . has gotten ten times more important since term limits came in during the 1990s."

2. How do corporations influence public policy? Congress has regulated corporate political activity since 1907, due, in part, on the perception that corporations have an outsized ability to influence public policy due to their wealth and resources. Some also consider political activity to be an illegitimate way to use corporate funds. Professor Jill E. Fisch studied how FedEx developed and used political capital from its founding in 1971 to 2000 when the FedEx had annual revenues of $24.7 billion and 245,000 employees worldwide. During that time FedEx built a reputation as an influential political player. FedEx did this by:

- political expenditures of $3.4 in "soft money" and PAC contributions between 1999–2000;

- lobbying expenditures in 2000 of $3,320,000;

- founder and CEO Fred Smith traveled to Washington monthly to meet with political officials and testify before Congress;

- Smith cultivated relationships with prominent political figures in Congress and several presidents, including Bill Clinton and George W. Bush;

- FedEx maintained a six-person government affairs office in Washington with a reputation for being "well informed" and "very accessible";

- Employed several political insiders, including former senators, on its board of directors;

- Employed several outside lobbying firms;

- Routinely allowed members of Congress to use its corporate jets when traveling, including fundraising events (which is allowed under federal law);

- Purchased the naming rights for the professional football stadium in Washington DC, where "the majority of lobbying is done for Federal Express;"

- regularly drafts legislation and provides research and other supporting information for government officials;

- Built coalitions and "rent chains," including customers and employees, to demonstrate broader support for its initiatives;

- Participated in industry groups such as the Air Transport Association ("ATA");

- Engaged in high profile charitable activities such as airlifting hay to drought-stricken South Carolina, delivering drilling equipment to Midland, Texas, to help save a child who fell down a well, assisting the American Red Cross during disasters and national emergencies, and even flying celebrity panda bears, Tian Tian and Mei Xiang, from China to the National Zoo in Washington.

After reviewing how FedEx used political influence to deregulate the air and ground shipping industry, Prof. Fisch concluded:

The FedEx case study demonstrates that the characterization of corporate political activity as a diversion of operating funds is, at best, naive. U.S. corporations operate within a complex legal infrastructure, and the regulatory environment is an integral part of market decisions for corporations as well as a key factor in their growth and strategic planning. FedEx, and indeed the entire air cargo industry, could not have gotten off the ground without air cargo deregulation. FedEx's ability to develop and serve its customer base was critically enhanced by the urgent letter exemption, which enabled it to deliver letters as well as freight. Noise standards, labor rules, and trucking regulation directly affected FedEx's operating costs, influencing the manner in which FedEx developed its business plan, affecting its pricing structure, and defining its key industry competitors.

Campaign finance scholars and the Supreme Court have isolated corporate political activity without considering the relationship of politics to the firm's business strategy. Corporate scholars may emphasize marketplace competition at the cost of overlooking nonmarket strategies. Yet, as the FedEx story shows, firm competition takes place both in the marketplace and in the political arena; the dynamics of one environment affect the other. Jill E. Fisch, "How do Corporations Play Politics? The FedEx Story," 58 *Vanderbilt L. Rev.* 1495 (2005).

3.   Given the FedEx example, how should campaign finance regulations be reformed assuming that corporate political activity is inevitable? Would it include a reporting mechanism to give a complete picture of a company's political activities and what they get for their efforts? Fisch suggests requiring Congress to provide, in a bill's legislative history, information on persons and groups that participated in the legislative process; and to incorporate political activity into the disclosure requirements applicable to publicly traded companies under the federal securities laws.

4.   Sometimes celebrities become the face of lobbying efforts. U2 lead singer Bono Vox's non-profit organization "One Action" saw a dramatic increase in lobbying expenditures in 2014. One Action lobbies influential policymakers to influence policies related to poverty and saving the lives of millions of people in the world's poorest countries. The organization spent over $2.25 million in one year on lobbying efforts—$1.3 million in the first half of 2014 alone. Some of the issues it advocated for included: HIV/AIDS, agriculture, vaccines, Feed the Future, The Foreign Aid Transparency and Accountability Act; the Electrify Africa Act; and the Energize Africa Water for the World Act. Kent Cooper, "Bono's One Action Ramps Up Lobbying," *Roll Call*, July 8, 2014.

3.   WHAT DOES A K STREET LOBBYING FIRM LOOK LIKE?

What does a Washington "K Street" lobbying firm look like? Where do the members go to school and what experience do they have before becoming lobbyists? The law firm Squire Patton Boggs has 45 offices in 20 countries. It is one of the largest law firms in the world by both employees and revenue. Its offices in Washington DC, London and Cleveland each have more than 100 lawyers. When the firm Squire Sanders merged with the Washington based firm Patton Boggs in 2014 it became the third largest lobbying firm in the U.S. The lobbying practice was managed by the legendary lawyer and lobbyist Thomas Hale Boggs Jr., until his death in 2014.

From 2003–2013, Patton Boggs was the largest U.S. lobbying firm by revenue. Patton Boggs expanded in 2010 when it bought the Breaux-Lott Leadership Group, which was founded by former U.S. Senators John Breaux (D-LA) and Trent Lott (R-MS).

As of 2021, the public policy practice group listed 75 members, with 54 of them based in Washington DC. The European members were based in London, Brussels, Prague and Berlin and included members of the UK Parliament, EU Parliament and Irish Parliament.

Squire Patton Boggs boasts four former members of Congress as members: former House Speaker John Boehner (R-OH), Joe Crowley (D-NY), Jack Kingston (R-GA), and Bill Shuster (R-PA). Other members include former Secretary of Transportation Rodney Slater and former ambassador Frank Wisner.

- How do the members of the Squire Patton Boggs break down by education, political party and prior experience?

Education	Bachelor's only	Master's Degree	Law Degree	JD & MA	PhD
	24	6	28	15	2

Political Connection	Republican	Democratic	Not Apparent
	20	16	33

Prior Work Experience	Senate	House	Senate & House	President/ Administration	Municipal & State	Foreign Government
	9	16	5	23	5	6

- There are more people with House experience right now, but that may be due to the addition of Speaker Boehner in September 2016, who brought along 5 of his former staffers.

- How do the members break down by gender? There are 53 men and 22 women.

- Where did the lawyers go to law school?

American University	New York University	University of Denver
Catholic University	The Ohio State University	University of Kansas
Columbia University	Regent University	University of Maryland
Cornell University	Santa Clara University	University of North Carolina
Emory University	Seton Hall University	University of Virginia
George Mason University	Tulane University	University of Wisconsin
Georgetown University	University of Alabama	Washington University of Law (St. Louis)
George Washington University	University of Arkansas	

- Lawyers typically hold the title of partner, associate and counsel.

- Non-lawyers typically hold the titles of principal, senior strategic advisor, public policy advisor, and public policy specialist.

- The global managing partner for the public policy group, Edward J. Newberry, was called the "King of K Street" by the *New York Times*.

- Interestingly, when the Squire web site gives the biography of public policy group members, it highlights the government experience of people holding a bachelor's degree 88% of the time. All of the members with a master's degree highlighted their prior government experience. Just 49% of the lawyers' biographies highlighted prior government experience.

4. SKILL DEVELOPMENT: TESTIFYING AT A LEGISLATIVE HEARING

One of the best ways to advocate for or against a bill continues to be testifying before the relevant legislative committees. In Congress, the number of witnesses on any given matter is limited and requires an invitation from the committee. Many states, however, allow anyone to attend a hearing offer written and oral testimony to the committee members and staff. Often the committee will establish rules for testimony such as limiting the amount of time for the witness and questioning by the committee. In Massachusetts, the committee chair will often limit oral testimony to just three minutes. Therefore, witnesses have to carefully plan how to best use that time to get the committee's attention, convey key information, and win support for their position.

TIPS FOR TESTIFYING BEFORE A LEGISLATIVE COMMITTEE
Nevada Legislative Counsel Bureau

Check the Schedule

Check the legislative website, with your legislative liaison, and with legislative staff to know when a bill is scheduled to be heard. Be advised—schedules can change quickly, especially in the final days of a legislative session.

Know the Process and Players

Before testifying, know who is sponsoring the bill, who supports or opposes the bill and why. Be familiar with the committee chairs, committee members, and legislative staff. Let the sponsor of the bill or key legislators know beforehand you are testifying on the bill.

Know the Purpose of your Testimony

Understand why you are testifying. Are you there to persuade, dissuade, provide expertise, or delay action on a bill? Know how to separate out the important points of your testimony to ensure they are heard.

Important

Triple check your facts and figures and be prepared to explain how you collected your data, especially if you have staff prepare remarks for you. Remember that what you say will become part of the public record. A person who knowingly misrepresents any fact when testifying in a committee meeting or in communications to a legislator preliminary to that meeting is guilty of a misdemeanor per *Nevada Revised Statutes* 218E.085(2).

A few more tips. . .

When you arrive, fill out the sign-in sheet and indicate if you wish to testify.

At the appropriate time, go to the witness table, turn on the microphone, and introduce yourself: "Chair, and members of the committee, my name is . . ."

Explain your position clearly and simply, and do not repeat earlier testimony.

Be brief (testimony may be limited to 3 minutes).

If you have written materials to present, bring enough copies for the committee members, for the committee secretary, other staff, and members of the public.

If you believe a change in the law is needed or some other action should be taken by the committee, be specific about your recommendation (for example, written material explaining changes to wording in the law are encouraged).

Be ready to answer questions from the committee members. If you don't know, say so. Say you will follow up with the information—and be sure to do so.

Check the committee deadline for providing a written copy of your testimony to the committee secretary (some committees require all written material to be submitted electronically 24 hours in advance).

GUIDELINES FOR PREPARING, WRITING, AND GIVING TESTIMONY

Citizen Advocacy Center
(http://www.citizenadvocacycenter.org/uploads/8/8/4/0/8840743/
guidelines_for_preparing_writing_and_giving_testimony.pdf)

Giving testimony is one of the most effective ways to educate legislators and policymakers about the impact, either positive or negative, that proposed legislation or legislative change might have. Legislators and other policymakers aren't always aware of all the implications a particular piece of legislation may have on their constituents. Oral testimony is very powerful, especially when the testifier speaks directly instead of reading from their written testimony. Your testimony should be short—no longer than 3 to 5 minutes. It is most effective when you speak from your own personal experience. As a general rule, testimonies should be delivered verbally and also submitted in writing.

It is best to type your testimony using a computer or like device from which you can print because you will be submitting copies of your testimony for distribution to your state legislators at the hearing. Bring enough copies of your prepared statement for the entire committee or task force. Be sure the committee or task force clerk has a copy for the official record of the hearing. Many speakers write down their speeches and read directly from that written text, which audiences find dull. Others forgo notes and memorize their speeches; but if they forget something, they often become completely lost and are unable to continue. The key to preparing notes for public speaking lies between these two extremes: notes remind the speaker about what to say, but don't tell the speaker how to say it.

Yet, the first step in offering effective testimony is to write down your speech. Here are some guidelines:

Write your speech. Construct an opening, well-organized paragraph, effective transitions, and a memorable closing. Pay attention to sentence structure and word choice.

Follow this outline for preparing your statement:

1)   Identify yourself and the organization you represent (if applicable)

2)   Greetings

3)   Clear presentation of your position: State your position as "for" or "against" the proposed bill; identify the bill name and number

4)   Factual arguments and data as evidence to support your position, if available

5)   Personal story or anecdotes to demonstrate your position. This is often the most powerful part

6)   Conclusion: Restate/review your position at the end of your testimony

7)   Thank the committee or task force for the opportunity to speak

Highlight the keywords in each sentence.

Rehearse your testimony! Read your speech out loud and make changes. If you stumble over a certain word or combination of words, choose alternatives that will be easier to say. Listen for the rhythm and flow of your speech and make changes so that your reading proceeds smoothly from start to finish.

Try reciting the speech from memory by referring to your highlighted transcript. Try to remember what to say based only on the keywords you've highlighted. If the keywords don't help you, find new ones.

Transfer only the keywords to a paper or notecards. Which you will use depends on the speaking situation and your own preferences.

Exceptions: Write out lengthy quotes, complex statistics or other information that must be exact on your notes. Read these word for word in your speech. In these situations, your audience will appreciate that you're taking the time to make sure you're accurate.

Use a sheet of paper (or 2 if you need more room). Put your notes on the lectern and occasionally glance down at your keywords. This will allow you to look out at your audience most of the time, which will keep them engaged.

- Don't use more sheets than necessary for your notes. The movement and sound of turning pages over during your speech will be distracting to your audience.

- When using paper for notes, organize the keywords in a way that makes sense to you. You may want to number them, list them under general headings or use different colors. Write the keywords large enough to keep you from having to lean down and squint in order to read them.

Practice your speech using your notes. Because you haven't memorized it, your speech will be a little different each time, but it will sound more natural than a memorized speech.

- Use the notes you create to practice. If you practice from an outline and then try to use a keyword sheet or notecards when you give your speech, you'll likely become flustered.

- If you can't deliver your speech smoothly and completely, make changes to your notes.

Think carefully before you talk. Use silence; it can be a great ally and cause the audience to hang off your next words, wondering what you are about to say. Don't be intimidated by silent moments.

Anticipate questions you might be asked and practice answering them.

ON THE DAY OF THE HEARING

Arrive early and sign up. Make sure you follow any procedures that have been published, and indicate that you wish to testify. Generally, speakers will testify in the same order as their names appear on the sign-up sheet.

If there is a microphone, speak directly into it (keep the mike about 6 inches from your mouth). If necessary, move or adjust the microphone. If you cannot be heard, your testimony will not be effective, regardless of how carefully your statement was prepared.

Do not repeat points made by speakers ahead of you. If all of the points you wanted to make have been made, tell the committee you agree with the testimony given by the preceding speakers and urge them to take the appropriate action.

Answer only those questions that you can answer correctly, and answer as clearly and succinctly as you can. Offer to find the answers to other questions and promptly get back to the committee members with the information.

Do not argue with members of the committee or with people giving opposing testimony.

C. REGULATING LOBBYISTS

Given their perceived negative influence on the legislative system and periodic high profile scandals involving lobbyists, good government advocates and policy makers often look for ways to better regulate lobbyists. Massachusetts enacted the first lobbying statute in 1890. Several other states passed similar laws between 1906–1909 due to information that some New York insurance companies were manipulating the legislative process in other states. This section will explore the various methods the states and federal government use to regulate lobbyists.

1. CASE STUDY: JACK ABRAMOFF AND TRIBAL CASINO GAMBLING

New lobbying restrictions are often driven by scandal. Legislative proposals have been put forward after Watergate, Ab-Scam, and most recently, the activities of Jack Abramoff.

From 1994–2004, Jack Abramoff was one of the most powerful lobbyists in Washington. His most lucrative clients were the "gambling tribes" of Native Americans, which he billed $82 million—sometimes for legitimate services, and other times for manufactured threats to the various tribes' businesses. He accomplished this through his many contacts in Congress and the White House, campaign contributions, trips, and promises of employment. In 2004, however, his schemes came to light and Abramoff and several of his associates went to prison. As Sen. John McCain (R-AZ) said, "What sets this tale apart, what makes it truly extraordinary is the extent and degree of the apparent exploitation."

Jack Abramoff graduated from Brandeis University in 1981 and Georgetown Law School in 1984. After law school he became the chairman of the College Republican National Committee (CRNC). At CRNC, Abramoff met and worked with future conservative activists Ralph Reed, Grover Norquist, and Adam Kidan. Although Abramoff took a break from Washington in the late 1980s to write and produce movies, the Republican wave during the 1994 mid-term elections gave the GOP control of Congress and drew Abramoff back to Washington DC.

Abramoff first worked for the lobbying firm of Preston Gates & Ellis, and later joined the mega law firm Greenberg Traurig, where he oversaw a team of two dozen lobbyists. His political connections, especially with House Majority Whip Rep. Tom DeLay (R-Texas), allowed Abramoff to quickly develop a blue-chip book of business: including Unisys, Tyco, and the government of the Northern Marianas Islands. In 1995, Abramoff signed the Mississippi Band of the Choctaw as a client, which needed help with a tax matter. Abramoff's success on the tax issue led to bigger projects concerning the tribe's casino revenue.

Abramoff's partner was communications specialist Michael Scanlon, who had been Rep. Tom DeLay's communication director. In 2000, Scanlon joined Abramoff's team at Preston Gates & Ellis. When Abramoff joined Greenberg Traurig in 2001, Scanlon formed his own public relations firm, Capitol Campaign Strategies.

"We are missing the boat. . .There are a ton of potential opportunities out there. There are 27 tribes which make more than $100 [million] a year . . . . We need to get moving on them."

E-mail from Abramoff to Scanlon.

Abramoff and Scanlon recruited six tribes with gambling interests as clients: Mississippi Band of Choctaw Indians, Agua Caliente Band of Cahuilla Indians in California, Saginaw Chippewa Indian Tribe in Michigan, the Chitimacha Tribe of Louisiana, the Coushatta Tribe of Louisiana, and the Tigua Indian Reservation in Texas.

In addition to traditional lobbying services, Abramoff and Scanlon set up a scheme to make millions of dollars from the tribes. Abramoff and Scanlon manufactured threats to the tribes' interests and pushing the clients to agree to pay them for more work and higher fees.

Native American tribes typically elect their leadership, and Abramoff and Scanlon spent a great deal of time and money attempting to elect officers who would hire or keep employing them. For example, they spent tens of thousands of dollars to swing the 2002 Agua Caliente tribal elections. Abramoff and Scanlon also supported candidates in a Saginaw Chippewas election, with the expectation that if their candidate won, they would "have millions." Bernie Sprague, sub-chief of the Saginaw Chippewas, testified in the fall of 2001 that Abramoff and Scanlon "smeared the reputations of other candidates running for Tribal Council." Their hand-picked slate was elected, winning seven seats on the Saginaw Chippewas Council. In an e-mail, Scanlon bragged, "We now control 9 out of the 12 seats on the council . . . hopefully we will be doing some more work for the tribe in the near future."

Abramoff not only charged the tribes lobbying fees but also urged them to hire Scanlon's public relations firm as a grass roots field organizer at hugely inflated prices. Scanlon, in turn, kicked back half of the money to Abramoff, who was thus able to conceal the funds from public disclosure and even from his law firm. They called this arrangement "gimme five."

The heart of the scheme was convincing the tribes that something was threatening their gambling businesses. In 2002 Abramoff stoked tribal fears about "racinos" legislation pending in the Michigan legislature. Abramoff emailed Chris Petras with the Saginaw Chippewa:

"Chris, I am getting worried about this. Last night we opened Stacks [a Pennsylvania Avenue restaurant owned by Abramoff] and there were some [White House] guys there. . . . They told me that there is a hearing coming up on this immediately, and they have heard that this is going to happen!!! . . . where is Scanlon on this? . . . We need to get him firing missiles. How do we move it faster? Please get the council focused on this as soon as you can."

Abramoff sent a copy to Scanlon, who messaged back: "I love you."

Scanlon should have loved Abramoff—over a five-year period, Scanlon billed six Native American tribes for more than $66.3 million and Abramoff pocketed $21 million of it.

Abramoff and Scanlon also used grass roots campaigns by Christian groups to secretly protect or threaten their clients. Abramoff got his old friend Ralph Reed, the former executive director of the Christian Coalition, to use his network of Christian groups to oppose casinos proposed by Abramoff clients' rival tribes. Reed's phone banks identified themselves as members of the Christian Research Network or Global Christian Outreach Network and urge voters to contact their representatives to oppose gambling. Since Reed could not openly take money from tribes involved in gambling, Abramoff funneled money from the tribes to Reed's consulting firm through his law firm, Grover Norquist's organization Americans for Tax Reform, and a shell corporation.

Over several years, Reed & Norquist received millions of dollars from Abramoff and Scanlon to run anti-gambling campaigns in the South. In one instance, Norquist collected at least $1.15 million from the Mississippi Choctaw that wanted to block competition from another gaming operation in Alabama. Norquist sent about $850,000 to the Alabama Christian Coalition and $300,0000 to Citizens Against Legalized Lottery, both associated with Reed, to lead the fight against gambling in Alabama. Abramoff used a similar pattern to help the Tiquas Tribe in Texas. In 2002, after a long court fight, Texas had won the right to shut down the Tiguas Tribe's 1,500 slot Speaking Rock Casino outside of El Paso, arguing that casino gambling was illegal in the state, even on nominally sovereign soil like that of an Native American reservation. The Tiguas reached out to Abramoff, who suggested inserting language in a bill by a friendly congressman that would override the Texas court decision. The Tiguas did not know that Abramoff and Scanlon had earlier sent $4 million to Ralph Reed to run a grass-roots operation to generate support for Attorney General John Cornyn's effort to change Texas law. Abramoff's original intent was to prevent the opening of a new casino outside of Houston that would threaten a Louisiana casino run by Abramoff's client, the Coushattas Tribe. When that effort spilled over to affect the Tiguas, Abramoff offered to take them on as a client, initially at no cost—to help the Tiguas. Abramoff's efforts to reopen Standing Rock were unsuccessful, but Abramoff and Scanlon still got $4.2 million from the Tiguas. A Tiguas spokesman later told a congressional panel it was one of "the most despicable acts of greed and fraud that I hope to never, ever see again."

In addition to creating threats to their clients, Abramoff and his lobbying team routinely "pumped up" their client's bills by tens of thousands of dollars a month. This scheme also required that money from clients be laundered as donations to tax-exempt groups and a variety of other charitable organizations created by Abramoff and Scanlon.

Abramoff's success as a lobbyist came from his access to key government officials. At one point, Abramoff opened a high-end restaurant and bar on Pennsylvania Avenue called "Signatures," which became the gathering place for many prominent Republicans. The restaurant sometimes hosted dozens of political fundraisers a week. Many lawmakers and staff ran up large bills with little pressure to pay. After the media noticed this arrangement a handful of lawmakers, including House Speaker Dennis Hastert, paid their long-overdue tabs. Abramoff's Native American clients were also billed thousands of dollars for meals and meetings at Signatures with public officials and other lobbyists.

Abramoff cultivated connections with both Republicans and Democrats through traditional methods such as campaign contributions, and some shadier routes.

Between 1999–2004, Abramoff and Scanlon directed nearly $4 million in funds from the tribes to lawmakers. Among these donations were:

Rep. Tom DeLay (R-TX) (House Majority Whip) $70,000
Sen. Conrad Burns (R-MT)
(Appropriations subcommittee chair) $141,590
Rep. Patrick Kennedy (D-RI)..$100,000
Sen. Harry Reid (D-NV) (Senate Majority Leader) $40,000
Sen. Thomas Daschle (D-SD) (Senate Majority Leader)...............$40,000
Rep. Richard Gephardt (D-MO) (House Democratic Leader) $32,500

In total, two-thirds of Abramoff's contributions went to Republicans and one-third was handed out to Democrats.

Each of the Congressmen offered a different rationale for the donations beyond Abramoff's involvement. Rep. Kennedy cited his family's long-standing commitment to Native American causes, the fact that he co-founded the Congressional Native American Caucus in 1997, and his personal relationship with the chief of the Mississippi Choctaw Tribe. Senator Harry Reid pointed out that he is also a member of the Senate Indian Affairs Committee. Sen. Daschle received donations from 64 Native American tribes, including the five represented by Abramoff, because his home state is home to nine tribes, and he had been a champion of Native American issues. Sen. Conrad Burns claimed his actions were consistent with his support for improving conditions for Native American tribes through his Appropriations subcommittee chairmanship.

Abramoff also won support from members of Congress by providing trips for them and their staffs. In 1999, Abramoff arranged a week-long visit to England and Scotland with Majority Leader DeLay, his wife and two aides. Later in the year Abramoff arranged a trip for DeLay's aides to the U.S. Open aboard a corporate jet belonging to his company SunCruz Casinos.

In 2001, Abramoff brought aides for Sen. Burns and Rep. Delay on a Super Bowl trip. The staffers flew to Tampa on a SunCruz corporate jet, treated to the game, and then a night of gambling on a SunCruz ship—including $500 in gambling chips.

Abramoff gave Rep. Bob Ney (R-FL) a golf trip to Scotland's St. Andrews Golf Course. Although initially paid for with Abramoff's credit card, which was a violation of House Rules, the trip was later reported as sponsored by the National Center for Public Policy Research, a think tank that had Abramoff on the board of directors.

Another valuable perk was tickets to sporting events or entertainment, especially the four luxury sports-stadium skyboxes Abramoff leased with clients' funds for $1 million a year. After Rep. J.D. Hayworth (R-Ariz.) helped Abramoff's efforts to exempt tribal casinos from labor laws, Hayworth used Abramoff's sports skyboxes five times from 1999 to 2001. Rep. Heyworth eventually reimbursed the Choctaw and Chitimacha $12,880.

Yet another way for Abramoff to reward members of Congress was to find employment for their spouses. One lobbying firm Abramoff referred lucrative clients to, Alexander Strategy Group, hired Rep. DeLay's wife Christine at Abramoff's request. Over four years she was paid $115,000 to determine the favorite charity of every member of Congress.

Abramoff and Scanlon made an enormous amount of money while representing the Native American tribes: $16 million in lobbying fees paid to Greenberg Traurig; $66 million in fees to Scanlon's firm, with Scanlon and Abramoff each receiving $21 million; and $87 million collected by Abramoff and Scanlon from Native American clients in just five years.

When the *Washington Post* reported some of Abramoff and Scanlon's activities in the winter of 2003, Greenberg Traurig demanded Abramoff's resignation and the Senate Indian Affairs Committee began a seven-month investigation.

In September 2004, Abramoff appeared before the Senate Indian Affairs Committee. Sen. Ben Nighthorse Campbell said Abramoff's activities showed not only "unbounded greed" but also bigotry and contempt for tribal officials by referring to them as "idiots" and "troglodytes" in e-mails. Abramoff reportedly "looked abashed," but did not answer, citing his right against self-incrimination. Sen. Byron L. Dorgan (D-N.D.) called the two men's activities "a cesspool of greed]. . . . a pathetic, disgusting example of greed run amok." Sen. Kent Conrad (D-N.D.) stated, "I think all of us know this is the most extraordinary pattern of abuse to come before this committee in the 18 years I've served here."

In November 2005, Scanlon pleaded guilty to conspiring to bribe a congressman and other public officials and agreed to pay back more than $19 million he fraudulently charged tribal clients. The Department of Justice investigation targeted several members of Congress including former Rep. Tom DeLay (R), Sen. Conrad Burns (R-Mont.), Rep. John T. Doolittle (R-Calif.), and Rep. Robert W. Ney (R-Ohio).

On January 3, 2006 Abramoff pleaded guilty to fraud, tax evasion and conspiracy to bribe public officials in a deal that required him to provide evidence about members of Congress. The statement of facts attached to the plea agreement stated Abramoff and Scanlon "offered and provided a stream of things of value to public officials in exchange for official acts," defrauding four tribal clients out of millions of dollars, evading taxes, to conspiring to bribe lawmakers, and to conspiring to induce former Capitol Hill staffers to violate the one-year ban on lobbying their former bosses.

Eventually 22 people were convicted of corruption or bribery or receiving bribes. Abramoff was sentenced to six years in prison. In 2010, Abramoff was released from Federal prison after serving four years. Abramoff's lobbying and scandals was the subject of two 2010 films: the documentary *Casino Jack and the United States of Money*, and the feature film *Casino Jack*.

Since his release, Abramoff has re-registered as a lobbyist and frequently speaks out against Washington, D.C. corruption and the lobbying community. In 2011, Abramoff released a memoir, *Capitol Punishment: The Hard Truth About Washington Corruption From America's Most Notorious Lobbyist* (2011). In the final chapter, Abramoff argues for lobbying reform, including barring members of Congress and their aides for life from becoming lobbyists.

Sources:

- "Information by Department of Justice," *U.S. v. Jack A. Abramoff*, January 3, 2006. (https://www.washingtonpost.com/wp-srv/politics/documents/abramoff_info_010306.pdf);

- " 'Gimme Five'—Investigation of Tribal Lobbying Matters," Report of U.S. Senate Committee on Indian Affairs, June 22, 2006. (https://www.govinfo.gov/content/pkg/CRPT-109srpt325/pdf/CRPT-109srpt325.pdf);

- Susan Schmidt, James V. Grimaldi, "The Fast Rise and Steep Fall of Jack Abramoff," *Washington Post*, December 29, 2005 (https://www.washingtonpost.com/wp-dyn/content/article/2005/12/28/AR2005122801588.html).

QUESTIONS & NOTES

1.   In the Ethics chapter, one commentator argued that legislative staff did not need clear rules of behavior, rather, if they did something wrong, the other legislative actors would punish them. Dean Allard argued that one of the virtues of lobbyists were that they kept other lobbyists honest. There are thousands of lobbyists in Washington DC—why did they not "blow the whistle" on Abramoff?

2.   Can "sunlight" (press coverage, disclosure rules, etc.) prevent lobbyists and public officials from acting unethically? What are the limits of exposure? Will these measures have a greater effect on Congress or the Administration?

3.   Other than criminal sanctions, what factors prevent lobbyists from either breaking the law or acting unethically?

4.   Nearly every aspect of what happens in Washington DC (not to mention state capitals) depends on personal relationships. These relationships often require reciprocity of "favors" be it information, access, employment, campaign contributions, etc. Abramoff argued that much of what he did was just "business as usual." Was it?

5.   Former lobbyist and law dean Nicholas Allard distinguished between Abramoff and most lobbyists: "Consider the myth that 'the system is rotten and all involved are corrupt' versus the reality that 'the system works as intended and most everyone involved, including public officials and lobbyists are hard-working, dedicated, and honest.' Are there exceptions? Of course. But the exceptions prove the rule, and are often examples of the law being enforced. Inevitably the bad apple gets caught and punished, like notorious convicted lobbyist Jack Abramoff, former Representatives Randy "Duke" Cunningham and William Jefferson. And that is why you know about them. They attract a lot of attention for the wrong reasons. Abramoff, for example, was not a lobbyist, he was a crook. He was running, in effect, a political Ponzi scheme, and Ponzi schemes always, inevitably, eventually collapse." Nicholas W. Allard, "The Seven Deadly Virtues of Lobbyists: What Lawyer Lobbyists Really Do," 13 *Election L.J.* 210, 211–19 (2014).

6.   In June 2020, Abramoff agreed to plead guilty to criminal conspiracy charges and a criminal violation of the 2007 Lobbying Disclosure Act; the first prosecution brought under the law passed largely due to Abramoff's crimes in the early 2000s. In 2017 Abramoff lobbied members of Congress on behalf of a California-based marijuana industry client without registering as a lobbyist. Abramoff was also charged with investor fraud for making false claims about a cryptocurrency he was promoting. See, Olga R. Rodriguez, "Lobbyist Abramoff Charged in Cryptocurrency Fraud Case," *US News*, June 25, 2020.

REGULATING LOBBYISTS: LAW, ETHICS, AND PUBLIC POLICY

Vincent R. Johnson, 16 *Cornell Journal of Law & Public Policy* 1 (2006)

CONCERNS ABOUT LOBBYING

Widespread concerns about the influence of lobbyists have been addressed only half-heartedly through legal regulation. At the federal, state, and local levels of American government, numerous rules have been adopted to govern the conduct of lobbyists. Yet, many of those laws are so weak or incomplete that they do little to advance the cause of good government. Even the reforms recently passed by Congress are said by lobbyists to contain "ample loopholes for those seeking to buy access to lawmakers, mainly through campaign fund-raising."

Citizens following media reports might easily conclude that the situation is hopeless. However, this unfortunate state of affairs reflects a lack of political will—and the powerful influence of lobbyists—more than uncertainty as to what should be done. There are valuable legal steps that can and should be taken to minimize the risks that lobbying will corrupt the exercise of governmental power. As this article demonstrates, for virtually every problem that one can identify relating to lobbyists, some legislative body, somewhere in the country, has already found a plausible solution.

It is important to remember that regulating lobbyists is a continuing task that faces every generation. Even when reforms are passed, they are often eroded by legal changes subsequently made to "loosen" the rules when public attention is focused elsewhere. For example, the ban on gifts recently enacted by the U.S. House of Representatives is reminiscent of reforms passed in the mid-1990s, which substantially tightened the rules on gifts, but were relaxed after just four years in force. Regulation of lobbyists is a never ending task, just as ethics in government is a goal never permanently achieved.

. . . .

E.   The Goals of Lobbyist Regulations

Lobbying regulations are not meant to discourage persons from exercising their right to petition the government, nor to harass those who take advantage of that right. Rather, carefully crafted lobbyist rules should address five concerns of great importance to democratic institutions. The rules governing lobbyists should ensure (1) that all persons have a fair opportunity to be heard by the government, (2) that government enjoys the confidence of the people, (3) that official decisions are based on accurate information, (4) that the citizenry knows how the government operates, and (5) that the performance of public business benefits from the wisdom of the community.

The first objective is sometimes referred to as the "level-playing-field" concern. America has long been deeply committed to this principle. The right to a level playing field is sometimes called equal protection of the laws, as set down by the Equal Protection Clause of the Fourteenth Amendment. . . . In the lobbying context, practices that improperly give some persons advantages over others (such as gifts to public officials) run afoul of the "level-playing-field" principle.

The second objective in regulating lobbyists is to preserve public confidence in political institutions by ensuring that they are fair not only in operation, but also in appearance. In other words, it is necessary to avoid the "appearance of corruption." Perceived corruption, like corruption itself, can destroy a democratic institution. Thus, lobbyist rules should restrict practices that create an appearance of impropriety, such as business transactions between legislators and lobbyists, the presence of lobbyists on the floor of the House or Senate, or service by a lobbyist as the treasurer for a legislator's re-election campaign.

The third goal of lobbyist rules is to guarantee that public decisions are based upon accurate information. In this, as in other contexts, the law "presupposes that right conclusions are more likely to be gathered out of a multitude of tongues," than from a single voice. To avoid misunderstandings, the First Amendment favors the dissemination of more information, not less. Consequently, government ethics rules should not only ban culpable falsehoods by lobbyists, but also seek to move the debate of public issues into public view, where arguments can be considered, contested, and judged on their merits. In addition, through disclosure requirements, ethics rules should assist public representatives in scrutinizing the petitioners who come before them. . . . .

The fourth goal in regulating lobbyists is to ensure that people have access to accurate information about how the government operates. This knowledge is an essential component of representative government. Otherwise, the citizenry cannot accurately evaluate the performance of their representatives or cast ballots at the voting booth reflecting that assessment. In the words of Judge J. Skelly Wright, "the public has an interest in knowing who is influencing or attempting to influence their public officers, for what purpose, the means adopted to that purpose, and the results achieved." These concerns animate the lobbyist registration and reporting requirements that have been adopted at the federal, state, and local levels.

Finally, as a fifth objective, lobbyist rules should not impede lobbyists and their clients from contributing to the effective resolution of public issues. Because the American public is often reluctant to provide funding for the staffing and expertise needed by legislative bodies, administrative agencies, and other organs of government, official decision makers frequently operate with minimal support. Indeed, "[c]ongressional staffs rarely have the resources to gather their own data and examples." Such obstacles are also present at the state and local levels. Lobbyists who provide clear arguments and accurate information to public servants can play an important role in closing the gap between needs and resources. Consequently, the rules governing lobbyists should not impede those practices that assist the government in doing its work.

. . .

III. THE LEGAL TOOLS FOR REGULATING LOBBYISTS

The legal tools for regulating lobbyists come in two basic varieties: prohibitions and disclosure requirements. Legal prohibitions identify practices that are impermissible, either on all occasions or beyond specified limits. Such rules may be used to prohibit false statements, limit gifts to public officials or employees, restrict the scope or frequency of revolving-door employment, or bar lobbyists from collecting contingent fees or exacting economic reprisals against legislators.

Disclosure requirements, in contrast, do not ban particular practices. Rather, they expose information to community scrutiny by making data available to the public. . . . While conceptually appealing, disclosure requirements are hard to implement because it is difficult to determine what information should be reported, who should be required to report, and how that information can be made available to the public in a timely fashion. As a result, some disclosure schemes are exceedingly complex and, as a result, lack the ethical clarity and efficacy that simpler rules might provide.

A. Prohibitions

1. False Statements

False statements of fact can distort the decision-making process. This is as true in politics as it is in business. In the commercial context, numerous rules protect consumers and entities from the harm that erroneous information can cause. Tort actions for fraud and negligent misrepresentation, along with statutory claims for deceptive trade practices, exist in virtually all jurisdictions. However, there is an important distinction between political speech and commercial speech. The latter is afforded less protection by the Constitution and is therefore more susceptible to legal regulation. With respect to political speech, the Supreme Court has recognized that the "erroneous statement is inevitable in free debate, and that it must be protected if the freedoms of expression are to have the 'breathing space' that they 'need . . . to survive.' " Thus, civil or criminal liability is not typically imposed (on lobbyists or others) for false statements related to matters of public concern absent proof of "actual malice." Actual malice requires evidence that the defendant acted with knowledge of the falsity or in reckless disregard for the truth.

Liability for deception further requires a provably false assertion of fact. A pure statement of opinion that does not imply false facts does not give rise to liability. Presumably, these constitutional principles apply just as readily to lobbyist regulations as in other areas of the law. For example, a lobbyist's deliberate misrepresentation of product test results might give rise to legal sanctions, since test results are a matter of fact. However, a lobbyist's views about whether a proposed law would be beneficial to consumers would be beyond legal reproach, if such statements were purely opinion.

Prohibitions against false statements of fact by lobbyists are an important tool for preventing abuse. The Code of Ethics of the American League of Lobbyists supports the view that honesty and integrity are essential aspects of effective lobbying. Thus, provisions at the state and local levels which bar false statements by lobbyists stand on solid ground in terms of ethical and business principles. However, if such legal rules do not expressly include a culpability requirement, presumably they must be applied in a manner that is consistent with the First Amendment and the actual malice standard. This is important, for it is often difficult to establish actual malice. Even so, prohibitions against false statements by lobbyists are an important tool for preventing abuse. First, a ban on misrepresentations by lobbyists is an essential symbol, without which the moral force of a law purporting to regulate lobbyists is seriously undercut. Second, such restrictions are readily understood by the public, urged by reformers, and invoked by government "watchdogs." Third, the nature of modern communication sometimes makes it possible to prove actual malice. Lobbyists often rely on extensive written material to make the case for their clients. Electronic messages, including email, and surreptitious recordings can often be used to prove what was said and to scrutinize those statements. Consequently, there may be sufficient evidence for a fact finder to determine whether misrepresentations of fact were culpably false.

One type of falsehood that commonly arises in the government context is the creation of a false appearance of public approval for a particular government action. This manufacturing of an artificial substitute for authentic grassroots support is sometimes referred to as "astroturfing." Such misrepresentations by lobbyists are banned in some states and cities. For example, a San Antonio ordinance provides that "[a] person who lobbies . . . shall not cause any communication to be sent to a city official in the name of any fictitious person or in the name of any real person, except with the consent of such real person."

. . . .

2.   Gifts, Meals, Entertainment, and Travel

When lobbyists bestow gifts upon public servants, there is both an actual risk and an appearance of impropriety. The risk is that the lobbyist's client will enjoy an unfair advantage because the offering will induce the official or employee to make a decision calculated to repay the favor, rather than based on the merits. Even if the recipient has not been influenced by the gift, the public will perceive that the lobbyist's client enjoys an unfair advantage vis a vis others. Consequently, the gift will diminish confidence in the government, making democracy less effective.

Two common types of gifts that lobbyists give to public servants are meals and entertainment. It is difficult to see why either of these practices should be tolerated. Where the meals or entertainment are extravagant—as in the case of weekends at resorts, skybox seats, or trips abroad—the ethical issues are obvious. Where the amounts spent are small—as in the case of lunches during a legislative session—the expenditures nevertheless erode the public's confidence in its elected representatives. It appears that the parties footing the bills enjoy privileged standing that is not available to others who fail to proffer such gratuities. At the federal level, members of Congress and other public officials and employees are paid a living wage. There is no reason to rely on lobbyists to feed, clothe, or entertain federal public servants. At the state and local levels, some public officials are not paid adequately, but the solution to that problem is to pay them fair compensation, not to rely on lobbyists to cover the deficiency.

Public servants should not be permitted to sell their time. While "a steak . . . might not 'buy' lawmakers, . . . it's almost certain to buy access [to them]." Recent figures for the Texas legislature show that "[s]pending on food, entertainment, and gifts . . . [amounted] to about $15,900 worth of perks for each of the 181 lawmakers—more than double their $7,200-a-year salary." Until recently, many members of Congress flew on corporate jets at heavily discounted rates, "a practice that gives precious access to lobbyists, who often go along for the trip." Such "[t]rips 'violate the principle of fairness. In order to get this special kind of access, you have to pay a lot of money.'" Recently, the House and Senate banned such travel. The public is right to be concerned about gifts to public officials and their staff members, for "[a] review of thousands of state records shows legislation is often introduced by powerful lawmakers after lobbyists spend lavishly on their campaigns and entertain them."

The best practice is to ban gifts from lobbyists entirely. A total ban is easy to understand and enforce. However, total bans on gifts are extremely difficult to enact or continue in force. . . . At the federal level, the House recently passed a total ban on gifts from lobbyists, but a similar ban had been the law just a decade earlier, only to be jettisoned for more lenient rules when that was politically feasible. The recent House reform was quickly followed by a similar reform in the Senate.

Absent a total ban, a dollar limitation can be imposed on gifts from lobbyists. Such a restriction can be enforced through disclosure requirements that compel recipients or their lobbyist-donors to reveal the source, nature, and value of gifts. However, disclosure is not a panacea. A study of privately funded congressional travel found that disclosure forms were often too vague or incomplete to determine whether the trip was legitimate.

. . .

Beyond the issue of whether there is political resolve to limit gifts from lobbyists lies an important issue of equitable dimensions. That issue is the question of how to define a "lobbyist" for purposes of applying the rule. Does the term "lobbyist" only refer to someone who is paid to petition the government on behalf of another, or does the term also include persons who volunteer their services to represent others, or even individuals who act on their own behalf in petitioning the government? What good reason could justify allowing individual citizens or volunteer surrogates seeking to influence legislation or official decisions to give gifts to public servants, if paid surrogates are restricted from freely doing so? Should not the same rules apply to each type of actor? There is a serious risk that a rule drafted too narrowly will be circumvented. For example, although lobbyists are now prohibited from paying for travel by members of Congress, their clients may do so if the trip is connected to the members' official duties. A recent study showed that during a six-year period, "[p]rivate groups, corporations or trade associations—many with legislation that could affect them pending before Congress—paid nearly $50 million . . . to send members of Congress and their staffers on at least 23,000 trips overseas and within the United States."

. . .

3.   Campaign Contributions and Fundraising

The great exception to limitations on gifts by lobbyists is lawful campaign contributions made or orchestrated by lobbyists. Campaign money often dwarfs lobbyists' expenditures on gratuities such as meals, travel, and entertainment. Like gifts, those contributions can be a way to buy access to legislators and perhaps votes. In some cases, "[r]egular contributors attend dozens of fund-raisers a year and become part of the 'circuit' of lobbyists around a cadre of lawmakers and their committees . . . . Contacts are made, relationships formed, and networks established." Occasionally, the intent of a contribution is blatant. In 1995, an Ohio congressman "passed [campaign contribution] checks from tobacco lobbyists to other congressmen on the House floor while lawmakers were considering ending a tobacco subsidy."

Not surprisingly, some states impose special limitations on campaign donations by lobbyists. Kentucky has a flat ban on campaign contributions. Alaska provides a slight exception to its ban when the lobbyist's contribution goes to the candidate from the district where the lobbyist will be eligible to vote on election day. . . . Unfortunately, laws in a number of states dilute the effectiveness of their restrictions by providing that a ban on campaign contributions applies only when the legislature is in session. These half-hearted reform efforts seem to assume that either legislators or voters have very short attention spans.

. . .

Some lobbying firms have formed their own political action committees (PACs), which presumably are more effective at achieving their clients' goals. However, PACs have the added advantage of making the sources of campaign donations less clear to political watchdogs. Such conduct appears to run afoul of laws prohibiting lobbyists from directly or indirectly collecting contributions for a candidate.

4.   Revolving-Door Employment

Perhaps no problem in government ethics is easier to understand, or more difficult to address effectively, than that posed by "revolving-door employment." The risk is obvious that a client represented by a public-servant-turned-lobbyist will have, or will appear to have, an unfair advantage in petitioning the government. This type of conduct poses a significant threat to the integrity of democratic institutions. Consequently, Congress and a number of state legislatures have enacted laws addressing revolving-door employment. Indeed, even cities, including some with otherwise weak ethics codes, commonly have revolving-door limitations prohibiting former public officials or employees from "representing" private parties before the government for specified periods of time. Depending on how the relevant terms are defined, these city ordinances may treat lobbying as a form of "representation" and thus limit revolving-door lobbying. Yet, despite such restrictions at all levels of government, "[s]ome of the most successful [lobbyists] are former lawmakers[,] or former aides to lawmakers[,] who cycle in and out of government."

The problem with most restrictions on revolving-door employment is that they apply for too short a period of time. For example, with respect to lobbying by former state legislators, six states only require a two-year moratorium, twenty states have only a one-year moratorium, and one state has a mere six month moratorium. Other states have no revolving-door restrictions at all. Retired or defeated members of Congress "must sit out one year before doing active lobbying, although they can offer 'guidance' at up to $500,000 a year." Needless to say, the connections legislators accrue during years of service often last far longer than a year or two. This is particularly true at the federal level, where turnover in Congress is minimal due to careful redistricting that aggressively protects incumbents.

. . .

Some reformers also advocate placing limits on the ability of lobbyists to be appointed to positions in government. For example, during recent efforts to strengthen the law in Georgia an amendment was proposed that would have prevented "the appointment of lobbyists for one year following the expiration of the lobbyist's registration 'to any state office, board, authority, commission, or bureau' that regulates the activities of a firm on whose behalf they had lobbied." The City of Austin, Texas, prohibits lobbyists from being appointed to a "city-established board, commission, or committee within three years of engaging in lobbying activity." As a matter of public policy, these regulations make good sense. The underlying concern is similar to an "administrative capture" scenario, where an administrative agency is dominated by those it is supposed to regulate and becomes less effective as a result. By limiting the ease with which lobbyists are able to move into appointed governmental positions, revolving-door limitations preserve a healthy distance between those who seek the aid of government and those who make decisions.

5.   Contingent-Fee Lobbying

Some lobbyist compensation arrangements pose more serious threats to the public interest than others. A lobbyist whose fee is contingent on success has a greater incentive to "win at all costs," in contrast to lobbyists who are paid an hourly fee, a lump-sum fee, or a monthly retainer. As a result, contingent fee arrangements may promote the use of "improper means, such as distorting relevant facts, to ensure success." Contingent fees, or "success fees," may also over-compensate lobbyists.

. . .

Numerous court decisions have condemned lobbyists' contingent fees. For example, more than 130 years ago in Trist v. Child, the Supreme Court held that a contingent-fee agreement to lobby a private bill through Congress was void and unenforceable. Justice Swayne's opinion for the Court condemned lobbying generally, and contingent-fee lobbying in particular, regardless of whether there was evidence of actual abuse. "Where the avarice of the agent is inflamed by the hope of a reward contingent upon success, and to be graduated by a percentage upon the amount appropriated, the danger of tampering in its worst form is greatly increased." Other Supreme Court cases have held that "[c]ontingent fee contracts to secure Government business for the employer of the recipient are invalid because of their tendency to induce improper solicitation of public officers and the exercise of political pressure."

However, "there are no modern federal cases dealing with contingency fee lobbying." While Trist and related cases have not been overruled, some have expressed doubt about their continuing validity. Congress' recent failure to enact a ban on contingent-fee lobbying led one law review article to conclude that "lobbyists are still free to receive contingency fees for lobbying members of Congress." However, "[m]ost states prohibit the payment of fees contingent on the outcome of legislation and or administrative action." The same is true of many cities.

Yet, in other contexts no such action has been taken. This void represents an opportunity for strengthening the rules governing the conduct of lobbyists. It is bad enough that lobbying firms sometimes solicit clients "with virtual guarantees that they . . . [can] deliver 'dollars for pennies' (or billions for millions)." . . .

6. Business Transactions with and Employment by Lobbyists

Business transactions represent another means by which public officials and employees can become indebted to lobbyists. "[F]ormer House speaker James Wright was routinely paid huge sums of money for speaking to lobbyists, who covered the expense by 'buying' signed copies of his book for all of their members." Such transactions create an appearance of impropriety, threaten to bias public officials in favor of the lobbyist's clients, and generally compromise the goal of a level playing field in public life. Such ethical problems are exacerbated when the transaction involves payment of an amount in excess of fair market value. One newspaper reported that a city councilman offered his vanity-press Frankenstein sequel for $500 per autographed copy, and that an appreciative lobbyist paid that amount. Indiana, quite sensibly, bars state officers and employees from receiving compensation for "the sale or lease of any property or service which substantially exceeds that which . . . [he or she] would charge in the ordinary course of business."

Despite the obvious problems associated with business transactions between lobbyists and public servants, various obstacles stand in the way of crafting an effective ban on fair-market-value transactions. For example, a member of a city council may also own a coffee shop. Should it be impermissible for a lobbyist who represents clients before the city council to patronize that member's coffee shop occasionally? What if the lobbyist patronizes the coffee shop every day, or recruits his or her clients and their friends to do business at the establishment? A rule banning de minimis business transactions probably serves no good purpose, but differentiating those purchases from ones that are objectionable is difficult. One possible approach would be to exclude "routine" transactions, or transactions that do not create an appearance of impropriety. However, such vague distinctions may be subject to challenge on the ground that they fail to provide clear notice of what is prohibited.

. . .

Sound principles of government ethics hold that public representatives should be prohibited from engaging in outside employment that conflicts with official duties. Legislators should not be permitted to work simultaneously for a lobbyist if the interests of the lobbyist's clients could be affected by the official actions of the legislator. . . .

7.   Reciprocal Favors

Basic principles of good government suggest that official power should not be used to unfairly advance or impede private interests. That rule is sometimes expressly set out in city or state ethics codes. These codes provide that a public servant shall "not enter into an agreement or understanding with any other person that official action by the official or employee will be rewarded or reciprocated by the other person, directly or indirectly." In addition, municipal ethics codes and other laws often state that a public official or employee shall not take official action that supports the economic interests of a person with whom that official or employee is negotiating to secure subsequent employment. These are sound principles upon which to base the conduct of public affairs. Presumably, they should apply even when—or perhaps especially when—the reciprocal favor would be traded with a lobbyist, or when the subsequent employment would be arranged by a lobbyist.

. . .

8.   Lobbying by Closely Related Persons

There is an obvious appearance of impropriety when a public servant is lobbied by a close family member, who is acting on behalf of a third party. In such circumstances, it appears to observers that the family member is selling access to the public servant. This harms public confidence in government almost as much as if the public official personally charged petitioners for the privilege of being heard.

Harm to confidence in government can also occur when an elected representative dates a lobbyist who is representing private clients on matters for which the representative has official responsibility. . . . Some lobbying firms also "openly hire the friends of a particular member in order to get the legislator's ear.". . . In addition, legislative staff members often move on to lobbying firms after leaving the public sector. These problems relating to privileged access are sometimes susceptible to legal solutions. A rule banning lobbying by "friends" would be unenforceably vague and unworkable. However, provisions prohibiting lobbying by relatives or former staffers could be written in sufficiently specific terms that would pass constitutional muster.

. . .

9.   Lobbyists as Campaign Treasurers, Consultants, and Staff

A variety of cozy relationships between lobbyists and candidates or officeholders have become prevalent in recent years. In some cases, candidates sometimes select lobbyists to serve as campaign treasurers or in other campaign positions. These relationships send the message that advancing a client's interests depends more upon campaign money than upon the merits of the matter in question. Quite sensibly, some states bar lobbyists from serving in a fundraising capacity. The rationale underlying these regulations is a desire to counteract the threat that fundraising lobbyists will crowd other voices out of the debate. Moreover, lobbyists are supposed to aid the legislative process by bringing "information to law makers, who often have small staffs that are young and insufficiently paid." Where the focus is predominantly on fundraising, cogent arguments about the merits become less important. This is also true where the fundraising involves not the public official's campaign, but charities and other private institutions favored by the official. Some states expressly prohibit lobbyists from engaging "in any charitable fund-raising activity at the request of an official or employee." Other states have more flexible rules. For example, Kentucky allows legislators and candidates to solicit contributions "on behalf of charitable, civic, or educational entities provided the solicitations are broad-based and are not directed solely or primarily at legislative agents [i.e., lobbyists]."

Some lobbying groups also provide campaign "consultants" to candidates. Those consultants can ultimately play a "key part in access and lobbying battles after candidates become elected public officials." For this reason, it becomes "hard to tell where lobbying end[s] and public service beg[ins]." Astute observers of government rightfully ask whether it is "ethical to have reciprocal relationships among consultants, lobbyists, and public officials [where] those alliances are not transparent and . . . seem to go against the public interest."

. . .

10.   Make-Work Legislative Proposals

Many states prohibit lobbyists from introducing legislation solely for the purpose of securing future employment either to ensure the law's passage or defeat. Such limitations share a common objective with ethics rules and other laws that prohibit attorneys and their clients from engaging in frivolous litigation. The goal in both of these contexts is to avoid wasting valuable public and private resources on initiatives that do not further legitimate purposes.

NOTES & QUESTIONS

1.   Notice how closely these suggestions track the issues in the Abramoff scandal.

2.   Which of these suggestions will be most effective? Which will be least effective? Do any of the suggested reforms trigger Constitutional concerns?

3.   "Revolving door" happens when a public official or employee leaves the public sector to become a lobbyist. Most states now mandate a legal waiting period before such a person can perform lobbying activities. These periods typically range between six months to two years, but starting on December 31, 2022 Florida will have the longest cooling off period in the country at six years. The National Council of State Legislatures provides a chart of state restrictions at: https://www.ncsl.org/research/ethics/50-state-table-revolving-door-prohibitions.aspx.

A 2016 study found that 25% of 1,275 U.S. House members and 29% of 254 U.S. Senators who left Congress between 1976 and 2012 registered as lobbyists.

Currently, federal ethics laws provide minimal protections against influence-peddling by former members of Congress. Former U.S. Representatives cannot lobby their ex-colleagues for one year and former Senators have a two-year ban.

Former lawmakers, however, can lobby executive agency personnel. They can also act as "consultants" and work with registered lobbyists on the best way to lobby lawmakers. Recently the House passed a bill that would have closed the consultant loophole. Other lawmakers have proposed even greater restrictions. Sen. Jon Tester (D-Mont.) proposed a five-year ban on lobbying for former members of Congress and the executive branch. Sen. Elizabeth Warren (D-Mass.) proposed permanently banning all elected officials from lobbying.

2.   DISCLOSURE & RESTRICTIONS

One of the most effective tools to regulate lobbyists is required disclosure of who is acting as a lobbyist, their activities, and who exactly is paying them and what they are expected to accomplish for the fee.

2 U.S.C.A. § 1603. REGISTRATION OF LOBBYISTS
(effective September 14, 2007)

(a) **Registration**

(1) General rule

No later than 45 days after a lobbyist first makes a lobbying contact or is employed or retained to make a lobbying contact, whichever is earlier, or on the first business day after such 45th day if the 45th day is not a business day, such lobbyist (or, as provided under paragraph (2), the organization employing such lobbyist), shall register with the Secretary of the Senate and the Clerk of the House of Representatives.

(2)   Employer filing

Any organization that has 1 or more employees who are lobbyists shall file a single registration under this section on behalf of such employees for each client on whose behalf the employees act as lobbyists.

(3)   Exemption

(A)   General rule. Notwithstanding paragraphs (1) and (2), a person or entity whose—

(i)   total income for matters related to lobbying activities on behalf of a particular client (in the case of a lobbying firm) does not exceed and is not expected to exceed $2,500; or

(ii)   total expenses in connection with lobbying activities (in the case of an organization whose employees engage in lobbying activities on its own behalf) do not exceed or are not expected to exceed $10,000, (as estimated under section 1604 of this title) in the quarterly period described in section 1604(a) of this title during which the registration would be made is not required to register under this subsection with respect to such client.

. . .

(b)   **Contents of registration.** Each registration under this section shall contain—

(1)   the name, address, business telephone number, and principal place of business of the registrant, and a general description of its business or activities;

(2)   the name, address, and principal place of business of the registrant's client, and a general description of its business or activities (if different from paragraph (1));

(3)   the name, address, and principal place of business of any organization, other than the client, that—

(A)   contributes more than $5,000 to the registrant or the client in the quarterly period to fund the lobbying activities of the registrant; and

(B)   actively participates in the planning, supervision, or control of such lobbying activities;

(4)   the name, address, principal place of business, amount of any contribution of more than $5,000 to the lobbying activities of the registrant, and approximate percentage of equitable ownership in the client (if any) of any foreign entity that—

(A)   holds at least 20 percent equitable ownership in the client or any organization identified under paragraph (3);

(B) directly or indirectly, in whole or in major part, plans, supervises, controls, directs, finances, or subsidizes the activities of the client or any organization identified under paragraph (3); or

(C) is an affiliate of the client or any organization identified under paragraph (3) and has a direct interest in the outcome of the lobbying activity;

(5) a statement of—

(A) the general issue areas in which the registrant expects to engage in lobbying activities on behalf of the client; and

(B) to the extent practicable, specific issues that have (as of the date of the registration) already been addressed or are likely to be addressed in lobbying activities; and

(6) the name of each employee of the registrant who has acted or whom the registrant expects to act as a lobbyist on behalf of the client and, if any such employee has served as a covered executive branch official or a covered legislative branch official in the 20 years before the date on which the employee first acted as a lobbyist on behalf of the client, the position in which such employee served.

NOTES & QUESTIONS

1.   Prof. Johnson writes: "Lobbying that occurs in the open is less objectionable than lobbying that occurs behind closed doors. Statements made in public by lobbyists can be scrutinized by others and challenged with competing facts and arguments. The resulting public debate is consistent with a healthy political process. In contrast, statements made by lobbyists that are hidden from public view cannot easily be probed or disputed. Consequently, inaccurate assertions may go uncontested. Lobbyist disclosure requirements reflect these concerns. As a result, statements made by lobbyists at public meetings, in publicly available documents, or through mass media are typically exempted from the definition of what constitutes lobbying. Such activities, as well as expenditures or income related thereto, normally do not need to be revealed. Vincent R. Johnson, "Regulating Lobbyists: Law, Ethics, and Public Policy," 16 *Cornell J.L. & Pub. Pol'y* 1 (2006).

2.   How effective are disclosure laws? Often it is difficult just to define what constitutes "lobbying:" "Disclosure laws typically incorporate intricate formulations that exclude from the definition of "lobbying" the activities of media outlets, churches, whistle blowers, persons responding to agency requests for public comment, individuals seeking to resolve problems related to government benefits, employment, or personal matters, certain governmental entities, and others. In addition to direct contacts with government officials or employees, disclosure laws regulate indirect or "grassroots" lobbying." Vincent R. Johnson, "Regulating Lobbyists: Law, Ethics, and Public Policy," 16 *Cornell J.L. & Pub. Pol'y* 1 (2006).

3.　　What would a useful disclosure regime include?

4.　　When Barack Obama was running for President he stated, "When I'm president of the United States, if you want to work for my administration, you can't leave my administration and then go lobby." Closing the "revolving door," where lobbyists join the administration and then go back to lobbying, was part of Obama's campaign promise to change to business as usual in Washington. He promised to not hire registered lobbyists and to impose new restrictions on people leaving his administration for the private sector. To get around these rules, many lobbyists who dreamed of a job with the Obama Administration unregistered as lobbyists. Further, many leaving the government work found loopholes that allowed them to perform the activities of a lobbyist without having to register.

By 2014, the Obama administration had hired more than 70 previously registered lobbyists, and many officials had left the government to become "consultants" doing things that would be thought of as lobbying activities. Another way to skirt the executive order was for a person to spend less than 20% or more of his or her time directly lobbying do not have to register.

From the time Obama took office until 2015, the number of registered lobbyists declined from 14,173 to 11,165. Those people did not have file any disclosure about their activities and clients under the Lobbying Disclosure Act. One K Street veteran said, "There is no doubt that there is this underground lobbying railroad where people aren't registered, but they are involved in advocating on behalf of clients." See, Kate Ackley, "Obama's Unlobbyists," *Roll Call*, April 28, 2014; Josh Gerstein, "How Obama failed to shut Washington's revolving door," *Politico*, December 31, 2015.

5.　　Craig Holman, a registered lobbyist with Public Citizen, said he'd like a professional investigative agency that could audit unregistered Washington policy advisers. "The solution to the problem is not to get rid of all these ethics requirements," Holman said. "The solution is to create an enforcement agency to enforce the law." See, Kate Ackley, "Obama's Unlobbyists," *Roll Call*, April 28, 2014. What are the pros and cons of this suggestion?

6.　　The U.S. House Clerk maintains a searchable database of lobbying activity. The lobbyist files a quarterly report for activity with each client. See, https://lobbyingdisclosure.house.gov/. For instance, if you search the activity of "The King of K Street" Edward Newberry's activity in 2020 you find four reports detailing his work for The Pebble Partnership. The proposed Pebble Mine would be a mile long and mile wide open pit copper and gold mine in Alaska. Environmentalists claim the Pebble Mine will destroy wetlands and 81 miles of Alaskan salmon streams. The Obama Administration stopped the mine's construction, only to have the Trump led EPA reverse course and allow it. In late 2020 the Army Corps of Engineers again halted the project. In 2020, Squire Patton Boggs reported that The Pebble Partnership paid the firm approximately $320,000 for the lobbying services of Newberry and four other lobbyists.

7. In a not-so-subtle response to Jack Abramoff becoming a lobbyist again, in late 2018 Congress passed the Justice Against Corruption on K Street Act of 2018 or the "JACK Act." This amendment to the Lobbying Disclosure Act (LDA) to requires lobbyists to disclose on registrations and quarterly activity reports whether the person has been convicted of a federal or state offense for bribery, extortion, embezzlement, taking kickbacks, tax evasion, fraud, conflicts of interest, making a false statement, perjury, or money laundering. See, https://lobbyingdisclosure.house.gov/Notice_re_JACK_Act.pdf. Is this a valuable change to the disclosure laws?

GAINING ACCESS: A STATE LOBBYING CASE STUDY
Trevor D. Dryer, 23 *Journal of Law & Politics* 283, 319–24 (2007)

The lobbyists I interviewed all believed (not surprisingly) that the reform proposals of recent years are largely ineffectual and quite costly. While nobody appeared to pine away for the days when lobbyists could personally funnel unlimited amounts of cash to legislators on behalf of wealthy clients, lobbyists thought that Proposition 34 and recent disclosure laws caused unnecessary work for them and an unnecessary expense for taxpayers. Under the current system, California law requires lobbyists to file quarterly lobbying reports disclosing campaign contributions they have made and any amount of money they have spent to influence members of the legislature. In order to provide accurate reporting, most of the lobbyists stated that they keep extensive logs about who they meet and whether anything of value was exchanged. These logs are tallied up in quarterly reports submitted to the California Fair Political Practice Commission, which publishes electronic versions on the Internet. These arduous reporting requirements, coupled with strict Assembly and Senate gift laws that prohibit gifts (including meals) with a value over $10, deters most lobbyist from directly giving to legislators. Despite these gift laws, lobbyists reported that they typically still meet over meals with legislators; the legislators just make sure to pick up their own tab. The lobbyists I interviewed believed that nearly all reports filed and posted on the Internet contain useless information, as lobbyists do not have anything to report either in the way of campaign contributions or money expended on activities.

Indeed, I surveyed the reports for the years 1999–2005 filed by the lobbyists I interviewed: on nearly all of the quarterly filings, the lobbyist listed that he or she had nothing to report. Although the California Secretary of State posts the names of all registered lobbyists, their employer, and their employer's clients on the web, it is impossible to tell from the mandatory reports who the lobbyists met and what was being discussed. One lobbyist summed up the position of virtually all of the interviewees: "All of this [disclosure] is a monumental waste of time. It's extremely bureaucratic . . . like trying to do your own taxes . . . you can do it, but to really do a good job, you have to spend hours." Most of the lobbyists did not advocate for eliminating the reporting and disclosure requirements altogether, but simply suggested simplification that would provide the public with what they termed "useful" information and create an incentive for lobbyists to conduct themselves above board. A small but significant group of respondents were openly hostile to reforms in general and were pessimistic that reforms could actually have a positive impact on the process. . . .

Some lobbyists stressed that that no matter what reforms are enacted, there will always be people willing to engage in illegal or ethically questionable activity. One lobbyist, citing the Jack Abramoff scandal, noted that, "Money in politics confuses who is your constituent. Campaigns are expensive and you buy votes by giving [legislators] the money to finance a campaign. Big political scandals will always happen." Another maintained that current laws against bribery and fraud were adequate. "Compared to many countries in the world, America's problems are remarkably benign. Bribery is still punished and the laws won't prevent things like Duke Cunningham and Jack Abramoff from happening."

. . .

Despite their somewhat pessimistic outlook on current attempts at reform, many of the lobbyists indicated that they thought beneficial reform was possible and would serve the public interest (by increasing lobbyist and legislator accountability). Many of the suggestions for reform centered on changes to the reporting system. Several lobbyists advocated moving to a real-time, searchable, web-based reporting system that would provide truly useful information to citizens, such as who lobbyists meet and what topics they discuss:"[The current reporting system] is a waste of taxpayer money and embarrassment to government. It's not timely. You need real time reporting on a weekly basis. Most firms track real time, and it could easily be sent in on weekly basis." "Disclosure makes sense. It would do a lot if we had an easy database to link up meetings with donations." "The current system just doesn't serve a public purpose that couldn't be more easily reached by a web-based system available to public real-time that reported just things that reporters or citizens are interested in—who is giving what money to what candidate and through or by whom. That's what we should focus on, yet the current [regime] doesn't do that at all."

. . .

Another respondent suggested simply regulating the time, manner, and place of speech without altering limitation on speech itself. Under such a system, the state would enact a law prohibiting giving, receiving, or arranging of campaign contributions while the legislature is in active session. In California, the Legislature is in active session from January to September. Even when the body is in session, the lobbyist explained, members attend almost daily fundraisers held at noon and in the evenings. "Everyone knows when various legislative deadlines are to get bills out of committee or to a full vote on the floor," he explained. "It's no coincidence that key fundraisers are set up five days or two weeks before the deadlines when almost every lobbyist or interest group has something they're trying to pass or kill. . . . There is all the incentive in the world [for the lobbyist] to show up with a happy face." He believed that forcing fundraising into the four-month period when the legislature is out of session would force both legislators and lobbyists to "focus on the long term" and remove some of the pressure to vote a certain way because of large donations the legislator just received. He further suggested that cabining fundraising would allow people to look at the legislative record for the previous session, which he felt would give fundraising a "decidedly different tone."

NOTES & QUESTIONS

1.   Mr. Dryer points out that while disclosure systems have flaws, they have worked well in other contexts such as in the SEC's regulation of the securities markets and nutritional labeling.

2.   How would reliance on disclosure rather than restrictions avoid Constitutional problems relating to judicial decisions on political giving and spending?

SCHICKEL V. DILGER

United States Court of Appeals, Sixth Circuit
925 F.3d 858 (6th Cir. 2019)

[Note: Appellant, Kentucky state senator John Schickel, alleged that several of Kentucky's campaign finance and ethics statutes violated their rights protected by the First and Fourteenth Amendments. Schickel, in part, challenged seven recent changes to the ethics laws regulating the conduct of legislators and lobbyists. These included:

A ban on lobbyists making campaign contributions to a legislative candidate and a prohibition on candidates from accepting these contributions;

a ban on political contributions by the employer of a lobbyist or a political action committee (PAC) during the legislative session;

a gift ban prohibiting a legislator or their spouse from accepting "anything of value" from a lobbyist or their employer: and

A prohibition on lobbyists from either serving as a campaign treasurer, or directly soliciting, controlling, or delivering a campaign contribution to a legislator or candidate.

The district court found that the laws burdened "core political speech" and curtailed freedom of association, requiring strict scrutiny of every ethics provision except the regular session contribution ban. The District Court upheld the regular session contribution ban but found the other ethics provisions unconstitutional. In discussing the gift ban the judge stated,

> As discussed, the scope of the gift ban is so broad that even a glass of water may be considered a violation. Plaintiffs argue that if water is an item of value, then so might be the heating of a building on a cold winter day, or air-conditioned cooling in the middle of the summer. Not knowing what otherwise mundane amenities may constitute something of "value" would cause hesitation on the part of a legislator if invited to a lobbyist's office to discuss a matter of importance.

The ruling, however, alarmed Kentucky's Attorney General, who called it a "very dangerous decision," that "opens the door for a significant amount of corruption." George Troutman, chairman of the Kentucky Legislative Ethics Commission, said that although it's hard to argue against a lawmaker accepting a cup of coffee from a lobbyist, "But, everybody being human beings, it may not stop at a cup of coffee. It may stop at a fancy dinner in the Caribbean." Sen. Schickel said state and federal prosecutors should go after lawmakers who accept bribes. Kentucky appealed the case to the 6th Circuit.]

COOK, CIRCUIT JUDGE.

. . .

We now examine the legislators' challenges to the constitutionality of the three ethics provisions that target their own conduct: the contribution ban, regular session contribution ban, and gift ban.

. . .

The legislators argue that limiting their receiving contributions burdens political speech. But contribution limits entail "only a marginal restriction upon the contributor's ability to engage in free communication," as they permit "the symbolic expression of support evidenced by a contribution but do[ ] not in any way infringe the contributor's freedom to discuss candidates and issues." *Buckley v. Valeo* (1976). As such, they are subject to closely drawn scrutiny, a "lesser but still 'rigorous standard of review.'" *McCutcheon v. FEC* (2014). And contribution *bans*—such as those enacted here—receive the same treatment. *FEC v. Beaumont* (2003) (expressly declining to apply strict scrutiny to a contribution ban).

The same goes for the gift ban. Restrictions on gift giving, like those on contributions, are marginal restrictions that do not in any way hinder lobbyists' or legislators' ability to discuss candidates or issues. Indeed, if contribution restrictions "lie closer to the edges than to the core of political expression," gifts of value hug the fringe. *See United States v. Ring*, 706

F.3d 460, 466 (D.C. Cir. 2013) ("[T]he First Amendment interest in giving hockey tickets to public officials is, at least compared to the interest in contributing to political campaigns, de minimis.").

C.   Applying Closely Drawn Scrutiny

Closely drawn scrutiny requires the Commonwealth to demonstrate that each provision furthers "a sufficiently important interest and employs means closely drawn to avoid unnecessary abridgement of associational freedoms." *McCutcheon*.

1.   Do the challenged provisions further a "sufficiently important" government interest?

The Commonwealth asserts a familiar interest for the ethics provisions: the prevention of actual quid pro quo corruption or its appearance. This interest has long been considered sufficiently important to justify regulating campaign contributions, and "may properly be labeled 'compelling,' so that [it] would satisfy even strict scrutiny." *McCutcheon*, 572 U.S. at 199.

It follows that this focus on preventing corruption or its appearance would also justify Kentucky's gift ban. *See Fla. Ass'n of Prof'l Lobbyists, Inc. v. Div. of Legislative Info. Servs. of the Fla. Office of Legislative Servs.*, (11th Cir. 2008). But having an undeniably important interest is not enough; Kentucky must still "demonstrate *how* its [ethics provisions] further[ ]" that interest.

To do so, Kentucky must show only "a cognizable *risk* of corruption"— a "*risk* of quid pro quo corruption or its appearance." *McCutcheon; see Citizens United v. FEC*, (2010) (noting that "restrictions on direct contributions are *preventative*" and that the *Buckley* Court "sustained limits on direct contributions in order to *ensure against* the reality or appearance of corruption") (emphases added). The threat of corruption must be more than "mere conjecture," and cannot be "illusory." But a state need not produce evidence of actual instances of corruption.

The Commonwealth's briefs describe a sordid history. In the wake of an infamous FBI investigation into public corruption in Kentucky that led to "the indictment and conviction of legislators, former legislators, and lobbyists for criminal misconduct," known as Operation BOPTROT, the state legislature enacted the Ethics Code. In the aftermath of BOPTROT, the public lost faith in its elected officials, and public standing plunged to an all-time low. Corruption was rampant and came cheap—in some cases, legislators accepted as little as $400 from lobbyists in exchange for influencing legislation.

Kentucky's stated interest "[is] neither novel nor implausible." The contribution ban—enacted against this backdrop and untouched by the 2014 amendments—plainly furthers Kentucky's anticorruption interest.

Its own supreme court agreed, rejecting several constitutional challenges to the Code's provisions by an employer of lobbyists and holding that the state demonstrated "a compelling interest in insuring the proper operation of a democratic government and deterring corruption, as well as the appearance of corruption." *Assoc. Indus. v. Kentucky (1995).*

The legislators argue that Operation BOPTROT involved only the horse racing industry, and therefore cannot serve as the basis for restrictions on all lobbyists. Given that lobbyists were caught up in BOPTROT, however, we find this argument specious. A state need not wait for the entanglement of every industry or every lobbyist in scandal before taking action.

Kentucky also demonstrated how the regular session contribution ban, created by the 2014 amendments, furthers this anticorruption interest. The risk of corruption stemming from contributions by employers of lobbyists or PACs *during* a regular session of the legislature "is common sense and far from illusory." The regular session runs, at most, from early January to March 30th (in odd-numbered years) or April 15th (in even-numbered years). Stifling direct contributions from two of the most powerful players in the political arena during these three or so months undoubtedly furthers Kentucky's interest in preventing the appearance of corruption.

In the years since the Code's enactment, history confirms that contributions from lobbyists, their employers, and PACs, as well as gifts from lobbyists, suggest quid pro quo corruption or its appearance.

Further, if lobbyists' employers and PACs were "free to contribute to legislators while pet projects sit before them, the temptation to exchange 'dollars for political favors' [would] be powerful." Even though PACs and lobbyists' employers may "have no intention of directly 'purchasing' favorable treatment, appearances may be otherwise." *Id.* Where "the conflict of interest is apparent [and] the likelihood of stealth great," we will not require Kentucky to "experience the very problem it fears before taking appropriate prophylactic measures."

As for the removal of the de minimis exception from the gift ban, we note that the Commonwealth enacted this exception at the same time as the contribution limit—in the immediate aftermath of the BOPTROT scandal. Removing the exception simply changed the limit on gifts from $100 to $0. Kentucky's choice to reduce the limit to $0, we think, "goes to whether the limit is sufficiently tailored, not whether [Kentucky] had a sufficiently important interest to justify setting any [gift] limit at all." But even if we required a showing that its decision to remove this exception furthers its anticorruption interest, Kentucky has done so.

As KLEC's representative explained, removing the de minimis exception—and the administrative blunders that accompanied it—helps prevent the appearance of corruption. To be sure, KLEC's representative admitted that the de minimis exception "had not developed into an ethics problem," but that it was an "administrative" and "public perception" problem. Administering the exception led to "incorrect reports that include[d] legislators who didn't even attend events or didn't eat or drink at the events but they're getting their name publicized." Faced with this issue, the legislature decided to entirely close this "loophole in the law" by "paint[ing] a brighter line for the General Assembly and the public to know that legislators are not taking anything of value."

Kentucky is not an outlier. Both before the district court and on appeal, Kentucky cited the laws and experiences of other states to justify the removal of the de minimis exception. The Commonwealth took this action after KLEC recommended it, grounding the recommendation on its research of governmental ethics issues, a task assigned to it by statute. Its research yielded plentiful and detailed newspaper accounts from across the country "supporting inferences of impropriety" arising from gifts of value, including several that discussed how lobbyists and their employers skirted de minimis exceptions with tickets to sporting events, rounds of golf, and cigars. In addition to its recommendation, KLEC compiled these news articles into Ethics . . .

Tellingly, perhaps, of the 138 members of the Kentucky General Assembly, only one member—the member who initiated this lawsuit— voted against the 2014 amendments that enacted the regular session ban and removed the de minimis exception. Just as the overwhelming seventy-four-percent statewide vote in favor of the contribution limits in *Shrink* helped demonstrate the state's interest, so too this landslide vote. Had the legislators made a showing of their own to cast doubt on the evidence presented here, Kentucky might have needed to show more. . But on this record, Kentucky adequately illustrated that these ethics provisions further the sufficiently important interest of preventing quid pro quo corruption or its appearance.

2.   Are the challenged provisions closely drawn?

To clear the second hurdle of the closely drawn test, a state must show it employed "means closely drawn to avoid unnecessary abridgment of associational freedoms." *McCutcheon.* This requires "a fit that is not necessarily perfect, but reasonable; that represents not necessarily the single best disposition but one whose scope is 'in proportion to the interest served,' . . . that employs not necessarily the least restrictive means but . . . a means narrowly tailored to achieve the desired objective." *Id.* In conducting such review, of course, we owe "proper deference to a [legislative] determination of the need for a prophylactic rule [to address] the evil of potential corruption." *Nat'l Conservative Political Action Comm.,* 470 U.S. at 500.

Contribution Ban. This provision prohibits a legislator from accepting a campaign contribution from a lobbyist. Not long ago, the Fourth Circuit applied closely drawn scrutiny and upheld a complete ban on campaign contributions by lobbyists. *Preston,* 660 F.3d at 729, 735–36. There, plaintiff argued that the provision was not closely drawn because the state "could have allowed for ... small donations ... without undermining its interest in preventing actual and perceived corruption." The court rejected this argument, reasoning that, in response to recent scandals, the legislature made the "rational judgment that a complete ban was necessary as a prophylactic to prevent not only actual corruption but also [its] appearance." *Id.* The court also emphasized that the ban aimed only at lobbyists "who, experience has taught, are especially susceptible to political corruption." *Id.* at 737. "This is both an important and a legitimate legislative judgment that '[c]ourts simply are not in the position to second-guess,' especially 'where corruption is the evil feared.' " *Id.* at 736 (citation omitted).

The Fourth Circuit's reasoning persuades us. Lobbyists' role undoubtedly sharpens the risk of corruption and its appearance. *See Wagner,* 793 F.3d at 22; To be sure, "[t]he role of a lobbyist is both legitimate and important to legislation and government decision making, but by its very nature, it is prone to corruption and therefore especially susceptible to public suspicion of corruption." *Preston,* 660 F.3d at 737. Indeed, contributions and gifts from lobbyists and others who have a "particularly direct financial interest in these officials' policy decisions pose a heightened risk of actual and apparent corruption, and merit heightened government regulation." *Ognibene,* 671 F.3d at 188; *see Preston,* 660 F.3d at 737 ("*Any payment* made by a lobbyist to a public official, whether a campaign contribution or simply a gift, calls into question the propriety of the relationship, and therefore North Carolina could rationally adjudge that it should ban *all* payments.").

We find no merit to the legislators' argument that only *recent* scandals justify a contribution ban. Courts do not require a recent scandal; indeed, the Supreme Court views contribution limits as *preventative* measures. *Citizens United,* 558 U.S. at 356 (noting the preventative nature of direct contribution restrictions because "the scope of such pernicious practices can never be reliably ascertained"). We do not require Kentucky "to experience the very problem it fears before taking appropriate prophylactic measures." *Ognibene,* 671 F.3d at 188.

Yes, a total ban presents a significant restriction. But under the closely drawn standard, "[e]ven a 'significant interference with protected rights' of political association may be sustained." *McCutcheon,* 572 U.S. at 197. While this ban dispenses with one means a legislator has to gather funds, it leaves open others less susceptible to the same risk of corruption or its appearance, and thus survives closely drawn scrutiny. *See Preston,* 660

F.3d at 734 (finding that the ban "serv[ed] only as a channeling device, cutting off the avenue of association and expression that is most likely to lead to corruption but allowing numerous other avenues of association and expression").

Regular Session Contribution Ban. This provision broadens the reach of the contribution ban; it prohibits a legislator from accepting campaign contributions from employers of lobbyists and PACs, though only during a regular legislative session. The district court upheld the ban, relying primarily on two cases. *See Bartlett,* 168 F.3d at 715–16 (finding a nearly identical ban closely drawn because it applied to only two of the "most ubiquitous and powerful players in the political arena," and did "nothing more than place a temporary hold" on the ability to contribute during the time when the risk of corruption is highest); *Kimbell,* 665 A.2d at 51 (finding a ban on contributions by lobbyists during active legislative sessions closely drawn because it focused on "a narrow period during which legislators could be, or could appear to be, pressured, coerced, or tempted into voting on the basis of cash contributions"). We agree.

First, this time-specific ban restricts less than would an absolute ban, *Lavin,* 689 F.3d at 548, and targets the time when the risk of quid pro quo corruption—especially its appearance—is highest, *Bartlett,* 168 F.3d at 716. Indeed, contributions to a legislator (or his challenger) when a legislator is poised to cast a favorable (or unfavorable) vote on a pet bill could cause Kentuckians to question whether the contribution motivated the vote. *See id.* ("[T]he temptation to exchange 'dollars for political favors' can be powerful."). For that reason, we assess this limited ban as permissible. As the Supreme Court emphasized, "the danger of corruption and the appearance of corruption apply with equal force to challengers and to incumbents," justifying "imposing the *same* fundraising constraints upon both." *Buckley,* 424 U.S. at 33, 96 S.Ct. 612 (emphasis added).

In addition to the time limitation, the Commonwealth limited the coverage of this ban to two of the "most ubiquitous and powerful players in the political arena." *Bartlett,* 168 F.3d at 716. Though these players can significantly inform the legislative process, "there remain powerful hydraulic pressures at play [that] can cause both legislators and lobbyists to cross the line." *Id.* The legislators take issue with the scope of this ban, arguing that it covers "[e]ach and every PAC," not just those that employ lobbyists, as was the case in *Bartlett.* 168 F.3d at 714. But Kentucky similarly limited the definition of what constitutes a PAC. As we noted over twenty years ago, the Kentucky General Assembly "explicitly narrow[ed] the definition of 'permanent committee' to encompass only those organizations which expressly advocate the election or defeat of clearly identified candidate(s)." *Terry,* 108 F.3d at 643.

The level of scandal uncovered by Operation BOPTROT, as well as the experiences of other states, provides more than "scant evidence" that lobbyists sometimes turn to employers and PACs to achieve their ends. *McConnell,* 540 U.S. at 232. Indeed, if we upheld the absolute ban on lobbyist contributions but struck down this restriction, we would be inviting the very circumvention proscribed by this provision. Because this provision "does nothing more than recognize that lobbyists"—and their employers and narrowly-defined PACs—"are paid to persuade legislators, not to purchase them," *Bartlett,* 168 F.3d at 718, and that contributions made by these power players during an active session are particularly likely to give rise to the appearance of corruption, we find this time-limited ban closely drawn.

Gift Ban. The gift ban provision prohibits a legislator or his spouse from soliciting, accepting, or agreeing to accept "anything of value" from a lobbyist or his employer. We again see no constitutional problem here. The gift ban does not prevent lobbyists and legislators from meeting to discuss pressing issues facing Kentuckians. To be sure, it does not forbid *any* interaction or the utterance of *any* word between the two. They may associate as often as they wish over a cup of coffee or dinner or baseball game. This law simply requires that, if they do, legislators pay their own way. A fair, reasonable way of preventing quid pro quo corruption and its appearance.

In addition, we reject the legislators' argument that permitting events where all legislators are invited and not requiring reporting of who attended such events makes these provisions underinclusive. This exception *permits* associations and facilitates speech between lobbyists and legislators without undercutting Kentucky's stated interest or abridging associational freedoms. Through this carve out, Kentucky encourages interactions that are less likely to raise concerns about actual or apparent corruption. Thus, this provision survives closely drawn review.

Having found these provisions closely drawn, we turn to examine the legislators' other arguments for striking down the gift ban—that it is content based, a violation of their right to equal protection, vague, and overbroad. As to each, we disagree.

D.   Content-Based Restriction on Speech

The legislators argue that the gift ban provision is a content-based restriction because it "targets gifts based on the identity of the giver." But speaker-based bans are not automatically content based or content neutral. Rather, because "[s]peech restrictions based on the identity of the speaker are all too often simply a means to control content," *Citizens United,* 558 U.S. at 340, such laws "demand strict scrutiny when the legislature's speaker preference reflects a content preference." To make this determination, we follow the framework set out by the Supreme Court in *Reed*, 135 S. Ct. at 2230.

A law reflects a content preference when it cannot be "justified without reference to the content of the regulated speech" or was "adopted by the government 'because of disagreement with the message [the speech] conveys.'" In making this determination, "[t]he government's purpose is the controlling consideration." *Ward*, 491 U.S. at 791. "[A] regulation that serves purposes unrelated to the content of expression is deemed neutral, even if it has an incidental effect on some speakers or messages but not others." *See McCullen v. Coakley*, 573 U.S. 464, 480. The gift ban provision passes this test.

Again, Kentucky's purpose was clear: To protect the integrity of the legislative process and avoid the reality or appearance that state legislation was being bought and sold. Such a purpose reflects a preference for a state legislature that maintains the trust of its citizens, not for the expression of certain content. *See McCullen*. Nor have the legislators offered any evidence that the provision was adopted by Kentucky "because of disagreement with the message [the speech] conveys." *Reed*, 135 S. Ct. at 2227. It applies to gifts that are "pecuniary or compensatory in value," regardless of whether they convey any message at all.

In *Reed*, the Court discussed speaker-based bans and explained that a law limiting the content of newspapers—and only newspapers—could not avoid strict scrutiny "simply because it could be characterized as speaker based." So too, a "content-based law that restricted the political speech of all corporations would not become content neutral just because it singled out corporations as a class of speakers." *Reed*, at bottom, teaches us to be wary of speaker-based restrictions that are nothing more than content-based restrictions in disguise. And wary we are. Kentucky's gift ban provision, however, serves an anticorruption purpose unrelated to the content of expression and is justified without any reference to the content of the gifts regulated. *See Ward*.

Since the gift ban provision is content neutral, it is "subject to an intermediate level of scrutiny." *Turner*, 512 U.S. at 642. Thus, just as the other First Amendment challenges here, we apply closely drawn scrutiny. *See Zimmerman*, 881 F.3d at 384–85 (rejecting argument that base contribution limit was content based and applying closely drawn scrutiny). Again, the Commonwealth has demonstrated that the gift ban advances its anticorruption interest and employs means closely drawn to do so, and therefore survives closely drawn review.

E. Equal Protection

The district court found that the gift ban violated lobbyists' right to equal protection because "[e]ven though lobbyists and their employers are not part of a suspect class, a law that treats them differently from other citizens is subject to the highest level of scrutiny when it seeks to suppress their political expression." It got there by relying on the Supreme Court's decision in *Austin v. Mich. Chamber of Commerce,* 494 U.S. 652 (1990), where the Court held that "[b]ecause the right to engage in political expression is fundamental to our constitutional system, statutory classifications impinging upon that right must be narrowly tailored to serve a compelling governmental interest." *Id.* at 666.

In *Citizens United,* the Court overruled *Austin* on the question of whether the government may, under the First Amendment, suppress political speech "based on the corporate identity of the speaker." But the Court did not express an intent to overturn *Austin*'s holding regarding the level of scrutiny applied to political expression, so it remains good law. *See Minn. Citizens Concerned for Life, Inc. v. Swanson,* 692 F.3d 864, 879–80 (8th Cir. 2012) (en banc) (explaining that *Citizens United* did not explicitly overrule the equal protection analysis in *Austin*). That said, several of our sister circuits express doubt as to whether *Austin* demands strict scrutiny in cases involving equal protection challenges to contribution limits.

. . .

As for this circuit, we've not yet considered the level of scrutiny to apply. From our review of other circuits' precedent, however, we agree that the best reading of *Austin,* especially considering the scope of its application, confines its holding to cases in which the First Amendment analysis itself requires strict scrutiny. *See Wagner,* 793 F.3d at 32. We have found no case where the Supreme Court applied strict scrutiny in examining an equal protection challenge when the First Amendment analysis itself did not require such scrutiny, *see id.,* and just as our sister circuits, we decline to be the first. Thus, we hold that closely drawn scrutiny, the tier of scrutiny applied to the First Amendment challenge, also applies to the equal protection challenge. The gift ban withstands such scrutiny.

NOTES & QUESTIONS

1.   The US Supreme Court denied Sen. Schickel's appeal of the 6th Circuits decision. *See, Schickel v. Troutman,* 140 S.Ct. 649 (2019).

2.   Massachusetts state Rep. Angelo Scaccia (D-Boston) served as the chair of the powerful Taxation Committee during the years 1991–1993. In 1991 he attended a Council of State Governments (CGS) conference in Hauppauge, New York. During the conference Scaccia, his wife and son attended a dinner thrown by tobacco lobbyist Theodore Lattanzio. The cost of the Scaccias' meals was $176. The next day Scaccia and his son went golfing with a group of tobacco lobbyists and Lattanzio paid for $112 for their golf fees. Two years later, Scaccia attended another conference, this time for insurance legislators on Florida's Amelia Island. John Hancock Mutual Life Insurance lobbyist F.

William Sawyer, brought Scaccia golfing twice and paid $193 to cover Scaccia's fees. Another insurance lobbyist paid $118 for Scaccia and his son's meals. The State Ethics Commission found that Scaccia and his family received nearly $600 in free meals and golf from lobbyists in violation the gratuity statute and imposed a $3,000 civil penalty.

Scaccia appealed the penalty to the Massachusetts Supreme Judicial Court, arguing that the commission failed to prove a link between the free meals and golf the lobbyists provided and any of his official acts.

The gratuity statute forbids giving offering or promising something of "substantial value" to a public official "for or because of any official act performed or to be performed," or for a public official to seek or accept something of value "for or because of any official act or act within his official responsibility performed or to be performed." A gratuity violation is, essentially, a lesser included offense of bribery, the difference being that bribery requires proof of "corrupt intent." Unlike bribery's two-way nexus, a gratuity violation can be either something given to an official as a reward for past action, to influence an official regarding a present action, or to induce an official to undertake a future action.

The SJC held that the Commission needed proof of a link to a particular official act, "not merely the fact that the official was in a position to take some undefined or generalized action, such as holding a hearing on proposed legislation that, if passed, could benefit the giver of the gratuity." The Court could not find that link in the record and, in fact, stated Scaccia took a position on legislation contrary to the insurance industry. The SJC overturned the gratuity violation. See, *Scaccia v. State Ethics Commission*, 431 Mass. 351 (2000).

Does this standard make sense given the role the chair plays in the legislative process?

3. LOBBYIST ETHICS

As lobbying grows as a profession and the methods of lobbying expand, ethical challenges will grow as well. In addition to the regulations above, there is a growing movement to provide ethics trainings to lobbyists. California Government Code § 86103 requires that lobbyists attend a day long ethics course once during each 2-year legislative session and certify the completion date with the California Secretary of State. Lawyers taking the course qualify for continuing legal education credits. Lobbyists are also beginning to develop ethical codes to self-regulate the practice.

CALIFORNIA CODE OF CONDUCT
California Institute of Governmental Advocates ("IGA")

The Institute of Governmental Advocates (IGA) is a voluntary, non-partisan association representing California lobbyists and lobbying firms.

IGA members subscribe to a voluntary code of conduct and professional ethics that go beyond what is required under the California Fair Political Practices Act.

1. OBLIGATIONS TO THE PUBLIC AND PARTICIPANTS OF THE GOVERNMENTAL DECISION-MAKING PROCESS:

1.1 All IGA members ("Members") acknowledge and accept the concept of owing an ethical obligation to the public and participants of the governmental decision-making process.

1.2 A Member owes members of the State Legislature and their staffs, the Governor and members of the Executive Administration, and all governmental employees an obligation of respect as legitimate and proper participants of the governmental decision-making process.

1.3 A Member has a duty to protect confidences when information is given to him or her with an expectation of confidentiality.

1.4 A Member owes participants of the governmental decision-making process an obligation not to mislead them. A Member owes participants of the governmental decision-making process an obligation to correct as quickly as practically possible any incorrect information that the Member provided them.

1.5 A Member owes participants of the governmental decision-making process an obligation to make every reasonable effort to become, and to stay, as informed as possible on the issues and process involved in the Member's activities.

1.6 A Member owes the public an obligation to make every reasonable effort to promote public understanding of the governmental decision-making process and the proper role of advocacy within that process.

1.7 A Member owes a public officeholder an obligation to inform the officeholder of the Member's planned opposition to a proposal by the officeholder prior to the Member's active opposition.

1.8 A Member owes participants of the governmental decision-making process an obligation to inform them of potential adverse effects of proposals to the extent that it can be adverse to known interests of those participants.

1.9 A Member owes the public and participants of the governmental decision-making process an obligation to immediately cease representing a client in a pursued objective and inform the client as quickly as practically possible of the Member's inability to continue representing the client in the pursued objective if it becomes known to the Member that the client's effort in the objective is purely harassment, taken out of spite, or otherwise not in good faith, or if the continued representation would violate applicable law or this Code.

2.   OBLIGATIONS TO THE CLIENT:

2.1 All Members acknowledge that he or she has ethical obligation to their clients.

2.2 A Member owes his client an obligation of understanding, knowledge, competence and continuing effort throughout the process of representation. A Member owes his client an obligation to make every reasonable effort to become, and to stay, as informed as possible on the issues and process involved in the objectives pursued by the Member on his client's behalf.

2.3 A Member owes his client an obligation that any assurances made by the Member to the client must be regarded as an obligation.

2.4 A Member owes his client an obligation to make all legal and ethical efforts to accomplish an objective pursued by the Member on his client's behalf. A Member owes his client an obligation to inform the client of the Member's inability to accomplish a pursued objective as quickly as practically possible after the Member has determined such inability.

2.5 A Member owes his client an obligation to fully inform the client of all material information accumulated and/or known by the Member relating to the objectives pursued by the Member on his client's behalf. A Member may also owe another party an obligation to protect such material information from the client as confidential. In such a case, the Member must exercise great care and wisdom in properly dealing with the situation and parties to whom the obligations are due.

2.6 A Member owes his client an obligation not to mislead the client. A Member owes his client an obligation to correct as quickly as practically possible any incorrect information that the Member has provided the client.

2.7 A Member owes his client an obligation to advise and counsel the client as to the proper course of conduct upon knowledge and/or suspicion of any contemplated action by the client related to the objectives pursued by the Member on his client's behalf which is contrary to applicable law, this Code, or the best interests of the client.

2.8 A Member owes his client an obligation not to pursue an objective if the Member's attitude, opinion or another obligation interferes with the duties to be assumed by the Member within the scope of the pursuit. A Member owes his client an obligation to immediately cease pursuing an objective on his client's behalf and inform the client as quickly as practically possible of the Member's inability to continue pursuing the objective if the Member's attitude, opinion, or another obligation interferes with the duties assumed by the Member within the scope of the pursuit.

2.9 A Member owes his client an obligation to avoid known or anticipated conflicts of interest arising from an inconsistent economic interest between the client and another client, the Member, an associate of the Member, a participant in a joint venture with the Member, or other persons or interests which share in any material way in the revenues of the Member. A Member owes his client an obligation to immediately inform the client of the existence or appearance of any such known or anticipated conflict. A Member owes his client an obligation to sever the relationship with the client if the existence or appearance of such a known or anticipated conflict between the client and the Member, an associate of the Member, a participant in a joint venture with the Member, or other persons or interests which share in any material way in the revenues of the Member cannot be resolved between the conflicted parties. A Member owes his client an obligation to sever subsequently-formed relationships with other clients who have or appear to have such a known or anticipated conflict with the client if the conflict cannot be resolved between the conflicted parties.

2.10 A Member owes his client an obligation to immediately cease pursuing an objective on his client's behalf and inform the client as quickly as practically possible of the Member's inability to continue pursuing the objective on his client's behalf if a physical, mental, or similar condition causes the Member to be unable to pursue the objective in an effective manner.

2.11 A Member owes his client an obligation not to charge fees incommensurate with the objectives pursued by the Member. A Member owes his client an obligation to return any charged fees incommensurate with the objectives pursued by the Member, unless the client has conducted himself in a manner which would render such a return of fees an inequity. A Member owes his client an obligation to return any charged fees unearned by the Member upon severing the relationship with the client, except fees charged solely for the purpose of insuring the availability of the Member.

2.12 A Member owes his client an obligation to include the subject of expenses in any contractual agreement between the Member and the client. A Member owes his client an obligation to only charge those expenditures made on behalf of the client and in furtherance of the objective pursued by the Member on his client's behalf, unless expressly agreed upon by the client to the contrary in the contractual agreement.

2.13 A Member owes his client an obligation to communicate to the client as quickly as practically possible any significant offers of compromise or settlement. A Member owes his client an obligation to decide within the understanding of the effort any significant offers of compromise or settlement on his client's behalf if it is practically impossible to timely communicate the offer to the client; and thereafter as quickly as practically possible communicate with the client the Member's decision.

3.   OBLIGATIONS TO OTHER GOVERNMENTAL ADVOCATES:

3.1 All Members acknowledge and accept the concept of owing an ethical obligation to each other, and all other lobbyists.

3.2 A Member owes other lobbyists an obligation to inform a fellow lobbyist if the Member is contacted by a potential client, and the Member knows, or should know, that the potential client is represented by the other lobbyist; and advise the potential client that the matter of potential employment should not be discussed without either involving the other lobbyist or severing that pre-existing relationship.

3.3 A Member owes other lobbyists an obligation not to mislead them if the Member chooses to provide them information. A Member owes other lobbyists an obligation to correct as quickly as practically possible any incorrect information that the Member has provided them.

3.4 A Member owes other lobbyists an obligation to inform any other lobbyist with whom the Member is in communication on a pursued objective on his client's behalf as to the specific interest the Member represents. A Member owes other lobbyists an obligation to clarify to any other lobbyist with whom the Member is in communication on a pursued objective on his client's behalf as to the specific interest the Member represents if the Member makes an appearance representing an interest other than the interest of which the Member originally apprised the other governmental member.

3.5 A Member owes other lobbyists an obligation to respect the positions advocated by other lobbyists, even those in conflict with the positions of the Member's client.

3.6 A Member owes other lobbyists an obligation to avoid acts or utterances which intentionally may have adverse economic effects upon the business of another governmental advocate.

3.7 A Member owes other lobbyists an obligation to inform a lobbyist of his or her client's interest on a pursued objective when his client's interest conflicts with the position advocated by the other governmental advocate and such communication will not compromise the client's interest.

The foregoing rules are a statement by IGA regarding the standards of conduct for lobbyists mutually agreed upon by the membership. These rules depend upon a general consensus of what the public, participants of the governmental decision-making process, clients, Members, and other lobbyists expect of Members in pursuing the objectives of their clients. In general, these rules abide by the venerable maxim that you should deal with others as you would have them deal with you.

NOTES & QUESTIONS

1.   Would you have included any further provisions or excluded any of the existing provisions? Why?

2.   Had Jack Abramoff belonged to this organization, which of the provisions, if any, would he have violated?

3.   How would this code be enforced? Unlike the ethical rules for attorneys which can be enforced by the state courts and bar associations, the IGA cannot prevent someone from registering and acting as a lobbyist.

4.   Should registered lobbyists be licensed and subject to discipline by the government for ethical violations? If so, what part of government would enforce the rules and hand out discipline?

CHAPTER 8

THE INTERPRETERS: AGENCIES & COURTS

■ ■ ■

A. AGENCIES

CHEVRON, U.S.A., INC. V. NATURAL RESOURCES DEFENSE COUNCIL, INC.

Supreme Court of the United States
467 U.S. 837 (1984)

JUSTICE STEVENS.

[Note: In this case, the Environmental Protection Agency changed its standards when implementing the Clean Air Act Amendments of 1977, specifically how to define the term "stationary source" to include a so-called "bubble concept" that environmental activists worried would lessen air quality.]

II.

When a court reviews an agency's construction of the statute which it administers, it is confronted with two questions. First, always, is the question whether Congress has directly spoken to the precise question at issue. If the intent of Congress is clear, that is the end of the matter; for the court, as well as the agency, must give effect to the unambiguously expressed intent of Congress. If, however, the court determines Congress has not directly addressed the precise question at issue, the court does not simply impose its own construction on the statute, as would be necessary in the absence of an administrative interpretation. Rather, if the statute is silent or ambiguous with respect to the specific issue, the question for the court is whether the agency's answer is based on a permissible construction of the statute.

"The power of an administrative agency to administer a congressionally created . . . program necessarily requires the formulation of policy and the making of rules to fill any gap left, implicitly or explicitly, by Congress." If Congress has explicitly left a gap for the agency to fill, there is an express delegation of authority to the agency to elucidate a specific provision of the statute by regulation. Such legislative regulations are given controlling weight unless they are arbitrary, capricious, or manifestly contrary to the statute. Sometimes the legislative delegation to an agency on a particular question is implicit rather than explicit. In such a case, a court may not substitute its own construction of a statutory provision for a reasonable interpretation made by the administrator of an agency.

We have long recognized that considerable weight should be accorded to an executive department's construction of a statutory scheme it is entrusted to administer, and the principle of deference to administrative interpretations.

"has been consistently followed by this Court whenever decision as to the meaning or reach of a statute has involved reconciling conflicting policies, and a full understanding of the force of the statutory policy in the given situation has depended upon more than ordinary knowledge respecting the matters subjected to agency regulations.

". . . If this choice represents a reasonable accommodation of conflicting policies that were committed to the agency's care by the statute, we should not disturb it unless it appears from the statute or its legislative history that the accommodation is not one that Congress would have sanctioned."

In light of these well-settled principles it is clear that the Court of Appeals misconceived the nature of its role in reviewing the regulations at issue. Once it determined, after its own examination of the legislation, that Congress did not actually have an intent regarding the applicability of the bubble concept to the permit program, the question before it was not whether in its view the concept is "inappropriate" in the general context of a program designed to improve air quality, but whether the Administrator's view that it is appropriate in the context of this particular program is a reasonable one. Based on the examination of the legislation and its history which follows, we agree with the Court of Appeals that Congress did not have a specific intention on the applicability of the bubble concept in these cases, and conclude that the EPA's use of that concept here is a reasonable policy choice for the agency to make.

. . .

The arguments over policy that are advanced in the parties' briefs create the impression that respondents are now waging in a judicial forum a specific policy battle which they ultimately lost in the agency and in the 32 jurisdictions opting for the "bubble concept," but one which was never waged in the Congress. Such policy arguments are more properly addressed to legislators or administrators, not to judges.

In these cases, the Administrator's interpretation represents a reasonable accommodation of manifestly competing interests and is entitled to deference: the regulatory scheme is technical and complex, the agency considered the matter in a detailed and reasoned fashion, and the decision involves reconciling conflicting policies. Congress intended to accommodate both interests, but did not do so itself on the level of specificity presented by these cases. Perhaps that body consciously desired the Administrator to strike the balance at this level, thinking that those with great expertise and charged with responsibility for administering the provision would be in a better position to do so; perhaps it simply did not consider the question at this level; and perhaps Congress was unable to forge a coalition on either side of the question, and those on each side decided to take their chances with the scheme devised by the agency. For judicial purposes, it matters not which of these things occurred.

Judges are not experts in the field, and are not part of either political branch of the Government. Courts must, in some cases, reconcile competing political interests, but not on the basis of the judges' personal policy preferences. In contrast, an agency to which Congress has delegated policy-making responsibilities may, within the limits of that delegation, properly rely upon the incumbent administration's views of wise policy to inform its judgments. While agencies are not directly accountable to the people, the Chief Executive is, and it is entirely appropriate for this political branch of the Government to make such policy choices—resolving the competing interests which Congress itself either inadvertently did not resolve, or intentionally left to be resolved by the agency charged with the administration of the statute in light of everyday realities.

When a challenge to an agency construction of a statutory provision, fairly conceptualized, really centers on the wisdom of the agency's policy, rather than whether it is a reasonable choice within a gap left open by Congress, the challenge must fail. In such a case, federal judges—who have no constituency—have a duty to respect legitimate policy choices made by those who do. The responsibilities for assessing the wisdom of such policy choices and resolving the struggle between competing views of the public interest are not judicial ones: "Our Constitution vests such responsibilities in the political branches."

We hold that the EPA's definition of the term "source" is a permissible construction of the statute which seeks to accommodate progress in reducing air pollution with economic growth. "The Regulations which the Administrator has adopted provide what the agency could allowably view as . . . [an] effective reconciliation of these twofold ends. . . ."

NOTES & QUESTIONS

1.   *Chevron* is one of the most studied cases in American law. As of late 2019, Chevron has been cited in 16,599 court cases and in 20,278 secondary sources such as law review articles and treatises.

2.   Several scholars and judges have advocated a broad reading of *Chevron*, with interpretive authority given to agencies rather than the judiciary. The agencies have expertise, institutional competence, and are closely involved in the legislative process. Prof. Shobe states, "Agency legislative history not only calls into question courts' institutional capacity to uncover congressional intent to delegate, but it also supports arguments, first expressed by Professors Mashaw and Strauss, that agencies may be better statutory interpreters than courts." Jarrod Shobe, "Agency Legislative History," 68 *Emory L.J.* 283 (2018).

"The Iron Triangle"

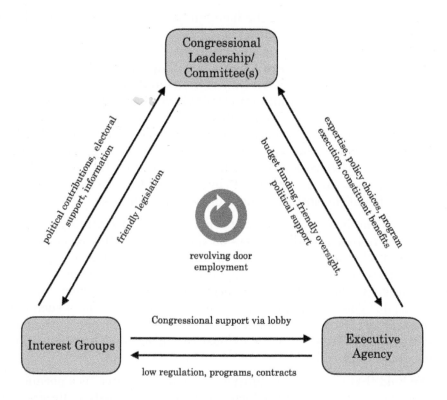

Political scientists have identified relationships between the legislature, agencies and interested special interests called "iron triangles." These complex relationships develop over time and provide an exchange of desirable services or outcomes, e.g., electoral support for friendly legislation and oversight.

NOTES & QUESTIONS

1.   Sanjiv Ahuja, chief executive officer of LightSquared, complained in a 2012 *Politico* article about the dysfunction that iron triangles can bring about in Washington DC.

The iron triangle that concerned Ahuja was the global positioning system industry. LightSquared had spent billions building a new wireless broadband network with the encouragement of the FCC. In 2011, however, the Space Based Positioning Navigation and Timing Executive Committee, a government panel that guides GPS policy, stood in the way to protect other players in the GPS industry. Ahuja points out that the vice chairman of the committee's advisory board sits on the board of company that spent over a million dollars lobbying against LightSquared's technology. The Executive Committee then adopted a testing regime favorable to GPS companies and excluded the input from LightSquared.

Ahuja wrote, "here the fox has been guarding the hen house," thereby stifling competition that would bring innovation along with better and cheaper cell service. Further, Ahuja argued, "The decision could also signal to entrepreneurs that they cannot count on the U.S. government to enforce the rule of law." See, "Lost in D.C.'s 'Iron Triangle,' " *Politico*, January 26, 2012.

2.   A month after this article appeared, the FCC proposed to suspend LightSquared's broadband activity because of claims that the company caused interference issues with satellite services. Three months later, LightSquared filed for bankruptcy. See, Mike Spector, Greg Bensinger, "LightSquared Pulls the Plug," *The Wall Street Journal*, May 14, 2012. In 2015, the company emerged from bankruptcy under a new name. What else could LightSquared do to protect its business?

OFFICE OF MANAGEMENT AND BUDGET CIRCULAR NO. A-19

(Revised September 20, 1979)

TO THE HEADS OF EXECUTIVE DEPARTMENTS AND ESTABLISHMENTS SUBJECT: Legislative coordination and clearance

1.   Purpose. This Circular outlines procedures for the coordination and clearance by the Office of Management and Budget (OMB) of agency recommendations on proposed, pending, and enrolled legislation. It also includes instructions on the timing and preparation of agency legislative programs.

. . .

6.   Agency legislative programs.

a.   Submission to OMB. Each agency shall prepare and submit to OMB annually its proposed legislative program for the next session of

Congress. If an agency has no legislative program, it should submit a statement to this effect.

b.   Purposes of legislative program submission. The essential purposes for requiring agencies to submit annual legislative programs are: (1) to assist agency planning for legislative objectives; (2) to help agencies coordinate their legislative program with the preparation of their annual budget submissions to OMB; (3) to give agencies an opportunity to recommend specific proposals for Presidential endorsement; and (4) to aid OMB and other staff of the Executive Office of the President in developing the President's legislative program, budget, and annual and special messages.

c.   Timing of submission to OMB.

(1)   Each agency shall submit its proposed legislative program to OMB at the same time as it initially submits its annual budget request as required by OMB Circular No. A-11. Timely submission is essential if the programs are to serve the purposes set forth in section 6b.

(2)   Items that are not included in an agency's legislative program and have significant upward budget impact will not be considered after the budget is prepared unless they result from circumstances not foreseeable at the time of final budget decisions.

d.   Number of copies. Each agency shall furnish 25 copies of its proposed legislative program to OMB. These copies will be distributed by OMB within the Executive Office of the President.

e.   Program content. Each agency shall prepare its legislative program in accordance with the instructions in Attachment A. Agency submissions shall include:

(1)   All items of legislation that an agency contemplates proposing to Congress (or actively supporting, if already pending legislation) during the coming session, including proposals to extend expiring laws or repeal provisions of existing laws. These items should be based on policy-level decisions within the agency and should take into account the President's known legislative, budgetary, and other relevant policies. Agencies' proposed legislative programs should identify those items of sufficient importance to be included in the President's legislative program.

(2)   A separate list of legislative proposals under active consideration in the agency that are not yet ready for inclusion in its proposed legislative program. For each item in this list, the agency should indicate when it expects to reach a policy-level decision and, specifically, whether it expects to propose the item in time for its consideration for inclusion in the annual budget under preparation.

(3)   A separate list of all laws or provisions of law affecting an agency that will expire between the date the program is submitted to OMB and the end of the two following calendar years, whether or not the agency plans to propose their extension.

(4)   All items in the submissions that are proposed, or expected to be proposed, for inclusion in the annual budget shall be accompanied by a tabulation showing amounts of budget authority and outlays or other measure of budgetary impact for the budget year and for each of the four succeeding fiscal years. See section 201(a)(5), (6), and (12) of the Budget and Accounting Act, 1921, as amended (31 U.S.C. 11(a)(12)). Criteria in OMB Circular No. A-11 shall be used in preparing these tabulations.

(5)   All items covered by section 6e(4) above shall also be accompanied by estimates of work-years of employment and of personnel required to carry out the proposal in the budget year and four succeeding fiscal years.

f.   Relationship to advice. Submission of a legislative program to OMB does not constitute a request for advice on individual legislative proposals. Such requests should be made in the manner prescribed in section 7 of this Circular.

. . .

i.   Drafting service. Agencies need not submit for clearance bills that they prepare as a drafting service for a congressional committee or a Member of Congress, provided that they state in their transmittal letters that the drafting service does not constitute a commitment with respect to the position of the Administration or the agency. Agencies shall advise OMB of these drafting service requests while the requests are being complied with, and supply a copy of the request, if in writing. A copy of each such draft bill and the accompanying letter should be furnished to OMB at the time of transmittal, together with an explanatory statement of what the bill would accomplish if that is not contained in the transmittal letter.

NOTES & QUESTIONS

1.   Professor Shobe points out that there is an informal legislative history where agencies unofficially communicate with Congress with phone calls and emails between staffers. These are likely the most frequent contacts between Congressional and agency personnel and outside the Office of Management and Budget's supervision. While judges would benefit from these key communications during the legislative process, it would be "difficult or impossible to gain access" to these communications, and even if they had the information, it would be difficult for judges make sense of it. The same is true of informal communications within Congress that would give valuable interpretive insights, such as conversations between committee staff and the drafters of the Offices of Legislative Counsel. J. Shobe, "Agency Legislative History," 68 *Emory L. J.* 283 (2018).

NORMS, PRACTICES, AND THE PARADOX OF DEFERENCE: A PRELIMINARY INQUIRY INTO AGENCY STATUTORY INTERPRETATION

Jerry L. Mashaw, 57 *Admin. L. Rev.* 501 (2005)

[Note: In this article, Professor Mashaw explores the differences between the methods courts and administrative agencies use to interpret statutes. Although interpretation by courts has been thoroughly studies, but this is not the case for agencies. Agencies must answer to both Congress and the President. Congress approves agency leaders and holds the power of the purse. Congress also regularly oversees the operations of agencies. The President can control agency actions through a range of methods: executive orders, signing statements, legislative proposals, public speeches, and private telephone calls. Professor Mashaw finds that given the institutional nature of the courts and agencies, and roles of each in the constitutional order, they naturally use different information and tools to read statutes. This creates an interesting paradox—"[f]ully legitimate judicial interpretation will conflict with fully legitimate agency interpretation." This is especially interesting given the *Chevron* doctrine where courts should defer to agency statutory interpretations under certain circumstances.]

A.   Constitutional Demands

In some sense, the position of agencies as "faithful agents" of the legislature has a constitutional clarity that exceeds that of the judiciary. While American courts must somehow balance their position as faithful agents of the Constitution and Congress, agencies seem to enjoy a less conflicted constitutional role: they are the executors of the President's constitutional responsibility to "take Care that the Laws be faithfully executed."

Continuous competition between Presidents and Congresses for control of administration is both a structural feature of the American Constitution and a stark fact of American political life. But, as a normative constitutional matter, it is generally not a good interpretive argument for an agency to say simply, "the President told me to interpret the statute that way." By contrast, "the statute made me do it," however empirically contestable in any particular instance, has the hallowed ring of constitutional legitimacy.

. . .

Statutes persist, while Presidents and Congresses change. In this context, the agency becomes the guardian or custodian of the legislative scheme as enacted. If agencies are meant to implement the statute, not the preferences of sitting Presidents or Senators or representatives, then to denude them of the use of legislative history as a defense against contemporary political importuning is to leave the statutory custodians naked before their enemies.

Hence, even if one believes that the use of legislative history has no constitutional consequences for courts—that is, that there is no constitutional basis for either restricting or requiring the use legislative history as a guide to a statutory meaning—one might take a different view with respect to agencies. They might, as a prudential matter, have a better chance of understanding the real political context, which is only partially revealed by legislative history as argued to courts in litigation. And, agencies might need to wrap themselves tightly in the blanket of pre-legislative congressional utterances in order to maintain the integrity of the statutory scheme in the face of powerful political controllers intent on wrenching statutory schemes loose from their historical, contextual foundations. In some instances, only the skillful deployment of legislative history will permit agencies to fulfill their constitutional role as faithful agents in the statute's implementation.

. . .

Prudential approaches to statutory interpretation. . . seem to have three major purposes: (1) Increasing the interpreter's capacity to avoid error; (2) Increasing or maintaining the legitimacy of the interpreter as an interpreter; and (3) Enhancing the interpreter's capacity to make its interpretations effective. All of these prudential considerations are relevant with respect to agency interpretation of statutes as well. They simply may press an agency in slightly different directions.

. . .

Table 1

Canons for Institutionally Responsible Statutory Interpretation

	Agency	Court
1. Follow presidential directions unless clearly outside your authority.	+*	−*
2. Interpret to avoid raising constitutional questions.	−	+
3. Use legislative history as a primary interpretive guide.	+	−
4. Interpret to give energy and breadth to all legislative programs within your jurisdiction.	+	−

5. Engage in activist lawmaking.	+	–
6. Respect all judicial precedent.	–	+
7. Interpret to lend coherence to the overall legal order.	–	+
8. Pay particular attention to the strategic parameters of interpretive efficiency.	+	–
9. Interpret to insure hierarchical control over subordinates.	+	–
10. Pay constant attention to your contemporary political milieu.	+	–
* "+" means appropriate; "–" inappropriate. Given my discussion, many of these notations might realistically be more nuanced, "++" or "+/–," or even "+/?," for example.		

. . .

B.   The Paradox of Deference

One reading of the analysis offered in this Article might see it as constructing what we might call a "deference paradox." Concern with agency interpretation as an autonomous enterprise has been motivated in substantial part by the prominence given to agency interpretation in the post-*Chevron* and now post-*Mead* world of deferential judicial review. Yet my construction of parallel universes of interpretive discourse on the foundation of divergent institutional roles seems to undermine the very possibility of an authentically deferential judicial posture. How can a court's determination of "ambiguity" or "reasonableness" at *Chevron*'s famous two analytical "steps" be understood as deferential when that determination emerges from the normative commitments and epistemological presumptions of "judging" rather "administering"? How could *Mead's* resuscitation of *Skidmore* deference make sense as deference at all when the discourse, to be persuasive, would presumably have to be within the terms of a judicial conversation about meaning that ignores, if not falsifies, the grounds upon which much administrative interpretive activity is appropriately and responsibly premised?

NOTES & QUESTIONS

1.   Agencies develop cultures of their own over time and pass that culture on to new employees. Professors Bob & Ann Seidman would have pointed out that they are institutions, made up of repetitive actions that tend to perpetuate the institution. How will that culture affect the agency's interpretation of legislation? How will it influence its relationship to the legislature?

2.   Professor Richard Pierce, in responding to Professor Mashaw, sees little difference between the ways in which courts and agencies interpret statutes, but perhaps more importantly, that agencies should be using the same interpretive process a court will use.

> [T]he agency should use the same "traditional tools of statutory construction" that it expects a reviewing court to use. If the agency uses a different method of interpretation—for example, if it relies on legislative history to a greater extent than a reviewing court as Strauss urges—it increases significantly the risk of judicial reversal without good reason.
>
> . . .
>
> I disagree with Strauss and Mashaw at the most fundamental level. Unlike Strauss and Mashaw, I do not believe that agencies are "the primary official interpreters of federal statutes." Rather, all agency statutory interpretations are subject to *de novo* review and potential rejection by a court through application of *Chevron* step one. Further, I do not believe that agencies should use methods of statutory interpretation that differ from the methods courts use. Accordingly, I do not see the conflicts between legitimate agency interpretations and legitimate court interpretations that trouble Mashaw. It is certainly true that agencies have the power to give meaning to ambiguous provisions in the statutes they administer, subject only to the deferential form of judicial review described in *Chevron* step two and *State Farm*. When agencies undertake that important task, however, they are not involved in the process of statutory interpretation. Instead, they are engaged in a policymaking process, the end result of which is to choose which of several linguistically plausible meanings to give ambiguous language to further the purposes of the statute the agency is implementing.

See, Richard J. Pierce, "How Agencies Should Give Meaning to the Statutes they Administer: A Response to Mashaw and Strauss," 59 *Admin. L. Rev.* 197 (2007).

AGENCY LEGISLATIVE HISTORY
Jarrod Shobe, 68 *Emory Law Journal* 283 (2018)

Agencies communicate with Congress during the legislative process in ways beyond drafting and revising legislation, yet these types of legislative communications have gone almost entirely unnoticed in legal literature. Agencies engage in various types of formal communications with Congress to express opinions about legislation, to raise issues with legislation, and to suggest changes to legislation. This section discusses various types of legislative analysis that agencies provide to Congress. The types of agency legislative history discussed here are not mutually exclusive, and often various types will exist for any bill.

1.   Section-by-Section Analyses

When agencies propose their own legislation to Congress, they often include a section-by-section analysis that explains the legislation in relatively plain-language terms and provides color and context to the statutory language. This is similar to congressional committee reports, which normally contain a similar section-by-section analysis of legislation. An agency-drafted section-by-section analysis can be important to understanding how Congress perceived the agency's proposed legislative language. It is now known that many members of Congress and their staff are more likely to read committee reports than legislative language. It may also be true that these same legislators and staff read an agency's plain-language section-by-section analysis more closely than an agency's proposed statutory text, which can be difficult to decipher because it often amends various portions of existing law and cross-references other statutory provisions. These section-by-section analyses therefore may be the best evidence of what Congress believes it is enacting when it adopts agency-drafted legislation.

Various agencies make their legislative proposals and accompanying section-by-section analyses publicly available. For example, the DoD's Office of Legislative Counsel posts its legislative proposals and section-by-section analyses on its website. The DoD has a sophisticated and coordinated legislative drafting process, due partially to the fact that Congress passes a yearly defense reauthorization bill that requires significant input from the DoD. The DoD proposes hundreds of pages of legislative language every year, and all of this legislative language is accompanied by a relatively plain-language section-by-section analysis of the purpose and function of the bill. It is likely that the DoD creates these section-by-section analyses for a reason: it knows that committee staff and members of Congress want a clear explanation of what the proposals do, which is hard to provide through relatively technical and dense legislative text.

2.   Views Letters

Views letters are an additional type of agency legislative analysis. Views letters are formal letters sent to Congress that state an agency's position on proposed legislation. These letters generally include a description of why the agency supports or opposes the legislation and what the agency believes the legislation will do. Sometimes an agency will also include technical comments as part of a views letter. For major pieces of legislation, an agency may send multiple views letters throughout the legislative process as the legislation evolves. Views letters sometimes provide direct insight into the meaning of statutory language. Even when they do not provide insight into specific language, they are helpful to establish what an agency has told Congress it believes the purpose and scope of the legislation is and to contextualize the relationship between the agency and Congress.

3.   Pre-Drafting Reports and Memos

Agencies also often send reports, letters, and memos to Congress early in the legislative process as Congress is contemplating legislation. Because these types of communications come before legislation is drafted, they can take a variety of forms and are often speculative and preliminary in nature. These communications are often focused on describing an issue that requires a legislative solution, so that Congress is aware of it, rather than attempting to resolve the issue. To the extent these communications propose resolutions, they often describe various potential solutions and explain the pros and cons of each without getting to the level of technical legislative language.

Because these types of communications tend to be relatively broad and are often sent to Congress long before legislation is drafted, they will usually be less useful than other types of agency legislative history and are very unlikely to be dispositive. To the extent they are useful, it will generally be as background to uncover the agency-Congress relationship and why Congress chose to legislate in the manner it did.

4.   Agency Testimony

Another way in which agencies participate in the legislative process is through testimony in congressional hearings. Congress regularly invites agencies to testify about particular issues or proposed legislation. This testimony is drafted within an agency the same way a legislative proposal would be: the relevant bureau creates a draft and then that draft goes through an internal agency clearance process and OMB clearance before it is submitted to Congress. This testimony is therefore meant to reflect official administration policy.

Scholars and judges already consider congressional hearings to be a type of legislative history, since hearings are almost always publicly available. However, scholars have not emphasized the importance of agency testimony. Because agencies are closely involved in drafting and revising legislation, their testimony is likely to be informative and accurate in explaining how legislation is intended to work. It is also very likely that committee members form their opinions on legislation based on how it is described by agencies and rely on representations made by agencies of how legislation will be carried out after enactment.

NOTES & QUESTIONS

How could the public and courts gain greater access to agency legislative documents? Professor Shobe suggests litigants using Freedom of Information Act requests, although that would require the requestor knowing what to ask for. Jarrod Shobe, "Agency Legislative History," 68 *Emory L.J.* 283 (2018).

Professor Shobe argues that the best solution to the accessibility of agency history problem could be courts only considering agency legislative history that Congress incorporates into its own legislative history such as a committee report statements in the Congressional Record. This rule would cause Congress to memorialize the agency legislative history that accurately reflects the "legislative deal," and would reduce litigation costs associated with obtaining agency documents. Agencies would also be incentivized to generate documents that "communicate honestly with Congress," rather than as an attempt to influence judges. Prof. Shobe believes that if Congress make it clear where they have relied on agency communications, courts could hold the agency accountable for the communications as it uses the law; even under new administrations or administrators, agency interpretations would have to more closely conform with the enacting Congress's intent. Jarrod Shobe, "Agency Legislative History," 68 *Emory L.J.* 283 (2018).

Case Study: The Consumer Financial Protection Bureau

In the early fall of 2019 Kathleen Kraninger, director of the Consumer Financial Protection Bureau (CFPB), had to decide what to do with the Bureau's consumer complaint database. To that point, the database had been available to the public—much to the disapproval of conservative policy makers and the financial industry alike. Once President Trump had the opportunity to appoint the leader of the CFPB, he chose Mick Mulvaney, his director of the powerful Office of Management and Budget (OMB) and one of the fiercest critics of the CFPB. When Mulvaney took over as Trump's Acting Chief of Staff, Trump named Kraninger, one of Mulvaney's OMB lieutenants, to lead the Bureau. Throughout the process of deciding what to do with the database, Ms. Kraninger had to consider many opinions of how she should proceed.

The Origins of the CFPB

The "Great Recession" began in late 2007—the worst financial crisis in the U.S. since the Great Depression. Over the next 18 months, the economy was in a shambles with 8.6 million people losing jobs and a peak unemployment rate of 10%. Real gross domestic product (GDP) fell by $650 billion and household net worth (the value of both stock markets and housing prices, fell $11.5 trillion. The causes of the Great Recession are complex, but it started with the collapse of subprime mortgage lending. Seemingly overnight credit disappeared for consumers and businesses alike.

During the early 2000s, Americans carried an increasing amount of debt. This was largely due to people buying real estate at increasingly higher amounts and financing the purchases with loans. Credit was easy to obtain, even for people with imperfect or bad credit. This credit market happened because of changed regulations, widespread irresponsible lending practices, and the ability of the financial industry to resell bad "subprime" loans to investors. Not all borrowers were irresponsible; many people took out unaffordable loans based on misleading claims by lenders about low payments. Even lenders that tried to act responsibly had to compete for business with other lenders who were willing to mislead consumers and cut corners.

When the lending market crashed, it affected nearly every homeowner. Even those people with a manageable amount of debt saw their property values plummet when their neighbors who were credit risks and were over-leveraged lost their homes to foreclosure. Everyone with credit cards saw interest rates increase and smaller available lines of credit. Retirement funds declined dramatically in value wiping out a significant amount of savings making the situation even more disastrous.

The financial industry itself was shaken to the core. Shortly after the crisis began, it became clear that even some of the oldest and largest investment banks, which were not regulated as closely as depository banks, were in danger. Lehman Brothers went bankrupt, and two other banks, Bear Stearns and Merrill Lynch, were sold for pennies on the dollar to more stable banks. Two other investment banks, Morgan Stanley and Goldman Sachs, which were also in danger of bankruptcy, reorganized as commercial banks. As commercial banks, they could access credit from the Federal Reserve, but had to comply with more federal regulations. One of the most difficult situations was what policy makers would do about American International Group (AIG), which had insured the mortgaged backed securities that were now worth little or nothing. AIG simply did not have the cash to pay its obligations when so many investors defaulted on these securities. Ultimately, the Federal government provided over $100 billion of public funds to major global financial institutions to cover AIG's obligations. While this probably saved the global economy from further damage, it sparked outrage by members of Congress and the public that large banks and companies, many of which acted irresponsibly, were "bailed out" by taxpayers.

While the immediate focus was on banking institutions, by mid 2009, policy makers started to focus on consumer protection. The brainchild of then Professor Elizabeth Warren, President Obama proposed a new agency to protect consumers from unfair, deceptive, and abusive financial practices. Financial institutions, which had been accountable in some fashion to seven different Federal agencies, would now be accountable to the new agency, which would better enforce consumer protection laws governing financial products and services. The President requested that Congress give the new agency the independence and funds needed to force gigantic financial companies into compliance with consumer laws.

In July 2010, President Obama signed the Dodd-Frank Wall Street Reform and Consumer Protection Act into law, which created the Consumer Financial Protection Bureau (CFPB) to regulate financial institutions with assets over $10 billion. The CFPB would have regulatory power, the ability to conduct investigations by issuing subpoenas, and take legal action to enforce consumer protection laws.

President Obama placed Prof. Warren in charge of setting up the new agency. Although most people expected her to become the first director of the agency, Republicans in Congress opposed the nomination. Pres. Obama then nominated Richard Cordray as the CFPB's director. In 2013, Warren was elected as a U.S. Senator for Massachusetts. During the 116th Congress (2019–2020), Senator Warren served on the Committee on Banking, Housing, & Urban Affairs.

To give the CFPB sufficient autonomy, the agency is funded not by Congress, but by the Federal Reserve, and its director is appointed to a five-year term. By design, the director does not report directly to the president, and can only be fired for "inefficiency, neglect of duty, or malfeasance."

As of 2017, the CFPB had fielded over 1.2 million complaints from consumers and provided $12 billion to 29 million people taken advantage of by the financial industry. Since its inception, the CFPB has:

- Fined Wells Fargo $185 million after its employees opened over 1 million accounts and nearly 600,000 credit cards in the names of Wells Fargo clients without their permission;

- Secured $92 million for nearly 17,000 service members harmed by a predatory loan scheme by Rome Finance;

- Ordered Navy Credit Union to pay a $5.5 million fine and pay $23 million to its victims for making false debt collection threats to active service members and retired veterans;

- Fined the for-profit Corinthian Colleges $550 million and ordered it to repay students $663 million after luring thousands of students into fraudulent student loans and using illegal debt collection tactics;

- Fined Ally Financial $18 million and ordered it to repay $80 million for the more than 235,000 minority borrowers after it charged them more for auto loans than white borrowers;

- Forced PNC Financial Services Group to compensate more than 75,000 African American and Hispanic borrowers $35 million after they were charged higher fees or interest rates based on their race;

- Ordered Bank of America to refund $727 million to more than a million customers who purchased add-on products for their credit cards that they never received;

- Made Citibank pay an estimated $700 million to roughly 7 million customers harmed by their illegal credit card practices and fined the bank $35 million.

The CFPB also protected consumers by launching a public database where people could research loan companies in 2015. The database also gave people a chance to log their concerns with banks, mortgage companies and debt collectors. Detailed complaints became public after a company responds or after 15 days.

From its inception, the database was a target for the financial services industry.

The Political Debate over CFPB

Despite its accomplishments, the CFPB has been politically controversial since its inception. Republican law makers and conservative commentators have claimed the CFPB's actions hurts consumer choice and economic growth. They have also complained that both Congress and the President are more limited in their ability to control the CFPB in contrast to other agencies. In 2016, CFPB critics challenged the Bureau's constitutionality due to its structure.

A 2018 lawsuit questioned the CFPB's constitutionality after the CFPB initiated an investigation into whether the Selia Law firm, which provided debt-relief services to consumers, violated telemarketing sales rules. When Seila Law did not comply with the CFPB's request for information and documents, the CFPB sued them in federal court. Seila Law, in turn, challenged the CFPB's constitutionality because its single director wields significant power but cannot be removed by the President for any reason. In 2019, the United States Court of Appeals for the District of Columbia ruled that CFPB's structure was unconstitutional. Independent agencies have been challenged before, but the Supreme Court upheld structures that insulate agency heads from political interference. For example, in *Humphrey's Executor v. United States* (1935) the Court upheld the structure of the Federal Trade Commission, where the President could only remove one of the five commissioners for cause.

CFPB Leadership Fight

In November 2017, the CFPB and White House engaged in a battle over who would lead the Bureau. When Richard Cordray resigned as CFPB's director, he appointed Leandra English as Acting Director. That same evening, President Trump appointed OMB director Mick Mulvaney, as the acting director of the CFPB.

Leandra English sued in the Federal District Court claiming that she was the CFPB's rightful acting director. The next Monday, both English and Mulvaney both showed up for work at the agency. Mulvaney brought donuts to the office for the staff.

Several powerful Democratic legislators—including Senator Elizabeth Warren, Senator Sherrod Brown, Senator Richard Durbin, Minority Leader Nancy Pelosi, and former Rep. Barney Frank (co-author of the Dodd-Frank Act) backed English. Still, the courts ruled against her and Mulvaney took control.

The leadership fight demonstrated how an independent agency tried to prevent its take-over by an administration that was openly hostile to not just its mission, but the agency's very existence. President Trump had already issued executive orders eliminating regulations for the financial sector, and the Republican controlled House of Representatives passed a bill that would dismantle the Dodd-Frank Act.

Mick Mulvaney served several roles in the Trump Administration. He was the director of the Office of Management and Budget (OMB) starting in February 2017 and continued in that role after taking over the CFPB. Mulvaney served in the South Carolina General Assembly from 2007 to 2011 and as a U.S. Representative from 2011 to 2017. As a congressman, Mulvaney was known for his fiscal conservatism and was a fierce opponent of the CFPB, which he once called a "sick, sad joke."

Talking about the CFPB database, Mulvaney stated that the agency shouldn't need to run a "Yelp for financial services, sponsored by the federal government." In 2018, Mulvaney called for public input on its consumer inquiry and complaint database. The announcement was widely seen as a sign that the agency would move to either discard the database or to make it private.

The American Bankers Association opposed the continued operation of the database due to "strongly expressed concerns about privacy implications and the CFPB's statutory authority to publish individualized complaint data." The Consumer Bankers Association stated, "For too long, the bureau's unverified compliant database has functioned to paint a picture of guilt through government press releases and statements, despite the CFPB reporting the overwhelming majority of complaints being self-corrected by banks." Financial services companies worried that the database caused irreversible damage to a company's reputation based on unsubstantiated complaints.

CFPB's advocates, however, feared a private database would limit the agencies' ability to address consumers' complaints. They argued a public database helps consumers make better informed decisions and helped the agency to identifying harmful practices.

In December 2018 Mulvaney became the President's Acting Chief of Staff, and one of his top lieutenants at OMB, Kathleen Kraninger, took over as the CFPB director. At OMB, Kraninger was a policy advocate director and oversaw the budgets for the Departments of Commerce, Justice, Homeland Security (DHS), Housing and Urban Development, Transportation (DOT), and Treasury, in addition to 30 other government agencies. Ms. Kraninger also worked in Congress as a clerk for the Senate and House Appropriations Subcommittees on Homeland Security. After the 9/11 terrorist attacks She was part of the team that set up the newly created Department of Homeland Security. Ms. Kraninger graduated magna cum laude from Marquette University and earned a law degree from Georgetown University Law Center.

As director, Kraninger stated, "Data security and data privacy is going to be a big focal point in terms of what the bureau collects, how it's used, how long it's stored, what information is appropriate to be shared among regulators."

In its Request for Information, the CFPB solicited information and comments on the following topics:

The Bureau is seeking feedback on all aspects of its consumer complaint and inquiry handling processes, including:

1.   Specific statutorily-permissible suggestions regarding how the Bureau currently allows consumers to submit complaints and inquiries, including:

a.   Should the Bureau require consumers to classify their submission affirmatively as a consumer complaint or inquiry prior to submission?

b.   How should the Bureau explain the difference between a consumer complaint and a consumer inquiry to consumers at the point of submission?

c.   Should the Bureau develop a process for companies to reclassify consumers' submissions? If so, what criteria should the Bureau establish to help companies differentiate consumer complaints from consumer inquiries?

2.   Specific statutorily-permissible suggestions regarding the Bureau's consumer complaint processes, including:

a.   The Bureau currently receives complaints via six channels: Website, referral from Federal and State entities/agencies, telephone, mail, fax, and email. Should the Bureau add or discontinue any channels for accepting complaints?

b.   Consistent with the Dodd-Frank Act's definition of "consumer," the Bureau currently allows consumers to authorize someone else (e.g., lawyer, advocate, power of attorney) to submit complaints on their behalf. Should the Bureau expand, limit, or maintain the ability of authorized third parties to submit complaints?

3.   Specific statutorily-permissible suggestions regarding the Bureau's consumer inquiry processes, including:

a.   The Bureau currently accepts consumer inquiries via telephone and mail. Should the Bureau add or discontinue any channels for accepting inquiries?

b.   Should the Bureau develop web chat systems to support consumers' submission of inquiries?

c.   Should the Bureau develop a process for companies to provide timely responses to consumer inquiries sent to them by the Bureau? If so, how should the Bureau balance its objective of providing timely and understandable information to consumers . . . with its objective of reducing unwarranted regulatory burden on companies?

d.   Should the Bureau publish data about consumer inquiries? If so, what types of data or analyses about consumer inquiries should be shared with the public?

The RFI returned 413 comments from private citizens and representatives of the financial industry. Many of the comments were short and supportive of the CFPB:

"The Consumer Financial Protection Bureau needs to be strengthened, not gutted. It is the job of government to protect American consumers from predatory commercial practices. The

Bureau's consumer complaint and inquiry practices should be maintained and, whenever possible, increased."

In contrast, the Independent Community Bankers of America ("ICBA") commented negatively on the CFPB's database. The ICBA testified that it was concerned with the Bureau's collection and control of data, particularly the "lack of written procedures and documentation for data intake and management."

A representative of the National Association of Federally-Insured Credit Unions argued that the database "gives a false impression that the CFPB has investigated complaints and determined that they are true. However, this is not the case, and the CFPB regularly publishes complaints that are not fully verified. Unfortunately, there is no process in place to assure that consumer complaints are fully vetted, and without an extra level of due diligence the database frequently operates as showcase for subjective criticism."

In early 2017, Rep. Matt Salmon (R-AZ) introduced "The CFPB Data Accountability Act," which according to Rep. Salmon, "improve the current database by requiring the CFPB to verify the facts of each complaint and present this information in an aggregated format so that consumers have better access to CFPB-collected data and can make better decisions about their financial futures."

While some wanted to reform the Consumer Financial Protection Bureau, others such as Sen. Ted Cruz, (R-TX), and Rep. John Ratcliffe (R-TX) filed bills to repeal Title X of the Dodd-Frank Wall Street Reform Act, which established the CFPB.

Sen. Cruz stated, "Don't let the name fool you, the Consumer Financial Protection Bureau does little to protect consumers. During the Obama administration, the CFPB grew in power and magnitude without any accountability to Congress and the people, and I am encouraged by the actions President Trump has begun to take to roll back the harmful impacts of an out-of-control bureaucracy,"

Rep. Ratcliffe said, "The past several years showed us precisely why massive swaths of federal regulations are never the right solution to help hard-working Americans. President Trump has made it clear he'll join us in our fight to dismantle Dodd-Frank and finally offer some relief to the small business owners throughout Texas and across the country who've been hit hardest by its devastating impact."

What are Director Kraninger's options in this situation and what should she do?

Appendix

12 United States Code—Banks & Banking (2018)

CHAPTER 53—Wall Street Reform and Consumer Protection

SUBCHAPTER V—Bureau of Consumer Financial Protection

§ 5511. Purpose, objectives, and functions

(a) Purpose

The Bureau shall seek to implement and, where applicable, enforce Federal consumer financial law consistently for the purpose of ensuring that all consumers have access to markets for consumer financial products and services and that markets for consumer financial products and services are fair, transparent, and competitive.

(b) Objectives

The Bureau is authorized to exercise its authorities under Federal consumer financial law for the purposes of ensuring that, with respect to consumer financial products and services—

(1) consumers are provided with timely and understandable information to make responsible decisions about financial transactions;

(2) consumers are protected from unfair, deceptive, or abusive acts and practices and from discrimination;

(3) outdated, unnecessary, or unduly burdensome regulations are regularly identified and addressed in order to reduce unwarranted regulatory burdens;

(4) Federal consumer financial law is enforced consistently, without regard to the status of a person as a depository institution, in order to promote fair competition; and

(5) markets for consumer financial products and services operate transparently and efficiently to facilitate access and innovation.

(c) Functions

The primary functions of the Bureau are—

(1) conducting financial education programs;

(2) collecting, investigating, and responding to consumer complaints;

(3) collecting, researching, monitoring, and publishing information relevant to the functioning of markets for consumer financial products and services to identify risks to consumers and the proper functioning of such markets;

(4) subject to sections 5514 through 5516 of this title, supervising covered persons for compliance with Federal consumer financial law, and taking

appropriate enforcement action to address violations of Federal consumer financial law;

(5) issuing rules, orders, and guidance implementing Federal consumer financial law; and

(6) performing such support activities as may be necessary or useful to facilitate the other functions of the Bureau.

(Pub. L. 111–203, title X, § 1021, July 21, 2010, 124 Stat. 1979.)

§ 5534. Response to consumer complaints and inquiries

(a) Timely regulator response to consumers

The Bureau shall establish, in consultation with the appropriate Federal regulatory agencies, reasonable procedures to provide a timely response to consumers, in writing where appropriate, to complaints against, or inquiries concerning, a covered person, including—

(1) steps that have been taken by the regulator in response to the complaint or inquiry of the consumer;

(2) any responses received by the regulator from the covered person; and

(3) any follow-up actions or planned follow-up actions by the regulator in response to the complaint or inquiry of the consumer.

(b) Timely response to regulator by covered person

A covered person subject to supervision and primary enforcement by the Bureau pursuant to section 5515 of this title shall provide a timely response, in writing where appropriate, to the Bureau, the prudential regulators, and any other agency having jurisdiction over such covered person concerning a consumer complaint or inquiry, including—

(1) steps that have been taken by the covered person to respond to the complaint or inquiry of the consumer;

(2) responses received by the covered person from the consumer; and

(3) follow-up actions or planned follow-up actions by the covered person to respond to the complaint or inquiry of the consumer.

(c) Provision of information to consumers

(1) In general

A covered person subject to supervision and primary enforcement by the Bureau pursuant to section 5515 of this title shall, in a timely manner, comply with a consumer request for information in the control or possession of such covered person concerning the consumer financial product or service that the consumer obtained from such covered person, including supporting written documentation, concerning the account of the consumer.

(2) Exceptions

A covered person subject to supervision and primary enforcement by the Bureau pursuant to section 5515 of this title, a prudential regulator, and any other agency having jurisdiction over a covered person subject to supervision and primary enforcement by the Bureau pursuant to section 5515 of this title may not be required by this section to make available to the consumer—

(A) any confidential commercial information, including an algorithm used to derive credit scores or other risk scores or predictors;

(B) any information collected by the covered person for the purpose of preventing fraud or money laundering, or detecting or making any report regarding other unlawful or potentially unlawful conduct;

(C) any information required to be kept confidential by any other provision of law; or

(D) any nonpublic or confidential information, including confidential supervisory information.

(d) Agreements with other agencies

The Bureau shall enter into a memorandum of understanding with any affected Federal regulatory agency regarding procedures by which any covered person, and the prudential regulators, and any other agency having jurisdiction over a covered person, including the Secretary of the Department of Housing and Urban Development and the Secretary of Education, shall comply with this section.

(Pub. L. 111–203, title X, § 1034, July 21, 2010, 124 Stat. 2008.)

Effective Date

Section effective on the designated transfer date, see section 1037 of Pub. L. 111–203, set out as a note under section 5531 of this title.

B. COURTS

1. TWO TYPES OF JUDGES

When a statute is disputed in court, there are two broad theories of statutory interpretation used by judges: intentionalism and the "new textualism."

The intentionalist judge reads unclear statutory language according to what the judge believes is the legislature's purpose in passing the law. This is often accomplished by looking at the "legislative history" of the statute, materials created during the legislative process, such as committee reports, legislator floor statements, and explanatory statements of conference committees.

The new textualist judge interprets statutory language by trying to determine the original meaning of the statutory language by scrutinizing the words and structure of the statute. If the textualist judge looks outside of the statute for guidance, it is for evidence of how the words were used in other contemporary statutes or understood when the statute was drafted. Legislative history evidence is employed only in a situation where the textual cues would lead to an absurd result.

MAKING OUR DEMOCRACY WORK

Justice Stephen Breyer, 2010 pp. 88–97

Ordinarily, cases that reach the Supreme Court involve ambiguous statutory language. When judges interpret that language, they look to the words that issue, to surrounding text, to the statute history, to legal traditions, to precedent, to the statute's purposes, and to its consequences evaluated in light of those purposes. Of these I find the last two—purposes and consequences—most helpful most often. I believe maintaining a strong workable relationship with Congress requires the Court to use these two tools to help unlock the meaning of a statutory text. A strong relationship, in turn, helps the nation's institutions, and the law, function well.

. . .

To determine a provision's purpose, the judge looks for the problem that Congress enacted the statue to resolve and asks how Congress expected the particular statutory words in question to help resolve that problem. The judge also examines the likely consequences of a proposed interpretation, asking whether they are more likely to further than to hinder achievement of the provision's purpose. In doing so, a judge may examine a wide range of relevant legislative materials. Furthermore, the judge can try to determine a particular provision's purpose even if no one in Congress said anything or even thought about the matter. In that case the judge (sometimes describing what he does in terms of the purpose of a hypothetical "reasonable legislator") will determine that hypothetical purpose in order to increase the likelihood that the Court's interpretation will further the more general purposes of the statute that Congress enacted.

. . .

Three sets of considerations, taken together, explain why I believe the Court is obliged to follow a purpose-oriented approach.

First, judicial consideration of a statute's purposes helps to further the Constitution's democratic goals. In a representative democracy, legislators must ultimately act in ways that voters find acceptable. But voters are unaware of the detailed language that legislators write. They can do no more than consider whether a legislator's work corresponds roughly to their own views, typically expressed in terms of general objectives, say peace, prosperity, healthy environment, and economizing.

A legislator whose statue furthers a popular objective will seek credit at election time—at least if the statute works reasonably well. But suppose the statute does not work well. Then whom should the voters blame? If courts have interpreted the statute in accordance with the legislator's purposes, there is no one to blame but the legislator. But if courts disregard the statute's purposes, it is much harder for the voter to know who is responsible when results go awry.

. . .

The more the court relies on text-based methods alone to interpret statutes, the easier it will be for legislators to avoid responsibility for a badly written statute simply by saying that the Court reach results they did not favor. The more the court seeks realistically to ascertain the purposes of a statue and it interprets its provisions in ways that further those purposes, the harder it will be for the legislator to escape responsibility for the statute's objectives, and the easier it will be for voters to hold their legislators responsible for their legislative decisions, including the consequences of the statutes for which they vote.

Second, a purpose-oriented approach helps individual statutes work better for those whom Congress intended to help.

. . .

Third, and most important, by emphasizing purpose of the Court will help Congress better accomplish its own legislative work. Congress does not, cannot, and need not write statutes that precisely and exhaustively explain where and how each of the statute's provisions will apply. For one thing, doing so would require too many words. Who wants statutory encyclopedias that spell out in excruciating detail all potential applications in all potential circumstances? Who could read them?

For another thing, linguistic imprecision, vagueness, and ambiguity are often useful, even necessary, statutory instruments. Congress may not know just how its statute should apply in future circumstances where it can see that future only dimly, and new situations will always emerge. Congress may want to consider only one aspect of a complex, detailed subject, an aspect that warrants a few general words that simply point a court in the right direction. Congress may want to use a general standard, such as "restraint of trade," while intending courts to develop more specific content on a case-by-case common-law basis. Or, the English language may lack words that succinctly express, say, the necessary quantitative measurement, as, for example, when Congress seeks to punish more severely those to commit "serious" or "violent" crimes.

In these circumstances, congressional drafting staffs may well use general or imprecise words while relying on committee reports, statements of members delivered on the floor of Congress, legislative hearings, and similar materials to convey intended purposes, hence meaning, scope, and reference. Congress can use that drafting system if, and only if, it can count on the courts to consider legislative purposes when interpreting statutes and look at the associated legislative materials to help determine legislative purpose. When courts do so, drafters, legislators, and judges can work together. They act in tandem with Congress, carrying out the legislators' objectives in even the most complex statutes, such as those dealing with bankruptcy, transit system mergers, or pension benefit guarantees.

A MATTER OF INTERPRETATION

Justice Antonin Scalia (1997) pp. 16–23

Statutory interpretation is such a broad subject that the substance of it cannot be discussed comprehensively here. It is worth examining a few aspects, however, if only to demonstrate the great degree of confusion that prevails. We can begin at the most fundamental possible level. So utterly unformed is the American law of statutory interpretation that not only is its methodology unclear, but even its very objective is. Consider the basic question: What are we looking for when we construe a statute?

You will find it frequently said in judicial opinions of my court and others that the judge's objective in interpreting a statute is to give effect to "the intent of the legislature." This principle, in one form or another, goes back at least as far as Blackstone. Unfortunately, it does not square with some of the (few) generally accepted concrete rules of statutory construction. One is the rule that when the text of a statute is clear, that is the end of the, matter. Why should that be so, if what the legislature intended, rather than what it said, is the object of our inquiry? In selecting the words of the statute, the legislature might have misspoken. Why not permit that to be demonstrated from the floor debates? Or indeed, why not accept, as proper material for the court consider, later explanations by the legislators—a sworn affidavit signed by the majority of each house, for example, as to what they really meant?

Another accepted rule of construction is that ambiguities in a newly enacted statue are to be resolved in such fashion as to make the statute, not only internally consistent, but also compatible with previously enacted laws. We simply assume, for purposes of our search for "intent," that the enacting legislature was aware of all those other laws. Well of course that is a fiction, and if we were really looking for the subjective intent of the enacting legislature we would more likely find it by paying attention to the text (and legislative history) of the new statute in isolation.

The evidence suggests that, despite frequent statements to the contrary, we do not really look for subjective legislative intent. We look for a sort of "objectified" intent—the intent that a reasonable person would gather from the text of the law, placed alongside the remainder of the corpus juris. As Bishop's old treatise nicely puts it, elaborating upon the usual formulation: "[T]he primary object of all rules for interpreting statutes is to ascertain the legislative intent; or, exactly the meaning which the subject is authorized to understand the legislature intended." And the reason we adopt the objectified version is, I think, that it is simply incompatible with democratic government, or indeed, even with fair government, to have the meaning of a law determined by what the lawgiver meant, rather than by what the lawgiver promulgated. That seems to me one step worse than the trick the emperor Nero was said to engage in: posting edicts high up on the pillars, so that they could not easily be read. Government by unexpressed intent is similarity tyrannical. It is the law that governs, not the intent of the law giver. That seems to me the essence of the famous American ideal set forth in the Massachusetts constitution: a government of laws, not of men. Men may intend what they will; but it is only the laws that they an act which bind us.

. . .

I agree with Justice Holmes's remark, quoted approvingly by Justice Frankfurter in his article on the construction of statutes: "Only a day or two ago—when counsel talked of the intention of a legislature, I was indiscreet enough to say I don't care what their intention was. I only want to know what the words mean." And I agree with Holmes's other remark, quoted approvingly by Justice Jackson: "We do not inquire what the legislature meant; we ask only what the statute means."

The philosophy of interpretation I have described above is known as textualism. In some sophisticated circles, it is considered simpleminded— "wooden," "unimaginative," "pedestrian." It is none of that. To be a textualist in good standing, one need not be too dull to perceive the broader social purposes that a statute is designed, or could be designed, to serve; or too hide bound to realize that new times require new laws. One need only hold the belief that judges have no authority to pursue those broader purposes or write those new laws.

Textualism should not be confused with so-called strict constructionism, a degraded form of textualism that brings the whole philosophy into disrepute. I am not a strict constructionist, and no one ought to be—though better that, I suppose, than a nontextualist. A text should not be construed strictly, and it should not be construed leniently; it should be construed reasonably, to contain all that it fairly means.

2. TOOLS OF INTERPRETATION

a. Ordinary Meaning & Statutory Context

The interpretive tool of first resort for judges is often the ordinary or plain meaning of the statutory text. This dates back to Blackstone, "Words are generally to be understood in their usual and most known signification, not so much regarding the propriety of grammar as their general and popular use." William Blackstone, COMMENTARIES *59.

In an analysis of three years of the Roberts Court a majority of the justices used textual cues and ordinary meaning along with Supreme Court precedent more often than any other interpretive tools. Anita S. Krishnakumar, "Statutory Interpretation in the Roberts Court's First Era: An Empirical and Doctrinal Analysis," 62 *Hastings L.J.* 221, 251 (2010).

If the legislature uses a word without defining it, judges will presume the legislature was using the common or popular meaning for the word. However, evidence the word has a specialized meaning in law or in another field can overcome the presumption. Often judges will "discover" meaning through their own understanding and introspection of a word. Another popular method is to refer to dictionary definitions to understand a word's usage, although the definitions may differ among different dictionaries or even in the same dictionary. Judges may also refer to popular literature, government materials, and in other laws to better understand the meaning of a word.

Critics of "ordinary meaning" argue that if a judge is using their own understanding of a word, they can impose their own policy preferences. See Ward Farnsworth et al., Ambiguity about Ambiguity: An Empirical Inquiry into Legal Interpretation, 2 *J. of Legal Analysis* 257, 259 (2010).

Courts also interpret words by looking at the term or phrase's statutory context. A judge may try to understand meaning by looking at the larger provision, the entire act, or other similar statutes. Justice Scalia and Bryan Garner include this practice as part of their "whole text canon." See, A. Scalia & B. Garner, READING LAW: THE INTERPRETATION OF LEGAL TEXTS at 167 (2012). Judges also find meaning when the legislature excludes language in one provision that is included elsewhere in the same statute.

Finally, judges may read words in the context of the statute's declarations of purpose, the way the entire statutory scheme was meant to function, or the practical consequences of one reading or another.

MOBLEY V. THE STATE
Supreme Court of Georgia
307 Ga. 59 (2019)

As we have explained before, "[w]hen we consider the meaning of a statute, we must presume that the General Assembly meant what it said and said what it meant." "To that end, we must afford the statutory text its plain and ordinary meaning, we must view the statutory text in the context in which it appears, and we must read the statutory text in its most natural and reasonable way, as an ordinary speaker of the English language would." "The common and customary usages of the words are important, but so is their context." "For context, we may look to other provisions of the same statute, the structure and history of the whole statute, and the other law—constitutional, statutory, and common law alike—that forms the legal background of the statutory provision in question."

b.   Canons of Construction

STATUTORY INTERPRETATION: THEORIES, TOOLS, AND TRENDS
Valerie C. Brannon, Congressional Research Service (Updated 2018)

Over time, courts have created the "canons of construction" to serve as guiding principles for interpreting statutes. The canons supply default assumptions about the way Congress generally expresses meaning, but are not "rules" in the sense that they must invariably be applied. A judge may decline to interpret a statute in accordance with any given canon if the canon's application is not justified in that case. Some judges, especially purposivists and some pragmatists, may even doubt the general validity of the canons as interpretive rules. However, the canons are widely used and defended. Just as the justifications for using the canons of construction vary, so may judges disagree on what qualifies as a valid canon, either as a matter of theory or historical fact. These disagreements will sometimes stem from a judge's individual theory of statutory interpretation. This report's Appendix combines two preeminent anthologies of the canons of construction, providing a list of the widely accepted canons of construction. However, even the authors of these prominent lists disagree about whether certain canons are valid. This report does not attempt to set out a definitive compilation of the canons of construction, but merely describes the canons generally, giving examples where appropriate.

Generally, legal scholars and judges divide the canons into two groups: semantic and substantive canons.

The semantic, or textual, canons represent "rules of thumb for decoding legal language." Because these canons focus on statutory text, they are often favored by textualists. The semantic canons frequently reflect the rules of grammar that govern ordinary language usage. Consequently, these rules may overlap with indicators of a provision's ordinary meaning—and indeed, some authors label the principle that words should be given their ordinary meaning as a semantic canon.

. . .

In contrast to the semantic canons, the substantive canons express "judicial presumption[s] . . . in favor of or against a particular substantive outcome." Some of these canons, primarily those that protect constitutional values, are frequently described as "clear statement rules" because courts will favor certain outcomes unless the statute makes a "clear statement" that unambiguously dislodges the presumption. The substantive canons "look to the legal consequences of interpretation rather than to linguistic issues alone." If a statute is susceptible to more than one meaning, they may tip the scale toward a particular result. Accordingly, invocation of the substantive canons frequently invites judicial disagreement. The canon of constitutional avoidance provides a good example of how even a well-established substantive canon can provoke debate. The canon of constitutional avoidance provides that if one plausible reading of a statute would raise "serious doubt" about the statute's constitutionality, a court should look for another, "fairly possible" reading that would avoid the constitutional issue. Thus, for instance, the constitutional-avoidance canon might lead a court to adopt a limiting construction of a statutory provision, if a broader interpretation would allow the government to exercise a constitutionally problematic amount of power.

. . .

[Note: the author has <u>underlined</u> and used SMALL CAPS for the most commonly used canons.]

Semantic Canons

1. **"Artificial-Person Canon"**: "The word person includes corporations and other entities, but not the sovereign."

2. *Casus Omissus*: A matter not covered by a statute should be treated as intentionally omitted (*casus omissus pro omisso habendus est*).

3. **"Conjunctive/Disjunctive Canon"**: "And" usually "joins a conjunctive list," combining items, while "or" usually joins "a disjunctive list," denoting alternatives.

4. <u>*EJUSDEM GENERIS*</u>: A general term that follows an enumerated list of more specific terms should be interpreted to cover only "matters similar to those specified."

5. <u>*EXPRESIO UNIUS*</u>: "The expression of one thing implies the exclusion of others (*expressio unius est exclusio alterius*)." This canon is strongest "when the items expressed are members of an 'associated group

or series,' justifying the inference that items not mentioned were excluded by deliberate choice, not inadvertence."

6.   "**Gender/Number Canon**": Usually, "the masculine includes the feminine (and vice versa) and the singular includes the plural (and vice versa)."

7.   "**General/Specific Canon**": Where two laws conflict, "the specific governs the general (*generalia specialibus non derogant*)." That is, "a precisely drawn, detailed statute pre-empts more general remedies," and conversely, "a statute dealing with a narrow, precise, and specific subject is not submerged by a later enacted statute covering a more generalized spectrum."

8.   "**General-Terms Canon**": "General terms are to be given their general meaning (*generalia verba sunt generaliter intelligenda*)."

9.   **Grammar Canon**: Statutes "follow accepted standards of grammar."

10.   "**Harmonious-Reading Canon**": "The provisions of a text should be interpreted in a way that renders them compatible, not contradictory."

11.   "**Irreconcilability Canon**": "If a text contains truly irreconcilable provisions at the same level of generality, and they have been simultaneously adopted, neither provision should be given effect."

12.   LEGISLATIVE HISTORY CANONS:

- "[C]lear evidence of congressional intent" gathered from legislative history "may illuminate ambiguous text."

- The most "authoritative source for finding the Legislature's intent lies in the Committee Reports on the bill."

- Floor statements, especially those made by a bill's sponsors prior to its passage, may be relevant, but should be used cautiously.

- "[T]he views of a subsequent Congress form a hazardous basis for inferring the intent of an earlier one."

13.   "**Mandatory/Permissive Canon**": "Shall" is usually mandatory and imposes a duty; "may" usually grants discretion.

14.   "**Nearest-Reasonable-Referent Canon**": "When the syntax involves something other than a parallel series of nouns or verbs, a prepositive or postpositive modifier normally applies only to the nearest reasonable referent."

15.   *NOSCITUR A SOCIIS*: "Associated words bear on one another's meaning . . . ."

16. **ORDINARY MEANING CANON**: Words should be given "their ordinary, everyday meanings," unless "Congress has provided a specific definition" or "the context indicates that they bear a technical sense."

17. **PLAIN MEANING RULE AND ABSURDITY DOCTRINE**: "Follow the plain meaning of the statutory text, except when a textual plain meaning requires an absurd result or suggests a scrivener's error."

18. **"Predicate-Act Canon"**: "The law has long recognized that the '[a]uthorization of an act also authorizes a necessary predicate act.'"

19. **"Prefatory-Materials" and "Titles-and-Headings" Canons**: Preambles, purpose clauses, recitals, titles, and headings are all "permissible indicators of meaning," though they generally will not be dispositive.

20. **Presumption of Consistent Usage**: "Generally, identical words used in different parts of the same statute are . . . presumed to have the same meaning." Conversely, "a material variation in terms suggests a variation in meaning."

21. **"Presumption of Nonexclusive 'Include'"**: "[T]he term 'including' is not one of all-embracing definition, but connotes simply an illustrative application of the general principle."

22. **"PRESUMPTION OF VALIDITY"**: "An interpretation that validates outweighs one that invalidates (*ut res magis valeat quam pereat*)." Stated another way, courts should construe statutes to have effect.

23. **"Proviso Canon"**: "A proviso," or "a clause that introduces a condition," traditionally by using the word "provided," "conditions the principal matter that it qualifies—almost always the matter immediately preceding."

24. **Punctuation Canon**: Statutes "follow accepted punctuation standards," and "[p]unctuation is a permissible indicator of meaning."

25. **Purposive Construction**: "[I]nterpret ambiguous statutes so as best to carry out their statutory purposes."

26. ***Reddendo Singula Singulis***: "[W]ords and provisions are referred to their appropriate objects . . . ."

27. **RULE AGAINST SURPLUSAGE**: Courts should "give effect, if possible, to every clause and word of a statute" so that "no clause is rendered 'superfluous, void, or insignificant.'"

28. **RULE OF THE LAST ANTECEDENT**: "[A] limiting clause or phrase . . . should ordinarily be read as modifying only the noun or phrase that it immediately follows . . . ."

29. **"Scope-of-Subparts Canon"**: "Material within an indented subpart relates only to that subpart; material contained in unindented text relates to all the following or preceding indented subparts."

30. **Series-Qualifier Canon**: " 'When there is a straightforward, parallel construction that involves all nouns or verbs in a series,' a modifier at the end of the list 'normally applies to the entire series.' "

31. **"Subordinating/Superordinating Canon"**: "Subordinating language (signaled by *subject to*) or superordinating language (signaled by *notwithstanding* or *despite*) merely shows which provision prevails in the event of a clash—but does not necessarily denote a clash of provisions."

32. **"Unintelligibility Canon"**: "[A] statute must be capable of construction and interpretation; otherwise it will be inoperative and void."

33. **"Whole-Text Canon"**: Courts "do not . . . construe statutory phrases in isolation; [they] read statutes as a whole."

Substantive Canons:

1. CANON OF CONSTITUTIONAL AVOIDANCE: "[W]here an otherwise acceptable construction of a statute would raise serious constitutional problems, the Court will construe the statute to avoid such problems unless such construction is plainly contrary to the intent of Congress."

2. **"Dog that Didn't Bark" Presumption**: A "prior legal rule should be retained if no one in legislative deliberations even mentioned the rule or discussed any changes in the rule."

3. FEDERALISM CANONS: Courts will generally require a clear statement before finding that a federal statute "alter[s] the federal-state balance." Thus, for example, courts require Congress to speak with "unmistakeable clarity" in order to "abrogate state sovereign immunity."

4. *In Pari Materia*: "[S]tatutes addressing the same subject matter generally should be read 'as if they were one law.' "

5. **"*Mens Rea* Canon"**: Courts should "presume that a criminal statute derived from the common law carries with it the requirement of a culpable mental state—even if no such limitation appears in the text— unless it is clear that the Legislature intended to impose strict liability." In the context of civil liability, "willfulness . . . cover[s] not only knowing violations of a standard, but reckless ones as well."

6. **Nondelegation Doctrine**: Courts should presume that "Congress does not delegate authority without sufficient guidelines."

7. **"Penalty/Illegality Canon"**: "[A] statute that penalizes an act makes it unlawful . . . ."

8.   **"Pending-Action Canon"**: "When statutory law is altered during the pendency of a lawsuit, the courts at every level must apply the new law unless doing so would violate the presumption against retroactivity."

9.   PRESUMPTION AGAINST EXTRATERRITORIALITY: Courts should presume, "absent a clear statement from Congress, that federal statutes do not apply outside the United States."

10. "PRESUMPTION AGAINST HIDING ELEPHANTS IN MOUSEHOLES": "Congress . . . does not alter the fundamental details of a regulatory scheme in vague terms or ancillary provisions—it does not, one might say, hide elephants in mouseholes."

11. PRESUMPTION AGAINST IMPLIED REPEALS: "[R]epeals by implication are not favored."

12. **Presumption Against Implied Right of Action**: Courts should not imply a private remedy "unless . . . congressional intent [to create a private remedy] can be inferred from the language of the statute, the statutory structure, or some other source." Without such intent, "a cause of action does not exist."

13. PRESUMPTION AGAINST RETROACTIVE LEGISLATION: "[C]ourts read laws as prospective in application unless Congress has unambiguously instructed retroactivity."

14. **Presumption Against Waiver of Sovereign Immunity**: A waiver of sovereign immunity "cannot be implied but must be unequivocally expressed."

15. PRESUMPTION FOR RETAINING THE COMMON LAW: " '[W]hen a statute covers an issue previously governed by the common law,' [courts] must presume that 'Congress intended to retain the substance of the common law.' "

16. **Presumptions in Favor of Judicial Process**: Courts sometimes require clear statements from Congress in order to bar judicial review of certain claims.

17. **"Presumption of Continuity"**: "Congress does not create discontinuities in legal rights and obligations without some clear statement."

18. PRESUMPTION OF LEGISLATIVE ACQUIESCENCE: "[A] long adhered to administrative interpretation dating from the legislative enactment, with no subsequent change having been made in the statute involved, raises a presumption of legislative acquiescence . . . ." This also applies to judicial interpretations of the statute. If Congress reenacts a statute without any change, it incorporates any settled judicial constructions of the statute "so broad and unquestioned that [a court] must presume Congress knew of and endorsed it." However, "[o]rdinarily, . . .

courts are slow to attribute significance to the failure of Congress to act on particular legislation."

19. **Presumption of Narrow Construction of Exceptions**: "An exception to a 'general statement of policy' is 'usually read . . . narrowly in order to preserve the primary operation of the provision.' "

20. "**Presumption of Purposive Amendment**": Courts should assume that Congress intends any statutory "amendment to have real and substantial effect."

21. "<u>REPEAL-OF-REPEALER CANON</u>": "The repeal or expiration of a repealing statute does not reinstate the original statute."

22. "**Repealability Canon**": "[O]ne legislature is competent to repeal any act which a former legislature was competent to pass; and . . . one legislature cannot abridge the powers of a succeeding legislature."

23. <u>RULE OF LENITY</u>: "Ambiguity in a statute defining a crime or imposing a penalty should be resolved in the defendant's favor."

3. LEGISLATIVE HISTORY

Despite the efforts of the "new textualists" to limit, if not eliminate, the use of legislative history as an interpretive tool, judges continue to examine the legislative documents related to a statute to understand the legislature's purpose or intent. Legislative history is the record of a legislature's deliberations and debates when creating statutory language. Why are some judges and legal academics so opposed to using legislative history? The best reason may be past cases where judges have misused, or perhaps misinterpreted, legislative history to achieve a result that was at odds with the plain statutory language.

One of Justice Scalia's favorite examples of the Court improperly deciding a case is *Church of the Holy Trinity v. United States*, 143 U.S. 457 (1892). In that case, a church in New York contracted the services of an English priest. The Alien Contract Labor Law of 1885, however, prohibited "the importation and migration of foreigners and aliens under contract or agreement to perform labor or service of any kind in the United States, its territories, and the District of Columbia."

The court held that a minister was not a foreign laborer under the statute even though he was a foreigner. The Court declared the United States, "a Christian people, and the morality of the country is deeply engrafted upon Christianity." Justice Brewer held that a principle of statutory construction that "a thing may be within the letter of the statute and yet not within the statute, because not within its spirit, nor within the intention of its makers."

Justice Scalia argued that courts should follow the text of a law rather than attempt to read exceptions into the law in accordance with the legislative intent calling the *Holy Trinity* decision as "nothing but an invitation to judicial lawmaking".

More recently, in *United Steelworkers v. Weber*, 443 U.S. 193, 201 (1979) the Court interpreted Title VII of the Civil Rights Act of 1964, which makes it unlawful for employers to discriminate because of race when hiring and training employees, to determine if the law prohibited a private employer from using an affirmative action plan to increase the number of Black trainees. Justice Brennan, writing for the majority, stated that a literal interpretation of the Act may forbid such plans, because White employees may not be accepted into the training program just because they were White. The Court did not adopt a "literal construction" but rather used the legislative history of Title VII to come to a different result. Justice Brennan cited the committee report and statements from senators and stated that the law sought to address racial injustice, could not be read to prohibit affirmative action efforts by the private sector.

More often than not, however, judges do not use legislative history to contradict a clear text, but as an aid to understand an ambiguous statute's purpose. As justice Kagan wrote in *Milner v. Dep't of the Navy*, 562 U.S. 562, 572 (2011), "Those of us who make use of legislative history believe that clear evidence of congressional intent may illuminate ambiguous text. We will not take the opposite tack of allowing ambiguous legislative history to muddy clear statutory language."

Judge Katzmann states that the "dominant mode of statutory interpretation over the past century" was that legislation is a purposive act and that judges shout read statutes in accord with Congress's purposes. Robert A Katzmann, JUDGING STATUTES p. 31. Purposivists emphasize that legislative history is the record of that process and judges should pay attention to those materials since it was the legislature created the policy and statutory language.

Textualists also claim to honor the legislature's supremacy by using the enacted text to understand the statute, rather than the committee reports and floor statements, which were a. never voted upon and may reflect the views of a minority of the legislature, b. may be conflicting, and c. is subject to manipulation. However, even textualist judges may also look to legislative history to when a term may have a specialized meaning or when a textual reading leads to an odd result.

The textualist critique of legislative history has had an effect on statutory interpretation. Judges are now more likely to use legislative history only in light of the statutory text.

What legislative history will be used most often or be deemed the most reliable? In her concurrence in *Dig. Realty Tr., Inc. v. Somers*, 138 S.Ct.

767, 782 (2018) Justice Sotomayor found that committee reports "are a particularly reliable source" of legislative history. By contrast, judges have traditionally found floor debates to be a weaker form of legislative history because it shows the purpose or intent of just an individual legislator. Another form of legislative history that judges will rely upon is legislative action amending an existing statute or bill. Courts will presume that the legislature intended amendments to have a real effect on the language. As Judge Katzmann writes,

> The task, as Senator [Orin] Hatch commented, is to draw upon legislative history "properly applied" in "reliable forms," and to separate the wheat from the chaff among legislative materials. For courts, that means, in part, having a better understanding of the legislative process and its rules, and appreciating the internal hierarchy of communications. Robert A Katzmann, JUDGING STATUTES p. 54.

Some legislative drafters worry about what will happen if an "intentionalist judge," one who looks for the legislature's intent in legislative history, is interpreting a statute. Arthur Rynearson writes that while the drafter "cannot prevent an intentionalist judge from resorting to legislative history," it is possible to assist such a judge to find intent in the statute instead. He suggests using:

- The long title as an abridged form of a "purposes" section;

- A findings section, especially if Congress' power to legislate depends on particular facts or circumstances;

- A purposes section tailored to the legislator's intent for the bill and in terms "that serve as the lowest common denominator of what is being expressed;" and

- Definitions, especially if they are amended later in the process to reflect an "interpretation, nuance, or 'spin'" that a legislative committee or key legislator gives a term or phrase.

See, Arthur Rynearson, LEGISLATIVE DRAFTING STEP-BY-STEP (2013) pp. 149–150.

C. INTERPRETATION IN PRACTICE

Judges may have a preferred method of interpretation, but they often will use a variety of available tools. In this case the Massachusetts Supreme Judicial Court uses plain meaning and contextual cues, various canons of interpretation, and legislative history. In the end the court still considers the statute ambiguous and uses the rule of lenity.

COMMONWEALTH V. MONTARVO

Supreme Judicial Court of Massachusetts
486 Mass. 535 (2020)

Colloquially referred to as the "three strikes" law, the habitual offender statute, G. L. c. 279, § 25, enhances the penalty for a defendant who, after two prior convictions resulting in State or Federal prison sentences of three or more years, receives a third felony conviction. This case requires us to determine whether § 25 (a) of the law allows sentencing judges to impose probation on defendants who fall within its ambit. We conclude that it does.

[Note: Defendant was convicted by a jury of assault and battery with a dangerous weapon and armed assault with intent to murder. Both convictions carried the possibility of habitual criminal sentencing enhancements. After trial, the judge found that the § 25 (a) enhancements applied to defendant and rejected the defendant's argument that the judge could impose probation rather than imprisonment.

The judge sentenced defendant to twenty years in prison.]

Because the issue whether a sentencing judge has discretion to impose probation under § 25 (a) is a matter of statutory interpretation, we review it *de novo*. As will become apparent, the question admits no easy answers.

1.   Section 25's text.

The Commonwealth and the defendant appear to agree that § 25 (a)'s text is unambiguous. They disagree about what the text unambiguously says; the Commonwealth argues that § 25 (a) clearly bars a judge from imposing probation, and the defendant argues the opposite. We disagree with both—the statute's text is ambiguous.

Legislative intent controls our interpretation of statutes. "To determine the Legislature's intent, we look to the words of the statute, construed by the ordinary and approved usage of the language, considered in connection with the cause of its enactment, the mischief or imperfection to be remedied and the main object to be accomplished." "We derive the words' usual and accepted meaning from sources presumably known to the statute's enactors, such as their use in other legal contexts and dictionary definitions." "Where the statutory language is clear and unambiguous, our inquiry ends."

a.   Plain language.

At first glance, G. L. c. 279, § 25 (a), seems to be unequivocal on the issue of sentencing discretion. The subsection reads:

"Whoever is convicted of a felony and has been previously twice convicted and sentenced to state prison or state correctional facility or a federal corrections facility for a term not less than [three] years by the commonwealth, another state or the United States, and who does not show that the person has been pardoned for either crime on the ground that the person was innocent, shall be considered a habitual criminal and *shall be punished by imprisonment in state prison or state correctional facility for such felony for the maximum term provided by law.*" (emphasis added).

Standing alone, the emphasized language (maximum term language) is clear: judges must sentence defendants convicted under § 25 (a) to the maximum term provided by the underlying offense. See *Commonwealth v. Tuitt*, (construing phrase "the maximum term provided by law" found in § 25 [a]'s predecessor to "preclude[ ] the possibility that the judge could have suspended all or any portion of the defendant's life sentence"). Probation appears to be unavailable.

The Commonwealth would have us stop our analysis here. A juxtaposition of the habitual offender's subsections, however, dispels the facial clarity of § 25 (a). See *Plymouth Retirement Bd. v. Contributory Retirement Appeal Bd.*, ("Even clear statutory language is not read in isolation"). Under G. L. c. 279, § 25 (b), if a defendant has been convicted twice before of one or more of certain offenses, then the defendant "shall be considered a habitual offender and shall be imprisoned in the state prison or state correctional facility for the maximum term provided by law for the offense enumerated . . . . No sentence imposed under this subsection shall be reduced or suspended nor shall such person so sentenced be eligible for probation, parole, work release or furlough or receive any deduction from such person's sentence for good conduct." (Emphasis added.)

Section 25 (a) makes no mention of disallowing probation, whereas § 25 (b) does. These are not two independent statutes, but rather two subsections of the same statute that were enacted simultaneously. When the Legislature includes a phrase in one subsection of a statute but not in another, this invites the "negative implication" that the phrase was purposefully excluded. See *Halebian v. Berv*, (maxim of negative implication teaches "that the express inclusion of one thing implies the exclusion of another"). See also *Field v. Mans* (U.S. 1995)(when "contrasting statutory sections [were] originally enacted simultaneously in relevant respects," then negative implication is "more apparently deliberate"). Examined in this light, the absence in § 25 (a) of any prohibition on probation leads to a straightforward conclusion: § 25 (b) bars a judge from imposing probation, whereas § 25 (a) does not.

The maxim of negative implication requires cautious application. Cautious application, however, does not mean no application. *Mans*, (maxim "is not illegitimate, but merely limited"). Context determines the maxim's application. A. Scalia & B.A. Garner, READING LAW: THE INTERPRETATION OF LEGAL TEXTS 107 (2012) ("Context establishes the conditions for applying the [maxim], but where those conditions exist, the [maxim] . . . validly describes how people express themselves and understand verbal expression"). The context here is how to address what would otherwise appear to be surplusage in the statute. See *Ropes & Gray LLP v. Jalbert* ("A statute should be construed so as to give effect to each word, and no word shall be regarded as surplusage").

b.   Surplusage. We cannot ignore that the same maximum term language that the Commonwealth contends eliminates sentencing discretion in § 25 (a) also appears in § 25 (b) alongside an explicit prohibition on probation. If the Legislature intended the maximum term language in § 25 (a) alone to bar probation, then it would not have needed anything more than this maximum term language in § 25 (b) in order to prohibit probation under that subsection. The addition of the words "nor should such person be so sentenced be eligible for probation" to § 25 (b) would have been unnecessary to achieve the intended meaning.

Three additional textual indications demonstrate that the Legislature intended the punishment imposed on the "habitual violent offenders" sentenced under § 25 (b) to be both more limited in its application and harsher once imposed than the penalties imposed under § 25 (a). First, whereas § 25 (b) "provides for enhanced penalties without parole for violent offenders who have two prior convictions from a list of nearly forty violent crimes," the predicate offenses for § 25 (a) have no violence requirement. Second, whereas the predicate offenses under § 25 (b) must have been separately prosecuted, the predicate offenses for § 25 (a) have no separate prosecution requirement. Third, whereas § 25 (d) requires that a judge warn a defendant who is either pleading or sentenced to one of § 25 (b)'s predicate offenses that this implicates § 25 (b)'s bar on probation, § 25 (a) has no analogous notice requirement.

The defendant would have us end our inquiry here, but the matter is not so simple. The question remains: If the maximum term language does not bar probation in § 25 (a), then what does it do? Just as the Commonwealth creates a surplusage problem in § 25 (b)by insisting that the maximum term language prohibits probation in § 25 (a), the defendant's argument that § 25 (a) allows for probation also renders a different part of § 25 (b) superfluous. For example, a judge may not impose a reduced sentence under § 25 (b). The maximum term language present in both § 25 (a) and § 25 (b), however, already appears to prohibit reduced sentences. Either the maximum term language does not mean what it says, or the prohibition on reduced sentences language in § 25 (b) is superfluous. Neither outcome is satisfactory.

Consequently, whichever way the plain language of G. L. c. 279, § 25, is read, some aspect of it is superfluous. Thus, we are left to conclude that the text of G. L. c. 279, § 25 (a), is ambiguous on the matter of probation.

2. Legislative history. Because the text of G. L. c. 279, § 25, is ambiguous, we turn next to the statute's legislative history.

The relevant history begins not in the halls of the Legislature but within our own case law. We held in *Commonwealth v. Zapata* that the Legislature's failure to include an express prohibition on probation in the home invasion statute, meant that judges retained discretion to impose probation on defendants sentenced under the statute. After surveying other statutes that prevent judges from imposing probation, we noted that "when the Legislature intends to bar probation, it knows how to say so explicitly."

In 2012, the Legislature amended G. L. c. 279, § 25. Prior to being amended, G. L. c. 279, § 25, read in its entirety:

> "Whoever has been twice convicted of crime and sentenced and committed to prison in this or another state, or once in this and once or more in another state, for terms of not less than three years each, and does not show that he has been pardoned for either crime on the ground that he was innocent, shall, upon conviction of a felony, be considered an habitual criminal and be punished by imprisonment in the state prison for the maximum term provided by law as a penalty for the felony for which he is then to be sentenced."

When the Legislature amended the law, it assigned, with minor linguistic changes, what once constituted the whole of the statute to § 25 (a). The Legislature also added three other new subsections, G. L. c. 279, § 25 (b)–(d). As already detailed, the Legislature included in § 25 (b), but not in § 25 (a), an express prohibition of probation.

"The Legislature is presumed to be aware of the prior state of the law as explicated by the decisions of this court." It is therefore not unreasonable to conclude that in amending the habitual offender statute, the Legislature added the express prohibition on probation and other sentencing options to § 25 (b) in response to the *Zapata* decision. In other words, despite the redundancy of including a prohibition on reduced sentences alongside the maximum term language in § 25 (b), the Legislature intended to foreclose the possibility of suspended sentences, probation, parole, work release, furlough, and deductions for good conduct under § 25 (b) while leaving these options available under § 25 (a).

Examination of a report from the amendment's conference committee further supports this conclusion. After the bill was reported out of the conference committee, members noticed that some of the language in § 25 (b) had been "incorrectly reported." The passage wrongly stated: "No sentence imposed under this section shall be reduced or suspended nor shall such person so sentenced be eligible for probation, parole, work release or furlough or receive any deduction from such person's sentence for good conduct" (emphasis added). The committee asked that "section" be changed to "subsection," which, as the final language of § 25 (b) shows, it was. Although the Legislature had an opportunity to apply the prohibition on probation to the entirety of G. L. c. 279, § 25, the Legislature deliberately chose to limit that prohibition to § 25 (b). We are bound by this choice.

3.   Rule of lenity. Although the legislative history of G. L. c. 279, § 25, supports the defendant's interpretation that probation is available under § 25 (a), the redundancy of adding all the express prohibitions to § 25 (b) remains. We thus conclude that G. L. c. 279, § 25, is ambiguous, and despite our tools of statutory interpretation, we are unable to resolve this ambiguity. "Under the rule of lenity, 'if we find that the statute is ambiguous or are unable to ascertain the intent of the Legislature, the defendant is entitled to the benefit of any rational doubt.' "This principle applies to sentencing as well as substantive provisions." Thus, we must read § 25 (a) to provide sentencing judges with the discretion to impose probation.

We acknowledge that this result, which has the effect of offering a sentencing judge in some cases a Hobson's choice between probation and a mandatory term of twenty years in prison, may appear "contrary to common sense."[12] Yet if this choice sounds familiar, that is because it is. In *Zapata*, we reached the same result. Despite the facial clarity of G. L. c. 265, § 18C, which proscribed that home invasion "shall be punished by imprisonment . . . for life or for any term of not less than twenty years," we held that probation was nonetheless available under the statute. We invited the Legislature to amend the law if we misinterpreted its intent— an invitation that, to this date, the Legislature has declined. Should the Legislature decide to do so, it may amend § 25 (a) to bar a judge from imposing probation. It need not look far for how to accomplish this goal.

NOTES & QUESTIONS

In 2018, the Tennessee Supreme Court decided *Coleman v. Olson* and stated:

> The primary goal of statutory interpretation is to carry out legislative intent without expanding or restricting the intended scope of the statute. In determining legislative intent, we first must look to the text of the statute and give the words of the statute "their natural and ordinary meaning in the context in which they appear and in

---

[12] That said, closer inspection of the facts in this case indicate some sense behind the result as applied here. The defendant could have been sentenced to the maximum term on the conviction of assault and battery with a dangerous weapon (ten years) and given probation on the conviction of armed assault with intent to murder (which carries a twenty-year maximum term), or vice versa. Indeed, public safety may be well served by having a habitual offender on probation once released from his committed sentence, as he or she transitions back into the community.

light of the statute's general purpose." When a statute's language is clear and unambiguous, we enforce the statute as written; we need not consider other sources of information. We apply the plain meaning of a statute's words in normal and accepted usage without a forced interpretation. We do not alter or amend statutes or substitute our policy judgment for that of the Legislature.

Did the Massachusetts Supreme Judicial Court do the same in this case?

1. USING AGENCY MATERIALS

As discussed earlier in this chapter, administrative agencies often work closely with the legislature to develop the law and then are often the first interpreters of the law. Agencies must interpret the law with very little precedent or official guidance, and to apply broadly rather than in the context of a case or controversy. Judges may look to agency interpretation to better understand the social problem Congress addressed by passing the statute. Judges may also give weight to how an agency interprets and applies statutory terms and provisions.

This is different from the "*Chevron* deference" to agency interpretation first announced in *Chevron U.S.A., Inc. v. Natural Resources Defense Council* (1984). Courts use *Chevron* deference when reviewing an agency interpretation of a statute that Congress empowered an agency to implement. If the statute is ambiguous, *Chevron* instructs the judge to give a reasonable agency interpretation controlling weight.

Professor Shobe's article below points out some of the ways courts utilize agency legislative history materials to influence their decisions. Justice Souter's decision in *United States v. Mead Co.* shows how the Supreme Court both limits *Chevron* deference yet may defer to agency decisions based on its expertise, known as *Skidmore* deference.

AGENCY LEGISLATIVE HISTORY
Jarrod Shobe, 68 *Emory Law Journal* 283 (2018)

In *Watkins v. Blinzinger*, Judge Easterbrook, a noted textualist, approached the question of whether personal injury awards are income for purposes of determining whether a family qualified for the Aid to Families with Dependent Children program. The language at issue in the case was drafted by the Department of Health and Human Services, which was charged with carrying out the program. As part of his analysis, Judge Easterbrook looked to a section-by-section analysis the agency provided to Congress—which the House committee also appended to its report—and to a summary of the draft bill that the Department provided with the legislative proposal. Although these documents were not dispositive, Judge Easterbrook used the section-by-section analysis to support his ruling in favor of the agency by showing that the agency's interpretation was in line with the stated purpose of the bill.

Courts have occasionally referenced agency views letters, generally where these letters were included in a congressional committee report. In *United States v. One Bell Jet Ranger II Helicopter*, a case over the potential forfeiture of a helicopter used to hunt big horn sheep, the Ninth Circuit considered whether the forfeiture provision of the Airborne Hunting Act was subject to judicial discretion or agency discretion. The Department of Interior claimed that under the statute it was up to the agency whether to seize the helicopter. The lower court ruled that it was in the court's discretion and decided that forfeiture was not warranted. To resolve the question the Ninth Circuit noted that the statutory language was proposed by the Department of Interior and looked to a views letter written by the Assistant Secretary of the Interior, which was included in the Senate report of the bill. The views letter advised the Senate that the language was intended "to confer upon the courts discretion to determine whether or not forfeiture of animals taken or equipment used in violation of the Act is appropriate in a particular case." The court noted the historic Supreme Court practice of granting deference where Congress enacts legislation proposed by an agency, but ruled against the agency's interpretation in this case, instead relying on "the statement made to Congress by the agency at the very time it presented its own amendment to the Congress as one it urged for adoption, as the more reliable."

. . .

[I]n *Lindahl v. Office of Personnel Management*, the Court considered both agency testimony and views letters in deciding in favor of the agency's interpretation. Congress had proposed a bill that would grant broad judicial review to determinations made by the Office of Personnel Management. The Court noted that in committee hearings on the proposed bill, OPM testified in opposition to the bill as written, and in response, the committee amended the statute to limit the scope of judicial review. The Director of OPM then sent both the House and Senate committees a views letter expressing support for the bill as amended, and these letters were included in the House and Senate committee reports. The Court relied on these statements to determine that Congress intended to restrict the scope of judicial review of OPM's determinations.

The Court has also considered letters sent from agencies to Congress in the pre-drafting stages of legislation, although less frequently than other types of agency legislative history and only where the pre-drafting documents turned out to be relevant to the legislative process. For example, in Thompson v. Thompson, the Justice Department, knowing that Congress was contemplating drafting legislation, sent a letter outlining a variety of legislative options to deal with parental kidnapping. This letter was referred to extensively in the congressional debates over the legislation, which is probably why the Court viewed it as reliable legislative history. The letter focused on two options: either granting jurisdiction to federal courts to enforce state custody decrees or imposing on states the duty to give full faith and credit to custody decrees of other states. The agency's letter discussed the pros and cons of each approach and ultimately argued in favor of leaving states to enforce custody decrees and against the federal approach. Although the enacted legislation did not preclude a federal cause of action, the Court relied on this letter to infer that Congress did not intend to allow a federal cause of action.

. . .

The Supreme Court has also used agency testimony to overturn agency interpretations. In *Piper v. Chris-Craft Industries, Inc.*, the Court looked to the testimony of the SEC Chairman during the legislative process to demonstrate the purpose of the legislation. In that case, the SEC argued that the legislation was intended to protect both tender offerors and shareholders. However, the Court looked to statements made by the SEC Chairman at the time the bill was being considered in Congress, which indicated that the legislation was targeted solely at shareholders and not tender offerors. By looking to the agency legislative history, the Court attempted to ensure that later political changes did not upset the legislative bargain that led to enactment a number of years before.

UNITED STATES V. MEAD CORP.

Supreme Court of the United States
533 U.S. 218 (2001)

JUSTICE SOUTER.

The question is whether a tariff classification ruling by the United States Customs Service deserves judicial deference. The Federal Circuit rejected Customs's invocation of *Chevron U.S.A. Inc. v. Natural Resources Defense Council, Inc.*, in support of such a ruling, to which it gave no deference. We agree that a tariff classification has no claim to judicial deference under *Chevron*, there being no indication that Congress intended such a ruling to carry the force of law, but we hold that under *Skidmore v. Swift & Co.*, the ruling is eligible to claim respect according to its persuasiveness.

. . .

Respondent, the Mead Corporation, imports "day planners," three-ring binders with pages having room for notes of daily schedules and phone numbers and addresses, together with a calendar and suchlike. The tariff schedule on point falls under the HTSUS heading for "[r]egisters, account books, notebooks, order books, receipt books, letter pads, memorandum pads, diaries and similar articles," HTSUS subheading 4820.10, which comprises two subcategories. Items in the first, "[d]iaries, notebooks and address books, bound; memorandum pads, letter pads and similar articles," were subject to a tariff of 4.0% at the time in controversy.

Between 1989 and 1993, Customs repeatedly treated day planners under the "other" HTSUS subheading. In January 1993, however, Customs changed its position, and issued a Headquarters ruling letter classifying Mead's day planners as "Diaries . . ., bound" subject to tariff under subheading 4820.10.20. That letter was short on explanation, but after Mead's protest, Customs Headquarters issued a new letter, carefully reasoned but never published, reaching the same conclusion. This letter considered two definitions of "diary" from the Oxford English Dictionary, the first covering a daily journal of the past day's events, the second a book including " 'printed dates for daily memoranda and jottings; also . . . calendars . . . .' ". Customs concluded that "diary" was not confined to the first, in part because the broader definition reflects commercial usage and hence the "commercial identity of these items in the marketplace." App. to Pet. for Cert. 34a. As for the definition of "bound," Customs concluded that HTSUS was not referring to "bookbinding," but to a less exact sort of fastening described in the Harmonized Commodity Description and Coding System Explanatory Notes to Heading 4820, which spoke of binding by " 'reinforcements or fittings of metal, plastics, etc.' " Id., at 45a.

Customs rejected Mead's further protest of the second Headquarters ruling letter, and Mead filed suit in the Court of International Trade (CIT). The CIT granted the Government's motion for summary judgment, adopting Customs's reasoning without saying anything about deference.

. . .

When Congress has "explicitly left a gap for an agency to fill, there is an express delegation of authority to the agency to elucidate a specific provision of the statute by regulation," Chevron, and any ensuing regulation is binding in the courts unless procedurally defective, arbitrary or capricious in substance, or manifestly contrary to the statute. . . . But whether or not they enjoy any express delegation of authority on a particular question, agencies charged with applying a statute necessarily make all sorts of interpretive choices, and while not all of those choices bind judges to follow them, they certainly may influence courts facing questions the agencies have already answered. "[T]he well-reasoned views of the agencies implementing a statute 'constitute a body of experience and informed judgment to which courts and litigants may properly resort for guidance,' " . . . and "[w]e have long recognized that considerable weight should be accorded to an executive department's construction of a statutory scheme it is entrusted to administer . . . ." The fair measure of deference to an agency administering its own statute has been understood to vary with circumstances, and courts have looked to the degree of the agency's care, its consistency, formality, and relative expertness, and to the persuasiveness of the agency's position, see *Skidmore*. Justice Jackson summed things up in *Skidmore v. Swift & Co.*:

> "The weight [accorded to an administrative] judgment in a particular case will depend upon the thoroughness evident in its consideration, the validity of its reasoning, its consistency with earlier and later pronouncements, and all those factors which give it power to persuade, if lacking power to control."

Since 1984, we have identified a category of interpretive choices distinguished by an additional reason for judicial deference. This Court in *Chevron* recognized that Congress not only engages in express delegation of specific interpretive authority, but that "[s]ometimes the legislative delegation to an agency on a particular question is implicit." Congress, that is, may not have expressly delegated authority or responsibility to implement a particular provision or fill a particular gap. Yet it can still be apparent from the agency's generally conferred authority and other statutory circumstances that Congress would expect the agency to be able to speak with the force of law when it addresses ambiguity in the statute or fills a space in the enacted law, even one about which "Congress did not actually have an intent" as to a particular result. When circumstances implying such an expectation exist, a reviewing court has no business rejecting an agency's exercise of its generally conferred authority to resolve a particular statutory ambiguity simply because the agency's chosen resolution seems unwise, but is obliged to accept the agency's position if Congress has not previously spoken to the point at issue and the agency's interpretation is reasonable.

We have recognized a very good indicator of delegation meriting *Chevron* treatment in express congressional authorizations to engage in the process of rulemaking or adjudication that produces regulations or rulings for which deference is claimed. It is fair to assume generally that Congress contemplates administrative action with the effect of law when it provides for a relatively formal administrative procedure tending to foster the fairness and deliberation that should underlie a pronouncement of such force. Thus, the overwhelming number of our cases applying *Chevron* deference have reviewed the fruits of notice-and-comment rulemaking or formal adjudication. That said, and as significant as notice-and-comment is in pointing to *Chevron* authority, the want of that procedure here does not decide the case, for we have sometimes found reasons for *Chevron* deference even when no such administrative formality was required and none was afforded. The fact that the tariff classification here was not a product of such formal process does not alone, therefore, bar the application of *Chevron*.

There are, nonetheless, ample reasons to deny *Chevron* deference here. The authorization for classification rulings, and Customs's practice in making them, present a case far removed not only from notice-and-comment process, but from any other circumstances reasonably suggesting that Congress ever thought of classification rulings as deserving the deference claimed for them here.

No matter which angle we choose for viewing the Customs ruling letter in this case, it fails to qualify under *Chevron*. On the face of the statute, to begin with, the terms of the congressional delegation give no indication that Congress meant to delegate authority to Customs to issue classification rulings with the force of law. We are not, of course, here making any global statement about Customs's authority, for it is true that the general rulemaking power conferred on Customs, authorizes some regulation with the force of law, or "legal norms," as we put it in *Haggar*, It is true as well that Congress had classification rulings in mind when it explicitly authorized, in a parenthetical, the issuance of "regulations establishing procedures for the issuance of binding rulings prior to the entry of the merchandise concerned," The reference to binding classifications does not, however, bespeak the legislative type of activity that would naturally bind more than the parties to the ruling, once the goods classified are admitted into this country. And though the statute's direction to disseminate "information" necessary to "secure" uniformity, ibid., seems to assume that a ruling may be precedent in later transactions, precedential value alone does not add up to *Chevron* entitlement; interpretive rules may sometimes function as precedents, and they enjoy no *Chevron* status as a class. In any event, any precedential claim of a classification ruling is counterbalanced by the provision for independent review of Customs classifications by the CIT; the scheme for CIT review includes a provision that treats classification rulings on par with the Secretary's rulings on "valuation, rate of duty, marking, restricted merchandise, entry requirements, drawbacks, vessel repairs, or similar matters." It is hard to imagine a congressional understanding more at odds with the *Chevron* regime.

It is difficult, in fact, to see in the agency practice itself any indication that Customs ever set out with a lawmaking pretense in mind when it undertook to make classifications like these. Customs does not generally engage in notice-and-comment practice when issuing them, and their treatment by the agency makes it clear that a letter's binding character as a ruling stops short of third parties; Customs has regarded a classification as conclusive only as between itself and the importer to whom it was issued, and even then only until Customs has given advance notice of intended change. Other importers are in fact warned against assuming any right of detrimental reliance.

Indeed, to claim that classifications have legal force is to ignore the reality that 46 different Customs offices issue 10,000 to 15,000 of them each year. Any suggestion that rulings intended to have the force of law are being churned out at a rate of 10,000 a year at an agency's 46 scattered offices is simply self-refuting. Although the circumstances are less startling here, with a Headquarters letter in issue, none of the relevant statutes recognizes this category of rulings as separate or different from others; there is thus no indication that a more potent delegation might have been understood as going to Headquarters even when Headquarters provides developed reasoning, as it did in this instance.

. . .

In sum, classification rulings are best treated like "interpretations contained in policy statements, agency manuals, and enforcement guidelines." They are beyond the *Chevron* pale.

To agree with the Court of Appeals that Customs ruling letters do not fall within *Chevron* is not, however, to place them outside the pale of any deference whatever. *Chevron* did nothing to eliminate *Skidmore's* holding that an agency's interpretation may merit some deference whatever its form, given the "specialized experience and broader investigations and information" available to the agency, and given the value of uniformity in its administrative and judicial understandings of what a national law requires.

There is room at least to raise a *Skidmore* claim here, where the regulatory scheme is highly detailed, and Customs can bring the benefit of specialized experience to bear on the subtle questions in this case: whether the daily planner with room for brief daily entries falls under "diaries," when diaries are grouped with "notebooks and address books, bound; memorandum pads, letter pads and similar articles;" and whether a planner with a ring binding should qualify as "bound," when a binding may be typified by a book, but also may have "reinforcements or fittings of metal, plastics, etc." A classification ruling in this situation may therefore at least seek a respect proportional to its "power to persuade." Such a ruling may surely claim the merit of its writer's thoroughness, logic, and expertness, its fit with prior interpretations, and any other sources of weight.

Underlying the position we take here, like the position expressed by Justice SCALIA in dissent, is a choice about the best way to deal with an inescapable feature of the body of congressional legislation authorizing administrative action. That feature is the great variety of ways in which the laws invest the Government's administrative arms with discretion, and with procedures for exercising it, in giving meaning to Acts of Congress. Implementation of a statute may occur in formal adjudication or the choice to defend against judicial challenge; it may occur in a central board or office or in dozens of enforcement agencies dotted across the country; its institutional lawmaking may be confined to the resolution of minute detail or extend to legislative rulemaking on matters intentionally left by Congress to be worked out at the agency level.

Although we all accept the position that the Judiciary should defer to at least some of this multifarious administrative action, we have to decide how to take account of the great range of its variety. If the primary objective is to simplify the judicial process of giving or withholding deference, then the diversity of statutes authorizing discretionary administrative action must be declared irrelevant or minimized. If, on the other hand, it is simply implausible that Congress intended such a broad range of statutory authority to produce only two varieties of administrative action, demanding either Chevron deference or none at all, then the breadth of the spectrum of possible agency action must be taken into account. Justice SCALIA's first priority over the years has been to limit and simplify. The Court's choice has been to tailor deference to variety. This acceptance of the range of statutory variation has led the Court to recognize more than one variety of judicial deference, just as the Court has recognized a variety of indicators that Congress would expect *Chevron* deference.

     * * *

Since the *Skidmore* assessment called for here ought to be made in the first instance by the Court of Appeals for the Federal Circuit or the CIT, we go no further than to vacate the judgment and remand the case for further proceedings consistent with this opinion.

NOTES & QUESTIONS

1.   Justice Scalia in dissent stated,

What was previously a general presumption of authority in agencies to resolve ambiguity in the statutes they have been authorized to enforce has been changed to a presumption of no such authority, which must be overcome by affirmative legislative intent to the contrary. And whereas previously, when agency authority to resolve ambiguity did not exist the court was free to give the statute what it considered the best interpretation, henceforth the court must supposedly give the agency view some indeterminate amount of so-called *Skidmore* deference. We will be sorting out the consequences of the *Mead* doctrine, which has today replaced the *Chevron* doctrine for years to come. I would adhere to our established jurisprudence, defer to the reasonable interpretation the Customs Service has given to the statute it is charged with enforcing, and reverse the judgment of the Court of Appeals.

2.   Should agency expertise be considered by a reviewing court when deciding these types of cases?

2.   CASE STUDY: FACEBOOK V. DUGUID

Noah Duguid began receiving text messages from Facebook in 2014 even though he did not have a Facebook account and never gave Facebook his cellphone number. Facebook has a policy of sending computer-generated text messages to users' cellphones when their accounts are accessed from an unknown device. After receiving many robotexts, Duguid asked Facebook to turn off the messages, and despite Facebook responding that the texts were now off, the texts continued. When Duguid complained again, and tried to reach a Facebook employee, he would get another automated response. In 2016, Duguid filed a federal class-action lawsuit and claimed Facebook was using an automatic telephone dialing system (ATDS) in violation of the Telephone Consumer Protection Act of 1991 (TCPA) and demanded Facebook pay $1,500 for each message it sent him.

Congress passed the TCPA as a reaction to the problem of robocalls and the law prohibits almost every robocall to cell phones unless the recipient gives consent.

The two types of outlawed robocalls are calls made using an ATDS, and calls using a prerecorded message. The TCPA defines an ATDS as a system that has the "capacity—(A) to store or produce telephone numbers to be called, using a random or sequential number generator; and (B) to dial such numbers." An exception allows legitimate businesses to make robocalls if the consumer consents by providing the company their cellphone number.

The Federal Communications Commission (FCC), which implements the TCPA, has stated that unless there is consent or an emergency, "it is unlawful to make any call using an [ATDS] . . . to any wireless telephone number." The prohibition applies to live calls using autodialers and text calls, and in both cases without regard to whether the consumer is charged for a call. On several occasions, the FCC has ruled automated devices that call thousands of stored numbers per minute are ATDSs regardless of whether they use number generators.

Facebook moved to dismiss the case because its automated system was not an ATDS since it did not use a random or sequential number generator. The district court agreed and dismissed the case.

Duguid appealed to the Ninth Circuit, which in a 2018 case held the definition of an ATDS included equipment that either makes automatic calls from lists of recipients or devices that generate numbers to be dialed, based on the statute's language and its "context and structure." The Ninth Circuit held Duguid's allegation that Facebook's system automatically dialed stored numbers was a valid claim under the TCPA. In other cases, the Second and Sixth Circuits agreed with the Ninth Circuit on this point, but the Seventh and Eleventh Circuits disagreed. Facebook appealed to the United States Supreme Court in 2020. Duguid's brief, partially written by Justice Scalia's long-time writing collaborator Bryan Garner, made several arguments as to why the TCPA's definition of an ATDS included devices that can "store" and "automatically dial" telephone numbers, even if the device does not "us[e] a random or sequential number generator."

BRIEF OF THE RESPONDENT, FACEBOOK, INC. V. DUGUID

Supreme Court of the United States
592 U.S. ___, 141 S.Ct. 193 (2020)

Brief of Respondent Noah Duguid

Argument

Like all exercises of statutory construction, determining whether the ATDS definition includes devices that automatically dial stored numbers as well as devices that generate numbers to be dialed requires a "fair reading" of the statutory language. *Bond v. United States*; Antonin Scalia & Bryan A. Garner, READING LAW: THE INTERPRETATION OF LEGAL TEXTS. Because the FCC has not yet exercised its regulatory authority to resolve the issue clearly, the Court must use standard statutory-construction tools to decide the "best reading," even if other readings are permissible. *Encino Motorcars, LLC v. Navarro*.

"As always," this task "begin[s] with the text of the statute," *Limtiaco v. Camacho*, including the words of the provision and its grammar, structure, context, subject matter, and evident purpose. See *Va. Uranium, Inc. v. Warren*. The Court's "duty is to give coherence to what Congress has done within the bounds imposed by a fair reading of legislation." *Achilli v. United States*. The fairest and best reading is that the TCPA applies to systems that automatically dial stored numbers.

I. The most straightforward reading is that "using a random or sequential number generator" describes how ATDS equipment "produces" numbers, not how it "stores" them.

A. Ordinary and technical meanings of "random number generator" and "sequential number generator" refer to means of producing numbers.

Construction of a statute starts with its "key words," *NLRB v. SW General, Inc.* Here, those key words reveal that a system that automatically dials stored numbers is an ATDS whether or not it uses a number generator.

The ATDS definition unambiguously applies to equipment that can: (A) either store or produce telephone numbers to be called; and (B) dial those numbers. Determining whether "using a random or sequential number generator" applies to both of the evidently alternative ways of satisfying the first requirement-storing numbers or producing them— requires applying principles of grammar to the meanings of the statutory words that dictate understanding of their grammatical relationships. Grammarians recognize that construction of a text often is "governed not by the rules of syntax but by the sense of the passage." Statutory interpretation likewise turns not on grammar alone, but on an understanding of how "the meaning of each word inform[s] the others," accounting for "a statute's full text, language as well as punctuation, structure, and subject matter." *U.S. Nat'l Bank of Or.* The commonsense meanings of the ATDS definition's key words signal that "using a random or sequential number generator" refers to how an ATDS produces-that is, generates-numbers, not how it stores them.

When "both the ordinary and technical meanings of [statutory words], as well as the statutory context in which the word[s] [are] found, lead to the [same] conclusion," there is no need to choose between them. *Taniguchi v. Kan Pac. Saipan, Ltd.* This is such a case: Both the ordinary and technical meanings of the crucial words and phrases store, produce, and using a generator-indicate that "using a generator" describes a way of producing numbers to be called, not of storing them.

Contemporaneous sources define a generator as "[o]ne that generates, causes, or produces." WEBSTER'S THIRD NEW INTERNATIONAL DICTIONARY UNABRIDGED (1976). The verb produce is so closely connected to the noun generator that it is hard to find a definition of the latter that doesn't include it. See, e.g., OXFORD ENGLISH DICTIONARY (2d Ed. 1989) In contrast, the verb store describes a very different activity: Its relevant meaning is "to leave or deposit in a . . . place for keeping, preservation or disposal" and, even more relevant, "to record (information) in an electronic device (as a computer) from which the data can be obtained as needed." THIRD NEW INTERNATIONAL DICTIONARY UNABRIDGED (1976). In common usage, then, using a number generator means producing numbers-it is unrelated to how they are stored.

When the TCPA was enacted, computer specialists understood the technical meaning of random number generator in exactly this way. For example, a 1992 book on the subject states that "[a] random number generator is a computer procedure that scrambles the bits of a current number or set of numbers to produce a new number, in such a way that the result appears to be randomly distributed among the possible set of numbers and independent of the previously generated numbers." George Marsaglia, "The Mathematics of Random Number Generators," 46 *Proceedings of Symposia in Applied Mathematics* 73 (1992). Meanwhile, a 1970 patent for a "pseudorandom sequence generator"-a form of number generator-specifically disclaimed the generator's having any capacity to store and specified that it is to be "connected to a serial storage device . . .

external to the generator." U.S. Patent No. 3633015 (patent description, col. 2, ll. 1, 21–22). Technical usage underscores that at the relevant time (as now) random and sequential number generators referred to ways of producing numbers, not means of storing them.

Moreover, when the TCPA was passed, the general meaning of an automatic dialing system was a device that called either stored lists of numbers or randomly or sequentially generated numbers. The acronym ADAD was used for "automatic dialing (and) announcing device." A 1978 California statute defined an ADAD in words that closely track the later federal statute's ATDS definition: "any automatic equipment which incorporates a storage capability of telephone numbers to be called or a random or sequential number generator capable of producing numbers to be called and the capability, working alone or in conjunction with other equipment, to disseminate a prerecorded message to the telephone number called." West's Ann. Cal. Pub. Util. Code § 2871.

. . .

Congress chose the same disjunctive phrase to cover devices that store numbers plus devices that produce them, together with a phrase defining how they are produced (using a random or sequential number generator) to satisfy the second alternative. The main difference between the TCPA's phrasing and that of the earlier references is that Congress economized by using "numbers to be called" only once to describe what an ATDS must store or produce instead of unnecessarily using the phrase twice. Such "economy of parallelism" is a common feature of legislative drafting. Bryan A. Garner, GUIDELINES FOR DRAFTING AND EDITING LEGISLATION 92 (2015) (explaining that "economy of parallelism" helps "eliminate repetition and verbiage"). The most natural inference is that Congress used fewer words to describe the same devices, not that it limited the definition by applying the adverbial phrase using a random or sequential number generator to a verb to which the phrase has no relationship in ordinary or technical usage.

. . .

B.   *The correct grammatical reading of the definition aligns with the semantic content of the words.*

The statutory sentence at issue may not be pretty, but its grammar, although complex, is readily discernible. No principles of construction require any reading that ignores the commonsense linkage between produce and using a number generator.

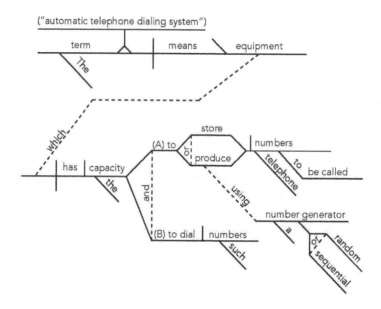

. . .

In *Advocate Health Care Network v. Stapleton*, the Court recognized that a statute may establish "relatively distinct" criteria that "likely . . . were designed to have standalone relevance,"—such as, here, the alternative capacities to store numbers or to produce them. In such a case, the most natural meaning of a modifying phrase that sensibly applies to one and not the other is that the modifier applies only to that one, regardless of how a reader might parse a grammatically similar sentence in which the modifier readily applied to both.

The most analogous canons of construction express the same insight: A court should carefully consider the fit between multiple verbs or nouns and modifiers that follow them rather than indiscriminately applying modifiers to terms to which they are not reasonably applicable.

The distributive-phrasing canon provides that in construing statutory language, courts should "appl[y] each expression to its appropriate referent." Scalia & Garner 214. Hence "[w]here a sentence contains several antecedents and several consequents," courts should "read them distributively and apply the words to the subjects which, by context, they seem most properly to relate." N. Singer & S. Singer, SUTHERLAND STATUTES AND STATUTORY CONSTRUCTION (rev. 7th ed. 2014).

. . .

Here, the meaning of generator matches up with produce but not with store. The sole difference is that only one of the verbs has a modifying adverbial of manner, so the "one-to-one matching" of expressions and referents that calls most forcefully for application of the distributive canon is absent. See *Encino Motorcars LLC*. But the principle that modifiers should be applied only to terms to which they properly relate solidly applies.

The last-antecedent canon leads to the same result. When a statute "include[s] a list of terms or phrases followed by a limiting clause," that "limiting clause or phrase . . . should ordinarily be read as modifying only the noun or phrase that it immediately follows," unless context dictates otherwise. *Lockhart v. United States*. This principle is especially applicable when it is a "heavy lift to carry the modifier across" all the entries in a list. One such circumstance is where a statute "does not contain items that readers are used to seeing listed together or a concluding modifier that readers are accustomed to applying to each of them." That description aptly characterizes the ATDS definition, which uses two verbs (store and produce) with distinct and unconnected meanings followed by a modifier that readers would be accustomed to applying to produce but not store.

          . . .

Ignoring these canons, Facebook mistakenly invokes the series-qualifier canon. That canon teaches that "[w]hen there is a straightforward, parallel construction that involves all nouns or verbs in a series, . . . a postpositive modifier normally applies to the entire series." Pet. Br. 23 (quoting Scalia & Garner, at 147). Facebook overlooks that the series qualifier canon "is highly sensitive to context." Scalia & Garner 150. It requires not only that nouns or verbs in a series have a parallel construction, but also that the modifier be "applicable as much to the first and other words as to the last." *Paroline v. United States*. The latter is absent here: The idea of "generating" is applicable to "producing" but not to "storing." In that circumstance, "the sense of the matter prevails: He went forth and wept bitterly does not suggest that he went forth bitterly." Scalia & Garner 150.

          . . .

Facebook's argument that the comma before the adverbial phrase clinches the case is equally wrong. As this Court has cautioned, "a purported plain-meaning analysis based only on punctuation is necessarily incomplete and runs the risk of distorting a statute's true meaning." *U.S. Nat'l Bank of Or*. The Solicitor General acknowledges another explanation for the comma: to avoid the appearance that using a random or sequential number generator modifies called. The comma tells the reader to look farther back to see what must be done using a number generator but does not tell the reader how far back. And it certainly does not dictate that the phrase must be read to require using a number generator to perform an operation-storing-that has nothing to do with number generation.

C. *Facebook's reading makes the words store or surplusage.*

The flaws in Facebook's textual argument go deeper than its failure to offer a coherent explanation of how *using a random or sequential number generator* sensibly applies to *storing* numbers. Facebook's construction would read the words store or out of the statute altogether, violating the principle that courts should not "adopt an interpretation of a congressional enactment which renders superfluous another portion of that same law." *Me. Cmty. Health Options v. United States.*

Under Facebook's reading, a number generator is an essential component of an ATDS because any ATDS must have the capacity to use a number generator to store or produce numbers to be called. Because a number generator's function is to produce numbers, any dialing equipment that has such a generator necessarily can produce telephone numbers to be called using that generator. So even if it were meaningful to speak of *storing* numbers using a number *generator*, any system that had that capacity would already qualify as an ATDS because of its capacity to *produce* numbers using a number generator. "Store or" would be wholly superfluous.

Facebook's reading, then, would nullify Congress's use of language providing two distinct alternative ways for equipment to satisfy the definition: having capacity to store numbers or to produce them. It would "transform [] . . . separate predicates into . . . synonyms describing the same predicate" for the statute's application. *Lockhart.* That result would disregard that "Congress used two terms because it intended each term to have a particular, nonsuperfluous meaning." *Bailey v. United States.* Reading *capacity to store* out of the statute would be especially anomalous given the common understanding when the statute was enacted that autodialers included both (1) devices that dialed from stored lists and (2) devices that generated random or sequential numbers. Facebook would ascribe to Congress the paradoxical intention of excluding the former from the ATDS definition even while choosing a term that has meaning only if they are included.

. . .

II. Applying the prohibition on unwanted robocalls to autodialers that do not use random or sequential number generators is consistent with the TCPA's structure, manifest purposes, and context.

All the considerations that go into reading a statute as a whole-its wording, overall structure, purposes, and context-reinforce that the ATDS definition encompasses autodialers that make robocalls to stored numbers without using number generators.

A.   *Congress drafted the robocalling prohibition to carry out the statute's broad privacy-protection goals.*

This Court has recognized that the TCPA's provisions, including its prohibition on unconsented-to calls to cellphones using an ATDS, broadly protect the public against "intrusive nuisance calls" that are "rightly regarded by recipients as 'an invasion of privacy.'" *Mims*. The statute reflects Congress's effort, over "nearly 30 years," to "fight [ ] back" against the robocalls that, despite the TCPA, still generate "a torrent of vociferous consumer complaints." *Barr*. As this Court has emphasized, the TCPA's "continuing broad prohibition of robocalls amply demonstrates Congress's continuing interest in consumer privacy." *Barr*.

The findings incorporated in the TCPA demonstrate Congress's broad concern about invasions of privacy attributable to the number and frequency of unwanted calls facilitated by autodialing technology. See TCPA § 2. Congress found that telemarketing "can be an intrusive invasion of privacy," and that "consumers are outraged over the proliferation of intrusive, nuisance calls." The robocalling prohibition was an integral part of the response to those concerns, not a surgical strike at the more limited problem posed by calls to random or sequential numbers.

Congress also recognized the need to balance individuals' privacy rights and "legitimate telemarketing practices." It struck that balance by permitting robocalls with the "prior express consent of the called party." Those provisions allow callers with a legitimate commercial or other relationship with the recipient to obtain permission to use automated calling methods, while preserving consumers' ability to avoid automated calls they consider intrusive.

. . .

Making the consent requirement's applicability turn on whether an autodialing system uses a number generator to *store* numbers to be called-as opposed to storing them using, say, a computer's hard drive or an external memory device-would fundamentally distort this statutory design. The statute's premise is that, absent consent, automatically dialed calls "are a nuisance and an invasion of privacy, regardless of the type of call." TCPA § 2(13). The statute's ban on robocalls to cellphones advances its stated objective of addressing the proliferation of such nuisance calls. TCPA § 2(12). Reading the statute to make the legality of a robocall to a cellphone depend on the caller's use of a number generator rather than on consent would disconnect the statute's congressionally enacted findings and objectives from its operation.

. . .

D.   The TCPA's historical context supports its application to systems that automatically dial stored numbers.

The context in which Congress enacted the TCPA confirms what the statute's language says: Congress wrote it to cover systems that store numbers to be called automatically, regardless of whether they use number generators. Contrary to Facebook's revisionist view, the statute's legislative history reflects a predominant concern not just about calls to random or sequential numbers, but about how "computer driven telemarketing tools have caused the frequency and number of unsolicited telemarketing calls [to] increase markedly." H.R. Rep. No. 102–317, at 6 (1991). When the statute was enacted, the proliferation of automated dialing systems driving that increase, which Congress acted to regulate, included (1) systems that called numbers stored in databases without using random or sequential number generators and (2) systems that dialed random or sequential numbers. Both types of automatically dialed calls formed the universe of activities that the statute addressed, and there is no reason to think that Congress intended to regulate only part of the problem it confronted.

The growing use of systems that automatically dialed stored numbers without using number generators formed the factual backdrop to Congress's action. The House Committee Report on the legislation describes telemarketers' increasing reliance on "telemarketing software that organizes information on current and prospective clients into databases" containing detailed information on consumers targeted for automatically dialed calls. H.R. Rep. No. 102–317, at 7 (1991). The Report detailed the emergence of a market "to develop and enhance telemarketing databases," id., as well as a growing industry supplying businesses with information allowing them to tailor databases to target automated telemarketing at chosen groups of consumers:

> Another market exists for companies that specialize in maintaining demographic and psychographic databases designed to provide businesses with a wealth of personal and lifestyle data on as many as 50 or 60 million people. Businesses routinely purchase data from multiple sources in an effort to create unique producter service-specific databases. And, the databases can be developed from multiple starting points: a name, address, or telephone number; a drivers license number or license plate; or a personal check or credit card number. H.R. Rep. No. 102–317

The Report also described another market providing businesses with confirmation of telephone numbers in their databases or, if those numbers have changed, "updating a company's file with new telephone numbers," for fees based on the number of telephone numbers input, confirmed, and changed. Id.

The use of such targeted databases to drive automatically dialed calls to stored telephone numbers derived from a wide range of sources-not just randomly or sequentially generated ones-was a key contributor to the central subject the TCPA addressed: the pervasive use of telephone marketing "due to the increased use of cost-effective telemarketing techniques." TCPA § 2(1); see also H.R. Rep. No. 102–317, at 6 ("[R]apidly decreasing telecommunications costs coupled with nationwide business use of sophisticated, computer driven telemarketing tools have caused the frequency and number of unsolicited telemarketing calls [to] increase markedly.").

The factual circumstances when the TCPA was enacted refute the suggestion that autodialers using random or sequential number generators were the exclusive or dominant technology of the day, or the primary drivers of the consumer "outrage[ ] over the proliferation of intrusive, nuisance calls" that the Act explicitly addressed. See TCPA, § 2(6). Calls using random or sequential number generators formed only one part of the universe of autodialed calls in 1991. See H.R. Rep. No. 102–317, at 10 (noting that telemarketers "often" called numbers sequentially); S. Rep. No. 102–178, at 2 ("some" autodialers dialed numbers sequentially). Those technologies were linked to a discrete problem: tying up lines of emergency facilities and businesses, see H.R. Rep. No. 102–317, at 10; S. Rep. No. 102–178, at 2, which is *one* of the concerns addressed by the TCPA's restrictions on autodialed calls. See 47 U.S.C. § 227(b)(1)(A)(i) (prohibiting ATDS calls to emergency telephone lines); id. § 227(b)(1)(D) (prohibiting ATDS calls that tie up multiple lines of a business). But the Act's central focus the proliferation of nuisance calls to consumers-was implicated by all forms of automatic dialing in use at the time. The nuisance that generated consumer outrage was the calls themselves, not the way computers stored numbers.

Likewise, the hearings leading to the legislation didn't focus principally on problems posed by autodialers that called random or sequential numbers. Their predominant focus was the sheer number of intrusive calls that autodialers facilitated-a concern unrelated to autodialers' use of number generators. See S. 1462, The Automated Tel. Consumer Prot. Act of 1991: Hearing Before the Subcomm. on Commc'ns of the S. Comm. on Commerce, Sci., & Transp., S. Hrg. 102–460, at 1 (1991).

The hearings highlighted that the quantity of calls was driven by all forms of autodialers. A leading consumer-privacy advocate informed the subcommittee about the telemarketing industry's increasing use of predictive dialers, which were already used by 30 to 40 percent of national telemarketing firms. The principal industry witness at the Senate hearing likewise acknowledged that autodialers were not limited to equipment using random or sequential dialing. Accordingly, he urged Congress not to "ban all unsolicited calls by automatic dialing," but instead to alter the draft legislation to ban or limit only "sequential and random dialing." Id. at 33; see also id. at 36. Congress did not take up that suggestion.

The factual context in which Congress acted sheds light on its choice not to define autodialers solely in terms of how they produced numbers to be dialed, but rather to include all systems capable of storing numbers and dialing them automatically. Far from aiming only at specific problems posed by calls to random and sequential numbers-which would not have necessitated any reference to a system's capacity to store numbers-Congress chose language that would apply to all technologies used to deluge cellphones with automated calls, including then-emerging technologies that did not employ number generation.

For that reason, when the FCC first addressed whether the TCPA's robocalling prohibition applies to calls from predictive dialers that do not use random or sequential number generation, the agency concluded that it does. See FCC, In re Rules, 18 FCC Rcd. at 14092 (2003); In re Rules & Regulations Implementing the Telephone Consumer Protection Act of 1991, 27 FCC Rcd. 15391, 15392 n.5 (2012). The FCC may not have articulated its reading of the statutory language clearly and consistently enough to merit deference under *Chevron, U.S.A., Inc. v. NRDC*. Nonetheless, the agency's longstanding view that limiting the statute to devices that use number generators would be inconsistent with its purposes and context merits respectful consideration. *Skidmore v. Swift & Co.*

NOTES & QUESTIONS

1.   Facebook summarized its argument as follows:

The plain text and basic rules of construction and grammar resolve this case. Congress defined an "automatic telephone dialing system" as "equipment which has the capacity-(A) to store or produce telephone numbers to be called, using a random or sequential number generator; and (B) to dial such numbers." 47 U.S.C. § 227(a)(1). Under ordinary rules of grammar and canons of construction, the phrase "using a random or sequential number generator" cannot be decoupled from the verb "store," but instead modifies both "store" and "produce."

That conclusion follows from a straightforward application of the series-modifier rule and is particularly clear given that the verbs "store" and "produce" are the only two verbs in the section and share a common direct object ("telephone numbers to be called") that *follows* "produce" and *precedes* the modifier "using a random or sequential number generator." Thus, at least *some* of what follows "produce" modifies both "store" and "produce." Otherwise, the statute would nonsensically prohibit calls made using a device with "the capacity— (A) to store . . . and (B) to dial such numbers," without ever explaining what is "store[d]" or what *"such* numbers" refers to. And the notion that only the direct object ("telephone numbers to be called"), but not the adverbial clause ("using a random or sequential number generator"), modifies "store" strains credulity and defies basic rules of grammar. If a college makes it "a violation of dorm rules to wash or dry your clothes using your roommates' access card," no one would think that college students were prohibited from washing their clothes, wholly apart from whether they did so using someone else's access card. But that is the nonsense that results from allowing only the direct object and not the adverbial phrase to modify both verbs.

The surrounding statutory text only reinforces the conclusion that "using a random or sequential number generator" modifies both "store" and "produce." First, only the plain-text reading gives effect to the critical feature that makes an "automatic telephone dialing system" automatic under the statute and distinguishes it from an ordinary phone-namely, the use of "a random or sequential number generator." What makes an ATDS automatic (and a distinct threat to emergency and other non-residential lines) is not the rudimentary capacity to store a number for later dialing-a capacity possessed in 1991 by ordinary telephones with a "speed-dial" feature-but the capacity to "us[e] a random or sequential number generator" to store or produce numbers. This reading aligns the definition of an ATDS with the specific concerns Congress identified and the specific conduct Congress prohibited, such as the use of an ATDS to tie up two business lines simultaneously. Finally, it aligns with Congress' stated intent to protect ordinary telephone users and businesses, not from each other, but from the abusive practices of telemarketers.

The Ninth Circuit's approach, by contrast, violates rules of punctuation, grammar, and statutory construction and raises serious First Amendment problems to boot. There is no basis in grammar or canons of construction for applying the adverbial "phrase 'using a random or sequential number generator' " to "modif[y] only the verb 'to produce,' and not the preceding verb, 'to store.' " Indeed, one of the few courts to follow the Ninth Circuit's lead admitted it is not one that "follows proper grammar." *Allan v. Pa. Higher Educ. Assistance Agency*, 968 F.3d 567, 572–73 (6th Cir. 2020). Decoupling the use of random- or sequential-number-generation technology from the verb "store" also carries the untenable consequence of extending the ATDS prohibitions to devices that pose none of the risks unique to random and sequential dialing that were Congress' target. Indeed, taken at face value, the prohibitions would cover calls from not just every modern smartphone, but from ordinary telephones with call-forwarding or speed-dial features that were already common in 1991.

Making matters worse, the practical and constitutional consequences of the Ninth Circuit's (mis)reading of the statute are untenable. The Ninth Circuit's opinion converts a statute designed to target the specialized technologies of telemarketers that posed distinct risks of tying up emergency numbers or business lines into one that penalizes wrong numbers. The Ninth Circuit's ATDS definition casts the net so widely that nearly everyone in the country risks $1,500-per-call statutory liability practically every time they attempt a phone call. That result is impossible to square with any fair reading of statutory text or legislative intent, and would convert a targeted statute into an unconstitutional dragnet. A statute that directly implicates the First Amendment cannot be interpreted to embrace the very antithesis of narrow tailoring. In short, there is no reason to accept the Ninth Circuit's strained interpretation and every reason to reject it. See, *Facebook v. Duguid*, 592 U.S. ___ (2020), Brief of Petitioner.

2.   A unanimous Supreme Court held for Facebook. Justice Sotomayor wrote:

Perhaps Duguid's interpretive approach would have some appeal if applying the traditional tools of interpretation led to a "linguistically impossible" or contextually implausible outcome. *Encino Motorcars, LLC v. Navarro*, 138 S.Ct. 1134, 1141 (2018); see also *Advocate Health Care Network v. Stapleton*, 137 S.Ct. 1652, 1661 (2017)(noting that a "sense of inconceivability" might "urg[e] readers to discard usual rules of interpreting text"). Duguid makes a valiant effort to prove as much, but ultimately comes up short. It is true that, as a matter of ordinary parlance, it is odd to say that a piece of equipment "stores" numbers using a random number "generator." But it is less odd as a technical matter. Indeed, as early as 1988, the U. S. Patent and Trademark Office issued patents for devices that used a random number generator to store numbers to be called later (as opposed to using a number generator for immediate dialing). Brief for Professional Association for Customer Engagement et al. as *Amici Curiae* 15–21. At any rate, Duguid's interpretation is contrary to the ordinary reading of the text and, by classifying almost all modern cell phones as autodialers, would produce an outcome that makes even less sense.

CHAPTER 9

LEGISLATIVE OVERSIGHT & INVESTIGATIVE HEARINGS

■ ■ ■

'It is the proper duty of a representative body to look diligently into every affair of government and to talk much about what it sees. It is meant to be the eyes and the voice, and to embody the wisdom and will of its constituents. Unless Congress have and use every means of acquainting itself with the acts and the disposition of the administrative agents of the government, the country must be helpless to learn how it is being served; and unless Congress both scrutinize these things and sift them by every form of discussion, the country must remain in embarrassing, crippling ignorance of the very affairs which it is most important that it should understand and direct. The informing function of Congress should be preferred even to its legislative function.'—Woodrow Wilson, *Congressional Government*, 303.

A. HISTORY OF LEGISLATIVE OVERSIGHT

One of a legislature's greatest powers is oversight of how the laws it passes are working, how the money it appropriates is spent and the activities of an ever growing and powerful executive branch.

A legislature's constant gathering of information falls into different, but overlapping, categories: oversight, where legislators review a law or program's effectiveness, or social issue. Regular hearings where legislators question executive branch officials also helps ensure that agencies are executing the law in a manner that the legislature intended, are generally good public policy and promote effective government operations. Investigative hearings usually concern possible wrongdoing by government officials or private citizens. For investigations, the legislature may create a select committee to hold hearings or a standing committee may investigate issues or agencies within its jurisdictions. The oversight or investigative hearings often lead to legislation to make adjustments or reform some aspect of the government or society.

The American legislative power to investigate grew out of British Parliamentary practice dating back centuries. In 1644 Lord Coke called Parliament, the "general Inquisitors of the realm."

The American colonial assemblies followed the English parliamentary tradition and investigated government departments and other matters of general concern. During the Indian war of 1722, the Massachusetts House of Representatives and Governor battled over the House's right to call two military officers to testify about a failed operation in what is now Maine. The House insisted that it was "not only their Privilege but Duty to demand of any Officer in the pay and service of this Government an account of his Management while in the Public Imploy." In 1742, the Pennsylvania Assembly summoned several witnesses to investigate riots connected to an election and requested the governor and judiciary punish those at fault.

Colonial governments considered the power to investigate, and punish those in contempt, as integral to the legislative power, perhaps explaining why the contempt power was only mentioned in two of the 13 original state constitutions. However, in the Massachusetts Constitution, John Adams was explicit that:

> The House of representatives . . .shall have authority to punish by imprisonment every person, not a member, who shall be guilty of disrespect to the house, by any disorderly or contemptuous behavior in its presence. MASS. CONST. ART. X.

Although the U.S. Constitution is silent on the subject of contempt, Congress has conducted investigations and punished non-compliance from the earliest days of the Republic.

The first recorded investigation by Congress came in 1792 when it investigated a failed military campaign led by Maj. General Arthur St. Clair. This case established both the right of Congress to investigate the executive branch and the concept of executive privilege.

In March 1792, a special House committee demanded papers and records for their investigation. President Washington consulted his Cabinet and decided that while Congress had a right to investigate and the President should turn over the papers permitted by the public good, the executive documents that may "harm the public" should remain confidential.

Ultimately, the committee exonerated St. Clair and placed the blame on the War department for poorly funding and supplying the troops. This investigation established Congressional authority to investigate presidents and their administrations.

While courts rarely, if ever, became involved in the scope of legislative investigatory power, members of Congress would occasionally argue for self-imposed limits. For example, during an investigation into the Bank of the United States in 1834, Rep. John Quincy Adams objected to an open-ended inquiry that would compel witnesses to testify and to produce such records as might be deemed necessary. Adams argued that "an unlimited investigation was not within the power of the House," and convinced the House to limit the investigating committee's power to inspecting the Bank's books and proceedings to determine whether the Bank's charter have been violated.

Since 1791 Congress has constantly used its oversight and investigatory powers to gather information needed for new legislation, to see how existing laws are working, to determine how much money should appropriate for each part of the government and the ever-growing list of programs, and for nearly every major scandal.

Some of the most high-profile Congressional investigations in U.S. history are:

- The Burning of Washington (1814)
- John Brown's Raid on Harper's Ferry (1859–1860)
- The Joint Committee on Reconstruction (1865–1867)
- The Ku Klux Klan and Racial Violence (1871–1872)
- The Credit Mobilier Scandal (1872–1873)
- The Teapot Dome Scandal (1922–1924)
- The Truman Committee on War Mobilization (1941–1944)
- The Kefauver Committee on Organized Crime (1950–1951)
- The Army-McCarthy Hearings (1954)
- Watergate (1973–1974)
- The Iran-Contra Hearings (1987)
- The 9/11 Commission (2002–2004)
- The Veterans Administration Scandal (2014–2015)

Two excellent (but old) articles on the history of legislative investigatory power are: James M. Landis, "Constitutional Limitations on the Congressional Power of Investigations," 40 *Harv. L. Rev.* 153 (1926) and C.S. Potts, "Power of Legislative Bodies to Punish for Contempt," 74 *U. Penn. L. Rev.* 691 (1925–1926). *Congress Investigates: A Critical and Documentary History* (Infobase Learning, 2011) provides detailed information on major Congressional investigations.

B. "GENERAL INQUISITORS OF THE REPUBLIC"

"The Senators and Representatives shall receive a Compensation for their Services, to be ascertained by Law, and paid out of the Treasury of the United States. They shall in all Cases, except Treason, Felony and Breach of the Peace, be privileged from Arrest during their Attendance at the Session of their respective

Houses, and in going to and returning from the same; and for any Speech or Debate in either House, they shall not be questioned in any other Place."

U.S. CONST. Art. I § 6

"A legislative body cannot legislate wisely or effectively in the absence of information respecting the conditions which the legislation is intended to affect or change; and where the legislative body does not itself possess the requisite information—which not infrequently is true—recourse must be had to others who do possess it. Experience has taught that mere requests for such information often are unavailing, and also that information which is volunteered is not always accurate or complete; so some means of compulsion are essential to obtain what is needed. All this was true before and when the Constitution was framed and adopted. In that period the power of inquiry—with enforcing process—was regarded and employed as a necessary and appropriate attribute of the power to legislate—indeed, was treated as inhering in it."

McGrain v. Daugherty, 273 U.S. 135, 174–175 (1927).

EASTLAND V. UNITED STATES SERVICEMEN'S FUND
Supreme Court of the United States
421 U.S. 491 (1975)

[Note: In this case, a Senate committee subpoenaed the bank records related to an organization opposed to the Vietnam War. The organization objected asserting the First Amendment protected the records since they were the equivalent of confidential membership lists. The Court of Appeals concluded that if the subpoena were obeyed respondents' First Amendment rights would be violated because the identities of donors was the goal of the subpoena. In addition, revealing the donors' identities would substantially decrease the organization's contributions.]

MR. CHIEF JUSTICE BURGER.

In early 1970 the Senate Subcommittee on Internal Security was given broad authority by the Senate to "make a complete and continuing study and investigation of . . . the administration, operation, and enforcement of the Internal Security Act of 1950 . . . ." The authority encompassed discovering the "extent, nature, and effect of subversive activities in the United States," and the resolution specifically directed inquiry concerning "infiltration by persons who are or may be under the domination of the foreign government . . . ." Pursuant to that mandate the Subcommittee began an inquiry into the activities of respondent United States Servicemen's Fund, Inc. (USSF).

USSF describes itself as a nonprofit membership corporation supported by contributions. Its stated purpose is "to further the welfare of persons who have served or are presently serving in the military." To accomplish its declared purpose USSF has engaged in various activities directed at United States servicemen. It established "coffeehouses" near domestic military installations, and aided the publication of "underground" newspapers for distribution on American military installations throughout the world. The coffeehouses were meeting places for servicemen, and the newspapers were specialized publications which USSF claims dealt with issues of concern to servicemen. Through these operations USSF attempted to communicate to servicemen its philosophy and attitudes concerning United States involvement in Southeast Asia. USSF claims the coffeehouses and newspapers became "the focus of dissent and expressions of opposition within the military toward the war in [Southeast Asia]."

In the course of its investigation of USSF, the Subcommittee concluded that a prima facie showing had been made of the need for further investigation, and it resolved that appropriate subpoenas, including subpoenas duces tecum could be issued. Petitioner Eastland, a United States Senator, is, as he was then, Chairman of the Subcommittee. On May 28, 1970, pursuant to the above authority, he signed a subpoena duces tecum, issued on behalf of the Subcommittee, to the bank where USSF then had an account. The subpoena commanded the bank to produce by June 4, 1970:

> "any and all records appertaining to or involving the account or accounts of [USSF]. Such records to comprehend papers, correspondence, statements, checks, deposit slips and supporting documentation, or microfilm thereof within [the bank's] control or custody or within [its] means to produce."

From the record it appears the subpoena was never actually served on the bank. In any event, before the return date, USSF and two of its members brought this action to enjoin implementation of the subpoena duces tecum.

The complaint named as defendants Chairman Eastland, nine other Senators, the Chief Counsel to the Subcommittee, and the bank. The complaint charged that the authorizing resolutions and the Subcommittee's actions implementing them were an unconstitutional abuse of the legislative power of inquiry, that the "sole purpose" of the Subcommittee investigation was to force "public disclosure of beliefs, opinions, expressions and associations of private citizens which may be unorthodox or unpopular," and that the "sole purpose" of the subpoena was to "harass, chill, punish and deter [USSF and its members] in their exercise of their rights and duties under the First Amendment and particularly to stifle the freedom of the press and association guaranteed by that amendment." The subpoena was issued to the bank rather than to USSF and its members, the complaint claimed, "in order to deprive [them] of their rights to protect their private records, such as the sources of their contributions, as they would be entitled to do if the subpoenas had been issued against them directly." The complaint further claimed that financial support to USSF is obtained exclusively through contributions from private individuals, and if the bank records are disclosed "much of that financial support will be withdrawn and USSF will be unable to continue its constitutionally protected activities."

For relief USSF and its members, the respondents, sought a permanent injunction restraining the Members of the Subcommittee and its Chief Counsel from trying to enforce the subpoena by contempt of Congress or other means and restraining the bank from complying with the subpoena. Respondents also sought a declaratory judgment declaring the subpoena and the Senate resolutions void under the Constitution. No damages claim was made.

. . .

We conclude that the actions of the Senate Subcommittee, the individual Senators, and the Chief Counsel are protected by the Speech or Debate Clause of the Constitution, Art. I, § 6, cl. 1, and are therefore immune from judicial interference. We reverse.

The question to be resolved is whether the actions of the petitioners fall within the "sphere of legitimate legislative activity." If they do, the petitioners "shall not be questioned in any other Place" about those activities since the prohibitions of the Speech or Debate Clause are absolute.

Without exception, our cases have read the Speech or Debate Clause broadly to effectuate its purposes. The purpose of the Clause is to insure that the legislative function the Constitution allocates to Congress may be performed independently.

"The immunities of the Speech or Debate Clause were not written into the Constitution simply for the personal or private benefit of Members of Congress, but to protect the integrity of the legislative process by insuring the independence of individual legislators." In our system "the clause serves the additional function of reinforcing the separation of powers so deliberately established by the Founders." The Clause is a product of the English experience. Due to that heritage our cases make it clear that the "central role" of the Clause is to "prevent intimidation of legislators by the Executive and accountability before a possibly hostile judiciary. That role is not the sole function of the Clause, however, and English history does not totally define the reach of the Clause. Rather, it "must be interpreted in light of the American experience, and in the context of the American constitutional scheme of government . . . ." Thus we have long held that, when it applies, the Clause provides protection against civil as well as criminal actions, and against actions brought by private individuals as well as those initiated by the Executive Branch.

The applicability of the Clause to private civil actions is supported by the absoluteness of the term "shall not be questioned," and the sweep of the term "in any other Place." In reading the Clause broadly we have said that legislators acting within the sphere of legitimate legislative activity "should be protected not only from the consequences of litigation's results but also from the burden of defending themselves." Just as a criminal prosecution infringes upon the independence which the Clause is designed to preserve, a private civil action, whether for an injunction or damages, creates a distraction and forces Members to divert their time, energy, and attention from their legislative tasks to defend the litigation. Private civil actions also may be used to delay and disrupt the legislative function. Moreover, whether a criminal action is instituted by the Executive Branch, or a civil action is brought by private parties, judicial power is still brought to bear on Members of Congress and legislative independence is imperiled. We reaffirm that once it is determined that Members are acting within the "legitimate legislative sphere" the Speech or Debate Clause is an absolute bar to interference.

III

In determining whether particular activities other than literal speech or debate fall within the "legitimate legislative sphere" we look to see whether the activities took place "in a session of the House by one of its members in relation to the business before it." More specifically, we must determine whether the activities are "an integral part of the deliberative and communicative processes by which Members participate in committee and House proceedings with respect to the consideration and passage or rejection of proposed legislation or with respect to other matters which the Constitution places within the jurisdiction of either House."

The power to investigate and to do so through compulsory process plainly falls within that definition. This Court has often noted that the power to investigate is inherent in the power to make laws because "[a] legislative body cannot legislate wisely or effectively in the absence of information respecting the conditions which the legislation is intended to affect or change." Issuance of subpoenas such as the one in question here has long been held to be a legitimate use by Congress of its power to investigate.

"[W]here the legislative body does not itself possess the requisite information—which not infrequently is true—recourse must be had to others who do possess it. Experience has taught that mere requests for such information often are unavailing, and also that information which is volunteered is not always accurate or complete; so some means of compulsion are essential to obtain what is needed."

It also has been held that the subpoena power may be exercised by a committee acting, as here, on behalf of one of the Houses. Without such power the Subcommittee may not be able to do the task assigned to it by Congress. To conclude that the power of inquiry is other than an integral part of the legislative process would be a miserly reading of the Speech or Debate Clause in derogation of the "integrity of the legislative process."

We have already held that the act "of authorizing an investigation pursuant to which . . . materials were gathered" is an integral part of the legislative process. The issuance of a subpoena pursuant to an authorized investigation is similarly an indispensable ingredient of lawmaking; without it our recognition that the act "of authorizing" is protected would be meaningless. To hold that Members of Congress are protected for authorizing an investigation, but not for issuing a subpoena in exercise of that authorization, would be a contradiction denigrating the power granted to Congress in Art. I and would indirectly impair the deliberations of Congress.

The particular investigation at issue here is related to and in furtherance of a legitimate task of Congress. On this record the pleadings show that the actions of the Members and the Chief Counsel fall within the "sphere of legitimate legislative activity." The Subcommittee was acting under an unambiguous resolution from the Senate authorizing it to make a complete study of the "administration, operation, and enforcement of the Internal Security Act of 1950 . . . ." That grant of authority is sufficient to show that the investigation upon which the Subcommittee had embarked concerned a subject on which "legislation could be had."

The propriety of making USSF a subject of the investigation and subpoena is a subject on which the scope of our inquiry is narrow. "The courts should not go beyond the narrow confines of determining that a committee's inquiry may fairly be deemed within its province." Even the most cursory look at the facts presented by the pleadings reveals the legitimacy of the USSF subpoena. Inquiry into the sources of funds used to carry on activities suspected by a subcommittee of Congress to have a potential for undermining the morale of the Armed Forces is within the legitimate legislative sphere. Indeed, the complaint here tells us that USSF operated on or near military and naval bases, and that its facilities became the "focus of dissent" to declared national policy. Whether USSF activities violated any statute is not relevant; the inquiry was intended to inform Congress in an area where legislation may be had. USSF asserted it does not know the sources of its funds; in light of the Senate authorization to the Subcommittee to investigate "infiltration by persons who are or may be under the domination of . . . foreign government," and in view of the pleaded facts, it is clear that the subpoena to discover USSF's bank records "may fairly be deemed within [the Subcommittee's] province."

We conclude that the Speech or Debate Clause provides complete immunity for the Members for issuance of this subpoena. We draw no distinction between the Members and the Chief Counsel. In *Gravel*, we made it clear that "the day-to-day work of such aides is so critical to the Members' performance that they must be treated as [the Members'] alter egos ...." Here the complaint alleges that the "Subcommittee members and staff caused the ... subpoena to be issued ... under the authority of Senate Resolution 366 ...." The complaint thus does not distinguish between the activities of the Members and those of the Chief Counsel. Since the Members are immune because the issuance of the subpoena is "essential to legislating," their aides share that immunity.

IV

Respondents rely on language in *Gravel v. United States*:

"[N]o prior case has held that Members of Congress would be immune if they executed an invalid resolution by themselves carrying out an illegal arrest, or if, in order to secure information for a hearing, themselves seized the property or invaded the privacy of a citizen. Neither they nor their aides should be immune from liability or questioning in such circumstances."

From this respondents argue that the subpoena works an invasion of their privacy, and thus cannot be immune from judicial questioning. The conclusion is unwarranted. The quoted language from Gravel referred to actions which were not "essential to legislating." For example, the arrest by the Sergeant at Arms was held unprotected in *Kilbourn v. Thompson*, because it was not "essential to legislating." Quite the contrary is the case with a routine subpoena intended to gather information about a subject on which legislation may be had.

Respondents also contend that the subpoena cannot be protected by the speech or debate immunity because the "sole purpose" of the investigation is to force "public disclosure of beliefs, opinions, expressions and associations of private citizens which may be unorthodox or unpopular." Respondents view the scope of the privilege too narrowly. Our cases make clear that in determining the legitimacy of a congressional act we do not look to the motives alleged to have prompted it. In *Brewster*, we said that "the Speech or Debate Clause protects against inquiry into acts that occur in the regular course of the legislative process and into the motivation for those acts." And in *Tenney v. Brandhove* we said that "[t]he claim of an unworthy purpose does not destroy the privilege." If the mere allegation that a valid legislative act was undertaken for an unworthy purpose would lift the protection of the Clause, then the Clause simply would not provide the protection historically undergirding it. "In times of political passion, dishonest or vindictive motives are readily attributed to legislative conduct and as readily believed." The wisdom of congressional approach or methodology is not open to judicial veto. Nor is the legitimacy of a congressional inquiry to be defined by what it produces. The very nature of the investigative function—like any research—is that it takes the searchers up some "blind alleys" and into nonproductive enterprises. To be a valid legislative inquiry there need be no predictable end result.

Finally, respondents argue that the purpose of the subpoena was to "harass, chill, punish and deter" them in the exercise of their First Amendment rights, and thus that the subpoena cannot be protected by the Clause. Their theory seems to be that once it is alleged that First Amendment rights may be infringed by congressional action the Judiciary may intervene to protect those rights; the Court of Appeals seems to have subscribed to that theory. That approach, however, ignores the absolute nature of the speech or debate protection and our cases which have broadly construed that protection.

> "Congressmen and their aides are immune from liability for their actions within the 'legislative sphere,' even though their conduct, if performed in other than legislative contexts, would in itself be unconstitutional or otherwise contrary to criminal or civil statutes."

For us to read the Clause as respondents suggest would create an exception not warranted by the language, purposes, or history of the Clause. Respondents make the familiar argument that the broad protection granted by the Clause creates a potential for abuse. That is correct, and in Brewster, supra, we noted that the risk of such abuse was "the conscious choice of the Framers" buttressed and justified by history. Our consistently broad construction of the Speech or Debate Clause rests on the belief that it must be so construed to provide the independence which is its central purpose.

This case illustrates vividly the harm that judicial interference may cause. A legislative inquiry has been frustrated for nearly five years, during which the Members and their aide have been obliged to devote time to consultation with their counsel concerning the litigation, and have been distracted from the purpose of their inquiry. The Clause was written to prevent the need to be confronted by such "questioning" and to forbid invocation of judicial power to challenge the wisdom of Congress' use of its investigative authority.

NOTES & QUESTIONS

1.   In their concurrence, Justices Marshall, Brennan and Stewart agreed with the Court that the Speech or Debate Clause protects the actions of the Senate petitioners in this case from judicial interference but wanted to

emphasize that the Clause does not entirely immunize a congressional subpoena from challenge by the party whose information is at issue. Justice Marshall wrote that the Speech or Debate Clause does not preclude "judicial review of their decisions in an appropriate case." A person does not "shed his constitutional right to withhold certain classes of information." If Congress cites a person for contempt, the witness may defend themselves in court on the basis of the constitutional right to withhold information from the legislature. The Speech or Debate Clause cannot be used to avoid meaningful review of constitutional objections to a subpoena simply because the subpoena is served on a third party. Justice Marshall points out that the USSF case did not fully decide the proper procedure, and who might be the proper parties to get before a court a constitutional challenge to a subpoena *duces tecum* issued to a third party.

2.   Should the Court have done more to have protect the Constitutional rights of persons served with a Congressional subpoena?

CONGRESSIONAL OVERSIGHT MANUAL
Congressional Research Service, January 16, 2020

Legal Tools Available for Oversight and Investigations

A review of congressional precedents indicates that there is no single method or set of procedures for engaging in oversight or conducting an investigation. Historically, congressional committees appeared to rely a great deal on public hearings and subpoenaed witnesses to gather information and accomplish their investigative goals. In more recent years, congressional committees have seemingly relied more heavily on staff level communication and contacts as well as other "informal" attempts at gathering information—document requests, informal briefings, interviews, etc.—before initiating the necessary formalistic procedures such as issuing committee subpoenas, holding on-the-record depositions, and/or engaging the subjects of inquiries in public hearings. This section discusses the formal process of issuing subpoenas, depositions, and holding committee hearings. This section also reviews Congress's authority to grant witnesses limited immunity for the purpose of obtaining information and testimony that may be protected by the Fifth Amendment's right against self-incrimination.

Subpoena Power

As a corollary to Congress's accepted oversight and investigative authority, the Supreme Court has determined that the issuance of subpoenas "has long been held to be a legitimate use by Congress of its power to investigate." *Eastland*, 421 U.S. 504. The Court has referred to the subpoena power as "an essential and appropriate auxiliary to the legislative function" *McGrain*, 273 U.S. at 174–175.

. . .

A properly authorized subpoena issued by a committee or subcommittee has the same force and effect as a subpoena issued by the parent house itself. Individual committees and subcommittees must be delegated the authority to issue subpoenas. Senate Rule XXVI(1) and House Rule XI(2)(m)(1) presently empower all standing committees and subcommittees to issue subpoenas requiring the attendance and testimony of witnesses and the production of documents. Special or select committees must be specifically delegated that authority by Senate or House resolution. The rules governing issuance of committee subpoenas vary by committee. Some committees require a full committee vote to issue a subpoena, while others empower the chairman to issue them unilaterally or with the concurrence of the ranking minority member.

Congressional subpoenas are served by the U.S. Marshal's office, committee staff, or the Senate or House Sergeants-at-Arms. Service may be effected anywhere in the United States. The subpoena power has been held to extend to aliens physically present in the United States. As will be discussed below, however, securing compliance of U.S. nationals and aliens living in foreign countries is more complex.

A witness seeking to challenge the legal sufficiency of a subpoena has limited remedies to defeat the subpoena even if it is found to be legally deficient. In order for a subpoena to be valid, the underlying investigation must meet the following general criteria, as articulated by the Supreme Court in *Wilkinson v. United States,* 365 U.S. 399, 408–409 (1961):

- The committee's investigation of the broad subject matter area must be authorized by Congress.

- The investigation must be pursuant to "a valid legislative purpose."

- The specific inquiries must be pertinent to the broad subject matter areas that have been authorized by Congress.

However, regardless of the subpoena's legal sufficiency, courts will generally not entertain a subpoena recipient's attempt to block a subpoena under the Speech or Debate Clause because the Constitution provides "an absolute bar to judicial interference" with such compulsory process. As a consequence, a witness's typical judicial recourse is to refuse to comply with the subpoena, risk being cited for contempt, and then challenge the legal sufficiency of the subpoena in the contempt prosecution.

Staff Deposition Authority

Committees often rely on informal staff interviews to gather information to prepare for investigative hearings. However, in recent years, congressional committees have also used staff-conducted depositions as a tool in exercising their investigatory power. On a number of occasions such specific authority has been granted pursuant to Senate and House resolutions. When granted, procedures for taking depositions may be issued, including provisions for notice (with or without a subpoena), transcription of the deposition, the right to be accompanied by counsel, and the manner in which objections to questions are to be resolved.

Staff depositions afford a number of significant advantages for committees engaged in complex investigations, including the ability to:

- obtain sworn testimony quickly and confidentially without the necessity of Members devoting time to lengthy hearings that may be unproductive because witnesses do not have the facts needed by the committee or refuse to cooperate;

- obtain testimony in private, which may be more conducive to candid responses than public hearings;

- verify witness statements that might defame or tend to incriminate third parties before they are repeated publicly;

- prepare for hearings by screening witness testimony in advance, which may obviate the need to call other witnesses;

- question witnesses outside of Washington, DC, without the inconvenience of conducting field hearings with Members present.

Moreover, Congress has enhanced the efficacy of the staff deposition process by re-establishing the applicability of criminal prohibition against false statements to statements made during congressional proceedings, including the taking of depositions.

Certain disadvantages may also inhere. Unrestrained staff may be tempted to engage in tangential inquiries. Also, depositions present a "cold record" of a witness's testimony and may not be as useful for Members as in-person presentations.

Hearings

House Rule XI(2) and Senate Rule XXVI(2) require that committees adopt written rules of procedure to be used in hearings and publish them in the Congressional Record. The failure to publish such rules has resulted in the invalidation of a perjury prosecution. Once properly promulgated, such rules are judicially cognizable and must be strictly observed. The House and many individual Senate committees require that all witnesses be given a copy of a committee's rules.

Both the House and the Senate have adopted rules permitting a reduced quorum for taking testimony and receiving evidence. House committees are required to have at least two Members present to take testimony. Senate rules allow the taking of testimony with only one Member in attendance. Most committees have adopted the minimum quorum requirement, and some require a higher quorum for sworn rather than unsworn testimony. For perjury purposes, the quorum requirement must be met at the time the allegedly perjured testimony is given, not at the beginning of the session. Reduced quorum requirement rules do not apply to authorizations for the issuance of subpoenas. Senate rules require a one-third quorum of a committee or subcommittee, while the House requires a quorum of a majority of the members unless a committee delegates authority for issuance to its chairman.

Senate and House rules limit the authority of their committees to meet in closed session. For example, the House requires testimony to be held in closed session if a majority of a committee or subcommittee determines that it "may tend to defame, degrade, or incriminate any person." Such testimony taken in closed session is normally releasable only by a majority vote of the committee. Similarly, confidential material received in a closed session requires a majority vote for release.

In most oversight and investigative hearings, the chair usually makes an opening statement. In the case of an investigative hearing, the opening statement is an important means of defining the subject matter of the hearing and thereby establishing the pertinence of questions asked of the witnesses. Not all committees swear in their witnesses, but a few committees require that all witnesses be sworn. Most committees leave the swearing of witnesses to the discretion of the chair. If a committee wishes the potential sanction of perjury to apply, it should, in accordance with the statute, administer an oath and swear in its witnesses. However, it should be noted that false statements not under oath are also subject to criminal sanctions.

A witness does not have the right to make a statement before being questioned, but the opportunity is usually accorded. Committee rules may prescribe the length of such statements and also require written statements be submitted in advance of the hearing. Questioning of witnesses may be structured so that members alternate for specified lengths of time. Questioning may also be conducted by staff at the committee's discretion. Witnesses may be allowed to review a transcript of their testimony and make non-substantive corrections.

The right of a witness to be accompanied by counsel is recognized by House rule and the rules of Senate committees. The House rule limits the role of counsel, who are to serve solely "for the purpose of advising [witnesses] concerning their constitutional rights." Some committees have adopted rules specifically prohibiting counsel from "coaching" witnesses during their testimony.

A committee has complete authority to control the conduct of counsel. Indeed, the House rules provide, "The chair may punish breaches of order and decorum, and of professional ethics on the part of counsel, by censure and exclusion from the hearings; and the committee may cite the offender to the House for contempt." Some Senate committees have adopted similar rules. There is no right of cross-examination of adverse witnesses during an investigative hearing. However, witnesses are entitled to a range of other constitutional protections, such as the Fifth Amendment right to avoid making self-incriminating statements, which are discussed in more detail below.

Congressional Immunity

The Fifth Amendment to the Constitution provides in part that "no person . . . shall be compelled in any criminal case to be a witness against himself." The privilege against self-incrimination is available to a witness in a congressional investigation. When a witness before a committee asserts this testimonial constitutional privilege, the committee may obtain a court order granting the witness immunity if two-thirds of the full committee votes for the order. Such an order compels the witness to testify and grants him or her immunity against the use of that testimony, and other information derived therefrom, in a subsequent criminal prosecution. The witness may still be prosecuted on the basis of other evidence.

Grants of immunity have occurred in a number of notable congressional investigations, including the investigations of Watergate (John Dean and Jeb Magruder) and Iran-Contra (Oliver North and John Poindexter). The decision to grant immunity involves a number of complex issues but is ultimately a strategic decision for Congress. As observed by Iran-Contra Independent Counsel Lawrence E. Walsh, "The legislative branch has the power to decide whether it is more important perhaps even to destroy a prosecution than to hold back testimony they need. They make that decision. It is not a judicial decision or a legal decision but a political decision of the highest importance."

In determining whether to grant immunity to a witness, a committee might consider, on the one hand, its need for the witness's testimony to perform its legislative, oversight, and informing functions and, on the other, the possibility that the witness's immunized congressional testimony could jeopardize a successful criminal prosecution.

Illustrative Subpoena

Subpena Duces Tecum

By Authority of the House of Representatives of the Congress of the United States of America

To ..Custodian.of.Documents.International.Brotherhood.of.Teamsters...............

You are hereby commanded to produce the things identified on the attached schedule before the Subcommittee on Oversight
and.Investigations. Committee on ...Education.and.the.Workforce...........

of the House of Representatives of the United States, of which the Hon. Pete.Hoekstra...........

.... is chairman, by producing such things in Room ...B-346A... of the

..........Rayburn.............. Building ...., in the city of Washington, on

..........March..17,.1998......, at the hour of ....5:00..p.m,..............

To .Any.staff.member.or.agent.of.the.Committee.on.Education.and.the.Workfor
       of the age of 18 years or older or to any United States Marshal
to serve and make return.

Witness my hand and the seal of the House of Representatives

of the United States, .at the city of Washington, this

.....10th..... day of ......March................., 19..98...

Peter Hoekstra

The Honorable Pete Hoekstra   *Chairman.*

Attest:

....
                                        Clerk.

GENERAL INSTRUCTIONS

1.   In complying with this Subpoena, you are required to produce all responsive documents that are in your possession, custody, or control, whether held by you or your past or present agents, employees, and representatives acting on your behalf. You are also required to produce documents that you have a legal right to obtain, documents that you have a right to copy or have access to, and documents that you have placed in the temporary possession, custody, or control of any third party. No records, documents, data or information called for by this request shall be

destroyed, modified, removed or otherwise made inaccessible to the Committee.

2.   In the event that any entity, organization or individual denoted in this subpoena has been, or is also known by any other name than that herein denoted, the subpoena shall be read to also include them under that alternative identification.

3.   Each document produced shall be produced in a form that renders the document susceptible of copying.

4.   Documents produced in response to this subpoena shall be produced together with copies of file labels, dividers or identifying markers with which they were associated when this subpoena was served. Also identify to which paragraph from the subpoena that such documents are responsive.

5.   It shall not be a basis for refusal to produce documents that any other person or entity also possesses non-identical or identical copies of the same document.

6.   If any of the subpoenaed information is available in machine-readable form (such as punch cards, paper or magnetic tapes, drums, disks, or core storage), state the form in which it is available and provide sufficient detail to allow the information to be copied to a readable format. If the information requested is stored in a computer, indicate whether you have an existing program that will print the records in a readable form.

7.   If the subpoena cannot be complied with in full, it shall be complied with to the extent possible, which shall include an explanation of why full compliance is not possible.

8.   In the event that a document is withheld on the basis of privilege, provide the following information concerning any such document: (a) the privilege asserted; (b) the type of document; (c) the general subject matter; (d) the date, author and addressee; and (e) the relationship of the author and addressee to each other.

9.   If any document responsive to this subpoena was, but no longer is, in your possession, custody, or control, identify the document (stating its date, author, subject and recipients) and explain the circumstances by which the document ceased to be in your possession, or control.

10. If a date set forth in this subpoena referring to a communication, meeting, or other event is inaccurate, but the actual date is known to you or is otherwise apparent from the context of the request, you should produce all documents which would be responsive as if the date were correct.

11. Other than subpoena questions directed at the activities of specified entities or persons, to the extent that information contained in

documents sought by this subpoena may require production of donor lists, or information otherwise enabling the re-creation of donor lists, such identifying information may be redacted.

12. The time period covered by this subpoena is included in the attached Schedule A.

13. This request is continuing in nature. Any record, document, compilation of data or information, not produced because it has not been located or discovered by the return date, shall be produced immediately upon location or discovery subsequent thereto.

14. All documents shall be Bates stamped sequentially and produced sequentially.

15. Two sets of documents shall be delivered, one set for the Majority Staff and one set for the Minority Staff. When documents are produced to the Subcommittee, production sets shall be delivered to the Majority Staff in Room B346 Rayburn House Office Building and the Minority Staff in Room 2101 Rayburn House Office Building.

. . .

SCHEDULE A

1. All organizational charts and personnel rosters for the International Brotherhood of Teamsters ("Teamsters" or "IBT"), including the DRIVE PAC, in effect during calendar years 1991 through 1997.

2. All IBT operating, finance, and administrative *manuals* in effect during calendar years 1991 through 1997, including, but not limited to those that set forth (1) operating policies, practices, and procedures; (2) internal financial practices and reporting requirements; and (3) authorization, approval, and review responsibilities.

3. All annual audit reports of the IBT for the years 1991 through 1996 performed by the auditing firm of Grant Thornton.

4. All IBT annual reports to its membership and the public for years 1991 through 1997, including copies of IBT annual audited financial statements certified to by independent public accountants.

5. All books and records showing receipts and expenditures, assets and liabilities, profits and losses, and all other records used for recording the financial affairs of the IBT including, journals (or other books of original entry) and ledgers including cash receipts journals, cash disbursements journals, revenue journals, general journals, subledgers, and workpapers reflecting accounting entries.

6. All Federal Income Tax returns filed by the IBT for years 1991 through 1997.

7.   All minutes of the General Board, Executive Board, Executive Council, and all Standing Committees, including any internal ethics committees formed to investigate misconduct and corruption, and all handouts and reports prepared and produced at each Committee meeting.

8.   All documents referring or relating to, or containing information about, any contribution, donation, expenditure, outlay, in-kind assistance, transfer, loan, or grant (from DRIVE, DRIVE E&L fund, or IBT general treasury) to any of the following entities/organizations:

a.   Citizen Action

b.   Campaign for a Responsible Congress

c.   Project Vote

d.   National Council of Senior Citizens

e.   Vote Now '96

f.   AFL-CIO

g.   AFSCME

h.   Democratic National Committee

i.   Democratic Senatorial Campaign Committee ("DSCC")

j.   Democratic Congressional Campaign Committee ("DCCC")

k.   State Democratic Parties

l.   Clinton-Gore '96

m.   SEIU

KILBOURN v. THOMPSON

Supreme Court of the United States
103 U.S. 168 (1880)

[Note: In 1876, Hallet Kilbourn was subpoenaed to testify before a Special House Committee to investigate the bankruptcy of Jay Cooke & Company and its investments into a questionable "real estate pool." The House resolution creating the committee stated that the United States was a creditor of the bankrupt firm because the Secretary of the Navy invested public funds with the firm. The House resolution also stated that the U.S. had lost its funds due to the bankruptcy and "the courts are now powerless by reason of said settlement to afford adequate redress to said creditors." Although Kilbourn, a real estate broker with knowledge of the investments, appeared before the Committee, he refused to answer any questions and did not provide the subpoenaed documents. Kilbourn denied "the right of the House to investigate private business arbitrarily," but stated that "if either the committee or the House would assert that the production of his private papers, or the revelation of his private business, would promote any public interest, or if any private individual would assert on oath that the papers asked for would lead to the detection of corruption, he would respond freely to all demands for information or papers." House Sergeant-At-Arms John G. Thompson took Kilbourn into custody. When Kilbourn continued to refuse to testify, the House held Kilbourn in contempt and ordered he be held in custody until he complied with the subpoena.

While in custody, a federal grand jury indicted Kilbourn for criminal contempt of Congress. This created a battle between the legislative branch and the executive/judicial branches. The U.S. marshal attempted to take custody of Kilbourn under orders from a Federal court, but the Sergeant-at-Arms refused. Finally the House authorized the Sergeant-at-Arms to obey the writ of habeas corpus. Kilbourn sued the House for false imprisonment.]

MR. JUSTICE MILLER, after stating the case, delivered the opinion of the court.

. . .

That the power to punish for contempt has been exercised by the House of Commons in numerous instances is well known to the general student of history, and is authenticated by the rolls of the Parliament. And there is no question but that this has been upheld by the courts of Westminster Hall. . . .

It is important, however, to understand on what principle this power in the House of Commons rests, that we may, see whether it is applicable to the two Houses of Congress, and, if it be, whether there are limitations to its exercise.

While there is, in the adjudged cases in the English courts, little agreement of opinion as to the extent of this power, and the liability of its exercise to be inquired into by the courts, there is no difference of opinion as to its origin. This goes back to the period when the bishops, the lords, and the knights and burgesses met in one body, and were, when so assembled, called the High Court of Parliament.

They were not only called so, but the assembled Parliament exercised the highest functions of a court of judicature, representing in that respect the judicial authority of the king in his Court of Parliament. While this body enacted laws, it also rendered judgments in matters of private right, which, when approved by the king, were recognized as valid. Upon the separation of the Lords and Commons into two separate bodies, holding their sessions in different chambers, and hence called the House of Lords and the House of Commons, the judicial function of reviewing by appeal the decisions of the courts of Westminster Hall passed to the House of Lords, where it has been exercised without dispute ever since. To the Commons was left the power of impeachment, and, perhaps, others of a judicial character, and jointly they exercised, until a very recent period, the power of passing bills of attainder for treason and other high crimes which are in their nature punishment for crime declared judicially by the High Court of Parliament of the Kingdom of England.

It is upon this idea that the two Houses of Parliament were each courts of judicature originally, which, though divested by usage, and by statute, probably, of many of their judicial functions, have yet retained so much of that power as enables them, like any other court, to punish for a contempt of these privileges and authority that the power rests.

. . .

We are of opinion that the right of the House of Representatives to punish the citizen for a contempt of its authority or a breach of its privileges can derive no support from the precedents and practices of the two Houses of the English Parliament, nor from the adjudged cases in which the English courts have upheld these practices. Nor, taking what has fallen from the English judges, and especially the later cases on which we have just commented, is much aid given to the doctrine, that this power exists as one necessary to enable either House of Congress to exercise successfully their function of legislation.

This latter proposition is one which we do not propose to decide in the present case, because we are able to decide it without passing upon the existence or non-existence of such a power in aid of the legislative function.

As we have already said, the Constitution expressly empowers each House to punish its own members for disorderly behavior. We see no reason to doubt that this punishment may in a proper case be imprisonment, and that it may be for refusal to obey some rule on that subject made by the House for the preservation of order.

So, also, the penalty which each House is authorized to inflict in order to compel the attendance of absent members may be imprisonment, and this may be for a violation of some order or standing rule on that subject.

Each House is by the Constitution made the judge of the election and qualification of its members. In deciding on these it has an undoubted right to examine witnesses and inspect papers, subject to the usual rights of witnesses in such cases; and it may be that a witness would be subject to like punishment at the hands of the body engaged in trying a contested election, for refusing to testify, that he would if the case were pending before a court of judicature.

The House of Representatives has the sole right to impeach officers of the government, and the Senate to try them. Where the question of such impeachment is before either body acting in its appropriate sphere on that subject, we see no reason to doubt the right to compel the attendance of witnesses, and their answer to proper questions, in the same manner and by the use of the same means that courts of justice can in like cases.

Whether the power of punishment in either House by fine or imprisonment goes beyond this or not, we are sure that no person can be punished for contumacy as a witness before either House, unless his testimony is required in a matter into which that House has jurisdiction to inquire, and we feel equally sure that neither of these bodies possesses the general power of making inquiry into the private affairs of the citizen.

. . .

In looking to the preamble and resolution under which the committee acted, before which Kilbourn refused to testify, we are of opinion that the House of Representatives not only exceeded the limit of its own authority, but assumed a power which could only be properly exercised by another branch of the government, because it was in its nature clearly judicial.

The Constitution declares that the judicial power of the United States shall be vested in one Supreme Court, and in such inferior courts as the Congress may from time to time ordain and establish. If what we have said of the division of the powers of the government among the three departments be sound, this is equivalent to a declaration that no judicial power is vested in the Congress or either branch of it, save in the cases specifically enumerated to which we have referred. If the investigation which the committee was directed to make was judicial in its character, and could only be properly and successfully made by a court of justice, and if it related to a matter wherein relief or redress could be had only by a judicial proceeding, we do not, after what has been said, deem it necessary to discuss the proposition that the power attempted to be exercised was one confided by the Constitution to the judicial and not to the legislative department of the government. We think it equally clear that the power asserted is judicial and not legislative.

The preamble to the resolution recites that the government of the United States is a creditor of Jay Cooke & Co., then in bankruptcy in the District Court of the United States for the Eastern District of Pennsylvania.

If the United States is a creditor of any citizen, or of any one else on whom process can be served, the usual, the only legal mode of enforcing payment of the debt is by a resort to a court of justice. For this purpose, among others, Congress has created courts of the United States, and officers have been appointed to prosecute the pleas of the government in these courts.

The District Court for the Eastern District of Pennsylvania is one of them, and, according to the recital of the preamble, had taken jurisdiction of the subject-matter of Jay Cooke & Co.'s indebtedness to the United

States, and had the whole subject before it for action at the time the proceeding in Congress was initiated. That this indebtedness resulted, as the preamble states, from the improvidence of a secretary of the navy does not change the nature of the suit in the court nor vary the remedies by which the debt is to be recovered. If, indeed, any purpose had been avowed to impeach the secretary, the whole aspect of the case would have been changed. But no such purpose is disclosed. None can be inferred from the preamble, and the characterization of the conduct of the secretary by the term 'improvident,' and the absence of any words implying suspicion of criminality repel the idea of such purpose, for the secretary could only be impeached for 'high crimes and misdemeanors.'

The preamble then refers to 'the real-estate pool,' in which it is said Jay Cooke & Co. had a large interest, as something well known and understood, and which had been the subject of a partial investigation by the previous Congress, and alleges that the trustee in bankruptcy of Jay Cooke & Co. had made a settlement of the interest of Jay Cooke & Co. with the associates of the firm of Jay Cooke & Co., to the disadvantage and loss of their numerous creditors, including the government of the United States, by reason of which the courts are powerless to afford adequate redress to said creditors.

Several very pertinent inquiries suggest themselves as arising out of this short preamble. How could the House of Representatives know, until it had been fairly tried, that the courts were powerless to redress the creditors of Jay Cooke & Co.? The matter was still pending in a court, and what right had the Congress of the United States to interfere with a suit pending in a court of competent jurisdiction? Again, what inadequacy of power existed in the court, or, as the preamble assumes, in all courts, to give redress which could lawfully be supplied by an investigation by a committee of one House of Congress, or by any act or resolution of Congress on the subject? The case being one of a judicial nature, for which the power of the courts usually afford the only remedy, it may well be supposed that those powers were more appropriate and more efficient in aid of such relief than the powers which belong to a body whose function is exclusively legislative. If the settlement to which the preamble refers as the principal reason why the courts are rendered powerless was obtained by fraud, or was without authority, or for any conceivable reason could be set aside or avoided, it should be done by some appropriate proceeding in the court which had the whole matter before it, and which had all the power in that case proper to be intrusted to any body, and not by Congress or by any power to be conferred on a committee of one of the two Houses.

The resolution adopted as a sequence of this preamble contains no hint of any intention of final action by Congress on the subject. In all the argument of the case no suggestion has been made of what the House of Representatives or the Congress could have done in the way of remedying the wrong or securing the creditors of Jay Cooke & Co., or even the United States. Was it to be simply a fruitless investigation into the personal affairs of individuals? If so, the House of Representatives had no power or authority in the matter more than any other equal number of gentlemen interested for the government of their country. By 'fruitless' we mean that it could result in no valid legislation on the subject to which the inquiry referred.

What was this committee charged to do?

To inquire into the nature and history of the real-estate pool. How indefinite! What was the real-estate pool? Is it charged with any crime or offence? If so, the courts alone can punish the members of it. Is it charged with a fraud against the government? Here, again, the courts, and they alone, can afford a remedy. Was it a corporation whose powers Congress could repeal? There is no suggestion of the kind. The word 'pool,' in the sense here used, is of modern date, and may not be well understood, but in this case it can mean no more than that certain individuals are engaged in dealing in real estate as a commodity of traffic; and the gravamen of the whole proceeding is that a debtor of the United States may be found to have an interest in the pool. Can the rights of the pool, or of its members, and the rights of the debtor, and of the creditor of the debtor, be determined by the report of a committee or by an act of Congress? If they cannot, what authority has the House to enter upon this investigation into the private affairs of individuals who hold no office under the government.

. . .

We are of opinion, for these reasons, that the resolution of the House of Representatives authorizing the investigation was in excess of the power conferred on that body by the Constitution; that the committee, therefore, had no lawful authority to require Kilbourn to testify as a witness beyond what he voluntarily chose to tell; that the orders and resolutions of the House, and the warrant of the speaker, under which Kilbourn was imprisoned, are, in like manner, void for want of jurisdiction in that body, and that his imprisonment was without any lawful authority.

At this point of the inquiry we are met by *Anderson v. Dunn* (6 Wheat. 204), which in many respects is analogous to the case now under consideration. Anderson sued Dunn for false imprisonment, and Dunn justified under a warrant of the House of Representatives directed to him as sergeant-at-arms of that body. The warrant recited that Anderson had been found by the House 'guilty of a breach of the privileges of the House, and of a high contempt of the dignity and authority of the same.' The warrant directed the sergeant-at-arms to bring him before the House, when, by its order, he was reprimanded by the speaker. Neither the warrant nor the plea described or gave any clew to the nature of the act which was held by the House to be a contempt. Nor can it be clearly ascertained from the report of the case what it was, though a slight inference may be derived from something in one of the arguments of counsel, that it was an attempt to bribe a member.

But, however that may be, the defence of the sergeant-at-arms rested on the broad ground that the House, having found the plaintiff guilty of a contempt, and the speaker, under the order of the House, having issued a warrant for his arrest, that *197 alone was sufficient authority for the defendant to take him into custody, and this court held the plea good.

It may be said that since the order of the House, and the warrant of the speaker, and the plea of the sergeant-at-arms, do not disclose the ground on which the plaintiff was held guilty of a contempt, but state the finding of the House in general terms as a judgment of guilty, and as the court placed its decision on the ground that such a judgment was conclusive in the action against the officer who executed the warrant, it is no precedent for a case where the plea establishes, as we have shown it does in this case by its recital of the facts, that the House has exceeded its authority.

This is, in fact, a substantial difference. But the court in its reasoning goes beyond this, and though the grounds of the decision are not very clearly stated, we take them to be: that there is in some cases a power in each House of Congress to punish for contempt; that this power is analogous to that exercised by courts of justice, and that it being the well-established doctrine that when it appears that a prisoner is held under the order of a court of general jurisdiction for a contempt of its authority, no other court will discharge the prisoner or make further inquiry into the cause of his commitment. That this is the general rule, though somewhat modified since that case was decided, as regards the relations of one court to another, must be conceded.

But we do not concede that the Houses of Congress possess this general power of punishing for contempt. The cases in which they can do this are very limited, as we have already attempted to show. If they are proceeding in a matter beyond their legitimate cognizance, we are of opinion that this can be shown, and we cannot give our assent to the principle that, by the mere act of asserting a person to be guilty of a contempt, they thereby establish their right to fine and imprison him, beyond the power of any court or any other tribunal whatever to inquire into the grounds on which the order was made. This necessarily grows out of the nature of an authority which can only exist in a limited class of cases, or under special circumstances; otherwise the limitation is unavailing and the power omnipotent. The tendency of modern decisions everywhere is to the doctrine that the jurisdiction of a court or other tribunal to render a judgment affecting individual rights, is always open to inquiry, when the judgment is relied on in any other proceeding.

. . .

We must, therefore, hold, notwithstanding what is said in the case of *Anderson v. Dunn*, that the resolution of the House of Representatives finding *Kilbourn* guilty of contempt, and the warrant of its speaker for his commitment to prison, are not conclusive in this case, and in fact are no justification, because, as the whole plea shows, the House was without authority in the matter.

NOTES & QUESTIONS

1.   In this case the Supreme Court established the so-called "*Kilbourn* Test," that limited the scope of investigations:

(a)   Inquiries must not "invade areas constitutionally reserved to the courts or the executive"

(b)   Inquiries must deal "with subjects on which Congress could validly legislate"

(c)   The resolution authorizing the investigation must specify "a congressional interest in legislating on that subject."

(d)   Where the inquiry can result in "no valid legislation," then the "Private affairs of individuals" are not valid targets for inquiry.

Is this a useful break with past Congressional practice to rebalance the powers divided among the three branches? Is this a workable test?

2.   The *Kilbourn* decision seems to severely limit Congress's power to obtain information and is still frequently cited when someone objects to a subpoena. However, nearly 50 years later, *McGrain v. Daugherty*, 273 U.S. 135 (1927) readdressed the *Kilbourn* test. Congress was investigating the Teapot Dome Scandal and the Justice Department's failure to investigate the matter. The most notorious government scandal until Watergate, the Teapot Dome scandal involved the bribery of Secretary of the Interior Albert Bacon Fall who leased Navy petroleum reserves at Teapot Dome in Wyoming and in California to oil companies at below market rates without competitive bidding. After the Congressional investigation, Fall became the first cabinet member to go to prison. During the investigation the Senate subpoenaed Mally Daugherty, brother of the former Attorney General Harry Daugherty, to testify before an investigating committee. When he failed to appear to testify he was arrested and convicted of contempt. The Court stated:

[*Kilbourn v. Thompson*] has been cited at times, and is cited to us now, as strongly intimating, if not holding, that neither house of Congress has power to make inquires and exact evidence in aid of contemplated legislation.

. . .

We are of opinion that the power of inquiry—with process to enforce it—is an essential and appropriate auxiliary to the legislative function. It was so regarded and employed in American Legislatures before the Constitution was framed and ratified. Both houses of Congress took this view of it early in their history-the House of Representatives with the approving votes of Mr. Madison and other members whose service in the convention which framed the Constitution gives special significance to their action-and both houses have employed the power accordingly up to the present time. . . .

We are further of opinion that the provisions are not of doubtful meaning, but, as was held by this court in the cases we have reviewed, are intended to be effectively exercised, and therefore to carry with them such auxiliary powers as are necessary and appropriate to that end.

The Court rejected the lower court's assertion that the investigation of a former attorney general would not lead to legislation but was judicial in nature. Although Congress may not have set out to create legislation, the Court found that the investigation into the administration of the Department of Justice could lead to legislation, and therefore, valid.

C. RIGHTS OF WITNESSES BEFORE CONGRESS

1. MCCARTHYISM

During the early to mid-1950s Sen. Joseph McCarthy (R-WI) used the power of Congress in an effort to identify communists undermining the United States, ruining many innocent lives in the process. Although a first term senator, Sen. McCarthy freely disregarded the Senate's rules and customs, and became known for threats, personal attacks, and the easy distortion of the truth.

The early to mid-20th century saw several "red scares" where Americans worried that an international communist movement would overthrow the U.S. government. The Russian Revolution in 1917 creating the Soviet Union, the Soviets' aggressive moves in Eastern Europe after World War II, and the Chinese Communist Party's takeover of China in 1949 all led some Americans to believe that the United States could not stop the spread of communism. Worse, many worried that communists were infiltrating key positions in the United States. In February 1950, Senator McCarthy delivered his infamous "Enemies from Within" speech to the Women's Republican Club in Wheeling, West Virginia:

This is a time of the Cold War. This is a time when all the world is split into two vast, increasingly hostile armed camps—a time of a great armaments race. Today we can almost physically hear the mutterings and rumblings of an invigorated god of war. You can see it, feel it, and hear it all the way from the hills of Indochina, from the shores of Formosa right over into the very heart of

Europe itself. . . . Today we are engaged in a final, all-out battle
between communistic atheism and Christianity. The modern
champions of communism have selected this as the time. And,
ladies and gentlemen, the chips are down—they are truly down.

. . .

As one of our outstanding historical figures once said, "When a
great democracy is destroyed, it will not be because of enemies
from without but rather because of enemies from within."

. . .

The reason why we find ourselves in a position of impotency is not
because our only powerful, potential enemy has sent men to
invade our shores, but rather because of the traitorous actions of
those who have been treated so well by this nation. It has not been
the less fortunate or members of minority groups who have been
selling this nation out, but rather those who have had all the
benefits that the wealthiest nation on earth has had to offer—the
finest homes, the finest college education, and the finest jobs in
government we can give.

This is glaringly true in the State Department. There the bright
young men who are born with silver spoons in their mouths are
the ones who have been worst. Now I know it is very easy for
anyone to condemn a particular bureau or department in general
terms. Therefore, I would like to cite one rather unusual case—
the case of a man who has done much to shape our foreign policy.
When Chiang Kai-shek was fighting our war, the State
Department had in China a young man named John S. Service.
His task, obviously, was not to work for the communization of
China. Strangely, however, he sent official reports back to the
State Department urging that we torpedo our ally Chiang Kai-
shek and stating, in effect, that communism was the best hope of
China. Later, this man—John Service—was picked up by the
Federal Bureau of Investigation for turning over to the
communists secret State Department information. Strangely,
however, he was never prosecuted. However, Joseph Grew, the
undersecretary of state, who insisted on his prosecution, was
forced to resign. Two days after, Grew's successor, Dean Acheson,
took over as undersecretary of state, this man—John Service—
who had been picked up by the FBI and who had previously urged
that communism was the best hope of China, was not only
reinstated in the State Department but promoted; and finally,
under Acheson, placed in charge of all placements and
promotions. Today, ladies and gentlemen, this man Service is on
his way to represent the State Department and Acheson in

Calcutta—by far and away the most important listening post in the Far East. Now, let's see what happens when individuals with communist connections are forced out of the State Department.

. . .

This, ladies and gentlemen, gives you somewhat of a picture of the type of individuals who have been helping to shape our foreign policy. In my opinion the State Department, which is one of the most important government departments, is thoroughly infested with communists. I have in my hand 57 cases of individuals who would appear to be either card-carrying members or certainly loyal to the Communist Party, but who nevertheless are still helping to shape our foreign policy. One thing to remember in discussing the communists in our government is that we are not dealing with spies who get 30 pieces of silver to steal the blueprints of new weapons. We are dealing with a far more sinister type of activity because it permits the enemy to guide and shape our policy.

This speech gave Sen. McCarthy national attention. Four months after his "Enemy From Within" speech, however, Sen. Margaret Chase Smith (R-ME) took to the Senate floor to denounce him. For weeks, Sen. McCarthy refused her repeated requests for evidence to back up his claims of communist infiltration of the U.S. government, especially because he was attacking officials she considered above suspicion. Sen. Smith had hoped a more senior senator would take the lead but noted there was a "great psychological fear" of offending McCarthy.

Sen. Chase said the United States Senate, with a reputation as the world's "greatest deliberative body" had been debased to "a forum of hate and character assassination." Sen. Smith lauded the right of every American to protest and hold unpopular beliefs and asked her fellow Republicans not to ride to political victory on the "Four Horsemen of Calumny—Fear, Ignorance, Bigotry, and Smear."

Sen. McCarthy dismissed Sen. Chase's criticism. When McCarthy became the chair of the Senate Committee on Government Operations' Permanent Subcommittee on Investigations in 1953, he now had the legal power to fully investigate communist influence within the press and the federal government, including the State Department, the U.S. Army, and the Government Printing Office.

Sen. McCarthy used the committee to relentlessly hunt for communists. He called hundreds of witnesses in both public and closed hearings. After not consulting the other committee members on hiring staff, the panel's three Democrats reigned in mid-1953. Republican senators stopped attending the hearings that were arranged at the last minute and often held outside of Washington DC. This left Sen. McCarthy and his chief counsel to run the hearings without check and able to question, harass and insult witnesses.

During this time, hundreds of Americans were accused of being "communists" or "communist sympathizers" either by Sen. McCarthy or the House Un-American Activities Committee. Innocent people in government, the entertainment industry, academics, and labor-union activists were accused, often based on inconclusive, questionable or exaggerated evidence. The accusations alone led to people losing their careers and reputation. Some people were even imprisoned.

In early 1954, McCarthy charged that the U.S. Army had poor security at a top-secret army facility. In response, the army claimed that Sen. McCarthy had improperly sought preferential treatment for a former aide who had been drafted. McCarthy temporarily gave up his chairmanship and the Committee held a three-month nationally televised set of hearings known as the Army-McCarthy hearings. During 36 days of televised hearings the public watched accusations of possible espionage at the Army Signal Corps Engineering Laboratories and allegations the Army had promoted a dentist who had refused to answer loyalty questions.

Attorney Joseph Welch represented the Army, and when Sen. McCarthy claimed during a hearing that one of Welch's legal associates had ties to a communist organization, Welch responded on national television, "Until this moment, Senator, I think I never really gauged your cruelty or your recklessness." When Sen. McCarthy tried to respond, Welch angrily interrupted, "Let us not assassinate this lad further, senator. You have done enough. Have you no sense of decency?"

This exchange marked the end of Sen. McCarthy's popularity and power. Shortly afterward, Edward R. Murrow, one of the most prominent journalists in America, condemned McCarthy's actions on television. He was censured by the Senate, ignored by the media, and died three years later at the age of 48. As Senator Robert C. Byrd (D-WV) said, "There was never quite anyone like McCarthy in the Senate, before or after; nor has this chamber ever gone through a more painful period."

WATKINS V. U.S.

Supreme Court of the United States
354 U.S. 178 (1957)

MR. CHIEF JUSTICE WARREN delivered the opinion of the Court.

This is a review by certiorari of a conviction under 2 U.S.C. s 192, 2 U.S.C.A. s 192 for 'contempt of Congress.' The misdemeanor is alleged to have been committed during a hearing before a congressional investigating committee. It is not the case of a truculent or contumacious witness who refuses to answer all questions or who, by boisterous or discourteous conduct, disturbs the decorum of the committee room. Petitioner was prosecuted for refusing to make certain disclosures which he asserted to be beyond the authority of the committee to demand. The controversy thus rests upon fundamental principles of the power of the Congress and the limitations upon that power. We approach the questions presented with conscious awareness of the far-reaching ramifications that can follow from a decision of this nature.

On April 29, 1954, petitioner appeared as a witness in compliance with a subpoena issued by a Subcommittee of the Committee on Un-American Activities of the House of Representatives. The Subcommittee elicited from petitioner a description of his background in labor union activities. He had been an employee of the International Harvester Company between 1935 and 1953. During the last eleven of those years, he had been on leave of absence to serve as an official of the Farm Equipment Workers International Union, later merged into the United Electrical, Radio and Machine Workers. He rose to the position of President of District No. 2 of the Farm Equipment Workers, a district defined geographically to include generally Canton and Rock Falls, Illinois, and Dubuque, Iowa. In 1953, petitioner joined the United Automobile Workers International Union as a labor organizer.

Petitioner's name had been mentioned by two witnesses who testified before the Committee at prior hearings. In September 1952, on Donald O. Spencer admitted having been a Communist from 1943 to 1946. He declared that he had been recruited into the Party with the endorsement and prior approval of petitioner, whom he identified as the then District Vice-President of the Farm Equipment Workers. Spencer also mentioned that petitioner had attended meetings at which only card-carrying Communists were admitted. A month before petitioner testified, one Walter Rumsey stated that he had been recruited into the Party by petitioner. Rumsey added that he had paid Party dues to, and later collected dues from, petitioner, who had assumed the name, Sam Brown. Rumsey told the Committee that he left the Party in 1944.

Petitioner answered these allegations freely and without reservation. His attitude toward the inquiry is clearly revealed from the statement he made when the questioning turned to the subject of his past conduct, associations and predilections:

'I am not now nor have I ever been a card-carrying member of the Communist Party. Rumsey was wrong when he said I had recruited him into the party, that I had received his dues, that I paid dues to him, and that I had used the alias Sam Brown.

'Spencer was wrong when he termed any meetings which I attended as closed Communist Party meetings.

'I would like to make it clear that for a period of time from approximately 1942 to 1947 I cooperated with the Communist Party and participated in Communist activities to such a degree that some persons may honestly believe that I was a member of the party.

'I have made contributions upon occasions to Communist causes. I have signed petitions for Communist causes. I attended caucuses at an FE convention at which Communist Party officials were present.

'Since I freely cooperated with the Communist Party I have no motive for making the distinction between cooperation and membership except the simple fact that it is the truth. I never carried a Communist Party card. I never accepted discipline and indeed on several occasions I opposed their position.

'In a special convention held in the summer of 1947 I led the fight for compliance with the Taft-Hartley Act by the FE-CIO International Union. This fight became so bitter that it ended any possibility of future cooperation.'

The character of petitioner's testimony on these matters can perhaps best be summarized by the Government's own appraisal in its brief:

'A more complete and candid statement of his past political associations and activities (treating the Communist Party for present purposes as a mere political party) can hardly be imagined. Petitioner certainly was not attempting to conceal or withhold from the Committee his own past political associations, predilections, and preferences. Furthermore, petitioner told the Committee that he was entirely willing to identify for the Committee, and answer any questions it might have concerning, 'those persons whom I knew to be members of the Communist Party,' provided that, 'to (his) best knowledge and belief,' they still were members of the Party * * *.'

The Subcommittee, too, was apparently satisfied with petitioner's disclosures. After some further discussion elaborating on the statement, counsel for the Committee turned to another aspect of Rumsey's testimony. Rumsey had identified a group of persons whom he had known as members of the Communist Party, and counsel began to read this list of names to petitioner. Petitioner stated that he did not know several of the persons. Of those whom he did know, he refused to tell whether he knew them to have been members of the Communist Party. He explained to the Subcommittee why he took such a position:

'I am not going to plead the fifth amendment, but I refuse to answer certain questions that I believe are outside the proper scope of your committee's activities. I will answer any questions which this committee puts to me about myself. I will also answer questions about those persons whom I knew to be members of the Communist Party and whom I believe still are. I will not, however, answer any questions with respect to others with whom I associated in the past. I do not believe that any law in this country requires me to testify about persons who may in the past have been Communist Party members or otherwise engaged in Communist Party activity but who to my best knowledge and belief have long since removed themselves from the Communist movement.

'I do not believe that such questions are relevant to the work of this committee nor do I believe that this committee has the right to undertake the public exposure of persons because of their past activities. I may be wrong, and the committee may have this power, but until and unless a court of law so holds and directs me to answer, I most firmly refuse to discuss the political activities of my past associates.'

The Chairman of the Committee submitted a report of petitioner's refusal to answer questions to the House of Representatives. The House directed the Speaker to certify the Committee's report to the United States Attorney for initiation of criminal prosecution. A seven-count indictment was returned. Petitioner waived his right to jury trial and was found guilty on all counts by the court. The sentence, a fine of $100 and one year in prison, was suspended, and petitioner was placed on probation.

An appeal was taken to the Court of Appeals for the District of Columbia. The conviction was reversed by a three-judge panel, one member dissenting. Upon rehearing en banc, the full bench affirmed the conviction with the judges of the original majority in dissent.

We start with several basic premises on which there is general agreement. The power of the Congress to conduct investigations is inherent in the legislative process. That power is broad. It encompasses inquiries concerning the administration of existing laws as well as proposed or possibly needed statutes. It includes surveys of defects in our social, economic or political system for the purpose of enabling the Congress to remedy them. It comprehends probes into departments of the Federal Government to expose corruption, inefficiency or waste. But, broad as is this power of inquiry, it is not unlimited. There is no general authority to expose the private affairs of individuals without justification in terms of the functions of the Congress. This was freely conceded by the Solicitor General in his argument of this case. Nor is the Congress a law enforcement or trial agency. These are functions of the executive and judicial departments of government. No inquiry is an end in itself; it must be related to, and in furtherance of, a legitimate task of the Congress. Investigations conducted solely for the personal aggrandizement of the investigators or to 'punish' those investigated are indefensible.

It is unquestionably the duty of all citizens to cooperate with the Congress in its efforts to obtain the facts needed for intelligent legislative action. It is their unremitting obligation to respond to subpoenas, to respect the dignity of the Congress and its committees and to testify fully with respect to matters within the province of proper investigation. This, of course, assumes that the constitutional rights of witnesses will be respected by the Congress as they are in a court of justice. The Bill of Rights is applicable to investigations as to all forms of governmental action. Witnesses cannot be compelled to give evidence against themselves. They cannot be subjected to unreasonable search and seizure. Nor can the First Amendment freedoms of speech, press, religion, or political belief and association be abridged.

. . .

In the decade following World War II, there appeared a new kind of congressional inquiry unknown in prior periods of American history. Principally this was the result of the various investigations into the threat of subversion of the United States Government, but other subjects of congressional interest also contributed to the changed scene. This new phase of legislative inquiry involved a broad-scale intrusion into the lives and affairs of private citizens. It brought before the courts novel questions of the appropriate limits of congressional inquiry. Prior cases, like *Kilbourn*, *McGrain* and *Sinclair*, had defined the scope of investigative power in terms of the inherent limitations of the sources of that power. In the more recent cases, the emphasis shifted to problems of accommodating the interest of the Government with the rights and privileges of individuals. The central theme was the application of the Bill of Rights as a restraint upon the assertion of governmental power in this form.

It was during this period that the Fifth Amendment privilege against self-incrimination was frequently invoked and recognized as a legal limit upon the authority of a committee to require that a witness answer its questions. Some early doubts as to the applicability of that privilege before a legislative committee never matured. When the matter reached this Court, the Government did not challenge in any way that the Fifth Amendment protection was available to the witness, and such a challenge could not have prevailed. It confined its argument to the character of the answers sought and to the adequacy of the claim of privilege.

A far more difficult task evolved from the claim by witnesses that the committees' interrogations were infringements upon the freedoms of the First Amendment. Clearly, an investigation is subject to the command that the Congress shall make no law abridging freedom of speech or press or assembly. While it is true that there is no statute to be reviewed, and that an investigation is not a law, nevertheless an investigation is part of lawmaking. It is justified solely as an adjunct to the legislative process. The First Amendment may be invoked against infringement of the protected freedoms by law or by lawmaking.

Abuses of the investigative process may imperceptibly lead to abridgment of protected freedoms. The mere summoning of a witness and compelling him to testify, against his will, about his beliefs, expressions or associations is a measure of governmental interference. And when those forced revelations concern matters that are unorthodox, unpopular, or even hateful to the general public, the reaction in the life of the witness may be disastrous. This effect is even more harsh when it is past beliefs, expressions or associations that are disclosed and judged by current standards rather than those contemporary with the matters exposed. Nor does the witness alone suffer the consequences. Those who are identified by witnesses and thereby placed in the same glare of publicity are equally subject to public stigma, scorn and obloquy. Beyond that, there is the more subtle and immeasurable effect upon those who tend to adhere to the most orthodox and uncontroversial views and associations in order to avoid a similar fate at some future time. That this impact is partly the result of non-governmental activity by private persons cannot relieve the investigators of their responsibility for initiating the reaction.

The Court recognized the restraints of the Bill of Rights upon congressional investigations in *United States v. Rumely*. The magnitude and complexity of the problem of applying the First Amendment to that case led the Court to construe narrowly the resolution describing the committee's authority. It was concluded that, when First Amendment rights are threatened, the delegation of power to the committee must be clearly revealed in its charter.

Accommodation of the congressional need for particular information with the individual and personal interest in privacy is an arduous and delicate task for any court. We do not underestimate the difficulties that would attend such an undertaking. It is manifest that despite the adverse effects which follow upon compelled disclosure of private matters, not all such inquiries are barred. *Kilbourn v. Thompson* teaches that such an investigation into individual affairs is invalid if unrelated to any legislative purpose. That is beyond the powers conferred upon the Congress in the Constitution. *United States v. Rumely* makes it plain that the mere semblance of legislative purpose would not justify an inquiry in the face of the Bill of Rights. The critical element is the existence of, and the weight to be ascribed to, the interest of the Congress in demanding disclosures from an unwilling witness. We cannot simply assume, however, that every congressional investigation is justified by a public need that overbalances any private rights affected. To do so would be to abdicate the responsibility placed by the Constitution upon the judiciary to insure that the Congress does not unjustifiably encroach upon an individual's right to privacy nor abridge his liberty of speech, press, religion or assembly.

Petitioner has earnestly suggested that the difficult questions of protecting these rights from infringement by legislative inquiries can be surmounted in this case because there was no public purpose served in his interrogation. His conclusion is based upon the thesis that the Subcommittee was engaged in a program of exposure for the sake of exposure. The sole purpose of the inquiry, he contends, was to bring down upon himself and others the violence of public reaction because of their past beliefs, expressions and associations. In support of this argument, petitioner has marshaled an impressive array of evidence that some Congressmen have believed that such was their duty, or part of it.

We have no doubt that there is no congressional power to expose for the sake of exposure. The public is entitled to be informed concerning the workings of its government. That cannot be inflated into a general power to expose where the predominant result can only be an invasion of the private rights of individuals. But a solution to our problem is not to be found in testing the motives of committee members for this purpose. Such is not our function. Their motives alone would not vitiate an investigation which had been instituted by a House of Congress if that assembly's legislative purpose is being served.

Petitioner's contentions do point to a situation of particular significance from the standpoint of the constitutional limitations upon congressional investigations. The theory of a committee inquiry is that the committee members are serving as the representatives of the parent assembly in collecting information for a legislative purpose. Their function is to act as the eyes and ears of the Congress in obtaining facts upon which the full legislature can act. To carry out this mission, committees and subcommittees, sometimes one Congressman, are endowed with the full power of the Congress to compel testimony. In this case, only two men exercised that authority in demanding information over petitioner's protest.

An essential premise in this situation is that the House or Senate shall have instructed the committee members on what they are to do with the power delegated to them. It is the responsibility of the Congress, in the first instance, to insure that compulsory process is used only in furtherance of a legislative purpose. That requires that the instructions to an investigating committee spell out that group's jurisdiction and purpose with sufficient particularity. Those instructions are embodied in the authorizing resolution. That document is the committee's charter. Broadly drafted and loosely worded, however, such resolutions can leave tremendous latitude to the discretion of the investigators. The more vague the committee's charter is, the greater becomes the possibility that the committee's specific actions are not in conformity with the will of the parent House of Congress.

The authorizing resolution of the Un-American Activities Committee was adopted in 1938 when a select committee, under the chairmanship of Representative Dies, was created. Several years later, the Committee was made a standing organ of the House with the same mandate. It defines the Committee's authority as follows:

> 'The Committee on Un-American Activities, as a whole or by subcommittee, is authorized to make from time to time investigations of (1) the extent, character, and objects of un-American propaganda activities in the United States, (2) the diffusion within the United States of subversive and un-American propaganda that is instigated from foreign countries or of a domestic origin and attacks the principle of the form of government as guaranteed by our Constitution, and (3) all other questions in relation thereto that would aid Congress in any necessary remedial legislation.'

It would be difficult to imagine a less explicit authorizing resolution. Who can define the meaning of 'un-American'? What is that single, solitary 'principle of the form of government as guaranteed by our Constitution'? There is no need to dwell upon the language, however. At one time, perhaps, the resolution might have been read narrowly to confine the Committee to the subject of propaganda. The events that have transpired in the fifteen years before the interrogation of petitioner make such a construction impossible at this date.

. . .

Combining the language of the resolution with the construction it has been given, it is evident that the preliminary control of the Committee exercised by the House of Representatives is slight or non-existent. No one could reasonably deduce from the charter the kind of investigation that the Committee was directed to make. As a result, we are asked to engage in a process of retroactive rationalization. Looking backward from the events that transpired, we are asked to uphold the Committee's actions unless it appears that they were clearly not authorized by the charter. As a corollary to this inverse approach, the Government urges that we must view the matter hospitably to the power of the Congress—that if there is any legislative purpose which might have been furthered by the kind of disclosure sought, the witness must be punished for withholding it. No doubt every reasonable indulgence of legality must be accorded to the actions of a coordinate branch of our Government. But such deference cannot yield to an unnecessary and unreasonable dissipation of precious constitutional freedoms.

. . .

It is, of course, not the function of this Court to prescribe rigid rules for the Congress to follow in drafting resolutions establishing investigating committees. That is a matter peculiarly within the realm of the legislature, and its decisions will be accepted by the courts up to the point where their own duty to enforce the constitutionally protected rights of individuals is affected. An excessively broad charter, like that of the House Un-American Activities Committee, places the courts in an untenable position if they are to strike a balance between the public need for a particular interrogation and the right of citizens to carry on their affairs free from unnecessary governmental interference. It is impossible in such a situation to ascertain whether any legislative purpose justifies the disclosures sought and, if so, the importance of that information to the Congress in furtherance of its legislative function. The reason no court can make this critical judgment is that the House of Representatives itself has never made it. Only the legislative assembly initiating an investigation can assay the relative necessity of specific disclosures.

. . .

In fulfillment of their obligation under this statute, the courts must accord to the defendants every right which is guaranteed to defendants in all other criminal cases. Among these is the right to have available, through a sufficiently precise statute, information revealing the standard of criminality before the commission of the alleged offense. Applied to persons prosecuted under s 192, this raises a special problem in that the statute defines the crime as refusal to answer 'any question pertinent to the question under inquiry.' Part of the standard of criminality, therefore, is the pertinency of the questions propounded to the witness.

The problem attains proportion when viewed from the standpoint of the witness who appears before a congressional committee. He must decide at the time the questions are propounded whether or not to answer. As the Court said in *Sinclair v. United States*, the witness acts at his peril. he is '* * * bound rightly to construe the statute.' An erroneous determination on his part, even if made in the utmost good faith, does not exculpate him if the court should later rule that the questions were pertinent to the question under inquiry.

It is obvious that a person compelled to make this choice is entitled to have knowledge of the subject to which the interrogation is deemed pertinent. That knowledge must be available with the same degree of explicitness and clarity that the Due Process Clause requires in the expression of any element of a criminal offense. The 'vice of vagueness' must be avoided here as in all other crimes. There are several sources that can outline the 'question under inquiry' in such a way that the rules against vagueness are satisfied. The authorizing resolution, the remarks of the chairman or members of the committee, or even the nature of the proceedings themselves, might sometimes make the topic clear. This case demonstrates, however, that these sources often leave the matter in grave doubt.

The first possibility is that the authorizing resolution itself will so clearly declare the 'question under inquiry' that a witness can understand the pertinency of questions asked him. The Government does not contend that the authorizing resolution of the Un-American Activities Committee could serve such a purpose. Its confusing breadth is amply illustrated by the innumerable and diverse questions into which the Committee has inquired under this charter since 1938. If the 'question under inquiry' were stated with such sweeping and uncertain scope, we doubt that it would withstand an attack on the ground of vagueness.

. . .

The most serious doubts as to the Subcommittee's 'question under inquiry,' however, stem from the precise questions that petitioner has been charged with refusing to answer. Under the terms of the statute, after all, it is these which must be proved pertinent. Petitioner is charged with refusing to tell the Subcommittee whether or not be knew that certain named persons had been members of the Communist Party in the past. The Subcommittee's counsel read the list from the testimony of a previous witness who had identified them as Communists. Although this former witness was identified with labor, he had not stated that the persons he named were involved in union affairs. Of the thirty names propounded to petitioner, seven were completely unconnected with organized labor. One operated a beauty parlor. Another was a watchmaker. Several were identified as 'just citizens' or 'only Communists.' When almost a quarter of the persons on the list are not labor people, the inference becomes strong that the subject before the Subcommittee was not defined in terms of Communism in labor.

. . .

The statement of the Committee Chairman in this case, in response to petitioner's protest, was woefully inadequate to convey sufficient information as to the pertinency of the questions to the subject under inquiry. Petitioner was thus not accorded a fair opportunity to determine whether he was within his rights in refusing to answer, and his conviction is necessarily invalid under the Due Process Clause of the Fifth Amendment.

We are mindful of the complexities of modern government and the ample scope that must be left to the Congress as the sole constitutional depository of legislative power. Equally mindful are we of the indispensable function, in the exercise of that power, of congressional investigations. The conclusions we have reached in this case will not prevent the Congress, through its committees, from obtaining any information it needs for the proper fulfillment of its role in our scheme of government. The legislature is free to determine the kinds of data that should be collected. It is only those investigations that are conducted by use of compulsory process that give rise to a need to protect the rights of individuals against illegal encroachment. That protection can be readily achieved through procedures which prevent the separation of power from responsibility and which provide the constitutional requisites of fairness for witnesses. A measure of added care on the part of the House and the Senate in authorizing the use of compulsory process and by their committees in exercising that power would suffice. That is a small price to pay if it serves to uphold the principles of limited, constitutional government without constricting the power of the Congress to inform itself.

NOTES & QUESTIONS

1. The federal statute for refusing to testify or cooperate with a Congressional investigation reads:

> Every person who having been summoned as a witness by the authority of either House of Congress to give testimony or to produce papers upon any matter under inquiry before either House, or any joint committee established by a joint or concurrent resolution of the two Houses of Congress, or any committee of either House of Congress, willfully makes default, or who, having appeared, refuses to answer any question pertinent to the question under inquiry, shall be deemed guilty of a misdemeanor, punishable by a fine of not more than $1,000 nor less than $100 and imprisonment in a common jail for not less than one month nor more than twelve months. 2 U.S.C.A. § 192

> As a direct result of the anti-communist effort, the House of Representatives adopted rules to protect the rights of witnesses in 1955. House Rule XI, clause 2(k) protects witnesses, especially during investigative hearings. Witnesses are provided with a copy of the committee rules and the House rules applicable to investigative hearings. Witnesses may also have counsel at the hearing to advise them of their constitutional rights. If evidence before the committee tends to defame, degrade, or incriminate a person, the committee may vote to meet in closed session. Committee must give a potentially incriminated person an opportunity to testify, and to consider the person's requests to subpoena additional witnesses.

2. House Rule XI clause 2(k)(3)–(4) provides for witnesses to have an attorney during Congressional hearings:

> (3) Witnesses at hearings may be accompanied by their own counsel for the purpose of advising them concerning their constitutional rights.

(4)   The chair may punish breaches of order and decorum, and of professional ethics on the part of counsel, by censure and exclusion from the hearings; and the committee may cite the offender to the House for contempt.

2.   CASE STUDY: PERFORMANCE ENHANCING DRUGS & ROGER CLEMENS

On February 13, 2008, former all-star baseball pitcher Roger Clemens was due to appear before the U.S. House Committee on Oversight and Government Reform. Congress had been investigating the use of performance enhancing drugs on and off for several years. In fact, Congressional pressure on the issue led Major League Baseball to commission an investigation and report by former U.S. Senator George Mitchell (D-Me) into the issue. When MLB released the Mitchell Report in December 2007, a shocking revelation came from Clemens's former trainer, Brian McNamee; he had personally provided performance enhancing drugs to Clemens. Immediately, Clemens angrily denied the allegations. Another result was the Oversight Committee refocusing on the use of PEDs in baseball.

Performance Enhancing Drugs in Baseball

The umbrella term "performance enhancing drugs" includes several types of steroids and human growth hormone. Anabolic steroids are an artificial version of the male hormone testosterone, which is often abused by athletes to promote muscle growth and enhance their physical performance. The Drug Enforcement Agency classifies steroids as a schedule III-controlled substance in accord with the Anabolic Steroid Control Act of 1990. Human growth hormone (HGH) is a protein naturally made by the pituitary gland. The body puts out the hormone in bursts following exercise, trauma, and sleep, and hormone production peaks during puberty and declines starting in middle age. For adults, the hormone boosts protein production, promotes the utilization of fat, interferes with the action of insulin, and raises blood sugar levels.

HGH is a prescription drug that is injected and can be of great physical benefit to people with a bona fide growth hormone deficiency. Hormone injections can protect patients from fractures, increases muscle mass, improves their capacity for exercise and reduces their risk of heart disease. HGH offers a shortcut for athletes who wish to enhance their performance on the field.

Performance enhancing drugs have been banned by the International Olympic Committee, Major League Baseball, the National Football League, and the World Anti-Doping Agency.

Major League Baseball has had drug policies since the early 1970s in response to the federal Comprehensive Drug Abuse Prevention and Control

Act of 1970. In 1971, MLB prohibited the use of prescription medicines without a valid prescription. Unfortunately, the Leagues policies were rarely enforced.

During the 1970s and 1980s the most popular drug for players was amphetamines, often called "greenies," which players used to improve concentration and boost energy. By 1985, MLB Commissioner Bowie Kuhn pushed for a stronger drug enforcement program, but this was consistently opposed by the Major League Baseball Players Association (MLBPA) as an infringement of player privacy. The MLBPA particularly opposed random drug testing and insisted that testing not happen as part of their collective bargaining agreement. Despite the fact that steroids were illegal without a doctor's prescription and MLB did not allow their use, the lack of testing meant the prohibition had little effect. In response to Congress passing the Anabolic Steroid Control Act of 1990, MLB explicitly included steroids in the league's drug policy in 1991.

The "Steroids Era"

Despite this new policy, 1991 marked the beginning of what would become known as a the "steroids era" in baseball. The era was interrupted by labor troubles. In 1994, MLB commissioner Bud Selig proposed the next collective bargaining agreement include a more effective drug program that listed steroids as prohibited substances with testing based on "reasonable cause." The MLBPA again rejected the program, and this issue, along with several other labor issues caused the baseball players to go on a strike that caused MLB to lose its entire postseason. This caused many resentful fans to stay away from ballparks in 1995. A dramatic increase in hitting power—especially the home run—was a lure for disaffected fans to come back to baseball. The high point of this era was a dramatic home run chase in 1998 where Mark McGwire of the St. Louis Cardinals and Sammy Sosa of the Chicago Cubs dueled with each other to break one of the most storied records in baseball—Roger Maris' 61 home runs in a season. Both McGwire and Sosa hit home runs that year at a pace previously unseen in professional baseball. Both men ultimately broke the 37-year-old record with McGwire hitting 70 home runs and Sosa hitting 66. That year, Roger Clemens, now playing for the Toronto Blue Jays, won his second consecutive Cy Young Award.

The first indication that something was amiss came when a reporter saw a bottle of a steroid precursor "Andro" (androstenedione) in McGwire's locker. While McGwire's use of the drug raised eyebrows, it was a legal over-the-counter supplement at the time. In fact, the sale of Andro and other similar products were available at "health stores" due to the Dietary Supplement Health & Education Act (DSHEA). Over-the-counter supplements were later banned by the FDA after it identified various health risks. They were valuable to players, however, as cover for the widespread use of anabolic steroids and other performance enhancing drugs.

Until 2001, the players became bigger, stronger, and more powerful hitters and pitchers, and in spite of it all no player was ever punished for PED violations. In 2001, Barry Bonds of the San Francisco Giants broke McGwire's home run record by hitting 73.

Finally, in 2002, the MLBPA agreed to a new CBA that prohibited the use of anabolic steroids and allowed some player drug testing. In 2003 there would be "survey testing" and if five percent or more of the players tested positive, mandatory testing would happen in 2004. Still, a player would only receive a 15-day suspension for a second offense. The best Commissioner Selig could say about the agreement was, "At least it was a start."

Scandals and the End of the Steroids Era

The Steroids Era unraveled in large part due to an investigation into a San Francisco company and the publication of a tell all book by former major leaguer Jose Canseco.

During the early 2000s IRS agent Jeff Novitsky investigated the Bay Area Laboratory Co-Operative (BALCO) and its owner Victor Conte for suspected illegal distribution of steroids, particularly to professional athletes. During the investigation, Novitsky discovered that BALCO was providing steroids to Barry Bonds through his trainer Greg Anderson. When Federal authorities raided BALCO and Anderson's apartment, they discovered evidence that Bonds had been on a program that included taking the steroid trenbolone, HGH, an anti-narcolepsy drug, and a female infertility drug.

In 2003, federal agents arrested Anderson and Conte for distributing steroids, and prosecutors had several baseball players, including Bonds, to testify before a grand jury. Unlawful possession of anabolic steroids is punishable by up to one year of imprisonment and a minimum fine of $1000, with stiffer penalties for repeat offenders. 21 U.S.C. § 844(a) (2004). Distribution of steroids is a felony and can lead to five years imprisonment and up to $250,000 in fines.

Prosecutors offered doping calendars, records, and blood samples seized from Anderson and Conte and questioned Bonds about them. He claimed that he did not know he was taking PEDs, but thought Anderson was administering flaxseed oil and arthritis cream.

In 2006, San Francisco Chronicle reporters Mark Fainaru-Wada and Lance Williams wrote *Game of Shadows*, about the BALCO scandal. They wrote that Bonds became jealous of the attention McGwire and Sosa received for the 1998 home run chase and decided to use steroids to enhance his own performance.

The prosecutors in this case did not pursue charges against players for using controlled substances, but only for not being truthful with investigators. Given the evidence that Bonds had knowingly taken steroids and HGH, Bonds was indicted for perjury and obstruction of justice in November 2007.

The second blow against professional baseball came in 2005 when Jose Canseco published his autobiography *Juiced: Wild Times, Rampant 'Roids, Smash Hits and How Baseball Got Big*. Canseco, who called himself "the Chemist" claimed that the use of performance enhancing drugs in baseball was widespread. He stated that he had personally injected several other all-stars with steroids including McGwire, Rafael Palmeiro, Ivan Rodriguez, and Juan Gonzalez. Although Canseco stated he never observed Clemens taking steroids, they had talked about the benefits of steroids. Rather he claimed that Clemens' amazing late career success was due to "working out harder."

Congressional Hearings

The BALCO investigation and Canseco's book were a wake-up call on PEDs in professional sports. President George W. Bush talked about the issue during his 2004 State of the Union Address, and prominent members of Congress warned both the MLB and the MLBPA that Congress may step in if they could not deal with the problem.

By 2005, the House Committee on Government Reform and Oversight held hearings on the affects professional athletes using steroids had on teenagers and "youth safety."

Along with the mother of a teenaged son who committed suicide due to steroid use, the Committee called McGwire, Sosa, Canseco, and Rafael Palmeiro to testify. While Canseco readily admitted his PED use, Sosa and Palmeiro both categorically denied using either steroids or HGH. When questioned about his use of drugs McGwire stated that he was "not there to talk about the past," and repeatedly invoked his Fifth Amendment rights to not answer questions. Sosa evaded questions by pretending that he had trouble understanding the questions or being able to answer in English. Perhaps the most dramatic part of the hearing came when Baltimore Orioles first baseman Rafael Palmeiro forcefully denied Canseco's allegations, pointed his finger at committee chair Rep. Tom Davis (R-Va.), and stated that he had "never used steroids. Period."

Two months after that statement Palmeiro tested positive for steroids and was suspended by MLB. Palmeiro denied intentionally taking PEDs, but the positive test results, in light of his testimony, was devastating.

The Committee also questioned Commissioner Selig and MLBPA head Donald Fehr. Committee members accused MLB of both ignoring and covering up PED use in the game. Congressional pressure caused

Commissioner Selig to hire former Senator George Mitchell (D-Me.) to do a full independent investigation on the issue.

The Mitchell Report

Senator Mitchell conducted a 20-month investigation and in December 2007 issued his report. He found evidence of steroid use by major league players since the mid 1980s, widespread abuse of PEDs in the game and recommended greater testing for violations.

Mitchell drew a tremendous amount of information from a former New York Mets employee, Kirk Radomski. In an investigation related to BALCO, IRS Agent Novitsky had raided Radomski's home and arrested him for distributing steroids in 2005. In 2007, Radomski agreed with prosecutors to plead guilty to one count of steroids distribution and one count of money laundering if he would cooperate with the Mitchell's investigation. Radomski told investigators that one of his customers was Roger Clemens' trainer Brian McNamee. McNamee in turn entered into an agreement with prosecutors to provide information on PEDs to Mitchell. McNamee subsequently met with Mitchell's investigators three times.

McNamee provided extensive information about Clemens' alleged use of PEDs while playing for the Toronto Blue Jays and New York Yankees. McNamee stated that in 1998, when the Blue Jays played in Florida, Clemens and McNamee attended a party at Jose Canseco's house where Clemens met with Canseco and an unidentified man. It was at the end of the Florida road trip where Clemens first approached McNamee about using steroids. McNamee stated that Clemens handed him a bottle of the steroid Anadrol-50 that Canseco had given him. Canseco, however, signed an affidavit denying McNamee's account and that Clemens never even attended the party in question.

McNamee advised Clemens against using the Anadrol-50, but injected Clemens with the steroid Winstrol four times over the next several weeks. In 2000, now with the Yankees, Clemens again wanted to use steroids and McNamee injected him "four to six times" with a version of testosterone and HGH that McNamee obtained from Radomski. This happened again in 2001. McNamee also told investigators that he provided PEDs to New York Yankee players Andy Pettitte and Chuck Knoblauch.

McNamee also saved physical evidence, including syringes and gauze he used when injecting Clemens, which he turned over to federal investigators. When asked why he saved these items, McNamee said that while he liked Clemens, he did not trust him; he saved the syringes to keep himself from being a fall guy.

When Mitchell released his report, Clemens immediately and strongly denied the allegations at a press conference, and sued McNamee for defamation. In a "60 Minutes" interview, Clemens said that McNamee's claims were "ridiculous," and that he had never used any banned substances. When asked if McNamee had injected him with any drugs, Clemens responded: "Lidocaine and B12. It's for my joints, and B12 I still take today."

On January 15, 2008, Mitchell testified before Congress on his findings and defended his reliance on McNamee's testimony since he could only face a legal penalty for perjury, giving him a significant incentive to tell the truth. Given Clemens' denials, the House Oversight and Government Reform Committee decided to subpoena McNamee, Clemens, Pettitte, and Knoblauch.

The Government Oversight Committee

Members/mandate/procedure

As a practical matter, the House Committee on Government Oversight & Reform consists of 41 members; 23 members from the majority and 18 from the minority party. According to Rule 9(b) of the Committee's rules, "A member may question witnesses only when recognized by the presiding member for that purpose. In accordance with House Rule XI, clause 2(j)(2), the five-minute rule shall apply during the questioning of witnesses in a hearing. The presiding member shall, so far as practicable, recognize alternately based on seniority of those majority and minority members present at the time the hearing was called to order and others based on their arrival at the hearing. After that, additional time may be extended at the direction of the presiding member." The only discussion of an attorney representing a witness during a hearing is found in Rule 16(b), "Representation by Counsel. When representing a witness or entity before the Committee or a subcommittee in response to a request or subpoena from the Committee, or in connection with testimony before the Committee or a subcommittee, counsel for the witness or entity must promptly submit to the Committee a notice of appearance specifying the following:(1) counsel's name, firm or organization, bar membership, and contact information including email; and (2) each client or entity represented by the counsel in connection with the proceeding."

Congressional testimony is normally given under oath and with immunity. The testimony cannot be used directly as evidence of criminal conduct if there should be further investigation or prosecution for criminal conduct.

Investigation

The Committee staff conducted its own investigation in preparation for a potential hearing. As is typical, Committee staff gathered affidavits and depositions from potential witnesses under oath. These included statements from McNamee, Pettitte, and Knoblauch.

Andy Pettitte, one of Clemens' best friends in baseball, provided a deposition where he corroborated McNamee's account and stated that Clemens admitted to Andy that he used HGH in either 1999 or 2000. Pettitte told his wife Laura about Clemens' admission and she signed an affidavit for the committee. Pettitte also stated that when Congress held its 2005 steroids hearing he asked Clemens what he would say if asked about his use of PEDs. At that time Clemens told Pettitte that it was his wife Debbie, and not him, who had used PEDs. Finally, Pettitte said that McNamee had told the truth about him. Knoblauch confirmed McNamee's story in a February 1, 2008 deposition.

During this investigation Clemens retained Rusty Hardin and Lanny Breuer as his attorneys. Rusty Hardin graduated from Wesleyan University and Southern Methodist University Law School. Between college and law school Hardin served as an Army officer in Vietnam and spent a year as a legislative assistant to Rep. Charles R. Jonas (R-NC). After 15 years as an assistant district attorney in Houston, Hardin entered private practice engaging in a civil and criminal trial practice at both the state and federal levels. In 1994, he was named chief trial counsel for the Whitewater Independent Counsel's Office. Lanny Breuer graduated from Columbia University and Columbia Law School. Breuer served as an assistant district attorney in Manhattan from 1985 to 1989. From 1997–1999, Mr. Breuer served as special counsel to President Bill Clinton, representing the White House in investigations by the Independent Counsel, Department of Justice, and Congress, and defending President Clinton in impeachment proceedings. In 2003, American Lawyer, named him one of the "Top 45 private lawyers under the age of 45 in the United States." In 2007, Washingtonian, named him one of thirty "Big Guns," a list of the top lawyers in Washington.

Hardin said, "Roger is willing to answer questions, including those posed to him while under oath. We hope to determine shortly if schedules and other commitments can accommodate the committee on that date."

According to the Committee's chief of staff Phil Barnett, Clemens turned down a chance to avoid testifying at the hearing.

The Committee's plan all along was to at the very least issue a report of their findings to the public. In fact, Committee chair Henry Waxman (D-Ca.) considered issuing their own findings in a report and not holding a hearing. Hardin asked the Committee staff, "Why do you need to issue a report now that you heard from everyone?" In lieu of a report Hardin suggested that the committee could just proclaim "victory on steroids" and hold an event with Clemens to denounce drugs. The committee declined because it felt compelled to draw conclusions as to whether Clemens' denials diminished the validity of the Mitchell's report.

Given the inevitability of a report, Clemens's wanted the opportunity to testify in public.

The Hearing

On the day of the hearing Clemens arrived at the Rayburn House Office Building with his attorneys Rusty Hardin and Lanny A. Breuer. Leading up to the hearing, Rusty Hardin noted the unusual influence the Mitchell Report had, "[t]hat a document created by a private citizen commissioned for a private corporation [is] turning the wheels of the justice system." In effect, a private citizen, based on the statements of a few players and employees of Major League Baseball could ruin the reputation of one of its greatest stars. Hardin and Breuer would sit behind their client while the Committee did their questioning.

Clemens would sit at a long table with the other two witnesses, Brian MacNamee and Charles Scheele, a representative of the Major League Baseball Commissioner. Clemens had a prepared statement to read at the beginning of the hearing:

> I appreciate the opportunity to tell this Committee and the public—under oath—what I have been saying all along: I have never used steroids, human growth hormone [HGH], or any other type of illegal performance enhancing drugs. I think these types of drugs should play no role in athletics at any level, and I fully support Senator Mitchell's conclusions that steroids have no place in baseball. However, I take great issue with the report's allegation that I used these substances. Let me be clear again: I did not.

McNamee was prepared to state, "During the time that I worked with Roger Clemens I injected him on numerous occasions with steroids and human growth hormone." McNamee would also state he had not been offered any "special treatment or consideration for fingering star players."

Clearly, these statements contradicted each other, with Clemens' statement at odds with the findings of the Mitchell Report, and other statements gathered by the Committee staff. Rep. Tom Davis (R-Va.) stated that either Clemens or McNamee was "lying in spectacular fashion."

Strangely, the hearing would become a partisan affair; Democrats including chairman Henry Waxman (D-Cal.) and longtime committee member Elijah Cummings (D-Md.) were ready to grill Clemens, and Republicans such as Rep. Dan Burton (R-Ind.) Virginia Foxx (R-NC), and Darrell Issa (R-Cal.) ready to cross-examine McNamee.

Skills Exercise

You are one of Rusty Hardin's associates and he has asked you to write a short memo in preparation for the Congressional hearing:

What issues, if any, need to be raised and discussed with the committee legal staff?

What should Hardin's role be during the hearing?

How should you prepare Clemens for the hearing?

Appendix A. Federal Statutes

Perjury 18 U.S. Code § 1621

Whoever—

(1) having taken an oath before a competent tribunal, officer, or person, in any case in which a law of the United States authorizes an oath to be administered, that he will testify, declare, depose, or certify truly, or that any written testimony, declaration, deposition, or certificate by him subscribed, is true, willfully and contrary to such oath states or subscribes any material matter which he does not believe to be true; or

(2) in any declaration, certificate, verification, or statement under penalty of perjury as permitted under section 1746 of title 28, United States Code, willfully subscribes as true any material matter which he does not believe to be true;

is guilty of perjury and shall, except as otherwise expressly provided by law, be fined under this title or imprisoned not more than five years, or both. This section is applicable whether the statement or subscription is made within or without the United States.

Statements or entries generally 18 U.S. Code § 1001

(a) Except as otherwise provided in this section, whoever, in any matter within the jurisdiction of the executive, legislative, or judicial branch of the Government of the United States, knowingly and willfully—

(1) falsifies, conceals, or covers up by any trick, scheme, or device a material fact;

(2) makes any materially false, fictitious, or fraudulent statement or representation; or

(3) makes or uses any false writing or document knowing the same to contain any materially false, fictitious, or fraudulent statement or entry;

shall be fined under this title, imprisoned not more than 5 years or, if the offense involves international or domestic terrorism (as defined in section 2331), imprisoned not more than 8 years, or both. If the matter relates to an offense under chapter 109A, 109B, 110, or 117, or section 1591, then the term of imprisonment imposed under this section shall be not more than 8 years.

(b) Subsection (a) does not apply to a party to a judicial proceeding, or that party's counsel, for statements, representations, writings or documents submitted by such party or counsel to a judge or magistrate in that proceeding.

(c) With respect to any matter within the jurisdiction of the legislative branch, subsection (a) shall apply only to—

(1) administrative matters, including a claim for payment, a matter related to the procurement of property or services, personnel or employment practices, or support services, or a document required by law, rule, or regulation to be submitted to the Congress or any office or officer within the legislative branch; or

(2) any investigation or review, conducted pursuant to the authority of any committee, subcommittee, commission or office of the Congress, consistent with applicable rules of the House or Senate.

Obstruction of proceedings 18 U.S. Code § 1505.

Whoever, with intent to avoid, evade, prevent, or obstruct compliance, in whole or in part, with any civil investigative demand duly and properly made under the Antitrust Civil Process Act, willfully withholds, misrepresents, removes from any place, conceals, covers up, destroys, mutilates, alters, or by other means falsifies any documentary material, answers to written interrogatories, or oral testimony, which is the subject of such demand; or attempts to do so or solicits another to do so; or

Whoever corruptly, or by threats or force, or by any threatening letter or communication influences, obstructs, or impedes or endeavors to influence, obstruct, or impede the due and proper administration of the law under which any pending proceeding is being had before any department or agency of the United States, or the due and proper exercise of the power of inquiry under which any inquiry or investigation is being had by either House, or any committee of either House or any joint committee of the Congress—

Shall be fined under this title, imprisoned not more than 5 years or, if the offense involves international or domestic terrorism (as defined in section 2331), imprisoned not more than 8 years, or both.

Appendix B. Roger Clemens' Major League Statistics

Table 1

Year	Team	Games	Wins	Losses	Earned Run Avg.	Innings Pitched	Strike outs	Awards
					Roger Clemens Pitching Stats			
1984	Red Sox	21	9	4	4.32	133.1	126	
1985	Red Sox	15	7	5	3.29	98.1	74	
1986	Red Sox	33	24	4	2.48	254.0	238	All-Star; Most Valuable Player; Cy Young Award
1987	Red Sox	36	20	9	2.97	281.2	256	Cy Young
1988	Red Sox	35	18	12	2.93	264.0	291	All-Star
1989	Red Sox	35	17	11	3.13	253.1	230	
1990	Red Sox	31	21	6	1.93	228.1	209	All-Star
1991	Red Sox	35	18	10	2.62	271.1	241	All-Star; Cy Young
1992	Red Sox	32	18	11	2.41	246.2	208	All-Star
1993	Red Sox	29	11	14	4.46	191.2	160	
1994	Red Sox	24	9	7	2.85	170.2	168	
1995	Red Sox	23	10	5	4.18	140.0	132	
1996	Red Sox	34	10	13	3.63	242.2	257	
1997	Blue Jays	34	21	7	2.05	264.0	292	All-Star; Cy Young
1998	Blue Jays	33	20	6	2.65	234.2	271	All-Star; Cy Young
1999	Yankees	30	14	10	4.60	187.2	163	
2000	Yankees	32	13	8	3.70	204.1	188	
2001	Yankees	33	20	3	3.51	220.1	213	All-Star; Cy Young
2002	Yankees	29	13	6	4.35	180.0	192	
2003	Yankees	33	17	9	3.91	211.2	190	All-Star
2004	Astros	33	18	4	2.98	214.1	218	All-Star; Cy Young
2005	Astros	32	13	8	1.87	211.1	185	All-Star
2006	Astros	19	7	6	2.30	113.1	102	
2007	Yankees	18	6	6	4.18	99.0	68	
24 Years		709	354	184	3.12	4,916.2	4,672	0

1

NOTES & QUESTIONS

1.   The general federal perjury statute requires willfulness or knowledge on the part of the witness; actual falsity in the statement; and materiality, meaning the false information is capable of influencing the tribunal. Adroit witnesses frequently avoid conviction under the statute by employing the

defenses of mistake, confusion, or inadequate memory. *United States v. Dunnigan*, 507 U.S. 87, 93 (1993).

2.   Just because a witness commits perjury or obstruction of justice does not necessarily mean the witness will be prosecuted. For example, the Oversight & Government Reform Committee did not recommend prosecution for Rafael Palmeiro because the evidence was "confusing and contradictory in many respects." See, P.J. Meitl, "The Perjury Paradox: The Amazing Under Enforcement of the Laws Regarding Lying to Congress," 25 *Quinnipiac L. Rev.* 547, 547–48 (2007). In fact, Meitl found only six examples of witnessed convicted of perjury connected to congressional testimony in the previous 60 years, perhaps with the result that lying to Congress has become accepted.

3.   Daniel Healey, "Fall of the Rocket: Steroids in Baseball and the Case Against Roger Clemens," 19 *Marq. Sports L. Rev.* 289 (2008) states "The Clemens hearing—and its unfolding aftermath—is the most prominent example of the very public manner in which the federal government is now meting out punishment to sports stars for past steroids-related indiscretions."

Is this type of a hearing "punishment?" The Supreme Court has stated that Congress is not a law enforcement agency, and therefore should not be acting as a prosecutor or court, powers reserved to the executive and judiciary. *U.S. v. Watkins*, 354 U.S. 178 (1957). Where do you draw the line between the informing function of Congress and the prosecutorial powers of the executive?

D. EXECUTIVE AGENCIES & INVESTIGATIONS

THE WHITE HOUSE, SEPTEMBER 28, 1994

Memorandum for all executive department and agency general counsels

FROM: LLOYD N. CUTLER, SPECIAL
COUNSEL TO THE PRESIDENT

SUBJECT: Congressional Requests to Departments and Agencies
for Documents Protected by Executive Privilege

The policy of this Administration is to comply with congressional requests for information to the fullest extent consistent with the constitutional and statutory obligations of the Executive Branch. While this Administration, like its predecessors, has an obligation to protect the confidentiality of core communications, executive privilege will be asserted only after careful review demonstrates that assertion of the privilege is necessary to protect Executive Branch prerogatives.

The doctrine of executive privilege protects the confidentiality of deliberations within the White House, including its policy councils, as well as communications between the White House and executive departments and agencies. Executive privilege applies to written and oral communications between and among the White House, its policy councils and Executive Branch agencies, as well as to documents that describe or prepares for such communications (e.g., "talking points"). This has been the view expressed by all recent White House Counsels. In circumstances involving communications relating to investigations of personal wrongdoing by government officials, it is our practice not to assert executive privilege, either, in judicial proceedings or in congressional investigations and hearings. Executive privilege must always be weighed against other competing governmental interests, including the judicial need to obtain relevant evidence, especially in criminal proceedings, and the congressional need to make factual findings for legislative and oversight purposes.

In the last resort, this balancing is usually conducted by the courts. However, when executive privilege is asserted against a congressional request for documents, the courts usually decline to intervene until after the other two branches have exhausted the possibility of working out a satisfactory accommodation. It is our policy to work out such an accommodation whenever we can, without unduly interfering with the President's need to conduct frank exchange of views with his principal advisors.

Historically, good faith negotiations between Congress and the Executive Branch have minimized the need for invoking executive privilege.

Executive privilege belongs to the President, not individual departments or agencies. It is essential that all requests to departments and agencies for information of the type described above be referred to the White House Counsel before any information is furnished. Departments and agencies receiving such request should therefore follow the procedures set forth below, designed to ensure that this Administration acts responsibly and consistently with respect to executive privilege issues, with due regard for the responsibilities and prerogatives of Congress:

First, any document created in the White House, including a White House policy council, or in a department or agency, that contains the deliberations of, or advice to or from, the White House, should be presumptively treated as protected by executive privilege. This is so regardless of the document's location at the time of the request or whether it originated in the White House or in a department or agency.

Second, a department or agency receiving a request for any such document should promptly notify the White House Counsel's Office, and direct any inquiries regarding such a document to the White House Counsel's Office.

Third, the White House Counsel's Office, working together with the department or agency (and, where appropriate, DOJ), will discuss the request with appropriate congressional representatives to determine whether a mutually satisfactory recommendation is available.

Fourth, if efforts to reach a mutually satisfactory accommodation are unsuccessful, and if release of the document would pass a substantial question of executive privilege, the Counsel to the President will consult with DOJ and other affected agencies to determine whether to recommend that the President invoke the privilege.

We believe this policy will facilitate the resolution of issues relating to disclosures to Congress and maximize the opportunity for reaching mutually satisfactory accommodations with Congress. We will of course try to cooperate with reasonable congressional requests for information in ways that preserve the President's ability to exchange frank advice with his immediate staff and the heads of the executive departments and agencies.

WHEN CONGRESS CHECKS OUT
Norman J. Ornstein and Thomas E. Mann, The Brookings Institute (2006)
https://www.brookings.edu/opinions/when-congress-checks-out/

Oversight depends on a vigorous, deliberative, and often combative process that involves both the executive and the legislative branches. The country's Founding Fathers gave each branch both exclusive and overlapping powers in the realm of foreign policy, according to each one's comparative advantage—inviting them, as the constitutional scholar Edwin Corwin has put it, "to struggle for the privilege of directing American foreign policy."

. . .

In the past six years, however, congressional oversight of the executive across a range of policies, but especially on foreign and national security policy, has virtually collapsed. The few exceptions, such as the tension-packed Senate hearings on the prison scandal at Abu Ghraib in 2004, only prove the rule. With little or no midcourse corrections in decision-making and implementation, policy has been largely adrift. Occasionally—as during the aftermath of Hurricane Katrina last year—the results have been disastrous.

. . .

Vigorous oversight was the norm until the end of the twentieth century. During the Korean War, a special committee chaired by then Senator Lyndon Johnson strongly criticized the Truman administration. According to the historian Bruce Schulman, it also "reduced waste, improved the efficiency of wartime agencies and reaffirmed the patriotism of administration officials—no trivial matter when [Senator Joseph] McCarthy and his allies saw every small mishap as evidence of disloyalty and subversion." In the 1970s, there were the Church committee investigations of intelligence failures and secret illegal surveillance. In the

1980s, joint congressional committees scrutinized the Iran-contra affair. In the 1990s, authorizing committees and appropriations committees in both houses reviewed military operations in Kosovo. When the Republicans took control of Congress under President Bill Clinton, overall oversight declined. (Joel Aberbach, a political scientist at the University of California, Los Angeles, has found that the overall number of oversight hearings in the House—excluding the appropriations committees— dropped from 782 during the first six months of 1983 to 287 during the first six months of 1997. The falloff in the Senate between 1983 and 1997 is just as striking: from 429 to 175.) But there were still some visible and aggressive investigations, albeit often driven by an obsession with scandal. But since George W. Bush has become president, oversight has all but disappeared. From homeland security to the conduct of the Iraq war, from allegations of torture at Abu Ghraib to the surveillance of domestic telephone calls by the National Security Agency (NSA), Congress has mostly ignored its responsibilities. The same is true of less publicized issues involving the United States and the rest of the world, including U.S. relations with trading partners and rivals, allies and adversaries. The year-and-a-half hiatus in the Republicans' control of the Senate, which came after 9/11 and during a nationwide surge in patriotism, did not noticeably reverse that pattern.

The numbers are striking. Examining reports of the House Government Reform Committee, the journalist Susan Milligan found just 37 hearings described as "oversight" in 2003–4, during the 108th Congress, down from 135 in 1993–94, during the last Congress dominated by Democrats. The House Energy and Commerce Committee produced 117 pages of activity reports on oversight during the 1993–94 cycle, compared with 24 pages during 2003–4. In the mid-1990s, the Republican Congress took 140 hours of testimony on whether President Clinton had used his Christmas mailing list to find potential campaign donors; in 2004–5, House Republicans took 12 hours of testimony on Abu Ghraib.

. . . .

A KILLER BLIND SPOT

Thursday, August 3, 2006, was a remarkable day in Congress. The Senate Armed Services Committee held an oversight hearing on Iraq featuring three star witnesses: General John Abizaid, the commander of U.S. Central Command; General Peter Pace, the chairman of the Joint Chiefs of Staff; and Defense Secretary Donald Rumsfeld. The hearing led the evening news, with footage of General Abizaid, echoed by General Pace, warning about the danger of a civil war in Iraq. Senator John McCain (R-Ariz.) asked both generals if they had foreseen that possibility a year earlier; both said no. Senator Hillary Clinton (D-N.Y.) recited to Secretary

Rumsfeld a litany of failures over the past three years; his first response was "Oh my goodness."

The frank and pessimistic admissions by two top generals and the tense moment of theater between Senator Clinton and Secretary Rumsfeld were striking indeed. But even more striking was the fact of the oversight hearing itself. Secretary Rumsfeld, when asked to testify, first brushed off the request, changing his mind only after Senator Clinton turned his refusal into a major public issue.

Oversight failures in regard to the Iraq war go back to before the beginning of the war. On June 15 of this year, the House of Representatives convened a debate over the war—which Democrats called a sham—to consider a nonbinding resolution about whether to stay the course or cut and run. It was the first formal discussion of the U.S. military role in Iraq since Congress voted to authorize the use of force in October 2002. And that was not much to brag about. As Thomas Ricks writes in Fiasco: The American Military Adventure in Iraq, "When the House debate began there was just one reporter in the press gallery. At their most intense points, the debates in both the House and Senate attracted fewer than 10 percent of each body's members." Unlike during the lead-up to the Persian Gulf War in 1990–91, there was little sustained discussion before the Iraq war. As Ricks puts it, "There were many failures in the American system that led to the war, but the failures in Congress were at once perhaps the most important and the least noticed." He adds, "There was little follow-up investigation or oversight. There were, for example, no hearings with returning division commanders."

Congress has also done little about the Bush administration's lack of any plan for the post-Saddam Hussein regime, its quashing of the State Department's planning, and its stunning failure to provide adequate armor to all U.S. troops. One senator said of the equipment problem, "There really is no excuse for this. Many in the military thought this would be a short conflict, and they did not want to lay out large sums of money for vehicles that would soon be superfluous. Some of the Pentagon officials said that there was only one manufacturer of the appropriate body armor, and the pipeline got clogged. If we had ridden herd on them regularly and publicly, it would have been different."

Thus, whatever intermittent oversight there has been so far has come from the media. On July 30, 2006, a front-page story in The *New York Times* reported that the U.S. Agency for International Development had engaged in "an accounting shell game" to hide huge cost overruns in the $1.4 billion reconstruction program in Iraq while "knowingly with[holding] information on schedule delays from Congress." The same day, The Washington Post showcased a major story, headlined "Report on Prewar Intelligence Lagging," about a long-promised oversight report from the

Senate Intelligence Committee on the Bush administration's use of intelligence in the lead-up to the war. Nine months earlier, responding to charges by committee Democrats that the report had been sidetracked for political reasons, the committee's chair, Pat Roberts (R-Kans.), had asserted it was near completion. The Washington Post story made clear Roberts' intention to delay its release until after the elections in November. (Pressure from Democrats and two Republican senators resulted in a partial release in September.)

These two articles underscored some of the reasons for the lack of oversight: the executive branch's willful denial of accurate and meaningful information to Congress, the growing partisan divide in Congress, and the reluctance of congressional Republicans to criticize the administration (especially Speaker of the House Dennis Hastert, of Illinois; Senate Majority Leader Bill Frist, of Tennessee; and House Armed Services Committee Chair Duncan Hunter, of California). But these accounts barely scratch the surface. Even more worrisome are the broader dynamic that has led to the sharp decline in Congress' influence over foreign policy and the policy failures that have occurred as a result.

CONTEMPT of CONGRESS

Since Congress has shown little appetite for any serious oversight or for using the power of the purse or pointed public hearings to call the executive branch to account, executive agencies that once viewed Congress with at least some trepidation now regard it with contempt.

In March 2003, the Senate Foreign Relations Committee slated a hearing to examine the post invasion planning for Iraq, with retired Lieutenant General Jay Garner, the first U.S. civilian administrator of Iraq, as the star witness. Garner canceled at the last minute, prompting the committee's chair, Richard Lugar (R-Ind.), to call the event a "fiasco." "He was not able to come to the [Senate] Dirksen Building, but could brief [reporters] in the Pentagon," Lugar told the National Journal. "On the face of it, it was ridiculous." A senator on the Senate Armed Services Committee told us that Chair John Warner (R-Va.) was apoplectic when Garner also stood up his committee. Last January, an hour into a Senate Appropriations Subcommittee hearing on mine safety, Chair Arlen Specter (R.-Pa.) asked the administration's top two mine-safety officials to stay for another hour to answer more questions. It was a routine request, but the two said they were too busy and, despite another more pointed appeal from Specter, abruptly rose and exited through a back door. Relating the incident, The *Washington Post's* Ruth Marcus reported that the Bush administration "thinks of congressional oversight as if it were a trip to the dentist, to be undertaken reluctantly and gotten over with as quickly as possible. Most astonishingly, it reserves the right simply to ignore congressional dictates that it has decided intrude too much on executive branch power."

Consider, too, the Senate Armed Services Committee hearing in May 2004 on torture at the Abu Ghraib prison, a crucial test for the Defense Department and the U.S. military. During Senator McCain's tough questioning about who was responsible, Rumsfeld said that the military brass with him had prepared a chart showing the chain of command. When one of the generals said they had forgotten to bring it, Rumsfeld said, "Oh my."

NOTES & QUESTIONS

1.   Mr. Ornstein and Mr. Mann ask why Congress has abandoned oversight and suggest:

- the loss of a strong identity for Congress as an institution, where majority party members "act as field lieutenants in the president's army" rather than members of a separate branch willing to criticize;

- members spending less time in Washington, limiting the time available for extended oversight hearings;

- an emphasis of members holding on to (or trying to overturn) small Congressional majorities, rather than attempting to govern;

- ideological polarization and the importance of majority control, which weakens the institutional incentives for oversight of the executive.

What reforms would you suggest to reinvigorate Congressional oversight?

2.   Mr. Ornstein and Mr. Mann point out the particular failures of Congress to oversee the creation of the Department of Homeland Security (DHS) after the 2001 terrorist attacks. The first years of DHS were difficult: management problems, including high turnover, a lack of focus, poor information management systems, and problems integrating the 22 existing agencies pulled into the new Department.

Mr. Ornstein and Mr. Mann called Congress' failure to oversee the DHS "crushing" because only Congress can push such a sprawling entity to address pressing problems and determine if the agency has the capacity to properly carry out its mission. For the first three years of DHS's existence, there was no functional oversight. When the House finally created the Select Committee on Homeland Security it still did not have legislative jurisdiction or control over the DHS budget. Unsurprisingly, DHS officials treated the impotent committee "with indifference or contempt." In 2005 the Committee became a permanent standing committee. In 2012, the Committee created the Subcommittee on Oversight, Investigations, & Management. What difference do you think this makes in the operations of the Department of Homeland Security?

3.   An analysis by Professors Doug Kriner and Eric Schickler shows the difference in how the House handles investigations when it is controlled by a different part from the President in addition to a general decline in investigative hearings since 1968. Prof. Kriner states, "Congress's ability to investigate the president has really become weaponized over the past few decades. When Congress is going after the president aggressively, you see an erosion of the president's support." See, Amelia Thomson-DeVeaux, "Trump Is Wrong. When The Opposition Party Runs The House, The President Gets Investigated." *FiveThirtyEight*, Feb. 7, 2019.

4.   When Congress authorized the American Relief Act in early 2021, sending billions of dollars in aid to state governments oversight was an important consideration. What role would state legislatures play in the expenditure of these funds? The Connecticut House of Representatives asserted a role for the Legislature in the Constitution State. In a 147–0 vote, the House passed a bill that would require the legislature to approve plans to distribute federal COVID aid, in a manner similar to the budget process, with the appropriations committees taking the lead. The bill also requires the governor's budget office report back to the legislature how the federal COVID aid was spent. Brenden Crowley, "House Legislators Vote 147–0 to Assert Legislative Oversight of Federal COVID Funds," *Ct Examiner*, March 16, 2021. It should be noted that the Connecticut House has 97 Democrats and 53 Republicans, and that the Governor is a Democrat.

Case Study: The Worst Hack in U.S. History

"This is crown jewels material. . .a gold mine for a foreign intelligence service. This is not the end of American human intelligence, but it's a significant blow."—Joel Brenner, former NSA Senior Counsel

On June 4, 2015, news broke of a cybersecurity incident at the U.S. Office of Personnel Management (OPM): OPM issued a press release reporting that approximately 4 million current and former federal employees' personally identifiable information had been compromised. In a closed-door briefing to Senators, FBI Director James Comey estimated that the number of impacted individuals was closer to 18 million—despite OPM publicly maintaining its initial figure.

By mid-June, officials confirmed a second, far more devastating breach: 21.5 million employees' security clearance background investigation documents—the Standard Form 86 (SF-86)—had been stolen. Prior to gaining a security clearance, an employee must complete a SF-86 that exhaustively documents their financial and employment history, mental health and substance abuse issues, and other potentially embarrassing information that could threaten the employee's security clearance. As FBI Director James Comey explained, "My SF-86 lists every place I've ever lived since I was 18, every foreign travel I've ever taken, all of my family, their addresses. So it's not just my identity that's affected. I've got siblings. I've got five kids. All of that's in there."

Two years later, following several congressional investigations into the circumstances surrounding the hacks, the FBI made its first, and only, arrest in connection with the attack. Pingan Yu, a Chinese national, was apprehended in August 2017 for allegedly selling the malicious software tool that hackers used to break into OPM's system. After spending 18 months in a federal detention center, Yu pled guilty and was sentenced to time served and ordered to pay $1.1 million in restitution. The U.S. deported him to China, where he resumed teaching computer science. The fallout from the breach continues, and the hackers who infiltrated OPM's systems remain at large.

The Hacks

For years OPM had been on notice that its computer system was vulnerable to attack. The OPM Inspector General had warned of security deficiencies in 2005, yet the office made no major changes in its systems or protocols. This lax security, compounded by OPM's failure to implement basic safeguards—such as multi-factor authentication—paved the way for an onslaught of cyber-attacks beginning in 2012.

While evidence of unauthorized access to OPM's network dates back to July 2012, OPM only became aware of adversarial activity in March 2014, when US-CERT notified the office of a data breach. Hackers ("Hacker 1") had successfully pillaged manuals, schematics, and other information regarding OPM's computer systems. Hoping to gain valuable counterintelligence information, OPM collaborated with US-CERT to monitor the attacker's activities, resolving to shut down its network only if needed.

While OPM continued to monitor Hacker 1, a second adversary ("Hacker 2") infiltrated OPM's systems by posing as an employee of a contractor who was performing background investigations for OPM. Using stolen credentials, Hacker 2 logged into OPM's system and created a backdoor into the network.

Meanwhile, OPM was growing increasingly concerned that Hacker 1 was close to obtaining FS-86 information on federal employees. Working with the Department of Homeland Security, OPM orchestrated a plan, dubbed "the Big Bang," to kick Hacker 1 out of its system. While the Big Bang successfully booted its target, Hacker 2 continued to move about OPM's system freely and undetected. From July through August 2014, Hacker 2 exfiltrated the same security clearance investigation files that OPM had feared Hacker 1 was targeting. Hacker 2 struck again in

December 2014, stealing additional personnel files. A third breach in early 2015 resulted in stolen fingerprint data.

On April 15, 2015—nine months after Hacker 2's first exfiltration attempts—OPM finally noticed that its systems had been compromised. At this point, OPM contracted with Cylance Inc., a cyber security firm, to determine the scope of the attack. Cylance's technology and know-how, had it been deployed earlier, could have thwarted Hacker 2 before it exfiltrated a treasure trove of secret information.

Congress Responds, and OPM Demurs

Congress responded to OPM's public admission of the incident with a flurry of hearings into the scope and ramifications of the breach: What quantity and type of data was stolen? How did this happen? Had it been preventable?

The majority of these congressional hearings were conducted within the House Oversight and Government Reform Committee. The first, held on June 16, 2015, revealed that the extent of the damage and collateral consequences were far more serious than OPM had publicly reported. In prepared testimony, OPM Director Katherine Archuleta opined that "there was a high degree of confidence that OPM systems related to background investigations of current, former, and prospective Federal government employees, and those for whom a federal background investigation was conducted, may have been compromised." OPM's Chief Information Officer Donna Seymour confirmed that SF-86 information had in fact been compromised, and, in a far more damning revelation, testified that security clearance adjudicative information had also been exfiltrated.

Far surpassing the scope of SF-86 data, adjudicative information is a catchall category comprising the results of background investigations into suitability for intelligence clearance and other sensitive government work. Topics of inquiry range from sexual behavior to evidence of foreign influence to potential pressure points for foreign exploitation. Records include polygraph tests and subject interviews as well as interviews with neighbors, employers, and current and former spouses. The depth and thoroughness of an adjudicative packet has the potential to compromise not only the subject, but any friends, family, or acquaintances caught in the scope of the investigation.

A second hearing was held on June 23, 2015 before the Senate Subcommittee on Financial Services and General Government Committee on Appropriations. At this hearing Director Archuleta took a defensive tone, arguing that OPM was not responsible for the data breaches. "If there is anyone to blame, it is the perpetrators." Archuleta further deflected responsibility by arguing that decades of underinvestment in OPM's IT systems prevented the Office from modernizing its systems. Democrats took the opportunity to call for budget increases to cover critical IT updates, while Republic lawmakers questioned the wisdom of this approach: "It's easy to suggest more money is the solution. . .But it is often the wrong choice, especially in situations like this where it appears that the problem is much greater than a lack of resources." Despite their disagreement, lawmakers on both sides of the aisle recognized that systemic deficiencies in cyber security were a rampant problem that needed to be urgently addressed.

A day later, Director Archuleta was called back before the House Committee on Oversight and Government Reform. This time, tensions flared between Archuleta and the FBI. She vehemently disputed the Bureau's assertion that 18 million current, former, and prospective government workers' personal information had been compromised, instead defending OPM's initial estimate that only 4.2 million individuals had been impacted. Her testimony prompted James Trainor, acting assistant director for the FBI's cyber division—who was not scheduled to testify—to speak up. The Bureau had obtained its data from an internal report prepared by OPM officials, he declared, holding up the briefing in his hand.

OPM's Chief Information Officer, Donna Seymour, also testified at the third hearing. She downplayed the importance of the stolen IT manuals—blueprints that outlined OPM's entire IT infrastructure—as mere outdated security documents. The Committee's final report detailing the OPM hack characterized her testimony as "mis[leading] the public about the significance of the data stolen in the 2014 attack."

A fourth hearing, held on July 8, 2015 in the House Committee on Science, Space, and Technology, continued to slam OPM with public admonitions that the Office had disregarded guidance and failed to prioritize computer network security. Questioning whether the OPM breach could be the tip of the iceberg, Chairman Lamar Smith (R-TX) declared that "this Committee will continue to demand answers about who is responsible for failing to keep Americans' sensitive information secure."

Three days later, Director Archuleta resigned following the Obama administration's public announcement that the OPM breaches exposed 22.1 million Americans' sensitive information.

Changes at OPM

In September 2016, the House Committee on Government Oversight and Reform issued its findings following a yearlong investigation into the circumstances that led up to the breach, OPM's response, and the Office's subsequent efforts to update its security systems.

Following the congressional hearings and recommendations, OPM hired a cyber security advisor and increased its IT modernization budget from $31 million to $87 million. These investments are intended to provide preventive monitoring of network servers and stronger firewalls to mitigate system vulnerabilities.

More significantly, OPM will no longer conduct background investigations. The Obama administration announced the creation of the National Background Investigations Bureau (NBIB), which will absorb OPM's Federal Investigative Services department. Although NBIB will continue to be housed within OPM, the Department of Defense has assumed the responsibility of security IT systems related to background investigations for security clearances. In 2019, the NBIB was transferred to the Defense Counterintelligence and Security Agency.

Since the attacks were publicly revealed, OPM has been hit with a wave of class actions lawsuits filed on behalf of the 21.5 million individuals whose data was compromised; those cases are still underway.

Malfeasance Leads to Broader Reforms

As Congress waded deeper into the root causes of the OPM fiasco, its investigation unveiled the daunting reality that cyber vulnerabilities permeate nearly every federal agency. The breaches at OPM served as a wakeup call, catalyzing both Congress and the executive branch into action. Internal reports cataloguing a history of lax security measures may no longer go unheeded; reforms to modernize and strengthen IT systems are long past due, and Congress is growing impatient.

Congress has begun to address the broader issue of cyber vulnerabilities throughout the federal government through enquires into other "high-impact" systems, examinations of federal agencies' abilities to detect and mitigate cyber incidents, and hearings to monitor implementation of the Federal Information Security Management Act (FISMA) and Federal Information Technology Acquisition Reform Act (FITARA)—legislative mandates that define a comprehensive framework to protect government information.

Congressional oversight of cyber information systems has also expanded to include scrutiny of other agencies beyond OPM. In November 2015, the House Oversight Committee grilled the Department of Education over its failure to heed repeated warnings that its IT system, which contained 139 million Social Security numbers, is patently insecure. The Committee on Oversight held a separate hearing to examine the Department of Veterans Affairs' compliance with FISMA and FITARA, and to ensure that the Department's IT security modernization program is accomplishing its target objectives.

These investigations have not been enthusiastically embraced by the agencies themselves, however. In the aftermath of the OPM hack, OPM, the Department of Homeland Security, and the Office of Management and Budget declined to attend a classified meeting of the House Armed Services

Committee, citing concerns that their closed-door conversations would be transcribed. The Committee's affronted chairman responded, "If they are unwilling to come and answer questions about the biggest national security data breach we've ever had, then that does not inspire greater confidence. . .So I'm sure we will pursue the matter with them again."

NOTES & QUESTIONS

1.   Should Congressional oversight be remedial or managerial? Hearings in this case did not take place until after the breaches were made public. Given the prior warnings about OPM's deficient security measures, as well as OPM's discovery of the first breach in March 2014, should Congress have stepped in earlier to oversee how OPM was running its IT operations?

2.   OPM Director Katherine Archuleta argued that a lack of adequate IT funding led to the data breaches. Is it fair for Congress to demand reforms and system overhauls without appropriating funds to accomplish its oversight goals?

3.   Does money play a role in oversight? To what degree can a Congressional committee influence agency policy by promising (or threatening) changes in funding?

4.   The House Committee on Oversight and Government Reform's OPM report included a detailed timeline of events around the breaches and highlighted the magnitude of OPM's failures. Considering that OPM is not an intelligence agency, should Congress have investigated why such sensitive data was housed in an office that had neither the capacity nor expertise to protect information critical to national security?

5.   What recourse does Congress have when agency personnel mislead committees during a hearing? Should Donna Seymour and Katherine Archuleta be held accountable for making false statements to Congress?

6.   Absent a subpoena, do committee chairs have the power to demand agencies' attendance at closed-door briefings? At public hearings?

7.   What are the particular problems that face Congress when overseeing the intelligence community? See, James A. Baker, "Intelligence Oversight," 45 *Harv. J. Legis.* 199 (2008).

E. CONGRESSIONAL OVERSIGHT & THE PRESIDENT

TRUMP V. MAZARS

Supreme Court of the United States
591 U.S. ___, 140 S.Ct. 2019 (2020)

CHIEF JUSTICE ROBERTS delivered the opinion of the Court.

Over the course of five days in April 2019, three committees of the U. S. House of Representatives issued four subpoenas seeking information about the finances of President Donald J. Trump, his children, and affiliated businesses. We have held that the House has authority under the Constitution to issue subpoenas to assist it in carrying out its legislative responsibilities. The House asserts that the financial information sought here—encompassing a decade's worth of transactions by the President and his family—will help guide legislative reform in areas ranging from money laundering and terrorism to foreign involvement in U. S. elections. The President contends that the House lacked a valid legislative aim and instead sought these records to harass him, expose personal matters, and conduct law enforcement activities beyond its authority. The question presented is whether the subpoenas exceed the authority of the House under the Constitution.

We have never addressed a congressional subpoena for the President's information. Two hundred years ago, it was established that Presidents may be subpoenaed during a federal criminal proceeding, *United States v. Burr* (1807) and earlier today we extended that ruling to state criminal proceedings, *Trump v. Vance* (2020). Nearly fifty years ago, we held that a federal prosecutor could obtain information from a President despite assertions of executive privilege, *United States v. Nixon* (1974), and more recently we ruled that a private litigant could subject a President to a damages suit and appropriate discovery obligations in federal court, *Clinton v. Jones* (1997).

This case is different. Here the President's information is sought not by prosecutors or private parties in connection with a particular judicial proceeding, but by committees of Congress that have set forth broad legislative objectives. Congress and the President—the two political branches established by the Constitution—have an ongoing relationship that the Framers intended to feature both rivalry and reciprocity. That distinctive aspect necessarily informs our analysis of the question before us.

I

A

Each of the three committees sought overlapping sets of financial documents, but each supplied different justifications for the requests.

The House Committee on Financial Services issued two subpoenas, both on April 11, 2019. App. 128, 154, 226. The first, issued to Deutsche Bank, seeks the financial information of the President, his children, their immediate family members, and several affiliated business entities. Specifically, the subpoena seeks any document related to account activity, due diligence, foreign transactions, business statements, debt schedules, statements of net worth, tax returns, and suspicious activity identified by Deutsche Bank. The second, issued to Capital One, demands similar financial information with respect to more than a dozen business entities associated with the President. The Deutsche Bank subpoena requests materials from "2010 through the present," and the Capital One subpoena covers "2016 through the present," but both subpoenas impose no time limitations for certain documents, such as those connected to account openings and due diligence.

According to the House, the Financial Services Committee issued these subpoenas pursuant to House Resolution 206, which called for "efforts to close loopholes that allow corruption, terrorism, and money laundering to infiltrate our country's financial system." Such loopholes, the resolution explained, had allowed "illicit money, including from Russian oligarchs," to flow into the United States through "anonymous shell companies" using investments such as "luxury high-end real estate." The House also invokes the oversight plan of the Financial Services Committee, which stated that the Committee intends to review banking regulation and "examine the implementation, effectiveness, and enforcement" of laws designed to prevent money laundering and the financing of terrorism. The plan further provided that the Committee would "consider proposals to prevent the abuse of the financial system" and "address any vulnerabilities identified" in the real estate market.

On the same day as the Financial Services Committee, the Permanent Select Committee on Intelligence issued an identical subpoena to Deutsche Bank—albeit for different reasons. According to the House, the Intelligence Committee subpoenaed Deutsche Bank as part of an investigation into foreign efforts to undermine the U. S. political process. Committee Chairman Adam Schiff had described that investigation in a previous statement, explaining that the Committee was examining alleged attempts by Russia to influence the 2016 election; potential links between Russia and the President's campaign; and whether the President and his associates had been compromised by foreign actors or interests. Chairman Schiff added that the Committee planned "to develop legislation and policy reforms to ensure the U. S. government is better positioned to counter future efforts to undermine our political process and national security."

Four days after the Financial Services and Intelligence Committees, the House Committee on Oversight and Reform issued another subpoena, this time to the President's personal accounting firm, Mazars USA, LLP. The subpoena demanded information related to the President and several affiliated business entities from 2011 through 2018, including statements of financial condition, independent auditors' reports, financial reports, underlying source documents, and communications between Mazars and the President or his businesses. The subpoena also requested all engagement agreements and contracts "[w]ithout regard to time."

Chairman Elijah Cummings explained the basis for the subpoena in a memorandum to the Oversight Committee. According to the chairman, recent testimony by the President's former personal attorney Michael Cohen, along with several documents prepared by Mazars and supplied by Cohen, raised questions about whether the President had accurately represented his financial affairs. Chairman Cummings asserted that the Committee had "full authority to investigate" whether the President: (1) "may have engaged in illegal conduct before and during his tenure in office," (2) "has undisclosed conflicts of interest that may impair his ability to make impartial policy decisions," (3) "is complying with the Emoluments Clauses of the Constitution," and (4) "has accurately reported his finances to the Office of Government Ethics and other federal entities." "The Committee's interest in these matters," Chairman Cummings concluded, "informs its review of multiple laws and legislative proposals under our jurisdiction."

B

Petitioners—the President in his personal capacity, along with his children and affiliated businesses—filed two suits challenging the subpoenas. They contested the subpoena issued by the Oversight Committee in the District Court for the District of Columbia, and the subpoenas issued by the Financial Services and Intelligence Committees in the Southern District of New York. In both cases, petitioners contended that the subpoenas lacked a legitimate legislative purpose and violated the separation of powers. The President did not, however, resist the subpoenas by arguing that any of the requested records were protected by executive privilege. For relief, petitioners asked for declaratory judgments and injunctions preventing Mazars and the banks from complying with the subpoenas. Although named as defendants, Mazars and the banks took no positions on the legal issues in these cases, and the House committees intervened to defend the subpoenas.

Petitioners' challenges failed. In Mazars, the District Court granted judgment for the House, and the D. C. Circuit affirmed. In upholding the subpoena issued by the Oversight Committee to Mazars, the Court of Appeals found that the subpoena served a "valid legislative purpose" because the requested information was relevant to reforming financial disclosure requirements for Presidents and presidential candidates. (internal quotation marks omitted). Judge Rao dissented. As she saw it, the "gravamen" of the subpoena was investigating alleged illegal conduct by the President, and the House must pursue such wrongdoing through its impeachment powers, not its legislative powers. Otherwise, the House could become a "roving inquisition over a co-equal branch of government."

In Deutsche Bank, . . . the Court of Appeals held that the Intelligence Committee properly issued its subpoena to Deutsche Bank as part of an investigation into alleged foreign influence over petitioners and Russian interference with the U. S. political process. That investigation, the court concluded, could inform legislation to combat foreign meddling and strengthen national security.

As to the subpoenas issued by the Financial Services Committee to Deutsche Bank and Capital One, the Court of Appeals concluded that they were adequately related to potential legislation on money laundering, terrorist financing, and the global movement of illicit funds through the real estate market. Rejecting the contention that the subpoenas improperly targeted the President, the court explained in part that the President's financial dealings with Deutsche Bank made it "appropriate" for the House to use him as a "case study" to determine "whether new legislation is needed."

Judge Livingston dissented, seeing no "clear reason why a congressional investigation aimed generally at closing regulatory loopholes in the banking system need focus on over a decade of financial information regarding this President, his family, and his business affairs."

. . .

II

The question presented is whether the subpoenas exceed the authority of the House under the Constitution. Historically, disputes over congressional demands for presidential documents have not ended up in court. Instead, they have been hashed out in the "hurly-burly, the give-and-take of the political process between the legislative and the executive."

[C]ongressional demands for the President's information have been resolved by the political branches without involving this Court. The Reagan and Clinton presidencies provide two modern examples:

During the Reagan administration, a House subcommittee subpoenaed all documents related to the Department of the Interior's decision whether to designate Canada a reciprocal country for purposes of the Mineral Lands Leasing Act. President Reagan directed that certain documents be withheld because they implicated his confidential relationship with subordinates. While withholding those documents, the administration made "repeated efforts" at accommodation through limited disclosures and testimony over a period of several months. Unsatisfied, the subcommittee and its parent committee eventually voted to hold the Secretary of the Interior in contempt, and an innovative compromise soon followed: All documents were made available, but only for one day with no photocopying, minimal note taking, and no participation by non-Members of Congress.

In 1995, a Senate committee subpoenaed notes taken by a White House attorney at a meeting with President Clinton's personal lawyers concerning the Whitewater controversy. The President resisted the subpoena on the ground that the notes were protected by attorney-client privilege, leading to "long and protracted" negotiations and a Senate threat to seek judicial enforcement of the subpoena. Eventually the parties reached an agreement, whereby President Clinton avoided the threatened suit, agreed to turn over the notes, and obtained the Senate's concession that he had not waived any privileges.

Congress and the President maintained this tradition of negotiation and compromise—without the involvement of this Court—until the present dispute. Indeed, from President Washington until now, we have never considered a dispute over a congressional subpoena for the President's records.

. . .

Congress has no enumerated constitutional power to conduct investigations or issue subpoenas, but we have held that each House has power "to secure needed information" in order to legislate. This "power of inquiry—with process to enforce it—is an essential and appropriate auxiliary to the legislative function." Without information, Congress would be shooting in the dark, unable to legislate "wisely or effectively." The congressional power to obtain information is "broad" and "indispensable." It encompasses inquiries into the administration of existing laws, studies of proposed laws, and "surveys of defects in our social, economic or political system for the purpose of enabling the Congress to remedy them."

Because this power is "justified solely as an adjunct to the legislative process," it is subject to several limitations. Most importantly, a congressional subpoena is valid only if it is "related to, and in furtherance of, a legitimate task of the Congress." The subpoena must serve a "valid legislative purpose," it must "concern[ ] a subject on which legislation 'could be had,' " . . . .

Furthermore, Congress may not issue a subpoena for the purpose of "law enforcement," because "those powers are assigned under our Constitution to the Executive and the Judiciary." Thus Congress may not use subpoenas to "try" someone "before [a] committee for any crime or wrongdoing." Congress has no " 'general' power to inquire into private affairs and compel disclosures," and "there is no congressional power to expose for the sake of exposure," "Investigations conducted solely for the personal aggrandizement of the investigators or to 'punish' those investigated are indefensible."

Finally, recipients of legislative subpoenas retain their constitutional rights throughout the course of an investigation. And recipients have long been understood to retain common law and constitutional privileges with respect to certain materials, such as attorney-client communications and governmental communications protected by executive privilege.

C

The President contends, as does the Solicitor General appearing on behalf of the United States, that the usual rules for congressional subpoenas do not govern here because the President's papers are at issue. They argue for a more demanding standard based in large part on cases involving the Nixon tapes—recordings of conversations between President Nixon and close advisers discussing the break-in at the Democratic National Committee's headquarters at the Watergate complex. The tapes were subpoenaed by a Senate committee and the Special Prosecutor investigating the break-in, prompting President Nixon to invoke executive privilege and leading to two cases addressing the showing necessary to require the President to comply with the subpoenas.

Those cases, the President and the Solicitor General now contend, establish the standard that should govern the House subpoenas here. Quoting Nixon, the President asserts that the House must establish a "demonstrated, specific need" for the financial information, just as the Watergate special prosecutor was required to do in order to obtain the tapes. And drawing on Senate Select Committee—the D. C. Circuit case refusing to enforce the Senate subpoena for the tapes—the President and the Solicitor General argue that the House must show that the financial information is "demonstrably critical" to its legislative purpose.

We disagree that these demanding standards apply here. Unlike the cases before us, Nixon and Senate Select Committee involved Oval Office communications over which the President asserted executive privilege. That privilege safeguards the public interest in candid, confidential deliberations within the Executive Branch; it is "fundamental to the operation of Government." As a result, information subject to executive privilege deserves "the greatest protection consistent with the fair administration of justice." We decline to transplant that protection root and branch to cases involving nonprivileged, private information, which by definition does not implicate sensitive Executive Branch deliberations.

The standards proposed by the President and the Solicitor General—if applied outside the context of privileged information—would risk seriously impeding Congress in carrying out its responsibilities. The President and the Solicitor General would apply the same exacting standards to all subpoenas for the President's information, without recognizing distinctions between privileged and nonprivileged information, between official and personal information, or between various legislative objectives. Such a categorical approach would represent a significant departure from the longstanding way of doing business between the branches, giving short shrift to Congress's important interests in conducting inquiries to obtain the information it needs to legislate effectively. Confounding the legislature in that effort would be contrary to the principle that:

> "It is the proper duty of a representative body to look diligently into every affair of government and to talk much about what it sees. It is meant to be the eyes and the voice, and to embody the wisdom and will of its constituents. Unless Congress have and use every means of acquainting itself with the acts and the disposition of the administrative agents of the government, the country must be helpless to learn how it is being served."

Legislative inquiries might involve the President in appropriate cases; as noted, Congress's responsibilities extend to "every affair of government." Because the President's approach does not take adequate account of these significant congressional interests, we do not adopt it.

The House meanwhile would have us ignore that these suits involve the President. Invoking our precedents concerning investigations that did not target the President's papers, the House urges us to uphold its subpoenas because they "relate[ ] to a valid legislative purpose" or "concern[ ] a subject on which legislation could be had." That approach is appropriate, the House argues, because the cases before us are not "momentous separation-of-powers disputes."

Largely following the House's lead, the courts below treated these cases much like any other, applying precedents that do not involve the President's papers. The Second Circuit concluded that "this case does not concern separation of powers" because the House seeks personal documents and the President sued in his personal capacity. The D. C. Circuit, for its part, recognized that "separation-of-powers concerns still linger in the air," and therefore it did not afford deference to the House. But, because the House sought only personal documents, the court concluded that the case "present[ed] no direct inter branch dispute."

The House's approach fails to take adequate account of the significant separation of powers issues raised by congressional subpoenas for the President's information. Congress and the President have an ongoing institutional relationship as the "opposite and rival" political branches established by the Constitution. As a result, congressional subpoenas directed at the President differ markedly from congressional subpoenas we have previously reviewed, and they bear little resemblance to criminal subpoenas issued to the President in the course of a specific investigation. Unlike those subpoenas, congressional subpoenas for the President's information unavoidably pit the political branches against one another.

Far from accounting for separation of powers concerns, the House's approach aggravates them by leaving essentially no limits on the congressional power to subpoena the President's personal records. Any personal paper possessed by a President could potentially "relate to" a conceivable subject of legislation, for Congress has broad legislative powers that touch a vast number of subjects. The President's financial records could relate to economic reform, medical records to health reform, school transcripts to education reform, and so on. Indeed, at argument, the House was unable to identify any type of information that lacks some relation to potential legislation.

Without limits on its subpoena powers, Congress could "exert an imperious controul" over the Executive Branch and aggrandize itself at the President's expense, just as the Framers feared. And a limitless subpoena power would transform the "established practice" of the political branches. Instead of negotiating over information requests, Congress could simply walk away from the bargaining table and compel compliance in court.

The House and the courts below suggest that these separation of powers concerns are not fully implicated by the particular subpoenas here, but we disagree. We would have to be "blind" not to see what "[a]ll others can see and understand": that the subpoenas do not represent a run-of-the-mill legislative effort but rather a clash between rival branches of government over records of intense political interest for all involved.

The interbranch conflict here does not vanish simply because the subpoenas seek personal papers or because the President sued in his personal capacity. The President is the only person who alone composes a branch of government. As a result, there is not always a clear line between his personal and official affairs. "The interest of the man" is often "connected with the constitutional rights of the place." Given the close connection between the Office of the President and its occupant, congressional demands for the President's papers can implicate the relationship between the branches regardless whether those papers are personal or official. Either way, a demand may aim to harass the President or render him "complaisan[t] to the humors of the Legislature." In fact, a subpoena for personal papers may pose a heightened risk of such impermissible purposes, precisely because of the documents' personal nature and their less evident connection to a legislative task. No one can say that the controversy here is less significant to the relationship between the branches simply because it involves personal papers. Quite the opposite. That appears to be what makes the matter of such great consequence to the President and Congress.

In addition, separation of powers concerns are no less palpable here simply because the subpoenas were issued to third parties. Congressional demands for the President's information present an interbranch conflict no matter where the information is held—it is, after all, the President's information. Were it otherwise, Congress could sidestep constitutional requirements any time a President's information is entrusted to a third party—as occurs with rapidly increasing frequency. Indeed, Congress could declare open season on the President's information held by schools, archives, internet service providers, e-mail clients, and financial institutions. The Constitution does not tolerate such ready evasion; it "deals with substance, not shadows."

Congressional subpoenas for the President's personal information implicate weighty concerns regarding the separation of powers. Neither side, however, identifies an approach that accounts for these concerns. For more than two centuries, the political branches have resolved information disputes using the wide variety of means that the Constitution puts at their disposal. The nature of such interactions would be transformed by judicial enforcement of either of the approaches suggested by the parties, eroding a "[d]eeply embedded traditional way[ ] of conducting government."

A balanced approach is necessary, one that takes a "considerable impression" from "the practice of the government," and "resist[s]" the "pressure inherent within each of the separate Branches to exceed the outer limits of its power,". We therefore conclude that, in assessing whether a subpoena directed at the President's personal information is "related to, and in furtherance of, a legitimate task of the Congress," courts must perform a careful analysis that takes adequate account of the separation of powers principles at stake, including both the significant legislative interests of Congress and the "unique position" of the President. Several special considerations inform this analysis.

First, courts should carefully assess whether the asserted legislative purpose warrants the significant step of involving the President and his papers. " '[O]ccasion[s] for constitutional confrontation between the two branches' should be avoided whenever possible." Congress may not rely on the President's information if other sources could reasonably provide Congress the information it needs in light of its particular legislative objective. The President's unique constitutional position means that Congress may not look to him as a "case study" for general legislation.

Unlike in criminal proceedings, where "[t]he very integrity of the judicial system" would be undermined without "full disclosure of all the facts," efforts to craft legislation involve predictive policy judgments that are "not hamper[ed] . . . in quite the same way" when every scrap of potentially relevant evidence is not available. While we certainly recognize Congress's important interests in obtaining information through appropriate inquiries, those interests are not sufficiently powerful to justify access to the President's personal papers when other sources could provide Congress the information it needs.

Second, to narrow the scope of possible conflict between the branches, courts should insist on a subpoena no broader than reasonably necessary to support Congress's legislative objective. The specificity of the subpoena's request "serves as an important safeguard against unnecessary intrusion into the operation of the Office of the President."

Third, courts should be attentive to the nature of the evidence offered by Congress to establish that a subpoena advances a valid legislative purpose. The more detailed and substantial the evidence of Congress's legislative purpose, the better. That is particularly true when Congress contemplates legislation that raises sensitive constitutional issues, such as legislation concerning the Presidency. In such cases, it is "impossible" to conclude that a subpoena is designed to advance a valid legislative purpose unless Congress adequately identifies its aims and explains why the President's information will advance its consideration of the possible legislation.

Fourth, courts should be careful to assess the burdens imposed on the President by a subpoena. We have held that burdens on the President's time and attention stemming from judicial process and litigation, without more, generally do not cross constitutional lines. But burdens imposed by a congressional subpoena should be carefully scrutinized, for they stem from a rival political branch that has an ongoing relationship with the President and incentives to use subpoenas for institutional advantage.

Other considerations may be pertinent as well; one case every two centuries does not afford enough experience for an exhaustive list.

When Congress seeks information "needed for intelligent legislative action," it "unquestionably" remains "the duty of all citizens to cooperate." Congressional subpoenas for information from the President, however, implicate special concerns regarding the separation of powers. The courts below did not take adequate account of those concerns. The judgments of the Courts of Appeals for the D. C. Circuit and the Second Circuit are vacated, and the cases are remanded for further proceedings consistent with this opinion.

CONGRESSIONAL OVERSIGHT OF THE WHITE HOUSE

Memorandum Opinion for the Counsel to the President
2021 WL 222744 (O.L.C.) (Jan. 8, 2021)

Congressional oversight of the White House is subject to greater constitutional limitations than oversight of the departments and agencies of the Executive Branch, in light of the White House staff's important role in advising and assisting the President in the discharge of his constitutional responsibilities, the need to ensure the independence of the Presidency, and the heightened confidentiality interests in White House communications.

January 8, 2021

MEMORANDUM OPINION FOR THE COUNSEL TO THE PRESIDENT

This memorandum opinion summarizes the principles and practices governing congressional oversight of the White House. The White House, as we use the term here, refers to those components within the Executive Office of the President ("EOP"), such as the White House Office and the National Security Council, whose principal function is to advise and assist the President in the discharge of the duties of his office. All three branches of government have recognized that the White House has a role and status distinct from the executive branch departments and agencies, and this Office has long recognized those distinctions to be critical to the development of principles and practices for congressional oversight addressed to the White House.

The Constitution vests all of "[t]he executive Power" in the President and charges him alone with the responsibility to "take Care that the Laws be faithfully executed." U.S. Const. art. II, § 1, cl. 1; id. § 3. In carrying out that charge, the President necessarily depends on "the assistance of subordinates," *Myers v. United States*, 272 U.S. 52, 117 (1926), most of whom are his appointed officials in the executive departments and agencies. Yet the size and complexity of modern federal administration have required the establishment of the White House as an organizational apparatus to directly support the President in the discharge of his responsibilities. White House personnel work in close proximity to the President and advise and assist him in the development of presidential policy, in supervising and guiding the affairs of the executive branch departments and agencies, and in communicating with Congress, the American public, and foreign governments.

The White House's important role in advising and assisting the President has special significance for congressional oversight. Each House of Congress has, as an adjunct to its legislative power, the constitutional authority to obtain information, a power typically carried out through its committees. But this investigative authority, often referred to as "oversight" authority, is subject to limitations. A congressional information request "is valid only if it is 'related to, and in furtherance of, a legitimate task of the Congress.'" *Trump v. Mazars USA, LLP*, 140 S. Ct. 2019, 2031 (2020) (quoting *Watkins v. United States*, 354 U.S. 178, 187 (1957)). Consequently, the Executive Branch must scrutinize the asserted legislative purpose underlying a congressional request by examining the objective fit between that purpose and the information sought. Because Congress may conduct oversight investigations only with respect to "'subject[s] on which legislation could be had,'" *id.* (quoting *Eastland v. U.S. Servicemen's Fund*, 421 U.S. 491, 506 (1975)), Congress may not conduct such investigations for the purpose of reviewing the discharge of functions exclusively entrusted to the President by the Constitution. *See, e.g., Assertion of Executive Privilege with Respect to Clemency Decision*, 23 Op. O.L.C. 1, 2 (1999) (Reno, Att'y Gen.) ("*Clemency Decision*").[1] It follows that the activities of White House advisers are less likely than the activities of the departments' and agencies' staffs to involve matters within Congress's oversight authority.

Even when Congress operates within the appropriate scope of its oversight authority, the Constitution places additional separation of powers constraints on inquiries directed at the White House. The Supreme Court has recognized the importance of "the Executive Branch's interests in maintaining the autonomy of [the Presidency] and safeguarding the confidentiality of its communications." *Cheney v. U.S. Dist. Ct.*, 542 U.S. 367, 385 (2004). These concerns are particularly acute with respect to White House advisers. Congressional oversight directed at the White House must be conducted in a way that protects the ability of the White House to function effectively in advising and assisting the President as he carries out his responsibilities under the Constitution.

Congressional inquiries are also constrained by the heightened confidentiality interests in White House communications. *See id.* At the core of those interests is the presidential communications component of executive privilege, which covers many White House communications involving presidential decision-making. Congressional inquiries directed to the White House must take account of the presumptive application of executive privilege to White House communications, as well as the

---

[1] This memorandum addresses Congress's authority to investigate in furtherance of its power to legislate. See *McGrain v. Daugherty*, 273 U.S. 135, 175 (1927). We do not consider Congress's parallel authority to obtain the information necessary to the discharge of its other powers, such as the House's power to impeach, although we have recognized that similar principles apply in those areas. *See, e.g., Exclusion of Agency Counsel from Congressional Depositions in the Impeachment Context*, 43 Op. O.L.C. ___, at *3 (Nov. 1, 2019) (recognizing "that a congressional committee must likewise make a showing of need that is sufficient to overcome [executive] privilege in connection with an impeachment inquiry"); Letter for Pat A. Cipollone, Counsel to the President, from Steven A. Engel, Assistant Attorney General, Office of Legal Counsel at 2 (Nov. 3, 2019) (recognizing that the immunity of certain presidential advisers from compelled congressional testimony "applies in an impeachment inquiry just as it applies in a legislative oversight inquiry").

President's interests in autonomy and independence. Even when the White House may have relevant information, these separation of powers and privilege concerns weigh in favor of Congress seeking available information first from the departments and agencies before proceeding with White House requests.[2]

. . .

B.   Validity of Subpoenas Issued to the White House

It is the Executive Branch's settled policy to work to accommodate congressional requests for information in a manner consistent with the Executive's constitutional and statutory obligations. Historically, however, congressional subpoenas to executive branch officials have raised a variety of separation of powers concerns. This section identifies and discusses a number of legal defects, several of which are discussed at greater length above, that have commonly arisen in subpoenas involving the White House. These limitations on Congress's oversight powers are rooted in the separation of powers and observing them serves to prevent Congress from "aggrandiz[ing] itself at the [Executive's] expense." *Mazars*, 140 S. Ct. at 2034.

Lack of Oversight Authority or Legitimate Legislative Purpose. As we have discussed, all congressional oversight inquiries must be conducted in support of Congress's legislative authority under Article I of the Constitution. See *id.* at 2031–32, 2035–36; *McGrain*, 273 U.S. at 177. A subpoena that seeks material or testimony on matters beyond Congress's legislative authority, such as the exercise of a constitutional power vested exclusively in the Executive Branch, is beyond Congress's oversight authority. See *Barenblatt*, 360 U.S. at 111–12.

Infringement of Presidential Autonomy and Confidentiality. Congressional inquiries to the White House are constrained by "the Executive Branch's interests in maintaining the autonomy of its office and safeguarding the confidentiality of its communications." *Cheney*, 542 U.S. at 385. In certain circumstances, compliance with a congressional subpoena directed at the White House may unduly impair the Executive's "ability to discharge its constitutional responsibilities." *Id.* at 382. For example, compliance with a subpoena that is excessively broad or intrusive might burden White House personnel to a degree that prevents them from effectively advising and assisting the President in the performance of his constitutional duties. In that circumstance, it would be unconstitutional to

---

[2]   Although this memorandum addresses the EOP components whose principal function is to advise and assist the President, many of the principles discussed here would apply as well to so-called "dual hat" presidential advisers in other components who "exercise substantial independent authority or perform other functions in addition to advising the President." *In re Sealed Case*, 121 F.3d 729, 752 (D.C. Cir. 1997). To the extent that Congress directs oversight efforts at activities implicating the advising "hat" of those officials, many of the same principles governing oversight would apply.

enforce such an unduly broad subpoena. Of course, the accommodation process serves to ensure that congressional requests are tailored or narrowed so as to avoid infringement of presidential autonomy and confidentiality while satisfying Congress's legitimate needs for relevant information.

NOTES & QUESTIONS

1. The Office of Legal Counsel's opinion also states:

Congress's authority to investigate in furtherance of its power to legislate has come to be known as its "oversight" authority, but that shorthand term does not imply a general authority to review the actions of the Executive Branch. Congress may direct the departments and agencies through the enactment of appropriate legislation, but the Constitution does not otherwise confer on Congress or its committees an authority to "oversee" or direct the Executive Branch in the conduct of its assigned duties and responsibilities under Article II. Rather, because Congress enjoys an implied power of investigation that "is 'justified solely as an adjunct to the legislative process,' it is subject to several limitations." *Mazars*, 140 S. Ct. at 2031 (quoting *Watkins*, 354 U.S. at 197). Two of these limitations have particular significance for congressional oversight of the White House. First, because a congressional oversight request "is valid only if it is 'related to, and in furtherance of, a legitimate task of the Congress,'" it "must serve a 'valid legislative purpose.'" Id. (quoting *Watkins*, 354 U.S. at 187; *Quinn v. United States*, 349 U.S. 155, 161 (1955)). Second, and relatedly, the scope of oversight authority is limited to subjects "on which legislation could be had," *McGrain*, 273 U.S. at 177, and therefore Congress "cannot inquire into matters which are within the exclusive province of one of the other branches of the Government," *Barenblatt v. United States*, 360 U.S. 109, 112 (1959), including any function committed exclusively to the President by the Constitution.[5]

---

[5] Congressional oversight authority may encompass inquiries into the Executive Branch's use of appropriated funds with respect to statutory programs as well as inquiries relevant to future appropriations. However, as *Barenblatt* makes clear, the fact that the President or the federal courts may rely upon appropriated funds to carry out their activities does not mean that everything they do falls within the scope of the oversight authority. Otherwise, no matter would fall within the "exclusive province of one of the other branches of the Government." *Barenblatt*, 360 U.S. at 112. Rather, "[s]ince Congress may only investigate into those areas in which it may potentially legislate or appropriate, it cannot inquire into matters which are within the [Executive's] exclusive province[.]" Id. at 111–12 (emphasis added). Therefore, the limits placed on Congress when conducting oversight pursuant to its general legislative power also apply to oversight conducted pursuant to its appropriations authority. While Congress may, pursuant to its appropriations authority, review manpower statistics and other non-substantive data regarding the resources that Presidents historically invest in areas of exclusive executive authority, Congress lacks the authority to inquire into the Executive's substantive decision-making in these areas.

Is this correct? If Congress does not have authority over agencies other than by legislation, does this lead to an "imperial presidency?" What other of the President's powers should be examined by the Congress?

CHAPTER 10

GLOSSARY

■ ■ ■

A

act: Legislation that has become law, either by the Governor's signature, the Governor's inaction within 10 days of receiving the bill or by legislative override of a Governor's veto. Each act has a chapter number indicating the order in which it became law during the then current year. (MA)

A public law enacted by the Texas Legislature. A bill that has been passed by both houses of the legislature and presented to the governor becomes law if it is signed by the governor, if it is not signed by the governor within a specified period of time, or if the governor vetoes the bill and the veto is overridden by a two-thirds vote in each house. (TX)

action: A description of a step that a bill undergoes as it moves through the legislative process. (TX)

action codes: Action Codes identify stages that condense detailed legislative action steps. (U.S.)

acts and resolves: A compilation of the bills and resolves that become law that are bound in a volume on a yearly basis. (MA)

adjourn: Formally end a meeting of a chamber or committee. (U.S.)

adjournment: The termination of a meeting. Adjournment occurs at the close of each legislative day upon completion of business, with the hour and day of the next meeting set before adjournment. (See RECESS.) (TX)

adjournment sine die: An adjournment that terminates an annual session of Congress. A "sine die" ("without day") adjournment sets no day for reconvening, so that Congress will not meet again until the first day of the next session. Under the Constitution, adjournment sine die (except when the next session is about to convene) requires the agreement of both chambers, accomplished through adoption of a concurrent resolution, which in current practice also authorizes leaders of either chamber to reconvene its session if circumstances warrant. (U.S.)

adoption: Approval or acceptance; usually applied to amendments or resolutions. (TX)

advice and consent: Procedure by which the senate gives approval or confirms appointments made by the governor to state offices. (TX)

amendment: A proposed change to a pending text (e.g., a bill, resolution, another amendment, or a treaty [or an associated resolution of ratification]). See also Proposed/offered Senate amendment and Submitted Senate amendment. (U.S.)

A proposed modification to a legislative document that is submitted by or on behalf of a committee or a legislator to a clerk and is considered on the floor. An amendment may be in the form of a redraft or a substitute. (MA)

Any proposed alteration to a bill or resolution as it moves through the legislative process. Amendments to a measure may be proposed by members in their assigned committees or by any member of a chamber during that chamber's second reading or third reading consideration of the measure. (TX)

amendment exchange: Also referred to as "amendments between the houses" or, colloquially, "ping-pong." A method for reconciling differences between the two chambers' versions of a measure by sending the measure back and forth between them until both have agreed to identical language. (U.S.)

amendment in the nature of a substitute: Amendment that seeks to replace the entire text of an underlying measure. (U.S.)

apportionment: The proportionate distribution of elected representation in the U.S. Congress among the states. (TX)

appropriation: An authorization by the legislature for the expenditure of money for a public purpose. In most instances, money cannot be withdrawn from the state treasury except through a specific appropriation. (TX)

author: The legislator who files a bill and guides it through the legislative process. (TX)

B

bicameral: Literally, "two chambers;" in a legislative body, having two houses (as in the House of Representatives and the Senate comprising the U.S. Congress). (U.S.)

biennial: Occurring every two years; a term applied to the scheduled regular session of the legislature. (TX)

bill: The primary form of legislative measure used to propose law. Depending on the chamber of origin, bills begin with a designation of either H.R. or S. Joint resolution is another form of legislative measure used to propose law. (U.S.) [**bill:** A type of legislative measure that requires passage by both chambers of the legislature and action by the governor. A bill is the primary means used to create and change the laws of the state. The term "bill" also is used generically in TLIS on the legislative intranet and in TLO on the Internet to refer to the various types of legislative measures that may be introduced during a legislative session. Bill types include: senate and house bills, senate and house joint resolutions, senate and house concurrent resolutions, and senate and house resolutions. (TX)

Document accompanying a petition, usually asking for legislative action on a particular matter. (MA)

bill analysis: A document prepared for all bills reported out of committee that explains in nonlegal language what a bill will do. A bill analysis may include background information on the measure, a statement of purpose, and a detailed analysis of the content of the measure. (TX)

bill summary: Upon introduction of a bill or resolution in the House or Senate, legislative analysts in the Congressional Research Service of the Library of Congress write a short summary that objectively describes the measure's significant provisions. Introduced version summaries are subject to length limitations as a matter of policy. When a measure receives action (e.g., it is reported from a committee or passed by the House or Senate), the analysts then write an expanded summary, detailing the measure's effect upon programs and current law. Bill summaries are written as a result of a congressional action and may not always correspond to a document published by the Government Publishing Office. A final public law summary is prepared upon enactment into law. Each summary description identifies the date and version of the measure, and indicates whether there have been amendments: e.g., Passed House amended (07/19/2013). (U.S.)

bipartisan: A term used to refer to an effort endorsed by both political parties or a group composed of members of both political parties. (TX)

budget resolution: A measure (provided for by the Congressional Budget Act of 1974, as amended) that sets forth a congressional budget plan, including aggregate budgetary levels, which may be enforced during the subsequent consideration of spending and revenue legislation. It is in the form of a concurrent resolution (e.g., an H.Con.Res or an S.Con. Res), not a law-making vehicle; as such, it is not submitted to the president. (U.S.)

by request: A designation on a measure indicating that the member has introduced the measure on behalf of someone else (e.g., the President or an executive branch agency), or pursuant to statutory requirements, and may not necessarily support its provision. See bills introduced by request. (U.S.)

C

calendar: Lists of measures, motions, and matters that are (or soon will become) eligible for consideration on the chamber floor; also, the official document that contains these lists and other information about the status of legislation and other matters. The House has four such calendars, published as one document; the Senate publishes two. (U.S.)

A list of bills or resolutions that is scheduled or eligible to be taken up for consideration on a specified date by the members of a chamber. (TX).

An agenda for each day of formal session; also called the orders of the day. There are 3 different calendars, a House calendar, a Senate calendar, and a Joint Session calendar. Calendars are available to legislative users and to the public on the General Court website. (MA)

calendar day: A day of the year on which the legislature may be in session. (TX)

called session: See SESSION.

caption: A statement that gives the legislature and public reasonable notice of the subject of a bill or resolution. For bills and joint resolutions, the first sentence of the text that summarizes the contents of the bill or resolution. For other types of resolutions, a brief description of the contents of the resolution. (TX)

chair: A legislator appointed to preside over a legislative committee. A traditional designation for the member currently presiding over a house of the legislature or one of its committees. (TX)

chamber: The place in which the senate or house of representatives meets. Also a generic way to refer to a house of the legislature. (TX)

chief clerk: The chief administrative officer of the house of representatives, who supervises the legislative departments of the house. The chief clerk is the custodian of all bills and resolutions in the possession of the house and is responsible for keeping a complete record of their introduction and all subsequent house actions taken on them throughout the legislative process. (TX)

cloture: The method by which a supermajority (typically, three-fifths) of the Senate may agree to limit further debate and consideration of a question (e.g., a bill, amendment, or other matter). Details of the procedural process are provided for in Rule XXII of the Senate standing rules. (U.S.)

coauthor: A legislator authorized by the primary author to join in the authorship of a bill or resolution. A coauthor must be a member of the chamber in which the bill was filed. (TX)

codification measure: Codification measures are not drafted in XML, therefore XML/HTML text formats should not be expected to be available from Congress.gov nor from FDsys. (U.S.)

committee/subcommittee: A panel (or subpanel) with members from the House or Senate (or both) tasked with conducting hearings, examining and developing legislation, conducting oversight, and/or helping manage chamber business and activities. (U.S.).

A group of legislators, appointed by the presiding officer of the house or the senate, to which proposed legislation is referred or a specific task is assigned. (TX)

One of 27 joint standing committees, one of 9 House standing committees, or one of 8 Senate standing committees. Committees and their membership sizes are set forth in the Rules and may be changed periodically. (MA)

committee chair: The member of the majority party on a committee who has formal responsibility over the panel's agenda and resources, presides at its meetings, and can, in some circumstances, act on the committee's behalf. (U.S.)

Committee of the Whole: A parliamentary device designed to allow greater participation in floor consideration of measures. It can be understood as the House assembled in a different form; it is a committee of the House composed of every Representative that meets in the House chamber. The House considers many major measures in the Committee of the Whole. (U.S.)

committee-related activity: A committee or subcommittee may interact with a bill in a variety of ways. Bills may be referred to or discharged from a committee by the full chamber. Committees markup bill texts, hold hearings to learn more about a topic, or may express legislative interest. Committees report legislation out to the full chamber recommending or disapproving consideration, or may report an original bill. (U.S.)

Committee on Bills in the Third Reading: A committee which is empowered to examine and make technical corrections to bills and resolves prior to their final reading in the Senate or House, to resolutions prior to their adoption and to amendments to bills, resolves and resolutions adopted by the other branch and which is before the body for concurrence. The Senate and House committees work closely with their respective counsels to prepare the legislative documents for floor action. (MA)

committee report: Document accompanying a measure reported from a committee. It contains an explanation of the provisions of the measure, arguments for its approval, votes held in markup, individual committee members' opinions, cost estimates, and other information. Committee reports are published in the congressional report document series. (U.S.).

The text of a bill or resolution and its required attachments that is prepared when the measure is reported from a committee for further consideration by the members of the chamber. The committee report includes the recommendations of the committee regarding action on the measure by the full house or senate and generally is necessary before a measure can proceed through the legislative process. (TX)

committee substitute: A complete, new bill or resolution recommended by a committee in lieu of the original measure. A committee will report a committee substitute rather than a bill with a large number of individual amendments when the committee wishes to make a substantial number of changes to the original measure. The committee substitute must contain the same subject matter as the original measure. (TX)

communications: Written statements, messages or petitions sent to the Congress by the President of the United States, executive branch officials, or state or local governments. Types of communications include executive communications, presidential messages, petitions and memorials. (U.S.)

companion bill: A bill filed in one chamber that is identical or very similar to a bill filed in the opposite chamber. Companion bills are used to expedite passage as they provide a means for committee consideration of a measure to occur in both houses simultaneously. A companion bill that has passed one house then can be substituted for the companion bill in the second house. (TX)

companion measure: Identical or substantially similar measures introduced in the other chamber. Identical bills, procedurally-related measures, and legislation with text similarities are other related bill types. (U.S.)

concurrence: When the originating chamber votes to accept, or concur in, the amendments made by the opposite chamber. (TX)

concurrent resolution: A form of legislative measure used for the regulation of business within both chambers of Congress, not for proposing changes in law. Depending on the chamber of origin, they begin with a designation of either H.Con.Res. or S.Con.Res. Joint resolutions and simple resolutions are other types of resolutions. (U.S.)

A type of legislative measure that requires passage by both chambers of the legislature and generally requires action by the governor. A concurrent resolution is used to convey the sentiment of the legislature and may offer a commendation, a memorial, a statement of congratulations, a welcome, or a request for action by another governmental entity. Concurrent resolutions are used also for administrative matters that require the concurrence of both chambers such as providing for adjournment or a joint session. These types of concurrent resolutions do not require action by the governor. (TX)

conferees: Members of the House and Senate appointed to a conference committee. Also sometimes called "managers." (U.S.)

conference committee: Temporary joint committee created to resolve differences between House-passed and Senate-passed versions of a measure. (U.S.)

A committee composed of five members from each house appointed by the respective presiding officers to resolve the differences between the house and senate versions of a measure when the originating chamber refuses to concur in the changes made by the opposite chamber. Upon reaching an agreement, the conferees issue a report that then is considered for approval by both houses. (TX)

A committee consisting of 3 members from each body appointed by the legislative leaders to resolve differences between the 2 bodies with regard to specific matter, with one senator and one representative acting as chairmen. Failure of the committee to agree or failure of 1 body to accept the committee's recommendation results in the appointment of a new conference committee. Usually the committees are made up of 2 members of the majority party and 1 member of the minority party from each body. (MA)

conference report: The document presenting an agreement reached by a joint temporary committee (a conference committee) appointed to negotiate a compromise between the House and Senate. Conference reports are published in the Congressional Record and also in the congressional report document series. (U.S.)

The text of a bill and its required attachments that is issued when a conference committee has completed its work in resolving the differences between the house and senate versions of a measure. (TX)

Congratulatory and Memorial Calendar: A list of congratulatory and memorial resolutions scheduled by the House Committee on Rules and Resolutions for consideration by the house that must be distributed to the members 24 hours before the house convenes. (TX)

congress (i.e., 2-year time-frame): When referring to a time-period (e.g., the 114th Congress which convened on January 6, 2015) rather than the legislative branch generally, a Congress is the national legislature in office (for approximately two years). It begins with the convening of a new Congress comprised of members elected in the most-recent election and ends with the adjournment sine die of the legislature (typically after a new election has occurred). (U.S.)

CBO / Congressional Budget Office: The Congressional Budget Office is a legislative branch agency that produces independent analyses of budgetary and economic issues to support the Congressional budget process. (U.S.)

Congressional Record: The Congressional Record is the official record of the proceedings and debates of the U.S. Congress. For every day Congress is in session, an issue of the Congressional Record is printed by the Government Publishing Office. Each issue summarizes the day's floor and committee actions and records all remarks delivered in the House and Senate. (U.S.)

Congressional report: Congressional reports originate from congressional committees and deal with proposed legislation or issues under investigation. Congress issues different types of reports, including committee reports, conference reports and executive reports.

Congressional reports may be issued by the House or Senate. Depending on the chamber of origin, report citations begin with the Congress number during which it was issued and either H. Rpt. or S. Rpt., and an accession number (e.g., 112 H. Rpt. 1). Congressional reports are compiled in the U.S. Congressional Serial Set. (U.S.)

CRS/Congressional Research Service: The Congressional Research Service (CRS) of the Library of Congress works exclusively for the United States Congress, providing policy and legal analysis to committees and Members of both the House and Senate, regardless of party affiliation. CRS provides Congress with analysis that is authoritative, confidential, objective, and non-partisan. (U.S.)

constituent: A citizen residing within the district of an elected representative. (TX)

Constitutional Amendment: A change to the state constitution. A constitutional amendment may be proposed by the legislature in the form of a joint resolution that must be adopted by both houses of the legislature by a two-thirds vote and be approved by a majority of the voters to become effective. (TX)

continuing resolution (continuing appropriation): An appropriations act (typically in the form of a joint resolution) that provides stop-gap (or full-year) funds for federal agencies and programs to continue operations when the regular (or annual) appropriations acts have not been enacted by the beginning of the fiscal year. (U.S.)

convene: To assemble or call to order the members of a legislative body. (TX)

cosponsor: Representatives or Senators who formally sign on to support a measure. Only the first-named Member is the sponsor, all others are cosponsors, even those whose names appeared on the measure at the time it was submitted. (U.S.)

A legislator who joins with the primary sponsor to guide a bill or resolution through the legislative process in the opposite chamber. A cosponsor must be a member of the opposite chamber from the one in which the bill was filed. (TX)

concurrence: Agreement by one branch with an action originating in the other branch.

Legislation that has become law, either by the Governor's signature, the Governor's inaction within 10 days of receiving the bill or by legislative override of a Governor's veto. Each act has a chapter number indicating the order in which it became law during the then current year.

Document accompanying a petition, usually asking for legislative action on a particular matter. (MA)

Council document number: The unique number assigned to a bill or resolution draft prepared by the Texas Legislative Council. If a filed bill or resolution has been prepared by the council, the number will appear in the lower left-hand corner of the document. (TX)

D

Daily Digest: A section of the _Congressional Record_ summarizing the day's floor and committee actions in each chamber, with page references to the verbatim accounts of floor actions. It also lists the measures scheduled for action during each chamber's next meeting and the announcements of upcoming committee meetings.

The Digest appears at the back of each daily _Record_. Its pages are separately numbered and preceded by the letter _D_. In the bound _Congressional Record_, all Daily Digests for a session are printed in a separate volume. (U.S.)

Daily House Calendar: A list of new bills and resolutions scheduled by the House Committee on Calendars for consideration by the house that must be distributed to the members 36 hours before the house convenes during regular sessions and 24 hours before the house convenes during special or called sessions. (TX)

district (representative): A geographic division of the state made on the basis of population and in accordance with conditions dictated by state and federal law for the purpose of equitable representation of the people in a legislative or other body. (TX)

division vote: A vote by any method other than voice vote that will give the presiding officer an indication of the members' preference without calling the roll. Traditional methods were show of hands, standing, or moving to opposite sides of the room. (TX)

duplicate bill: A bill that is identical to a bill filed in the same chamber. (TX)

E

election: The process of choosing government officials by a vote of the citizens. (TX)

enactment: Final passage of a bill by the House or Senate. All bills must be enacted in the House first. After a bill is enacted by the Senate it is "laid before the Governor". (MA)

emergency preamble: A preamble to a bill setting forth the facts constituting an emergency, and the statement that the law is necessary for the immediate preservation of the public peace, health, safety or convenience. Matters with emergency preambles become law immediately upon approval by the Governor. To make a matter effective immediately or upon a date certain less than 90 days either the Governor may attach an emergency letter or the legislature may attach a preamble. The legislature must adopt an emergency preamble "on enactment", i.e., after the bill is engrossed in both branches, by a two-thirds vote. (MA)

enacted: Made into law. (U.S.) To pass a law. (TX)

enacting clause: A clause required by the Texas Constitution to precede the body of each bill. The enacting clause follows the caption and must read as follows: "Be it enacted by the Legislature of the State of Texas:". (TX)

en bloc: "All together." Sometimes a committee or congressional chamber will agree to act concurrently on multiple measures (e.g., bills) or matters (e.g., nominations), thereby considering them "en bloc." (U.S.)

engrossed: The stage in a bill's legislative progress when it has been passed by the chamber in which it was filed and all amendments to the bill have been incorporated into the text of the bill, which is then forwarded to the second house for consideration. (TX)

engrossed bill or resolve: Final version of a bill or resolve before the House or Senate for final action after being prepared on special parchment by the Legislative Engrossing Division and certified by the clerk. (MA)

engrossed measure: Official copy of a measure as passed by one chamber, including the text as amended by floor action. (U.S.)

enrolled measure: Final official copy of a measure as passed in identical form by both chambers and then printed on parchment for presentation to the President. (U.S.)

The stage in a bill's legislative progress when it has been passed by both chambers of the legislature in identical form and is prepared for signature by the presiding officers of both houses. If the bill is not passed in identical form by both houses, any changes made by the opposite chamber must be accepted by the originating chamber or a conference committee report must be adopted by both chambers before the bill may be enrolled. (TX)

executive business: Nominations and treaties submitted by the president to the Senate for its "Advice and Consent;" the Senate treats such business separately from its legislative business. (U.S.)

Executive Calendar: The list of treaties and nominations that are (or soon will become) eligible for consideration by the full Senate; also, the official document that contains these lists and other information about the status of items of executive business. (U.S.)

executive communication: Written statement or petition presented to Congress by the Executive Branch or other organization that may affect appropriations. (U.S.)

executive report: A written committee report accompanying a matter of executive business (treaty or nomination) reported by the committee. (U.S.)

executive session: A period under Senate rules during which executive business is considered on the floor. Legislation is considered only in legislative session, with its own distinct rules and practices; the Senate may go back and forth between legislative and executive session, even within the course of a day. (U.S.)

ex officio: Used to refer to a member of a governmental body who holds his or her position on that body as the result of holding another governmental position. (TX)

F

federal depository library: Libraries where congressional and other federal publications are available for free public use. (U.S.)

filed: The stage in a bill's legislative progress when it is given a bill number and introduced into the legislative process. Members of the house of representatives file bills with the chief clerk of the house. Senators file bills with the secretary of the senate. (TX)

filibuster: In the Senate, the use of dilatory or obstructive tactics to delay or block passage of a measure by preventing it from coming to a vote. (U.S.)

first reading: See **reading**. (TX)

fiscal note: An estimate, prepared by the Legislative Budget Board, of the probable costs that will be incurred as an effect of a bill or joint resolution. (TX)

fiscal year: A 12-month period at the end of which accounts are reconciled. The fiscal year for state agencies in Texas begins on September 1 of each year and ends on August 31 of the following year. (TX)

floor: A traditional term for the meeting chamber of either house. (TX)

floor action: Action taken by either house on a bill reported by a committee. Subject to rules adopted by the respective house, its members may propose amendments, enter debate, seek to promote or prevent a bill's passage, and vote on its final passage in that house. (TX)

formal meeting: A meeting of a house committee or subcommittee during which official action may be taken on any measure or matter before the committee or subcommittee. (TX)

formal session: Meeting to consider and act upon reports of committees, messages from the Governor, petitions, orders, enactments, papers from the other branch, matters in the Orders of the Day (calendar) which are generally required to be made available for formal sessions and various other matters which may be controversial in nature and during which roll call votes may be taken. (MA)

G

General Laws: Legislative acts applying generally to the Commonwealth and its citizens. (MA)

germaneness: The requirement that an amendment be closely related—in terms of the precise subject or purpose, for example—to the text it proposes to amend. House rules require amendments to be germane; Senate rules apply this restriction only in limited circumstances. (U.S.)

gerrymander: To divide a state, county, or other political subdivision into election districts in an unnatural manner to give a political party or ethnic group advantage over its opponents. (TX)

GPO/Government Publishing Office: Government Publishing Office is a legislative branch agency that provides publishing and dissemination services for the official and authentic government publications to Congress, federal agencies, federal depository libraries, and the American public. (U.S.)

H

hearing: A formal meeting of a congressional committee (or subcommittee) to gather information from witnesses for use in its activities (that is, the development of legislation, oversight of executive agencies, investigations into matters of public policy, or Senate consideration of presidential nominations). See also, committee-related activity. (U.S.)

hold: A request by a Senator to his or her party leader to delay floor action on a measure (e.g., bill) or matter (e.g., nomination), to be consulted on its disposition, and/or an indication that he or she would object to a unanimous consent request to consider said item of business or otherwise delay or obstruct consideration. (U.S.)

hopper: A wooden box on the House floor into which measures are dropped for formal introduction. (U.S.)

House and Senate rules: Rules of order and procedure adopted by that branch at the beginning of each biennial session. (MA)

House of Representatives: The lower house of the Texas Legislature, consisting of 150 members elected from districts of roughly equal population, all of whom are elected every two years for two-year terms. (TX)

House Rules Committee: A committee in the House that, among other things, is responsible for reporting out "special rules"—simple resolutions that propose to the House tailored terms for debate and amendment of a measure on the House floor. (U.S.)

I

identical bill: A bill that is word-for-word identical to another bill. Bills are characterized as identical to each other at the introduced stage only, even though a later (e.g., reported or passed) version of a bill might meet the same criteria for text similarity. Companion measures, procedurally-related measures, and legislation with text similarities are other related bill types. (U.S.)

informal sessions: Meetings designated by the Speaker of the House and Senate President to consider reports of committees, enactments, papers from the other branch, amendments and various other matters which are of a noncontroversial nature. Any session may be declared an informal session with prior notice given or in cases of an emergency. (MA)

initiative petition: Request by a specified number of voters to submit a constitutional amendment or law to the General Court and, if not approved, to the people for approval or rejection. The petition is introduced into the General Court if signed by a number of citizens equaling 3 per cent of the entire vote for Governor in the preceding gubernatorial election. If a proposed initiative law fails to pass the General Court, additional signatures are required to place it on the ballot. A proposed initiative constitutional amendment approved by at least one quarter of the General Court, sitting in joint sessions by 2 consecutively-elected General Courts, can be placed on the ballot. (MA)

intent calendar: A list of bills and resolutions for which senators have filed with the secretary of the senate written notice to suspend the regular order of business for consideration. Normally, a bill may not be brought up for consideration by the full senate unless it is listed on the Intent Calendar. (TX)

interim: The period between regular legislative sessions. (TX)

interim committee: A group of legislators appointed by the presiding officer of the house or senate when the legislature is not in session that studies a particular issue or group of issues for the purpose of making recommendations to the next legislature. (TX)

international agreement: Legal agreements the United States enters into with other States or international organizations; they may take the form of an executive agreement entered into by the executive branch (but not submitted to the Senate for its advice and consent) or the form of a treaty. (U.S.)

introduced: Used to refer to the version of a bill or resolution as it was filed in the house or the senate. (TX)

J

joint committee: Twenty-seven committees, generally consisting of 6 senators and 11 representatives, responsible for holding public hearings and reporting on all legislative matters referred to them. (MA)

A committee composed of members from each house appointed by the respective presiding officers. Joint committees normally are created by special proclamation issued by the speaker and lieutenant governor for the purpose of studying a particular issue or group of issues when the legislature is not in session. Joint committees rarely, if ever, are created during a session, and house and senate rules do not permit bills and resolutions to be referred to a joint committee. (TX)

joint explanatory statement: Statement appended to a conference report explaining the conference agreement and the intent of the conferees. Sometimes called a "statement of managers." (U.S.)

joint resolution: A form of legislative measure used to propose changes in law, or to propose an amendment to the U.S. Constitution. Depending on the chamber of origin, they begin with a designation of either H.J.Res. or S.J.Res. Concurrent resolutions and simple resolutions are other types of resolutions. Bill is another form of legislative measure used to propose law. (U.S.)

A type of legislative measure that requires passage by both chambers of the legislature but does not require action by the governor. A joint resolution is used to propose amendments to the Texas Constitution, to ratify amendments to the U.S. Constitution, or to request a convention to propose amendments to the U.S. Constitution. Before becoming effective, the provisions of joint resolutions proposing amendments to the Texas Constitution must be approved by the voters of Texas. (TX)

Joint Rule 10: Rule ordering that all matters referred to joint committees (except for the Joint Committee on Health Care Financing) be reported out of committees by the third Wednesday in March of the second annual session and within 30 days on all matters referred to them on or after the third Wednesday in February of the second annual session of the General Court. (MA)

joint rules: Rules for the governing of the 2 bodies that are adopted by both branches. (MA)

journal: The constitutionally-mandated record of certain House and Senate actions, including motions offered, votes taken, and amendments agreed to. Unlike the Congressional Record, it does not contain remarks delivered in the House and Senate. (U.S.)

The official publication that records the legislative proceedings of each chamber, including record vote information. The journal of each house is printed daily in pamphlet form and subsequently compiled and indexed for publication in bound volumes after the conclusion of a regular or special session of the legislature. (TX)

jurisdiction: A set of policy issues that fall under the purview of a specific committee (or subcommittee); full committee jurisdiction is set by chamber standing rules and precedents. (U.S.)

L

laid before the governor: Presentment of a bill before the Governor for his action after the bill has been engrossed and enacted or reenacted by both branches. The Governor has 10 days beginning on the day after presentment to either sign the bill, let it become law without his signature, return the bill to its branch of origin with a recommended amendment (except for reenacted bills) or veto the bill. (MA)

lame duck: An elected official who has been defeated for re-election or who has chosen not to run for re-election but whose current term has not yet expired. (TX)

last action: The description of the most recent step a bill has gone through in the legislative process. (TX)

lay on table: To temporarily lay aside the consideration of a specific bill, resolve, report, amendment or motion. If laid on the table, consideration is postponed until a subsequent motion taking the item off the table succeeds. A motion to lay on the table can be made only in the Senate. (MA)

legislative action steps: Each chamber produces detailed, chamber-specific legislative action steps. Each step has a number code. U.S. Congress Legislative Status Steps is a depiction of the steps in relation to the codes. It was published in 1975 within a committee print titled The Bill Status System for the United States House of Representatives. See also, major action. (U.S.)

legislative day: That period from convening after an adjournment until the next adjournment. The house or the senate may convene for a daily session in the morning, recess for lunch, and adjourn that same evening, completing a legislative day on the same calendar day. However, if a chamber recesses at the end of the day, that particular legislative day continues until the next time the chamber adjourns. (TX)

LIV/Legislative Indexing Vocabulary: The Legislative Indexing Vocabulary (LIV) was the Congressional Research Service (CRS) thesaurus for subject searching in databases of the Library of Congress from 1973 to 2008. This controlled vocabulary provided access via specific subjects to legislative material, public policy literature, and CRS products. With increased availability of electronic full text of documents and accompanying search capabilities, the level of detail employed by LIV became unnecessary and work began to modernize and streamline the pool of vocabulary terms assigned by CRS analysts to classify and group legislation. Those efforts resulted in the far more compact list of legislative subject terms, in use since 2009. (U.S.)

legislative interest: A label used by committees to identify bills that were not formally referred to the committee but which the committee expresses jurisdictional or provisional interest in. See also, committee-related activity. (U.S.)

legislative subject term: The legislative subject term vocabulary consists of approximately 1,000 subjects, geographic entities, and organization names. CRS may assign one or many terms to describe a measure's substance and effects. The legislative subject term vocabulary is consistently used for all bills and resolutions introduced since 2009 (111th Congress).

Terms assigned to a bill can be seen from the "View All Subjects" link to the right of each bill's overview. Find Bills by Subject and Policy Area provides subject term search guidance. See also, policy area term. (U.S.)

legislature: The lawmaking body of the State of Texas. It consists of two chambers, the house of representatives and the senate. The Texas Legislature convenes in regular session at noon on the second Tuesday in January of each odd-numbered year for no more than 140 days. (TX)

list of items eligible for consideration: Prepared by the chief clerk of the house, upon request of the speaker, when the volume of legislation warrants (normally during the last few weeks of a regular session). The list must be distributed six hours before it may be considered and contains: (1) house bills with senate amendments eligible to be considered; (2) senate bills for which the senate has requested the appointment of a conference committee; and (3) conference committee reports eligible to be considered. (TX)

lobby: The act of a person or group of persons (lobbyists) seeking to present their views on an issue to the members of the legislature and its committees and working for the passage or defeat of proposed legislation. (TX)

Local and Uncontested Calendar: A list of local or noncontroversial bills scheduled by the Senate Committee on Administration for consideration by the senate that must be distributed to the senators by noon of the day preceding the day the calendar is to be considered. (TX)

Local, Consent, and Resolutions Calendar: A list of local or noncontroversial bills scheduled by the House Committee on Local and Consent Calendars for consideration by the house that must be distributed to the members 48 hours before the house convenes. (TX)

M

majority: A number of members that is greater than half of the total membership of a group and that has the power to make decisions binding on the whole. There are two types of majorities that may be required for legislative approval of bills and other actions—a simple majority and an absolute majority. A simple majority consists of more than half of those members present and voting. An absolute majority consists of more than half of those members entitled to vote, whether present or absent. (TX)

markup: Meeting by a committee or subcommittee during which committee members offer, debate, and vote on amendments to a measure. See also, committee-related activity. (U.S.)

measure: A legislative vehicle: a bill, joint resolution, concurrent resolution, or simple resolution. (U.S.)

memorial: Written statement or petition presented to Congress by the legislature of a state or territory that may affect the proceedings of a committee or Congress in general. Memorials may be referred by a Member of the House of Representatives. The Senate does not differentiate between memorials and petitions. (U.S.)

money bill: A bill that transfers money or property from the people to the Commonwealth, i.e., a bill that imposes a tax. These bills must be taken up in the House first. (MA)

motion: A formal suggestion presented to a legislative body for action by one of its members while the body is meeting. (TX)

motion to proceed to consider: A motion in the Senate, which, if agreed to by a majority of those present and voting, brings a measure (e.g., bill) or matter (e.g., nomination) before the chamber for consideration. Often referred to simply as a "motion to proceed." (U.S.)

motion to recommit: In the House, a motion offered by a member of the minority party at the end of floor consideration that, if adopted in its simple form, returns the measure to legislative committee. If combined with "instructions to report back forthwith," the motion effectively provides one last opportunity for a minority party member to offer an amendment to the measure. In the Senate, the motion may be offered at other times during consideration of a measure, and is not a prerogative of a member of the minority party; it may also be used as a means of offering an amendment. (U.S.)

motion to table: A non-debatable motion in the House and Senate (and in their committees) by which a simple majority may agree to negatively and permanently dispose of a question (e.g., an amendment). (U.S.)

N

NARA/National Archives and Records Administration: After the President signs a bill into law, it is delivered to NARA's Office of the Federal Register where editors assign a public law number. (U.S.)

nomination: The president's formal submission of an individual's name, and the federal government position to which he or she is proposed to be appointed, for Senate consideration and potential confirmation. (U.S.)

nonpartisan: Free from party domination. (TX)

notes: Legislative analysts in the Congressional Research Service of the Library of Congress may supplement a bill record with a brief note when the title, text, or actions require explanation beyond the information immediately available. Such explanations might alert the user to a text anomaly, note that the bill is a vehicle for a rapidly moving measure, include links to additional documents, or aid in the interpretation of the measure's context. (U.S.)

O

official title: A bill's sponsor designates an official title which may be amended in the course of legislative action. Bills may also have short titles. The more complex a bill becomes, the more likely the bill is to acquire additional titles. See also, popular title and short title. (U.S.)

omnibus bill: A bill regarding a single subject that combines many different aspects of that subject. (TX)

order: Formal motion in writing, not requiring the Governor's signature, which is temporary in nature and is used to establish investigative committees, to change rules and for other parliamentary actions. (MA)

ordered reported: Committee's formal action of agreeing to report a measure or matter to its chamber. See also, reported. (U.S.)

orders of the day (calendar): Listing of most matters to be considered by the Senate and the House at each formal sitting. (MA)

original bill: An introduced bill that embodies a text approved in a committee markup but not formally introduced prior to the markup. Senate committees are authorized to report original bills within their jurisdictions in addition to reporting measures that have been introduced and referred to them; some House committees also have authority to originate certain measures. See also, committee-related activity. (U.S.)

outside section: A section of an appropriation bill that may deal with an existing line item in an appropriation, but may also amend an existing law or create a new law (MA)

override: To overturn the Governor's veto by a two-thirds vote of the members present in both the House and Senate. (MA)

To set aside or annul, as to override a veto. (TX)

P

pairing: A procedure for voting whereby, under a formal agreement between two members, a member who will be present for a vote agrees with a member who will be absent for a vote that the member who is present will not vote but will be "present, not voting." When two members are paired, the journal reflects how each member would have voted. Two members may be paired only if one would have voted "aye" and one would have voted "nay" on a particular measure or motion. (TX)

parliamentarian: Nonpartisan staff officials (one in each chamber, assisted by deputies and assistants) who provide expert advice and assistance to the presiding officer and to members on the application and interpretation of chamber rules, precedents, and practices (including referral of measures to committee). (U.S.)

partitioned nomination: A presidential nomination (PN) with multiple nominees may be partitioned by the Senate if the nominees follow a different confirmation path. Partitions are identified with a suffix; for example, PN230-1 (114th Congress) and PN230-2 (114th Congress). Searching on a PN number in Congress.gov, such as PN230, without a partition designation will retrieve all partitions of a partitioned nomination. (U.S.)

party caucus/conference: The official organization comprised of all members of a political party serving within a congressional chamber (e.g., the Senate Republican Conference, the House Democratic Caucus, etc.). (U.S.)

passage: Approval of a measure by the full body. (TX)

pass a resolve: Final passage of a resolve by the House or Senate. (MA)

petition: Written statement from any entity other than a state legislature—boards, commissions, cities, towns, individuals—that may affect the proceedings of a committee or Congress in general. The Senate does not differentiate between petitions and memorials. (U.S.)

A request describing the nature of the proposed legislation and the objects sought by it, signed by the primary sponsor and a petitioner or multiple petitioners, and accompanied by a draft of the bill or resolve embodying the legislation proposed. (MA)

ping-pong: See amendment exchange. (U.S.)

pocket veto: A veto resulting from the Governor's failure to sign a bill following prorogation or dissolution of the General Court. Because the session has ended, the bill will not automatically become law after 10 days and the General Court has no opportunity to override the veto. (MA)

point of order: A member's statement to the presiding officer that the chamber (or committee) is taking action contrary to the rules or precedents, and a demand that they be enforced. (U.S.)

A motion calling attention to a breach of the procedural rules. (TX)

A challenge to the breach of order or rule. (MA)

policy area term: The policy area term vocabulary consists of 32 legislative policy areas. One term, which best describes an entire measure, is assigned to every bill or resolution. The policy area term vocabulary is consistently used for all bills and resolutions introduced since 1995 (104th Congress). Policy Area terms display to the right of the bill Overview. Find Bills by Subject and Policy Area provides subject term search guidance. See also, legislative subject term. (U.S.)

popular title: An informal, unofficial name for legislation that may be assigned by the House, Senate, or CRS to improve access. Popular titles are usually not found within official legislative texts (e.g., the Patient Protection and Affordable Care Act is commonly known as the health care reform bill). (U.S.)

prefiling: Filing of bills and other proposed legislation prior to the convening of a session of the legislature. (TX)

presidential message: Written statement presented to the Congress, such as the President's Budget or the State of the Union address. (U.S.)

President of the Senate: The presiding officer of the senate. The state constitution provides that the lieutenant governor serves as the president of the senate. (TX)

previous question: Non-debatable motion, available in the House and its legislative committees, which, when agreed to, cuts off further debate, prevents the offering of additional amendments, and brings the pending matter to an immediate vote. (U.S.)

private bill: In contrast to public bills (which apply to public matters and deal with individuals only by classes), a private bill proposes to provide benefits that are restricted to one or more specified individuals (including corporations or institutions), typically when no other legal remedy is available. The Legislative Subject term "Private Legislation" is assigned to measures proposed to provide benefits that are restricted to one or more specified individuals. Measures with a Legislative Subject term assignment "Private Legislation" usually do not get a Policy Area term assignment. See also, private laws. (U.S.)

privilege of the floor: Permission to view the proceedings from the floor of the chamber rather than from the public gallery. (TX)

privileged nomination: Certain nominations entitled to expedited procedures, pursuant to S.Res. 116 (112th Congress). (U.S.)

pro forma session: A daily session of either chamber held chiefly to avoid the occurrence of either a recess of more than three days within the annual session or an adjournment sine die (either of which would constitutionally require the consent of the other chamber). Pro forma sessions are typically short, with no business, or very little, conducted. (U.S.)

pro tempore or **pro tem:** Temporarily; literally, for the time. The term is used particularly to apply to a temporary presiding officer of either the house or the senate. (TX)

procedurally-related measure: Legislation that affects consideration of other legislation (e.g., a rule for consideration, a bill ordered to be reported or passed in lieu of another measure). Identical bills, companion measures, and legislation with text similarities are other related bill types. (U.S.)

proposal: Document accompanying a petition or a committee redraft introducing legislative amendments to the Constitution of the Commonwealth. (MA)

proposed/offered Senate amendment: A Senate amendment is proposed or offered when a Senator has been recognized by the presiding officer, sends his/her amendment to the desk (or identifies an amendment already at the desk), and the amendment is read by the clerk. The amendment becomes pending before the Senate, and remains pending until disposed of by the Senate. Occasionally the term "called up" is used in lieu of "proposed" or "offered." Both proposed and submitted amendments are numbered and printed in the Congressional Record. (U.S.)

prorogation: Formal motion in writing, not requiring the Governor's signature, which is temporary in nature and is used to establish investigative committees, to change rules and for other parliamentary actions. Termination of a legislative year by agreement of the Governor and both legislative bodies. (MA)

public hearing: A meeting of a house or senate committee or subcommittee during which public testimony may be heard and formal action may be taken on any measure or matter before the committee or subcommittee. (TX)

Q

quorum: Minimum number of members of a chamber (or committee) required for the transaction of certain types of business. (U.S.)

Twenty-one members in the Senate; 81 members in the House. Quorum is established by the Constitution. (MA)

The number of members required to conduct business. Two-thirds of the elected members constitute a quorum in each house. A majority of the appointed members of a committee forms a quorum for the purpose of conducting committee business. (TX)

quorum call: Action to formally ascertain the presence of the minimum number of members required to transact business. In the Senate, quorum calls are also commonly used as a sort of "time out" in floor proceedings without recessing the chamber. (U.S.)

R

ranking member: The most senior (though not necessarily the longest-serving) member of the minority party on a committee (or subcommittee). The ranking member typically oversees minority committee staff and may coordinate involvement of the minority party committee members in committee activities. (U.S.)

reading: The presentation of a bill before either house by the recital of the caption of the bill. The Texas Constitution requires that every bill be read in each house on three separate days. Until a bill is finally passed, it will be in the process of a first, second, or third reading. The first reading of a bill is the point in the process when the bill is referred to committee by the appropriate presiding officer. The second reading of a bill is the first point in the process when the entire membership of a chamber has the opportunity to debate the bill and amend it by majority vote. The third reading of a bill is the next point in the process when the entire membership of a chamber may debate a bill and the final opportunity the members of a chamber have to offer amendments to the bill. (TX)

recess: A temporary termination of a meeting. Recesses are called for short breaks (e.g., for lunch or dinner) or occasionally at the close of a daily session to allow the legislative day to continue into the next calendar day. (See **adjournment**) (TX)

Temporary delay in proceedings. (MA)

recess appointment: A temporary presidential appointment, during a recess of the Senate, of an individual to a federal government position, where such appointment usually requires the advice and consent of the Senate. (U.S.)

reconsideration: A procedure by which the house, senate, or one of its committees may, after approval by majority vote, repeat the vote on an action previously taken to either annul or reaffirm the action. (TX)

Motion to reconsider a vote on action previously taken. Any member may propose reconsideration and, if the motion prevails, the matter is voted on again. A motion to reconsider must be moved prior to entering upon the Orders of the Day on the next legislative session. (MA)

record vote: A listing of the individual vote of each member of a committee or the full house or senate on a particular motion or measure. (TX)

redistricting: A geographical division of the state into congressional, state representative, senatorial, or other legislative districts on the basis of the relative distribution of the state's total population. District boundaries are redrawn every 10 years following the publication of the U.S. census to ensure an appropriate number of districts of approximately equal population. (TX)

referendum petition: A petition signed by a specified number of voters to repeal a law enacted by the legislature and requesting that the legislation be suspended until the vote is taken. (MA)

referral: Assignment of a measure to a committee or committees (or subcommittees) for potential consideration. See also, committee-related activity. (U.S.)

regular session: See **session.** (TX)

related bill: A related bill may be a companion measure, an identical bill, a procedurally-related measure, or one with text similarities. Bill relationships are identified by the House, the Senate, or CRS, and refer only to same-Congress measures. (U.S.)

reported: Formal submission of a measure by a committee to its parent chamber or by a subcommittee to its parent committee. See also, ordered reported. See also, committee-related activity. (U.S.)

reserved bill number: In recent Congresses, the resolution specifying House internal rules of procedure includes reserving bill numbers for assignment by the Speaker. In the 112th Congress (2011–2012) the practice was extended to reserve additional bill numbers for assignment by the Minority Leader. Resolutions with "Numbering of Bills" sections include: H.Res.5 [114], H.Res.5 [113], H.Res.5 [112], H.Res.5 [111], H.Res.6 [110], H.Res.5 [109], H.Res.5 [108], H.Res.5 [107]. In the Senate, some of the lowest bills numbers are reserved for leadership. (U.S.)

resolution: A formal expression of opinion or decision, other than a proposed law, that may be offered for approval to one or both houses of the legislature by a member of the house or senate. (TX)

Documents which may or may not accompany a petition expressing an opinion of the sentiment of one or both branches of the General Court, used for congratulations, for memorializing the Congress of the United States regarding public questions, etc. Resolutions do not require the Governor's signature. (MA)

resolution of ratification: A resolution by which the Senate, if supported by a vote of two-thirds, formally gives its advice and consent to a treaty, thereby empowering the President to proceed with ratification of the treaty. (U.S.)

resolve: Document accompanying a petition, usually asking for legislative action of a temporary or immediate nature; e.g., establishing temporary investigative commissions. Resolves do require the Governor's signature to the same extent as an act. (MA)

roll call vote: A vote that records the individual position of each Member who voted. Such votes occurring on the House floor (by the "yeas and nays" or by "recorded vote") are taken by electronic device. The Senate has no electronic voting system; in such votes, Senators answer "yea" or "nay" as the clerk calls each name aloud. Each vote is compiled by clerks and receives a roll call number (referenced in Congress.gov as a "Record Vote" [Senate] or "Roll no." [House]). See Roll Call Votes by the U.S. Congress. (U.S.)

report of Committees: Recommendation on a legislative matter by the committee to which it was referred. (MA)

S

second reading: See **reading**. (TX)

Secretary of the Senate: The chief administrative officer of the senate, responsible for the day-to-day operations of the senate and its departments. (TX)

Senate: The upper house of the Texas Legislature, consisting of 31 members elected from districts of roughly equal population, one-half of whom are elected every two years for four-year terms. (TX)

Senate Agenda: The document prepared daily for the senators and the public that contains the following information: (1) the Intent Calendar; (2) a list of senate bills returned from the house with amendments; (3) the status of bills in conference committee; (4) the Local and Uncontested Calendar; (5) gubernatorial appointments reported favorably from the Committee on Nominations and awaiting confirmation by the senate; (6) committee hearings scheduled, with a list of measures to be considered by the committees; (7) the regular order of business, listing bills that have been reported favorably from committee; (8) miscellaneous announcements; (9) senate floor action from the previous day; (10) senate committee action from the previous day; and (11) morning call items of business. (TX)

Senate and House Journals: Records of proceedings in each chamber for each legislative day, including matters considered, amendments offered and votes taken. (MA)

Sergeant at Arms: An officer of the house or senate charged with maintaining order and carrying out the directives of the presiding officers and the members. (TX)

session: The period during which the legislature meets. There are two types of sessions. The regular session convenes every two years and may last no more than 140 days. A called session, commonly referred to as a special session, is so designated because it must be called by the governor. A called or special session may last no more than 30 days. (TX)

short title: In addition to an official title, a bill may be assigned one or more short titles upon introduction, committee or chamber action, or enactment. Short titles may name all or portions of the bill's content. In a display of titles, those that describe the entirety of the bill version appear under a bolded heading (e.g., Short Titles as Passed House), followed by those, if any, that describe portions of the bill. Short titles may change as the bill moves through the legislative process. See also, official title and popular title. (U.S.)

simple resolution: A form of legislative measure introduced and potentially acted upon by only one congressional chamber and used for the regulation of business only within the chamber of origin. Depending on the chamber of origin, they begin with a designation of either H.Res. or S.Res. Joint resolutions and concurrent resolutions are other types of resolutions. (U.S.)

The type of legislative measure that is considered only within the chamber in which it is filed. It can offer a commendation, a memorial, a statement of congratulations, a welcome, or another statement of legislative sentiment. (TX)

sine die: Literally, "without day." The term is used to signify the final adjournment of a session of a legislative body. The body adjourns sine die when it adjourns without appointing a day on which to appear or assemble again. (TX)

slip law: The initial publication of a measure that has become law. Slip laws are made available online within days after enactment through the U.S. Government Publishing Office (GPO) and are used until the law is published in a more permanent form. Public and private laws are then reprinted by number in the Statutes at Large, and public laws later incorporated into the U.S. Code. (U.S.)

Speaker of the House: The presiding officer of the house of representatives elected from and by the membership of the house at the beginning of each regular session. (TX)

special law: Legislative act applying to a particular county, city, town or district, individual or group of individuals and not general in nature. (MA)

special rule: A resolution reported by the Rules Committee that, if agreed to by the House, sets the terms for debating and amending a specified measure or measures. (U.S.)

special session: See **session.** (TX)

sponsor: A Representative or Senator who introduces or submits a bill or other measure. (U.S.)

The legislator who guides the bill through the legislative process after the bill has passed the originating chamber. The sponsor must be a member of the opposite chamber of the one in which the bill was filed. (TX)

standing committee: A committee created in the rules of either house that meets during the legislative session or an interim to consider and report on measures referred or tasks assigned to it by the respective presiding officers. (TX)

star print: Star prints are corrected re-prints of congressional publications. Star prints supersede the original print of a report or document. Corrected re-prints may be identifiable by one or more stars, and sometimes the words "Star Print," at the lower left-hand corner of official paper and PDF title pages or covers. Web-friendly bill texts display stars in the top left margin (e.g., Star print of 114SRes22). (U.S.)

subcommittee: A group of committee members, appointed by the chair of a committee of the house or the senate, to which proposed legislation is referred or a specific task is assigned. (TX)

subject: There are three separate and distinct subject term vocabularies used to facilitate finding bills by subject. See policy area term, legislative subject term, and LIV—Legislative Indexing Vocabulary. (U.S.)

submitted Senate amendment: An amendment is submitted when a senator files his/her amendment at the desk with the clerk for possible future consideration by the Senate. A submitted amendment is not pending until it is formally proposed/offered by a senator. The term "filed" is sometimes used in lieu of "submitted." Both proposed and submitted amendments are numbered and printed in the Congressional Record. (U.S.)

supermajority: A term sometimes used for a vote on a matter that requires approval by more than a simple majority of those members present and voting, with a quorum being present; also referred to as extraordinary majority. (U.S.)

Supplemental House Calendar: The primary agenda followed by the house during its deliberations. It is prepared by the House Committee on Calendars and is required to be distributed two hours before the house convenes. The Supplemental House Calendar contains: (1) measures passed to third reading on the previous day; (2) measures on the Daily House Calendar for a previous day that were not reached for consideration; (3) measures on the Daily House Calendar for the current day; and (4) postponed business from a previous day. (TX)

suspension of the rules: In the House, a procedure that streamlines consideration of a measure with wide support by prohibiting floor amendments, limiting debate to 40 minutes, and requiring a two-thirds majority for passage. Although rarely used, the Senate may also suspend various rules by a vote of two-thirds following one day's written notice. (U.S.)

T

text similarities: Legislation that is substantially similar in both text and meaning. Relationships indicated on this basis also include cases where language of one measure is found intact in another, often larger, measure. Identical bills, companion measures, and procedurally-related measures are other related bill types. (U.S.)

third reading: See **reading** (TX)

title: See official title, popular title, and short title. (U.S.)

treaty: An agreement negotiated and signed by the executive that enters into force if it is approved by a two-thirds vote in the Senate, and is subsequently ratified by the President.

treaty document: The text of a treaty as submitted to the Senate by the executive branch, as well as letters of transmittal from the President and the Secretary of State, and accompanying background documentation. (U.S.)

U

unanimous consent agreement: In the Senate, a proposal that, if agreed to, establishes the procedural guidelines for considering a measure or matter on the floor. If any member objects to such a request, it is not agreed to. Also sometimes called a "UC agreement" or a "time agreement." (U.S.)

unanimous consent request: A proposal that all members (of a chamber or committee) agree to set aside one or more chamber or committee rules to take some action otherwise not in order. If any member objects to such a request, it is not agreed to. (U.S.)

V

veto: Presidential disapproval of a bill or joint resolution presented to him for enactment into law. If a president vetoes a bill, it can become law only if the House and Senate separately vote (by two-thirds) to override the veto. A less common form of presidential veto—a pocket veto—occurs if Congress has adjourned without the possibility of returning and the president does not sign the measure within the required 10-day (excluding Sundays) period. (U.S.)

Governor's objection in writing to legislation enacted by the General Court. The legislation is returned to its branch of origin. (MA)

The rejection of an enrolled bill by the governor. (TX)

voice vote: A vote during which the presiding officer will request the members who are voting in favor of a measure or motion to respond collectively by saying "aye" and those who are voting against the measure or motion to respond collectively by saying "nay." (TX)

W

work session: A meeting of a house committee or subcommittee during which the members may only discuss measures or matters before the committee or subcommittee. Public testimony cannot be heard and formal action cannot be taken during a work session. (TX)

Sources:

- MA: Massachusetts Drafting Guide (Adopted in part from "Massachusetts Legislative Procedure and History," by Mary Ann Neary, MCLE 2002).

- U.S.: Library of Congress (https://www.congress.gov/help/legislative-glossary#glossary_jointresolution).

- TX: Texas Legislature Website (https://tlc.texas.gov/glossary).

INDEX

References are to Pages